Rick S

ROME

Rick Steves & Gene Openshaw

2013

CONTENTS

East Rome

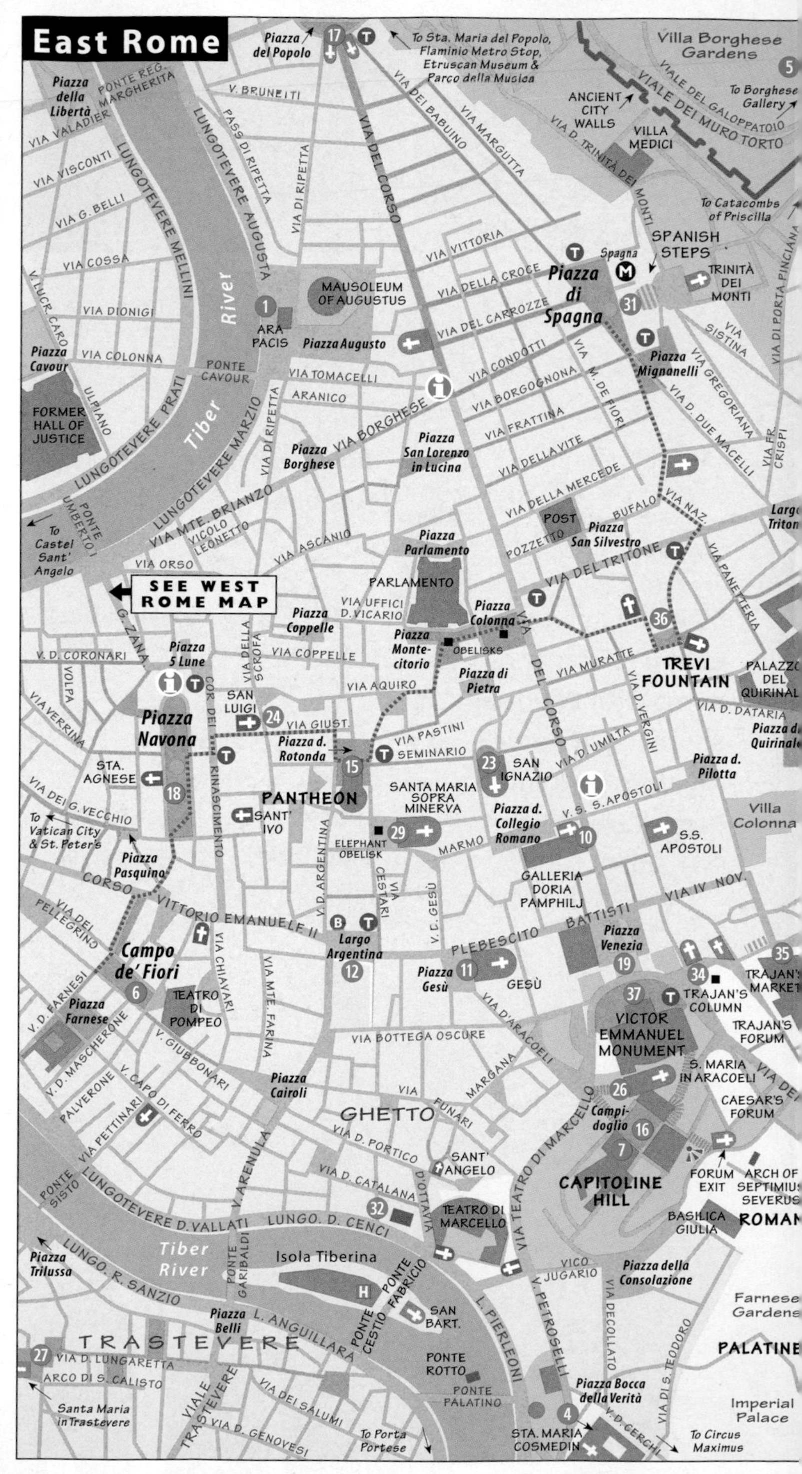

Piazza del Popolo
To Sta. Maria del Popolo, Flaminio Metro Stop, Etruscan Museum & Parco della Musica
Villa Borghese Gardens
To Borghese Gallery
ANCIENT CITY WALLS
VIALE DEL GALOPPATOIO
VIALE DEI MURO TORTO
VILLA MEDICI
VIA D. TRINITÀ DEI MONTI
To Catacombs of Priscilla
SPANISH STEPS
Spagna
Piazza di Spagna
TRINITÀ DEI MONTI
VIA DI PORTA PINCIANA
VIA SISTINA
Piazza Mignanelli
VIA GREGORIANA
VIA D. DUE MACELLI
VIA FR. CRISPI
Piazza della Libertà
PONTE REG. MARGHERITA
VIA VALADIER
V. BRUNETTI
VIA DEI BABUINO
VIA MARGUTTA
VIA DEL CORSO
PASS DI RIPETTA
VIA DI RIPETTA
LUNGOTEVERE AUGUSTA
LUNGOTEVERE MELLINI
VIA VISCONTI
VIA G. BELLI
VIA COSSA
V. LUCR. CARO
VIA DIONIGI
VIA COLONNA
Piazza Cavour
River
Tiber
ARA PACIS
MAUSOLEUM OF AUGUSTUS
Piazza Augusto
VIA VITTORIA
VIA DELLA CROCE
VIA DEL CARROZZE
VIA CONDOTTI
VIA BORGOGNONA
VIA FRATTINA
VIA DELLA VITE
VIA DELLA MERCEDE
V. M. DE FIORI
PONTE CAVOUR
VIA TOMACELLI
ARANICO
FORMER HALL OF JUSTICE
ULPIANO
LUNGOTEVERE PRATI
LUNGOTEVERE MARZIO
VIA BORGHESE
Piazza Borghese
Piazza San Lorenzo in Lucina
PONTE UMBERTO I
To Castel Sant' Angelo
VIA MTE. BRIANZO
VICOLO LEONETTO
VIA ASCANIO
VIA ORSO
Piazza Parlamento
POST
BUFALO
VIA NAZ.
Piazza San Silvestro
POZZETTO
VIA DEL TRITONE
Largo Triton
VIA PANETTERIA
SEE WEST ROME MAP
PARLAMENTO
VIA UFFICI D. VICARIO
Piazza Colonna
Piazza Coppelle
Piazza Montecitorio
OBELISKS
G. ZANA.
V. D. CORONARI
Piazza 5 Lune
VIA DELLA SCROFA
VIA COPPELLE
VIA MURATTE
TREVI FOUNTAIN
PALAZZO DEL QUIRINAL
VIA D. DATARIA
Piazza di Pietra
VIA DEL CORSO
VIA D. VERGINI
VOLPA
VIA VERRINA
Piazza Navona
COR. DEI RINASCIMENTO
SAN LUIGI
VIA AQUIRO
VIA GIUST.
VIA PASTINI
SEMINARIO
Piazza d. Rotonda
Piazza d. Quirinale
VIA D. UMILTA
Piazza d. Pilotta
STA. AGNESE
SAN IGNAZIO
PANTHEON
SANTA MARIA SOPRA MINERVA
V. S. S. APOSTOLI
VIA DEI G. VECCHIO
To Vatican City & St. Peter's
SANT' IVO
Piazza d. Collegio Romano
Villa Colonna
S.S. APOSTOLI
ELEPHANT OBELISK
MARMO
Piazza Pasquino
V. D. ARGENTINA
VIA CESTARI
V. L. GESÙ
GALLERIA DORIA PAMPHILJ
VIA IV NOV.
CORSO VITTORIO EMANUELE II
VIA DEI PELLEGRINO
BATTISTI
Piazza Venezia
Campo de' Fiori
VIA CHIAVARI
VIA MTE. FARINA
Largo Argentina
PLEBESCITO
Piazza Gesù
GESÙ
TRAJAN'S MARKET
TEATRO DI POMPEO
V. D. FARNESI
Piazza Farnese
TRAJAN'S COLUMN
VIA D'ARACOELI
VICTOR EMMANUEL MONUMENT
TRAJAN'S FORUM
V. D. MASCHERONE
V. GIUBBONARI
VIA BOTTEGA OSCURE
V. CAPO DI FERRO
PALVERONE
Piazza Cairoli
VIA FUNARI
MARGANA
S. MARIA IN ARACOELI
VIA DEI
CAESAR'S FORUM
GHETTO
VIA PETTINARI
V. ARENULA
VIA D. PORTICO
SANT' ANGELO
VIA TEATRO DI MARCELLO
Campidoglio
PONTE SISTO
LUNGOTEVERE D. VALLATI
VIA D. CATALANA
D'OTTAVIA
CAPITOLINE HILL
FORUM EXIT
ARCH OF SEPTIMIUS SEVERUS
LUNGO. D. CENCI
TEATRO DI MARCELLO
BASILICA GIULIA
ROMAN
Piazza Trilussa
Tiber River
PONTE GARIBALDI
Isola Tiberina
PONTE FABRICIO
VICO JUGARIO
Piazza della Consolazione
LUNGO. R. SANZIO
SAN BART.
L. PIERLEONI
V. PETROSELLI
VIA DECOLLATO
Farnese Gardens
Piazza Belli
L. ANGUILLARA
PONTE CESTIO
VIA DI S. TEODORO
TRASTEVERE
PALATINE
VIA D. LUNGARETTA
PONTE ROTTO
ARCO DI S. CALISTO
PONTE PALATINO
Piazza Bocca della Verità
Santa Maria in Trastevere
VIALE TRASTEVERE
VIA DEI SALUMI
VIA D. GENOVESI
To Porta Portese
V. D. CERCHI
Imperial Palace
STA. MARIA COSMEDIN
To Circus Maximus

SIGHTS

1. Ara Pacis
2. Arch of Constantine
3. Baths of Diocletian
4. Bocca della Verità
5. To Borghese Gallery
6. Campo de' Fiori
7. Capitoline Museums
8. Capuchin Crypt
9. Colosseum
10. Galleria Doria Pamphilj
11. Gesù Church
12. Largo Argentina
13. Nat'l Museum of Rome
14. Palatine Hill (Entrance)
15. Pantheon
16. Piazza del Campidoglio
17. Piazza del Popolo
18. Piazza Navona
19. Piazza Venezia
20. Roman Forum (Entrance)
21. St. Peter-in-Chains Church
22. San Clemente Church
23. San Ignazio Church
24. San Luigi dei Francesi Ch.
25. Sta. Maria della Vittoria Ch.
26. Santa Maria in Aracoeli Ch.
27. Santa Maria in Trastevere Ch.
28. Santa Maria Maggiore Ch.
29. Sta. Maria sopra Minerva Ch.
30. Santa Susanna Church
31. Spanish Steps
32. Synagogue & Jewish Museum
33. Termini Train Station
34. Trajan's Column
35. Trajan's Market & Museum of the Imperial Forums
36. Trevi Fountain
37. Victor Emmanuel Monument

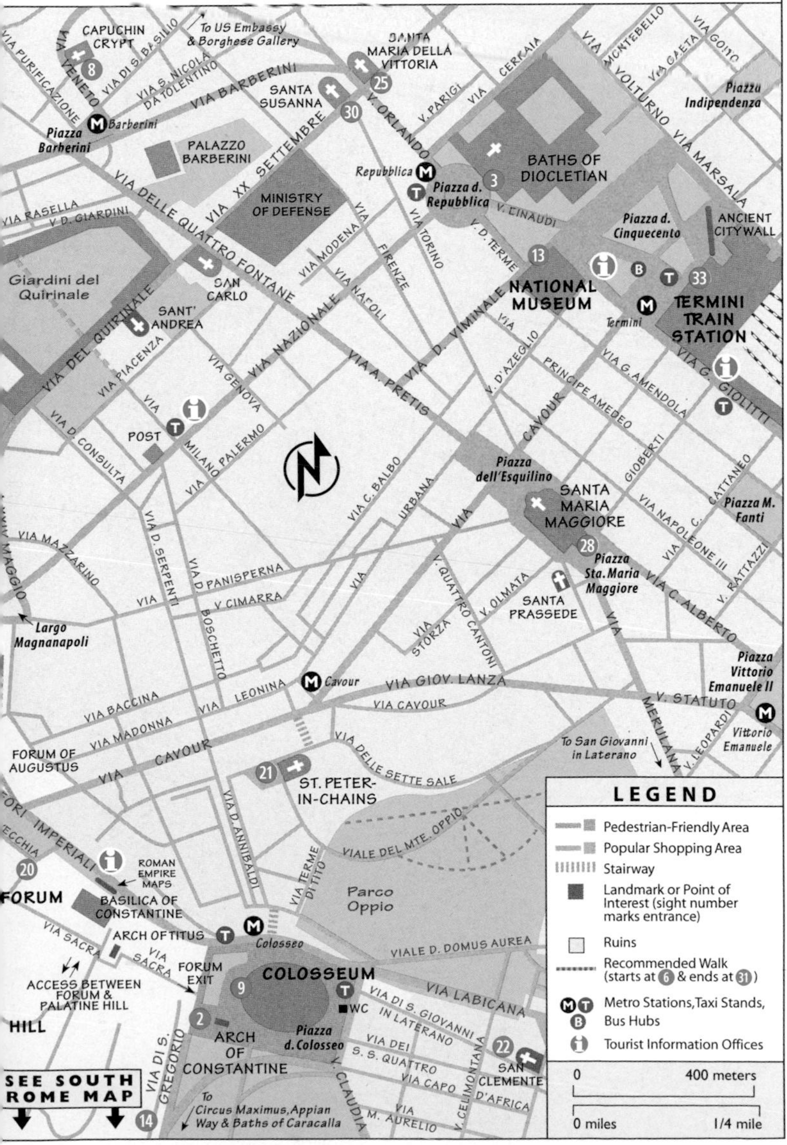

LEGEND

- Pedestrian-Friendly Area
- Popular Shopping Area
- Stairway
- Landmark or Point of Interest (sight number marks entrance)
- Ruins
- Recommended Walk (starts at 6 & ends at 31)
- M T B Metro Stations, Taxi Stands, Bus Hubs
- i Tourist Information Offices

0 — 400 meters

0 miles — 1/4 mile

SEE SOUTH ROME MAP

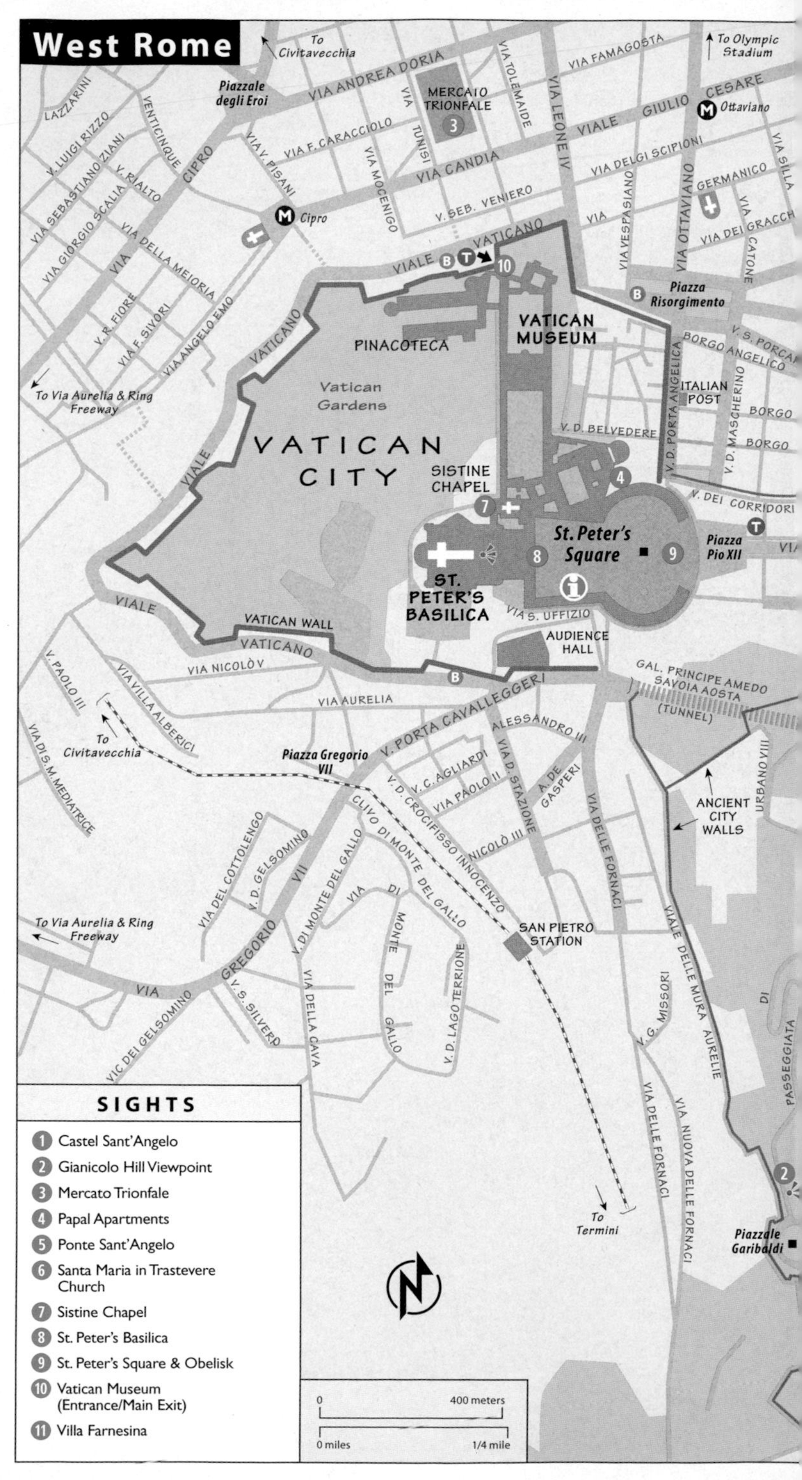
West Rome
VATICAN CITY
Vatican Gardens
PINACOTECA
VATICAN MUSEUM
SISTINE CHAPEL
ST. PETER'S BASILICA
St. Peter's Square
Piazza Pio XII
Piazza Risorgimento
ITALIAN POST
AUDIENCE HALL
VATICAN WALL
MERCATO TRIONFALE
Piazzale degli Eroi
Piazza Gregorio VII
SAN PIETRO STATION
ANCIENT CITY WALLS
GAL. PRINCIPE AMEDO SAVOIA AOSTA (TUNNEL)
Piazzale Garibaldi
Ottaviano
Cipro
To Civitavecchia
To Olympic Stadium
To Via Aurelia & Ring Freeway
To Termini
VIA ANDREA DORIA
VIALE GIULIO CESARE
VIA CANDIA
VIA LEONE IV
VIA OTTAVIANO
VIALE VATICANO
VIA AURELIA
V. PORTA CAVALLEGGERI
VIA GREGORIO VII
VIA DELLE FORNACI
VIALE DELLE MURA AURELIE
SIGHTS
1 Castel Sant'Angelo
2 Gianicolo Hill Viewpoint
3 Mercato Trionfale
4 Papal Apartments
5 Ponte Sant'Angelo
6 Santa Maria in Trastevere Church
7 Sistine Chapel
8 St. Peter's Basilica
9 St. Peter's Square & Obelisk
10 Vatican Museum (Entrance/Main Exit)
11 Villa Farnesina
0 400 meters
0 miles 1/4 mile

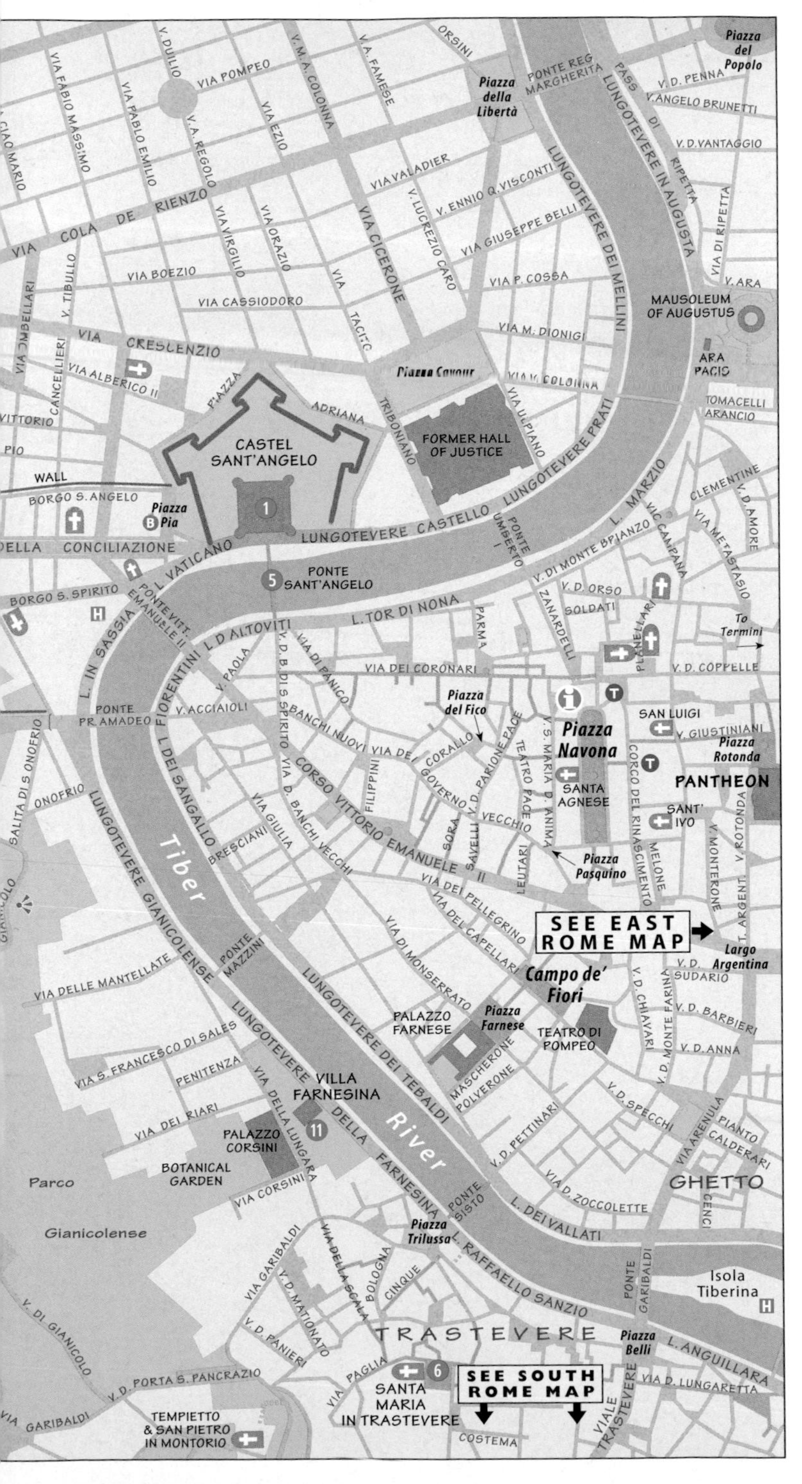
CASTEL SANT'ANGELO
Piazza del Popolo
Piazza della Libertà
Piazza Cavour
FORMER HALL OF JUSTICE
MAUSOLEUM OF AUGUSTUS
ARA PACIS
PONTE SANT'ANGELO
Piazza Pia
Piazza del Fico
Piazza Navona
SANTA AGNESE
SAN LUIGI
Piazza Rotonda
PANTHEON
SANT' IVO
Piazza Pasquino
SEE EAST ROME MAP
Largo Argentina
Campo de' Fiori
PALAZZO FARNESE
Piazza Farnese
TEATRO DI POMPEO
VILLA FARNESINA
PALAZZO CORSINI
BOTANICAL GARDEN
Parco Gianicolense
Tiber River
GHETTO
Isola Tiberina
Piazza Trilussa
TRASTEVERE
Piazza Belli
SANTA MARIA IN TRASTEVERE
SEE SOUTH ROME MAP
TEMPIETTO & SAN PIETRO IN MONTORIO
To Termini
VIA COLA DI RIENZO
VIA CRESCENZIO
VIA CICERONE
LUNGOTEVERE IN AUGUSTA
LUNGOTEVERE CASTELLO
LUNGOTEVERE PRATI
LUNGOTEVERE DEI MELLINI
CONCILIAZIONE
BORGO S. SPIRITO
BORGO S. ANGELO
L. TOR DI NONA
VIA DEI CORONARI
CORSO VITTORIO EMANUELE II
VIA GIULIA
LUNGOTEVERE DEI TEBALDI
LUNGOTEVERE GIANICOLENSE
LUNGOTEVERE DELLA FARNESINA
L. RAFFAELLO SANZIO
L. DEI VALLATI
L. ANGUILLARA
VIA DELLA LUNGARA
VIA GARIBALDI
VIALE TRASTEVERE
PONTE SISTO
PONTE GARIBALDI
PONTE MAZZINI
PONTE PR. AMADEO
PONTE UMBERTO I
PONTE VITT. EMANUELE II
PONTE REG. MARGHERITA

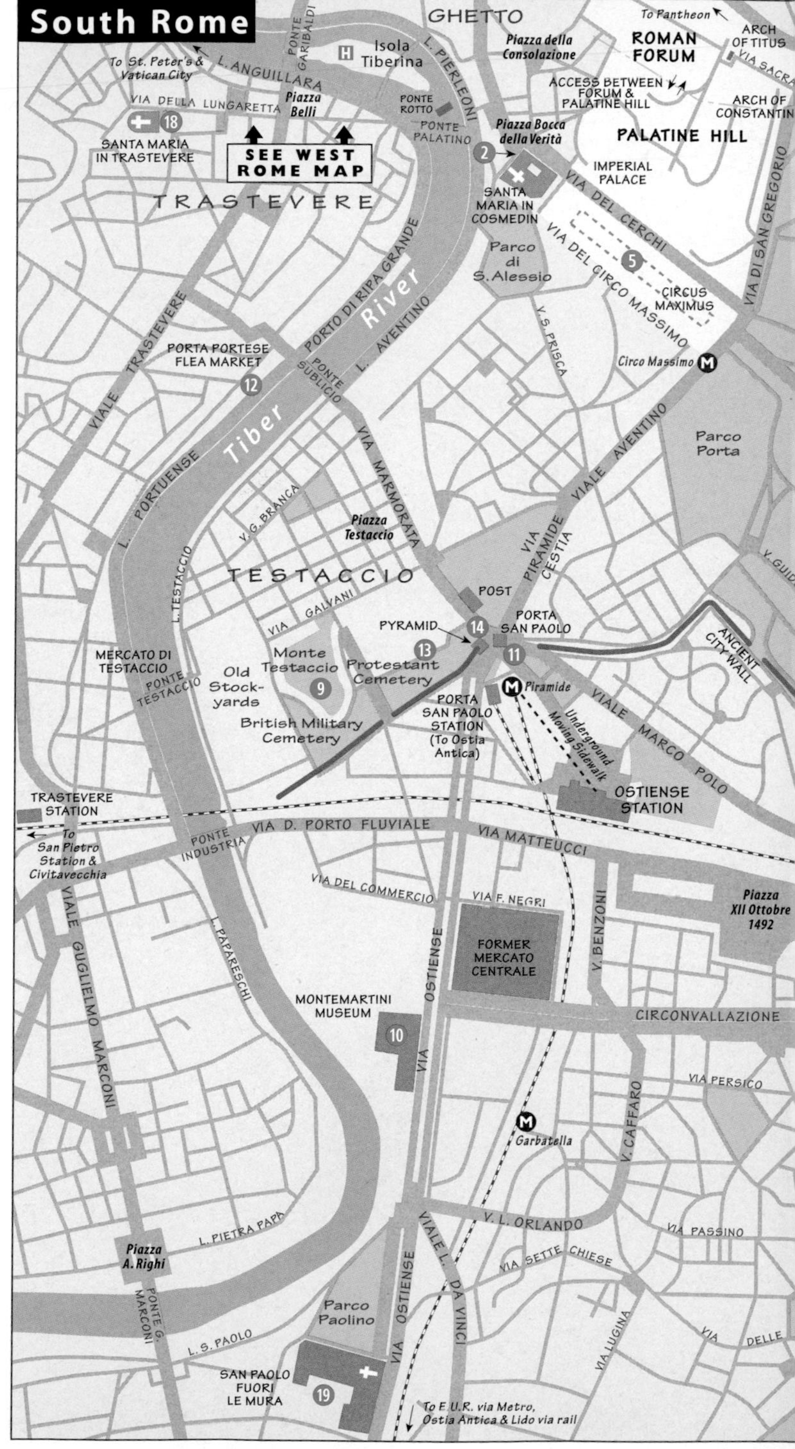

South Rome
GHETTO
To Pantheon
ARCH OF TITUS
ROMAN FORUM
VIA SACRA
Piazza della Consolazione
ACCESS BETWEEN FORUM & PALATINE HILL
ARCH OF CONSTANTIN
PALATINE HILL
Piazza Bocca della Verità
IMPERIAL PALACE
To St. Peter's & Vatican City
L. ANGUILLARA
PONTE GARIBALDI
Isola Tiberina
L. PIERLEONI
VIA DELLA LUNGARETTA
Piazza Belli
PONTE ROTTO
PONTE PALATINO
SANTA MARIA IN TRASTEVERE
SEE WEST ROME MAP
TRASTEVERE
SANTA MARIA IN COSMEDIN
VIA DEL CERCHI
VIA DI SAN GREGORIO
Parco di S. Alessio
VIA DEL CIRCO MASSIMO
CIRCUS MAXIMUS
VIALE TRASTEVERE
PORTO DI RIPA GRANDE
River
L. AVENTINO
V. S. PRISCA
PORTA PORTESE FLEA MARKET
PONTE SUBLICIO
Circo Massimo
Tiber
L. PORTUENSE
VIA MARMORATA
VIALE AVENTINO
Parco Porta
V. G. BRANCA
Piazza Testaccio
VIA PIRAMIDE CESTIA
V. GUIDO
L. TESTACCIO
TESTACCIO
POST
VIA GALVANI
PYRAMID
PORTA SAN PAOLO
ANCIENT CITY WALL
MERCATO DI TESTACCIO
Monte Testaccio
Protestant Cemetery
PONTE TESTACCIO
Old Stock-yards
Piramide
VIALE MARCO POLO
British Military Cemetery
PORTA SAN PAOLO STATION (To Ostia Antica)
Underground Moving Sidewalk
TRASTEVERE STATION
OSTIENSE STATION
To San Pietro Station & Civitavecchia
PONTE INDUSTRIA
VIA D. PORTO FLUVIALE
VIA MATTEUCCI
VIA DEL COMMERCIO
VIA F. NEGRI
VIALE GUGLIELMO MARCONI
Piazza XII Ottobre 1492
L. PAPARESCHI
VIA OSTIENSE
FORMER MERCATO CENTRALE
V. BENZONI
MONTEMARTINI MUSEUM
CIRCONVALLAZIONE
VIA PERSICO
V. CAFFARO
Garbatella
V. L. ORLANDO
L. PIETRA PAPA
VIA PASSINO
Piazza A. Righi
VIA SETTE CHIESE
VIALE L. DA VINCI
VIA OSTIENSE
PONTE G. MARCONI
Parco Paolino
VIA LUGINA
VIA DELLE
L. S. PAOLO
SAN PAOLO FUORI LE MURA
To E.U.R. via Metro, Ostia Antica & Lido via rail
2
5
12
14
13
11
9
10
18
19

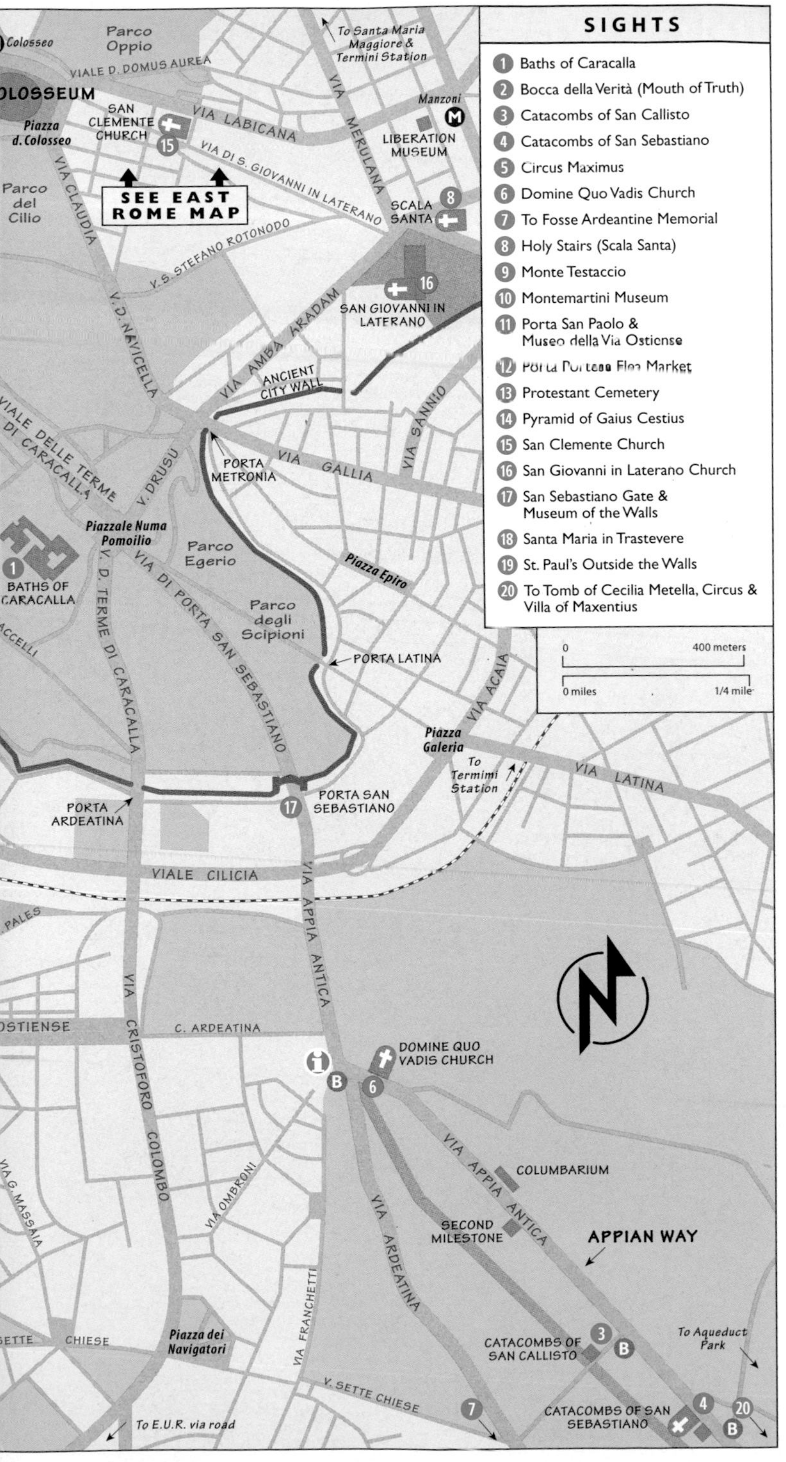
SIGHTS
1 Baths of Caracalla
2 Bocca della Verità (Mouth of Truth)
3 Catacombs of San Callisto
4 Catacombs of San Sebastiano
5 Circus Maximus
6 Domine Quo Vadis Church
7 To Fosse Ardeantine Memorial
8 Holy Stairs (Scala Santa)
9 Monte Testaccio
10 Montemartini Museum
11 Porta San Paolo & Museo della Via Ostiense
12 Porta Portese Flea Market
13 Protestant Cemetery
14 Pyramid of Gaius Cestius
15 San Clemente Church
16 San Giovanni in Laterano Church
17 San Sebastiano Gate & Museum of the Walls
18 Santa Maria in Trastevere
19 St. Paul's Outside the Walls
20 To Tomb of Cecilia Metella, Circus & Villa of Maxentius
0 400 meters
0 miles 1/4 mile
Colosseo
Parco Oppio
To Santa Maria Maggiore & Termini Station
VIALE D. DOMUS AUREA
COLOSSEUM
SAN CLEMENTE CHURCH
VIA LABICANA
Manzoni
LIBERATION MUSEUM
Piazza d. Colosseo
VIA DI S. GIOVANNI IN LATERANO
VIA MERULANA
Parco del Cilio
SEE EAST ROME MAP
SCALA SANTA
VIA CLAUDIA
V. S. STEFANO ROTONODO
SAN GIOVANNI IN LATERANO
VIA AMBA ARADAM
V. D. NAVICELLA
ANCIENT CITY WALL
VIA SANNIO
VIALE DELLE TERME DI CARACALLA
PORTA METRONIA
VIA GALLIA
V. DRUSO
Piazzale Numa Pomoilio
Parco Egerio
Piazza Epiro
BATHS OF CARACALLA
VIA DI PORTA SAN SEBASTIANO
Parco degli Scipioni
V. D. TERME DI CARACALLA
PORTA LATINA
VIA ACAIA
Piazza Galeria
To Termini Station
VIA LATINA
PORTA ARDEATINA
PORTA SAN SEBASTIANO
VIALE CILICIA
V. PALES
VIA APPIA ANTICA
OSTIENSE
C. ARDEATINA
VIA CRISTOFORO COLOMBO
DOMINE QUO VADIS CHURCH
VIA APPIA ANTICA
COLUMBARIUM
VIA G. MASSAIA
VIA OMBRONI
VIA ARDEATINA
SECOND MILESTONE
APPIAN WAY
VIA FRANCHETTI
SETTE CHIESE
Piazza dei Navigatori
CATACOMBS OF SAN CALLISTO
To Aqueduct Park
V. SETTE CHIESE
CATACOMBS OF SAN SEBASTIANO
To E.U.R. via road

Italy
SWITZERLAND
LIECH.
Vaduz
Bern
Luzern
Lake Luzern
Murten
Fribourg
Spiez
Interlaken
Lausanne
Lake Geneva
Montreux
Gimmelwald
BERNER OBERLAND
GLACIER EXPRESS
TICINO
St. Moritz
Samedan
Pontresina
BERNINA EXPRESS
Glurns
BRENNER PASS
Vipiteno
REIFENSTEIN CASTLE
Merano
Castelrotto
Bolzano
TRENTINO ALTO ADIGE
Trento
Riva
Saas Fee
Domodossola
Locarno
Lago di Como
MATTERHORN
Zermatt
Lugano
Menaggio
Varenna
Bellagio
Chamonix
AIGUILLE DU MIDI
MONT BLANC
Breuil-Cervinia
Courmayeur
Pré-St Didier
Aosta
AOSTA
Lago Maggiore
Lago Lugano
Stresa
Chiasso
Como
Lecco
Lago d'Iseo
Lago di Garda
Bergamo
Orio al Serio
Lago di Orta
Malpensa
Monza
Linate
Milan
Brescia
Sirmione
Verona
Vicenza
Desenzano
Catullo
LOMBARDY
Mantua
Adige
Modane
Po
Turin
Cremona
Piacenza
Po
PIEDMONT
LE MARCHE
EMILIA
Parma
Modena
Asti
Alba
Barolo
Briançon
Santa Margherita Ligure
Reggio Emilia
ROMAGNA
Bologna
MONTE VISO
Cuneo
Genoa
LIGURIA
Camogli
SAN FRUTTUOSO
Portofino
Sestri Levante
Levanto
Monterosso
Vernazza
CINQUE TERRE
ITALY
APUAN ALPS
COLLE DI TONDA PASS
Savona
Finale
La Spezia
Carrara
Alassio
Porto-venere
Pistoia
Amerigo Vespucci
FRANCE
Viareggio
Lucca
Florence
Ventimiglia
MONACO
Pisa
Arno
CHIANTI
Nice
Villefranche
Antibes
Cannes
Galileo
Ligurian Sea
Livorno
San Gimignano
Volterra
TUSCANY
Siena
St-Tropez
COTE D'AZUR
Capraia
Montalcino
VIA AURELIA
Prombino
Porto-ferraro
Grosseto
Elba
Bastia
Monte Argentario
L'Ile Rousse
To Marseille, France
CORSICA (France)
Tyrrhenian
See Tuscany & Umbria detail map
Ajaccio
Propriano
Mediterranean Sea
Bonifacio
Maddalena
S.Teresa
EMERALD COAST
Asinara
Olbia
Porto Torres
Sassari
SARDINIA (Italy)
GROTTO OF NEPTUNE
A-1
A-3
A-2
A-12
A-9
A-40
A-5
A-4
A-8
A2
A-43
A-32
A-7
A-21
A-6
A-26
A-15
A-13
A-22
A-10
A-11
S-68
S-22

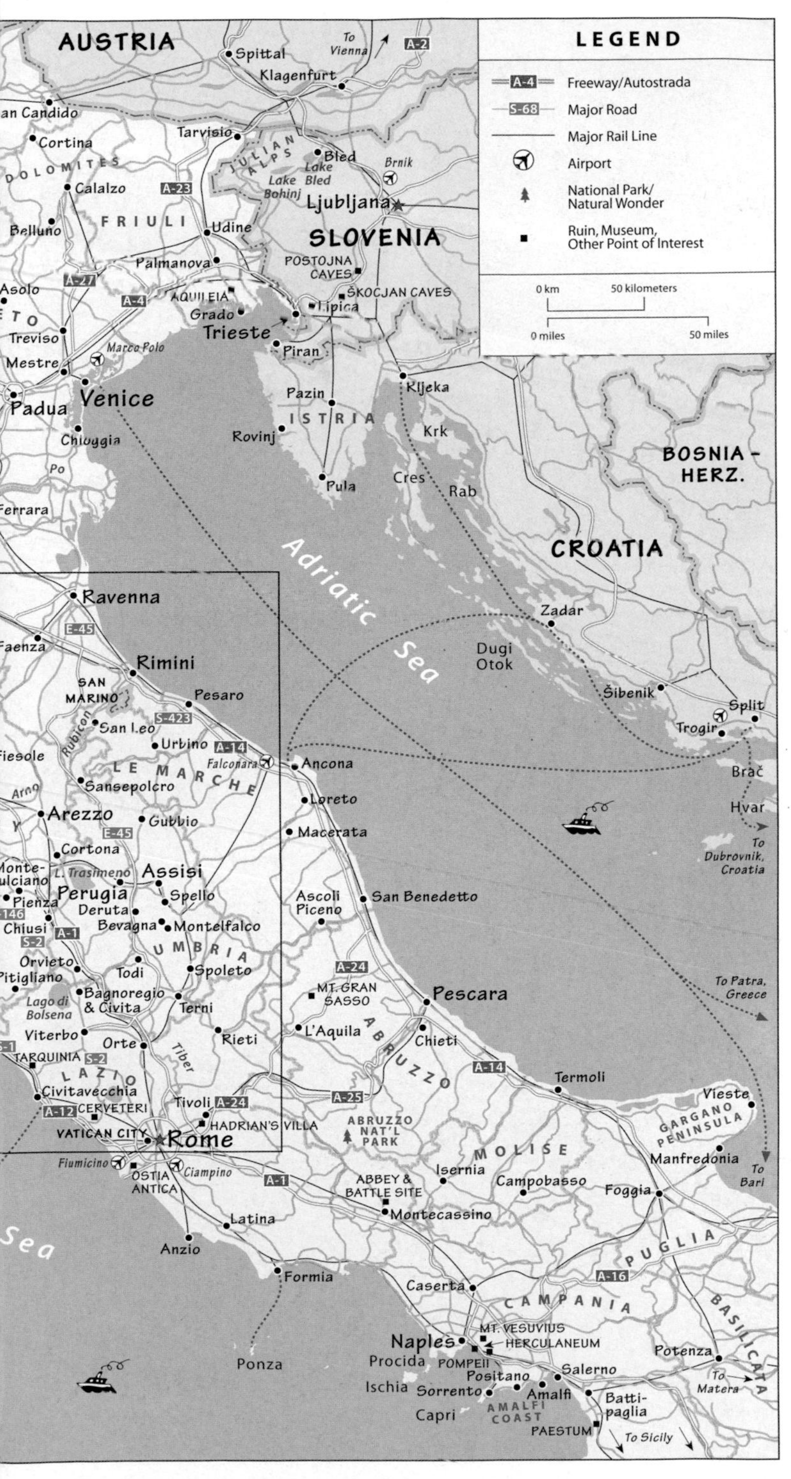

AUSTRIA
LEGEND
A-4 Freeway/Autostrada
S-68 Major Road
Major Rail Line
Airport
National Park/ Natural Wonder
Ruin, Museum, Other Point of Interest
0 km
50 kilometers
0 miles
50 miles
To Vienna
Spittal
Klagenfurt
San Candido
Cortina
DOLOMITES
Calalzo
Belluno
FRIULI
Tarvisio
JULIAN ALPS
Bled
Lake Bled
Lake Bohinj
Brnik
Ljubljana
SLOVENIA
Udine
Palmanova
POSTOJNA CAVES
ŠKOCJAN CAVES
Lipica
AQUILEIA
Grado
Trieste
Piran
Asolo
Treviso
Marco Polo
Mestre
Padua
Venice
Chioggia
Po
Ferrara
Pazin
ISTRIA
Rovinj
Pula
Rijeka
Krk
Cres
Rab
BOSNIA-HERZ.
CROATIA
Adriatic Sea
Zadar
Dugi Otok
Šibenik
Split
Trogir
Brač
Hvar
To Dubrovnik, Croatia
To Patra, Greece
To Bari
Ravenna
Faenza
Rimini
SAN MARINO
Pesaro
Rubicon
San Leo
Urbino
Fiesole
LE MARCHE
Falconara
Ancona
Loreto
Macerata
Arno
Sansepolcro
Arezzo
Gubbio
Cortona
Montepulciano
L. Trasimeno
Assisi
Perugia
Spello
Pienza
Deruta
Bevagna
Montelfalco
Chiusi
UMBRIA
Orvieto
Todi
Spoleto
Pitigliano
Bagnoregio & Civita
Lago di Bolsena
Terni
Viterbo
Orte
Rieti
Tiber
TARQUINIA
LAZIO
Civitavecchia
CERVETERI
Tivoli
HADRIAN'S VILLA
VATICAN CITY
Rome
Fiumicino
Ciampino
OSTIA ANTICA
Ascoli Piceno
San Benedetto
MT. GRAN SASSO
Pescara
L'Aquila
ABRUZZO
Chieti
Termoli
ABRUZZO NAT'L PARK
Vieste
GARGANO PENINSULA
MOLISE
Manfredonia
Isernia
Campobasso
Foggia
ABBEY & BATTLE SITE
Montecassino
Latina
Anzio
Sea
Formia
PUGLIA
Caserta
CAMPANIA
BASILICATA
MT. VESUVIUS
HERCULANEUM
Naples
POMPEII
Procida
Potenza
Ponza
Positano
Salerno
Ischia
Sorrento
Amalfi
To Matera
Battipaglia
Capri
AMALFI COAST
PAESTUM
To Sicily

National Museum of Rome

Roman Forum

Dining near the Pantheon

Rick Steves'®

ROME

2013

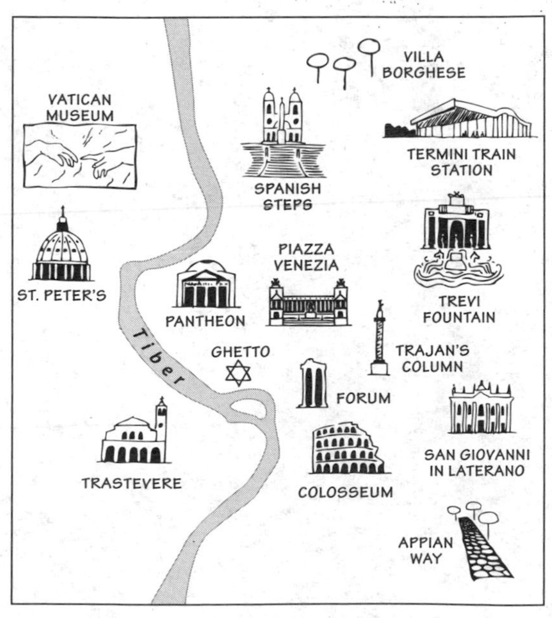

INTRODUCTION

Rome is magnificent and brutal at the same time. It's a showcase of Western civilization, with astonishingly ancient sights and a modern vibrancy. But if you're careless, you'll be run down or pick-pocketed. And with the wrong attitude, you'll be frustrated by the kind of chaos that only an Italian can understand. On my last visit, a cabbie struggling with the traffic said, *"Roma chaos."* I responded, *"Bella chaos."* He agreed.

While Paris is an urban garden, Rome is a magnificent tangled forest. If your hotel provides a comfortable refuge; if you pace yourself; if you accept—and even partake in—the siesta plan; if you're well-organized for sightseeing; and if you protect yourself and your valuables with extra caution and discretion, you'll love it. (And Rome is much easier to live with if you can avoid the mid-summer heat.)

For me, Rome is in a three-way tie with Paris and London as Europe's greatest city. Two thousand years ago the word "Rome" meant civilization itself. Everything was either civilized (part of the Roman Empire, Latin- or Greek-speaking) or barbarian. Today, Rome is Italy's political capital, the capital of Catholicism, and the center of the ancient world, littered with evocative remains. As you peel through its fascinating and jumbled layer you'll find Rome's buildings, cats, laundry, traffic, and 2.7 mill people endlessly entertaining. And then, of course, there ar stupendous sights.

Visit St. Peter's, the greatest church on earth, and Michelangelo's 448-foot-tall dome, the world's tallest. Lear thing about eternity by touring the huge Vatican Museu find the story of creation—bright as the day it was paint restored Sistine Chapel. Do the "Caesar Shuffle" thro Rome's Forum and Colosseum. Savor Europe's mos

Map Legend

Viewpoint	Airport	Tunnel
Entrance	Taxi Stand	Pedestrian Zone
Tourist Info	Tram Stop	Railway
Restroom	Bus Stop	Ferry/Boat Route
Castle	Metro Stop	Tram
Church	Parking	Stairs
Statue/Point of Interest	Mtn. Pass	Walk/Tour Route
	Park	Trail

Use this legend to help you navigate the maps in this book.

building, the Borghese Gallery, and take an early evening "Dolce Vita Stroll" down Via del Corso with Rome's beautiful people. Enjoy an after-dark walk from Campo de' Fiori to the Spanish Steps, lacing together Rome's Baroque and bubbly nightspots. Dine well at least once.

About This Book

Rick Steves' Rome 2013 is a personal tour guide in your pocket. Better yet, it's actually two tour guides in your pocket: The co-author of this book is Gene Openshaw. Since our first "Europe through the gutter" trip together as high school buddies in the 1970s, Gene and I have been exploring the wonders of the Old World. An inquisitive historian and lover of European culture, Gene wrote most of this book's self-guided museum tours and neighborhood walks. Together, Gene and I keep this book current (though for simplicity, from this point "we" will shed our respective egos and become "I").

In this book, you'll find the following chapters:

Orientation to Rome includes specifics on public transportation, helpful hints, local tour options, easy-to-read maps, and tourist information. The "Planning Your Time" section suggests a -chedule for how to best use your limited time.

Sights in Rome describes the top attractions and includes -, hours, location, and contact information.

The **Self-Guided Walks and Tours** lead you through the -of Rome, connecting the great monuments and atmospheric - You'll tour the Colosseum, Roman Forum, Palatine Hill, Forum, Capitoline Museums, and the Pantheon. You'll -ilgrimage churches, including the grandest of all—St. -'ll see the Vatican Museum, Borghese Gallery, National - Rome, St. Peter-in-Chains Church, and Baths of

Key to This Book

Updates

This book is updated every year—but once you pin down Italy, it wiggles. For the latest, visit www.ricksteves.com/update. For a valuable list of reports and experiences—good and bad—from fellow travelers, check www.ricksteves.com/feedback.

Abbreviations and Times

I use the following symbols and abbreviations in this book:

Sights are rated:

▲▲▲	**Don't miss**
▲▲	**Try hard to see**
▲	**Worthwhile if you can make it**
No rating	**Worth knowing about**

Tourist information offices are abbreviated as **TIs**, and bathrooms are **WCs.** To categorize accommodations, I use a **Sleep Code** (described on page 328).

Like Europe, this book uses the **24-hour clock.** It's the same through 12:00 noon, then keep going: 13:00, 14:00, and so on. For anything over 12, subtract 12 and add p.m. (14:00 is 2:00 p.m.).

When giving **opening times,** I include both peak season and off-season hours if they differ. So, if a museum is listed as "May-Oct daily 9:00-16:00," it should be open from 9:00 a.m. until 4:00 p.m. from the first day of May until the last day of October (but expect exceptions).

If you see a ✪ symbol near a sight listing, it means that sight is described in far greater detail elsewhere—either with its own self-guided tour, or as part of a self-guided walk.

For **transit** or **tour departures,** I first list the frequency, then the duration. So, a train connection listed as "2/hour, 1.5 hours" departs twice each hour and the journey lasts an hour and a half.

Diocletian. You'll explore Trastevere, the heart of the crusty, colorful neighborhood across the river; learn about the Jewish Ghetto, the city's medieval Jewish quarter; and take a spin on the ancient Appian Way.

Sleeping in Rome describes my favorite hotels, from good-value deals to cushy splurges, mainly in several convenient (and for Rome, relatively quiet) neighborhoods near the sights.

Eating in Rome serves up a range of options, from inexpensive cafés to fancy restaurants.

Rome with Children includes my top recommendations for keeping your kids (and you) happy in Rome.

Shopping in Rome gives you tips for shopping painlessly and enjoyably, without letting it overwhelm your vacation or ruin your budget.

Nightlife in Rome is your guide to fun, including concerts, nightclubs, and my Dolce Vita Stroll.

Rome Connections lays the groundwork for your smooth arrival and departure, covering transportation by train, bus, car, plane, and cruise ship, with detailed information on Rome's two airports (Fiumicino and Ciampino) and its two train stations (the main Termini station and smaller Tiburtina).

Day Trips cover nearby sights: Ostia Antica (includes self-guided tour), Tivoli, Naples, and Pompeii.

The **Roman History** chapter takes you on a whirlwind tour through the ages, covering three millennia from ancient Rome to the city today.

The **appendix** is a traveler's tool kit, with telephone tips, useful phone numbers, the basics on transportation in Italy, recommended books and films, a festival list, a climate chart, a handy packing checklist, a hotel reservation form, and Italian survival phrases.

Browse through this book and choose your favorite sights. Then have a great trip! Traveling like a temporary local, you'll get the absolute most out of every mile, minute, and dollar. As you visit places I know and love, I'm happy you'll be meeting my favorite Romans.

Planning

This section will help you get started planning your trip—with notes on trip costs, when to go, and things to know before you take off.

Travel Smart

Many people visit Rome and think it's a chaotic mess. They feel that any attempt at efficient travel is futile. This is dead wrong—and expensive. Rome, which seems as orderly as spilled spaghetti, actually functions well. Only those who understand this and travel smart can enjoy Rome on a budget.

This book can save you lots of time and money. But to have an "A" trip, you need to be an "A" student. Read it all before your trip, noting holidays, specifics on sights, and days when sights are closed. For instance, to see the Borghese Gallery, you must reserve ahead. If you go to the Vatican Museum on a Sunday, you'll run smack into closed doors, or—if it's the last Sunday of the month—huge crowds. You can wait an hour to buy a ticket at the Colosseum, or save time by ordering your ticket online or at the nearby Palatine Hill. Day-tripping to Ostia Antica on Monday is bad news. A smart trip is a puzzle—a fun, doable, and worthwhile challenge.

Be sure to mix intense and relaxed periods in your itinerary. Every trip—and every traveler—needs slack time (picnics, laundry, people-watching, and so on). Pace yourself. Assume you will return.

Get online at Internet cafés or your hotel, and buy a phone card or carry a mobile phone: You can find tourist information, learn the latest on sights (special events, English tour schedule, etc.), book tickets and tours, make reservations, reconfirm hotels, research transportation connections, and keep in touch with your loved ones.

Enjoy the friendliness of the Romans. Connect with the culture. Set up your own quest for the best piazza, church facade, or gelato. Slow down and be open to unexpected experiences. Ask questions—most locals are eager to point you in their idea of the right direction. Keep a notepad in your pocket for organizing your thoughts. Wear your money belt, learn the currency, and figure out how to estimate prices in dollars. Those who expect to travel smart, do.

Trip Costs

Six components make up your trip costs: airfare, surface transportation, room and board, sightseeing/entertainment, shopping/miscellany, and gelato.

Airfare: A basic round-trip US-to-Rome (or even cheaper, to Milan) flight should cost, on average, about $1,000-1,800 total, depending on where you fly from and when (cheaper in winter).

Surface Transportation: For a typical one-week visit, allow $60 to $100 for taxis (which can be shared by up to four people); if you opt for buses and the Metro, figure about $25 per person. The cost of round-trip transportation to day-trip destinations ranges from minimal (a few dollars to get to Tivoli or Ostia Antica) to affordable ($60 for second-class train tickets for a day trip to Naples and Pompeii). For a one-way trip between Rome's main airport and the city center, allow $20 per person by train or about $65 by taxi (can be shared by up to 4 people). For information on train travel and car rental, see the appendix.

Room and Board: You can manage comfortably in Rome in 2013 on $140 a day per person for room and board. This allows $15 for lunch, $25 for dinner, and $100 for lodging (based on two people splitting the cost of a $200 double room that includes breakfast). If you've got more money, I've listed great ways to spend it. Students and tightwads can enjoy Rome for as little as $65 a day ($35 for a hostel bed, $30 for meals and snacks).

Sightseeing and Entertainment: Figure about $17-21 per

Rome Almanac

Population: Approximately 2.7 million people

Currency: Euro (€)

Nickname: The Eternal City

City Layout: Rome, the capital of Italy, is divided into 22 rioni (districts). Of the famous seven hills of Rome, you're most likely to see Palatine Hill (birthplace of the legendary founders of the city, Romulus and Remus) and Capitoline Hill (topped by museums and a Michelangelo-designed square).

Best Viewpoints: From the rooftop of the Victor Emmanuel Monument (via the Rome from the Sky elevator) and the top of the dome of St. Peter's Basilica.

Best Strolls: Two major thoroughfares are opened to pedestrians and closed to traffic at certain times: Via del Corso in the early evening (Mon-Sat around 17:00-19:00, earlier afternoon on Sun) and Via dei Fori Imperiali on Sunday evening only.

Tourist Tracks: The Colosseum attracts 3.9 million visitors every year. About €3,000 is collected from the Trevi Fountain daily.

Culture Count: Rome is composed almost entirely of indigenous Italians; only 9.5 percent of its residents are immigrants, mostly from Poland, Ukraine, and Albania. Rome's population is largely Roman Catholic (90 percent).

Average Roman: The average Roman is 43 years old, has 1.3 children, and will live until the age of 80. Romans consume enough wine to average one bottle per person per day.

major sight (Colosseum, Vatican Museum), $2 for minor ones (church treasuries), and $30 for splurge experiences (such as concerts). An overall average of $20 per day works for most people. Don't skimp here. After all, this category is the driving force behind your trip—you came to sightsee, enjoy, and experience Rome.

Shopping and Miscellany: Figure $2 per postcard and $6 per coffee, soft drink, and gelato. Shopping can vary in cost from nearly nothing to a small fortune. Good budget travelers find that this category has little to do with assembling a trip full of lifelong and wonderful memories.

When to Go

Rome's best travel months (also busiest and most expensive) are April, May, June, September, October, and early November. These months combine the convenience of peak season with pleasant weather.

The most grueling thing about travel in Rome is the summer heat in July and August, when temperatures can soar to the high 90s and pricier hotels discount their rooms. Fortunately air-conditioning is the norm in all but the cheapest hotels (though it's generally available only from June through September).

Spring and fall can be cool, and many hotels do not turn on their heat. Rome is fine in winter—cold and crisp with temperatures in the 40s and 50s (for more information, see the climate chart in the appendix). Off-season has none of the sweat and stress of the tourist season, but sights may have shorter hours, lunchtime breaks, and fewer activities. Confirm your sightseeing plans locally, especially when traveling off-season.

Know Before You Go

Your trip is more likely to go smoothly if you plan ahead. Check this list of things to arrange while you're still at home.

You need a **passport**—but no visa or shots—to travel in Italy. You may be denied entry into certain European countries if your passport is due to expire within three to six months of your ticketed date of return. Get it renewed if you'll be cutting it close. It can take up to six weeks to get or renew a passport (for more on passports, see www.travel.state.gov). Pack a photocopy of your passport in your luggage in case the original is lost or stolen.

Book rooms in advance, particularly during peak season (spring and fall) and any major **holidays** (see page 491).

The **Borghese Gallery** requires advance reservations; book at least a week ahead in high season (see page 241 for instructions). At the **Vatican Museum,** lines are extremely long—skip the ticket-buying line altogether by reserving an entry time on their website (see page 207).

Call your **debit and credit card companies** to let them know the countries you'll be visiting, ask about fees, request your PIN (it will be mailed to you), and more. See page 12 for details.

If you plan to hire a **local guide,** reserve ahead by email. Popular guides can get booked up.

Do your homework if you want to buy **travel insurance.** Compare the cost of the insurance to the likelihood of your using it and your potential loss if something goes wrong. Also, check whether your existing insurance (health, homeowners, or renters) covers you and your possessions overseas. For more information, see www.ricksteves.com/insurance.

Check the **Rick Steves guidebook updates** page for the latest news about Rome (www.ricksteves.com/update).

If you're bringing a **mobile device,** download any apps you might want to use on the road, such as translators, maps, and transit schedules. Be sure to check out **Rick Steves Audio Europe,**

Rome vs. Milan: A Classic Squabble

In Italy, the North and South bicker about each other, hurling barbs, quips, and generalizations. All the classic North/South traits can be applied to Rome (the government capital) and Milan (the business capital). Although the differences have become less pronounced lately, the sniping continues.

The Milanese say the Romans are lazy. Roman government jobs come with short hours—cut even shorter by too many coffee breaks, three-hour lunches, chats with colleagues, and phone calls to friends and relatives. Milanese contend that *Roma ladrona* (Rome the big thief) is a parasite that lives off the taxes of people up North. Until recently, there was a strong Milan-based movement seriously promoting secession from the South.

Romans, meanwhile, dismiss the Milanese as uptight workaholics with nothing else to live for—gray like their foggy city. Romans do admit that in Milan, job opportunities are better and based on merit. And the Milanese grudgingly concede that the Romans have a gift for enjoying life.

While Rome is more of a family city, Milan is the place for high-powered singles on the career fast track. Milanese yuppies

featuring audio tours of Rome's major sights, hours of travel interviews on Rome, and more (via www.ricksteves.com/audioeurope, iTunes, Google Play, or the Rick Steves Audio Europe smartphone app; for details, see page 27).

If you're planning on **renting a car** in Italy, you'll need your driver's license. An International Driving Permit is required (see page 481). Driving is prohibited in some city centers; obey the signage or risk getting a huge fine (see page 484).

If you're taking an **overnight train** (especially between Rome and Paris), and you need a couchette *(cuccetta)* or sleeper—and you *must* leave on a certain day—consider booking it in advance through a US agent (such as www.raileurope.com), even though it may cost more than buying it in Italy. Other Italian trains, like the high-speed ES trains, require a seat reservation, but it's usually possible to make arrangements in Italy just a few days ahead. (For more on train travel, see the Rome Connections chapter and www.ricksteves.com/rail.)

Because **airline carry-on restrictions** are always changing, visit the Transportation Security Administration's website

mix with each other...not the city's long-time residents. Milan is seen as inward-looking and wary of foreigners, and Rome as fun-loving, tolerant, and friendly. In Milan, bureaucracy (like social services) works logically and efficiently, while in Rome, accomplishing even small chores can be exasperating. In Rome, everything—from finding a babysitter to buying a car—is done through friends. In Milan, while people are not as willing to discuss their personal matters, they are generous and active in charity work.

Milanese find Romans vulgar. The Roman dialect is considered one of the coarsest in the country. Much as they try, Milanese just can't say, "Damn your dead relatives" quite as effectively as the Romans. Still, they enjoy Roman comedians and love to imitate the accent.

The Milanese feel that Rome is dirty and Roman driving nerve-wracking. But despite the craziness, Rome maintains a genuine village feel. People share family news with their neighborhood grocer. Milan lacks people-friendly piazzas, and entertainment comes at a high price. But in Rome, *la dolce vita* is as close as the nearest square, and a full moon is enjoyed by all.

(www.tsa.gov/travelers) for an up-to-date list of what you can bring on the plane with you...and what you have to check.

Practicalities

Emergency and Medical Help: In Italy, dial 113 for English-speaking police help. To summon an ambulance, call 118. If you get sick, do as the Romans do and go to a pharmacist for advice. Or ask at your hotel for help. They'll know the nearest medical and emergency services.

Theft or Loss: To replace a passport, you'll need to go in person to an embassy (see page 469). If your credit and debit cards disappear, cancel and replace them (see "Damage Control for Lost Cards" on page 13). File a police report, either on the spot or within a day; it's required if you submit an insurance claim for lost or stolen railpasses or travel gear, and can help with replacing your passport or credit and debit cards. For more information, see www.ricksteves.com/help. Precautionary measures can minimize the effects of loss—back up your photos and other files frequently.

Time Zones: Italy, like most of continental Europe, is generally six/nine hours ahead of the East/West Coasts of the US. The exceptions are the beginning and end of Daylight Saving Time: Europe "springs forward" the last Sunday in March (two weeks after most of North America) and "falls back" the last Sunday in October (one week before North America). For a handy online converter, try www.timeanddate.com/worldclock.

Business Hours: Traditionally, Italy uses the siesta plan, though many businesses have adopted the government's recommended 8:00 to 14:00 workday. In tourist areas, shops are open longer. People usually work from about 9:00 to 13:00 and from 15:30 to 19:00. Stores are usually closed on Sunday, and often on Monday. Banking hours are generally Monday through Friday 8:30 to 13:30 and 15:30 to 16:30, but they can vary wildly.

Saturdays are virtually weekdays, with earlier closing hours. Sundays have the same pros and cons as they do in the US: Sightseeing attractions are generally open, while shops and banks are closed. City traffic is light. Rowdy evenings are rare on Sundays.

Watt's Up? Europe's electrical system is 220 volts, instead of North America's 110 volts. Most newer electronics (such as laptops, battery chargers, and hair dryers) convert automatically, so you won't need a converter, but you will need an adapter plug with two round prongs, sold inexpensively at travel stores in the US. Avoid bringing older appliances that don't automatically convert voltage; instead, buy a cheap replacement in Europe.

Discounts: Reduced price tickets *(ridotto)* are not listed in this book. However, many sights offer discounts for youths (up to age 18), students (with proper identification cards, www.isic.org), families, seniors (loosely defined as retirees or those willing to call themselves a senior), and groups of 10 or more. While youth and senior discounts are technically only for EU residents, Americans who ask sometimes get the same discounts.

Money

This section offers advice on how to pay for purchases on your trip (including getting cash from ATMs and paying with plastic), dealing with lost or stolen cards, VAT (sales tax) refunds, and tipping.

What to Bring

Bring both a credit card and a debit card. You'll use the debit card at cash machines (ATMs) to withdraw local cash for most purchases, and the credit card to pay for larger items. Some travelers carry a third card, in case one gets demagnetized or eaten by a temperamental machine.

Exchange Rate

1 euro (€) = about $1.40

To convert prices in euros to dollars, add about 40 percent: €20 = about $28, €50 = about $70. (Check www.oanda.com for the latest exchange rates.) Just like the dollar, one euro is broken down into 100 cents. You'll find coins ranging from €0.01 to €2, and bills ranging from €5 to €500.

Look carefully at any €2 coin you get in change. Some unscrupulous merchants give out similar-looking gold-rimmed old 500-lire coins (worth $0) instead of €2 coins (worth $2.80). You have been warned!

For an emergency reserve, bring several hundred dollars in hard cash in easy-to-exchange $20 bills. Avoid using currency exchange booths (lousy rates and/or outrageous fees); if you have foreign currency to exchange, take it to a bank. Don't use traveler's checks—they're not worth the fees and long waits at slow banks.

Cash

Cash is just as desirable in Europe as it is at home. Small European businesses (hotels, restaurants, shops, etc.) prefer that you pay your bills with cash. Some vendors will charge you extra for using a credit card, and some won't take credit cards at all. Cash is the best—and sometimes only—way to pay for bus fare, taxis, and local guides.

Throughout Italy, ATMs (which locals call a *bancomat*) are the standard way for travelers to get cash. Most ATMs in Italy are located outside of a bank. Try to use the ATM when the branch is open; if your card is munched by a machine, you can immediately go inside for help. Stay away from "independent" ATMs such as Travelex, Euronet, or Forex, which charge huge commissions and have terrible exchange rates.

To withdraw money from an ATM, you'll need a debit card (ideally with a Visa or MasterCard logo for maximum usability), plus a PIN code. Know your PIN code in numbers; there are only numbers—no letters—on European keypads. For security, it's best to shield the keypad when entering your PIN at an ATM. Although you can use a credit card for ATM transactions, it's generally more expensive (and only makes sense in an emergency) because it's considered a cash advance rather than a withdrawal.

When using an ATM, try to withdraw large sums of money to reduce the number of per-transaction bank fees you'll pay. If the machine refuses your request, try again and select a smaller amount (some cash machines limit the amount you can withdraw—don't take it personally). If that doesn't work, try a different machine. Also, be aware that some ATMs will tell you to take your cash within 30 seconds; if you don't, your cash will be sucked back into the machine...and you'll have a hassle trying to get it from the bank.

It's easier to pay for purchases with smaller bills; if the ATM gives you big bills, try to break them at a bank or larger store.

To keep your cash safe, wear a money belt—a pouch with a strap that you buckle around your waist like a belt, and tuck under your clothes.

Keep your cash, credit cards, and passport secure in your money belt, and carry only a day's spending money in your front pocket. Pickpockets target tourists. A money belt provides peace of mind, allowing you to carry lots of cash safely. Don't waste time every few days tracking down a cash machine—withdraw a week's worth of money, stuff it in your money belt, and travel!

Credit and Debit Cards

For purchases, Visa and MasterCard are more commonly accepted than American Express. Just like at home, credit or debit cards work easily at larger hotels, restaurants, and shops. I typically use my debit card to withdraw cash to pay for most purchases. I use my credit card only in a few specific situations: to book hotel reservations by phone, to make major purchases (such as car rentals, plane tickets, and long hotel stays), and to pay for things near the end of my trip (to avoid another visit to the ATM). While you could use a debit card to make most large purchases, using a credit card offers a greater degree of fraud protection (because debit cards draw funds directly from your account).

Ask Your Credit- or Debit-Card Company: Before your trip, contact the company that issued your debit or credit cards.

• Confirm your card will work overseas, and alert them that you'll be using it in Europe; otherwise, they may deny transactions if they perceive unusual spending patterns.

• Ask for the specifics on transaction **fees.** When you use your credit or debit card—either for purchases or ATM withdrawals—you'll often be charged additional "international transaction" fees of up to 3 percent (1 percent is normal) plus $5 per transaction. If your card's fees are too high, consider getting a card just for your trip: Capital One (credit cards only, www.capitalone.com) and most credit unions have low-to-no international fees.

• If you plan to withdraw cash from ATMs, confirm your daily **withdrawal limit** (€300 is usually the maximum), and if necessary, ask your bank to adjust it (withdrawal limits are set by your bank, but foreign banks or ATMs often also set maximum withdrawal amounts). Some travelers prefer a high limit that allows them to take out more cash at each ATM stop, while others prefer to set a lower limit in case their card is stolen.

• Get your bank's **emergency phone number** in the US (but not its 800 number) to call collect if you have a problem.

• Ask for your credit card's **PIN** in case you encounter Europe's "chip-and-PIN" system; since they're unlikely to tell you your PIN over the phone, allow time for the bank to mail it to you.

Chip and PIN: If your card is declined for a purchase in Europe, it may be because of chip and PIN, which requires cardholders to punch in a PIN instead of signing a receipt. While chip and PIN is not yet common in Italy, much of Europe is adopting it. Some merchants rely on it exclusively. When you're using your card, if you're prompted to enter your PIN but don't know it, ask if the cashier can swipe your card and print a receipt for you to sign instead; if not, just pay cash. You're most likely to encounter chip and PIN at automated payment machines, such as those at train and subway stations, toll roads, parking garages, luggage lockers, bike-rental kiosks, and self-serve gas pumps. If a machine won't take your card, look for a cashier nearby who can make your card work, or see if one of the machines takes cash.

Those who are concerned can apply for a chip card in the US (though I think it's overkill). The best of the lot is the no-annual-fee GlobeTrek Visa, offered by Andrews Federal Credit Union in Maryland (open to all US residents; see www.andrewsfcu.org). Less desirable options are Travelex's prepaid Cash Passport card (requires $250 minimum to preload with pounds or euros, comes with a bad exchange rate, and works only at places that accept MasterCard) or the chip cards offered by major US banks such as Chase, Citi, Bank of America, US Bank, and Wells Fargo (require a hefty annual fee and don't always work in offline transactions).

Dynamic Currency Conversion: If merchants offer to convert your purchase price into dollars (called dynamic currency conversion, or DCC), refuse this "service." You'll pay even more in fees for the expensive convenience of seeing your charge in dollars.

Damage Control for Lost Cards

If you lose your credit, debit, or ATM card, you can stop people from using your card by reporting the loss immediately to the respective global customer-assistance centers. Call these 24-hour US numbers collect: Visa (tel. 303/967-1096), MasterCard (tel. 636/722-7111), and American Express (tel. 623/492-8427). European toll-free numbers (listed by country) can also be found at the websites for Visa and MasterCard.

At a minimum, you'll need to know the name of the financial institution that issued you the card, along with the type of card (classic, platinum, or whatever). Providing the following information allows for a quicker cancellation of your missing card: full card number, whether you are the primary or secondary cardholder, the cardholder's name exactly as printed on the card, billing address, home phone number, circumstances of the loss or theft, and identification verification (your birth date, your mother's maiden name, or your Social Security number—memorize this, don't carry a copy). If you are the secondary cardholder, you'll also need to provide the primary cardholder's identification-verification details. You can generally receive a temporary card within two or three business days in Europe (see www.ricksteves.com/help for more).

If you report your loss within two days, you typically won't be responsible for any unauthorized transactions on your account, although many banks charge a liability fee of $50.

Tipping

Tipping in Italy isn't as automatic and generous as it is in the US, but for special service, tips are appreciated, if not expected. As in the US, the proper amount depends on your resources, tipping philosophy, and the circumstances, but some general guidelines apply.

Restaurants: The "service" charge *(servizio)* is generally already included in your bill. If you're pleased with the service, you can round up the bill by a euro or two per person (though some Italians don't add this additional tip). For more on tipping in restaurants, see page 345.

Taxis: To tip the cabbie, round up. For a typical ride, round up to the next euro on the fare (to pay a €4.50 fare, give €5). If the cabbie hauls your bags and zips you to the airport to help you catch your flight, you might want to toss in a little more. But if you feel like you're being driven in circles or otherwise ripped off, skip the tip.

Special Services: Tour guides at sights sometimes hold out their hands for tips after they give their spiel. If I've already paid for the tour, I don't tip extra, unless they've really impressed me. At hotels, if you let the porter carry your luggage, it's polite to give them a euro for each bag (another reason to pack light). If you like to tip maids, leave a euro per overnight at the end of your stay.

In general, if someone in the service industry does a super job for you, a small tip (the equivalent of a euro or two) is appropriate...but not required.

When in doubt, ask. If you're not sure whether (or how much) to tip for a service, ask your hotelier or the TI; they'll fill you in on how it's done on their turf.

Getting a VAT Refund

Wrapped into the purchase price of your Italian souvenirs is a Value-Added Tax (VAT) of 21 to 23 percent. You're entitled to get most of that tax back if you purchase more than €155 (about $220) worth of goods at a store that participates in the VAT-refund scheme. Typically, you must ring up the minimum at a single retailer—you can't add up your purchases from various shops to reach the required amount.

Getting your refund is usually straightforward and, if you buy a substantial amount of souvenirs, well worth the hassle. If you're lucky, the merchant will subtract the tax when you make your purchase. (This is more likely to occur if the store ships the goods to your home.) Otherwise, you'll need to:

Get the paperwork. Have the merchant completely fill out the necessary refund document, called a "cheque." You'll have to present your passport. Get the paperwork done before you leave the store to ensure you'll have everything you need (including your original sales receipt).

Get your stamp at the border or airport. Process your cheque(s) at your last stop in the EU (for instance, at the airport) with the customs agent who deals with VAT refunds. Before checking in for your flight, find the local customs office, and be prepared to stand in line. It's best to keep your purchases in your carry-on for viewing, but if they're too large or dangerous (such as knives), have your purchases easily accessible in the bag you're about to check, ready to show the customs agent. You're not supposed to use your purchased goods before you leave. If you show up at customs wearing your new leather shoes, officials might look the other way—or deny you a refund.

Collect your refund. You'll need to return your stamped document to the retailer or its representative. Many merchants work with a service, such as Global Blue (www.global-blue.com) or Premier Tax Free (www.premiertaxfree.com), which have offices at major airports, ports, or border crossings (either before or after security, probably strategically located near a duty-free shop). These services, which extract a 4 percent fee, can refund your money immediately in cash or credit your card (within two billing cycles). If the retailer handles VAT refunds directly, it's up to you to contact the merchant for your refund. You can mail the documents from home, or quicker, from your point of departure (using a stamped, addressed envelope you've prepared or one that's been provided by the merchant). You'll then have to wait—it can take months.

Customs for American Shoppers

You are allowed to take home $800 worth of items per person duty-free, once every 30 days. You can also bring in duty-free a liter of alcohol. As for food, you can take home many processed and packaged foods: vacuum-packed cheeses, dried herbs, jams, baked goods, candy, chocolate, oil, vinegar, mustard, and honey. However, fresh fruits and vegetables and most meats are not allowed. Any liquid-containing foods must be packed in checked luggage, a potential recipe for disaster. To check customs rules and duty rates, visit www.cbp.gov.

Sightseeing

Sightseeing can be hard work. Use these tips to make your visits to Rome's finest sights meaningful, fun, efficient, and painless.

Plan Ahead

Set up an itinerary that allows you to fit in all your must-see sights. For a one-stop look at opening hours, see "Rome at a Glance" (page 56; also see "Daily Reminder" on page 25). Most sights keep stable hours, but you can easily confirm the latest by checking their websites or asking at the local TI.

If you'll be visiting during a holiday, find out if a particular sight will be open by phoning ahead or checking its website. And don't put off visiting a must-see sight—you never know when a place will close unexpectedly for a holiday, strike, or restoration. If you want to see the Borghese Gallery, make reservations in advance (see page 241). It's smart to reserve for the Vatican Museum (see page 207) as well.

When possible, visit the major sights in the morning (when your energy is best) and save other activities for the afternoon. Hit the highlights first, then go back to other things if you have the stamina and time.

Going at the right time helps avoid crowds. This book offers tips on specific sights. Try visiting the sight very early, at lunch, or very late. Evening visits are usually peaceful with fewer crowds.

Study up. To get the most out of the self-guided tours and sight descriptions in this book, read them before you visit.

At Sights

Here's what you can typically expect:

Some important sights such as the Vatican Museum have metal detectors or conduct bag searches that will slow your entry, while others require you to check daypacks and coats. They'll be kept safely. If you have something you can't bear to part with, stash it in a pocket or purse. To avoid checking a small backpack, carry it under your arm like a purse as you enter. From a guard's point of view, a backpack is generally a problem while a purse is not.

Flash photography is often banned, but taking photos without a flash is usually allowed. Look for signs or ask. Flashes damage oil paintings and distract others in the room. Even without a flash,

How Was Your Trip?

Were your travels fun, smooth, and meaningful? If you'd like to share your tips, concerns, and discoveries, please fill out the survey at www.ricksteves.com/feedback. I value your feedback. Thanks in advance—it helps a lot.

a handheld camera will take a decent picture (or you can buy postcards or posters at the museum bookstore).

Be prepared to pay cash for the admission fee; a few sights may not take credit cards. Museums may have special exhibits in addition to their permanent collections. Some exhibits are included in the entry price, while others come at an extra cost (which you may have to pay even if you don't want to see the exhibit).

Expect changes—artwork can be on tour, on loan, out sick, or shifted at the whim of the curator. To adapt, pick up any available free floor plans as you enter, and ask the museum staff if you can't find a particular item. Say the title or artist's name, or point to the photograph in this book and ask, *"Dov'è?"* (doh-VEH, meaning "Where is?").

Many sights rent audioguides, which generally offer excellent recorded descriptions in English (about $4). If you bring along your own pair of headphones and a Y-jack, you can sometimes share an audioguide with your travel partner and save money. I've produced free downloadable audio tours of the major sights in Rome (see page 27).

Guided tours in English are most likely to occur during peak season (usually €4-10 and ranging widely in quality). Some sights also run short films featuring their highlights and history. These are generally well worth your time. I make it standard operating procedure to ask when I arrive at a sight if there is a film in English.

In museums, art is dated with *sec* for *secolo* (century, often indicated with Roman numerals), A.C. (for *Avanti Cristo,* i.e., before Christ) and D.C. (for *Dopo Cristo,* a.k.a. A.D.). OK?

Important sights have an on-site café or cafeteria (usually a good place to rejuvenate during a long visit). The WCs at many sights are free and generally clean (but it's smart to carry tissues in case a WC runs out of TP).

Many sights sell postcards and guidebooks that highlight their attractions. Before you leave, scan the postcards and thumb through the biggest guidebook (or skim its index) to be sure you haven't overlooked something that you'd like to see.

Most sights stop admitting people 30-60 minutes before closing time, and some rooms close early (often about 45 minutes before the actual closing time). Guards usher people out, so don't save the best for last.

Every sight or museum offers more than what is covered in this book. Use the information in this book as an introduction—not the final word.

Find Religion

Churches offer some amazing art (usually free), a cool respite from heat, and a welcome seat.

A modest dress code—no bare shoulders or shorts for anyone, even kids—is enforced at the Vatican City (St. Peter's Basilica and Vatican Museum) and at Rome's major churches, such as St. Paul's Outside the Walls, but is often overlooked elsewhere. If you're caught by surprise, you can improvise, using maps to cover your shoulders and a jacket for your knees. (I wear a super-lightweight pair of long pants rather than shorts for my hot and muggy big-city Italian sightseeing.)

Some churches have coin-operated audioboxes that describe the art and history; just set the dial on English, put in your coins, and listen. Coin boxes near a piece of art illuminate the art (and present a better photo opportunity). I pop in a coin whenever I can. It improves my experience, is a favor to other visitors trying to appreciate a great piece of art in the dark, and is a little contribution to that church and its work. Whenever possible, let there be light.

Traveling as a Temporary Local

We travel all the way to Italy to enjoy differences—to become temporary locals. You'll experience frustrations. Certain truths that we find "God-given" or "self-evident," such as cold beer, ice in drinks, bottomless cups of coffee, hot showers, and bigger being better, are suddenly not so true. One of the benefits of travel is the eye-opening realization that there are logical, civil, and even better alternatives. A willingness to go local ensures that you'll enjoy a full dose of Italian hospitality.

Europeans generally like Americans. But if there is a negative aspect to Italians' image of Americans, it's that we are big, loud, aggressive, impolite, rich, and a bit naive. Think about the rationale behind "crazy" Italian decisions. For instance, many hoteliers turn off the heat in early April and can't turn on air-conditioning until June. The point is to conserve energy, and it's mandated by the Italian government. You could complain about being cold or hot...or bring a sweater in winter, and in summer, be prepared to sweat a little like everyone else.

While Italians, flabbergasted by our Yankee excesses, say in disbelief, *"Mi sono cadute le braccia!"* ("I throw my arms down!"), they nearly always afford us individual travelers all the warmth we deserve.

Judging from all the happy feedback I receive from travelers who have used this book, it's safe to assume you'll enjoy a great, affordable vacation—with the finesse of an independent, experienced traveler.

Thanks, and *buon viaggio!*

Back Door Travel Philosophy

From *Rick Steves' Europe Through the Back Door*

Travel is intensified living—maximum thrills per minute and one of the last great sources of legal adventure. Travel is freedom. It's recess, and we need it.

Experiencing the real Europe requires catching it by surprise, going casual..."Through the Back Door."

Affording travel is a matter of priorities. (Make do with the old car.) You can eat and sleep—simply, safely, and enjoyably—anywhere in Europe for $120 a day plus transportation costs. In many ways, spending more money only builds a thicker wall between you and what you traveled so far to see. Europe is a cultural carnival, and time after time, you'll find that its best acts are free and the best seats are the cheap ones.

A tight budget forces you to travel close to the ground, meeting and communicating with the people. Never sacrifice sleep, nutrition, safety, or cleanliness to save money. Simply enjoy the local-style alternatives to expensive hotels and restaurants.

Connecting with people carbonates your experience. Extroverts have more fun. If your trip is low on magic moments, kick yourself and make things happen. If you don't enjoy a place, maybe you don't know enough about it. Seek the truth. Recognize tourist traps. Give a culture the benefit of your open mind. See things as different, but not better or worse. Any culture has plenty to share.

Of course, travel, like the world, is a series of hills and valleys. Be fanatically positive and militantly optimistic. If something's not to your liking, change your liking.

Travel can make you a happier American, as well as a citizen of the world. Our Earth is home to seven billion equally precious people. It's humbling to travel and find that other people don't have the "American Dream"—they have their own dreams. Europeans like us, but with all due respect, they wouldn't trade passports.

Thoughtful travel engages us with the world. In tough economic times, it reminds us what is truly important. By broadening perspectives, travel teaches new ways to measure quality of life.

Globetrotting destroys ethnocentricity, helping us understand and appreciate other cultures. Rather than fear the diversity on this planet, celebrate it. Among your most prized souvenirs will be the strands of different cultures you choose to knit into your own character. The world is a cultural yarn shop, and Back Door travelers are weaving the ultimate tapestry. Join in!

ORIENTATION TO ROME

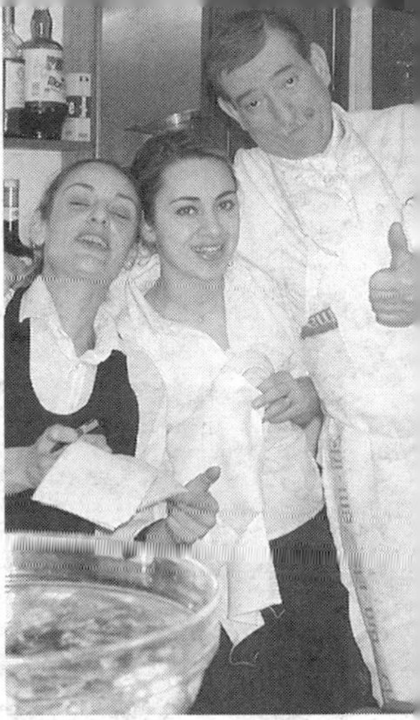

Sprawling Rome actually feels manageable once you get to know it. The old core, with most of the tourist sights, sits in a diamond formed by Termini train station (in the east), the Vatican (west), Villa Borghese Gardens (north), and the Colosseum (south). The Tiber River runs through the diamond from north to south. In the center of the diamond sits Piazza Venezia, a busy square and traffic hub. It takes about an hour to walk from Termini Station to the Vatican.

Think of Rome as a series of neighborhoods, huddling around major landmarks.

Ancient Rome: In ancient times, this was home for the grandest buildings of a city of a million people. Today, the best of the classical sights stand in a line from the Colosseum to the Forum to the Pantheon.

Pantheon Neighborhood: The Pantheon anchors the neighborhood I like to call the heart of Rome. It stretches eastward from the Tiber River through Campo de' Fiori and Piazza Navona, past the Pantheon to the Trevi Fountain.

Vatican City: Located west of the Tiber, it's a compact world of its own, with two great, huge sights: St. Peter's Basilica and the Vatican Museum.

North Rome: With the Spanish Steps, Villa Borghese Gardens, and trendy shopping streets (Via Veneto and the "shopping triangle"), this is a more modern, classy area.

East Rome: This includes the area around Termini Station, with its many recommended hotels and public-transportation connections. Nearby is the neighborhood I call "Pilgrim's Rome," with several prominent churches dotting the area south of the station.

South Rome: South of Vatican City is Trastevere, the seedy, colorful, wrong-side-of-the-river neighborhood that provides

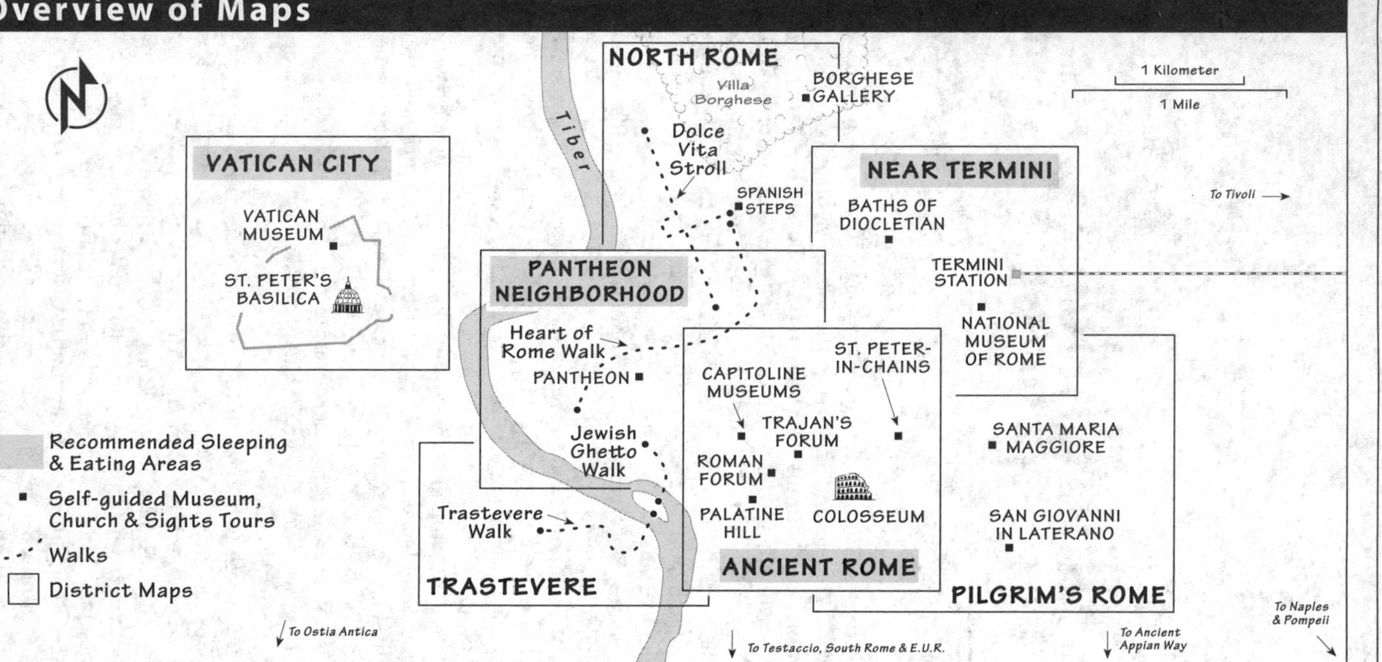
Overview of Maps
NORTH ROME
Villa Borghese
BORGHESE GALLERY
1 Kilometer
1 Mile
Tiber
Dolce Vita Stroll
VATICAN CITY
VATICAN MUSEUM
ST. PETER'S BASILICA
SPANISH STEPS
NEAR TERMINI
BATHS OF DIOCLETIAN
To Tivoli
TERMINI STATION
PANTHEON NEIGHBORHOOD
Heart of Rome Walk
PANTHEON
NATIONAL MUSEUM OF ROME
ST. PETER-IN-CHAINS
CAPITOLINE MUSEUMS
TRAJAN'S FORUM
Jewish Ghetto Walk
ROMAN FORUM
SANTA MARIA MAGGIORE
Recommended Sleeping & Eating Areas
Self-guided Museum, Church & Sights Tours
Walks
District Maps
Trastevere Walk
PALATINE HILL
COLOSSEUM
SAN GIOVANNI IN LATERANO
ANCIENT ROME
TRASTEVERE
PILGRIM'S ROME
To Ostia Antica
To Testaccio, South Rome & E.U.R.
To Ancient Appian Way
To Naples & Pompeii

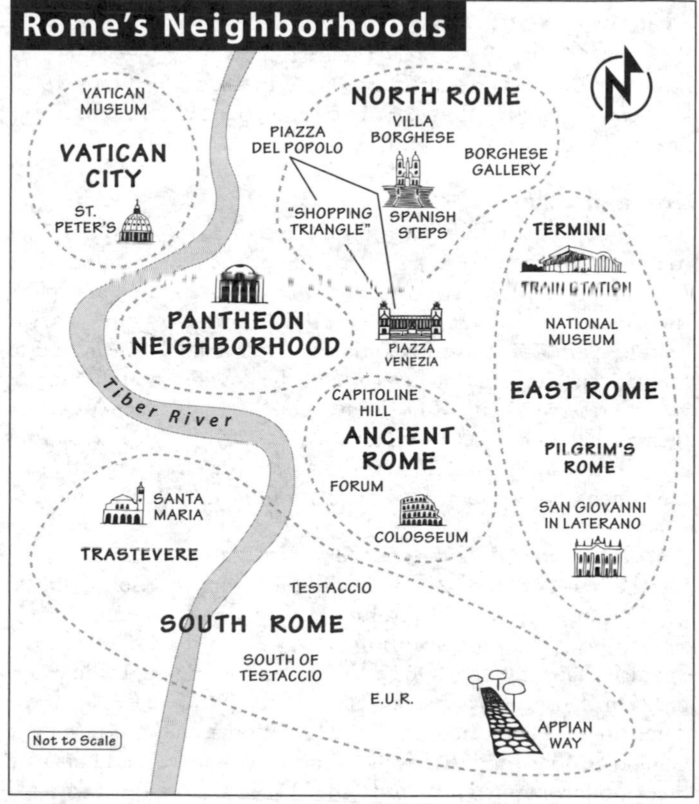

a look at village Rome. It's the city at its crustiest—and perhaps most "Roman." Across the Tiber River, directly south of the city center, are the gritty/colorful Testaccio neighborhood, the 1930s suburb of E.U.R., and the Appian Way, home of the catacombs.

Within each of these neighborhoods, you'll find elements from the many layers of Rome's 2,000-year history: the marble ruins of ancient times; tangled streets of the medieval world; early Christian churches; grand Renaissance buildings and statues; Baroque fountains and church facades; 19th-century apartments; and 20th-century boulevards choked with traffic.

Since no one is allowed to build taller than St. Peter's dome, and virtually no buildings have been constructed in the city center since Mussolini got distracted in 1938, Rome has no modern skyline. The Tiber River is basically ignored—after the last floods (1870), the banks were built up very high, and Rome turned its back on its naughty river.

Planning Your Time

After considering Rome's major tourist sights, I've covered just my favorites. You won't be able to see all of these, so don't try—you'll keep coming back to Rome. After several dozen visits, I still have a healthy list of excuses to return.

Rome in a Day

Some people actually try to "do" Rome in a day. Crazy as that sounds, if all you have is a day, it's one of the most exciting days Europe has to offer. Start at 8:30 at the Colosseum. Then explore the Forum, hike over Capitoline Hill, and cap your "Caesar Shuffle" with a visit to the Pantheon. After a quick lunch, taxi to the Vatican Museum (the lines usually die down mid-afternoon, or you can reserve a visit online in advance). See the Vatican Museum, then St. Peter's Basilica (open until 19:00 April-Sept). Taxi back to Campo de' Fiori to find dinner. Finish your day lacing together all the famous floodlit spots (see my Heart of Rome Walk chapter).

Rome in Two to Three Days

On the first day, do the "Caesar Shuffle" from the Colosseum to the Forum, then over Capitoline Hill to the Pantheon. After a siesta, join the locals strolling from Piazza del Popolo to the Spanish Steps (see the "Dolce Vita Stroll" in the Nightlife chapter). On the second day, see Vatican City (St. Peter's, climb the dome, tour the Vatican Museum). Have dinner on the atmospheric Campo de' Fiori, and then walk to the Trevi Fountain and Spanish Steps (following my Heart of Rome Walk). With a third day, add the Borghese Gallery (reservations required) and the National Museum of Rome.

Rome in Seven Days

Rome is a great one-week getaway. Its sights can keep even the most fidgety traveler well entertained for a week.

Day 1: Do the "Caesar Shuffle" from the Colosseum to the Forum, Trajan's Column, Capitoline Hill, and Pantheon.

Day 2: Morning—National Museum of Rome and the nearby Baths of Diocletian. Afternoon—"Dolce Vita Stroll" and shopping.

Day 3: Vatican City—St. Peter's Basilica, dome climb, and Vatican Museum (for tips on avoiding lines, see page 208).

Day 4: Side-trip to Ostia Antica (closed Mon). In the evening, take my recommended Heart of Rome Walk from Campo de' Fiori to the Spanish Steps.

Day 5: Borghese Gallery (reservation required) and Pilgrim's

Daily Reminder

Sunday: These sights are closed: the Vatican Museum (except for the last Sunday of the month, when it's free and even more crowded), Villa Farnesina, and the Catacombs of San Sebastiano. In the morning, the Porta Portese flea market hops, and the old center is delightfully quiet. Via dei Fori Imperiali is closed to traffic and fun to stroll.

Monday: Many sights are closed, including the National Museum of Rome, Borghese Gallery, Capitoline Museums, Catacombs of Priscilla, Museum of the Imperial Forum (includes Trajan's Market and Trajan's Forum), Castel Sant'Angelo, Ara Pacis, Montemartini Museum, E.U.R.'s Museum of Roman Civilization, Etruscan Museum, Museum of the Liberation of Rome, MAXXI, some Appian Way sights (Tomb of Cecilia Metella; Circus and Villa of Maxentius; and the San Sebastiano Gate and Museum of the Walls), Ostia Antica, and Villa d'Este (at Tivoli).

Major sights that are open include the Colosseum, Forum, and Vatican Museum, among others. Churches are open as usual. The Baths of Caracalla close early in the afternoon.

Tuesday: All sights are open in Rome. This isn't a good day to side-trip to Naples because its Archaeological Museum is closed.

Wednesday: All sights are open, except the Catacombs of San Callisto. St. Peter's Basilica may be closed in the morning for a papal audience.

Thursday/Friday: All sights are open.

Saturday: Most sights are open in Rome, except for the Synagogue and Jewish Museum.

Rome: the churches of San Giovanni in Laterano, Santa Maria Maggiore, and San Clemente (see Pilgrim's Rome Tour chapter).

Day 6: Side-trip to Naples and Pompeii.

Day 7: You choose—Hadrian's Villa, Appian Way with catacombs, E.U.R., Castel Sant'Angelo, Testaccio sights, Baths of Caracalla, Capuchin Crypt, shopping, or more time at the Vatican.

Overview

Tourist Information

Rome has two tourist information offices and several TI kiosks. The TI offices are at the airport (Terminal 3, daily 9:00-18:30) and Termini train station (daily 8:00-21:00, 100 yards down track 24, look for signs). Little kiosks (generally open daily 9:30-19:00)

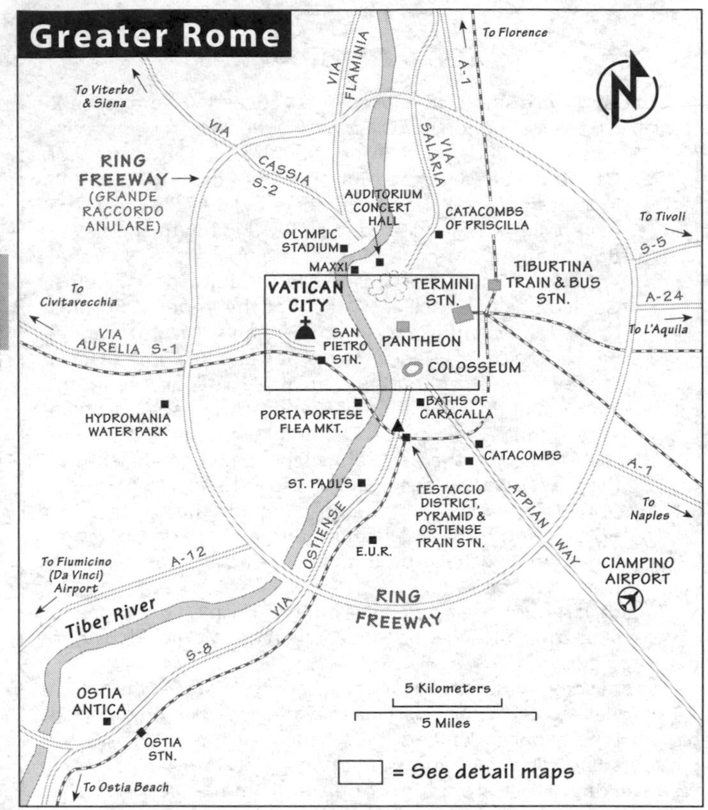

are near the Forum (on Piazza del Tempio della Pace), on Via Nazionale (at Palazzo delle Esposizioni), near Castel Sant'Angelo (at Piazza Pia), near Piazza Navona (at Piazza delle Cinque Lune), and near the Trevi Fountain (at Via del Corso and Via Minghetti). The TI's website is http://en.turismoroma.it. The TIs don't offer room-booking services. If a commercial info-center offers to book you a room, just say no—you'll save money by booking direct.

At any TI, ask for a city map and a listing of sights and hours (in the free *Evento* booklet with English-language pages listing the month's cultural events). Your hotel will have a freebie map and may also have the free *Evento* booklet, saving you a trip to the TI if that's all you need. The best map I found is published by Rough Guide (€9 in bookstores).

Rome's single best source of up-to-date tourist information is its **call center,** with English-speakers on staff. Dial 06-0608 (answered daily 9:00-21:00, press 2 for English, www.060608.it).

Several English-oriented **websites** provide insight into events and daily life in the city: www.inromenow.com (light tourist info

Rick Steves Audio Europe

If you're bringing a mobile device, be sure to check out **Rick Steves Audio Europe,** where you can download free audio tours and hours of travel interviews (via the Rick Steves Audio Europe smartphone app, www.ricksteves.com/audioeurope, iTunes, or Google Play).

My self-guided **audio tours** are user-friendly, easy to follow, fun, and informative, covering the Colosseum, Roman Forum, Pantheon, St. Peter's Basilica, Sistine Chapel, Trastevere neighborhood, Jewish Ghetto, Ostia Antica, and Pompeii. Compared to live tours, my audio tours are hard to beat: Nobody will stand you up, the quality is reliable, you can take the tour exactly when you like, and they're free.

Rick Steves Audio Europe also offers a far-reaching library of intriguing **travel interviews** with experts from around the globe.

on lots of topics), www.wantedinrome.com (events and accommodations), and http://rome.angloinfo.com (on living in and moving to Rome).

Arrival in Rome

For a rundown of Rome's train stations and airports, see the Rome Connections chapter.

Helpful Hints

Sightseeing Tips: Avid sightseers can save money by buying the Roma Pass (see page 50), available at TIs and participating sights—buy one before visiting the Colosseum or Forum, and you can skip the long lines there. If you want to see the Borghese Gallery, remember to reserve ahead (see page 241). To bypass the long Vatican Museum line, reserve an entry time online (see page 207 for details).

Internet Access: If your hotel doesn't offer free or cheap Internet access, your hotelier can point you to the nearest Internet café.

Bookstores: These stores (all open daily except Anglo American and Open Door) sell travel guidebooks, including mine. The first two are chains, while the others have a more personal touch. **Borri Books** is at Termini Station, and **Feltrinelli International** has two branches (at Largo Argentina, and just off Piazza della Repubblica at Via Vittorio Emanuele Orlando 84, tel. 06-482-7878). **Anglo American Bookshop** has great art and history sections (closed all day Sun and Mon morning, a few blocks south of Spanish Steps at Via della Vite 102, tel. 06-679-5222). **Libreria Fanucci** has a small selection but is centrally located (a block toward the Pantheon from Piazza Navona at Piazza Madama 8, tel. 06-686-1141). In Trastevere, Irishman Dermot at the **Almost Corner Bookshop** stocks an Italian-interest section (Via del Moro 45, tel. 06-583-6942), and the **Open Door Bookshop** carries the only used books in English in town (closed Sun, Via della Lungaretta 23, tel. 06-589-6478).

Laundry: Your hotelier can direct you to the nearest launderette. The **ondablu** chain usually comes with Internet access; one of their more central locations is near Termini Station (€2/hour, about €8 to wash and dry a 15-pound load, usually open daily 8:00-22:00, Via Principe Amedeo 70b, tel. 06-474-4647).

Travel Agencies: You can get train tickets and railpass-related reservations and supplements at travel agencies (at little or no additional cost), avoiding a trip to a train station. Your hotelier will know of a convenient agency nearby.

Updates to this Book: Check www.ricksteves.com/update for any significant changes that have occurred since this book was printed.

Dealing with (and Avoiding) Problems

Theft Alert: While violent crime is rare in the city center, petty theft is rampant. With sweet-talking con artists meeting you at the station, well-dressed pickpockets on buses, and thieving gangs of children at the ancient sites, Rome is a gauntlet of rip-offs. Although it's not as bad as it was a few years ago, and pickpockets don't want to hurt you—they usually just want your money—green or sloppy tourists will be scammed. Thieves strike when you're distracted. Don't trust kind strangers. Keep nothing important in your pockets. Be most on guard while boarding and leaving buses and subways. Thieves crowd the door, then stop and turn while others crowd and push from behind. You'll find less crowding and commotion—and less risk—waiting for the end cars of a subway rather than the middle cars. The sneakiest thieves pretend to be well-dressed businessmen (generally with something in their hands), or tourists wearing fanny packs and toting cameras and even Rick Steves guidebooks.

Scams abound: Don't give your wallet to self-proclaimed "police" who stop you on the street, warn you about counterfeit (or drug) money, and ask to see your cash. If a bank machine eats your ATM card, see if there's a thin plastic insert with a tongue hanging out that thieves use to extract it.

If you know what to look out for, fast-fingered moms with babies and gangs of children picking the pockets and handbags of naive tourists are not a threat, but an interesting, albeit sad, spectacle. Pickpockets troll through the tourist crowds around the Colosseum, Forum, Vatican, and train and Metro stations. Watch them target tourists who are overloaded with bags or distracted with a video camera. The kids look like beggars and hold up newspapers or cardboard signs to confuse their victims. They scram like stray cats if you're on to them.

Reporting Losses: To report lost or stolen items, file a police report (at Termini Station, with *polizia* at track 11 or with Carabinieri at track 20; offices are also at Piazza Venezia). You'll need the report to file an insurance claim for lost gear, and it can help with replacing your passport—first file the police report, then call your embassy to make an appointment (US embassy: Tel. 06-46741, Via Vittorio Veneto 121, www.usembassy.it). For information on how to report lost or stolen credit cards, see page 13.

Emergency Numbers: Police—tel. 113. Ambulance—tel. 118.

Pedestrian Safety: Your main safety concern in Rome is crossing streets safely. Use extreme caution. Scooters don't need to stop at red lights, and even cars exercise what drivers call the "logical option" of not stopping if they see no oncoming traffic. Each year, as noisy gasoline-powered scooters are replaced by electric ones, the streets get quieter (hooray) but more dangerous for pedestrians. Follow locals like a shadow when you cross a street (or spend a good part of your visit stranded on curbs). When you do cross alone, don't be a deer in the headlights. Find a gap in the traffic and walk with confidence while making eye contact with approaching drivers—they won't hit you if they can tell where you intend to go.

Staying/Getting Healthy: The siesta is a key to survival in summertime Rome. Lie down and contemplate the extraordinary power of gravity in the Eternal City. I drink lots of cold, refreshing water from Rome's many drinking fountains (the Forum has three).

There's a pharmacy (marked by a green cross) in every neighborhood. Pharmacies stay open late in Termini Station (daily 7:30-22:00) and at Piazza dei Cinquecento 51 (open 24 hours daily, next to Termini Station on the corner of Via Cavour, tel. 06-488-0019).

Embassies can recommend English-speaking doctors. Consider MEDline, a 24-hour home-medical service; doctors speak English and make calls at hotels for €150 (tel. 06-808-0995). Anyone is entitled to free emergency treatment at public hospitals. The hospital closest to Termini Station is Policlinico Umberto 1 (entrance for emergency treatment on

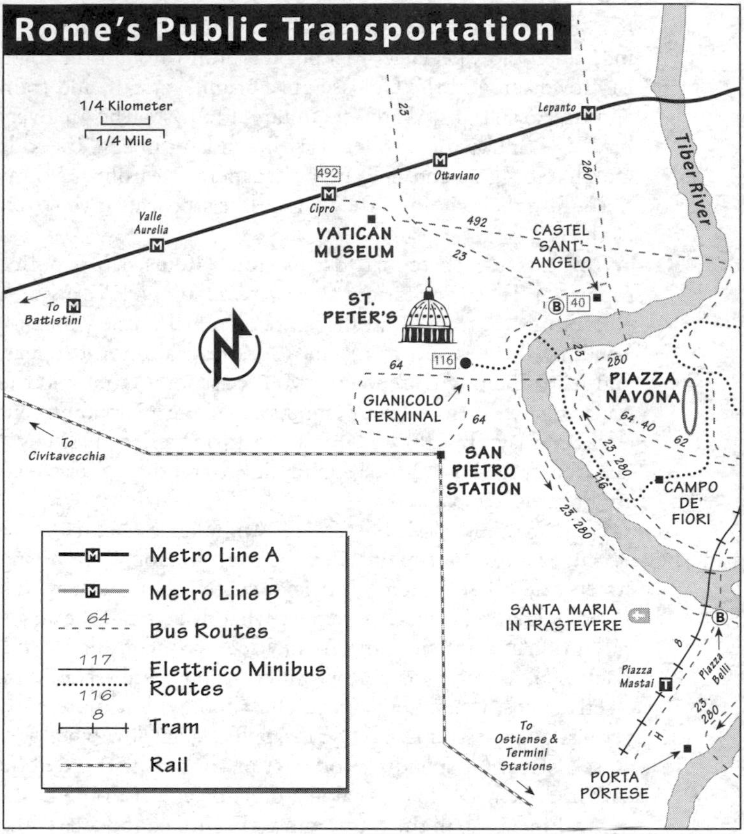

Rome's Public Transportation

1/4 Kilometer
1/4 Mile
To Battistini
Valle Aurelia
Cipro
492
Ottaviano
Lepanto
23
280
Tiber River
VATICAN MUSEUM
492
23
CASTEL SANT' ANGELO
40
ST. PETER'S
116
64
GIANICOLO TERMINAL
64
To Civitavecchia
SAN PIETRO STATION
PIAZZA NAVONA
64, 40
62
23, 280
116
CAMPO DE' FIORI
23, 280
SANTA MARIA IN TRASTEVERE
8
Piazza Mastai
Piazza Belli
23, 280
H
To Ostiense & Termini Stations
PORTA PORTESE

Metro Line A
Metro Line B
64 Bus Routes
117 / 116 Elettrico Minibus Routes
8 Tram
Rail

Via Lancisi, translators available, Metro: Policlinico). Readers report that the staff at Santa Susanna Church, home of the American Catholic Church in Rome, offers useful advice and medical referrals (see page 78).

Getting Around Rome

Sightsee on foot, by city bus, by Metro, or by taxi. I've grouped your sightseeing into walkable neighborhoods. Make it a point to visit sights in a logical order. Needless backtracking wastes precious time.

The public transportation system, which is cheap and efficient, consists primarily of buses, a few trams, and the two underground subway (Metro) lines. Consider it part of your Roman experience.

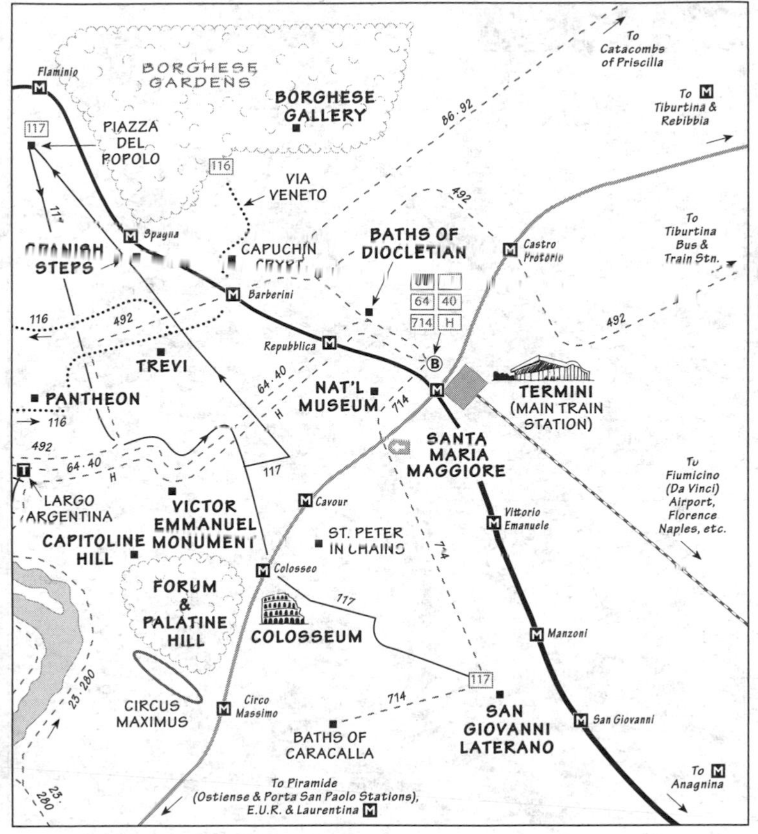

The walking-tour company, Rome Walks, has produced an orientation video to Rome's transportation system; find it on You Tube by searching for "Understanding Rome's Public Transport."

For information, visit www.atac.roma.it, which has a useful route planner in English, or call 06-57003.

Buying Tickets

All public transportation uses the same ticket. It costs €1.50 and is valid for one Metro ride—including transfers underground—plus unlimited city buses and *elettrico* buses during a 100-minute period. Passes good on buses and the Metro are sold in increments of one day (€6, good until midnight), three days (€16.50), one week (€24, about the cost of three taxi rides), and one month (€35, valid for a calendar month).

You can purchase tickets and passes at some newsstands, tobacco shops (*tabacchi*, marked by a black-and-white *T* sign), and major Metro stations and bus stops, but not on board. It's smart to

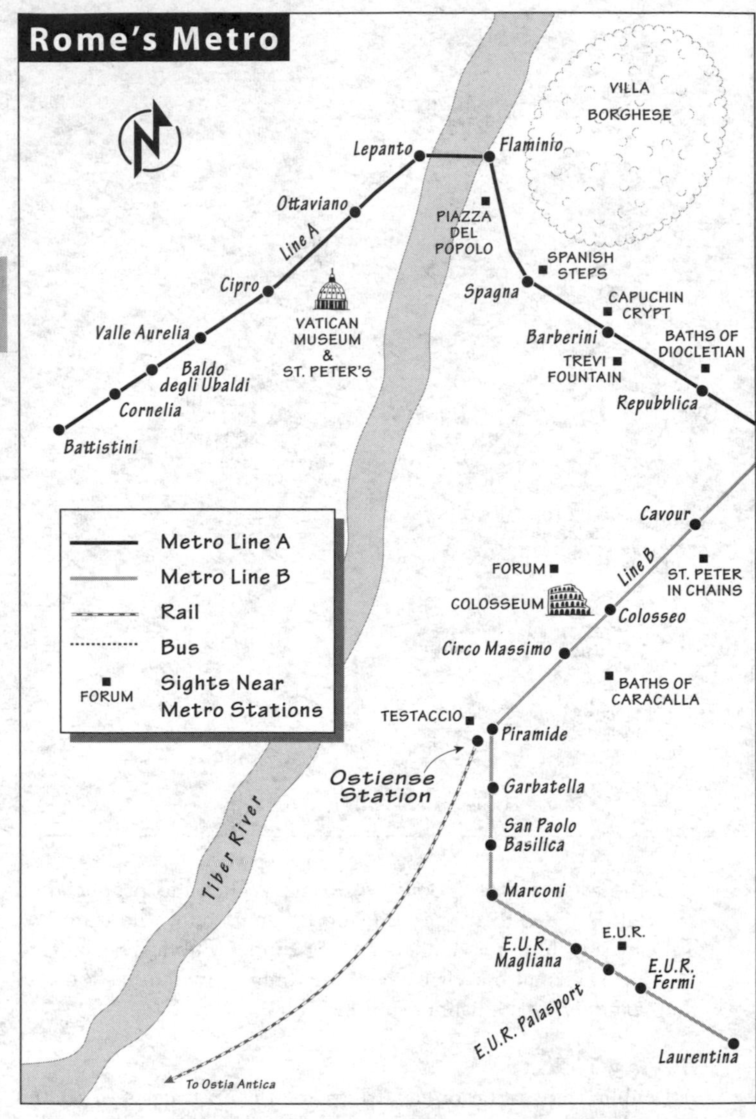

stock up on tickets early, or to buy a pass or a Roma Pass (which includes a three-day transit pass—see page 50). That way, you don't have to run around searching for an open tobacco shop when you spot your bus approaching. Metro stations rarely have human ticket-sellers, and the machines are often either broken or require exact change (it helps to insert your smallest coin first).

Validate your ticket by sticking it in the Metro turnstile (magnetic-strip-side up, arrow-side first) or in the machine when you

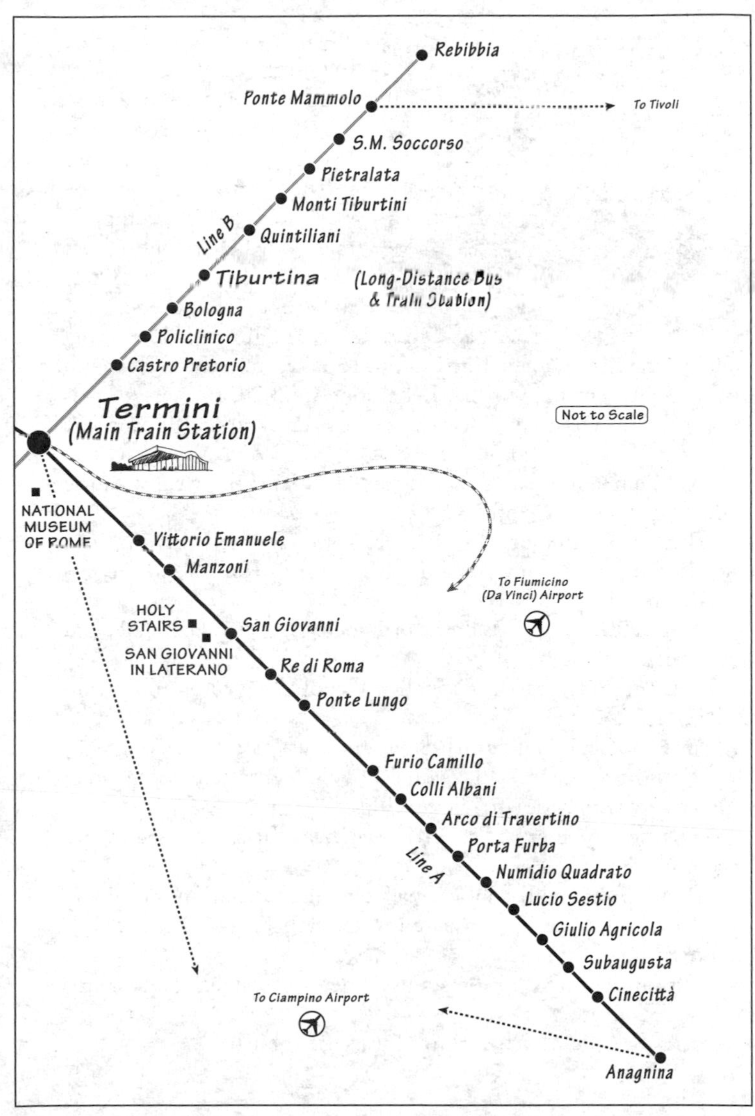

board the bus (magnetic-strip-side down, arrow-side first)—watch others and imitate. It'll return your ticket with your expiration time printed. To get through a Metro turnstile with a transit pass or Roma Pass, use it just like a ticket (on buses, however, you need to validate your pass only if that's your first time using it).

By Metro

The Roman subway system (Metropolitana, or "Metro") is simple,

with two clean, cheap, fast lines—A and B—that intersect at Termini Station. The Metro runs from 5:30 to 23:30 (Fri-Sat until 1:30 in the morning). The subway's first and last compartments are generally the least crowded (and the least likely to harbor pickpockets).

You'll notice lots of big holes in the city as a new line is built. Line C, from the Colosseum to Largo Argentina, will likely be done in 2020. Because of this construction, you may find the system closed at 21:00 on some nights.

While much of Rome is not served by its skimpy subway, the following stops are helpful:

Termini (intersection of lines A and B): Termini Station, shuttle train to airport, National Museum of Rome, and recommended hotels

Repubblica (line A): Baths of Diocletian, Via Nazionale, and recommended hotels

Barberini (line A): Capuchin Crypt, Trevi Fountain, and Villa Borghese

Spagna (line A): Spanish Steps and classy shopping area

Flaminio (line A): Piazza del Popolo, start of recommended "Dolce Vita Stroll" down Via del Corso

Ottaviano (line A): St. Peter's Basilica, Vatican Museum, and recommended hotels

Tiburtina (line B): Tiburtina train and bus station

Colosseo (line B): Colosseum, Roman Forum, bike rental, and recommended hotels

Piramide (line B): Protestant Cemetery, Testaccio, and trains to Ostia Antica

E.U.R. (line B): Mussolini's futuristic suburb

By Bus

The Metro is handy, but it won't get you everywhere—take the bus. Bus routes are clearly listed at the stops. TIs usually don't have bus maps, but with some knowledge of major stops, you won't necessarily need one (though if you do want a route map, find one printed inside the free-at-hotels

Bus Bravado

Zip around Rome by bus like a local by using the following tips to read bus signs.

The sign in the photo shows the three buses (#40, #60, and #64) that stop at the "Nazionale" stop. If you're asking yourself the following questions, it's got answers.

❶ **Where am I?** You're at the bus stop *(fermata)* called Nazionale (at the cross-street Torino; the cross-street differentiates this Nazionale stop from others nearby).

❷ **Which buses stop here?** Three do: #40, #60, and #64. Notice the arrow—it shows which direction the bus is headed.

❸ **Where is the bus going?** Bus #64, for example, starts its journey at "Termini" (Termini Station), goes to Repubblica, and then arrives at Nazionale—this stop. (Find "Nazionale," with the box around it.) From here, the #64 continues to "Pza Venezia" (Piazza Venezia), "Argentina" (Largo Argentina), makes several more stops, and ends its journey at "Pza Stz S. Pietro" (Piazza Stazione San Pietro). Easy.

Scan the list to see if any of these buses stops at your destination. If you don't see a particular street or piazza, look for a major landmark where you can transfer—such as Largo Argentina, Piazza Venezia, or Termini Station. Note that if your destination is listed *above* your current bus stop, you need to cross the street to catch the bus going in the other direction.

❹ **When will my bus come?** The bottom of the sign lists the first and last departure times from the beginning of the route. *"Lun./ven."* means it runs on weekdays, *"sab."* means Saturday, and *"fest."* means Sundays and holidays.

Will pickpockets take my wallet? Probably, if you read this entire sidebar at the bus stop without paying attention to your surroundings.

ORIENTATION

Evento magazine, or buy it from tobacco shops).

Buses—especially the touristy #40 and #64—are havens for thieves and pickpockets. Assume any commotion is a thief-created distraction. If one bus is packed, there's likely a second one on its tail with far fewer crowds and thieves. Once you know the bus system, you'll find it's easier than searching for a cab.

Tickets have a barcode and must be stamped on the bus in the yellow box with the digital readout (be sure to retrieve your ticket). Validate your ticket as you board (magnetic-strip-side down, arrow-side first), otherwise you're cheating. While relatively safe, riding without a stamped ticket on the bus is stressful. Inspectors fine even innocent-looking tourists €50. There's no need to validate a transit pass or Roma Pass on the bus, unless your pass is new and hasn't yet been stamped elsewhere in the transit system. Bus etiquette (not always followed) is to board at the front or rear doors and exit at the middle.

Regular bus lines start running at about 5:30, and during the day they run every 5-10 minutes. After 23:30, and sometimes earlier (such as on Sundays), buses are less frequent but still dependable. Night buses are also reliable, and are marked with an *N* and an owl symbol on the bus-stop signs.

These are the major bus routes:

Bus #64: This bus cuts across the city, linking Termini Station with the Vatican, stopping at Piazza della Repubblica (sights), Via Nazionale (recommended hotels), Piazza Venezia (near Forum), Largo Argentina (near Pantheon), St. Peter's Basilica (get off just past the tunnel), and San Pietro Station. Ride it for a city overview and to watch pickpockets in action. The #64 can get horribly crowded.

Bus #40: This express bus, which mostly follows the #64 route (but branches off on the Vatican side of the river), is especially helpful—fewer stops and crowds.

The following three routes conveniently connect Trastevere with other parts of Rome:

Bus #H: This express bus, linking Termini Station and Trastevere, makes a few stops on Via Nazionale (for Trastevere, get off at Piazza Belli, just after crossing the Tiber River).

Bus #8: This tram connects Largo Argentina with Trastevere (get off at Piazza Belli).

Buses #23 and #280: These link the Vatican with Trastevere and Testaccio, stopping at the Vatican Museum (nearest stop is Via Leone IV), Castel Sant'Angelo, Trastevere (Piazza Belli), Porta

Portese (Sunday flea market), and
Testaccio).

Other useful routes include:

Bus #62: Largo Argentina to St.

Bus #81: San Giovanni in Later
Piazza Risorgimento (Vatican).

Buses #85 and #87: Piazza Ve
Clemente, and San Giovanni in Laterano.

Bus #492: Travels east-west acros , connecting Tiburtina (train and bus stations), Largo Santa Susanna (near Piazza della Repubblica), Piazza Barberini, Piazza Venezia, Largo Argentina, Piazza Cavour (Castel Sant'Angelo), and Piazza Risorgimento (St. Peter's Basilica and Vatican).

Bus #714: Termini Station, Santa Maria Maggiore, San Giovanni in Laterano, Terme di Caracalla (Baths of Caracalla), and on to E.U.R.

***Elettrico* Minibuses:** Two cute *elettrico* minibuses that wind through the narrow streets of old and interesting neighborhoods are great for transport or simple joyriding. ***Elettrico* #116** runs through the medieval core of Rome: Ponte Vittorio Emanuele II (near Castel Sant'Angelo) to Campo de' Fiori, Pantheon, Piazza Barberini, and the southern edge of the scenic Villa Borghese Gardens. ***Elettrico* #117** connects San Giovanni in Laterano, Colosseo, Via dei Serpenti, Trevi Fountain, Piazza di Spagna, and Piazza del Popolo—and vice versa. Where Via del Corso hits Piazza del Popolo, a #117 is usually parked and ready to go. Riding it from here to the end of the line, San Giovanni in Laterano, makes for a fine joyride that leaves you, conveniently, at a great sight.

By Taxi

I use taxis in Rome more often than in other cities. They're reasonable and useful for efficient sightseeing in this big, hot metropolis.

Taxis start at €2.80, then charge about €1.30 per kilometer (surcharges: €1 on Sun, €3 for nighttime hours of 22:00-7:00, one regular suitcase or bag rides free, tip by rounding up to the nearest euro). Sample fares: Termini Station to Vatican-€10; Termini Station to Colosseum-€6; Colosseum to Trastevere-€7 (or look up your route at www.worldtaximeter.com). Three or four companions with more money than time should taxi almost everywhere.

It's tough to wave down a taxi in Rome, especially at night.

axi stand by asking a passerby or a clerk in a shop, *rmata dei taxi?"* (doh-VEH OO-nah fehr-MAH-tah AHK-see). Some taxi stands are listed on my maps. To ime and energy, have your hotel or restaurant call a taxi for ou; the meter starts when the call is received (generally adding a euro or two to the bill). To call a cab on your own, dial 06-4994 or 06-6645. It's routine for Romans to ask the waiter in a restaurant to call a taxi when they ask for the bill. The waiter will tell you how many minutes you have to enjoy your coffee.

Beware of corrupt taxis. A common cabbie scam is to take your €20 note, drop it, and pick up a €5 note (similar color), claiming that's what you gave him. To avoid this scam, pay in small bills; if you only have a large bill, show it to the cabbie as you state its face value.

If hailing a cab on the street, be sure the meter is restarted when you get in (should be around €2.80, or around €5 if you or your hotelier phoned for the taxi). Many meters show both the fare and the time elapsed during the ride—and some tourists pay €10 for an eight-and-a-half-minute trip (more than the fair meter rate).

When you arrive at the train station or airport, beware of hustlers conning naive visitors into unmarked, rip-off "express taxis." Only use official taxis, with a *taxi* sign and phone number marked on the door. By law, they must display a multilingual official price chart. If you have any problems with a taxi, point to the chart and ask the cabbie to explain it to you. Making a show of writing down the taxi number (to file a complaint) can motivate a driver to quickly settle the matter.

If you take a Rome city cab from Fiumicino Airport to anywhere in central Rome within the old city walls, the cost should be €48 (covering up to four people and their bags); however, every year some readers report being ripped off. The catch is that cabbies *not* based in Rome or Fiumicino can charge €70. At the airport, look specifically for a Rome city cab, with the "SPQR" shield on the door. By law, they can charge only €48 for the ride (still, be sure to establish the price before you get in).

Tired travelers arriving at the airport will likely find it less stressful to take an airport shuttle van to their hotel, or catch the train to Termini Station and take the Metro or a cheaper taxi from there (see page 388 for details on getting from the airport to downtown Rome via taxi, shuttle, or train).

By Bike

Biking in the big city of Rome can speed up sightseeing or simply be an enjoyable way to explore. Though Roman traffic can be stressful, Roman drivers are respectful of cyclists. Still, use caution and never assume the right of way. The best rides are on small streets in the city center. A bike path along the banks of the Tiber River makes a good 20-minute ride (easily accessed from the ramps at Porta Portese and Ponte Regina Margherita near Piazza del Popolo). Get a bike with a well-padded seat—the little stones that pave Roman streets are unforgiving.

Top Bike Rental and Tours is professionally run by Roman bike enthusiasts who want to show off their city. Your rental comes with a handy map that suggests a route and indicates less-trafficked streets. Owner Ciro also offers four-hour-long English-only guided tours around the city and the Ancient Appian Way; check his website for days and times (rental: €15/day, 10 percent discount with this book, best to reserve in advance via email; bike tours: start at €35, reservations required; daily 10:00-19:00, leave ID for deposit, from Santa Maria Maggiore go up Via dell'Olmata and turn left at the end of the block, Via dei Quattro Cantoni 40, tel. 06-488-2893, www.topbikerental.com, info@topbikerental.com).

Cool Rent, near the Colosseo Metro stop, is cheaper but less helpful (€3/hour, €10/day, 3-person bike cart €10/hour, daily 9:30-20:00, driver's license or other ID for deposit, 10 yards to the right as you exit the Metro). A second outlet is just off Via del Corso (on Largo di Lombardi, near corner of Via del Corso and Via della Croce, mobile 388-695-9303, Sasin). You can also rent a bike at the Appian Way (see Ancient Appian Way Tour chapter).

Tours

Walking Tours

Finding the best guided tours in Rome is challenging. Local guides are good but pricey. Tour companies are cheaper, but quality and organization are unreliable. To sightsee on your own, download my series of free audio tours that illuminate some of Rome's top sights and neighborhoods (see sidebar on page 27 for details).

If you do hire a private Italian guide, consider organizing a group of four to six people from your hotel to split the cost (€180 for a half-day tour); this ends up costing about the same per person as going on a scheduled tour from one of the walking-tour companies listed below (about €25, generally expat guides).

Local Guides—I've worked with each of these licensed independent local guides. They're worth every euro. They speak excellent English and enjoy tailoring tours to your interests. Their prices (roughly €50/hour) flex with the day, season, and demand. Arrange your date and price by email.

Francesca Caruso loves to teach and share her appreciation of her city, and has contributed generously to this book

Is the Pope Catholic?

Rome's tour guides, who introduce tourists to the city's great art and Christian history, field a lot of interesting questions and comments from their groups. Here are a few of their favorites:

- Oh, to be here in Rome... where our Lord Jesus walked.
- Is this where Christ fought the lions?
- Who's the guy on the cross?
- This guy who made so many nice things, Rene Sance, who is he? (Say it fast, and you'll get the gist.)

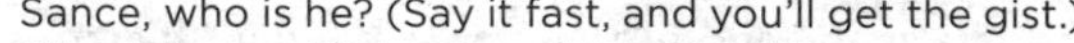

- Was John Paul II the son of John Paul I?
- What's the Sistine Chapel worth in US dollars?
- How did Michelangelo get Moses to pose for him?
- What's Michelangelo doing now?
- (Upon seeing the arrow-pierced St. Sebastian) Oh, you Italians had problems with the Indians, too.

(francescainroma@gmail.com). Popular with my readers, Francesca understandably books up quickly; if she's busy, she'll recommend one of her colleagues. **Carla Zaia** is an engaging expert on all things Roman (mobile 349-759-0723, carlaromeguide@gmail.com). **Cristina Giannicchi** has an archaeology background (mobile 338-111-4573, www.crisacross.com, crisgiannicchi@gmail.com). **Sara Magister** is a Roman with a doctorate in art history and author of a book on Renaissance Rome (mobile 339-379-3813, a.magister@iol.it). **Giovanna Terzulli** is a personable, knowledgeable art historian (terzulli@tiscali.it). **Alessandra Mazzoccoli** is experienced, easygoing, and good with all ages (alemazzoccoli@gmail.com). Italian-American **Sean Finelli,** known as "The Roman Guy," offers several walking tours and a trip-planning service (www.theromanguy.com).

Walking-Tour Companies—Rome has many highly competitive tour companies, each offering a series of themed walks through various slices of Rome. Three-hour guided walks generally cost €25-30 per person. Guides are usually native English speakers, often American expats. Tours are limited to small groups, geared to American tourists, and given in English only. I've listed some here, but without a lot of details on their offerings. Before your trip, spend some time on these companies' websites to get to know your options, as each company has a particular teaching and guiding personality. Some are highbrow, and others are less scholarly. It's sometimes required, and always smart, to book a spot in advance (easy online). I must add that we get a lot of negative feedback on some of these tour companies. Readers report that their advertising can be misleading, and scheduling mishaps are common.

Context Rome's walking tours are more intellectual than most, designed for travelers with longer-than-average attention spans. They are more expensive than others and are led by "docents" rather than guides (tel. 06-9672-7371, US tel. 800-691-6036, www.contextrome.com). **Enjoy Rome** offers a number of different walks and a website filled with helpful information (Via Marghera 8a, tel. 06-445-1843, www.enjoyrome.com, info@enjoyrome.com). **Rome Walks** has put together several particularly creative itineraries (mobile 347-795-5175, www.romewalks.com, info@romewalks.com, Annie). **Roman Odyssey** gives readers of this book a 10 percent discount on their walks (tel. 06-580-9902, mobile 328-912-3720, www.romanodyssey.com, Rahul). **Through Eternity** offers travelers with this book a 10 percent discount on most tours and a 20 percent discount on its Underground Rome; book through their website for the best discount (tel. 06-700-9336, mobile 347-336-5298, www.througheternity.com, office@througheternity.com, Rob). **Walks of Italy** has fun guides who lead a variety of good walks for groups no bigger than 12 people at a time (10 percent discount for readers of this book, US tel. 202/684-6916, Italian mobile 334-974-4274, www.walksofitaly.com, Jason Spiehler).

For **food-oriented walking tours,** see page 357.

Hop-on, Hop-off Bus Tours

Several different agencies, including the ATAC public bus company, run hop-on, hop-off tours around Rome. These tours are constantly evolving and offer varying combinations of sights. You can grab one (and pay as you board) at any stop; Termini Station and Piazza Venezia are handy hubs. Although the city is perfectly walkable and traffic jams can make the bus dreadfully slow, these open-top bus tours remain popular.

Trambus 110 seems to be the best. Operated by the ATAC city-bus lines, it offers an orientation tour on big red double-decker buses with an open-air upper deck. In less than two hours, you'll have 80 sights pointed out to you (with a next-to-worthless recorded narration). While you can hop on and off, the service can be erratic (mobbed midday, not ideal in bad weather), and

it can be very slow in heavy traffic. It's best to think of this as a two-hour quickie orientation with scant information and lots of images. Stops include Ara Pacis, Piazza Cavour, St. Peter's Square, Corso Vittorio Emanuele (for Piazza Navona), Piazza Venezia, Colosseum, and Via Nazionale. Bus #110 departs every 20 minutes. You can catch it at any stop, including Termini Station. Buy the ticket as you board (runs daily April-Oct 8:30-20:30, shorter hours off-season, single tour-€12, 48-hour ticket-€18, tel. 800-281-281, www.trambusopen.com).

Archeobus is an open-top bus, also operated by ATAC, that runs twice hourly from Termini Station out to the ancient Appian Way (with stops at the Colosseum, Baths of Caracalla, San Callisto, San Sebastiano, and the Tomb of Cecilia Metella). This is a handy way to see the sights down this ancient Roman road, but it can be frustrating for various reasons—sparse narration, sporadic service, and not ideal for hopping on and off (€15, €25 combo-ticket with Trambus 110, ticket valid 48 hours, 1.5-hour loop, daily 9:00-16:30, less frequent off-season, from Termini Station and Piazza Venezia, tel. 800-281-281, www.trambusopen.com). A similar bus laces together all the Christian sights.

Car and Minibus Tours

Autoservizi Monti Concezio, run by gentle, capable, and English-speaking Ezio, offers private cars or minibuses with driver/guides (car-€40/hour, minibus-€45/hour, 3-hour minimum for city sightseeing, long rides outside Rome are more expensive, mobile 335-636-5907 or 349-674-5643, www.tourservicemonti.it, info@tourservicemonti.it).

Miles & Miles Private Tours is a family-run company offering a number of tours (all explained on their website) in Mercedes minibuses and cars, all with good English-speaking driver/guides (€60/hour for up to 8 people, 5-hour minimum, Rick Steves readers booking direct get a 10 percent discount off any web prices they offer, mobile 331-466-4900, www.milesandmiles.net, info@milesandmiles.net, Francesco answers the mobile phone, while Kimberly—an American—runs their office). They can also provide unguided long-distance transportation; if traveling with a small group or a family from Rome to Florence or the Amalfi Coast, consider paying extra to turn the trip into a memorable day tour with door-to-door service.

Weekend Tour Packages for Students in Rome

Andy Steves (Rick's son) runs Weekend Student Adventures, offering experimental three-day weekend tours for €200-300, designed for American students studying abroad; see www.wsaeurope.com for details on tours of Rome and other great cities.

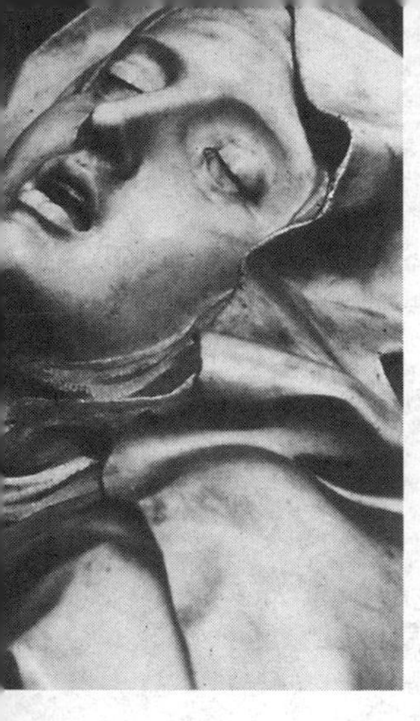

SIGHTS IN ROME

I've clustered Rome's sights into walkable neighborhoods, some quite close together (see the "Rome's Neighborhoods" map on page 23). Save transit time by grouping your sightseeing according to location. For example, the Colosseum and the Forum are a few minutes' walk from Capitoline Hill; a 15-minute walk beyond that is the Pantheon. I like to tour these sights in one great day, starting at the Colosseum and ending at the Pantheon.

Don't let the length of my descriptions determine your sightseeing priorities. In this chapter, Rome's most important sights have the shortest listings and are marked with a ✪. These sights are covered in much more detail in one of the tours included in this book. Check www.ricksteves.com/update for any significant changes that have occurred since this book was printed.

To connect some of the most central sights, follow my Heart of Rome Walk (see the chapter of the same name), which takes you from Campo de' Fiori to the Trevi Fountain and Spanish Steps. This walk is most enjoyable in the evening—after the churches and museums have closed, when the evening air and lit-up fountains show off Rome at its most magical. To join the parade of people strolling down Via del Corso every evening, take my "Dolce Vita Stroll" (see the end of the Nightlife in Rome chapter).

Price Hike Alert: Some of Rome's sights have found a clever way to squeeze more money out of visitors. They host a special exhibit that few tourists really care to see, and require you to pay extra for your ticket, even if all you want to see is the permanent collection. This means admission fees jump by about €3. Expect this practice at the Capitoline Museums, National Museum of Rome, Ara Pacis, and others.

The prices I've listed here include these obligatory temporary exhibits. Come expecting this higher price...and consider yourself lucky if you happen to visit on the rare occasion when you can get in for less.

Ancient Rome

The core of ancient Rome, where the grandest monuments were built, is between the Colosseum and Capitoline Hill. Among the ancient forums, a few modern sights have popped up.

The Colosseum and Nearby

▲▲▲Colosseum (Colosseo)—This 2,000-year-old building is the classic example of Roman engineering. Used as a venue for entertaining the masses, this colossal, functional stadium is one of Europe's most recognizable landmarks. Whether you're playing gladiator or simply marveling at the remarkable ancient design and construction, the Colosseum gets a unanimous thumbs-up.

Cost and Hours: €12 comboticket includes Roman Forum and Palatine Hill—see page 51, open daily 8:30 until one hour before sunset, last entry one hour before closing, audioguide-€5.50, Metro: Colosseo, tel. 06-3996-7700, http://archeoroma.beniculturali.it/en.

✪ See the Colosseum Tour chapter.

▲Arch of Constantine—This well-preserved arch, which stands between the Colosseum and the Forum, commemorates a military coup and, more importantly, the acceptance of Christianity by the Roman Empire. When the ambitious Emperor Constantine (who had a vision that he'd win under the sign of the cross) defeated his rival Maxentius in A.D. 312, Constantine became sole emperor of the Roman Empire and legalized Christianity. The arch is free to see—always open and viewable.

✪ See page 116 of the Colosseum Tour chapter.

▲St. Peter-in-Chains Church (San Pietro in Vincoli)—Built in the fifth century to house the chains that held St. Peter, this church is most famous for its Michelangelo statue. Check out the much-venerated chains under the high altar, then focus on mighty

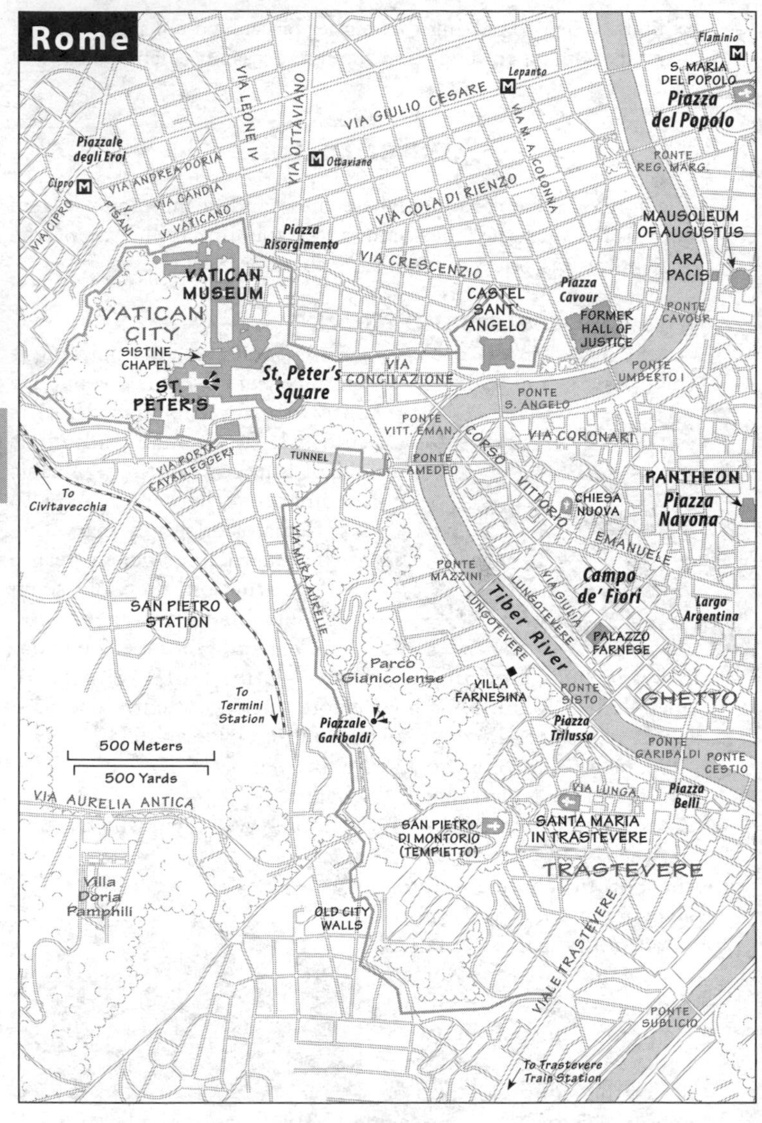

Moses. (Note that this isn't the famous St. Peter's Basilica, which is at Vatican City.)

Cost and Hours: Free, daily April-Sept 8:00-12:30 & 15:00-19:00, Oct-March 8:00-12:30 & 15:00-18:00, modest dress required; the church is a 10-minute uphill walk from the Colosseum, or a shorter, simpler walk from the Cavour Metro stop.

✪ See the St. Peter-in-Chains Tour chapter.

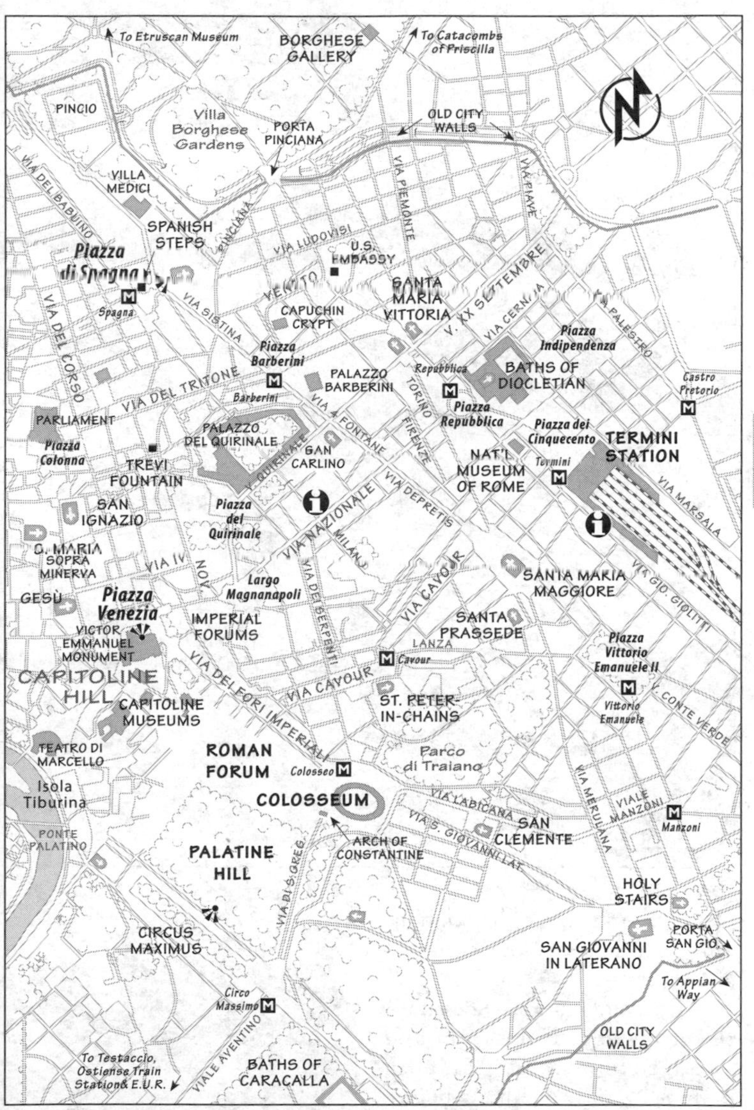

SIGHTS

The Roman Forum and Nearby

▲▲▲Roman Forum (Foro Romano)—This is ancient Rome's birthplace and civic center, and the common ground between Rome's famous seven hills. As just about anything important that happened in ancient Rome happened here, it's arguably the most important piece of real estate in Western civilization. While only a few fragments of that glorious past remain, history-seekers find

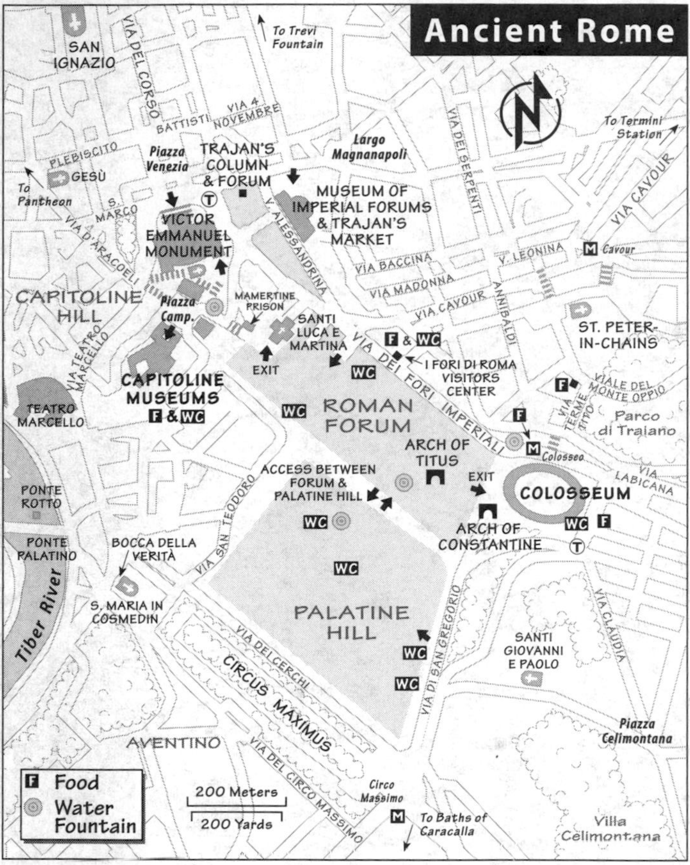

Ancient Rome

plenty to ignite their imaginations amid the half-broken columns and arches.

Cost and Hours: €12 combo-ticket includes Colosseum and Palatine Hill—see page 51, open daily 8:30 until one hour before sunset, last entry one hour before closing, audioguide-€5, Metro: Colosseo, tel. 06-3996-7700, http://archeoroma.beniculturali.it/en.

✪ See the Roman Forum Tour chapter.

▲▲Palatine Hill (Monte Palatino)—The hill overlooking the Forum was the home of the emperors and now contains a museum, scant (but impressive when understood) remains of imperial palaces, and a view of the Circus Maximus.

Cost and Hours: €12 combo-ticket includes Roman Forum and Colosseum—see page 51, open same hours as Forum and Colosseum, audioguide-€5, Metro: Colosseo.

✪ See the Palatine Hill Tour chapter.

Mamertine Prison—This 2,500-year-old cistern-like prison is where, according to Christian tradition, the Romans imprisoned Saints Peter and Paul. Though it was long a charming and historic sight, its artifacts have been removed, and today it's run by a commercial tour-bus company charging €10 for a cheesy "multimedia" walk-through. Don't go in. Instead, stand outside and imagine how this dank cistern once housed prisoners of the emperor. Amid fat rats and rotting corpses, unfortunate humans awaited slow deaths. It's said that a miraculous fountain sprang up inside so Peter could convert and baptize his jailers, who were also subsequently martyred. Before the commercial ruination of this sacred and ancient site, on the walls you could read lists of notable prisoners (Christian and non-Christian) and the ways they were executed: *strangolati, decapitato, morto per fame* (died of hunger). The sign by the Christian names read, "Here suffered, victorious for the triumph of Christ, these martyr saints." Today this sight itself has been martyred by a city apparently desperate to monetize its heritage.

▲Trajan's Column, Market, and Museum of the Imperial Forums—This grand column is the best example of "continuous narration" that we have from antiquity (free, always open and viewable, on Piazza Venezia across the street from Victor Emmanuel Monument). The market ruins are viewable for free from Via dei Fori Imperiali. Paying the admission fee gets you inside Trajan's Market, Trajan's Forum, and the Museum of the Imperial Forums. The museum features discoveries from the forums of emperors Julius Caesar, Augustus, Nerva, and Trajan, with fragments of statues and a slideshow that reconstructs how the forum looked in each emperor's time.

Cost and Hours: Museum—€11, Tue-Sun 9:00-19:00, closed Mon, last entry one hour before closing, audioguide-€3.50, entrance is uphill from the column on Via IV Novembre 94, tel. 06-0608, www.mercatiditraiano.it.

✪ See the Trajan's Forum Tour chapter.

Bocca della Verità—The legendary "Mouth of Truth" at the Church of Santa Maria in Cosmedin draws a playful crowd. Stick your hand in the mouth of the gaping stone face in the porch wall. As the legend goes (and was popularized by the 1953 film *Roman*

SIGHTS

Tips on Sightseeing in Rome

These tips will help you use your time and money efficiently, making the Eternal City seem less eternal and more entertaining. For general advice on sightseeing, see page 16.

Passes

Roma Pass: Rome offers several sightseeing passes to help you save money. For most visitors, the Roma Pass (www.romapass.it) is the clear winner. The Roma Pass costs €30 and is valid for three days, covering public transportation and free or discounted entry to Roman sights. You get free admission to your first two sights (where you also get to skip the ticket line) and then a discount on the rest within the three-day window. Sights covered (or discounted) by the pass include the following: Colosseum/Palatine Hill/Roman Forum, Borghese Gallery (though you still must make a reservation), Capitoline Museums, Castel Sant'Angelo, Montemartini Museum, Ara Pacis, Museum of Roman Civilization, Etruscan Museum, Baths of Caracalla, Trajan's Market, and some of the Appian Way sights. The pass also covers four branches of the National Museum of Rome, considered as a single "sight": Palazzo Massimo (the most important of the lot), Crypta Balbi (medieval art), Palazzo Altemps (sculpture collection), and Museum of the Bath (ancient inscriptions).

If you'll be visiting any two of the major sights in a three-day period, get the pass. It's sold at participating sights, TIs, and many tobacco shops or newsstands (look for a *Roma Pass* sign; all should offer the same price). Try to buy it at a less crowded TI or sight (you can buy it at a sight even if you don't intend to use it there). Don't bother to order it online—you have to physically pick up the pass in Rome, which negates any time-saving advantage.

Validate your Roma Pass by writing your name and validation date on the card. Then insert it directly into the turnstile at your first two (free) sights. At other sights, show it at the ticket office to get your reduced *(ridotto)* price—about 30 percent off.

To get the most of your pass, visit the two most expensive sights first—for example, the Colosseum (€12) and the National Museum (€10). Definitely use it to bypass the long ticket-buying line at the Colosseum. For sights that normally sell a combined ticket (such as the Colosseum/Palatine Hill/Roman Forum or the National Museum branches), visiting the combined sight counts as a single entry.

The Roma Pass comes with a three-day transit pass. Write your name and birth date on the transit pass, validate it on your first bus or Metro ride by passing it over a sensor at a turnstile or validation machine (look for a yellow circle), and you can take unlimited rides within Rome's city limits until midnight of the third day.

The TI's other passes—Roma & Più Pass ("Rome & More") and the Archeologia Card—are generally not worth the trouble for most tourists.

Combo-Ticket for Colosseum, Forum, and Palatine Hill: A €12 combo-ticket covers these three adjacent sights (no individual tickets are sold per sight). The combo-ticket allows one entry per sight and is valid for two days. Note that these sights are also covered by the Roma Pass. To avoid ticket-buying lines at the Colosseum and Forum, purchase your combo-ticket or Roma Pass at the lesser-visited Palatine Hill. Between the combo-ticket or Roma Pass, the pass is the better deal, unless you're planning on seeing only the sights covered by the combo-ticket.

Top Tips

Museum Reservations: The marvelous Borghese Gallery requires reservations in advance (for specifics, see page 241). You can reserve online to avoid long lines at the Vatican Museum (see page 207).

Opening Hours: Rome's sights have notoriously variable hours from season to season. Get a current listing of opening times—ask for the free booklet *Evento* at a TI or your hotel. Or check online at www.060608.it/en (find "Cultural Heritage" in the menu under "Culture and Leisure"; search by using the Italian names of sights). On holidays, expect shorter hours or closures.

Churches: Many churches, which have divine art and free entry, open early (around 7:00-7:30), close for lunch (roughly 12:00-15:00), and close late (about 19:00). Kamikaze tourists maximize their sightseeing hours by visiting churches before 9:00 or late in the day and, during the siesta, seeing major sights that stay open all day (St. Peter's, Colosseum, Forum, Capitoline Museums, Pantheon, and National Museum of Rome). Dress modestly for church visits.

Picnic Discreetly: Public drinking and eating is not allowed at major sights, though the ban has proven difficult to enforce. To avoid the risk of being fined, choose an empty piazza for your picnic, or keep a low profile.

Miscellaneous Tips: I carry a plastic water bottle and refill it at Rome's many public drinking spouts. Because public restrooms are scarce, use toilets at museums, restaurants, and bars.

Holiday, starring Gregory Peck and Audrey Hepburn), if you're a liar, your hand will be gobbled up. The mouth is only accessible when the church gate is open, but it's always (partially) visible through the gate, even when closed. If the church itself is open, step inside to see one of the few unaltered medieval church interiors in Rome. Notice the mismatched ancient columns and beautiful cosmatesque floor—a centuries-old example of recycling.

Cost and Hours: €0.50, daily 9:30-17:50, closes earlier off-season, Piazza Bocca della Verità, near the north end of Circus Maximus.

Capitoline Hill

Of Rome's famous seven hills, this is the smallest, tallest, and most famous—home of the ancient Temple of Jupiter and the center of city government for 2,500 years. There are several ways to get to the top of Capitoline Hill. If you're coming from the north (from Piazza Venezia), take Michelangelo's impressive stairway to the right of the big, white Victor Emmanuel Monument. Coming from the southeast (the Forum), take the steep staircase near the Arch of Septimius Severus. From near Trajan's Forum along Via dei Fori Imperiali, take the winding road. All three converge at the top, in the square called Campidoglio (kahm-pee-DOHL-yoh).

▲Piazza del Campidoglio (Capitoline Hill Square)—This square atop the hill, once the religious and political center of ancient Rome, is still the home of the city's government. In the 1530s, the pope called on Michelangelo to re-establish this square as a grand center. Michelangelo placed the ancient equestrian statue of Marcus Aurelius as the square's focal point. Effective. (The original statue is now in the adjacent museum.) The twin buildings on either side are the Capitoline Museums. Behind the replica of the statue is the mayoral palace (Palazzo Senatorio).

Michelangelo intended that people approach the square from his grand stairway off Piazza Venezia. From the top of the stairway, you see the new Renaissance face of Rome, with its back to the Forum. Michelangelo gave the buildings the "giant order"—

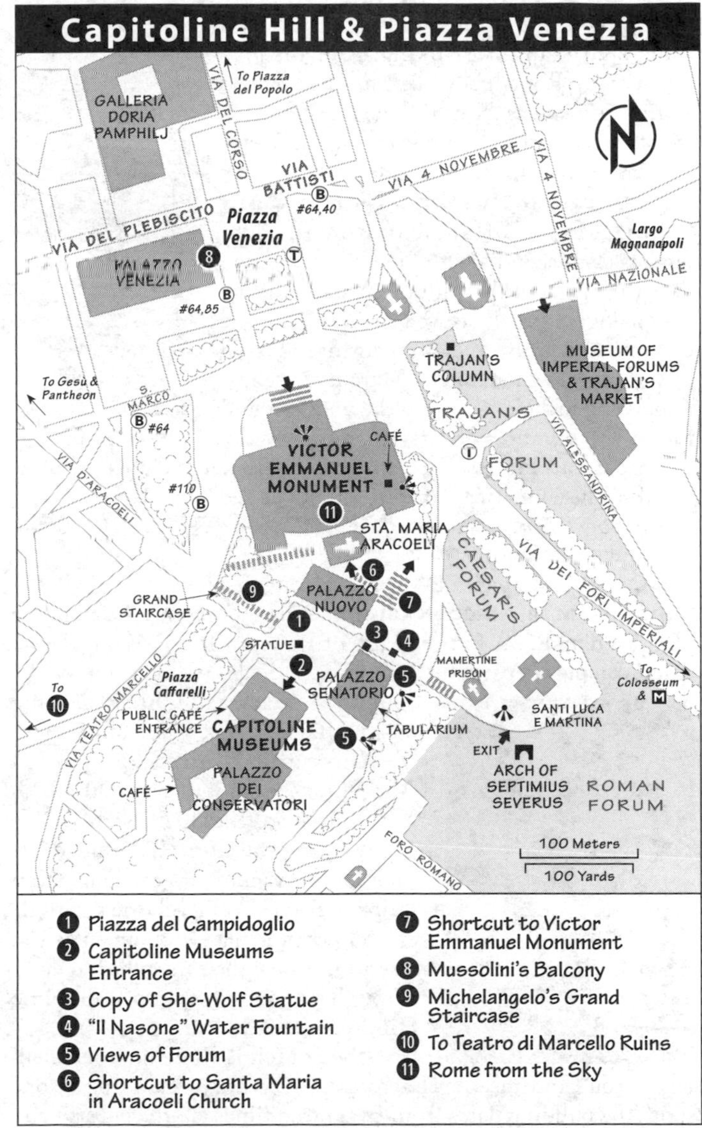

huge pilasters make the existing two-story buildings feel one-storied and more harmonious with the new square. Notice how the statues atop these buildings welcome you and then draw you in.

The terraces just downhill (past either side of the mayor's palace) offer grand views of the Forum. To the left of the mayor's palace is a copy of the famous she-wolf statue on a column. Farther down is *il nasone* ("the big nose"), a refreshing water fountain (see

photo). Block the spout with your fingers, and water spurts up for drinking. Romans joke that a cheap Roman boy takes his date out for a drink at *il nasone.* Near the she-wolf statue is the staircase leading to a shortcut to the Victor Emmanuel Monument (see sidebar).

▲▲Capitoline Museums (Musei Capitolini)—Some of ancient Rome's most famous statues and art are housed in the two palaces that flank the equestrian statue in the Campidoglio. You'll see the Dying Gaul, the original she-wolf, and the original version of the equestrian statue of Marcus Aurelius. Admission includes access to the underground vacant Tabularium, with its panoramic overlook of the Forum.

Cost and Hours: €12, €14 combo-ticket includes Montemartini Museum, Tue-Sun 9:00-20:00, closed Mon, last entry one hour before closing, audioguide-€5, tel. 06-8205-9127 or 06-0608, www.museicapitolini.org.

✪ See the Capitoline Museums Tour chapter.

Santa Maria in Aracoeli Church—The church atop Capitoline Hill is old and dear to the hearts of Romans. It stands on the site where Emperor Augustus (supposedly) had a premonition of the coming of Mary and Christ standing on an "altar in the sky" *(ara coeli).*

Cost and Hours: Free, daily April-Oct 9:00-12:30 & 15:00-18:30, Nov-March 9:00-12:30 & 14:30-17:30.

Visiting the Church: While dedicated pilgrims climb up the long, steep staircase from street level (the right side of Victor Emmanuel Monument as you face it), savvy sightseers prefer to enter through the shortcut atop Capitoline Hill (see sidebar).

The church is Rome in a nutshell, where you can time-travel across 2,000 years by standing in one spot. The building dates from Byzantine times (sixth century) and was expanded in the 1200s. Inside, the mismatched columns (red, yellow, striped, fluted) and marble floor are ancient, plundered from many different monuments. The medieval world is evident in the gravestones beneath your feet. The early Renaissance is featured in beautiful frescoes by Pinturicchio (first chapel on the right from the main entrance), with their 3-D perspective and natural landscapes. The coffered ceiling celebrates the Christian victory

Shortcut to the Victor Emmanuel Monument and Aracoeli Church

A clever shortcut lets you go directly from Piazza del Campidoglio, the square atop Capitoline Hill, to Santa Maria in Aracoeli Church and an upper level of the Victor Emmanuel Monument, avoiding long flights of stairs. Facing the square's equestrian statue, head to the left, climbing the wide set of stairs near the she-wolf statue. Midway up the stairs (at the column), turn left to reach the back entrance to the Aracoeli Church. To reach the Victor Emmanuel Monument, pass the column and continue to the top of the steps, pass through the iron gate, and enter the small unmarked door at #13 on the right. You'll soon emerge on a café terrace that leads to the monument and the Rome from the Sky elevator.

over the Ottoman Turks (Battle of Lepanto, 1571), with thanks to Mary (in the center of the ceiling). The chandeliers in the nave hint at the elegance of Baroque. Napoleon's occupying troops used the building as a horse stable. But like Rome itself, it survived and retained its splendor.

The church comes alive at Christmastime. Romans hike up to enjoy a manger scene *(presepio)* assembled every year in the second chapel on the left. They stop at the many images of the Virgin (e.g., the statue in the marble gazebo to the left of the altar), who made an appearance to the pagan Augustus so long ago. And, most famously, they venerate a wooden statue of the baby Jesus (Santo Bambino), displayed in a chapel to the left of the altar. Though the original statue was stolen in 1994, the copy continues this longtime Roman tradition.

The daunting 125-step staircase up Capitoline Hill to the entrance was once climbed—on their knees—by Roman women who wished for a child. Today, they don't...and Italy has Europe's lowest birthrate.

Rome at a Glance

▲▲▲**Colosseum** Huge stadium where gladiators fought. **Hours:** Daily 8:30 until one hour before sunset: April-Sept until 19:15, Oct until 18:30, off-season closes as early as 16:30. See page 45.

▲▲▲**Roman Forum** Ancient Rome's main square, with ruins and grand arches. **Hours:** Same hours as Colosseum. See page 47.

▲▲▲**Pantheon** The defining domed temple. **Hours:** Mon-Sat 8:30-19:30, Sun 9:00-18:00, holidays 9:00-13:00, closed for Mass Sat at 17:00 and Sun at 10:30. See page 60.

▲▲▲**St. Peter's Basilica** Most impressive church on earth, with Michelangelo's *Pietà* and dome. **Hours:** Church—daily April-Sept 7:00-19:00, Oct-March 7:00-18:00, often closed Wed mornings; dome—daily April-Sept 8:00-18:00, Oct-March 8:00-17:00. See page 63.

▲▲▲**Vatican Museum** Four miles of the finest art of Western civilization, culminating in Michelangelo's glorious Sistine Chapel. **Hours:** Mon-Sat 9:00-18:00. Closed on religious holidays and Sun, except last Sun of the month (open 9:00-14:00). May be open some Fri nights by online reservation only. Hours are subject to change. See page 64.

▲▲▲**Borghese Gallery** Bernini sculptures and paintings by Caravaggio, Raphael, and Titian in a Baroque palazzo. Reservations mandatory. **Hours:** Tue-Sun 9:00-19:00, closed Mon. See page 67.

▲▲▲**National Museum of Rome** Greatest collection of Roman sculpture anywhere. **Hours:** Tue-Sun 9:00-19:45, closed Mon. See page 77.

▲▲**Palatine Hill** Ruins of emperors' palaces, Circus Maximus view, and museum. **Hours:** Same as Colosseum. See page 48.

▲▲**Capitoline Museums** Ancient statues, mosaics, and expansive view of Forum. **Hours:** Tue-Sun 9:00-20:00, closed Mon. See page 54.

▲▲**Ara Pacis** Shrine marking the beginning of Rome's Golden Age. **Hours:** Tue-Sun 9:00-19:00, closed Mon. See page 74.

▲▲**Dolce Vita Stroll** Evening passeggiata, where Romans strut their stuff. **Hours:** Roughly Mon-Sat 17:00-19:00 and Sun afternoons. See page 73.

SIGHTS

▲▲**Catacombs** Underground tombs, mainly Christian, some outside the city. **Hours:** Generally open 10:00-12:00 & 14:00-17:00. See pages 73 and 95.

▲**Arch of Constantine** Honors the emperor who legalized Christianity. **Hours:** Always viewable. See page 45.

▲**St. Peter-in-Chains** Church with Michelangelo's Moses. **Hours:** Daily 8:00-12:30 & 15:00-19:00, until 18:00 in winter. See page 45.

▲**Trajan's Column, Market, and Museum of the Imperial Forums** Tall column with narrative relief, and museum with entry to Trajan's Market. **Hours:** Column always viewable; museum open Tue-Sun 9:00-19:00, closed Mon. See page 49.

▲**Piazza del Campidoglio** Square atop Capitoline Hill, designed by Michelangelo, with a museum, grand stairway, and Forum overlooks. **Hours:** Always open. See page 52.

▲**Victor Emmanuel Monument** Gigantic edifice celebrating Italian unity, with Rome from the Sky elevator ride up to 360-degree city view. **Hours:** Monument open daily 9:30-18:30; elevator open Mon-Thu 9:30-18:30, Fri-Sun 9:30-19:30. See page 58.

▲**Trevi Fountain** Baroque hot spot into which tourists throw coins to ensure a return trip to Rome. **Hours:** Always flowing. See page 62.

▲**Castel Sant'Angelo** Hadrian's Tomb turned castle, prison, papal refuge, now museum. **Hours:** Tue-Sun 9:00-19:30, closed Mon. See page 65.

▲**Capuchin Crypt** Decorated with the bones of 4,000 Franciscan friars. **Hours:** Daily 9:00-12:00 & 15:00-18:00. See page 69.

▲**Baths of Diocletian** Once ancient Rome's immense public baths, now a Michelangelo church. **Hours:** Mon-Sat 7:00-18:30, Sun 7:00-19:30, closed to sightseers during Mass. See page 77.

▲**Santa Maria della Vittoria** Church with Bernini's swooning St. Teresa in Ecstasy. **Hours:** Mon-Sat 8:30-12:00 & 15:30-18:00, Sun 15:30-18:00. See page 77.

Piazza Venezia

This vast square, dominated by the big, white Victor Emmanuel Monument, is a major transportation hub and the focal point of modern Rome. (The square has been dug up for years—Metro line C is under construction, and when anything of archaeological importance is uncovered, progress is interrupted, hence the canopied site on the square today.) With your back to the monument (you'll get the best views from the terrace by the guards and eternal flame), look down Via del Corso, the city's axis, surrounded by Rome's classiest shopping district. In the 1930s, Benito Mussolini whipped up Italy's nationalistic fervor from a balcony above the square (it's the less-grand balcony on the left). He gave 64 speeches from this balcony, including the declaration of war in 1940. This Early Renaissance building (with hints of medieval showing with its crenellated roof line) was the seat of Mussolini's fascist government. Fascist masses filled the square screaming, "Four more years!"—or something like that. Mussolini created the boulevard Via dei Fori Imperiali (to your right) to open up views of the Colosseum in the distance to impress his visiting friend Adolf Hitler. Mussolini lied to his people, mixing fear and patriotism to push his country to the right and embroil the Italians in expensive and regrettable wars. In 1945, they shot Mussolini and hung him from a meat hook in Milan. (Former Prime Minister Silvio Berlusconi's headquarters are still located—thought-provokingly—just behind Mussolini's. That explains all the security on Via del Plebiscito.)

With your back still to the monument, circle around the left side, and look down into the ditch on your left to see the ruins of an ancient apartment building from the first century A.D.; part of it was transformed into a tiny church (faded frescoes and bell tower). Rome was built in layers—almost everywhere you go, there's an earlier version beneath your feet. (The hop-on, hop-off Trambus 110 stops just across the busy intersection from here.)

Continuing on, you reach two staircases leading up Capitoline Hill. One is Michelangelo's grand staircase up to the Campidoglio. The longer of the two leads to the Santa Maria in Aracoeli Church, a good example of the earliest style of Christian churches (described earlier). The contrast between this climb-on-your-knees ramp to God's house and Michelangelo's elegant stairs illustrates the changes Renaissance humanism brought civilization.

From the bottom of Michelangelo's stairs, look right several blocks down the street to see a condominium actually built upon the surviving ancient pillars and arches of Teatro di Marcello.

▲Victor Emmanuel Monument—This oversize monument to Italy's first king, built to celebrate the 50th anniversary of the country's unification in 1861, was part of Italy's push to overcome

the new country's strong regionalism and create a national identity. The scale of the monument is over-the-top: 200 feet high, 500 feet wide. The 43-foot-long statue of the king on the horse is one of the biggest equestrian statues in the world. The king's moustache forms an arc five feet long, and a person could sit within the horse's hoof. At the base of this statue, Italy's Tomb of the Unknown Soldier (flanked by Italian flags and armed guards) is watched over by the goddess Roma (with the gold mosaic background).

With its gleaming white sheen (from a recent scrubbing) and enormous scale, the monument provides a vivid sense of what Ancient Rome looked like at its peak—imagine the Forum filled with shiny, grandiose buildings like this one. It's also lathered in symbolism meant to connect the modern city and nation with its grand past: The eternal flames are reminiscent of the Vestal Virgins and the ancient flame of Rome. And it's crowned by glorious chariots like those that topped the ancient Arch of Constantine.

Locals have a love/hate relationship with this "Altar of the Nation." Many Romans regret its unfortunate, clumsy location atop precious antiquities. Others consider it a reminder of the challenge that followed the creation of the modern nation of Italy: actually creating "Italians."

The "Vittoriano" (as locals call it) is open and free to the public. You can simply climb the front stairs, or go inside from one of several entrances: midway up the monument through doorways flanking the central statue, on either side at street level, and at the base of the colonnade (two-thirds of the way up, near the shortcut from Capitoline Hill). The little-visited **Museum of the Risorgimento** fills several floors with displays (well-described in English) on the movement and war that led to the unification of Italy in 1870. A section on the lower east side hosts temporary exhibits of minor works by major artists (free to enter museum, exhibits around €10, tel. 06-322-5380, www.comunicareorganizzando.it/home.asp). A café is at the base of the top colonnade, on the monument's east side.

Best of all, the monument offers a grand view of the Eternal City. You can climb the stairs to the midway point for a decent view, keep climbing to the base of the colonnade for a better view, or, for the best view, ride the **Rome from the Sky** elevator, which zips you from the top of the stair climb (at the back of the monument) to the rooftop for the grandest, 360-degree view of the center of Rome—even better than from the top of St. Peter's dome. Once on top, you stand on a terrace between the monument's two chariots. You can look north up Via del Corso to Piazza del Popolo, west to the dome of St. Peter's Basilica, and south to the Roman Forum and Colosseum. Helpful panoramic diagrams describe the skyline, with powerful binoculars available for zooming in on particular sights. It's best in late afternoon, when it's beginning to cool off and Rome glows.

Cost and Hours: Monument—Free, daily 9:30-18:30, a few WCs scattered throughout, tel. 06-679-3598. Elevator—€7, Mon-Thu 9:30-18:30, Fri-Sun 9:30-19:30, ticket office closes 45 minutes earlier, WC at entrance, tel. 06-6920-2049; follow *ascensori panoramici* signs inside the Victor Emmanuel Monument or take the shortcut from Capitoline Hill (no elevator access from street level).

Pantheon Neighborhood

Besides being home to ancient sights and historic churches, this neighborhood gives Rome its urban-village feel. Wander narrow streets, sample the many shops and eateries, and gather with the locals in squares marked by bubbling fountains. Exploring is especially good in the evening, when the restaurants bustle and streets are jammed with foot traffic.

For a self-guided walk of this neighborhood, from Campo de' Fiori to the Trevi Fountain, ✪ see the Heart of Rome Walk chapter.

▲▲▲Pantheon—For the greatest look at the splendor of Rome, antiquity's best-preserved interior is a must. Built two millennia ago, this influential domed temple served as the model for Michelangelo's dome of St. Peter's and many others.

Cost and Hours: Free, Mon-Sat 8:30-19:30, Sun 9:00-18:00, holidays 9:00-13:00, closed for Mass Sat at 17:00 and Sun at 10:30, audioguide-€5, tel. 06-6830-0230.

✪ See the Pantheon Tour chapter.

▲▲Churches near the Pantheon—For more information on the following churches, see the latter half of my Pantheon Tour chapter. Modest dress is recommended.

The **Church of San Luigi dei Francesi** has a magnificent chapel painted by Caravaggio (free, daily 10:00-12:30 & 15:00-19:00 except closed Thu afternoon, between the Pantheon and the north end of Piazza Navona). The only Gothic church in Rome is

the **Church of Santa Maria sopra Minerva,** with a little-known Michelangelo statue, *Christ Bearing the Cross* (free, Mon-Fri 7:00-19:00, Sat-Sun 8:00-12:30 & 15:30-19:00, on a little square behind Pantheon, to the east). The **Church of San Ignazio,** several blocks east of the Pantheon, is a riot of Baroque illusions with a false dome (free, Mon-Sat 7:30-19:00, Sun 9:00-19:00). A few blocks away, across Corso Vittorio Emanuele, is the rich and Baroque **Gesù Church,** headquarters of the Jesuits in Rome (free, daily 7:00-12:30 & 16:00-19:45, interesting daily service at 17:30—see page 176 for details).

Leaving the Gesù Church, head two blocks down Corso Vittorio Emanuele, and you'll hit Largo Argentina, an excavated square facing the boulevard, about four blocks south of the Pantheon. Stroll around this square and look into the excavated pit at some of the oldest ruins in Rome. Julius Caesar was assassinated near here. The far (west) side of the square is a refuge for cats—volunteers care for some 250 of them (www.romancats.com).

▲Galleria Doria Pamphilj—This underappreciated gallery, in the heart of the old city, offers a rare chance to wander through

a noble family's lavish rooms with the prince who calls this downtown mansion home. Well, almost. Through an audioguide, the prince lovingly narrates his family's story as you tour the palace and its world-class art.

Cost and Hours: €10.50, includes worthwhile 1.5-hour audioguide, daily 10:00-17:00, last entry 45 minutes before closing, elegant café, from Piazza Venezia walk 2 blocks up Via del Corso to #305, tel. 06-679-7323, www.dopart.it/roma.

Visiting the Galleria: The story begins upstairs in the grand entrance hall (Salone del Poussin), wallpapered with French landscapes. In the adjoining throne room, you'll see a portrait of Pope Innocent X (1574-1655), patriarch of the Pamphilj (pahm-FEEL-yee) family. His wealth and power flowed to his nephew, who built the palace—a cozy relationship that inspired the word "nepotism" (*nepotem* is Latin for "nephew"). The family eventually married into English nobility, which is why today's prince speaks the Queen's English. You'll visit the red velvet room, the green living room, and the mirror-lined ballroom that once hosted music by resident composers Scarlatti and Handel. Along the way, the prince tells charming family secrets, like when he and his sister were scolded for roller-skating through the palace.

Past the bookshop is the painting collection. (Major works have a number to dial up audioguide information.) Don't miss Velázquez's intense, majestic, ultra-realistic portrait of the family founder, Innocent X. It stands alongside an equally impressive bust of the pope by Bernini. Stroll through a mini-Versailles-like hall of mirrors to more paintings, including works by Titian and Raphael. Finally, relax along with Mary, Joseph, and Jesus, and let the angel serenade you in Caravaggio's *Rest on the Flight to Egypt.*

Piazza di Pietra (Piazza of Stone)—The square was actually a quarry set up to chew away at the abandoned Temple of Hadrian, dedicated to the emperor responsible for building the Pantheon (look for his bust and a model of the temple in a window on the square). You can still see the holes that hungry medieval scavengers chipped into the columns to steal the metal pins that held the slabs together. Look over the railing to see ground level 1,900 years ago (two blocks toward Via del Corso from Pantheon).

▲Trevi Fountain—The bubbly Baroque fountain, worth ▲▲ by night, is a minor sight to art scholars...but a major nighttime

gathering spot for teens on the make and tourists tossing coins. The coins tourists deposit daily are collected to feed Rome's poor.

✪ See the Heart of Rome Walk chapter.

Palazzo del Quirinale—This presidential palace, the former home of several popes and the Italian royal family, feels like a combination White House/Palace of Versailles. Guided tours—on Sundays only—take you through its opulent public rooms. Named after the highest of Rome's seven hills, the square in front offers fine views of St. Peter's Basilica.

Cost and Hours: €5, Sun 8:30-12:00 only—closed rest of the week, expect a line, square always open, 200 yards east and up the hill from Trevi Fountain on Piazza del Quirinale, tel. 06-46991, www.quirinale.it.

SIGHTS

Vatican City

Vatican City, the world's smallest country, contains St. Peter's Basilica (with Michelangelo's exquisite *Pietà*) and the Vatican Museum (with Michelangelo's Sistine Chapel). A helpful **TI** is just to the left of St. Peter's Basilica as you're facing it (Mon-Sat 8:30-18:15, closed Sun, tel. 06-6988-1662, Vatican switchboard tel. 06-6982, www.vatican.va). The entrances to St. Peter's and to the Vatican Museum are a 15-minute walk apart (follow the outside of the Vatican wall, which links the two sights). The nearest Metro stop—Ottaviano—still involves a 10-minute walk to either sight. For information on Vatican tours, post offices, and the pope's schedule, see page 184.

Modest dress is required of men, women, and children throughout Vatican City, even outdoors. Otherwise, the Swiss Guard can turn you away. Cover your shoulders; bring a light jacket or cover-up if you're wearing a tank top. Wear long pants instead of shorts. Skirts or dresses should extend below your knee.

▲▲▲St. Peter's Basilica (Basilica San Pietro)—There is no doubt: This is the richest and grandest church on earth. To call it

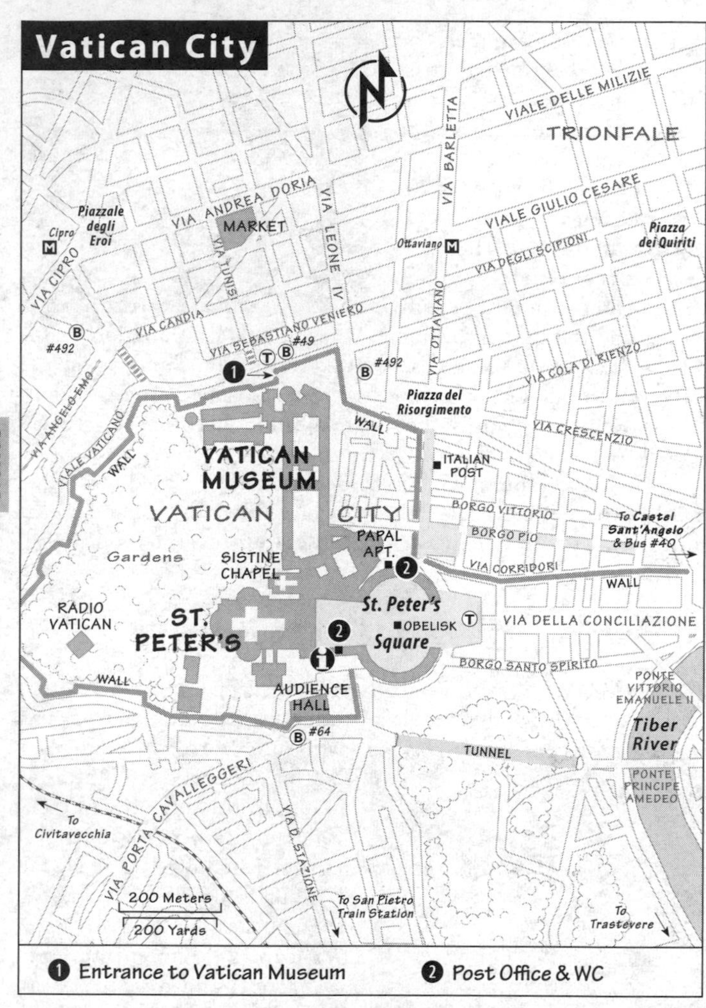

vast is like calling Einstein smart.

Cost and Hours: Free, daily April-Sept 7:00-19:00, Oct-March 7:00-18:00. The church closes on Wednesday mornings during papal audiences. Masses occur daily throughout the day. Audioguides can be rented near the checkroom (€5 plus ID, for church only, daily 9:00-17:00). The view from the dome is worth the climb (€7 for elevator to roof, then take stairs; €6 to climb stairs all the way; allow an hour to go up and down, daily April-Sept 8:00-18:00, Oct-March 8:00-17:00, www.saintpetersbasilica.org).

✪ See the St. Peter's Basilica Tour chapter.

▲▲▲Vatican Museum (Musei Vaticani)—The four miles of displays in this immense museum—from ancient statues to Christian frescoes to modern paintings—culminate in the Raphael Rooms and Michelangelo's glorious Sistine Chapel.

Cost and Hours: €15 plus optional €4 reservation fee, Mon-Sat 9:00-18:00, last entry at 16:00 (though the official closing time is 18:00, the staff starts ushering you out at 17:30), closed on religious holidays and Sun except last Sun of the month (when it's free, more crowded, and open 9:00-14:00, last entry at 12:30); may be open Fri nights May-July and Sept-Oct 19:00-23:00 (last entry at 21:30) by online reservation only. Hours are subject to constant change and frequent holidays; check http://mv.vatican.va for current times. Lines are extremely long in the morning—go in the afternoon, or skip the ticket-buying line altogether by reserving an entry time on their website. A €7 audioguide is available (ID required).

✪ See the Vatican Museum Tour chapter.

Near Vatican City

▲Castel Sant'Angelo—Built as a tomb for the emperor, used through the Middle Ages as a castle, prison, and place of last refuge for popes under attack, and today a museum, this giant pile of ancient bricks is packed with history.

Cost and Hours: €8.50, Tue-Sun 9:00-19:30, closed Mon, last entry one hour before closing, near Vatican City, Metro: Lepanto or bus #40 or #64, tel. 06-681-9111, www.castelsantangelo.beniculturali.it.

Background: Ancient Rome allowed no tombs—not even the emperor's—within its walls. So Emperor Hadrian grabbed the

most commanding position just outside the walls and across the river and built a towering tomb (c. A.D. 139) well within view of the city. His mausoleum was a huge cylinder (210 by 70 feet) topped by a cypress grove and crowned by a huge statue of Hadrian himself riding a chariot. For nearly a hundred years, Roman emperors (from Hadrian to Caracalla, in A.D. 217) were buried here.

In the year 590, the archangel Michael appeared above the mausoleum to Pope Gregory the Great. Sheathing his sword, the angel signaled the end of a plague. The fortress that was Hadrian's mausoleum eventually became a fortified palace, renamed for the "holy angel."

Castel Sant'Angelo spent centuries of the Dark Ages as a fortress and prison, but was eventually connected to the Vatican via an elevated corridor at the pope's request (1277). Since Rome was repeatedly plundered by invaders, Castel Sant'Angelo was a handy place of last refuge for threatened popes. In anticipation of long sieges, rooms were decorated with papal splendor (you'll see paintings by Carlo Crivelli, Luca Signorelli, and Andrea Mantegna). In 1527, during a sack of Rome by troops of Charles V of Spain, the pope lived inside the castle for months with his entourage of hundreds (an unimaginable ordeal, considering the food service at the top-floor bar).

Visiting the Castle: Touring the place is a stair-stepping workout. After you walk around the entire base of the castle, take the small staircase down to the original Roman floor (following the route of Hadrian's funeral procession). In the atrium, study the model of the mausoleum as it was in Roman times. Imagine being surrounded by a veneer of marble, and the niche in the wall filled with a towering "welcome to my tomb" statue of Hadrian. From here, a ramp leads to the right, spiraling 400 feet. While some of the fine original brickwork and bits of mosaic survive, the marble veneer is long gone (notice the holes in the wall that held it in place).

At the end of the ramp, a bridge crosses over the room where the ashes of the emperors were kept. From here, the stairs continue out of the ancient section and into the medieval structure (built atop the mausoleum) that housed the papal apartments. Don't miss the Sala del Tesoro (Treasury), where the wealth of the Vatican was locked up in a huge chest. (*Do* miss the 58 rooms of the military museum.) From the pope's piggy bank, a narrow flight of stairs leads to the rooftop and perhaps the finest view of Rome anywhere (pick out landmarks as you stroll around). From the safety of this dramatic vantage point, the pope surveyed the city in times of siege. Look down at the bend of the Tiber, which for 2,700 years has cradled the Eternal City.

Ponte Sant'Angelo—The bridge leading to Castel Sant'Angelo was built by Hadrian for quick and regal access from downtown to his tomb. The three middle arches are actually Roman originals and a fine example of the empire's engineering expertise. The statues of angels (each bearing a symbol of the passion of Christ—nail, sponge, shroud, and so on) are Bernini-designed and textbook Baroque. In the Middle Ages, this was the only bridge in the area that connected St. Peter's and the Vatican with downtown Rome. Nearly all pilgrims passed this bridge to and from the church.

Its shoulder-high banisters recall a tragedy: During a Jubilee Year festival in 1450, the crowd got so huge that the mob pushed out the original banisters, causing nearly 200 to fall to their deaths.

Today, as through the ages, pilgrims cross the bridge, turn left, and set their sights on the Vatican dome. Around the year 1600, they would have also set their sights on a bunch of heads hanging from the crenellations of the castle. Ponte Sant'Angelo was infamous as a place for beheadings (banditry in the countryside was rife). Locals said, "There are more heads at Castel Sant'Angelo than there are melons in the market."

North Rome

Borghese Gardens and Via Veneto

▲Villa Borghese Gardens—Rome's semi-scruffy three-square-mile "Central Park" is great for its shade and for people-watching plenty of modern-day Romeos and Juliets. The best entrance is at the head of Via Veneto (Metro: Barberini, then 10-minute walk up Via Veneto and through the old Roman wall at Porta Pinciana, or catch a cab to Via Veneto—Porta Pinciana). There you'll find a cluster of buildings with a café, a kiddie arcade, and bike rental (€4/hour). Rent a bike or, for romantics, a pedaled rickshaw *(riscio)*. Bikes come with locks to allow you to make sightseeing stops. Follow signs to discover the park's cafés, fountains, statues, lake, great viewpoint over Piazza del Popolo, and prime picnic spots. Some sights require paid admission, including Rome's zoo, the National Gallery of Modern Art (which holds 19th-century art; not to be confused with MAXXI, described later), and the Etruscan Museum described below.

▲▲▲Borghese Gallery (Galleria Borghese)—This plush museum, filling a cardinal's mansion in the park, offers one of Europe's most sumptuous art experiences. You'll enjoy a collection of world-class Baroque sculpture, including Bernini's *David* and his excited statue of Apollo chasing Daphne, as well as paintings by Caravaggio, Raphael, Titian, and Rubens. The museum's slick, mandatory reservation system keeps crowds to a manageable size.

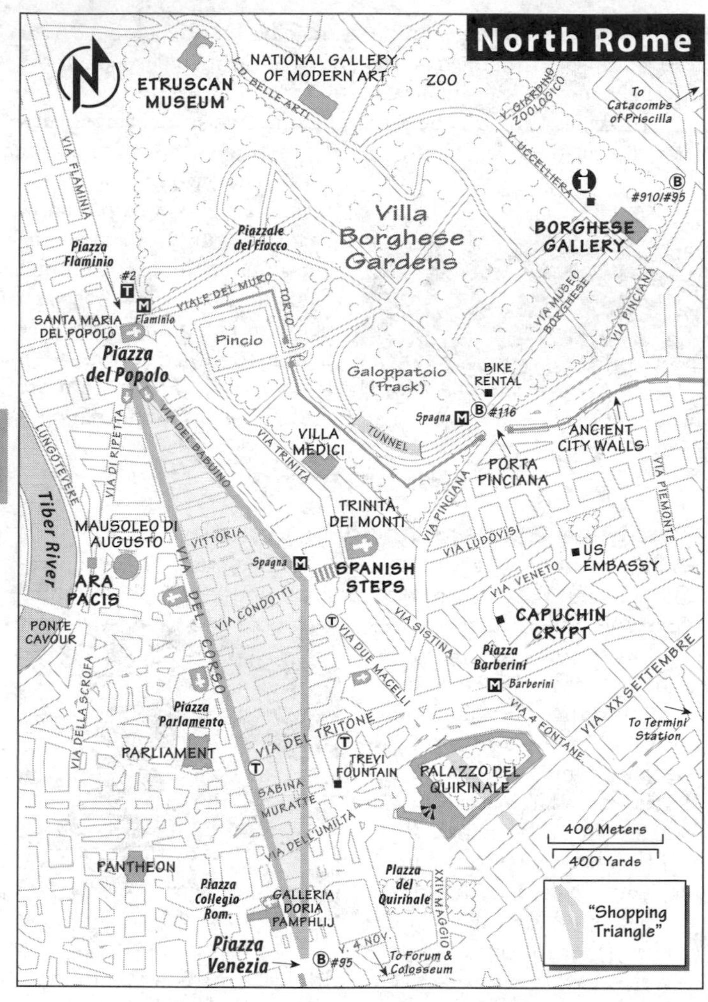

Cost and Hours: €12.50, price includes basic €2 reservation fee, credit cards accepted, Tue-Sun 9:00-19:00, closed Mon, ticket office closes one hour before museum. Reservations are mandatory and easy to get in English online (www.ticketeria.it) or by calling 06-32810. Reserve a minimum of several days in advance for a weekday visit, or at least a week ahead for weekends. The 1.5-hour audioguide (€5) is excellent.

For more on reservations, as well as a self-guided tour, ✪ see the Borghese Gallery Tour chapter.

Etruscan Museum (Villa Giulia Museo Nazionale Etrusco)—The fascinating Etruscan civilization thrived in Italy around 600 B.C., when Rome was an Etruscan town. The Villa Giulia (a fine

Renaissance palace in the Villa Borghese Gardens) hosts a museum that tells the story. The displays are clean and bright, with good English information.

Cost and Hours: €8, Tue-Sun 8:30-19:30, closed Mon, last entry one hour before closing, good English information, 20-minute walk from Borghese Gallery, Piazzale di Villa Giulia 9, tel. 06-322-6571.

Visiting the Museum: A map of the Etruscan world (in room I) shows the Etruscans centered from Rome northward (in modern-day Tuscany and Umbria), co-existing with neighboring civilizations like the Greeks and Phoenicians. Find key Etruscan cities (Vulci, Tarquinia, Cerveteri) where the museum's treasures were unearthed. Farther along, a painted, room-sized tomb from Tarquinia (room 8, down the spiral staircase) shows how Etruscans buried their dead along with their possessions, thus preserving these objects. Stroll through room after room of cases with vases—pottery painted either red-on-black or black-on-red. The star of the museum is the famous "husband and wife sarcophagus" (Il Sarofago degli Sposi, room 12)—a dead couple seeming to enjoy an everlasting banquet from atop their tomb (sixth century B.C. from Cerveteri). Room 13b has a few gold sheets from Pyrgi, with inscriptions in two languages—the "Etruscan Rosetta Stone" that has helped scholars decipher their odd language.

Upstairs on the mezzanine, pass through the long hall of small, mostly bronze objects (statuettes and mirrors). Continuing up to the second floor, you can ogle the gold jewelry of the sophisticated, luxury-loving Etruscans (room 24). Room 25 displays the well-known terra-cotta statue, the Apollo of Veio, which stood atop Apollo's temple. The smiling god welcomes Hercules, while his mother Latona stands nearby cradling baby Apollo.

Via Veneto—In the 1960s, movie stars from around the world paraded down curvy Via Veneto, one of Rome's glitziest nightspots. Today it's still lined with the city's poshest hotels and the US Embassy, but any hint of local color has faded to bland.

▲Capuchin Crypt—If you want to see artistically arranged bones, this is the place. The crypt is below the Church of Santa Maria della Immacolata Concezione at Via Veneto 27, just up from Piazza Barberini. Plans are in the works for a new museum which will incorporate the crypt. If it's open by the time of your visit, expect more artifacts, different hours, and a higher admission price.

Cost and Hours: €1 donation, daily 9:00-12:00 & 15:00-18:00, modest dress required, no photos, turn off mobile phones,

Metro: Barberini, tel. 06-487-1185.

Visiting the Crypt: The bones of more than 4,000 friars who died between 1528 and 1870 are in the basement, all lined up in a series of six crypts for the delight—or disgust—of the always-wide-eyed visitor.

The Crypt of the Resurrection (#1), with a painting of Jesus bringing Lazarus back to life, sets the theme of your visit: the Christian faith in resurrection.

The next room (#2) is the bone-less chapel. This is part of a church, and the monks sometimes hold somber services here.

In the Crypt of the Skulls (#3), look close on the central wall to find the hourglass with wings. Yes, time on earth flies. Between crypts #3 and #4, look up to see the jaunty skull with a shoulder-blade bowtie.

The Crypt of the Hips (#4) is named for the canopy of wavy hipbones with vertebrae bangles over its central altar.

In the large Crypt of the Tibia and Fibia (#5), niches are inhabited by Capuchin friars, whose robes gave the name to the brown coffee with the frothy white cowl. (Unlike monks, who live apart from society, the Capuchins are friars, who depend on charity and live among the people, and are part of the Franciscan order.) In this chapel we see the Franciscan symbol: the bare arm of Christ and the robed arm of a Franciscan friar embracing the faithful. Above that is a bony crown. And below, in dirt brought from Jerusalem 400 years ago, are 18 graves with simple crosses.

In the last room, the Crypt of the Three Skeletons (#6), the ceiling is decorated by a skeleton with a grim-reaper scythe, and scales weighing the "good deeds and the bad deeds so God can judge the soul"—illustrating the Catholic doctrine of earning salvation through good works. The clock with no hands, on the ceiling above the aisle, is a symbol: It means that life goes on forever, once led into the afterlife by "Sister Death." The chapel's bony chandelier and the stars and floral motifs made by ribs and vertebrae are particularly inspired. Finally, look down to read the macabre, monastic, thought-provoking message that serves as the moral of the story: "We were what you are...you will become what we are now."

As you leave (humming "the foot bone's connected to the..."), pick up a few of Rome's most interesting postcards—the proceeds support Capuchin mission work. Head back outside, where it's not just the bright light that provides contrast with the crypt. Within a few steps are the US Embassy, Hard Rock Cafe, and fancy Via Veneto cafés, filled with the poor and envious keeping an eye out for the rich and famous.

Piazza del Popolo—This vast oval square marks the traditional north entrance to Rome. From ancient times until the advent of trains and airplanes, this was just about any visitor's first look at Rome. Today the square, known for its symmetrical design and its art-filled churches, is the starting point for the city's evening *passeggiata* (see the "Dolce Vita Stroll" at the end of the Nightlife in Rome chapter).

In 1480, Pope Sixtus IV recognized that the ramshackle medieval city was making a miserable first impression on pilgrims who walked here from all over Europe (similar to the Muslim pilgrimage to Mecca). He authorized city planners to appropriate property (establishing "eminent domain"), demolish old buildings, and create straight streets to accommodate traffic. This was the first of several papal campaigns to spruce up the square and make it a suitable entrance for the grand city.

From the Flaminio Metro stop, pass through the third-century Aurelian Wall via the Porta del Popolo, and look south. The 10-story obelisk in the center of the square once graced the temple of Ramses II in Egypt and the Roman Circus Maximus racetrack. The obelisk was brought here in 1589 as one of the square's beautification projects. (The oval shape dates from the early 19th century.) At the south side of the square, twin domed churches mark the spot where three main boulevards exit the square and form a trident. The central boulevard (running between the churches) is Via del Corso, which since ancient times has been the main north-south drag through town, running to Capitoline Hill (the governing center) and the Forum. The road to the right led to the Vatican, and the road to the left led to the big pilgrimage churches of San Giovanni in Laterano and Santa Maria Maggiore. With the help of this *tridente,* pilgrims arriving without a good Rome guidebook knew just where to go. The three churches on Piazza del Popolo are all dedicated to Mary, setting the right tone.

Along the north side of the square (flanking the Porta del Popolo) are two 19th-century buildings that give the square its pleasant symmetry: the Carabinieri station and the Church of Santa Maria del Popolo.

Two large fountains grace the sides of the square—Neptune to the west and Roma to the east (marking the base of Pincio Hill).

Though the name Piazza del Popolo means "Square of the People" (and it is a popular hangout), the word was probably derived from the Latin *populus,* after the poplar trees which once stood here.

Church of Santa Maria del Popolo—One of Rome's most overlooked churches, this features two chapels with top-notch art and a facade built of travertine scavenged from the Colosseum. The church is brought to you by the Rovere family, which produced two popes, and you'll see their symbol—the oak tree and acorns—throughout.

Cost and Hours: Free, Mon-Sat 7:00-12:00 & 16:00-18:30, Sun 8:00-13:30 & 16:30-19:30, often partially closed to accommodate its busy schedule of Masses, on north side of Piazza del Popolo—as you face the gate in the old wall from the square, the church entrance is to your right.

SIGHTS

Visiting the Church: Go inside. The Chigi Chapel (second on the left) was designed by Raphael and inspired (as Raphael was) by the Pantheon. Notice the Pantheon-like dome, pilasters, and capitals. Above in the oculus, God looks in, aided by angels who power the eight known planets. Raphael built the chapel for his wealthy banker friend Agostino Chigi, buried in the pyramid-shaped tomb in the wall to the right of the altar. Later, Chigi's great-grandson hired Bernini to make two of the four statues, and Bernini delivered a theatrical episode. In one corner, Daniel straddles a lion and raises his praying hands to God for help. Kitty-corner across the chapel, an angel grabs Habbakuk's hair and tells him to go take some food to poor Daniel.

In the Cerasi Chapel (left of altar), Caravaggio's *The Conversion on the Way to Damascus* shows Paul sprawled on his back beside his horse while his servant looks on. The startled future saint is blinded by the harsh light as Jesus' voice asks him, "Why do you persecute me?" In the style of the Counter-Reformation, Paul receives his new faith with open arms.

In the same chapel, Caravaggio's *Crucifixion of St. Peter* is shown as a banal chore; the workers toil like faceless animals. The light and dark are in high contrast. Caravaggio liked to say, "Where light falls, I will paint it."

▲▲Dolce Vita Stroll—All over the Mediterranean world, people are out strolling in the early evening. Rome's *passeggiata* is both elegant (with chic people enjoying fancy window shopping in the grid of streets around the Spanish Steps) and a little crude (with young people on the prowl). Watching the spectacle is a key Rome experience; I recommend following the action on Piazza del Popolo and along the Via del Corso (roughly Mon-Sat 17:00-19:00 and Sun afternoons; for more, see the "Dolce Vita Stroll" in the Nightlife in Rome chapter).

▲▲Catacombs of Priscilla (Catacombe di Priscilla)—Of the countless catacombs honeycombing the ground just outside the ancient city walls, only five are open to the public. While most tourists and nearly all tour groups go out to the ancient Appian Way to see the famous catacombs of San Sebastiano and San Callisto, the Catacombs of Priscilla (on the other side of town) are less commercialized and crowded, and just feel more intimate, as catacombs should.

Cost and Hours: €8, Tue-Sun 8:30-12:00 & 14:30-17:00, closed Mon, last entry 30 minutes before closing, closed one random month a year—check website or call first, tel. 06-8620-6272, www.catacombepriscilla.com.

Getting There: The catacombs are northeast of Termini train station (at Via Salaria 430), far from the center (a €15 taxi ride) but well-served by buses (20-30 minutes). From Termini, take bus #92 or #86 from Piazza Cinquecento. From Piazza Venezia and along Via del Corso, take bus #63 or #630. Tell the driver "Piazza Crati" and "kah-tah-KOHM-bay" and he'll let you off near Piazza Crati (at the Nemorense/Crati stop). From there, walk through the little market in Piazza Crati, then down Via di Priscilla (about 5 minutes). The entrance is in the orange building on the left at the top of the hill.

Visiting the Catacombs: The Catacombs of Priscilla likely originated as underground tombs for Christians, who'd meet to worship in the wealthy Christian's home that was on this spot. As poor people couldn't generally afford a nice plot in a cemetery, they would dig graves at a generous person's home...and dig and dig.

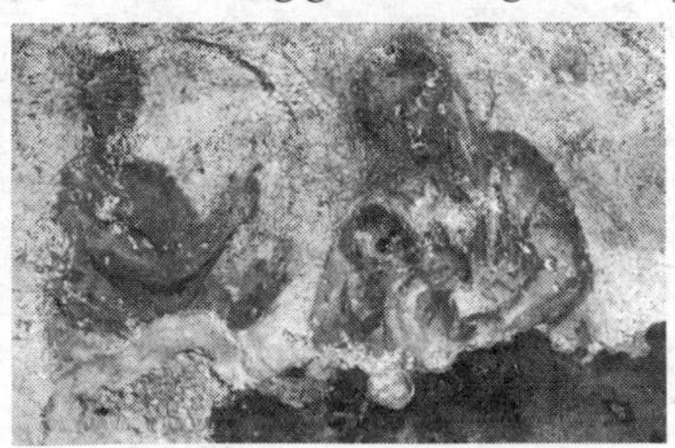

At the Catacombs of Priscilla, you enter from a convent and explore the result of 250 years of tunneling that occurred from the second to the fifth centuries. Visits are by 30-minute guided tour only (English-language tours go whenever a small group gathers—generally every 20 minutes or so). You'll see a few thousand of the 40,000 niches carved here, along with some beautiful frescoes, including what is considered the first depiction of Mary nursing the baby Jesus.

As in other catacombs, some of the tunnels date from an earlier quarry. Volcanic tuff, the stone ancient Rome was built with, works great for burial niches—it's easy to dig and dries hard when exposed to air.

For more information on catacombs, ✪ see the Ancient Appian Way Tour chapter.

MAXXI—Rome's "National Museum of Art of the 21st Century" is the big news on the museum scene here—as you can imagine it would be, after the 10 years and €150 million it took to make it happen. This complex, designed by Zaha Hadid and billed as Italy's "first national museum dedicated to contemporary creativity," is a playful concrete and steel structure filled with bizarre installations. Like many contemporary art museums, it's notable more for the building than the art inside. To me, it comes off as a second-rate Pompidou Center. While not to my taste, it's one of the few places in the city where fans of contemporary architecture can see the latest trends. Since it's away from the center, consider combining it with a walk around fellow "starchitect" Renzo Piano's Auditorium to see how the city continues to evolve (15-minute walk, from MAXXI follow Via Guido Reni to tram #2 stop and keep going; see page 380).

Cost and Hours: €11, Tue-Sun 11:00-19:00, Thu and Sat until 22:00, closed Mon, last entry one hour before closing; no permanent collection, several rotating exhibits throughout the year—preview on their site; tram #2 from Piazza del Popolo to Piazza Apollo Doro, Via Guido Reni 4a, tel. 06-322-5178, www.fondazionemaxxi.it.

From the Spanish Steps to the Ara Pacis

▲Spanish Steps—The wide, curving staircase, culminating with an obelisk between two Baroque church towers, makes for one of Rome's iconic sights. Beyond that, it's a people-gathering place. By day, the area hosts shoppers looking for high-end fashions; on warm evenings, it attracts young people in love with the city. For more, ✪ see the Heart of Rome Walk chapter.

"Shopping Triangle"—The triangular-shaped area between the Spanish Steps, Piazza Venezia, and Piazza del Popolo (along Via del Corso, see map on page 68) contains Rome's highest concentration of upscale boutiques and fashion stores.

▲▲Ara Pacis (Altar of Peace)—On January 30, 9 B.C., soon-to-be-emperor Augustus led a procession of priests up the steps and into this newly built "Altar of Peace." They sacrificed an animal on

the altar and poured an offering of wine, thanking the gods for helping Augustus pacify barbarians abroad and rivals at home. This marked the dawn of the Pax Romana (c. A.D. 1-200), a Golden Age of good living, stability, dominance, and peace *(pax)*. The Ara Pacis (AH-rah PAH-chees) hosted annual sacrifices by the emperor until the area was flooded by the Tiber River. Buried under silt, it was abandoned and forgotten until the 16th century, when various parts were discovered and excavated. Mussolini gathered the altar's scattered parts and reconstructed them here in 1938. In 2006, the Altar of Peace reopened to the public in a striking modern building. As the first new building allowed to be built in the old center since 1938, it's been controversial, but its quiet, air-conditioned interior may have signaled the dawn of another new age in Rome.

Cost and Hours: €7.50, tightwads can look in through huge windows for free; Tue-Sun 9:00-19:00, closed Mon, last entry one hour before closing; €3.50 audio tour available as free download at www.arapacis.it, good WC downstairs. The Ara Pacis is a long block west of Via del Corso on Via di Ara Pacis, on the east bank of the Tiber near Ponte Cavour, Metro: Spagna; a 10-minute walk down Via dei Condotti, tel. 06-0608.

➲ **Self-Guided Tour:** Start with the model in the museum's lobby. The Altar of Peace was originally located east of here, along today's Via del Corso. The model shows where it stood in relation to the Mausoleum of Augustus (now next door) and the Pantheon. (The Ara Pacis originally faced west; now it faces east. The compass directions given here match the altar's current orientation, but be aware that some art-history books and even the Ara Pacis website may describe it using the original—and opposite—orientation.)

Entrance (East) Side: Approach the Ara Pacis and look through the doorway to see the raised altar. This simple structure has just the basics of a Roman temple: an altar for sacrifices surrounded by cubicle-like walls that enclose a consecrated space. Its well-preserved reliefs celebrate Rome's success. After a sacrifice, the altar was washed, and the blood flowed out drain holes still visible at the base of the walls. Flanking the doorway are (badly damaged) reliefs of Rome's legendary founders—Romulus and Remus—being suckled by the she-wolf (left) and bearded Aeneas (right), who's pouring a wine offering and preparing to sacrifice a sow.

North Side: This relief probably depicts the parade of dignitaries who consecrated the altar. Near the head is Augustus (his body sliced in two vertically by missing stone), honored with a crown of laurel leaves, having just conquered parts of Spain and Gaul. Augustus is followed by a half-dozen bigwigs and priests (with spiked hats) and the man shouldering the sacrificial axe. Next comes Agrippa (wearing the hood of a priest), Augustus' right-hand man in battles against Mark Antony and Cleopatra. Agrippa married Augustus' daughter, Julia—their little son, Gaius, tugs on his dad's toga while turning to look at Livia, Augustus' wife. When Agrippa died, Gaius was adopted and named as successor by Augustus. Gaius also died young, making the next in line Tiberius, Livia's son by a first marriage, shown standing next to his mother. Confused? Find these names and other descendants of Julius Caesar on the genealogical chart in the museum lobby.

Before proceeding farther around the altar, look out the window to see the overgrown Mausoleum of Augustus and his family, once capped with a dome of earth, elegant spruces, and statues of the emperor. To the left is an example of Mussolini's fascist architecture—intended to remind Italians of their imperial Roman roots. Note the travertine, brick, low-relief propaganda, stony inscriptions, Roman numerals, and cold rationality. (Locals don't like it.) This area was the Field of Mars, Rome's only neighborhood continuously inhabited since ancient times.

West Side: The altar's back door is flanked with reliefs celebrating the two things Augustus brought to Rome: peace (goddess Roma as a conquering Amazon, right side) and prosperity (fertility goddess surrounded by children, plants, and animals). For a closer look at details from the various reliefs, see the model downstairs.

South Side: Leading the parade of senators is a *lictor*—a ceremonial bodyguard—carrying the *fasces*. This bundle of sticks symbolized how unity brings strength, and it gave us the modern word "fascism." The reliefs feature the first official portrayal of women and children in a public monument.

Beneath the parade, notice the elaborate floral relief that runs all the way around the Ara Pacis. Acanthus tendrils spiral out, forming decorative garlands, intertwining with ivy, laurel, and more. Swans with outstretched wings hide among the patterns. Some 50 plants are blooming in this display of abundance. Imagine the altar as it once was, standing in an open field, painted in bright colors—a mingling of myth, man, and nature.

▲Fausto delle Chiaie (Fausto of the Beach)—This eccentric fellow (who's likely more sane than the rest of us) is a self-appointed part of the Ara Pacis. Fausto's installation art, usually strewn along the curb that runs between the Ara Pacis and Mausoleum of Augustus, aims to take you to a different dimension. Though he sits next to the local art academy, he stresses that the proximity is merely a coincidence. Charming Fausto speaks English and reminds you that his "plastic secretary" (a tip box) is at the end of the curb. He may be mini compared to the nearby museum, but for me, he's more entertaining than the MAXXI.

East Rome

Near Termini Train Station

These sights are within a 10-minute walk of the train station. By Metro, use the Termini stop for the National Museum and the Repubblica stop for the rest.

▲▲▲National Museum of Rome (Museo Nazionale Romano Palazzo Massimo alle Terme)—The National Museum's main branch, at Palazzo Massimo, houses the greatest collection of ancient Roman art anywhere, including busts of emperors and a Roman copy of the Greek Discus Thrower.

Cost and Hours: €10 combo-ticket covers three other branches—all skippable, Tue-Sun 9:00-19:45, closed Mon, last entry 45 minutes before closing, audioguide-€5, about 100 yards from train station, Metro: Repubblica or Termini, tel. 06-3996-7700, http://archeoroma.beniculturali.it/en.

✪ See the National Museum of Rome Tour chapter.

▲Baths of Diocletian (Terme di Diocleziano)—Around A.D. 300, Emperor Diocletian built the largest baths in Rome. This sprawling meeting place—with baths and schmoozing spaces to accommodate 3,000 bathers at a time—was a big deal in ancient times. While much of it is still closed, the best part is open: the Church of Santa Maria degli Angeli, once the great central hall of the baths, later transformed into a church, with help from Michelangelo.

Cost and Hours: Free, Mon-Sat 7:00-18:30, Sun 7:00-19:30, closed to sightseers during Mass, faces Piazza della Repubblica.

✪ See the Baths of Diocletian Tour chapter.

▲Church of Santa Maria della Vittoria—This church houses Bernini's statue, the swooning *St. Teresa in Ecstasy*. Inside the church, you'll find St. Teresa to the left of the altar. Teresa has just been stabbed with God's arrow of fire. Now, the angel pulls it out and watches her reaction. Teresa swoons, her eyes roll up, her hand goes limp, she parts her lips...and moans. The smiling, cherubic angel understands just how she feels. Teresa, a 16th-century Spanish nun, later talked of the "sweetness" of "this intense pain," describing her

oneness with God in ecstatic, even erotic, terms.

Bernini, the master of multimedia, pulls out all the stops to make this mystical vision real. Actual sunlight pours through the alabaster windows, bronze sunbeams shine on a marble angel holding a golden arrow. Teresa leans back on a cloud and her robe ripples from within, charged with her spiritual arousal. Bernini has created a little stage-setting of heaven. And watching from the "theater boxes" on either side are members of the family who commissioned the work.

Cost and Hours: Free, pay €0.50 for light, Mon-Sat 8:30-12:00 & 15:30-18:00, Sun 15:30-18:00, about 5 blocks northwest of Termini train station on Largo Susanna, Metro: Repubblica.

Santa Susanna Church—The home of the American Catholic Church in Rome, Santa Susanna holds Mass in English daily at 18:00 and on Sunday at 9:00 and 10:30. They arrange papal audience tickets (see page 185), and their excellent website contains tips for travelers and a list of convents that rent out rooms.

Cost and Hours: Free, daily 9:00-12:00 & 16:00-18:00, Via XX Settembre 15, near recommended Via Firenze hotels, Metro: Repubblica, tel. 06-4201-4554, www.santasusanna.org.

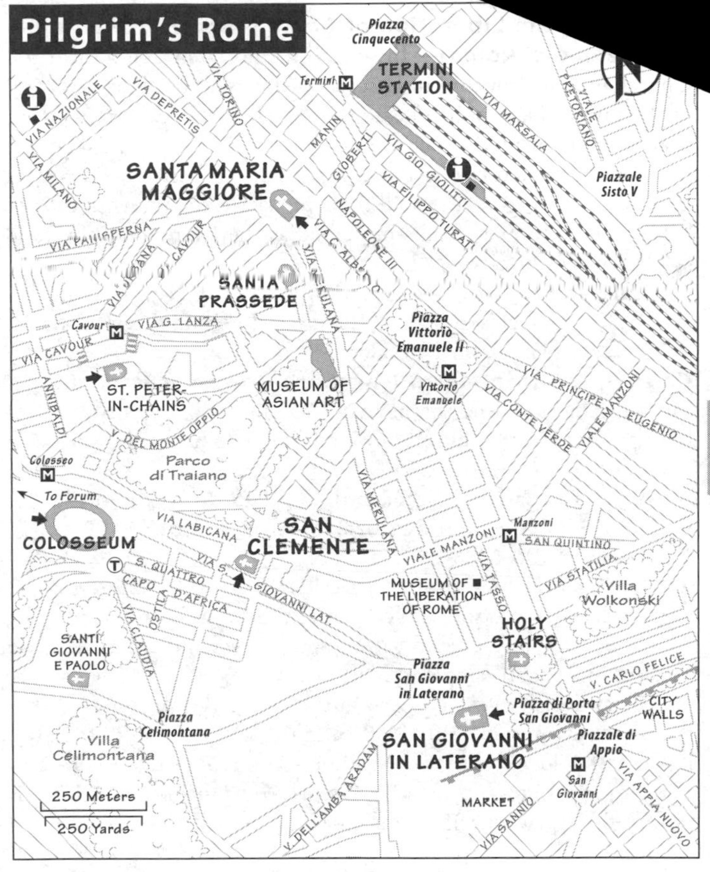

Pilgrim's Rome

East of the Colosseum (and south of Termini train station) are several venerable churches that Catholic pilgrims make a point of visiting. Near one of the churches is a small WWII museum. For more on these churches, ✪ see the Pilgrim's Rome Tour chapter.

Church of San Giovanni in Laterano—Built by Constantine, the first Christian emperor, this was Rome's most important church through medieval times. A building alongside the church houses the Holy Stairs (Scala Santa) said to have been walked up by Jesus, which today are ascended by pilgrims on their knees.

Cost and Hours: Free, church—daily 7:00-18:30; Holy Stairs—daily April-Sept 6:15-12:00 & 15:30-18:45, Oct-March 6:15-12:00 & 15:00-18:15; audioguide-€5; Piazza di San Giovanni in Laterano, Metro: San Giovanni, or bus #85 or #87; tel. 06-6988-6409.

... Rome (Museo Storico della ... small memorial museum, near the ... Laterano, is housed in the prison wing ... headquarters of occupied Rome. Other ... sheet to help, there's little in English. Still, ... in resistance movements and the Nazi occupatio... ng visit. You'll see a few artifacts, many photos of heroe... couple of cells preserved as they were found on June 4, 1944, ...hen the city was liberated.

Cost and Hours: Free, Tue-Sun 9:30-12:30, Tue and Thu-Fri also 15:30-19:30, closed Mon and Aug, just behind the Holy Stairs at Via Tasso 145; tel. 06-700-3866.

Church of Santa Maria Maggiore—Some of Rome's best-surviving mosaics line the nave of this church built as Rome was falling. The nearby Church of Santa Prassede has still more early mosaics.

Cost and Hours: Free, daily 7:00-19:00, audioguide-€5, Piazza Santa Maria Maggiore, Metro: Termini or Vittorio Emanuele, tel. 06-6988-6802.

▲Church of San Clemente—Besides visiting the church itself, with frescoes by Masolino, you can also descend into the ruins of an earlier church. Descend yet one more level and enter the eerie remains of a pagan temple to Mithras.

Cost and Hours: Upper church—free, lower church—€5, both open Mon-Sat 9:00-12:30 & 15:00-18:00, Sun 12:00-18:00, last entry to lower church 20 minutes before closing; Via di San Giovanni in Laterano, Metro: Colosseo, or bus #85 or #87; tel. 06-774-0021, www.basilicasanclemente.com.

South Rome

The area south of the center contains some interesting but widely scattered areas, from Trastevere to the Jewish Quarter to Testaccio to E.U.R. Most sights appear on the color map of South Rome at the beginning of this book.

Trastevere and Nearby

Trastevere is the colorful neighborhood across *(tras)* the Tiber *(Tevere)* River. Trastevere (trahs-TAY-veh-ray) offers the best look at medieval-village Rome. The action unwinds to the chime of the church bells. Go there and wander. Wonder. Be a poet. This is Rome's Left Bank. For a self-guided tour, ✪ see the Trastevere Walk chapter.

This proud neighborhood was long a working-class area. Now that it's becoming trendy, high rents are driving out the source of so much color. Still, it's a great people scene, especially at night. Stroll the back streets (for restaurant recommendations, see the Eating in Rome chapter).

To reach Trastevere by foot from Capitoline Hill, cross the Tiber on Ponte Fabricio to Isola Tiberina; from there, Ponte Cestio takes you to Trastevere. You can also take tram #8 from Largo Argentina, or bus #H from Termini and Via Nazionale (get off at Piazza Belli). From the Vatican (Piazza Risorgimento), it's bus #23 or #271.

Linking Trastevere with the Heart of Rome Walk: You can walk from Trastevere to Campo de' Fiori to link up with the beginning of my Heart of Rome Walk (see chapter of same name): From Trastevere's church square (Piazza di Santa Maria), take Via del Moro to the river and cross at Ponte Sisto, a pedestrian bridge that has a good view of St. Peter's dome. Continue straight ahead for one block. Take the first left, which leads down Via di Capo di Ferro through the scary and narrow darkness to Piazza Farnese, with the imposing Palazzo Farnese. Michelangelo contributed to the facade of this palace, now the French Embassy. The fountains on the square feature huge one-piece granite hot tubs from the ancient Roman Baths of Caracalla. One block from there (opposite the palace) is the atmospheric square, Campo de' Fiori.

SIGHTS

▲Church of Santa Maria in Trastevere—One of Rome's oldest church sites, a basilica was erected here in the fourth century, when Christianity was legalized. It is said to have been the first church in Rome dedicated to the Virgin Mary. The structure you see today dates mainly from the 12th century. Its portico (covered area just outside the door) is decorated with fascinating fragments of stone—many of them lids from catacomb burial niches—and filled with early Christian symbolism. The church is on Piazza di Santa Maria. While today's fountain is from the 17th century, there has been a fountain here since Roman times.

Cost and Hours: Free, daily 7:30-21:00.

▲Villa Farnesina—Here's a unique opportunity to see a sumptuous Renaissance villa in Rome decorated with Raphael paintings. It was built in the early 1500s for the richest man in Renaissance Europe, Siennese banker Agostino Chigi. Architect Baldassare

Peruzzi's design—a U-shaped building with wings enfolding what used to be a vast garden—successfully blended architecture and nature in a way that both ancient and Renaissance Romans loved. Orchards and flower beds flowed down in terraces from the palace to the riverbanks. Later construction of modern embankments and avenues robbed the garden of its grandeur, leaving it with a more melancholy charm.

Kings and popes of the day depended on generous loans from Agostino Chigi, whose bank had more than 100 branches in places as far-flung as London and Cairo. This villa was the meeting place of aristocrats, artists, beautiful women, and philosophers.

Cost and Hours: €5; Mon and Sat 9:00-17:00, Tue-Fri 9:00-14:00, closed Sun, last entry 20 minutes before closing; across the river from Campo de' Fiori, a short walk from Ponte Sisto and a block behind the river at 230 Via della Lungara; tel. 06-6802-7268, www.villafarnesina.it.

➲ **Self-Guided Tour:** Enjoy the best bits of the villa with this commentary.

• *Begin in room 1.*

Loggia of Galatea: Note the ceiling painted by Peruzzi, showing the position of the signs of the horoscope at the exact moment of Agostino's birth (21:30, November 29, 1466). The room's claim to fame is Raphael's painting of the nymph Galatea (on the wall by the entrance door). She shuns the doting attention of the ungainly one-eyed giant Polyphemus (in the niche to the left, painted by another artist) and speeds away in the company of her rambunctious entourage on a chariot led by dolphins. She turns back and looks up, amused by the cyclops' crude love song (which, I believe, was "I Only Have Eye for You"). The trigger-happy cupids and lusty, entwined fauns and nymphs announce the pagan spirit revived in Renaissance Rome. All the painting's lines of sight (especially the cupids' arrows) point to the center of the work, Galatea's radiant face. Galatea is considered Raphael's vision of female perfection—not a portrait of an individual woman, but a composite of his many lovers in an idealized vision.

• *Continue into room 2.*

Loggia of Psyche: This room was painted by Raphael and his assistants. Imagine it without the glass windows, as a continuation of the garden outside, where plays were performed to entertain Agostino's guests. Raphael's two ceiling frescoes were painted to look like tapestries (complete with ruffled edges), suspended from the ceiling by garlands, making the room appear to be an open bower. View the frescoes from the top, with your back to the garden. The ceiling shows episodes in the myth of a lovely mortal woman, Psyche, who caught the eye of the winged boy-god Cupid (Eros). See the loving couple at the far left end, at the base of the ceiling. The big ceiling fresco on the left depicts the gods of Olympus gathered to plan a series of ordeals to test whether Psyche is worthy to marry a god. (Find Hercules with white beard and club, and Dionysius pouring the wine.) The other shows the happy ending, as Cupid (boy with wings) and Psyche (to his left, in topless robe) stand before Zeus to celebrate their wedding feast attended by the pantheon of gods.

The whole setting—the room by the gardens, the subject of the frescoes, the fleshy bodies—has an erotic subtext. At the time, Raphael was having a passionate affair with the celebrated Fornarina (the "baker's daughter," who lived down the street). Agostino, noticing that his painter was constantly interrupting his workday to be with her, had the girl kidnapped so that Raphael would finally concentrate. But production slowed even more, as Raphael was depressed. Agostino gave up and had the Fornarina move in with Raphael to keep him company as he happily resumed work in this cheery room. The room's imagery abounds with images both phallic and yonic (the female counterpart of phallic). Next to the ripe and split-open cantaloupe (right end, base of ceiling), find the gourd wearing a condom.

• *Upstairs, accessed from the stairway near the entrance, is the...*

Room of the Perspectives: Peruzzi, another trendsetter, painted this room. Walls seem to open onto views and perspectives that actually correspond with what lies outside. The insulting-to-Catholics graffiti (for example, on the wall at the far end) date from 1527, when Protestant mercenaries sent by Charles V sacked the city.

Agostino had his wedding banquet in this room. His parties were the talk of the town. On one occasion, he invited his guests in the (now lost) dining loggia overlooking the Tiber to toss the gold and silver dishes they had just used into the river. (The banker had nets conveniently placed just below the river's surface.)

The small chamber at the end of the Room of the Perspectives was the **bedroom.** The painting on the wall depicts the wedding of Alexander the Great and Roxanne. Roxanne has the features of Agostino's bride, and the bed is the jewel-encrusted ebony bed that received Agostino and his bride here in this room. On the entrance wall, find the three-arched ruins of the Basilica of Constantine in the Forum. The room was painted by Il Sodoma, a devoted fan of Michelangelo and one of the artists who was canned when Raphael took over the decoration of the papal apartments at the Vatican. Had that not happened, the Raphael Rooms at the Vatican might have looked like this.

Agostino had famous affairs with the most beautiful courtesans of his day. He eventually settled down, but his wild-living descendants didn't, and—in the space of a couple of generations—the Chigi family lost its fabulous fortune.

Gianicolo Hill Viewpoint—From this park atop a hill, the city views are superb, and the walk to the top holds a treat for architecture buffs. Start at Trastevere's Piazza di San Cosimato, and follow Via Luciano Manara to Via Garibaldi, at the base of the hill. Via Garibaldi winds its way up the side of the hill to the Church of San Pietro in Montorio. To the right of the church, in a small courtyard, is the Tempietto by Donato Bramante. This tiny church, built to commemorate the martyrdom of St. Peter, is considered a jewel of Italian Renaissance architecture.

Continuing up the hill, Via Garibaldi connects to Passeggiata del Gianicolo. From here, you'll find a pleasant park with panoramic city views. Ponder the many Victorian-era statues, including that of baby-carrying, gun-wielding, horse-riding Anita Garibaldi. She was the Brazilian wife of the revolutionary General Giuseppe Garibaldi, who helped forge a united Italy in the late 19th century.

Near Trastevere: Jewish Quarter

From the 16th through the 19th centuries, Rome's Jewish population was forced to live in a cramped ghetto at an often-flooded bend of the Tiber River. While the medieval Jewish ghetto is long gone, this area—just across the river and toward Capitoline Hill from Trastevere—is still home to Rome's synagogue and fragments of its Jewish heritage. For more on this neighborhood, ✪ see the Jewish Ghetto Walk chapter.

Synagogue (Sinagoga) and Jewish Museum (Museo Ebraico)—Rome's modern synagogue stands proudly on the spot where the medieval Jewish community was sequestered for more than 300 years. The site of a historic visit by Pope John Paul II, this synagogue features a fine interior and a museum filled with artifacts of Rome's Jewish community. Modest dress is required. The only way to visit the synagogue—unless you're here for daily prayer service—is with a tour.

Cost and Hours: €10 ticket includes museum and guided hourly tour of synagogue; mid-June-mid-Sept Sun-Thu 10:00-19:00, Fri 10:00-16:00, closed Sat; mid-Sept-mid-June Sun-Thu 10:00-17:00, Fri 9:00-14:00, closed Sat; last entry 45 minutes before closing, English tours usually at :15 past the hour, 30 minutes, check schedule at ticket counter; on Lungotevere dei Cenci, tel. 06-6840-0661, www.museoebraico.roma.it. Walking tours of the Jewish Ghetto are conducted at least once a day except Saturday.

SIGHTS

Testaccio

In the gritty Testaccio neighborhood, several fascinating but lesser sights cluster at the Piramide Metro stop between the Colosseum and E.U.R. (This is a quick and easy stop as you return from E.U.R., or when changing trains en route to Ostia Antica.)

Working-class since ancient times, the Testaccio neighborhood has recently gone trendy-bohemian. Visitors wander through an awkward mix of yuppie and proletarian worlds, not noticing—but perhaps sensing—the "Keep Testaccio for the Testaccians" graffiti.

Pyramid of Gaius Cestius—An Egyptian-style pyramid from ancient Rome stands next to the Piramide Metro stop. The Mark Antony/Cleopatra scandal (c. 30 B.C.) brought exotic Egyptian styles into vogue. A rich Roman magistrate, Gaius Cestius, had this pyramid built as his tomb, complete with a burial chamber inside. Made of brick covered in marble, the 90-foot structure was completed in just 330 days (as stated in its Latin inscription). While smaller than actual Egyptian pyramids, its proportions are correct. It was later incorporated into the Aurelian Wall, and it now stands as a marker to the entrance of Testaccio.

Porta San Paolo and Museo della Via Ostiense—This formidable gate (also next to the Piramide Metro stop) is from

the Aurelian Wall, begun in the third century under Emperor Aurelian. The wall, which encircled the city, was 12 miles long and averaged about 26 feet high, with 14 main gates and 380 72-foot-tall towers. Most of what you'll see today is circa A.D. 400, but the barbarians reconstructed the gate later, in the sixth century.

Inside the gate is a tiny free museum (find entrance near pyramid; open Tue and Thu 9:00-13:30 & 14:30-16:30, Wed and Fri-Sat 9:00-13:30, some Sun 9:00-13:30, closed Mon). The museum offers a free ramble along the ramparts, plus exhibits on Ostia Antica, Rome's ancient port (for more information, see the Ostia Antica Day Trip chapter). You'll see models of the ancient city and its famed hexagonal harbor, and of the Ostian Way—the straight Roman road that paralleled the curvy Tiber for 15 miles from Rome to the sea.

For more on the Aurelian Wall, visit the San Sebastiano Gate and Museum of the Walls (described in my ✪ Ancient Appian Way Tour chapter).

Protestant Cemetery—The Cemetery for the Burial of Non-Catholic Foreigners (Cimitero Acattolico per gli Stranieri al Testaccio) is a tomb-filled park, running along the wall just beyond the pyramid. The cemetery is also the only English-style landscape

Keats and Shelley on Mortality

Ponder mortality along with Keats and Shelley, with these excerpts from their poetry:

From Keats' "Ode to a Nightingale"
Adieu! adieu! thy plaintive anthem fades
Past the near meadows, over the still stream,
Up the hill-side; and now 'tis buried deep
In the next valley-glades:
Was it a vision, or a waking dream?
Fled is that music:—Do I wake or sleep?

From Shelley's "Adonais: An Elegy on the Death of John Keats"
I weep for Adonais—he is dead!
Oh, weep for Adonais! though our tears
Thaw not the frost which binds so dear a head!
...I am borne darkly, fearfully, afar;
Whilst, burning through the inmost veil of Heaven,
The soul of Adonais, like a star,
Beacons from the abode where the Eternal are.

(rolling hills, calculated vistas) in Rome, and a favorite spot for a quiet stroll. From the Piramide Metro stop, walk between the pyramid and the Roman gate on Via Persichetti/Via Marmorata. Across the street, notice the beige travertine post office from 1932. This is textbook Mussolini-era fascist architecture; the huge X design on the stairwells celebrates the 10th anniversary of the dictator's reign.

Then go left on Caio Cestio to the gate of the cemetery. Originally, none of the Protestant epitaphs were allowed to make any mention of heaven. Signs direct visitors to the graves of notable non-Catholics who died in Rome since 1738. Many of the buried were diplomats. And many, such as the poets Percy Shelley (1792-1822) and John Keats (1795-1821), were from the Romantic Age. They came on the Grand Tour and—"captivated by the fatal charms of Rome," as Shelley wrote—never left.

Head 90 degrees left to find Keats' tomb, in the far corner. Keats died in his twenties, unrecognized. He wanted to be unnamed on a tomb that read, "Young English Poet, 1821. Here lies one whose name was writ in water." (To see Keats' tomb when the cemetery is closed, look through the tiny peephole on Via Caio Cestio, 10 yards off Via Marmarata.) Shelley's tomb is straight ahead from the entrance, up the hill, at the base of the stubby tower.

There are cats everywhere. At the pyramid, look down and to the right to find Matilde Talli's cat hospice. Volunteers use donations to care for these "Guardians of the Departed" who "provide loyal companionship to these dead," and who even have their own website (as posters nearby explain).

Cost and Hours: €3 suggested donation—leave in box by entrance, Mon-Sat 9:00-17:00, Sun 9:00-13:00, last entry 30 minutes before closing, staff at info office can help you find specific graves, www.cemeteryrome.it.

Monte Testaccio—The area surrounding this small hill is a popular nightlife spot (as you leave the cemetery, turn left and continue two blocks down Caio Cestio). The hill, actually a 115-foot-tall ancient trash pile, is made of broken *testae*—earthenware jars mostly used to haul oil 2,000 years ago, when this was a gritty port warehouse district. For 500 years, rancid oil vessels were discarded here. Slowly, Rome's lowly eighth hill was built. Because the caves dug into the hill stay cool, trendy bars, clubs, and restaurants compete with gritty car-repair places for a spot. The neighborhood was once known for a huge slaughterhouse and a Roma (Gypsy) camp that squatted inside an old military base. Now it's home to the Testaccio Village (a site for summer concerts and techno raves—dead until late at night, when it thrives), a weekend farmers' market, and a branch of the MACRO contemporary art gallery (Metro: Piramide).

Testaccio Market and Neighborhood—The covered and colorful Mercato di Testaccio is a focal point of the neighborhood. It recently moved to a more modern and "hygienic" location—many fear that it's lost some of its edgy charm. Still, it's a good look at one of the many neighborhood markets where locals do their daily shopping (Mon-Sat until 13:00, across from Monte Testaccio on Via Galvani). Testaccio has long been the neighborhood of slaughterhouses, and its restaurants are renowned for their ability to cook up the least palatable part of the animals...the "fifth quarter." The rest of the neighborhood is slowing gentrifying, with high-end shoe and clothing boutiques appearing alongside the traditional merchants.

South of Testaccio

▲Montemartini Museum (Musei Capitolini Centrale Montemartini)—This museum houses a dreamy collection of 400 ancient statues, set evocatively in a classic 1932 electric power plant, among generators and *Metropolis*-type cast-iron machinery. While the art is not as famous as the collections you'll see downtown, the effect is fun and memorable—and you'll encounter absolutely no tourists. If you're tackling Rome with kids, this museum is ideal: It's uncrowded and cool, immersed in an old power plant, with art placed at kid-level.

Cost and Hours: €7.50, €14 combo-ticket with Capitoline Museums, Tue-Sun 9:00-19:00, closed Mon, last entry 30 minutes before closing, look for red banner marking Via Ostiense 106, a short walk from Metro: Garbatella, tel. 06-574-8030, www.centralemontemartini.org.

▲St. Paul's Outside the Walls (Basilica San Paolo Fuori le Mura)—This was the last major construction project of Imperial Rome (c. A.D. 380) and the largest church in Christendom until St. Peter's.

Cost and Hours: Free, daily 7:00-18:30, modest dress code enforced, dry audioguide-€5 plus ID, Via Ostiense 186, Metro: San Paolo, exit the Metro station following *via Ostiense* sign, and look for the church's round tower, www.basilicasanpaolo.org.

➲ **Self-Guided Tour:** After a tragic 19th-century fire, St. Paul's was rebuilt in the same general style and size as the original. The column-lined courtyard leading up to the church is typical of early Christian churches—the first version of St. Peter's Basilica also had this kind of welcoming zone.

Step inside and feel as close as you'll get in the 21st century to experiencing a monumental Roman basilica. Marvel at the ceiling, and imagine building it with those massive wood beams in A.D. 380.

Alabaster windows light the vast interior. It feels sterile, but in a good way—as if you're already in heaven. Along with St. Peter's Basilica, San Giovanni in Laterano, and Santa Maria Maggiore, this church is, legally speaking, part of the Vatican rather than Italy. The triumphal arch leading to the altar has a fifth-century mosaic of Christ raising his hand in blessing. He's flanked by the four evangelists (in symbolic animal guise) and, in

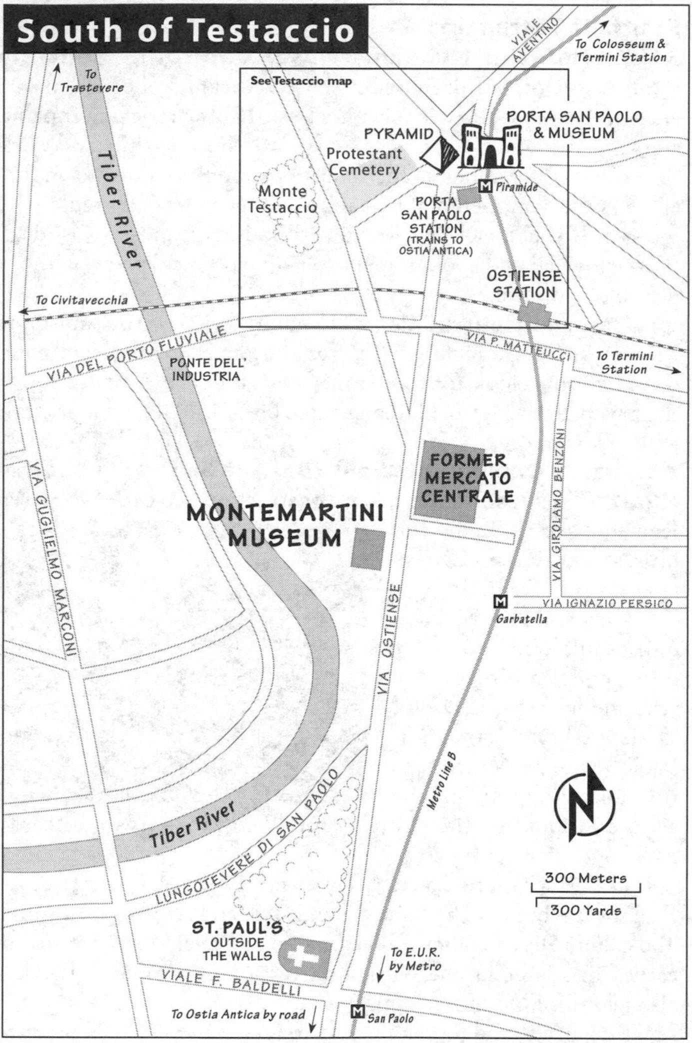

South of Testaccio

To Trastevere
See Testaccio map
VIALE AVENTINO
To Colosseum & Termini Station
PORTA SAN PAOLO & MUSEUM
PYRAMID
Protestant Cemetery
Monte Testaccio
Piramide
PORTA SAN PAOLO STATION (TRAINS TO OSTIA ANTICA)
OSTIENSE STATION
Tiber River
To Civitavecchia
VIA DEL PORTO FLUVIALE
PONTE DELL' INDUSTRIA
VIA P. MATTEUCCI
To Termini Station
FORMER MERCATO CENTRALE
VIA GIROLAMO BENZONI
MONTEMARTINI MUSEUM
VIA GUGLIELMO MARCONI
VIA OSTIENSE
Garbatella
VIA IGNAZIO PERSICO
Metro Line B
Tiber River
LUNGOTEVERE DI SAN PAOLO
300 Meters
300 Yards
ST. PAUL'S OUTSIDE THE WALLS
VIALE F. BALDELLI
To E.U.R. by Metro
To Ostia Antica by road
San Paolo

white, the mysterious 24 elders of the Apocalypse. At the bottom of the arch are the two early followers of Jesus who, according to tradition, came to Rome to spread the Gospel and ended up dying for it: St. Peter (right) carries the keys to the kingdom of heaven, and St. Paul holds a sword symbolizing the pierc-

ing truth. Over the altar is a multicolored marble canopy (13th century). A 20-foot-tall Easter candlestick (c. 1170) stands to the right.

The church is built upon the supposed grave of St. Paul. According to tradition, Paul was decapitated two miles from this spot. His head was preserved at San Giovanni in Laterano, and his body was buried here under the altar. In 2006, archaeologists unearthed a sarcophagus with early inscriptions identifying it as Paul's. Today, you can descend a few steps in front of the altar to see the exposed end of Paul's supposed stone coffin, and look down through the glass floor to see the remains of the earlier basilica.

Ringing the upper part of the church are round mosaic portraits of 265 popes, from St. Peter (the first one in the right transept) to the present. Find the recent popes to the right of the altar—not in the nave, but farther to the right, under the arches of the dim right aisle. You'll see globetrotting John Paul II *(Jo Paulus II)* and progressive John XXIII, who oversaw the Vatican II changes of the 1960s. A portrait of Pope #265—Benedict XVI—was recently installed, alongside blank medallions for future popes.

The peaceful 13th-century cloister (€4) has elegant Romanesque columns and arches, and fragments of early Christian/Roman sarcophagi.

E.U.R.

In the late 1930s, Italy's dictator, Benito Mussolini, planned an international exhibition to show off the wonders of his fascist society. But these wonders brought us World War II, and Il Duce's celebration never happened. The unfinished mega-project was completed in the 1950s, and today it houses government offices and big, obscure museums filled with important, rarely visited relics.

If Hitler and Mussolini had won the war, our world might look like E.U.R. (AY-oor). Hike down E.U.R.'s wide, pedestrian-mean boulevards. Patriotic murals, aren't-you-proud-to-be-an-extreme-right-winger pillars, and stern squares decorate the soulless planned grid and stark office blocks. Boulevards named for Astronomy, Electronics, Social Security, and Beethoven are more exhausting than inspirational.

Despite its grim past, E.U.R. is now an up-and-coming place with young people and trendy cafés. It's worth a trip for its Museum of Roman Civilization (described later). And because a few landmark buildings of Italian modernism are located here and

Mussolini and Imperial Rome

Benito Mussolini incorporated much from ancient Rome during his dictatorship. His military was organized according to Roman terminology (divided into legions and run by centurions and consuls). The salute with the right arm raised, flat palm down (later used by the Nazis), was also Roman. More hygienic and quicker than a handshake, it fit the dynamic character of fascism.

While the classical values of power and discipline were stressed in the rhythmic march of military parades, convincing the Italians of the need for order was a challenge even to Mussolini. He claimed it wasn't impossible to govern the Italian people...just useless.

Mussolini's title, Il Duce, was from the Latin *dux*—a generic term for leader. When chanted by crowds and carved onto monuments, it likely fueled Mussolini's belief that he was carrying out extraordinary historical missions like Caesar and Augustus before him.

For his fascist symbol, rather than the she-wolf or eagle, Mussolini used the *lictor's fasces*—an ax belonging to a Roman officer, with rods tied around the handle, carried in front of magistrates as a sign of authority. This was aimed at destroying the popular image of Italy as a joyous, carefree country and for promoting a new image of austerity and order. In ancient times, the ax stood for decapitation, the rods for flogging.

Fascist architecture, like ancient architecture, used a monumental scale, with arches, bold statues, and rhetorical inscriptions—resulting in an austere and impersonal feel that's generally disliked by Romans today.

In spite of his supposed passion for ancient Rome, Mussolini had a dreadful approach to archaeology. He would isolate a major monument and destroy everything around it. Sections of the Imperial Forums were sacrificed to build the wide street, Via dei Fori Imperiali, from Piazza Venezia to the Colosseum. A famous fountain by the Colosseum that had survived almost 2,000 years was torn down without another thought.

there, E.U.R. has become an important destination for architecture buffs.

The Metro skirts E.U.R. with three stops (10 minutes from the Colosseum). Use E.U.R. Magliana for the "Square Colosseum" and E.U.R. Fermi for the Museum of Roman Civilization. Consider walking 30 minutes from the palace to the museum through the center of E.U.R.

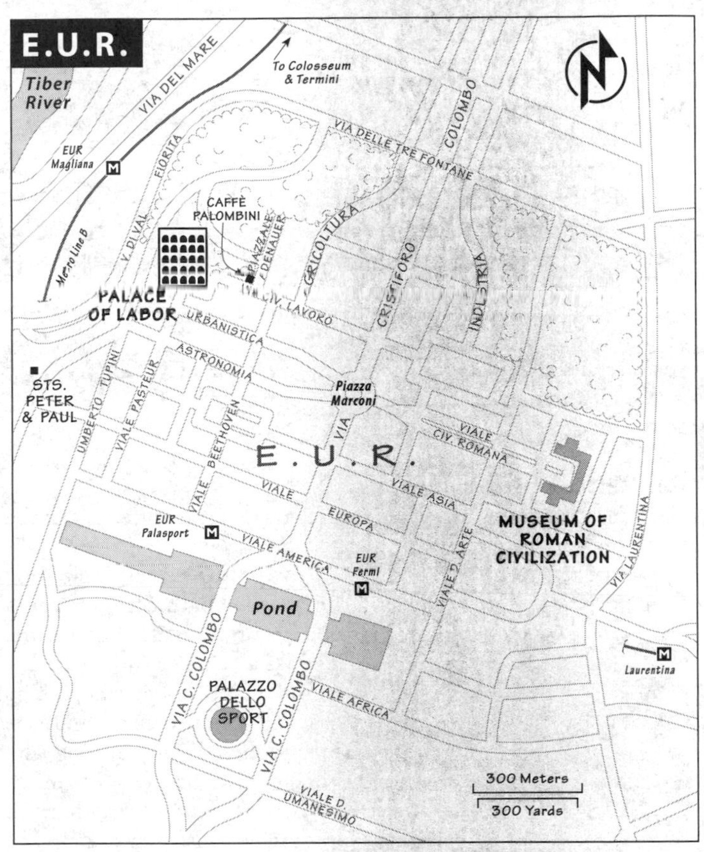

Palace of the Civilization of Labor (Palazzo della Civiltà del Lavoro)—From the Magliana Metro stop, stairs lead uphill to this epitome of fascist architecture. With its giant no-questions-asked patriotic statues and its black-and-white simplicity, this is E.U.R.'s tallest building and key landmark. It's understandably nicknamed the "Square Colosseum." Closed to the public while they decide how to use it, it's still interesting to walk around. Downhill, in front of the palace, Caffè Palombini is a popular institution for lunch or a drink (daily 7:00-22:00; good gelato, pastries, and snacks; Piazzale Adenauer 12, tel. 06-591-1700).

▲Museum of Roman Civilization (Museo della Civiltà Romana)—With dozens of rooms of plaster casts and models illustrating the greatness of classical Rome, this vast and heavy museum gives a strangely lifeless, close-up look at Rome. Each room has a theme, from military tricks to musical instruments. One long hall is filled with casts of the reliefs of Trajan's Column. The highlight is the huge scale model of Constantine's Rome, circa

A.D. 300. The Planetarium and Astronomical Museum are mostly of interest to children—so don't bother with the €9.50 combo-ticket unless you have kids.

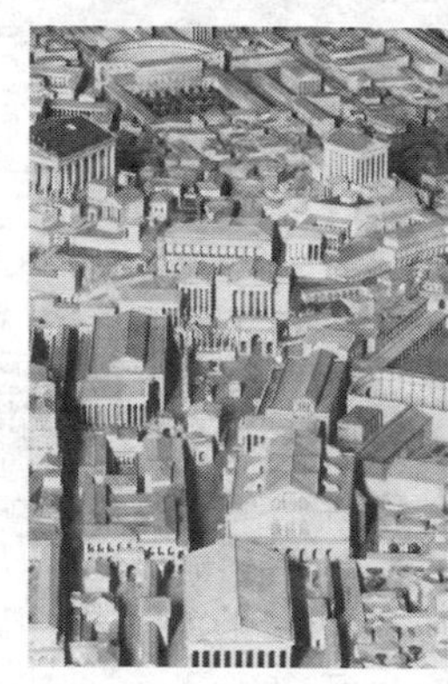

Cost and Hours: €7.50, sometimes €9 with special exhibits, Tue-Sun 9:00-14:00, closed Mon, last entry one hour before closing, Piazza G. Agnelli; leave the E.U.R. Fermi Metro station on Via America, head toward McDonald's, and at T-intersection, turn left and go uphill three blocks to Via dell'Arte—you'll see its colonnade on the right; to return to the city center, access the Metro entrance across the street, tel. 06-5422-0919, www.museociviltaromana.it.

Ancient Appian Way

Southeast of the city center lie several ancient sights that make the trek here worthwhile.

Baths of Caracalla (Terme di Caracalla)—Inaugurated by Emperor Caracalla in A.D. 216, this massive bath complex could accommodate 1,600 visitors at a time. Today it's just a shell—a huge shell—with all of its sculptures and most of its mosaics moved to museums. You'll see a two-story roofless brick building surrounded by a garden, bordered by ruined walls. The two large rooms at either end of the building were used for exercise. In between the exercise rooms was a pool flanked by two small mosaic-floored dressing rooms. Niches in the walls once held statues. The baths' statues are displayed elsewhere: For example, the immense *Toro Farnese* (a marble sculpture of a bull surrounded by people) snorts in Naples' Archaeological Museum.

In its day, this was a remarkable place to hang out. For ancient Romans, bathing was a social experience. The Baths of Caracalla functioned until Goths severed the aqueducts in the sixth century. In modern times, grand operas are performed here.

Cost and Hours: €6, includes the Tomb of Cecilia Metella and the Villa dei Quintili on the Appian Way, Mon 9:00-14:00, Tue-Sun 9:00 until one hour before sunset (19:00 in summer, 16:30 in winter), last entry one hour before closing, audioguide-€5, good €8 guidebook; Metro: Circus Maximus, plus a 5-minute walk south along Via delle Terme di Caracalla; bus #714 from Termini train station or bus #118 from the Appian Way—see the end of my

Ancient Appian Way Tour; tel. 06-3996-7700.

▲Appian Way—For a taste of the countryside around Rome and more wonders of Roman engineering, take the four-mile trip from the Colosseum out past the wall to a stretch of the ancient Appian Way, where the original pavement stones are lined by several interesting sights. Ancient Rome's first and greatest highway, the Appian Way once ran from Rome to the Adriatic port of Brindisi, the gateway to Greece. Today you can walk (or bike) some stretches of the road, rattling over original paving stones, past crumbling monuments that once lined the sides. The Tomb of Cecilia Metella and the Circus of Maxentius are the two most impressive pagan sights. Just a few hundred yards away are two major Christian catacombs (briefly described next); of the two catacombs, which is the best to visit? All in all, they're both quite similar, and either one will fit the bill.

For more on all of these sights, ✪ see the Ancient Appian Way Tour chapter.

▲▲Catacombs of San Sebastiano—A guide leads you underground through the tunnels where early Christians were buried. You'll see faded frescoes and graffiti by early-Christian tag artists. Besides the catacombs themselves, there's a historic fourth-century basilica with holy relics.

Cost and Hours: €8, includes 35-minute tour, 2/hour, Mon-Sat 10:00-17:00, closed Sun and mid-Nov-mid-Dec, last entry 30 minutes before closing, Via Appia Antica 136, tel. 06-785-0350, www.catacombe.org.

▲▲Catacombs of San Callisto—The larger of the two sets of catacombs, San Callisto also is the more prestigious, having been the burial site for several early popes.

Cost and Hours: €8, includes 30-minute tour, at least 2/hour, Thu-Tue 9:00-12:00 & 14:00-17:00, closed Wed and Feb, Via Appia Antica 110, tel. 06-5130-1580 or 06-513-0151, www.catacombe.roma.it.

HEART OF ROME WALK

From Campo de' Fiori to the Spanish Steps

Rome's most colorful neighborhood features narrow lanes, intimate piazzas, fanciful fountains, and some of Europe's best people-watching. During the day, this walk shows off the colorful Campo de' Fiori market and trendy fashion boutiques as it meanders past major monuments such as the Pantheon and the Spanish Steps.

But, when the sun sets, unexpected magic happens. A stroll in the cool of the evening brings out all the romance of the Eternal City. Sit so close to a bubbling fountain that traffic noise evaporates. Jostle with kids to see the gelato flavors. Watch lovers straddling more than the bench. Jaywalk past *polizia* in flak-proof vests. And marvel at the ramshackle elegance that softens this brutal city for those who were born here and can't imagine living anywhere else. These are the flavors of Rome, best tasted after dark.

Orientation

Length of This Walk: Allow anywhere from one to three hours for this mile-long walk, depending on whether you linger (yes, do) and tour the Pantheon (another good idea).

When to Go: This walk works well at any time. By day, you can enjoy Campo de' Fiori's morning market and sightsee the Pantheon and surrounding churches. But it's most engaging after dark, when the fountains are lit and the cool evening air brings locals out for the *passeggiata* (for more on this Italian tradition, see the sidebar on page 381).

Getting There: Campo de' Fiori is a few blocks west of Largo Argentina, a major transportation hub. Buses #40, #64, and #492 stop at both Largo Argentina and along Corso Vittorio Emanuele II, a long block north of Campo de' Fiori. A taxi from Termini Station costs about €8.

Pantheon: Free, Mon-Sat 8:30-19:30, Sun 9:00-18:00, holidays 9:00-13:00, closed for Mass Sat at 17:00 and Sun at 10:30.

Other Options: This walk is equally pleasant in reverse order. You could ride the Metro to the Spanish Steps and finish at Campo de' Fiori, near many recommended restaurants. To lengthen this walk, you could start in Trastevere; see directions on page 290.

The Walk Begins

• *Start this walk at Campo de' Fiori, my favorite outdoor dining room (especially after dark—see page 359 in the Eating in Rome chapter).*

Campo de' Fiori

One of Rome's most colorful spots, this bohemian piazza hosts a fruit and vegetable **market** in the morning, cafés in the evening, and pub-crawlers at night. In ancient times, the "Field of Flowers" was an open meadow. Later, Christian pilgrims passed through on their way to the Vatican, and a thriving market developed.

Lording over the center of the square is a statue of **Giordano Bruno,** an intellectual heretic who was burned on this spot in 1600. When the statue of Bruno was erected in 1889, riots overcame Vatican protests against honoring a heretic. Bruno faces his nemesis, the Vatican Chancellory (the big white building just outside the far-right corner of the square), while his pedestal reads, "And the flames rose up." Check out the reliefs on the pedestal for scenes from Bruno's trial and execution. Even today, this neighborhood is known for its free spirit and occasional demonstrations.

Campo de' Fiori is the product of centuries of unplanned urban development. At the east end of the square (behind Bruno), the ramshackle apartments are built right into the old outer wall of ancient Rome's mammoth Theater of Pompey. This entertainment complex covered several city blocks, stretching from here to Largo Argentina. Julius Caesar was assassinated in the Theater of Pompey, where the Senate was renting space.

The square is lined with and surrounded by fun eateries. Bruno faces the **Forno** (in the left corner of the square). Step in, at least to observe the frenzy as pizza is sold hot out of the oven. You can order *un etto* (100 grams, an average serving) by pointing, then take your snack to the counter to pay. The many bars lining the square are fine for drinks and watching the scene. On weekend

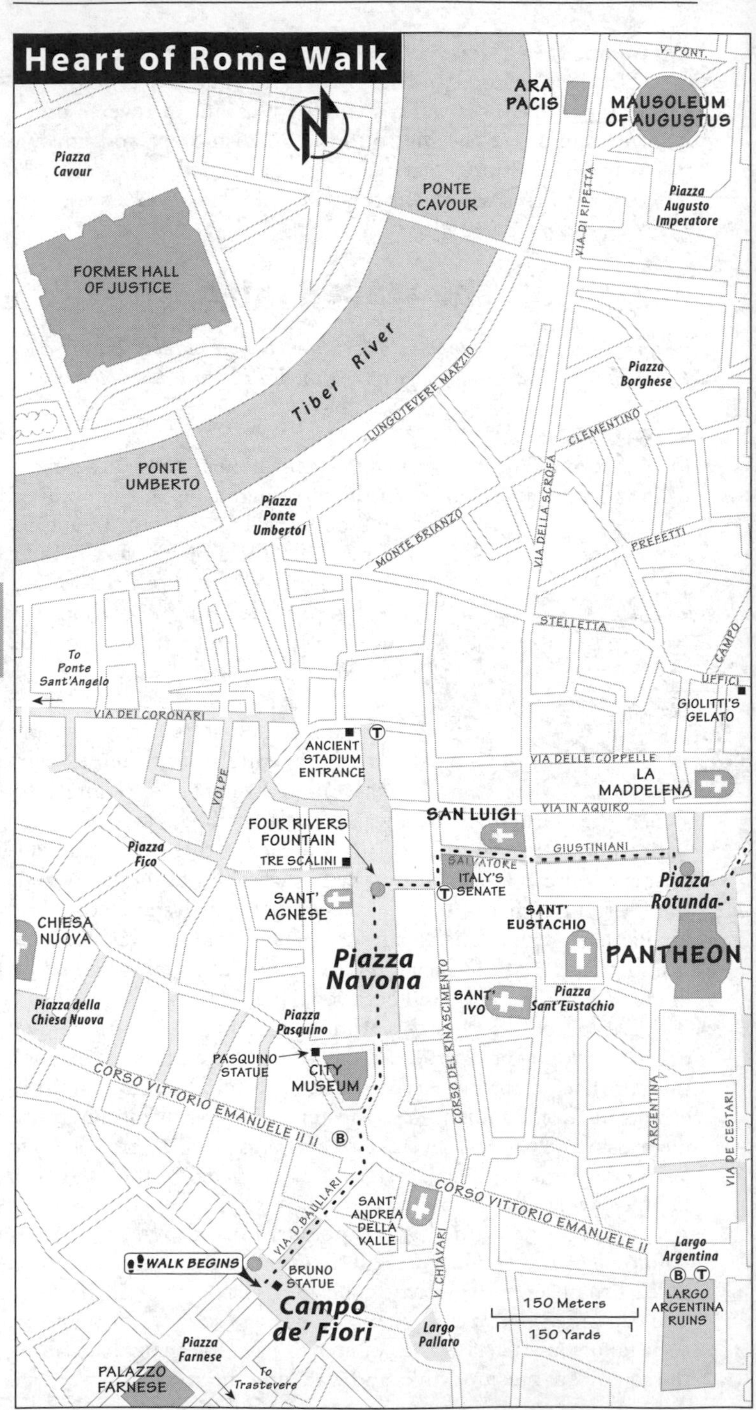
Heart of Rome Walk
ARA PACIS
MAUSOLEUM OF AUGUSTUS
V. PONT.
Piazza Cavour
PONTE CAVOUR
VIA DI RIPETTA
Piazza Augusto Imperatore
FORMER HALL OF JUSTICE
Tiber River
LUNGOTEVERE MARZIO
Piazza Borghese
CLEMENTINO
PONTE UMBERTO
Piazza Ponte Umberto I
MONTE BRIANZO
VIA DELLA SCROFA
PREFETTI
STELLETTA
CAMPO
UFFICI
To Ponte Sant'Angelo
VIA DEI CORONARI
GIOLITTI'S GELATO
ANCIENT STADIUM ENTRANCE
VIA DELLE COPPELLE
LA MADDELENA
VOLPE
SAN LUIGI
VIA IN AQUIRO
FOUR RIVERS FOUNTAIN
GIUSTINIANI
Piazza Fico
TRE SCALINI
SALVATORE
ITALY'S SENATE
Piazza Rotunda
SANT' AGNESE
SANT' EUSTACHIO
CHIESA NUOVA
PANTHEON
Piazza Navona
SANT' IVO
Piazza Sant'Eustachio
Piazza della Chiesa Nuova
Piazza Pasquino
CORSO DEL RINASCIMENTO
PASQUINO STATUE
CITY MUSEUM
CORSO VITTORIO EMANUELE II
ARGENTINA
VIA DE CESTARI
VIA D. BAULLARI
SANT' ANDREA DELLA VALLE
CORSO VITTORIO EMANUELE II
Largo Argentina
WALK BEGINS
BRUNO STATUE
V. CHIAVARI
LARGO ARGENTINA RUINS
Campo de' Fiori
150 Meters
150 Yards
Largo Pallaro
Piazza Farnese
PALAZZO FARNESE
To Trastevere

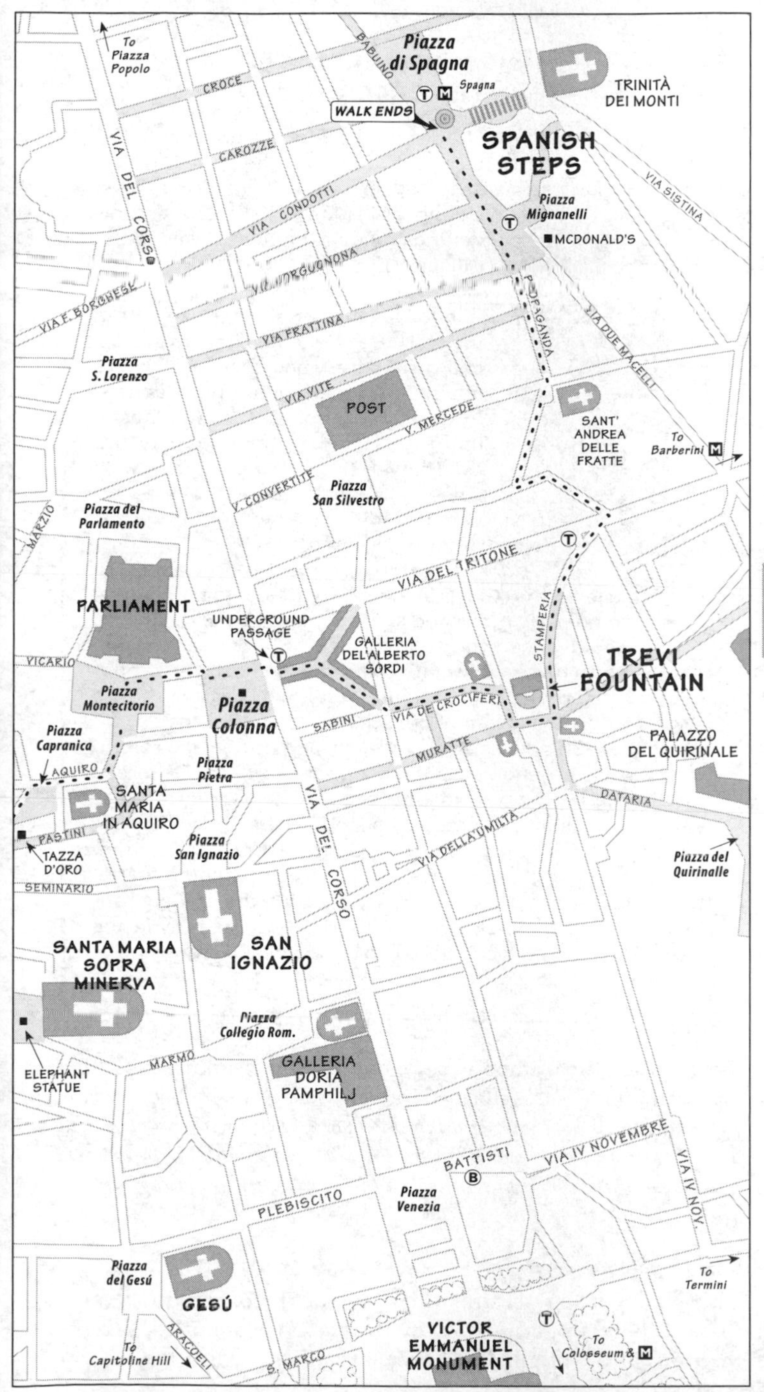

To Piazza Popolo
Piazza di Spagna
Spagna
TRINITÀ DEI MONTI
WALK ENDS
SPANISH STEPS
CROCE
CAROZZE
VIA DEL CORSO
VIA CONDOTTI
VIA SISTINA
Piazza Mignanelli
MCDONALD'S
VIA F. BORGHESE
VIA FRATTINA
PROPAGANDA
VIA DUE MACELLI
Piazza S. Lorenzo
VIA VITE
POST
V. MERCEDE
SANT' ANDREA DELLE FRATTE
To Barberini
V. CONVERTITE
Piazza San Silvestro
Piazza del Parlamento
MARZIO
VIA DEL TRITONE
PARLIAMENT
UNDERGROUND PASSAGE
GALLERIA DEL'ALBERTO SORDI
STAMPERIA
TREVI FOUNTAIN
VICARIO
Piazza Montecitorio
Piazza Colonna
SABINI
VIA DE CROCIFERI
MURATTE
PALAZZO DEL QUIRINALE
Piazza Capranica
AQUIRO
Piazza Pietra
SANTA MARIA IN AQUIRO
DATARIA
PASTINI
TAZZA D'ORO
Piazza San Ignazio
VIA DELLA UMILTÀ
Piazza del Quirinalle
SEMINARIO
SAN IGNAZIO
SANTA MARIA SOPRA MINERVA
Piazza Collegio Rom.
ELEPHANT STATUE
MARMO
GALLERIA DORIA PAMPHILJ
VIA IV NOVEMBRE
BATTISTI
VIA IV NOV.
PLEBISCITO
Piazza Venezia
Piazza del Gesú
GESÚ
To Termini
ARACOELI
To Capitoline Hill
S. MARCO
VICTOR EMMANUEL MONUMENT
To Colosseum &

Giordano Bruno (1548-1600)

Lauded as a martyr to free thought and reviled as an intellectual con man and heretic, the philosopher-priest Bruno has a legacy only a Roman could love. Details of his life are sketchy, and his writings range from the sublime to the ridiculous.

The young Dominican priest was nonconformist and outspoken from the start. He had to flee Italy to avoid a charge of heresy and spent most of his adult life wandering Europe's capitals. In Geneva, he joined the Calvinists, until he was driven out for his unorthodox views. In London, he met with Queen Elizabeth, who found him subversive. In Germany, the Lutherans excommunicated him.

In his writings, Bruno claimed to have discovered the "Clavis Magna" (Great Key) to training the human memory. He published satirical plays tweaking Church morals. He advanced the still-heretical (Copernican) notion that the earth revolved around the sun and speculated about other inhabited planets in the universe. All his works show a vast-ranging mind aware of the scientific trends of the day.

In 1593, Bruno was arrested by the Inquisition and sent to Rome, where he languished in prison for six years. (Tortured? Lost in bureaucracy? No one knows.) The exact charge against him remains debated by historians.

Bruno was sentenced to death by fire. He replied, "Perhaps you who pronounce this sentence are more fearful than I who receive it." On February 17, 1600, the civil authorities led him to the stake on Campo de' Fiori. As they lit the fire, he was offered a crucifix to hold. He pushed it away.

nights, when the Campo is packed with beer-drinking kids, this medieval square is transformed into one vast Roman street party.

• *If Bruno did a hop, step, and jump forward, then turned right on Via dei Baullari and marched 200 yards, he'd cross the busy Corso Vittorio Emanuele; then, continuing another 150 yards on Via Cuccagna, he'd find...*

Piazza Navona

This oblong square retains the shape of the original racetrack that was built around A.D. 80 by the emperor Domitian. (To see the ruins of the original entrance, exit the square at the far—or

north—end, then take an immediate left, and look down to the left 25 feet below the current street level.) Since ancient times, the square has been a center of Roman life. In the 1800s, the city would flood the square to cool off the neighborhood.

The **Four Rivers Fountain** in the center is the most famous fountain by the man who remade Rome in Baroque style, Gian Lorenzo Bernini. Four burly river gods (representing the four continents that were known in 1650) support an Egyptian obelisk. The water of the world gushes everywhere. The Nile has his head covered, since the headwaters were unknown then. The Ganges holds an oar. The Danube turns to admire the obelisk, which Bernini had moved here from a stadium on the Appian Way. And Uruguay's Río de la Plata tumbles backward in shock, wondering how he ever made the top four. Bernini enlivens the fountain with horses plunging through the rocks and exotic flora and fauna from these newly discovered lands. Homesick Texans may want to find the armadillo. (It's the big, weird, armor-plated creature behind the Plata river statue.)

The Plata river god is gazing upward at the **Church of St. Agnes,** worked on by Bernini's former student-turned-rival, Francesco Borromini. Borromini's concave facade helps reveal the dome and epitomizes the curved symmetry of Baroque. Tour guides say that Bernini designed his river god to look horrified at Borromini's work. Or maybe he's shielding his eyes from St. Agnes' nakedness, as she was stripped before being martyred. But either explanation is unlikely, since the fountain was completed two years before Borromini even started work on the church.

Piazza Navona is Rome's most interesting night scene, with street music, artists, fire-eaters, local Casanovas, ice cream, and outdoor cafés that are worthy of a splurge if you've got time to sit and enjoy Italy's human river.

• Leave Piazza Navona directly across from Tre Scalini (famous for its rich chocolate ice cream), and go east down Corsia Agonale, past rose peddlers and palm readers. Jog left around the guarded building (where Italy's senate meets), and follow the brown sign to the Pantheon, which is straight down Via del Salvatore.

The Pantheon

Sit for a while under the portico of the Pantheon (romantically floodlit and moonlit at night).

The 40-foot, single-piece granite columns of the Pantheon's entrance show the scale the ancient Romans built on. The columns support a triangular Greek-style roof with an inscription that says "M. Agrippa" built it. In fact, it was built *(fecit)* by Emperor Hadrian (A.D. 120), who gave credit to the builder of an earlier structure. This impressive entranceway gives no clue that the greatest wonder of the building is inside—a domed room that inspired later domes, including Michelangelo's St. Peter's and Brunelleschi's Duomo (in Florence).

If it's open, pop into the Pantheon for a look around. If you have extra time, consider detouring to several interesting churches near the Pantheon. For more information, ✪ see the Pantheon Tour chapter.

• With your back to the Pantheon, veer to the right, uphill toward the yellow sign that reads Casa del Caffè *at the Tazza d'Oro coffee shop on Via Orfani.*

From the Pantheon to the Trevi Fountain

Tazza d'Oro Casa del Caffè, one of Rome's top coffee shops, dates back to the days when this area was licensed to roast coffee beans. Locals come here for a shot of espresso or, when it's hot, a refreshing *granita di caffè con panna* (coffee slush with cream).

• Continue up Via Orfani to...

Piazza Capranica is home to the big, plain Florentine Renaissance-style Palazzo Capranica (directly opposite as you enter the square). Big shots, like the Capranica family, built towers on their palaces—not for any military use, but just to show off.

Egyptian Obelisks

Rome has 13 obelisks, more than any other city in the world. In Egypt, they were connected with the sun god Ra (like stone sun rays) and the power of the pharaohs. The ancient Romans, keen on exotic novelty and sheer size, brought the obelisks here and set them up in key public places as evidence and celebration of their occupation of Egypt. Starting from the 1580s, Rome's new rulers—the popes—relocated the obelisks, often topping them with Christian crosses so they came to acquire yet another significance that guaranteed their survival: the triumph of Christianity over all other religions.

The tallest (105 feet) and the most ancient (16th century B.C.) is the one by San Giovanni in Laterano. It once stood in the Circus Maximus next to its sister, which now marks the center of Piazza del Popolo.

The obelisks were carved out of single blocks of granite. Imagine the work, with only man and horsepower, first to quarry them and set them up in Egypt, then—after the Romans came along—to roll them on logs to the river or the coast, sail (or row) them in special barges across the Mediterranean and up the Tiber, and finally hoist them up.

Rome wasn't above cheap imitations, however: A couple of the obelisks are ancient Roman copies. The one at the top of the Spanish Steps has spelling mistakes in the hieroglyphics.

• *Leave the piazza to the right of the palace, heading down Via in Aquiro.*

The street Via in Aquiro leads to a sixth-century B.C. **Egyptian obelisk** taken as a trophy by Augustus after his victory in Egypt over Mark Antony and Cleopatra. The obelisk was set up as a sundial. Follow the zodiac markings to the well-guarded front door. This is Italy's **parliament building,** where the lower house meets; you may see politicians, political demonstrations, and TV cameras.

• *To your right is Piazza Colonna, where we're heading next—unless you like gelato...*

A one-block detour to the left (past Albergo Nazionale) brings you to Rome's most famous *gelateria*. **Giolitti's** is cheap for takeout or elegant and splurge-worthy for a sit among classy locals (open daily until past midnight, Via Uffici del Vicario 40); get your gelato in a cone *(cono)* or cup *(coppetta)*.

Piazza Colonna features a huge second-century column. Its reliefs depict the victories of Emperor Marcus Aurelius over the barbarians. When Marcus died in A.D. 180, the barbarians began to get the upper hand, beginning Rome's long three-century fall. The big, important-looking palace houses the headquarters for the prime minister's cabinet.

Noisy **Via del Corso** is Rome's main north-south boulevard. It's named for the Berber horse races—without riders—that took place here during Carnevale. This wild tradition continued until the late 1800s, when a series of fatal accidents (including, reportedly, one in front of Queen Margherita) led to its cancellation. Historically the street was filled with meat shops. When it became one of Rome's first gas-lit streets in 1854, these butcher shops were banned and replaced by classier boutiques, jewelers, and antiques dealers. Nowadays the northern part of Via del Corso is closed to traffic, and for a few hours every evening it becomes a wonderful parade of Romans out for a stroll (see the "Dolce Vita Stroll" in the Nightlife in Rome chapter).

• *Cross Via del Corso to enter a big palatial building with columns, which houses the Galleria Alberto Sordi shopping mall (with convenient WCs). Inside, take the fork to the right and exit at the back. (If you're here after 22:00, when the mall is closed, circle around the right side of the Galleria on Via dei Sabini.) Once out the back, head up Via de Crociferi, to the roar of the water, lights, and people at the...*

Trevi Fountain

The Trevi Fountain shows how Rome took full advantage of the abundance of water brought into the city by its great aqueducts. This watery Baroque avalanche by Nicola Salvi was completed in 1762. Salvi used the palace behind the fountain as a theatrical back-

drop for the figure of "Ocean," who represents water in every form. The statue surfs through his wet kingdom—with water gushing from 24 spouts and tumbling over 30 different kinds of plants—while Triton blows his conch shell.

The magic of the square is enhanced by the fact that no streets directly approach it. You can hear the excitement as you draw near, and then—*bam!*—you're there. The scene is always lively, with lucky Romeos clutching dates while unlucky ones clutch beers. Romantics toss a coin over their shoulder, thinking it will give them a wish and assure their return to Rome. That may sound silly, but every year I go through this tourist ritual...and it actually seems to work.

Take some time to people-watch (whisper a few breathy *bellos* or *bellas*) before leaving. There's a peaceful zone at water level on the far right.

• *From the Trevi Fountain, we're 10 minutes from our next stop, the Spanish Steps. Just use a map to get there, or follow these directions: Facing the Trevi Fountain, go forward, walking along the right side of the fountain on Via della Stamperia. Cross busy Via del Tritone. Continue 100 yards and veer right at Via delle Fratte, a street that changes its name to Via Propaganda before ending at the...*

Spanish Steps

Piazza di Spagna, with the very popular Spanish Steps, is named for the Spanish Embassy to the Vatican, which has been here for 300 years. It's been the hangout of many Romantics over the years (Keats, Wagner, Openshaw, Goethe, and others). In the 1700s, British aristocrats on the "Grand Tour" of Europe came here to ponder Rome's decay. The British poet John Keats pondered his mortality, then died of tuberculosis at age 25 in the pink building on the right side of the steps. Fellow Romantic Lord Byron lived across the square at #66.

The **Sinking Boat Fountain** at the foot of the steps, built by Bernini or his father, Pietro, is powered by an aqueduct. Actually, all of Rome's fountains are aqueduct-powered; their spurts are determined by the water pressure provided by the various aqueducts. This one, for instance, is much weaker than Trevi's gush.

The piazza is a thriving scene at night. Window-shop along Via Condotti, which stretches away from the steps. This is where Gucci and other big names cater to the trendsetting jet set. It's clear that the main sight around here is not the famous steps, but the people who sit on them.

• *Our walk is finished. If you'd like to reach the top of the steps sweat-free, take the free elevator just outside the Spagna Metro stop (to the left, as you face the steps; elevator closes at 21:00). A free WC is underground in the piazza near the Metro entrance, by the middle palm tree (10:00–19:30). The nearby McDonald's (as you face the Spanish Steps, go right one block) is big and lavish, with a salad bar and WC. When you're ready to leave, you can zip home on the Metro (usually open until 23:30, Fri–Sat until 1:30 in the morning) or grab a taxi at either the north or south side of the piazza.*

COLOSSEUM TOUR

Colosseo

Rome has many layers—modern, Baroque, Renaissance, Christian. But let's face it: "Rome" is Caesars, gladiators, chariots, centurions, *"Et tu, Brute,"* trumpet fanfares, and thumbs-up or thumbs-down. That's the Rome we'll look at. Our "Caesar Shuffle" begins with the downtown core of ancient Rome, the Colosseum. A logical next stop is the Roman Forum, just next door (and the next chapter).

Orientation

Cost: €12 combo-ticket covers both the Colosseum and the Roman Forum/Palatine Hill; also covered by the Roma Pass. The combo-ticket is valid for two consecutive days, but once your ticket is scanned for either the Colosseum or the Forum/Palatine Hill (grouped as one sight for the purposes of the ticket), you can't re-enter that sight (even the next day).

Hours: The Colosseum, Roman Forum, and Palatine Hill are all open daily 8:30 until one hour before sunset: April-Sept until 19:15, Oct until 18:30, Nov-mid-Feb until 16:30, mid-Feb-mid-March until 17:00, mid-March-late March until 17:30; last entry one hour before closing. Tel. 06-3996-7700, http://archeoroma.beniculturali.it/en.

Avoiding Lines: Crowds tend to be thinner (and lines shorter) in the afternoon (especially after 15:00 in summer); this is also true at the Forum.

You can save lots of

time by buying your combo-ticket in advance, having the Roma Pass, booking a guided tour, or renting an audioguide or videoguide. Here are the options:

1. Buy your combo-ticket (or Roma Pass) at the less-crowded Palatine Hill entrance, 150 yards away on Via di San Gregorio (facing the Forum, with Colosseum at your back, go left down the street). You can also buy a Roma Pass at the tobacco shop in the Colosseo Metro station, the I Fori di Roma visitors center on Via dei Fori Imperiali (see page 121), or other sights around town. It should cost the same no matter where you buy it. (Avoid buying your ticket or Roma Pass at the Forum, which also tends to have lines.)

2. Buy a combo-ticket online at www.ticketclic.it (€1.50 booking fee, not changeable). The "free tickets" you'll see listed are valid only for EU citizens with ID.

3. Pay to join an official guided tour, or rent an audioguide or videoguide (see "Tours," facing page). This lets you march right up to the Colosseum's guided visits *(Visite Guidate)* desk, thus bypassing the ticket lines. Even if you don't use the device or accompany the guided tour, the extra cost might be worth it just to skip the ticket line.

4. Hire a private walking-tour guide. Guides of varying quality linger outside the Colosseum, offering tours that allow you to skip the line. Be aware that these private guides may try to mislead you into thinking the Colosseum lines are longer than they really are. For more on this option, see "Tours" on the facing page.

Restoration: The arena is being cleaned from top to bottom, given permanent lighting, and outfitted with new shops and services. Long-range plans include building a free-standing ticket booth outside the Colosseum. These ongoing renovations, scheduled to last several years, may affect your visit.

Warning: Beware of the **greedy gladiators.** For a fee, the incredibly crude, modern-day gladiators snuff out their cigarettes and pose for photos. They're officially banned from panhandling in this area, but you may still see them, hoping to intimidate easy-to-swindle tourists into paying too much money for a photo op. (If you go for it, €4-5 for one photo usually keeps them appeased.) Also, look out for **pickpockets** and con artists in this prime tourist spot.

Getting There: The Colosseo Metro stop on line B is just across the street from the monument. Bus #60 is handy for hotels near Via Firenze and Via Nazionale. Bus #87 links Largo Argentina with the Colosseum.

Getting In: If you need to buy a ticket or sign up for a guided tour, follow the signs for the appropriate line. With a combo-ticket or Roma Pass in hand, look for signs for *ticket holders* or *Roma Pass*, allowing you to bypass the long lines.

Tours: A dry but fact-filled **audioguide** is available just past the turnstiles (€5.50/2 hours). A handheld **videoguide** senses where you are in the site and plays related video clips (€6).

Official **guided tours** in English depart nearly hourly between 10:00 and 17:00, and last 45-60 minutes (€5 plus Colosseum ticket, purchase inside the Colosseum near the ticket booth marked *Visite Guidate;* if you're lost, ask a guard to direct you to the desk).

Private guides stand outside the Colosseum looking for business (€25-30/2-hour tour of the Colosseum, Palatine Hill, and Forum). If booking a private guide, make sure that your tour will start right away and that the ticket you receive covers all three sights: the Colosseum, Forum, and Palatine Hill.

You can also download this chapter as a free Rick Steves **audio tour** (see page 27).

A 1.5-hour **behind-the-scenes tour** takes you through restricted areas, including underground passageways and the third floor, which are off-limits to regular Colosseum visitors. It's generally offered April-Nov only, and closes during and after bad weather, as the underground passageways flood easily. While interesting, this tour certainly isn't essential to appreciating the Colosseum. It's operated by Pierreci, a private company; to book, contact them at least a day in advance (€8 plus Colosseum ticket, www.pierreci.it, call 06-3996-7700 during business hours: Mon-Fri 9:00-18:00, Sat 9:00-14:00, closed Sun, no same-day reservations). After dialing, wait for English instructions on how to reach a live operator, then reserve a time and pre-pay with a credit card. Without a reservation, you can try to join the next available tour (may be in Italian): Once you have your Colosseum entrance ticket and are at the turnstiles, look for the tour meeting point just past the ticket desk; pay the guide directly.

Length of This Tour: Allow an hour.

With Limited Time: With a single glance, you can basically see the entire interior. It's not necessary to go upstairs or circle the place.

Services: For tips on where to eat, drink, and find a WC in the area, see the sidebar on page 114.

The Tour Begins

Exterior

• *View the Colosseum from the Forum fence, across the street from the Colosseo Metro station.*

Built when the Roman Empire was at its peak in A.D. 80, the Colosseum represents Rome at its grandest. The Flavian Amphitheater (the Colosseum's real name) was an arena for gladiator contests and public spectacles. When killing became a spectator sport, the Romans wanted to share the fun with as many people as possible, so they stuck two semicircular theaters together to create a freestanding amphitheater. The outside (where slender cypress trees stand today) was decorated with a 100-foot-tall bronze statue of Nero that gleamed in the sunlight. In a later age, the colossal structure was nicknamed a "coloss-eum," the wonder of its age. It could accommodate 50,000 roaring fans (100,000 thumbs).

The Romans pioneered the use of concrete and the rounded arch, which enabled them to build on this tremendous scale. The exterior is a skeleton of 3.5 million cubic feet of travertine stone. (Each of the pillars flanking the ground-level arches weighs five tons.) It took 200 ox-drawn wagons shuttling back and forth every day for four years just to bring the stone here from Tivoli. They stacked stone blocks (without mortar) into the shape of an arch, supported temporarily by wooden scaffolding. Finally, they wedged a keystone into the top of the arch—it not only kept the arch from falling, it could bear even more weight above. Iron pegs held the larger stones together—notice the small holes that pockmark the sides.

The exterior says a lot about the Romans. They were great engineers, not artists, and the building is more functional than beautiful. (If ancient Romans visited the US today as tourists, they might send home postcards of our greatest works of "art"—freeways.) While the essential structure of the Colosseum is Roman, the four-story facade is decorated with mostly Greek columns—Doric-like Tuscan columns on the ground level, Ionic on the second story, Corinthian on the next level, and at the top, half-columns with a mix of all three. Originally, copies of Greek statues stood in the arches of the middle two stories, giving a veneer of sophistication to this arena of death.

Only a third of the original Colosseum remains. Earthquakes destroyed some of it, but most was carted off as easy pre-cut stones for other buildings during the Middle Ages and Renaissance.

• *To enter, line up in the correct queue: the one for ticket buyers, or the one for those who already have a ticket or Roma Pass (plus people looking to take a guided tour or rent an audio- or videoguide). The third line is for groups. Once past the turnstiles, there may be signs directing you*

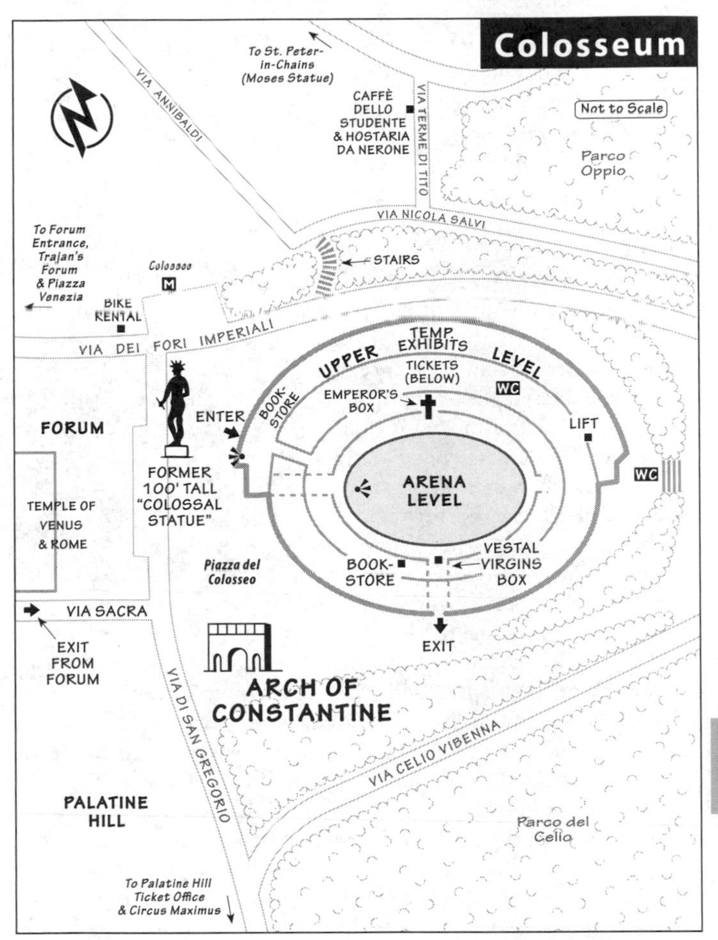

on a specific visitors' route. Follow the flow of traffic, making your way into the arena.

Interior

Entrances and Exits

As you walk through passageways and up staircases, admire the ergonomics. Fans could pour in through ground-floor entrances; there were 76 numbered ones in addition to the emperor's private entrance on the north side. Your ticket was a piece of pottery (or possibly wood or bone), marked with your entrance, section, row, and seat number. You'd pass by concession stands selling fast food and souvenirs, such as wine glasses with the names of famous gladiators. A hallway leading to the seats was called a *vomitorium*. At exit time, the Colosseum would "vomit" out its contents, giving us the English word. It's estimated that all 50,000 fans could enter and exit in 15 minutes.

• *Soon you'll spill out into the arena. Wherever you end up—upstairs or downstairs, at one side of the arena or the other—just take it all in and get oriented. The tallest side of the Colosseum (with the large Christian cross) is the north side.*

Arena

The games took place in this oval-shaped arena, 280 feet long by 165 feet wide. The ratio of length to width is 5:3, often called the golden ratio. Since the days of the Greek mathematician Pythagoras, artists considered that proportion to be ideal, with almost mystical properties. The Colosseum's architects apparently wanted their structure to embody the perfect 5-by-3 mathematical order they thought existed in nature.

When you look down into the arena, you're seeing the underground passages beneath the playing surface (which can only be visited on a private tour). The arena was originally covered with a wooden floor, then sprinkled with sand (*arena* in Latin). The bit of reconstructed floor gives you an accurate sense of the original arena level and the subterranean warren where animals and prisoners were held. As in modern stadiums, the spectators ringed the playing area in bleacher seats that slanted up from the arena floor. Around you are the big brick masses that supported the tiers of seats.

A variety of materials were used to build the stadium. Look around. Big white travertine blocks stacked on top of each other formed the skeleton. The pillars for the bleachers were made with a shell of brick, filled in with concrete. Originally the bare brick was covered with marble columns or ornamental facing, so the interior was a brilliant white (they used white plaster for the upper-floor cheap seats).

The Colosseum's seating was strictly segregated. At ringside, the emperor, senators, Vestal Virgins, and VIPs occupied marble seats with their names carved on them (a few marble seats have been restored, at the east end). The next level up held those of noble birth. The level tourists now occupy was for ordinary free Roman

citizens, called plebeians. Up at the very top (a hundred yards from the action), there were once wooden bleachers for the poorest people—foreigners, slaves, and women.

The top story of the Colosseum is mostly ruined—only the north side still retains its high wall. This was not part of the original three-story structure, but was added around A.D. 230 after a fire necessitated repairs. Picture the awning that could be stretched across the top of the stadium by armies of sailors. Strung along horizontal beams that pointed inward to the center, the awning only covered about a third of the arena—so those at the top always enjoyed shade, while many nobles down below roasted in the sun.

Looking into the complex web of passageways beneath the arena, you can imagine how busy the backstage action was. Gladiators strolled down the central passageway, from their warm-up yard on the east end to the arena entrance on the west. Some workers tended wild animals. Others prepared stage sets of trees or fake buildings, allowing the arena to be quickly transformed from an African jungle to a Greek temple. Props and sets were hauled up to arena level on 80 different elevator shafts via a system of ropes and pulleys. (You might be able to make out some small rectangular shafts, especially near the center of the arena.) That means there were 80 different spots from which animals, warriors, and stage sets could pop up and magically appear.

The games began with a few warm-up acts—dogs bloodying themselves attacking porcupines, female gladiators fighting each other, or a one-legged man battling a dwarf. Then came the main event—the gladiators.

"Hail, Caesar! *(Ave, Cesare!)* We who are about to die salute you!" The gladiators would enter the arena from the west end, parade around to the sound of trumpets, acknowledge the Vestal Virgins (on the south side), then stop at the emperor's box (supposedly marked today by the cross that stands at the "50-yard line" on the north

Modern Amenities in the Ancient World

The area around the Colosseum, Forum, and Palatine Hill is rich in history, but pretty barren when it comes to food, shelter, and WCs. Here are a few options:

The Colosseum has a few crowded **WCs** inside. A nice, big WC is behind (east of) the structure (facing ticket entrance, go clockwise; WC is under stairway). If you can wait, the best WCs in the area are at Palatine Hill—at the Via di San Gregorio entrance, outside the stadium, in the museum, and in the Farnese Gardens. The Forum also has one WC at the entrance and another near the Temple of Vesta (#8 on map on page 122).

Because the area's **eating** options are limited, consider assembling a small picnic. The Colosseo Metro stop has forgettable €5 hot sandwiches. Snack stands on street corners sell overpriced drinks, sandwiches, fruit, and candy. If you prefer to dine in, you'll find a few restaurants behind the Colosseum (with expansive views of the structure), several recommended places within a few blocks (no views but a better value—see page 367), and a cluster of places near the Forum's main entrance (where Via Cavour spills into Via dei Fori Imperiali).

To refill your **water** bottle, stop at one of the water fountains in the area. You'll find them along a few city streets, as well as inside the Forum and Palatine Hill.

A nice oasis is the free visitors center, **I Fori di Roma,** located near the Forum entrance. It's across Via dei Fori Imperiali and a bit east, toward the Colosseum. It has a small café, a WC, and a few exhibits.

If your sightseeing takes you as far as **Capitoline Hill,** you'll find services at the Capitoline Museums, including a nice view café (see page 152).

side—although no one knows for sure where it was). They would then raise their weapons, shout, and salute—and begin fighting. The fights pitted men against men, men against beasts, and beasts against beasts. Picture 50,000 screaming people around you (did gladiators get stage fright?), and imagine that they want to see you die.

Some gladiators wielded swords, protected only with a shield and a heavy helmet. Others represented fighting fishermen, with a net to snare opponents and a trident to spear them. The gladiators were usually slaves, crimi-

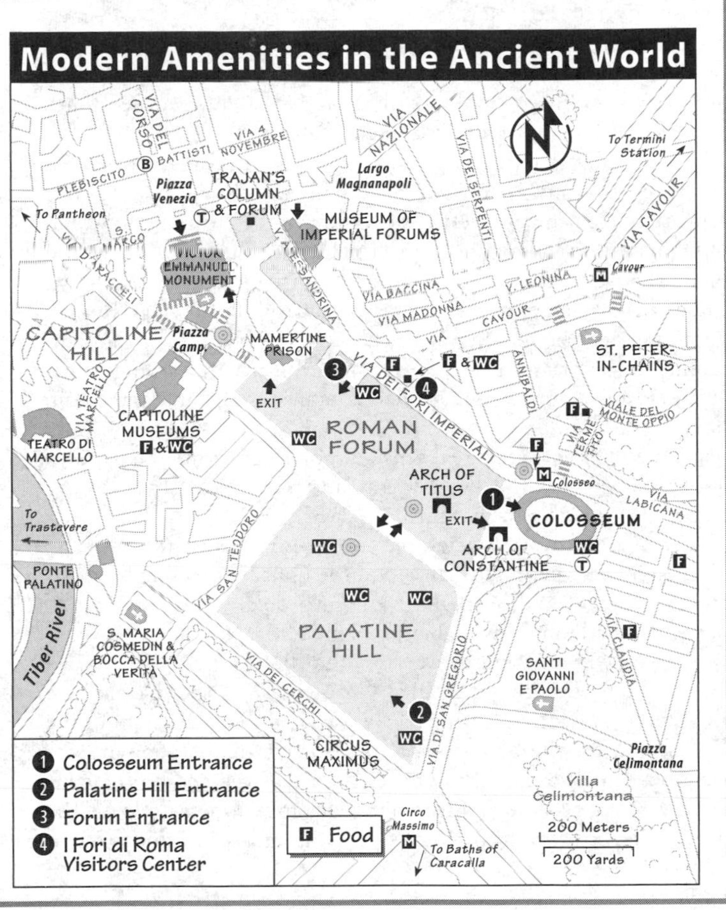

nals, or poor people who got their chance for freedom, wealth, and fame in the ring. They learned to fight in training schools, then battled their way up the ranks. The best were rewarded like our modern sports stars, with fan clubs, great wealth, and, yes, product endorsements.

The animals came from all over the world: lions, tigers, and bears (oh my!), crocodiles, elephants, and hippos (not to mention exotic human "animals" from the "barbarian" lands). They were kept in cages beneath the arena floor, then lifted up in the elevators. Released at floor level, animals would pop out from behind blinds into the arena—the gladiator didn't know where, when, or by what he'd be attacked. Many a hapless warrior met his death here, and he never knew what hit him. (This brought howls of laughter from the hardened fans in the cheap upper seats, who had a better view of the action.)

Nets ringed the arena to protect the crowd. The stadium was inaugurated with a 100-day festival in which 2,000 men and 9,000 animals were killed. Colosseum employees squirted perfumes around the stadium to mask the stench of blood.

If a gladiator fell helpless to the ground, his opponent would approach the emperor's box and ask: Should he live or die? Sometimes the emperor left the decision to the crowd, who would judge based on how valiantly the man had fought. They would make their decision: thumbs-up or thumbs-down. Consider the value of these games in placating and controlling the huge Roman populace. Seeing the king of beasts—a lion—slain by a gladiator reminded the masses of man's triumph over nature. Seeing exotic animals from Africa heralded their conquest of distant lands. And having the thumbs-up or thumbs-down authority over another person's life gave them a real sense of power. Imagine the psychological boost the otherwise downtrodden masses felt when the emperor granted them this thrilling decision.

Did they throw Christians to the lions as in the movies? Christians were definitely thrown to the lions, made to fight gladiators, crucified, and burned alive...but probably not here in this particular stadium. Maybe, but probably not.

Rome was a nation of warriors that built an empire by conquest. The battles fought against Germans and other barbarians, Egyptians, and strange animals were played out daily here in the Colosseum for the benefit of city-slicker bureaucrats, who got vicarious thrills by watching brutes battle to the death. The contests were always free, sponsored by the government to bribe the people's favor or to keep Rome's growing masses of unemployed rabble off the streets.

• *With these scenes in mind, wander around, then check out the upper level. There are stairs on both the east and west sides, as well as an elevator at the east end (only accessible to those who really need it). The upper deck offers more colossal views of the arena, plus a bookstore and temporary exhibits. Wherever you may Rome, find a spot at the west end of the upper deck, where you can look out over some of the sights nearby.*

Views from the Upper Level

• *Start your visual tour with the big, white, triumphal arch.*

Arch of Constantine

If you are a Christian, were raised a Christian, or simply belong to a so-called "Christian nation," ponder this arch. It marks one of the great turning points in history: the military coup that made Christianity mainstream. In A.D. 312, Emperor Constantine defeated his rival Maxentius in the crucial Battle of the Milvian

Bridge. The night before, he had seen a vision of a cross in the sky. Constantine—whose mother and sister had already become Christians—became sole emperor and legalized Christianity. With this one battle, a once-obscure Jewish sect with a handful of followers became the state religion of the entire Western world. In A.D. 300, you could be killed for being a Christian; a century later, you could be killed for not being one. Church enrollment boomed.

The restored arch is like an ancient museum. It's decorated entirely with recycled carvings originally made for other buildings. By covering it with exquisite carvings of high Roman art—works that glorified previous emperors—Constantine put himself in their league. Hadrian is featured in the round reliefs, with Marcus Aurelius in the square reliefs higher up. The big statues on top are of Trajan and Augustus. Originally, Augustus drove a chariot similar to the one topping the modern Victor Emmanuel II Monument. Fourth-century Rome may have been in decline, but Constantine clung to its glorious past.

Surrounding Hills

Looking southwest, beyond the Arch of Constantine, you see Palatine Hill, dotted with umbrella pines. To the right of the Arch of Constantine is the road called Via Sacra ("Sacred Way"), once Rome's main street. It heads west up an incline toward the Arch of Titus (you can just make out its white top from here). That marks the head of the Forum, the religious, political, and commercial heart of ancient Rome (covered in the next chapter).

The Colosseum was built between three of Rome's legendary seven hills: Palatine (to the southwest), Esquiline (to the north), and Caelian (to the south). The Colosseum stands on land where the notorious Emperor Nero once had his sumptuous Golden House, which stretched from the Arch of Titus, across the valley, and up onto Esquiline Hill. After the house was replaced by the Colosseum, Nero's statue (or colossus) became the Colosseum's 100-foot-tall doorman.

• *Looking west, in the direction of the Forum, you'll see some ruins sitting atop a raised, rectangular-shaped hill. (You can recognize the hill by some door-like openings cut into the hill's support wall.) The ruins—consisting of an arched alcove made of brick and backed by a church bell tower—are all that remain of the once-great...*

Temple of Venus and Rome

At 100 feet tall, this temple atop a pedestal was one of the most prominent temples in Rome—and also its biggest. The size of a football field, it once covered the entire hill. The style of the temple was Greek—surrounded by white columns and topped with a triangular pediment above the entrance. Today, the perimeter of the complex is still visible, marked by a few massive white columns, six feet thick.

The main ruin in the center—the tall brick arch with a cross-hatched ceiling—was once the *cella,* or sacred chamber of the temple. Here sat two monumental statues, back to back. Venus, the goddess of love, faced the Colosseum. The goddess called Roma Aeterna faced the Forum. The pair of statues symbolized the birth and eternal destiny of the race of people meant to endure forever. The goddesses' Latin names were written in the twin *cella*s. On one side it read "Roma" and on the other, "Amor." Roma and Amor—a perfectly symmetrical palindrome, showing how Rome and Love were meant to go together. In ancient times, newlyweds ascended the staircase from the Colosseum (some parts are still visible) to the temple to ask Venus and Roma Aeterna to bring them good luck. These days, Roman couples get married at the church with the bell tower to ensure themselves love and happiness for eternity.

The temple was designed by Hadrian, the second-century emperor and amateur architect who also designed the Pantheon. Hadrian's design was critiqued by Rome's best-known architect, who complained that the huge statues would be so cramped they'd bump their heads if they stood up. Hadrian listened patiently to the criticism...then had the architect killed.

For a closer-up look at the Temple of Venus and Rome, you can access the ruins from within the Roman Forum.

The Colosseum's Legacy: A.D. 500 to the Present

With the coming of Christianity to Rome, the Colosseum and its deadly games slowly became politically incorrect. However, some gladiator contests continued here sporadically until they were completely banned in A.D. 435. Animal hunts continued a few decades longer. As the Roman Empire dwindled and the infrastructure crumbled, the stadium itself was neglected. Finally, around A.D. 523—after nearly 500 years of games—the last animal was slaughtered, and the Colosseum shut its doors.

For the next thousand years, the structure was inhabited by various squatters. It was used for makeshift apartments or shops, as a church, a cemetery, and as a refuge during invasions and riots. Over time, the Colosseum was eroded by wind, rain, and the strain of gravity. Earthquakes weakened it, and a powerful quake in 1349 toppled the south side.

More than anything, the Colosseum was dismantled by the Roman citizens themselves, who carted off pre-cut stones to be reused for palaces and churches, including St. Peter's. The marble facing was pulverized into mortar, and 300 tons of iron brackets were pried out and melted down, resulting in the pockmarking you see today.

After centuries of neglect, a series of 16th-century popes took pity on the pagan structure. In memory of the Christians who may (or may not) have been martyred here, they shored up the south and west sides with bricks and placed the big cross on the north side of the arena.

Today, the Colosseum links Rome's glorious past with its vital present. Major political demonstrations begin or end here, providing protesters with an iconic backdrop for the TV cameras. On Good Friday, the pope comes here to lead pilgrims as they follow the Stations of the Cross.

The legend goes that as long as the Colosseum shall stand, the city of Rome shall also stand. For nearly 2,000 years, the Colosseum has been the enduring symbol of Rome, the Eternal City.

• *The Roman Forum is 100 yards to the right of the arch. You can enter it through the Forum entrance on Via dei Fori Imperiali or from the Palatine Hill entrance along Via di San Gregorio—see the map on page 122. (Note that what looks like an entrance gate up Via Sacra is currently exit-only.) If you're ready for a visit, turn to the next chapter.*

ROMAN FORUM TOUR

Foro Romano

The Forum was the political, religious, and commercial center of the city. Rome's most important temples and halls of justice were here. This was the place for religious processions, political demonstrations, elections, important speeches, and parades by conquering generals. As Rome's empire expanded, these few acres of land became the center of the civilized world.

Orientation

Cost: €12 combo-ticket covers both the Roman Forum/Palatine Hill (grouped as one sight for the purposes of the ticket) and the Colosseum; also covered by the Roma Pass. The combo-ticket is valid two consecutive days, but once your ticket is scanned for either the Forum/Palatine Hill or the Colosseum, you can't re-enter that sight (even the next day).

Hours: The Roman Forum, Colosseum, and Palatine Hill are all open daily 8:30 until one hour before sunset: April-Sept until 19:15, Oct until 18:30, off-season closing time can be as early as 16:30—for specifics, see "Hours" on page 107; last entry one hour before closing.

Avoiding Lines: See "Avoiding Lines" on page 107.

Getting There: The closest Metro stop is Colosseo. The Forum has two entrances. The main entrance is on Via dei Fori Imperiali ("Road of the Imperial Forums"). From the Colosseo Metro stop, walk away from the Colosseum on Via dei Fori Imperiali to find the low-profile Forum ticket office (look closely), located where Via Cavour spills into Via dei Fori Imperiali.

The other entrance is at the Palatine Hill ticket office on Via di San Gregorio—after buying your ticket, take the path to the right (not up the hill), and wind around to enter the

Forum at the Arch of Titus.

Information: A free visitors center (called I Fori di Roma), located across Via dei Fori Imperiali from the Forum's main entrance, has a TI (which sells the Roma Pass), bookshop, small café, WCs, and a film (daily 9:30-18:30). A bookstore is at the Forum entrance. Vendors outside sell *Rome: Past and Present* books with plastic overlays that restore the ruins (includes DVD; smaller book marked €15, prices soft, so offer €10). Info office tel. 06-3996-7700, http://archeoroma.beniculturali.it/en.

Tours: An unexciting yet informative **audioguide** helps decipher the rubble (€5/2 hours, €7 version includes Palatine Hill and lasts 3 hours, must leave ID), but you'll have to return it to one of the Forum entrances instead of being able to exit directly to Capitoline Hill or the Colosseum. Official **guided tours** in English might be available (inquire at ticket office). You can download this chapter as a free Rick Steves **audio tour** (see page 27).

Length of This Tour: Allow 1.5 hours.

With Limited Time: Walk from the Arch of Titus to the Arch of Septimius Severus. Don't miss the Basilica of Constantine hiding behind the trees.

Services: WCs are at the main entrance and in the middle of the Forum, near #8 on the map. For information on food and other WCs in the area, see the sidebar on page 114.

Plan Ahead: The ancient paving at the Forum is uneven; wear sturdy shoes. I carry a water bottle and refill it at the Forum's public drinking fountains.

The Tour Begins

• *Start at the Arch of Titus (Arco di Tito). It's the white triumphal arch that rises above the rubble on the east end of the Forum (closest to the Colosseum). Stand at the viewpoint alongside the arch and gaze over the valley known as the Forum.*

Overview

The Forum is a rectangular valley running roughly east (the Colosseum end) to west (Capitoline Hill, with its bell tower). The rocky path at your feet is Via Sacra. It leads from the Arch of Titus, through the trees, past the large brick Senate building, through the

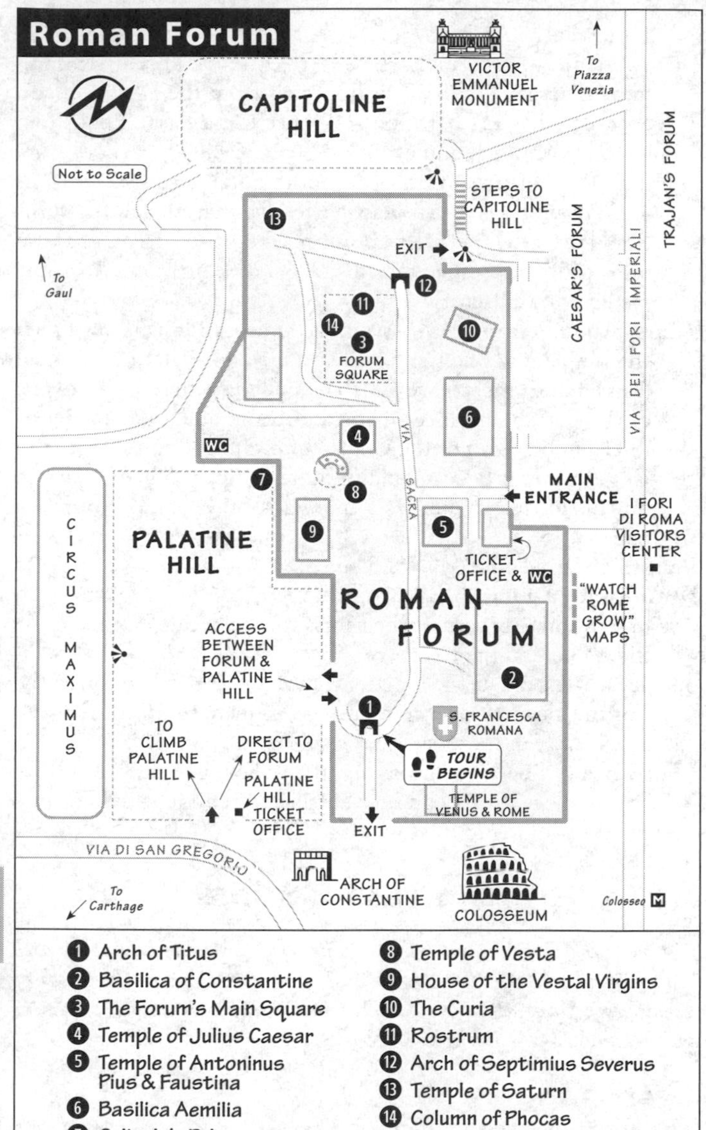
Roman Forum
Not to Scale
CAPITOLINE HILL
VICTOR EMMANUEL MONUMENT
To Piazza Venezia
TRAJAN'S FORUM
STEPS TO CAPITOLINE HILL
CAESAR'S FORUM
VIA DEI FORI IMPERIALI
EXIT
To Gaul
FORUM SQUARE
VIA SACRA
WC
MAIN ENTRANCE
I FORI DI ROMA VISITORS CENTER
PALATINE HILL
CIRCUS MAXIMUS
TICKET OFFICE & WC
"WATCH ROME GROW" MAPS
ROMAN FORUM
ACCESS BETWEEN FORUM & PALATINE HILL
S. FRANCESCA ROMANA
TO CLIMB PALATINE HILL
DIRECT TO FORUM
PALATINE HILL TICKET OFFICE
TOUR BEGINS
TEMPLE OF VENUS & ROME
EXIT
VIA DI SAN GREGORIO
ARCH OF CONSTANTINE
COLOSSEUM
To Carthage
Colosseo M
1 Arch of Titus
2 Basilica of Constantine
3 The Forum's Main Square
4 Temple of Julius Caesar
5 Temple of Antoninus Pius & Faustina
6 Basilica Aemilia
7 Caligula's Palace
8 Temple of Vesta
9 House of the Vestal Virgins
10 The Curia
11 Rostrum
12 Arch of Septimius Severus
13 Temple of Saturn
14 Column of Phocas

triumphal arch at the far end, and up Capitoline Hill. The hill to your left (with all the trees) is Palatine Hill.

Picture being here when a conquering general returned to Rome with crates of booty. The valley was full of gleaming white buildings topped with bronze roofs. The Via Sacra—Main Street of the Forum—would be lined with citizens waving branches and carrying torches. The trumpets would sound as the parade began. First came porters, carrying chests full of gold and jewels. Then a parade of exotic animals from the conquered lands—elephants, giraffes, hippopotamuses—for the crowd to "ooh" and "ahh" at. Next came the prisoners in chains, with the captive king on a wheeled platform so the people could jeer and spit at him. Finally, the conquering hero himself would drive down in his four-horse chariot, with rose petals strewn in his path. The whole procession would run the length of the Forum and up the face of Capitoline Hill to the Temple of Saturn (the eight big columns midway up the hill—#13 on the map in this chapter), where they'd place the booty in Rome's coffers. Then they'd continue up to the summit to the Temple of Jupiter (only ruins of its foundation remain today) to dedicate the victory to the King of the Gods.

❶ Arch of Titus (Arco di Tito)

The Arch of Titus commemorated the Roman victory over the province of Judaea (Israel) in A.D. 70. The Romans had a reputation as benevolent conquerors who tolerated the local customs and rulers. All they required was allegiance to the empire, shown by worshipping the emperor as a god. No problem for most conquered people, who already had half a dozen gods on their prayer lists anyway. But Israelites believed in only one god, and it wasn't the emperor. Israel revolted. After a short but bitter war, the Romans defeated the rebels, took Jerusalem, destroyed their temple (leaving only the foundation wall—today's revered "Wailing Wall"), and brought home 50,000 Jewish slaves...who were forced to build this arch (and the Colosseum).

Roman propaganda decorates the inside of the arch, where a relief shows the emperor Titus in a chariot being crowned by the goddess Victory. (Thanks to modern pollution, they both look like they've been through the wars.) The other side shows booty from the sacking of the temple in Jerusalem—soldiers carrying a Jewish menorah and other plunder. The two (unfinished) plaques

Rome: Republic and Empire
(500 B.C.–A.D. 500)

Ancient Rome spanned a thousand years, from about 500 B.C. to A.D. 500. During that time, Rome expanded from a small tribe of barbarians to a vast empire, then dwindled slowly to city size again. For the first 500 years, when Rome's armies made her ruler of the Italian peninsula and beyond, Rome was a republic governed by elected senators. Over the next 500 years, a time of world conquest and eventual decline, Rome was an empire ruled by a military-backed dictator.

Julius Caesar bridged the gap between republic and empire. This ambitious general and politician, popular with the people because of his military victories and charisma, suspended the Roman constitution and assumed dictatorial powers in about 50 B.C. A few years later, he was assassinated by a conspiracy of senators. His adopted son, Augustus, succeeded him, and soon "Caesar" was not just a name but a title.

Emperor Augustus ushered in the Pax Romana, or Roman peace (A.D. 1-200), a time when Rome reached her peak and controlled an empire that stretched even beyond Eurail—from England to Egypt, Turkey to Morocco.

on poles were to have listed the conquered cities. Look at the top of the ceiling. Constructed after Titus' death, the relief shows him riding an eagle to heaven, where he'll become one of the gods.

The brutal crushing of the A.D. 70 rebellion (and another one 60 years later) devastated the nation of Israel. With no temple as a center for their faith, the Jews scattered throughout the world (the Diaspora). There would be no Jewish political entity again for almost two thousand years, until modern Israel was created after World War II.

• *Walk down Via Sacra into the Forum. After about 50 yards, turn right and follow a path uphill to the three huge arches of the...*

❷ Basilica of Constantine (a.k.a. Basilica Maxentius)

Yes, these are big arches. But they represent only one-third of the original Basilica of Constantine, a mammoth hall of justice. The arches were matched by a similar set along the Via Sacra side (only a few squat brick piers remain). Between them ran the central hall, which was spanned by a roof 130 feet high—about 55 feet higher than the side arches you see. (The stub of brick you see sticking

up began an arch that once spanned the central hall.) The hall itself was as long as a football field, lavishly furnished with colorful inlaid marble, a gilded bronze ceiling, and statues, and filled with strolling Romans. At the far (west) end was an enormous marble statue of Emperor Constantine on a throne. (Pieces of this statue, including a hand the size of a man, are on display in Rome's Capitoline Museums.)

The basilica was begun by the emperor Maxentius, but after he was trounced in battle (see page 116), the victor Constantine completed the massive building. No doubt about it, the Romans built monuments on a more epic scale than any previous Europeans, wowing their "barbarian" neighbors.

• Now stroll deeper into the Forum, downhill along Via Sacra, through the trees. Many of the large basalt stones under your feet were walked on by Caesar Augustus 2,000 years ago. Pass by the only original bronze door still swinging on its ancient hinges (the green door at the Tempio di Romolo, on the right—if it happens to be open, peek in), and continue between ruined buildings until Via Sacra opens up to a flat, grassy area.

❸ The Forum's Main Square

The original Forum, or main square, was this flat patch about the size of a football field, stretching to the foot of Capitoline Hill. Surrounding it were temples, law courts, government buildings, and triumphal arches.

Rome was born right here. According to legend, twin brothers Romulus (Rome) and Remus were orphaned in infancy and raised by a she-wolf on top of Palatine Hill. Growing up, they found it hard to get dates. So they and their cohorts attacked the nearby Sabine tribe and kidnapped their women. After they made peace, this marshy valley became the meeting place and then the trading center for the scattered tribes on the surrounding hillsides.

The square was the busiest and most crowded—and often the seediest—section of town. Besides the senators, politicians, and currency exchangers, there were even sleazier types—souvenir hawkers, pickpockets, fortune-tellers, gamblers, slave marketers, drunks, hookers, lawyers, and tour guides.

The Forum is now rubble, but imagine it in its prime: blindingly brilliant marble buildings with 40-foot-high columns and shining metal roofs; rows of statues painted in realistic colors; processional chariots rattling down Via Sacra. Mentally replace tourists in T-shirts with tribunes in togas. Imagine the buildings towering and the people buzzing around you while an orator gives a rabble-rousing speech from the Rostrum. If things still look like just a pile of rocks, at least tell yourself, "But Julius Caesar once leaned against these rocks."

• At the near (east) end of the main square (the Colosseum is to the east) are the foundations of a temple now capped with a peaked wood-and-metal roof.

❹ Temple of Julius Caesar (Tempio del Divo Giulio, or Ara di Cesare)

Julius Caesar's body was burned on this spot (under the metal roof) after his assassination. Peek behind the wall into the small apse area, where a mound of dirt usually has fresh flowers—given to remember the man who, more than any other, personified the greatness of Rome.

Caesar (100-44 B.C.) changed Rome—and the Forum—dramatically. He cleared out many of the wooden market stalls and began to ring the square with even grander buildings. Caesar's house was located behind the temple, near that clump of trees. He walked right by here on the day he was assassinated ("Beware the Ides of March!" warned a street-corner Etruscan preacher).

Though he was popular with the masses, not everyone liked Caesar's urban design or his politics. When he assumed dictatorial powers, he was ambushed and stabbed to death by a conspiracy of senators, including his adopted son, Brutus *("Et tu, Brute?")*.

The funeral was held here, facing the main square. The citizens gathered, and speeches were made. Mark Antony stood up to say (in Shakespeare's words), "Friends, Romans, countrymen, lend me your ears. I come to bury Caesar, not to praise him." When Caesar's body was burned, the citizens who still loved him threw anything at hand on the fire, requiring the fire department to come put it out. Later, Emperor Augustus dedicated this temple in his name, making Caesar the first Roman to become a god.

• *Behind and to the left of the Temple of Julius Caesar are 10 tall columns. These belong to the...*

❺ Temple of Antoninus Pius and Faustina

The Senate built this temple to honor Emperor Antoninus Pius (A.D. 138-161) and his deified wife, Faustina. The 50-foot-tall Corinthian (leafy) columns must have been awe-inspiring to out-of-towners who grew up in thatched huts. Although the temple has been inhabited by a church, you can still see the basic layout—a staircase led to a shaded porch (the columns), which admitted you to the main building (now a church), where the statue of the god sat. Originally, these columns supported a triangular

Religion in Ancient Rome

Religion in ancient Rome was all about the *pax deorum* (peace, or pact, with the gods) that guaranteed the prosperity of the incredibly superstitious Romans. To appease the fickle gods, they performed elaborate rituals at lavish temples and shrines. Romans had a god for every moment of their days and each important event in their lives. While the Romans adopted the Greek pantheon, they also embraced the gods from many of the people they came into contact with, sometimes using elaborate ceremonies to persuade these new gods to "move" to Rome. Scholars estimate Romans had about 30,000 gods to keep happy. In this high-maintenance religion, there was Cunina, the goddess who protected cradles; Statulinus, to help children stand up; and Fabulina, for their first words. Fornax was the oven god, Pomona the fruit-tree goddess, Sterculinus the manure god, and Venus Cloacina the sewer goddess.

Priests interpreted the will of the gods by studying the internal organs of sacrificed animals, the flight of birds, and prophetic books. A clap of thunder was enough to postpone a battle.

Astrology, magic rites, the cult of deified emperors, house gods, and the near-deification of ancestors permeated Roman life. But all these gods didn't quite do it for the Romans—they were gradually replaced by the rise of monotheistic religions from the East. In A.D. 313, Emperor Constantine legalized and embraced Christianity. By 390, the Christian God was the only legal god in Rome.

pediment decorated with sculptures.

Picture these columns, with gilded capitals, supporting brightly painted statues in the pediment, and the whole building capped with a gleaming bronze roof. The stately gray rubble of today's Forum is a faded black-and-white photograph of a 3-D Technicolor era.

The building is a microcosm of many changes that occurred after Rome fell. In medieval times, the temple was pillaged. Note the diagonal cuts high on the marble columns—a failed attempt by scavengers to cut through the pillars to pull them down for their precious stone. (They used vinegar and rope to cut the marble...but because vinegar also eats through rope, they abandoned the attempt.) In 1550, a church was housed inside the ancient temple. The green door shows the street level at the time of Michelangelo. The long staircase was underground until excavated in the 1800s.

• *There's a ramp next to the Temple of A. and F. Walk halfway up it and look to the left to view the...*

❻ Basilica Aemilia

A basilica was a covered public forum, often serving as a Roman hall of justice. In a society that was as legal-minded as America is today, you needed a lot of lawyers—and a big place to put them. Citizens came here to work out matters such as inheritances and building permits, or to sue somebody.

Notice the layout. It was a long, rectangular building. The stubby columns all in a row form one long, central hall flanked by two side aisles. Medieval Christians required a larger meeting hall for their worship services than Roman temples provided, so they used the spacious Roman basilica as the model for their churches. Cathedrals from France to Spain to England, from Romanesque to Gothic to Renaissance, all have the same basic floor plan as a Roman basilica.

• *Return again to the Temple of Julius Caesar. To the right of the temple are the three tall Corinthian columns of the Temple of Castor and Pollux. Beyond that is Palatine Hill—the corner of which may have been...*

❼ Caligula's Palace (a.k.a. Palace of Tiberius)

Emperor Caligula (ruled A.D. 37-41) had a huge palace on Palatine Hill overlooking the Forum. It actually sprawled down the hill into the Forum (some supporting arches remain in the hillside).

Caligula was not a nice person. He tortured enemies, stole senators' wives, and parked his chariot in handicap spaces. But Rome's luxury-loving emperors only added to the glory of the Forum, with each one trying to make his mark on history.

• *To the left of the Temple of Castor and Pollux, find the remains of a small white circular temple.*

❽ Temple of Vesta

This is perhaps Rome's most sacred spot. Rome considered itself one big family, and this temple represented a circular hut, like the kind that Rome's first families lived in. Inside, a fire burned, just as in a Roman home. And back in the days before lighters and butane, you never wanted your fire to go out. As long as the sacred flame burned, Rome would stand. The flame was tended by priestesses known as Vestal Virgins.

• *Around the back of the Temple of Vesta, you'll find two rectangular brick pools. These stood in the courtyard of the...*

❾ House of the Vestal Virgins

The Vestal Virgins lived in a two-story building surrounding a long central courtyard with two pools at one end. Rows of statues depicting leading Vestal Virgins flanked the courtyard. This place was the model—both architecturally and sexually—for medieval convents and monasteries.

Chosen from noble families before they reached the age of 10, the six Vestal Virgins served a 30-year term. Honored and revered by the Romans, the Vestals even had their own box opposite the emperor in the Colosseum. The statues that line the courtyard honor dutiful Vestals.

As the name implies, a Vestal took a vow of chastity. If she served her term faithfully—abstaining for 30 years—she was given a huge dowry and allowed to marry. But if they found any Virgin who wasn't, she was strapped to a funeral car, paraded through the streets of the Forum, taken to a crypt, given a loaf of bread and a lamp...and buried alive. Many women suffered the latter fate.

• Return to the Temple of Julius Caesar and head to the Forum's west end (opposite the Colosseum). As you pass alongside the big open space of the Forum's main square, consider how the piazza is still a standard part of any Italian town. It has reflected and accommodated the gregarious and outgoing nature of the Italian people since Roman times.

Stop at the big, well-preserved brick building (on right) with the triangular roof. Look in at...

⑩ The Curia (Senate House)

The Curia was the most important political building in the Forum. While the present building dates from A.D. 283, this was the site of Rome's official center of government since the birth of the republic. (Ongoing archaeological work may restrict access to the Curia, as well as the Arch of Septimius Severus—described later—and the exit to Capitoline Hill.) Three hundred senators, elected by the citizens of Rome, met here to debate and create the laws of the land. Their wooden seats once circled the building in three tiers; the Senate president's podium sat at the far end. The marble floor is from ancient times. Listen to the echoes in this vast room—the acoustics are great.

Rome prided itself on being a republic. Early in the city's history, its people threw out the king and established rule by elected representatives. Each Roman citizen was free to speak his mind and have a say in public policy. Even when emperors became the supreme authority, the Senate was a power to be reckoned with. The Curia building is well-preserved, having been used as a church since early Christian times. In the 1930s, it was restored and opened to the public as a historic site. (Note: Although Julius Caesar was assassinated in "the Senate," it wasn't here—the Senate was temporarily meeting across town.)

A statue and two reliefs inside the Curia help build our mental image of the Forum. The statue, made of porphyry marble in about A.D. 100 (with its head, arms, and feet now missing), was a tribute to an emperor, probably Hadrian or Trajan. The two relief panels may have decorated the Rostrum. Those on the left show people (with big stone tablets) standing in line to burn their debt records following a government amnesty. The other shows the distribution of grain (Rome's welfare system), some buildings in the background, and the latest fashion in togas.

• Go back down the Senate steps and find the 10-foot-high wall just to the left of the big arch, marked...

Rome Falls

Remember that Rome lasted 1,000 years—500 years of growth, 200 years of peak power, and 300 years of gradual decay. The fall had many causes, among them the barbarians who pecked away at Rome's borders. Christians blamed the fall on moral decay. Pagans blamed it on Christians. Socialists blamed it on a shallow economy based on the spoils of war. (Republicans blamed it on Democrats.) Whatever the reasons, the far-flung empire could no longer keep its grip on conquered lands, and it pulled back. Barbarian tribes from Germany and Asia attacked the Italian peninsula and even looted Rome itself in A.D. 410, leveling many of the buildings in the Forum. In 476, when the last emperor checked out and switched off the lights, Europe plunged into centuries of ignorance, poverty, and weak government—the Dark Ages.

But Rome lived on in the Catholic Church. Christianity was the state religion of Rome's last generations. Emperors became popes (both called themselves "Pontifex Maximus"), senators became bishops, orators became priests, and basilicas became churches. The glory of Rome remains eternal.

⓫ Rostrum (Rostri)

Nowhere was Roman freedom more apparent than at this "Speaker's Corner." The Rostrum was a raised platform, 10 feet high and 80 feet long, decorated with statues, columns, and the prows of ships (rostra).

On a stage like this, Rome's orators, great and small, tried to draw a crowd and sway public opinion. Mark Antony rose to offer Caesar the laurel-leaf crown of kingship, which Caesar publicly (and hypocritically) refused while privately becoming a dictator. Men such as Cicero railed against the corruption and decadence that came with the city's newfound wealth. In later years, daring citizens even spoke out against the emperors, reminding them that Rome was once free. Picture the backdrop these speakers would have had—a mountain of marble buildings piling up on Capitoline Hill.

In front of the Rostrum are trees bearing fruits that were sacred to the ancient Romans: olives (provided food, light, and preservatives), figs (tasty), and wine grapes (made a popular export product).

• *The big arch to the right of the Rostrum is the...*

⓬ Arch of Septimius Severus

In imperial times, the Rostrum's voices of democracy would have been dwarfed by images of the empire, such as the huge six-story-high Arch of Septimius Severus (A.D. 203). The reliefs commemorate the African-born emperor's battles in Mesopotamia. Near ground level, see soldiers marching captured barbarians back to Rome for the victory parade. Despite Severus' efficient rule, Rome's empire was crumbling under the weight of its own corruption, disease, decaying infrastructure, and the constant attacks by foreign "barbarians."

• *Pass underneath the Arch of Septimius Severus and turn left. If the path is blocked, backtrack toward the Temple of Julius Caesar and around the square. On the slope of Capitoline Hill are the eight remaining columns of the...*

⓭ Temple of Saturn

These columns framed the entrance to the Forum's oldest temple (497 B.C.). Inside was a humble, very old wooden statue of the god Saturn. But the statue's pedestal held the gold bars, coins, and jewels of Rome's state treasury, the booty collected by conquering generals.

• *Standing here, at one of the Forum's first buildings, look east at the lone, tall...*

⓮ Column of Phocas—Rome's Fall

This is the Forum's last monument (A.D. 608), a gift from the powerful Byzantine Empire to a fallen empire—Rome. Given to commemorate the pagan Pantheon's becoming a Christian church, it's like a symbolic last nail in ancient Rome's coffin. After Rome's 1,000-year reign, the city was looted by Vandals, the population of a million-plus shrank to about 10,000, and the once-grand city center—the Forum—was abandoned, slowly covered up by centuries of silt and dirt. In the 1700s, an English historian named Edward Gibbon overlooked this spot from Capitoline Hill. Hearing Christian monks

singing at these pagan ruins, he looked out at the few columns poking up from the ground, pondered the decline and fall of the Roman Empire, and thought, "Hmm, that's a catchy title...."

• *From here, you have several options:*

1. *Exiting past the Arch of Titus lands you at the Colosseum (see Colosseum Tour chapter).*
2. *Exiting past the Arch of Septimius Severus leads you to the stairs up to Capitoline Hill (described on page 52).*
3. *The Forum's main entrance spills you back out onto Via dei Fori Imperiali (for Trajan's Column, Market, and Museum of the Imperial Forums; see Trajan's Forum Tour chapter).*
4. *From the Arch of Titus, you can climb Palatine Hill to the top and start the Palatine Hill Tour—see the next chapter.*

PALATINE HILL TOUR

Monte Palatino

While many tourists consider Palatine Hill just extra credit after the Forum, it offers an insight into the greatness of Rome that's well worth the effort. (And, if you're visiting the Colosseum or Forum, you've got a ticket whether you like it or not.) Palatine Hill is jam-packed with history—"the huts of Romulus," the huge Imperial Palace, a view of the Circus Maximus—but there's only the barest skeleton of rubble left to tell the story. This tour will enable the thoughtful sightseer to bring those remains to life. Palatine Hill is ideal for those who want to get away from the crowds and discover the romantic, melancholy essence of ruins. Become a 19th-century poet or a painter on the Grand Tour, meditating on the destiny of once-great civilizations, and wander through the remains of the palaces that Nature seems to have reclaimed for herself.

Orientation

Cost: €12 combo-ticket covers both the Roman Forum/Palatine Hill (grouped as one sight for the purposes of the ticket) and the Colosseum; also covered by the Roma Pass. The combo-ticket is valid two consecutive days, but once your ticket is scanned for either the Forum/Palatine Hill or the Colosseum, you can't re-enter that sight (even the next day).

Hours: The Palatine Hill, Roman Forum, and Colosseum are all open daily 8:30 until one hour before sunset: April-Sept until 19:15, Oct until 18:30, off-season closing time can be as early as 16:30—for specifics, see "Hours" on page 107; last entry one hour before closing, tel. 06-3996-7700, http://archeoroma.beniculturali.it/en. The House of Augustus, a minor stop on this tour, is usually closed Tue and Thu; on other days it has shorter hours than the rest of the site (11:00-18:15, at the latest).

Getting There: The closest Metro stop is Colosseo. The entrance is on Via di San Gregorio (facing the Forum with the Colosseum at your back, it's down the street to your left). You can also enter Palatine from within the Roman Forum—just climb the hill from the Arch of Titus.

Tours: Audioguides cost €5/2 hours (€7 version includes Roman Forum and lasts 3 hours, must leave ID). Guided tours in English might be available (inquire at the ticket booth).

Length of This Tour: Allow 1.5 hours.

With Limited Time: Don't miss the stadium or the view of the Circus Maximus. If lines are long, skip the House of Augustus.

Services: WCs are rare in the Colosseum-Roman Forum-Palatine Hill area. Your best (though still meager) options are here at Palatine Hill, where you'll find WCs at the ticket office when you enter, up the hill near the stadium, at the museum in the center of the site, and hiding among the orange trees in the Farnese Gardens. For restaurants in the area, see the sidebar on page 114.

The Tour Begins

• *Start on top of the hill at the Palatine Museum (Museo Palatino, see photo; the museum is #6 on the map). To get there from the entrance, take the stairs on the left and follow the path up. Walk past the stadium and some more ruins to the one modern building on the crest of the hill. It's the big, gray, 1930s-style building that houses the museum. We'll visit the museum later. For now, grab a stone and sit with your back to the museum to orient yourself, facing in the direction of the Forum (roughly north).*

The Imperial Palace

You're sitting at the center of what was once a huge palace, the residence of emperors for three centuries. Orgies, royal weddings, assassinations, concerts, intrigues, births, funerals, banquets, and the occasional Tupperware party took place within these walls. What walls? The row of umbrella pines about 200 yards to the east (to your right) now marks one edge of the palace. The reconstructed brick tower (at about 11 o'clock) was the northwest corner. The palace also stretched behind you (the area behind the museum)

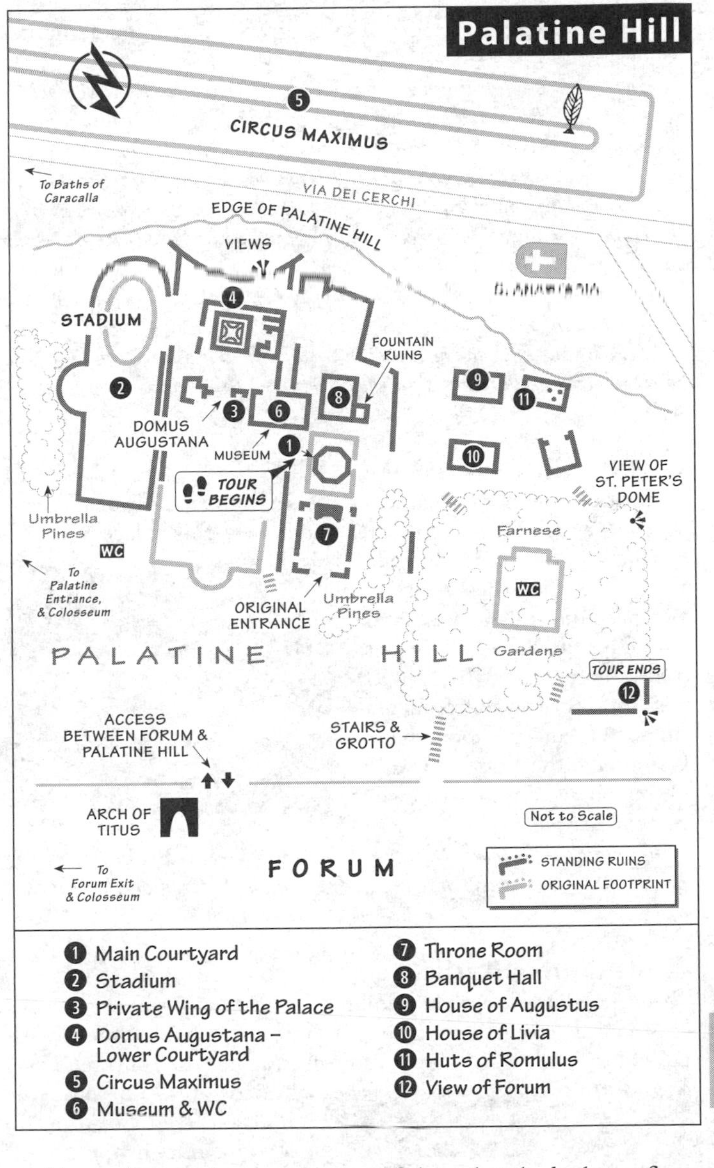

and beneath you, since some parts of the palace had a lower floor. (Right now, you're standing not on the original palace's ground level, but several floors up.)

The area in front was the official wing of the palace; behind were the private quarters. All in all, it made for a cozy little 150,000-square-foot pad.

The palace was built by Emperor Domitian in about A.D. 81.

A poet of the day described it as so grand that it "made Jupiter jealous."

• *Now proceed, following the map for this 12-stop tour. As you walk, you'll see colorful marble scraps all over Palatine Hill. Flashy building stone was used to boast of the power and vastness of the empire. Citizens knew that the Numidian yellow marble was from Tunisia, the veined Cipollino marble (with swirling designs like an onion) was from the island of Euboea in Greece, and the pink granite was from Aswan in Egypt. This was all sliced and laid out in fine pavement and wall designs, enjoyed by those who could only be thankful they were on the winning team.*

With your back to the museum, head left to a big rectangular field with an octagonal brick design in the center—the main courtyard of the palace.

❶ Main Courtyard (Peristilio)

The brick octagon was a sunken fountain in the middle of an open-air courtyard. Like many fine Roman homes, this palace was built around an oasis of peace where you could enjoy the sun, catch the precious rain, and listen to the babble of moving water. The courtyard was lined with columns (notice the fragments) supporting an arcade for shade. Originally, the floor and walls of the courtyard were faced with colorful marble.

• *The palace's stadium is 100 yards behind you (to the east), near the long row of pine trees. Belly up to the railing and look down on the elliptical track.*

❷ Stadium (Stadio)

This cigar-shaped, sunken stadium (500 feet long) was the palace's rec room. It looks like a racetrack, but it just held gardens with paths for strolling. The oval running track at the south end was added later. The emperor had a raised box on the 50-yard line, in the curved apse across from you. At the north end were changing rooms, and the marble fragments that litter the ground once held up an arcade.

• *Now, walk through the arch in the wall to the right and imagine the...*

PALATINE HILL

❸ Private Wing of the Palace (Domus Augustana)

The area between the stadium and the museum held the private rooms of the emperor and his extended family. Today, a lone umbrella pine on a mound marks the courtyard of this wing. To the left are the brick ruins of the Domus.

Wander southward under the arches and through the maze of brick rooms (many of them reconstructed), noticing...

- The typical Roman building method: Build a rectangular shell of brick, fill it with concrete, then finish it with either plaster (you'll see an occasional faded fresco) or slabs of marble. The small, round pockmarks on many walls show where the marble was fastened.
- The square holes in the walls that held wooden beams, used for scaffolding during construction and maintenance, for shelves, and for wooden floors.

- Over the doorways, the bricks in the walls that form the pattern of an arch. These "blind arches" were structural elements that allowed the walls to be built higher. The iron bar clamps are recent additions and hold the crumbling walls together.
- Niches and apses that once held statues. Every family had their own household gods and displayed small images of these guardian spirits, as well as busts of honored ancestors.
- The fragments of columns, reliefs, and sculpture scattered about that suggest the wealth of this great palace.

Finally, notice the floor plan—a complex fantasyland maze of small, private, sometimes even curved rooms.

• *In the south part of the Domus Augustana, you can look down on the ruins of the lower story.*

❹ Domus Augustana—Lower Courtyard

This open-air courtyard has the concave-convex remains of a large fountain that must have been a marvel. Try to mentally reconstruct the palace that surrounded this fountain. The emperors could look down on it from the upper story (where you're standing) or view it from the rooms around it on the lower story, where the emperor

and his family ate their meals in private.

The lower story was built into the slope of the hill. The southern part of the palace was an extension of the hillside, supported beneath your feet by big arches.

• *Continue to the southern edge of the hill (directly behind the museum), overlooking a long, wide grassy field—what once was the Circus Maximus. Lean over the railing and you might be able to make out the concave shape of the palace's southern facade.*

❺ Circus Maximus

If the gladiator show at the Colosseum was sold out, you could always get a seat at Circus Max. In an early version of today's demolition derby, Ben-Hur and his fellow charioteers once raced recklessly around this oblong course.

The chariots circled the cigar-shaped mound in the center (notice the lone cypress tree that now marks one end of the mound). Bleachers (now grassy banks) originally surrounded the track (see artist's reconstruction, below).

The track was 1,300 feet long, while the whole stadium measured 2,130 feet by 720 feet and seated—get this—250,000 people. The wooden bleachers once collapsed during a race, killing thousands.

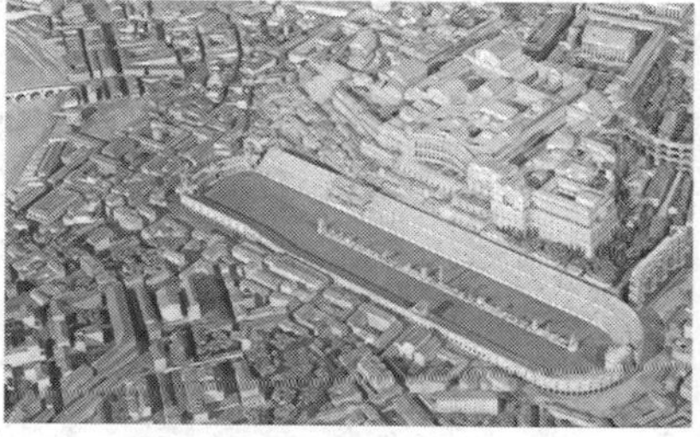

The horses began at a starting gate at the west end (to your right), while the public entered at the other end. Races consisted of seven laps (about 3.5 miles total). In such a small space, collisions and overturned chariots were common. The charioteers were usually poor, lowborn people who used this dangerous sport to get rich and famous. Some succeeded. Most died.

The public was crazy about the races. There were 12 per day, 240 days a year. Four teams dominated the competition—Reds, Whites, Blues, and Greens—and every citizen was fanatically devoted to one of them. Obviously, the emperors had the best seats in the house: Built into the palace's curved facade was a box overlooking the track. For their pleasure, emperors occasionally had the circus floor carpeted with designs in colored powders.

Picture the scene: intact palace; emperor watching; a quarter of a million Romans cheering, jeering, and furiously betting. Horses raced here for more than a thousand years. The track dates from 300 B.C., and the spectacles continued into the Christian era, until A.D. 549, despite Church disapproval.

From this viewpoint, looking to the left, you can see the ruins of the Baths of Caracalla (not worth touring if you've seen Palatine) rising above the trees a half-mile away. About a mile beyond that, Appian Way led from a grand gate in the ancient wall, past the catacombs, to Brindisi.

• *Turn around and head back toward the museum.*

❻ Museum (Museo Palatino)

The museum contains statues and frescoes that help you imagine the luxury of the imperial Palatine. To the left after you enter, pause at the statue of "Magna Mater" on her throne. This Great Mother brought life and fertility to the Roman people, who worshipped her at the nearby Temple of Cybele. Her arms and foot were destroyed by time, but there was always a cavity where her head should be—this was a standard Roman device in which interchangeable heads could be inserted. In this case, the Magna Mater's "head" was actually a sacred black cone-shaped meteorite that caused astonishment when it fell from the sky.

Also on this floor, room V holds frescoes and statues from the time of Augustus and fine decorative terra-cotta panels. Room VII has a bust of the notorious Emperor Nero ("Nerone") and exquisite marble-inlay work. In room VIII is a statue fragment of a river god's stomach. And finally, back near the entrance is a large headless statue of a Muse that once decorated the Hippodrome.

There's more in the basement (go back outside, down the stairs, and into the doorway directly below the staircase). Room II holds a model of the eighth-century B.C. Iron Age huts of Romulus that we'll see later in the tour. (There's also a 21st-century WC nearby.)

• *From the museum, begin circling the main courtyard (with its octagonal fountain) counterclockwise. When the path turns left, follow it to the first opening, marked by the squat brick pillar with a stubby column on top. Step into the...*

❼ Throne Room

The nerve center of an empire that controlled some 50 million people from England to Africa, this was the official seat of power. The curved apse of the largest brick stump (there's now a plaque on it) marks the spot where the emperor sat on his throne for official business.

Imagine being a Roman citizen summoned by the emperor. You'd enter the palace through the main doorway (now a gap) at

the far (Forum) end of the room, having climbed up three flights of a monumental staircase. The floor and walls dazzled with green, purple, red, white, and yellow marble. Along the walls were 12 colossal statues of Roman gods. The ceiling towered seven stories overhead. On either side were doorways leading to a basilica and the emperor's private temple.

You'd approach the emperor, who sat on a raised throne in the apse, dressed in royal purple, with a crown of laurel leaves on his head and a scepter cradled in his arm. Big braziers burned on either side, throwing off a flickering light. As you approached, you'd raise your arm to greet him, saying, *"Ave, Cesare!"* The words would echo through the great hall.

Now imagine yourself as emperor. Stand on the small white stone marking the location of the throne (a few feet in front of the plaque), and look out over your palace. (The ceiling was a barrel vault sitting upon towers as high as the brick tower in the distance to the left.)

• *Continue circling the main courtyard counterclockwise until it dead-ends at the...*

❽ Banquet Hall (Triclinium)

The floor of the banquet room had a hollow space beneath it (you can see the two-foot gap between the two original floors). Slaves stoked fires from underground stoves to heat the floor with forced air. At the far end of the room, the platform and curved apse mark the spot where the emperor ate while looking down on his subjects. Guests could look into the adjoining room, where an elliptical-shaped fountain (see the brick remains) spurted for their amusement.

Here, the wealthiest Romans enjoyed the spoils that poured into Rome from its vast empire. Reclining on a couch, waited on by slaves, you'd order bowls of larks' tongues or a roast pig stuffed with live birds, then wash it down with wine. If you were full but tempted by yet another delicacy, you could call for a feather, vomit, and start all over. Dancing dark-skinned slaves from Egypt or flute players from Greece entertained. If you fancied one, he or she was yours—the bedrooms were just down the hall.

Or so went the stories. In fact, many emperors were just and simple men, continuing the old Roman traditions of hard work and moderate tastes. But just as many were power-mad scoundrels who used their authority to indulge their every desire.

• *From the Banquet Hall, backtrack a few steps and work your way west through openings in the low brick wall to exit the palace.*

Archaeological Zone and Gardens

• *As you leave the palace, you'll run into a railing overlooking the ruins of the House of Livia (rarely open). Circle clockwise around the ruins and down the ramp. You're near the homes (once joined together) of Rome's first emperor and his wife. Because the space is so small, and the frescoes so fragile, only five visitors at a time are allowed to enter—and for just five minutes. Find the queue for the House of Augustus. The wait is usually about 15 to 30 minutes.*

❾ House of Augustus (Casa di Augusto)

Augustus, a.k.a. Octavian, the first emperor, lived in this house (and the neighboring House of Livia) with his wife. This relatively modest dwelling, dating from before Octavian became emperor, is a far cry from the later Imperial Palace that was built on top. The three humble rooms with their finely restored frescoes are well worth the wait. See rooms vibrantly painted with fake columns and arches, and with fake windows that once looked out on illusionary landscapes. Climb the steps outside to see a fourth room. You'll see that Livia and Augustus had little of the lavish marble found in most homes of the wealthy.

Augustus was a modest man who believed in traditional Roman values. His wife and daughter wove the clothes he wore. He slept in the same small bedroom for 40 years. He burned the midnight oil in his study, where he read and wrote his memoirs. Augustus set a standard for emperors' conduct that would last... until his death.

Augustus wanted to be the new Romulus, building his house adjacent to the home of the mythological founder of Rome.

• *After exiting the House of Augustus, see if the House of Livia is open (it probably isn't). If it is, you could take a free 20-minute tour, offered alternately in Italian and English—you may want to take whichever tour leaves first, as there's some English info inside. Otherwise, peek inside through the dirty windows.*

⑩ House of Livia (Casa di Livia)

Augustus' wife Livia lived here during her first marriage. After she married Augustus (and after he became Rome's ruler), they merged their two homes into a larger but still modest complex.

Your visit includes the former entrance hall—a high-ceilinged room with a few faded frescoes in purple, yellow, blue, and white. The best-preserved ones are in the central alcove, the room known as the *tablinum*, where guests were received. The *tablinum*'s right wall depicts the god Mercury (on the right side of the scene), arriving to kill the giant Argus (left) and kidnap the nymph Io (center) so Jupiter can ravish her. Frescoes in the alcove to the right of the *tablinum* show a columned portico draped with garlands. The left alcove has delicate Pompeiian-style designs.

Why do scholars think these ruins were Livia's house? Because they found her honorific name, "Julia Augusta," inscribed on the lead pipes now displayed in the *tablinum*.

• *Make your way to the nearby section of ruins, protected by a large metal roof. Cozy up to the railing to see ruined walls and foundations.*

⑪ The Huts of Romulus ("Romulean Huts")

Looking down into this pit filled with big blocks of stone, you can make out some elliptical and rectangular shapes carved into the stony ground. These are the partial outlines of huts from about 850 B.C. Some have holes that oncc held the wooden posts of round thatched huts.

According to legend, Romulus and Remus (see photo of statue on page 155) were children of the first Vestal Virgin. For complicated family reasons, she was executed and her babies were set adrift on the flooding Tiber River, eventually washing ashore at the foot of Palatine Hill. In a cave just downhill from here, a shepherd discovered them being suckled by a mother wolf. He took them home—maybe right here—and raised them as his own. When Romulus grew up, he killed his brother and built a square wall (Roma Quadrata) on the hilltop, thus founding the city of Rome.

For centuries, the Romans believed this myth. They honored the wolf's cave (called the "Lupercale," where every February 15 men dressed up in animal skins and whipped women), as well as the spot where Romulus was said to have lived. Lo and behold, in the 1940s, these huts were unearthed, and the legend became history. Archaeologists are still at it, and the more they dig, the more they find to confirm the legends. A nearby cave discovered in 2007—ornamented with seashells, colored marble, and a wolf mosaic—may be that original Lupercale. (It's not open to the public, and dissenting archaeologists believe it's a temple to water nymphs.)

Here at Rome's birthplace, reflect on the rise of this great culture—from thatched huts to the modest House of Augustus to the massive Imperial Palace of Domitian, with its stadium and view over the Circus Maximus. It's no wonder that the hill's name gave us our English word "palace."

• *Climb a few steps to the summit of the hill, and walk among the trees of the Farnese Gardens. Start making your way toward the Forum.*

⓬ View of Forum Fit for an Emperor

Finish your tour with a stroll through the Renaissance gardens of the Farnese family. Walk past the foundations of the House of Tiberius—Livia's son by her first husband—who became emperor after Augustus. Continue on, admiring the exotic plants, fountains, underground grotto, and pavilions. When you see the incredible view of the Forum from the end of the gardens, you'll know why Palatine Hill was Rome's best address.

• *To exit, wind down Palatine Hill to the Forum, ending up at the Arch of Titus.*

TRAJAN'S FORUM TOUR

Fori Imperiali

Rome peaked under Emperor Trajan (ruled A.D. 98-117) when the empire stretched from England to the Sahara, from Spain to the Fertile Crescent. A triumphant Trajan returned to Rome with his booty and shook it all over the city. He extended the Forum by building his own commercial, political, and religious center nearby, complete with temples, law courts, squares lined with shops, and a monumental column covered with detailed carvings that tell the story of one of his most famous conquests. This column, Trajan's Market, and the Museum of the Imperial Forums are the highlights of this tour. Much of Trajan's Forum (the broad expanse of really ruined ruins) can be seen quickly on your way to visit other nearby sights.

Orientation

Length of This Tour: Allow 30 minutes if you're viewing the column and market from the street, and another hour if you pay admission to enter the museum and market ruins.

With Limited Time: Snap a photo of Trajan's Column and move on.

When to Go: On Sunday afternoons, busy Via dei Fori Imperiali, which runs alongside the ruins, is closed to car traffic, making for a more pleasant viewing experience.

Getting There: Trajan's Column is just a few steps off Piazza Venezia (a hub for major bus routes #40, #64, #85, and #87) on Via dei Fori Imperiali, across the street from the Victor Emmanuel Monument. Trajan's Market can be entered only through the Museum of the Imperial Forums at Via IV Novembre 94 (up the staircase from Trajan's Column). Trajan's Forum stretches southeast of the column toward the Colosseo

Metro stop and the Colosseum itself.

Trajan's Column: It's free and viewable at all times.

Trajan's Market: You can view it for free from Via dei Fori Imperiali, but wandering through the market is possible only with paid admission to the Museum of the Imperial Forums.

Museum of the Imperial Forums: €11, includes entry to the market ruins, Tue-Sun 9:00-19:00, closed Mon, last entry one hour before closing, tel. 06-0608, www.mercatiditraiano.it. Skip the museum's slow, dry €3.50 audioguide. You'll find some English descriptions within the museum.

The Tour Begins

Trajan's Column

Rising 140 feet and decorated with a spiral relief of 2,500 figures trumpeting Trajan's exploits, this is the world's grandest column from antiquity. At one point, the ashes of Trajan and his wife were held in the base, and the sun glinted off a polished bronze statue of Trajan at the top. (Today, St. Peter is on top.) Built as a stack of 17 marble doughnuts, the column is hollow (note the small window slots) with a spiral staircase inside, leading up to the balcony.

The relief unfolds like a scroll, telling the story of Trajan's conquest of Dacia (modern-day Romania). It starts at the bottom with a trickle of water that becomes a river and soon picks up boats full

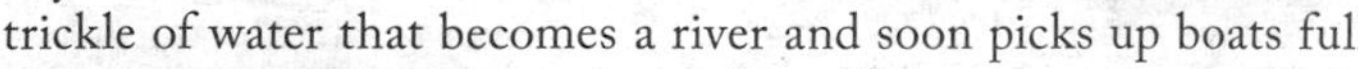

of supplies. Then come the soldiers themselves, who spill out from the gates of the city. A river god (bottom band, south side) surfaces to bless the journey. Along the way (second band), they build roads and forts to sustain the vast enterprise, including (third band, south side) Trajan's half-mile-long bridge over the Danube, the longest for a thousand years. (Find the three tiny crisscross rectangles representing the wooden span.) Trajan himself (fourth band, in military skirt with toga over his arm) mounts a podium to fire up the troops. They hop into a Roman galley ship (fifth band) and head off to fight the valiant Dacians in the middle of a forest (eighth band). Finally, at the very top, the Romans hold a sacrifice to give thanks for the victory, while the captured armor is displayed on the pedestal.

Originally, the entire story was painted in bright colors—and

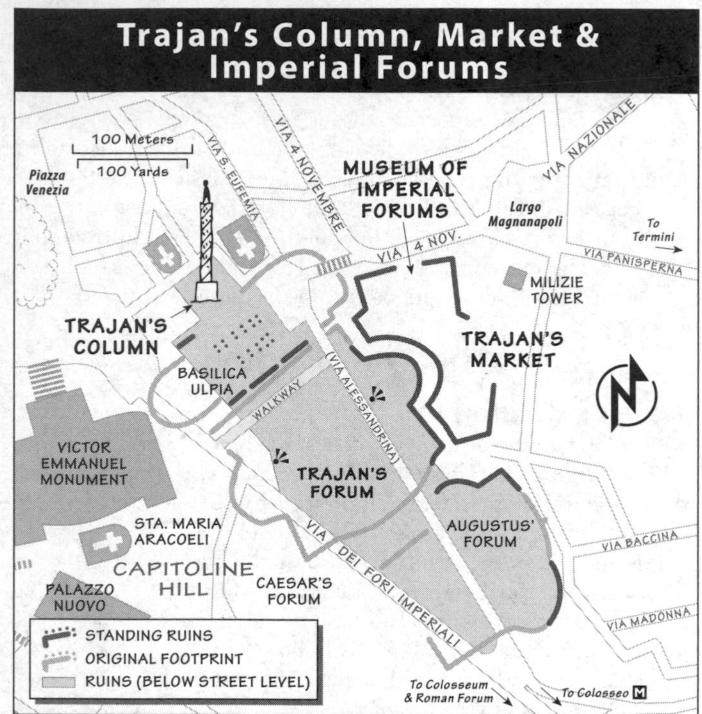

plans are afoot to re-create the column's colors with bright lights on weekend nights. If you were to unwind the scroll, it would stretch over two football fields—it's far longer than the frieze around the Greek Parthenon. (An unscrolled copy is in E.U.R.'s Museum of Roman Civilization; see page 93.)

Trajan's conquest of the Dacians was Rome's last and greatest foreign conquest. It produced Trajan's Forum, which stood for centuries as a symbol of a truly cosmopolitan civilization.

• *You can view Trajan's Market for free from Via dei Fori Imperiali. To walk around inside the market, you must pay admission and enter through the Museum of the Imperial Forums (described on the next page).*

Trajan's Market (Mercati di Traiano)

Nestled into the cutaway curve of Quirinal Hill is the semicircular brick complex of Trajan's Market. It was likely part shopping mall, part warehouse, and part administration building. Or, as some archaeologists have recently suggested, it may have contained mostly government offices.

For now the conventional wisdom holds that at ground level, the 13 tall (shallow) arches housed shops selling fresh fruit, veg-

etables, and flowers to people who passed by on the street. The 26 arched windows (above) lit a covered walkway lined with shops that sold wine and olive oil. On the roof (now lined with a metal railing) ran a street that likely held still more shops, making about 150 in all. Shoppers could browse through goods from every corner of Rome's vast empire—exotic fruits from Africa, spices from Asia, and fish-and-chips from Londinium.

Above the semicircle, the upper floors of the complex housed bureaucrats in charge of a crucial element of city life: doling out free grain to unemployed citizens, who lived off the wealth plundered from distant lands. Better to pacify them than risk a riot. Above the offices, at the very top, rises a tower added in the Middle Ages.

The market was beautiful and functional, filling the space of the curved hill perfectly and echoing the curved side of the Forum's main courtyard. (The wall of rough volcanic stones on the ground once extended into a semicircle.) Unlike most Roman buildings, the brick facade wasn't covered with plaster or marble. The architect liked the simple contrast between the warm brick and the white stone lining the arches and windows.

• *If you want to walk around the market—worth it only for those with a good imagination, stamina for stairs, or a Masters in Food Distribution—you'll have to pay to enter the museum, which also has exhibits about the entire site. Otherwise, skip ahead to "The Rest of Trajan's Forum."*

Museum of the Imperial Forums (Museo dei Fori Imperiali)

The museum, housed in buildings from Trajan's Market, features discoveries from forums built by several different emperors. Though its collection of statues is not impressive compared to Rome's other museums, it's well-displayed, and it's your only chance to get up close to Trajan's Market and Forum. Skip the detail-oriented audioguide and focus on the big picture to mentally resurrect the fabulous forums.

Each emperor commissioned a series of public piazzas—surrounded by temples, civic buildings, businesses, and markets—that stood in a line from the Colosseum to Trajan's Column. Julius Caesar built the first one (46 B.C.), figuring that the old Roman Forum was not a big enough public space for the expanding city. Over the next 150 years, it was added onto by Augustus (2 B.C.),

Vespasian (A.D. 75), Nerva (A.D. 97), and Trajan (A.D. 112).

Start with the introductory slideshow that virtually reconstructs the forums and Vespasian's Temple of Peace. Next, see the statues and broken columns that once decorated the sites. A caryatid (a female statue serving as a column) from the Forum of Augustus stands in the museum's entryway, alongside a bearded mask of Giove (Jupiter). Nearby, a bronze foot is all that's left of a larger-than-life Winged Victory that adorned Augustus' Temple of Mars the Avenger.

Upstairs, a section on Julius Caesar's Forum displays baby Cupids (the son of Venus and Mars) carved from the pure white stone that would eventually adorn all of Rome—Carrara marble.

The rest of the upstairs is dedicated to the Forum of Augustus. A model of the Temple of Mars and some large column fragments give a sense of the enormous scale. You'll see a reconstruction of the hand of the 40-foot statue of Augustus that once stood in his forum.

From here, you can descend to the ground level for a close-up look at Trajan's Market (described earlier). As you walk by the shops in the welcome shade of the arcade, you'll get a better sense of how inviting the market must have been in its heyday. Walking along the curved top of Trajan's Market, you'll enjoy expansive views of Trajan's Forum, other forums in the distance, and the modern Victor Emmanuel Monument.

• *Look down into the ruins of Trajan's Forum, either from atop Trajan's Market or from a viewpoint along Via dei Fori Imperiali.*

The Rest of Trajan's Forum (Foro di Traiano)

Trajan's Forum starts at Trajan's Column and runs about 120 yards southeast toward the Colosseum. It's mostly rubble today, except for Trajan's Market rising up the flank of Quirinal Hill.

In Roman times, you would have entered at the Colosseum end through a triumphal arch and been greeted in the main square by a large statue of the soldier-king on a horse. Continuing on, you'd enter the Basilica Ulpia (the gray granite columns near Trajan's Column), the largest law court of its day. Finally, at the far end, you would have found Trajan's Column, flanked by two libraries that contained the world's knowledge in Greek and Latin. Balconies on the libraries gave close-up looks at the upper reliefs of the column, in case anyone doubted the outcome of Trajan's war.

Trajan's Forum was a crucial expansion of the old Roman Forum, which was too small and ceremonial to fill the commercial needs of a booming city of more than a million people. It trumped the forums of previous Romans (the adjacent forums of Julius Caesar, Augustus, and Vespasian). Built with the staggering haul of gold plundered from Dacia, this was the largest forum ever—its opulence astounded even the jaded Romans.

To build his forum, Trajan literally moved mountains. He cut away a ridge that once connected the Quirinal and Capitoline hills, creating this valley. Trajan's Column marks the hill's original height—140 feet.

• *The tour is over. You are just a toga's toss from many other sights of ancient Rome. From here, you can cross over to the other side of busy Via dei Fori Imperiali and visit the Capitoline Hill sights, the Roman Forum, or the Colosseum that looms in the distance*

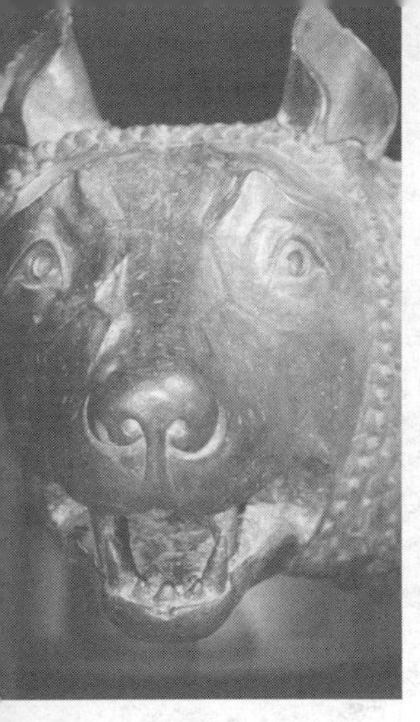

CAPITOLINE MUSEUMS TOUR

Musei Capitolini

This enjoyable museum complex claims to be the world's oldest, founded in 1471 when a pope gave ancient statues to the citizens of Rome. Perched on top of Capitoline Hill, its two buildings (Palazzo dei Conservatori and Palazzo Nuovo) are connected by an underground passage that leads to the Tabularium and panoramic views of the Roman Forum. (For directions on a climb-saving shortcut to the nearby Victor Emmanuel Monument and Santa Maria in Aracoeli Church, see the sidebar on page 55.)

Orientation

Cost: €12, €14 combo-ticket includes Montemartini Museum. Single tickets drop to €7.50 and combo-tickets to €10.50 with no temporary exhibits.

Hours: Tue-Sun 9:00-20:00, closed Mon, last entry one hour before closing.

Getting There: It sits atop Capitoline Hill (*Campidoglio* in Italian), housed in two buildings that flank the square. Buy tickets and enter at the Palazzo dei Conservatori (on your right as you face the equestrian statue).

Information: You'll find some English descriptions within the museum. Tel. 06-8205-9127 or 06-0608, www.museicapitolini.org.

Audioguide: The €5 audioguide is good.

Length of This Tour: Allow two hours.

With Limited Time: Focus on the Palazzo dei Conservatori (skip the Tabularium and Palazzo Nuovo).

Baggage Check: Free (mandatory for bags larger than a purse).

Cuisine Art: A great view café, called **Caffè Capitolino,** is upstairs in Palazzo dei Conservatori (enter from inside museum; also has exterior entrance for the public—facing museum entrance, go to your right around the building to Piazza Caffarelli and through door #4; see map on next page). The pavilion on the terrace outside offers full service; inside is self-service (pay first, then take receipt to bar; good salads and toasted sandwiches). Piazza Caffarelli is a fine place for a snooze or a picnic.

Starring: The original she-wolf statue, Marcus Aurelius, the Dying Gaul, the Boy Extracting a Thorn, and Forum views.

The Tour Begins

• *Begin at the square on top of Capitoline Hill.*

Overview

Capitoline Hill's main square (Piazza del Campidoglio), home to the museum, began in ancient Rome as a religious center, the site of temples to the gods Jupiter, Juno, and Minerva. In the 16th century, Michelangelo transformed the square from pagan to papal, while adding a harmonious and refined Renaissance touch. (For more on the square, see page 52.)

The museum's layout—with two different buildings connected by an underground passage—can be confusing, but this self-guided tour is easy to follow.

You'll enter at the Palazzo dei Conservatori (on your right as you face the equestrian statue), cross underneath the square (beneath the Palazzo Senatorio, the mayoral palace, not open to public—see photo), and exit from the Palazzo Nuovo (on your left).

Palazzo dei Conservatori

• *After your ticket is checked, enter the courtyard.*

In the courtyard, enjoy the massive chunks of Constantine: his head, hand, and foot. When intact, this giant held the place of honor in the Basilica of Constantine in the Forum. Also in the courtyard are reliefs of conquered peoples—not in chains, but new members of an expansive empire.

• *Go up the staircase (the one to the left of the entrance, not the one in the courtyard). On the landing, find...*

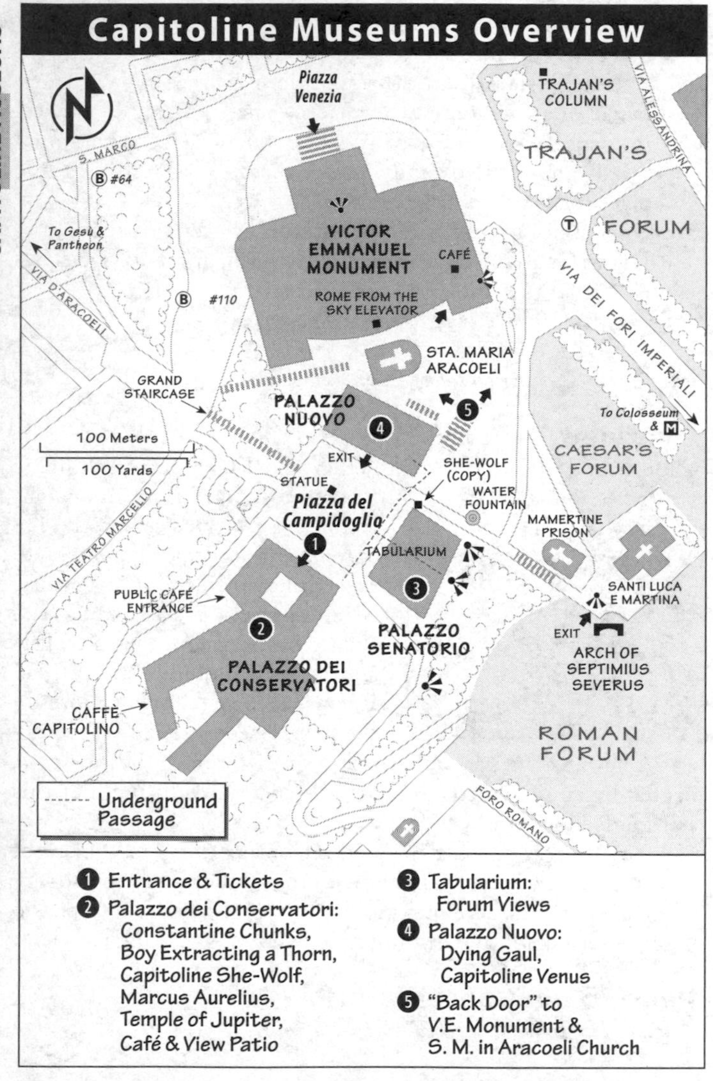

Reliefs of Second-Century Imperial Grandeur

These four fine reliefs show great moments in an emperor's daily grind. Find Marcus Aurelius overseeing preparations to sacrifice a bull (with even the bull looking on curiously) on Capitoline Hill. Also find Marcus Aurelius in an equestrian pose (like the bronze statue in Piazza del Campidoglio), with his hand out, offering clemency to his vanquished foes. The detail, with expressive faces and banners blowing in the wind, is impressive. In the relief showing Marcus Aurelius in his chariot, someone's missing...it's

Commodus, his wicked son (Russell Crowe's nemesis in *Gladiator*). After the assassination of Commodus, his memory was damned, so images of him were erased (or, in this case, chiseled out).

• *Continue up the stairs to the first floor. Go through two large frescoed rooms and through the doorway on the right of the far wall to find...*

Boy Extracting a Thorn *(Spinario)*

He's just a boy, intent only on picking a thorn out of his foot. As he bends over to reach his foot, his body sticks out at all angles, like a bony chicken wing. He's even scuffed up, the way small boys get. At this moment, nothing matters to him but that splinter. Our lives are filled with these mundane moments (when we'd give anything for tweezers) rarely captured in art.

Art scholars speculate that the boy's head, tilted unnaturally down, and his body are from two separate statues spliced together.

• *In the next room is the...*

Capitoline She-Wolf

The original bronze she-wolf suckles the twins Romulus and Remus. This symbol of Rome is ancient, though the wolf statue itself (long thought to be Etruscan from the fifth century B.C.) was made in the 13th century, and the boys are an invention of the 14th century. Look into the eyes of the wolf. An animal looks back, with ragged ears, sharp teeth, and staring eyes. This wild animal, teamed with the wildest creatures of all—hungry babies—makes a powerful symbol for the tenacious city/empire of Rome.

• *Continue to the next room.*

From Michelangelo to Medusa

Along with a bust of Michelangelo, this room contains Bernini's

anguished bust of Medusa—with writhing snakes on her head. This goes way beyond a bad hair day.

• *Pass through three small rooms containing the Artemis of Efenina, followed by Greek red-figured vases (and the elevator up to the café). Continue straight to a set of seven stairs and follow them up to the next room to discover the remarkable bust of...*

Commodus as Hercules

This arrogant emperor brat used to run around the palace in animal skins. Here, he wears a lion's head over his own and drapes the lion's paws over his chest. This lion king made a bad emperor (ruled A.D. 180-192).

• *As you are looking at Commodus, directly behind you is his dad, the Emperor...*

Marcus Aurelius (C. A.D. 176)

This is the greatest surviving equestrian statue of antiquity. Marcus Aurelius was a Roman philosopher-emperor (ruled A.D. 161-180) known more for his *Meditations* than his prowess on the battlefield. Notice that he doesn't use stirrups. An Asian invention, those newfangled devices wouldn't arrive in Europe for another 500 years.

Christians in the Dark Ages thought that the statue's hand was raised in blessing, which probably led to their misidentifying him as Constantine, the first Christian emperor. While most pagan statues were destroyed by Christians, "Constantine" was spared. It has graced several prominent locations in medieval Rome, including the papal palace at San Giovanni in Laterano.

In 1538, this gilded bronze statue was placed in the center of the Campidoglio (directly outside the museum), and Michelangelo was hired to design the buildings around it with the statue as the centerpiece. A few years ago, the statue was moved inside and restored, while the copy you see outside today was placed on the square.

Also in the room are a gilded Hercules and more hunks—head, finger, and a globe—of another statue of Constantine. (Or was it the Emperor Sylvestrus Stalloneus?)

• *Descend the ramp to the wall of blocks from the...*

Temple of Jupiter

This is part of the foundation of the ancient Temple of Jupiter (Giove), once the most impressive in Rome. Find the scale model of the temple (1:40) to get a sense of its size and where you stand in relation to the ruins.

The King of the Gods resided atop Capitoline Hill in this once-classy 10,000-square-foot temple, which was perched on a podium and lined with Greek-style columns, overlooking downtown Rome. The most important rites were performed here, and victory parades through the Forum ended here. The famous temple, known as the Capitolium, gave the hill its name. Replicas of this building were erected in every Roman city. The temple was begun by Rome's last king (the Tarquin), and its dedication in 509 B.C. marks the start of the Roman Republic.

All that remains of the temple today are these ruined foundation stones, made of volcanic tuff, an easily carved rock commonly used in Roman construction. Although there are hundreds of these blocks here, they represent only a portion of the immense foundation, which is only a fraction of the temple itself. In its prime, the temple rose two stories above our heads. Inside stood a statue of the god of thunder wielding a lightning bolt. The temple was refurbished a number of times over the centuries, often after damage by...lightning bolts.

• *Before heading for the Tabularium and Palazzo Nuovo, consider a break in the café. To do this, backtrack to the room with the Greek red-figured vases (near Michelangelo and Medusa), where you'll find the elevator up to the second floor. The café's huge outdoor view patio overlooks the domes of Rome, representing the religion that remained after Rome fell. When you're ready, go back downstairs to Marcus Aurelius.*

If Marcus trotted a few steps forward, turned left, and went to the end of the hall, he'd find a staircase. Go downstairs two flights, to the basement—the piano sotteraneo. *Then cross underneath the square through the long passageway filled with ancient inscriptions. Near the far end, turn right and climb a set of stairs into the...*

Tabularium

Built in the first century B.C., these sturdy vacant rooms once held the archives of ancient Rome. The word Tabularium comes from "tablet," on which Romans wrote their laws.

The rooms offer a stunning head-on view over the Forum, giving you a more complete picture of the sprawl of ancient Rome. Panning left to right, find the following landmarks: Arch of Septimius Severus, Arch of Titus (in the distance), the lone Column of Phocas, the three columns of the Temple of Castor and Pollux, the three columns (closer to you) of the Temple of Vespasiano, and the eight columns of the Temple of Saturn.

Now do an about-face and look up to see a huge white hunk of carved marble, an overhang from Temple of Vespasiano.

• *Find more views from this vantage point, plus the remains of another temple, then leave the Tabularium by going back down the stairs. Turn right and go up three flights of stairs. You're now on the first floor of the...*

Palazzo Nuovo

• *From the top of the stairs, the first room you encounter is room VIII—the "Hall of the Gaul"—with one of the museum's most famous pieces.*

Dying Gaul

A first-century B.C. copy of a Greek original, this was sculpted to celebrate the Greeks' victory over the Galatians. It may have been part of a larger sculpture group, a portion of which is across town in the Palazzo Altemps (a branch of the National Museum of Rome).

Wounded in battle, the dying Gaul holds himself upright, but barely. Minutes earlier, before he was stabbed in the chest, he'd been in his prime. Now he can only watch helplessly as his life ebbs away. His sword is useless against this last battle. With his messy hair, downcast eyes, and crumpled position, he poignantly reminds us that every victory also means a defeat.

• *In the next few rooms, take a quick look at...*

Ancient Roman Statues and Busts

A reddish faun glories in grapes and life, oblivious to the loss of his penis (at least he still has his tail). The statue, found among a couple of dozen pieces in Hadrian's Villa, was skillfully restored. Check out the chandeliered ceilings in this room and elsewhere; this building is truly a *palazzo* (palace).

The next room, the large hall, features more sculpture from Hadrian's Villa (and elsewhere). Notice the Wounded Amazon (near the window) undoing her delicate dress. This is a Roman copy of a fifth-century B.C. Greek original by Polycletus.

Roll through two rooms lined with busts—the Hall of Philosophers (Socrates, Homer, Euripides, Cicero, and many more) and the Hall of Emperors (Constantine's mom Helena sits center stage, resting after her journey to Jerusalem to find Christ's cross). In this 3-D yearbook of ancient history, there are few labels. The only purple bust is Caracalla. Infamous for his fervent brutality, he instructed his portraitists to stress his meanness. Directly across on the lower shelf, the smallest bust—of Emperor Gordiano (ruled A.D. 238-244)—is one of the finest of late antiquity. His expression shows the concerns and consternation of a ruler whose empire is in decline. In this room you can find classic expressions of confidence, brutality, and anguish—human drama through the ages. Don't miss the delicate elegance of the first-century A.D. woman with the complex hairdo by the window.

• *Enter the hallway and start down the hall. The small octagonal room on your left contains one of the museum's treasures.*

Capitoline Venus

This is a Roman copy of a fourth-century B.C. Greek original by the master Praxiteles. Venus, leaving the bath, is suddenly aware that someone is watching her. As she turns to look, she reflexively covers up (nearly). Her blank eyes hold no personality or emotion. Her fancy hairstyle is the only complicated thing about her. She is simply beautiful—generically erotic.

• *Head to the last room on the left before the stairs. Displayed on the wall is the...*

Mosaic of Doves

Four doves perch on the rim of a bronze bowl as one drinks water from the bowl. Minute bits make up this small, exquisite work. Found in the center of a floor in one of the rooms in Hadrian's

Villa, this second-century A.D. mosaic was based on an earlier work done, of course, by the Greeks.

We all know that ancient Rome was grand. But the art in this museum tells us that its culture was exquisite as well.

• *To exit, head down the stairs to the ground floor, and follow signs to the* uscita. *If you checked a bag, cross the courtyard to retrieve it.*

ST. PETER-IN-CHAINS TOUR

San Pietro in Vincoli

Michelangelo—the world's greatest sculptor—died having failed to complete his greatest work, the tomb of Pope Julius II. Today, you can visit the powerful remains of that unfinished masterpiece, including the famous statue of Moses, housed in a historic church that also contains Peter's chains.

Orientation

Cost: Free.

Hours: Daily April-Sept 8:00-12:30 & 15:00-19:00, Oct-March 8:00-12:30 & 15:00-18:00.

Dress Code: Modest dress is required.

Getting There: The church is a 10-minute uphill walk north of the Colosseum. From the Colosseo Metro stop, take the escalator just inside the station exit (following *S. Pietro in Vincoli* signs), then work your way slowly uphill. There's also a staircase 50 yards east of the station. For a shorter walk, use the Cavour Metro stop; from that station, go downhill on Via Cavour a half-block, then climb the steep pedestrian staircase called Via di San Francesco di Paola, which leads right to the church. If asking for directions, say "San Pietro in Vincoli" (sahn pee-AY-troh een VEEN-koh-lee). From the outside, St. Peter-in-Chains' rounded arches and columns look more like a Renaissance loggia than a church.

Length of This Tour: Allow 30 minutes.

Photography: Generally, photos without flash are allowed in Rome's churches. Bring €0.50 coins to light Moses and the tomb.

Eating: See the recommended eateries listed on page 367.

The Tour Begins

• *In the far-right corner of the church, you'll find a wall full of marble statues. In the center sits...*

Michelangelo's *Moses* (1515)

Moses has just returned from meeting face-to-face with God. Now he senses trouble back home. Slowly he turns to see his followers worshipping a golden calf. As his anger builds, he glares at them. His physical strength is symbolic of his moral and spiritual fortitude as a leader of his people. His powerful left leg tucks under and tenses, as he's just about to spring up out of his chair and punish the naughty Children of Israel with the Ten Commandments under his arm. Enjoy the cascading beard, one of the greatest in art history.

And if he did stand up, this statue would be 13 feet tall, nearly the height of Michelangelo's famous *David*. This Charlton Heston-with-horns is interesting in photographs... and awe-inspiring when confronted in person. His bare, muscular arms exude power. Michelangelo completed the statue after practicing for four years painting the seated prophets on the Sistine ceiling.

Like other Michelangelo statues, *Moses* is both at rest (seated) and in motion (his tensed leg, turning head, and nervous fingers). This restlessness may reflect Michelangelo's Neo-Platonic belief that the soul is the claustrophobic prisoner of the body. Or it's the statue itself fighting to emerge from the stone around it. A fanciful legend says that Michelangelo, frustrated at trying to bring God's statue into existence, hit *Moses* with his hammer (causing the scar on *Moses'* right knee), imploring, "Now, speak!"

The horns are the crowning touch. In medieval times, the Hebrew word for "rays of light" (halo) was mistranslated as "horns." Michelangelo knew better but wanted to give the statue an air of *terribilità*, a kind of scary charisma possessed by Moses, Pope Julius II...and Michelangelo. This Moses radiates the smoldering *terribilità* of a borderline-abusive father.

The Tomb Today

In 1542, remnants of the tomb project were brought to the St. Peter-in-Chains church and pieced together by Michelangelo's assistants. What we see today is a far cry from the original design,

The Tomb of Pope Julius II

Moses sits on the bottom level of a three-story marble wall filled with statues. This is a puny, cobbled-together version of what was to have been a grand tomb for Pope Julius II.

In 1505, Pope Julius II hired young Michelangelo to build his tomb, a huge monument to be placed in St. Peter's Basilica.

An excited Michelangelo sketched designs for a three-story wedding-cake mountain of marble studded with 48 statues and bronze reliefs, and topped with a huge statue of the egomaniacal pope. *Moses* was to have been placed on an upper level on the right-hand corner, looking away from the monument.

Michelangelo traveled to Carrara, selected 100 tons of marble for the project, and started working. Then Julius changed his mind. He ordered Michelangelo to paint the Sistine Chapel instead. Michelangelo knocked it off in a mere four years so that he could return to his true masterwork. Michelangelo would spend 30 years of his life working in fits and starts on the tomb. But when Julius died (1513), the funding for the project petered out, and Michelangelo eventually moved on to other things. Julius was buried in a simple grave in St. Peter's Basilica at the Vatican.

which was to have been fully three-dimensional and five times as big. Some of the best statues ended up elsewhere, such as the *Prisoners* in Florence and the *Slaves* in the Louvre. Though the assistants had Michelangelo's original instruction manual, they were trying to assemble it with most of the parts missing.

Moses and the Louvre's *Slaves* are the only statues Michelangelo personally completed for the project. Flanking *Moses* are the Old Testament sister-wives of Jacob, Leah (to our right) and Rachel, both begun by Michelangelo but probably finished by pupils. On the second story, a Madonna and Child stand above a reclining, thoughtful-looking Pope Julius II on a coffin.

The sheer variety of decoration we see here gives us a glimpse of the tomb's original scope—nearly 50 statues laced together with Pompeii-esque garlands and proto-Baroque scrolls.

Michelangelo went to his grave thinking that he'd wasted the best years of his life on the tomb. Today, we can only reconstruct it in our minds, imagining a monument intended to exceed (according to Giorgio Vasari) "every ancient or imperial tomb ever made."

The Church

Founded in 440, it's one of Rome's oldest, built to house Peter's chains. Though the church was greatly changed in 1475, the 20 Doric columns flanking the wide nave are from the original church. The central ceiling painting (c. 1700) shows the chains—with their miraculous curative powers in action—healing someone possessed by demons, on the steps of St. Peter's Basilica in the Vatican.

• *On the altar is a gold-and-glass case, containing what tradition claims to be...*

Peter's Chains

There are actually two different sets of chains, linked together. One set are said to have held Peter when he and Paul were in the Mamertine Prison in Rome (near the Forum).

The other dates from when Herod jailed Peter in Jerusalem (Acts 12; see the scene frescoed on the left wall of the apse). During the night, "Peter was sleeping between two soldiers, bound with chains, while sentries were guarding the doors. And behold, an angel of the Lord appeared and a light shone in the cell. The angel struck Peter on the side and woke him, saying, 'Get up quickly.' And the chains fell off his hands." The angel led Peter, who thought he was dreaming, out of the prison to safety. (Raphael's depiction of this is in the Vatican Museum.)

In the waning days of ancient Rome, the Jerusalem chains ended up here as a gift from the Eastern empress to her son-in-law, the Western emperor (as depicted in the fresco on the right wall of the apse).

According to tradition, when the Jerusalem chains arrived and were paired with the Mamertine chains, the two sets—chink!—joined together miraculously.

PANTHEON TOUR

The Roman Temple and Nearby Churches

If your imagination is fried from trying to reconstruct ancient buildings out of today's rubble, visit the Pantheon, Rome's best-preserved monument. Engineers still admire how the Romans built such a mathematically precise structure without computers, fossil fuel-run machinery, or electricity. (Having unlimited slave power didn't hurt.) Stand under the Pantheon's solemn dome to gain a new appreciation for the sophistication of these ancient people.

Several interesting churches are clustered nearby, easy to visit after you tour the Pantheon.

Orientation

Length of This Tour: Allow a half-hour to see the Pantheon and at least another hour to visit all the nearby churches.

With Limited Time: The essential Pantheon can be seen in a glance. The four nearby churches are far less important.

When to Go: Try to get to the Pantheon first thing in the morning: While it's jammed with people midday, you'll have it all to yourself before 9:00. (If you're touring nearby churches immediately afterward, save the Church of San Luigi dei Francesi for last, as it doesn't open until 10:00.)

Getting There: To reach the Pantheon neighborhood, you can walk (it's a 15-minute walk from Capitoline Hill), take a taxi, or catch a bus. Buses stop at a chaotic square called Largo Argentina, a few blocks south of the Pantheon—from here you can walk north on either Via dei Cestari or Via di Torre Argentina to the Pantheon. Buses #40 and #64 carry tourists and pickpockets frequently between the Termini train station and Vatican City (#492 serves the same areas via a different route). Bus #87 connects to the Colosseum. The *elettrico* minibus #116 runs between Campo de' Fiori and Piazza Barberini via the Pantheon. The most dramatic approach is on foot coming from Piazza Navona along Via Giustiniani, which spills directly into Piazza della Rotonda, offering the classic Pantheon view (✪ see the Heart of Rome Walk chapter).

Pantheon: Free, Mon-Sat 8:30-19:30, Sun 9:00-18:00, holidays 9:00-13:00, closed for Mass Sat at 17:00 and Sun at 10:30. Tel. 06-6830-0230.

Church of San Luigi dei Francesi: Free, daily 10:00-12:30 & 15:00-19:00 except closed Thu afternoon, good €3 booklet, www.saintlouis-rome.net. Bring coins to light the Caravaggios.

Gesù Church: Free, daily 7:00-12:30 & 16:00-19:45, interesting daily service at 17:30, www.chiesadelgesu.org.

Church of Santa Maria sopra Minerva: Free, Mon-Fri 7:00-19:00, Sat-Sun 8:00-12:30 & 15:30-19:00.

Church of San Ignazio: Free, Mon-Sat 7:30-19:00, Sun 9:00-19:00.

Dress Code: Modest dress is recommended for the churches near the Pantheon.

Audioguides: The Pantheon has a €5 audioguide that lasts 25 minutes (€8/2 people). You can download the Pantheon portion of this chapter as a free Rick Steves audio tour (see page 27).

Services: The nearest WCs are at bars and cafés on the Pantheon's square.

Photography: It's allowed—even with flash—in the Pantheon, but no flash is allowed in the nearby churches.

Eating: Restaurants abound. Several reasonable eateries are a block or two north up Via del Pantheon. You can picnic on the steps of the fountain or along the Pantheon's walls. While picnicking is forbidden under the Pantheon's portico, I enjoy discreetly munching a sandwich at the base of a column. Some of Rome's best gelato is nearby. For restaurant recommendations, see page 364.

Drinks: A drinking fountain spurts near the obelisk in Piazza della Rotonda. For those who prefer their liquids caffeinated, two of Rome's most venerable (and busiest) coffee shops are just steps away: **Tazza d'Oro Casa del Caffè** (their icy *granita di caffè con panna* is heaven on a hot day, Via degli Orfani 84) and **Bar Sant'Eustachio** (they add sugar to their coffee drinks unless you request otherwise, Piazza di Sant'Eustachio 82).

Overview

The Pantheon is the centerpiece of this tour, and is a must-see on any visit to Rome. The second part of this tour features several nearby churches with art by Michelangelo and Caravaggio, and connections with Galileo, St. Ignatius, and the Jesuit order.

The Tour Begins

• Start the tour at the top of the square called Piazza della Rotonda, with cafés and restaurants around the edges and an obelisk-topped fountain in the center. You're looking at...

The Pantheon

Exterior

The Pantheon was a Roman temple dedicated to all *(pan)* of the gods *(theos)*. The original temple was built in 27 B.C. by Augustus' son-in-law, Marcus Agrippa. In fact, the inscription below the triangular **pediment** proclaims in Latin, "Marcus Agrippa, son of Lucio, three times consul made this." But after a couple of fires, the structure we see today was completely rebuilt by the emperor Hadrian around A.D. 120. Some say that Hadrian, an amateur architect (and voracious traveler), helped design it.

The Pantheon looks like a pretty typical temple from the outside, but this is perhaps the most influential building in art history. Its dome was the model for the Florence cathedral dome, which launched the Renaissance, and for Michelangelo's dome of St. Peter's, which capped it all off. Even the US Capitol in Washington, DC, was inspired by this dome.

The **portico** is Greek in style, logically because Hadrian was a Grecophile. (He grew a beard to look like a Greek philosopher, bucking the beardless tradition of Rome's 13 previous emperors.) This fine porch is a visual reminder of the great debt Roman culture owed to the Greeks. Fittingly, you cross this Greek space to enter a purely Roman space, the rotunda. The columns are huge and unadorned, made from 40-foot-high single pieces of red-gray granite rather than the standard stacks of cylindrical pieces. They were quarried in Egypt, then shipped down the Nile and across the Mediterranean to Rome. They were then fitted with leafy Corinthian capitals, the Greek order that was most popular among Romans. They are sequoia huge—it takes the outstretched arms of four large tourists to encircle one column.

• Before passing through the portico, notice the two huge, empty niches flanking the door—once filled with towering statues of emperors. Look up at the porch roof, and imagine the ceiling covered in its original bronze plating. It was removed in the 17th century by a scavenging pope from the Barberini family, inspiring the well-known quip, "What

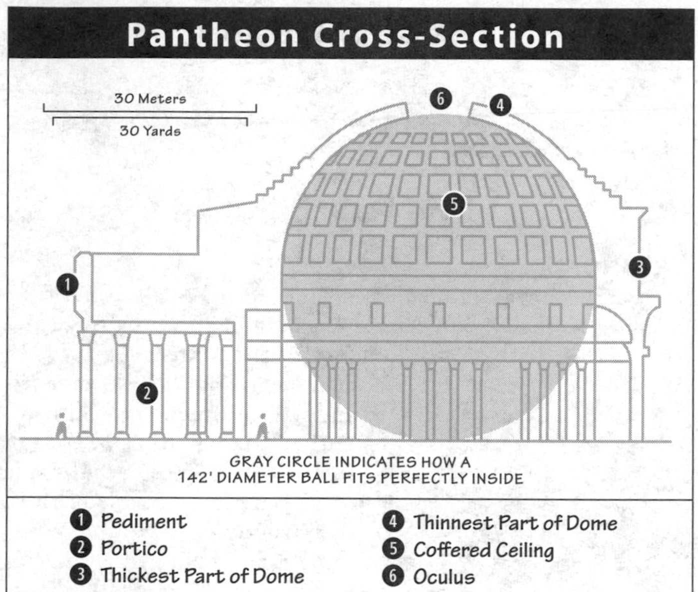

the barbarians didn't do, the Barberini did." Melted down, some of the bronze was used to build the huge bronze canopy over the altar at St. Peter's. Now pass through the giant ***bronze door****—a copy of the original. Take a seat and take it all in.*

Interior

The dome, which was the largest made until the Renaissance, is set on a circular base. The mathematical perfection of this dome-on-a-base design is a testament to Roman engineering. The dome is as high as it is wide—142 feet from floor to rooftop and from side to side. To picture it, imagine a basketball wedged inside a wastebasket so that it just touches bottom.

The dome—clean and feeling loftier than ever—is made from concrete (a Roman invention) that gets lighter and thinner as it reaches the top. The base of the dome is 23 feet thick and made from heavy concrete mixed with travertine, while near the top, it's less than five feet thick and made with a lighter volcanic rock (pumice) mixed in. Note the square indentations in the surface of the dome. This **coffered ceiling** reduces the weight of the dome without compromising strength. The walls are strengthened by brick relieving arches ("blind" arches)—visible in the exposed

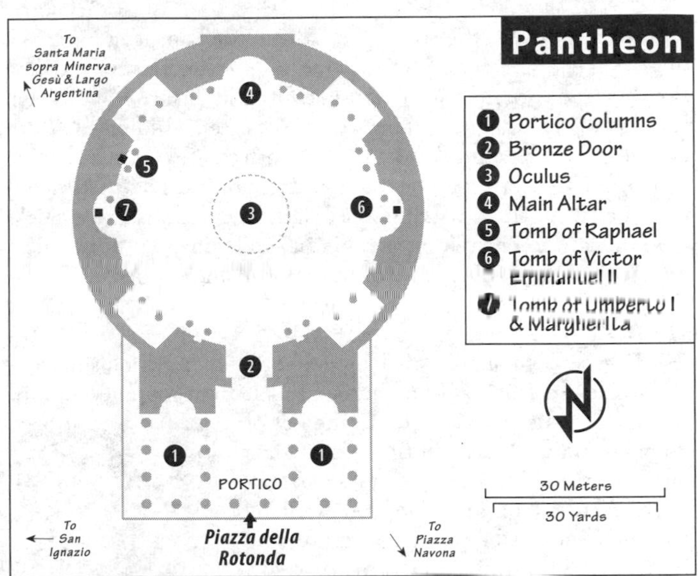

brickwork in a few of the interior niches and easy to see outside.

Both Brunelleschi and Michelangelo studied this dome before building their own (in Florence and the Vatican, respectively). Remember, the grandiose vision for St. Peter's Basilica was to place the dome of the Pantheon atop the Forum's Basilica of Constantine.

At the top, the **oculus,** or eye-in-the-sky, is the building's only light source. It's completely open and almost 30 feet across. The 1,800-year-old floor—with 80 percent of its original stones surviving—has holes in it and slants toward the edges to let the rainwater drain. Though some of the floor's marble has been replaced, the design—alternating circles and squares—is original.

In ancient times, this was a one-stop-shopping temple where you could worship any of the major gods whose statues decorated the niches. Entering the temple, Romans came face-to-face with a larger-than-life statue of Jupiter, the King of the Gods, where the

altar stands today. After the fall of Rome, the Pantheon became a Christian church (from "all the gods" to "all the martyrs"), which saved it from architectural cannibalism and ensured its upkeep through the Dark Ages. (The year 2009 was the building's 1,400th anniversary as a church.) In the seventh century, a Byzantine emperor stripped the dome's interior of its original golden-tile ceiling. The twin grilled windows just right of the altar (at 2 o'clock) are a modern re-creation of the original and, along with the inlaid marble floor, give you a sense of the colorful ancient decor.

Tombs

While its ancient statuary is long gone, the interior holds decorative statues and the tombs of famous people from more recent centuries. The artist Raphael lies to the left of the main altar, which is in the lighted glass niche (pictured here). Above him is a statue of the Madonna and Child that Raphael himself commissioned for his tomb. The Latin inscription on his tomb reads, "In life, Nature feared to be outdone by him. In death, she feared she too would die."

You'll also see the tombs of modern Italy's first two kings. To the right is Victor Emmanuel II (*"Padre della Patria,"* father of his country); to the left is Umberto I (son of the father). These tombs are a hit with royalists. In fact, a guard often stands by a guestbook in which visitors can register their support for these two kings' now-controversial family, the Savoys (see sidebar on opposite page). And finally, under Umberto lies his queen, Margherita...for whom the classic pizza Margherita (mozzarella, tomato sauce, and basil) was named in 1889.

The Pantheon is the only ancient building in Rome continuously used since its construction. When you leave, notice that the building is sunken below current street level, showing how the rest of the city has risen on 20 centuries of rubble.

The Pantheon also contains the world's greatest Roman column. There it is, spanning the entire 142 feet from heaven to earth—the pillar of light from the oculus.

• *Leaving the Pantheon, take a moment to enjoy the square facing it. Piazza della Rotonda has been a gathering place for 2,000 years. Its slope illustrates the literal "rise of Rome." Imagine in past centuries when there was a fish and chicken market in the portico. In an 18th-century urban beautification project, the fountain and obelisk were added. Feel the vibrancy of the piazza culture, which goes back to ancient Rome.*

The Italian Royal Family... in Switzerland

From Italy's unification in 1870 to the end of World War II, the country had four kings, all members of the Savoy family. One of Europe's oldest royal families (from the 10th century), the Savoia had long ruled the kingdom of Piedmont (in present-day northern Italy).

In 1946, the Italians voted for a republic and sent the Savoia into exile. Until 2002, a law proclaimed that no male Savoia could set foot on Italian soil. That's why only the first two kings are buried in the Pantheon (the last two died in exile).

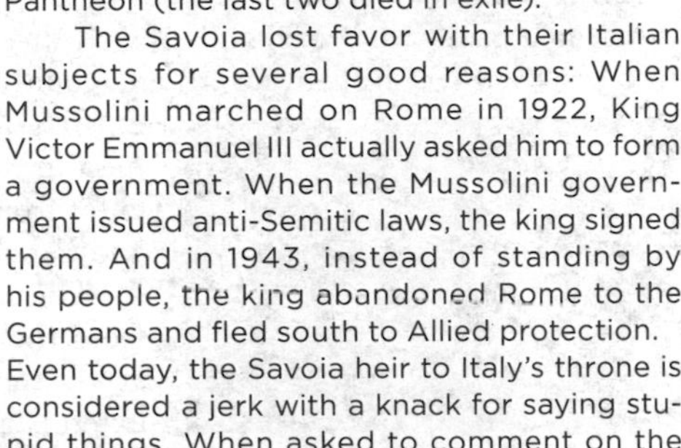

The Savoia lost favor with their Italian subjects for several good reasons: When Mussolini marched on Rome in 1922, King Victor Emmanuel III actually asked him to form a government. When the Mussolini government issued anti-Semitic laws, the king signed them. And in 1943, instead of standing by his people, the king abandoned Rome to the Germans and fled south to Allied protection. Even today, the Savoia heir to Italy's throne is considered a jerk with a knack for saying stupid things. When asked to comment on the racist laws signed by his grandfather, he candidly answered that he was too young at the time so he did not need to apologize, and, he said, the laws were not really all that bad. When the Savoia were allowed back into Italy in 2002, their first mistake was to visit the pope rather than the president of the republic. And while they live in stunning wealth in Switzerland, they still complain that Italy owes them more of the family riches. In 2007 their lawyers claimed that the Italian government should pay the family at least €260 million for damages as a result of their exile.

Churches near the Pantheon

Many visitors just see the Pantheon and leave. But consider visiting one or more of these four unique churches, all less than 10 minutes' walk from the Pantheon (see map for locations). If you're budgeting your energy, here's a quick rundown on what each has to offer: San Luigi houses several stunning Caravaggio paintings. The Gesù is packed with ornate art and Jesuit history. Santa Maria sopra Minerva, Rome's only Gothic church, has a Michelangelo sculpture and St. Catherine's tomb. Finally, San Ignazio is full of Baroque perspective illusions that will leave your head spinning.

Church of San Luigi dei Francesi

This is the French national church in Rome. Outside, check out the salamander, symbol of François I, the French king who brought Leonardo (and the Renaissance) north, from Italy to France. The stylized fleur-de-lis symbols found all over the interior are the emblem of French royalty. The one truly *magnifique* sight is the chapel in the far-left corner, which was decorated by Caravaggio. This church makes a great little detour between the Pantheon and nearby Piazza Navona.

• *In the Caravaggio chapel, first look to the left wall.*

The Calling of St. Matthew

Matthew (old man with beard) and his well-dressed, tax-collecting cronies sit in a dingy Roman tavern and count the money they've extorted. Suddenly, two men in robes and bare feet enter from the right—Jesus and Peter. Jesus' "Creation-of-Adam" hand emerges from the darkness to point at Matthew. A shaft of light extends the gesture, lighting up the face of Matthew, who points to himself, *Last Supper*-style, to ask, "You talkin' to me?" Jesus came to convince Matthew to leave his sleazy job and preach Love. Matthew did.

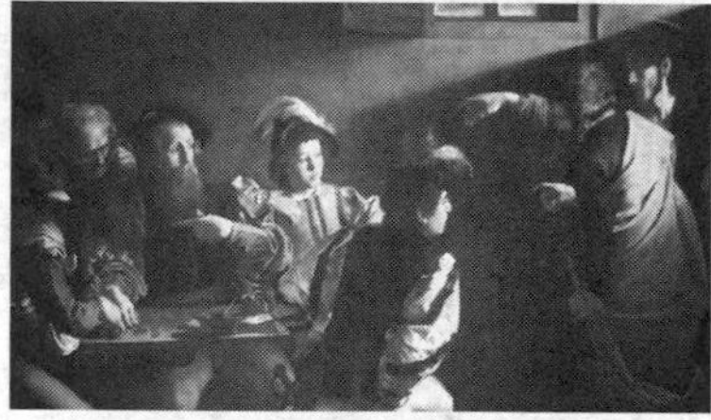

In this, his first large-scale work, 29-year-old Caravaggio (1571-1610) shocked critics and clerics by showing a holy scene in a down-to-earth location. Lower-class people in everyday clothes were his models; his setting was a dive bar (which he knew well). Christ's teeny gold halo is the only hint of the supernatural, as Caravaggio makes a bold proclamation—that miracles are natural events experienced in a profound way.

• *Now look to the center wall.*

The Inspiration of St. Matthew

Matthew followed Christ's call, traveled with him, and (supposedly) wrote Jesus' life story (the Gospel according to Matthew). Here, Matthew is hard at work when he's interrupted by an angel with a few suggestions. This sets the scene in motion. Matthew kneels on a stool, which is just about to fall out of the painting and into our zone. Matthew's bald head, wrinkled face, and grizzled beard make him an all-too-human saint. Even the teen angel

Churches near the Pantheon

lacks a holy glow—he just hangs there. Caravaggio paints a dark background, then shines a dramatic spotlight on the few things that tell the story.

• *Finally, check out the right wall.*

The Martyrdom of St. Matthew

Matthew lies prone, while a truly scary man straddles him and brandishes a sword. The bystanders shrink away from this angry executioner. Caravaggio shines his harsh third-degree spotlight on Matthew and the killer, who are the focus of the painting. The other figures

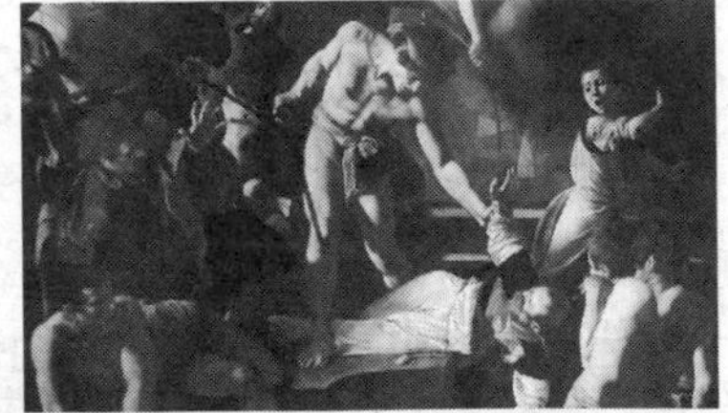

swirl around them in a circle (with the executioner's arm as the radius). Matthew, who thought he had given up everything to follow Christ, now gives up his life as well. He is as open as a crucifix, accepting his fate, and reaching for a palm frond—symbolic of victory over death. The bearded face in the background (to the left of the executioner's shoulder) is a self-portrait of Caravaggio, observing the violence without getting involved.

When the chapel was unveiled in 1600, Caravaggio's ultra-realism shocked Rome. Although he died only 10 years later, his uncompromising details, emotional subjects, odd compositions, and dramatic lighting set the tone for later Baroque painters.

Gesù Church

The center of the Jesuit order and the best symbol of the Catholic Counter-Reformation, the Gesù (jay-zoo) is packed with over-blown art and underappreciated history. Consider seeing this church en route to Capitoline Hill.

Exterior

The facade looks ho-hum, like a thousand no-name Catholic churches scattered from Europe to Southern California...until you realize that this was the first, the model for the others. Its scroll-like shoulders were revolutionary, breaking up the rigid rectangles of Renaissance architecture and signaling the coming of Baroque. The travertine stone facade has been cleaned but—with its sponge-like properties and Rome's pollution—it will be black again soon enough.

The adjacent building, to the right of the church—called Camere of St. Ignatius—is where Ignatius of Loyola, the founder of the Jesuits, lived, worked, and died (Mon-Sat 16:00-18:00, Sun 10:00-12:00).

• *Step inside the Gesù Church, grab a seat, and look up at the huge painting on the ceiling (or take advantage of the neck-saving mirror).*

Interior

❶ Ceiling Fresco and Stucco—*The Triumph of the Name of Jesus* (Il Baciccio)

The church's sunroof opens, and we can see right up to heaven. A glowing cross with the initials "I.H.S." (from the Latinized Greek, "Jesus Savior of Mankind," adopted as the seal of the Society of Jesus) astounds the faithful and sends the infidels plunging downward. The twisted tangle of bodies—the damned—spill over the

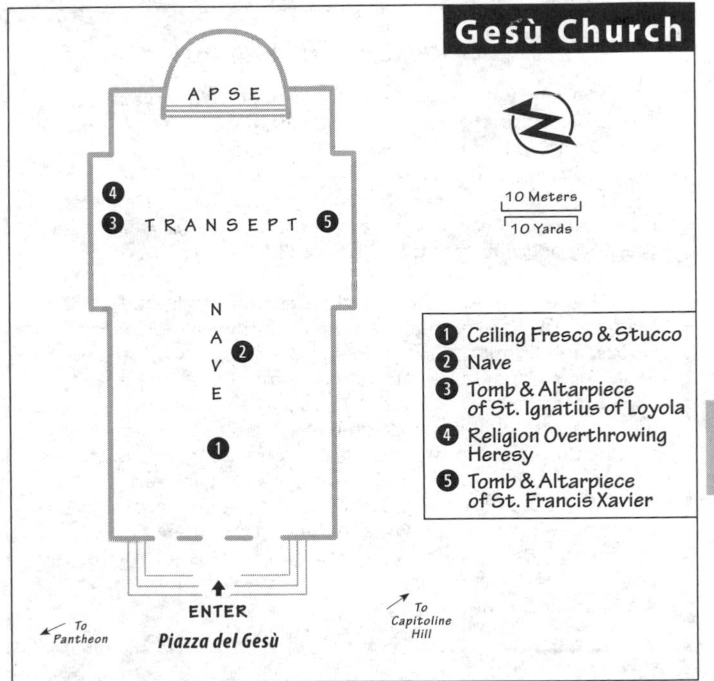

edge of the painting's frame on their way to hell. The painted bodies mingle with 3-D stucco bodies and a riot of decoration in a classic example of Baroque multimedia.

During the Counter-Reformation, when Catholics fought Protestants for the hearts and minds of the world's Christians, art was a powerful propaganda weapon. The moral here is clear—hell is the fate of Protestant heretics who dared to pervert the true teachings of Jesus.

❷ The Nave

When the church was originally built (1568), the walls were white and the decor was simple. It was designed for what the Jesuits did best—teaching. The Jesuits wanted to educate Catholics to prepare them for the onslaught of pesky, probing Protestant questions. The church's nave is like one big lecture hall, with no traditional side aisles.

In the 1500s, the best way to keep Protestants from stealing your church members was to reason with them. By the 1600s, it was easier to kill them, and so the Thirty Years' War raged across Europe. The church became crusted over with the colorful, bombastic, jingoistic Baroque we see today.

• *Now look toward the left transept.*

The Spectacle of Baroque

At 17:30 every day, a 20-minute service takes place at the Tomb of St. Ignatius in the Gesù Church (all are welcome). During this time, a statue of Ignatius, housed behind the altarpiece painting, is unveiled.

The service starts with recorded music—"Kyrie eleison" ("Lord, have mercy"). Then a recorded voice (in Italian) tells the story of Ignatius and his impact, illustrated by spotlighting different parts of the tomb.

The service is squarely in the Baroque tradition—a multimedia extravaganza that combines painting, sculpture, music, words, and lighting effects. (Don't expect Hollywood-quality SFX—this is "spectacle" on a small, semi-cheesy scale.)

The ceremony is meant to tap into the heart, not the head, encouraging an emotional response to the faith. As the service unfolds, look around the church at its glorious art and architecture. Don't reflect. Be awed, amazed, moved.

At 17:45, church attendants turn a crank, and the altarpiece painting slowly lowers, revealing the gleaming statue of Ignatius in his ta-da pose. After a few closing words, the choir finishes with "Gloria in excelsis Deo" ("Glory to God in the highest"). Amen.

❸ Tomb and Altarpiece of St. Ignatius of Loyola (left transept)

A big altarpiece with towering columns and topped with statues of the Trinity marks the burial spot of the humble war veteran who founded the Jesuit order.

In the center of this altarpiece, you'll see a painting (by Andrea Pozzo) of Ignatius receiving his call. Behind the painting rests a gleaming statue of the saint, who spreads his arms wide and gazes up, receiving a vision from on high. But you won't be able to see it unless you come at 17:30 (see sidebar).

Ignatius (1491-1556) was a Spanish soldier during the era of conquistadors. Then, at age 30, he was struck down by a cannonball. While convalescing, he was seized by the burning desire to change his life. He wandered Europe and traveled to Jerusalem. He meditated with monks. He lived in a cave. At 33, he enrolled in a school for boys to fill in the knowledge he'd missed. He studied in Paris and Rome. Finally, after almost two decades of learning and seeking, he found a way to combine his military training with his spiritual aspirations.

In 1540, the pope gave approval to Ignatius and his small band of followers—the Society of Jesus (Jesuits). These monks, organized like a military company, vowed complete obedience to their "General" and placed themselves at the service of the pope. Their mission: to be intellectual warriors doing battle with heretics. They were in the right place at the right time—Ignatius and Martin Luther were almost exact contemporaries.

Ignatius' body lies in the small coffin beneath the statue (near ground level). This simple, intense man might have been embarrassed by the lavish memorial to him, with its silver, gold, green marble, and lapis lazuli columns. Above the painting of Ignatius, a statue of God stands near a lapis lazuli globe (under the sunburst, the biggest in the world) and gestures as though to say, "Go and spread the Word to every land"...which the Jesuits tried to do.

• *Look at the marble statue group to the right of Ignatius.*

❹ Religion Overthrowing Heresy

This statue (and a similar one to the left of Ignatius) shows the Church as an angry nun hauling back with a whip and just spanking a bunch of miserable Protestants. The man with the serpent (Luther) is being stepped upon while the angry cherub rips pages out of a heretical book. Not too subtle.

The Jesuits earned a reputation for unfeeling dedication to truth above all else. Their weapons were words, ideas, and critical reasoning. They taught and defended the recently revamped doctrines of the Council of Trent (a reaction against—and a response to—the Reformation, 1545-1563).

• *Now view the right transept.*

❺ Tomb and Altarpiece of St. Francis Xavier

This was also the Age of Discovery, when Spain and Portugal were colonizing and Christianizing the world, using force if necessary. Francis Xavier joined a Portuguese expedition and headed out to convert the heathens. His right hand, with which he baptized and healed, is encased in a glass reliquary above his tomb. Francis touched down in Africa, India, Indonesia, China, and Japan. Along the way, he learned new languages and customs, trying to communicate a strange, monotheistic religion to puzzled polytheists.

The Jesuit Legacy

The Jesuits produced some great, open-minded thinkers, from the poet Gerard Manley Hopkins to modern mystic Pierre Teilhard de Chardin.

The great sculptor Bernini attended this church. He honored the Jesuit Robert Bellarmine (1542-1621) with a bust, which is sometimes on display in the Gesù Church. Bellarmine, a theologian at the height of Catholic-Protestant differences, was a voice of reason in the often bitter controversy. He's best known as the man who ordered Galileo to stop teaching the Copernican theory, though he was actually a moderating influence in the debate.

Because of their spiritual fervor, the Jesuits caught flack for being closed-minded. In the 1700s, several countries expelled them, and finally the pope even banned the Society (1773). Chastened, they were brought back (1814), and today they fill the staff of many a Catholic college.

He had been on the road for more than a decade (1552) when he died on an island off China (see the dim painting over the altar). Thanks largely to the tireless evangelizing of zealous Jesuits such as Francis, Catholicism became a truly worldwide religion.

Church of Santa Maria sopra Minerva

From the outside, survey the many layers of Rome: An Egyptian obelisk sits on a Baroque elephant (by Bernini) in front of a Gothic church built over *(sopra)* a pre-Christian, pagan Temple of Minerva.

Before stepping in, notice the high-water-mark plaques *(alluvione)* on the wall to the right of the door. Each time the Tiber River flooded, it left silt, which contributed to the slow and steady geological rise of Rome. Inside, you'll see that the lower parts of some frescoes were lost to floods. After the last great flood, in 1870, Rome built the present embankments along the river, finally breaking the spirit of the mighty Tiber.

Nave

This is the only Gothic church you'll see in Rome. The ceiling has pointed crisscross arches in a starry, luminous blue sky, and the nave is lit by rows of round stained-glass windows. When this Dominican church was built, Gothic was the rage in northern

Europe, with large windows to let in the light—though churches in Italy were so colorful there was less emphasis on colored glass. During the Middle Ages, Rome was almost a ghost town, and what little was built during this time was later gussied up in the Baroque style. The lack of Baroque excess in this church (in spite of its over-the-top, 19th-century renovation) is a refreshing exception.

Main Altar

The body of St. Catherine of Siena lies under the altar (her head is in Siena). In the 1300s, this Italian nun was renowned for her righteousness and her visions of a mystical marriage with Jesus. Her impassioned letters convinced the pope to return from France to Rome, thus saving Italy from untold chaos. Behind her, two Medici popes are buried: Leo X, the son of Lorenzo the Magnificent and the man who excommunicated Martin Luther, and his cousin Clement VII.

In 1634, a frail 70-year-old Galileo knelt at this altar on the way to his trial before the Inquisition in the church's monastery. Facing the fierce Dominican lawyers, he renounced his heretical belief that the earth moved around the sun. (Legend has it that as he walked out, he whispered, "But it *does* move.")

• *Left of the altar stands a little-known Michelangelo statue...*

Christ Bearing the Cross (1519-1520)

Note Jesus' athletic body, a striking contrast to the docile Jesus of medieval art. This sculpture shares the same bulging biceps as the Christ in Michelangelo's *The Last Judgment* in the Sistine Chapel. Christ's pose is slightly twisted, with one leg forward in typical *contrapposto* style, leaning on a large cross along with the symbols of the Crucifixion. Originally, Christ was buck naked, but later prudish Counter-Reformation censors gave him his bronze girdle.

This statue was Michelangelo's second attempt—he was forced to abandon a first effort due to a flaw in the block of Carrara marble. In this version, he left parts—including the face—to be finished by an apprentice, who took the liberty of working on and botching the feet and hands. This ineptitude led him to be replaced by yet another sculptor who finally finished the job. Michelangelo, disturbed that anyone would mess up his work, offered to redo the sculpture, but apparently the patrons were pleased. One contemporary said, "The knees alone are worth more than all of Rome together."

The tomb of the great early Renaissance painter (and Dominican brother) Fra Angelico ("Beato Angelico 1387-1455") is farther to the left, just up the three stairs.

Over in the right (south) transept, pop in a coin for light, and enjoy a Filippino Lippi fresco showing scenes of the life of the great Dominican scholar St. Thomas Aquinas (big man in blue and white). In the central scene, Thomas—seeming to interrupt the Annunciation—presents the chapel's patron to Mary. Above, circling an ascended Mary, is a frolicking carousel of heavenly musicians—notice the delightful instruments. Meanwhile, on the right wall, Thomas displays a book to show everyone the true dogma, causing a heretic to slump defeated at his feet.

• *Exit the church via its rear door (behind the Michelangelo statue), walk down tiny Fra Angelico lane, turn left, and walk to the next square. On your right, you'll find the last church on our tour.*

Church of San Ignazio

This church is a riot of Baroque illusions. Find a seat in the nave and look up at the large colorful ceiling fresco. ❶ St. Ignatius, whom we met in the Gesù Church, was the founder of the Jesuits, a disciplined Catholic teaching order charged with spreading the word of God around a world that was rapidly being "discovered." Here you see him (a small figure perched on a cloud in the center) having a ❷ vision of Christ with the Cross. Heavenly light from the vision bounces off his chest, and the rays beam to the four corners of the earth (including ❸ America, to the left, depicted as a bare-breasted Native American maiden spearing naked men). This fresco epitomizes pure Baroque drama, with perspective illusions that fool the eye into thinking the fresco is an extension of the church architecture. Note how the actual columns of the church are extended into the two-dimensional fresco. Now fix your eyes on the ❹ arch at the far

end of the painting. Walk up the nave, and watch the arch grow and tower over you.

Before you reach the center of the church, stop at the small yellow disc (near the last row of pews) on the floor, and look up into the central (black) dome. Keeping your eye on the dome, walk under and past it. Building project runs out of money? Hire an artist to paint a fake, flat dome.

Now take a moment to survey the art in general, appreciating the tricks of the trade. For example, in the right transept, you can drop in on an explosive scene. The curtain is pulled back for the theatrical tomb of Pope Gregory XV—textbook bombastic Baroque. With trumpet fanfare and the stony curtain flapping in the spiritual wind, the pope springs with jubilation into eternal life.

Back outside, the church faces a headquarters of the Carabinieri police force (this station deals with art theft—a major problem in a country with so much to protect), forming Piazza San Ignazio, a square with several converging streets that has been compared to a stage set. Sit on the church steps, admire the theatrical yellow backdrop, and watch the "actors" enter one way and exit another, in the human opera that is modern Rome.

• *From here it's a short walk to the left down Via del Seminario back to the Pantheon. Or go right, cross busy Via del Corso, and follow the crowds to the Trevi Fountain.*

ST. PETER'S BASILICA TOUR

Basilica San Pietro

St. Peter's is the greatest church in Christendom. It represents the power and splendor of Rome's 2,000-year domination of the Western world. Built on the memory and grave of the first pope, St. Peter, this is where the grandeur of ancient Rome became the grandeur of Christianity.

Orientation

Cost: Free entry to basilica and crypt. Dome climb-€6 if you take the stairs all the way up, or €7 to ride an elevator partway (to the roof), then climb to the top of the dome (for details, see "Dome Climb," later). Museum-Treasury-€6.

Hours: The **church** is open daily April-Sept 7:00-19:00, Oct-March 7:00-18:00. It closes on Wednesday mornings during papal audiences.

Mass is held daily, generally in Italian and in the south (left) transept, though other possible locations are the apse and the Blessed Sacrament Chapel (on right side of nave). Mass is typically scheduled on Mon-Sat at 8:30, 9:00, 10:00, 11:00, 12:00, and 17:00 (in Latin, in the apse); and on Sun and holidays at 9:00, 10:30 (in Latin), 11:30, 12:15, 13:00, 16:00, and 17:45. Confirm the schedule and location on site, or go to www.vatican.va (click on "Basilicas and Papal Chapels" link).

The **Museum-Treasury** is open daily April-Sept 9:00-18:15, Oct-March 9:00-17:15. The **crypt** is open daily 9:00-16:00. The **dome** is open to climbers daily April-Sept 8:00-18:00, Oct-March 8:00-17:00, last entry 30 minutes before closing.

When to Go: The best time to visit the church is early (before 10:00) or late; at 17:00, when the church is fairly empty, sunbeams can work their magic, and the late-afternoon Mass fills the place with spiritual music. The downside to visiting late is that the area around the altar and beyond is often roped off from around 16:00 to prepare for Mass. Still, the shorter line, smaller crowds, and ambience might make it worthwhile.

Avoiding Lines: The security-checkpoint lines can get quite long and there's no reliable way to avoid them (thankfully, they move relatively quickly). Occasionally, St. Peter's is accessible from the Vatican Museum (though the museum comes with its own long lines, which can be avoided if you reserve your entry time). If you visit the Vatican Museum first, pray that the shortcut from the Sistine Chapel directly to St. Peter's is open (depends on crowd levels—see page 209 for specifics).

Dress Code: No shorts, above-the-knee skirts, or bare shoulders (this applies to men, women, and children). Attendants strictly enforce this dress code, even in hot weather. Carry a cover-up, if necessary.

Getting There: Take the Metro to Ottaviano, then walk 10 minutes south on Via Ottaviano. There are several good bus options: The #40 express bus drops off at Piazza Pio, next to Castel Sant'Angelo—a 10-minute walk to St. Peter's. The more crowded bus #64 is convenient for pickpockets and stops just outside St. Peter's Square to the south (get off the bus after it crosses the Tiber, at the first stop past the tunnel; backtrack toward the tunnel and turn left when you see the rows of columns). Bus #492 heads through the center of town, stopping at Largo Argentina, and gets you near Piazza Risorgimento (get off when you see the Vatican walls). A taxi from Termini train station to St. Peter's costs about €11.

Information: The TI on the left (south) side of the square is excellent (Mon-Sat 8:30-18:15, closed Sun, free Vatican and church map). Tel. 06-6988-1662, www.saintpetersbasilica.org (detailed map available online).

Tours: The Vatican TI conducts free 1.5-hour tours of **St. Peter's** (depart from TI Mon-Fri 14:15, plus Tue and Thu 9:45, confirm schedule at TI, tel. 06-6988-1662). Audioguides can be rented near the checkroom (€5 plus ID, for church only, daily 9:00-17:00). Or you can download this chapter as a free Rick Steves audio tour (see page 27).

To see St. Peter's original grave, you can take a **Scavi "Excavations"** tour into the Necropolis (€12, 1.5 hours, ages 15 and older only, no photos). Book at least two months in advance by phone (tel. 06-6988-5318), email (scavi@fsp.va), or fax (06-6987-3017), following the detailed instructions at www.vatican.va (search on "Excavations Office"); no response means they're booked up.

Vatican City

This tiny independent country of little more than 100 acres, contained entirely within Rome, has its own postal system, armed guards, helipad, mini-train station, and radio station (KPOP). It also has two huge sights: St. Peter's Basilica (with Michelangelo's *Pietà*) and the Vatican Museum (with the Sistine Chapel). Politically powerful, the Vatican is the religious capital of 1.1 billion Roman Catholics. If you're not a Catholic, become one for your visit.

The pope is both the religious and secular leader of Vatican City. For centuries, locals referred to him as "King Pope." Italy and the Vatican didn't always have good relations. In fact, after unification (in 1870), when Rome's modern grid plan was built around the miniscule Vatican, it seemed as if the new buildings were designed to be just high enough so no one could see the dome of St. Peter's from street level. Modern Italy was created in 1870, but the Holy See didn't recognize it as a country until 1929, when the pope and Mussolini signed the Lateran Pact, giving sovereignty and a few nearby churches to the Vatican.

Like every European country, Vatican City has its own versions of the euro coin (with a portrait of Pope Benedict XVI and, before him, of Pope John Paul II). You're unlikely to find one in your pocket, though, as they are snatched up by collectors before falling into circulation.

Post Offices: The Vatican postal service is famous for its stamps, which you can get from offices on St. Peter's Square (next to TI or between the columns just before the security checkpoint) or in the Vatican Museum (Mon-Sat 8:30-18:30, closed Sun). Vatican stamps are good throughout Rome, but to use the Vatican's mail service, you need to mail your cards from the Vatican; write your postcards ahead of time. (Note that the Vatican won't mail cards with Italian stamps.)

Seeing the Pope: Your best chances for a sighting are on Sunday or Wednesday. The pope usually gives a blessing at noon on Sunday from his apartment on St. Peter's Square (except in July and August, when he speaks at his summer residence at

Dome Climb (Cupola): You can take the elevator or stairs to the roof (231 steps), then climb another 323 steps to the top of the dome. The entry to the elevator is just outside the basilica on the north side of St. Peter's (near the secret exit from the Sistine Chapel). Look for signs to the cupola. For more on the dome, see the end of this chapter.

Vatican Gardens: If you want to walk through the Vatican Gardens, you must book a tour online at least two days in advance at http://biglietteriamusei.vatican.va. No response means they're booked up (€31, 2 hours, usually daily except

Castel Gandolfo, 25 miles from Rome, reachable by train from Rome's Termini train station). St. Peter's is easiest (just show up) and, for most, enough of a "visit." Those interested in a more formal appearance (though not more intimate) can get a ticket for the Wednesday general audience (at 10:30) when the pope, arriving in his Popemobile, greets and blesses the crowds at St. Peter's from a canopied platform on the square (except in winter, when he speaks at 10:30 in the 7,000-seat Paulo VI Auditorium, next to St. Peter's Basilica). If you only want to see St. Peter's but not the pope—avoid these times (the basilica closes during papal audiences and crowds are substantial).

For the Wednesday audience, while anyone can observe from a distance, you need a (free) ticket to get close to the papal action (and get a seat). To find out the pope's schedule and request a ticket, see www.vatican.va (click on the "Prefecture of the Papal Household" link) or call 06-6988-3114.

The American Catholic Church in Rome, Santa Susanna, lets you order tickets online (free, no booking fee but donations appreciated) for the Wednesday general audience. Pick up your reserved tickets, or check for last-minute availability, at the church the Tuesday before the audience between 17:00 and 18:45 (consider staying for the 18:00 English Mass) or Wednesday morning between 7:00 and 8:30 (Via XX Settembre 15, near recommended Via Firenze hotels, Metro: Repubblica, tel. 06-4201-4554—charming Rosanna speaks English, details at www.santasusanna.org).

Probably less convenient—unless you're already at the basilica—is getting a ticket at St. Peter's Square from the Vatican guards at their station at the bronze doors (open Tue 12:00-19:30; last-minute tickets may be available Wed morning—just join the line). It's under the "elbow" of Bernini's colonnade, on the right side of the square as you face the basilica (#6 on the map on page 189).

While many visitors come hoping for a more intimate audience, private audiences ended with the death of Pope John Paul II. Pope Benedict doesn't do them.

Wed and Sun, includes entry to Vatican Museum; tours start at 9:30 or 10:00 at Vatican Museum tour desk). Roma Cristiana's open-bus tours of the gardens can usually be booked on short notice (€15, 1 hour, 2/hour Mon-Tue and Thu-Sat 8:00-13:00, best to reserve a couple days in advance but same-day availability possible, Opera Romana Pellegrinaggi office in front of St. Peter's Square, Piazza Pio XII 9, tel. 06-6989-6380 or 06-698-961).

Length of This Tour: Allow one hour, plus another hour if you climb the dome (or a half-hour to the roof).

With Limited Time: Stroll the nave, glance up at the dome and down at the marker of St. Peter's tomb. Don't miss the *Pietà*. Skip the crypt and the dome climb.

Baggage Check: The free bag check (mandatory for bags larger than a purse or daypack) is outside the basilica (to the right as you face the entrance) and just inside the security checkpoint.

Services: WCs are to the right and left on St. Peter's Square (just outside the security checkpoint and exit), near baggage storage down the steps on the right side of the entrance, and on the roof. **Drinking fountains** are at the obelisk and near WCs. **Post offices** are next to the TI and just outside the security checkpoint (you can buy stamps and postcards and drop them into a postbox).

Starring: Michelangelo, Bernini, St. Peter, a heavenly host...and, occasionally, the pope.

Background

Nearly 2,000 years ago, St. Peter's oval-shaped "square" was the site of Nero's Circus—a huge, cigar-shaped Roman chariot racecourse. The Romans had no marching bands, so for halftime entertainment they killed Christians. This persecuted minority was forced to fight wild animals and gladiators, or they were simply crucified. Some were tarred up, tied to posts, and burned—human torches to light up the evening races.

One of those killed here, in about A.D. 65, was Peter, Jesus' right-hand man, who had come to Rome to spread the message of love. At his own request, Peter was crucified upside down, because he felt unworthy to die as his master had. His remains were buried in a cemetery located where the main altar in St. Peter's is today. For 250 years, these relics were quietly and secretly revered.

Peter had been recognized as the first "pope," or bishop of Rome, from whom all later popes claimed their authority as head of the Church. When Christianity was finally legalized in 313, the Christian emperor Constantine built a church on the site of Peter's martyrdom. "Old St. Peter's" lasted 1,200 years (A.D. 329-1500).

By the time of the Renaissance, Old St. Peter's was falling apart and was considered unfit to be the center of the Western Church. The new, larger church we see today was begun in 1506 by the architect Bramante. He was succeeded by Michelangelo and a number of other architects, each with his own designs. Later, Carlo Maderno took Michelangelo's Greek cross-shaped church and lengthened it, adding a long nave. As the construction proceeded, the new church rose around the old one (see diagram on opposite page). The project was finally finished 120 years later, and Old St. Peter's was dismantled and carried out of the new church. (A few

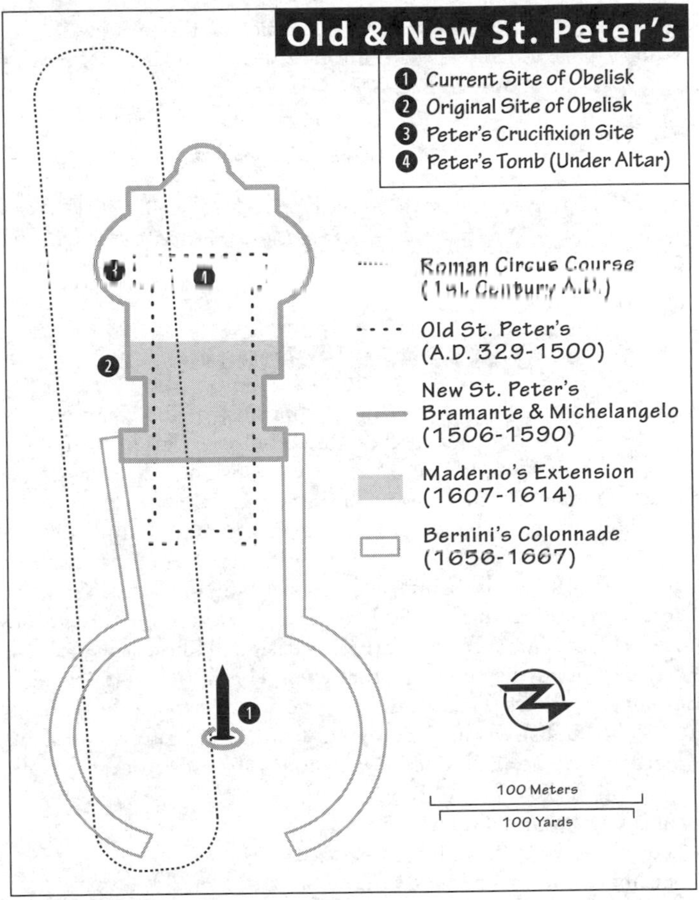

Old & New St. Peter's

1. Current Site of Obelisk
2. Original Site of Obelisk
3. Peter's Crucifixion Site
4. Peter's Tomb (Under Altar)

Roman Circus Course (1st Century A.D.)

Old St. Peter's (A.D. 329-1500)

New St. Peter's Bramante & Michelangelo (1506-1590)

Maderno's Extension (1607-1614)

Bernini's Colonnade (1656-1667)

100 Meters

100 Yards

bits survive from the first church: the central door, some columns in the atrium, eight spiral columns around the tomb from the Jerusalem Temple, the venerated statue of Peter, and Michelangelo's *Pietà*.)

Michelangelo designed the magnificent dome. Unfortunately, although it soars above St. Peter's, it's barely visible from the center of the square because of Maderno's extended nave. To see the entire dome, you'll need to step outside the open end of the square, where in the 1930s Benito Mussolini opened up the broad boulevard, finally letting people see the dome that had been hidden for centuries by the facade. Though I don't make a habit of thanking fascist dictators, in this case I'll make an exception: *"Grazie, Benito."*

The Tour Begins

• *Ideally, you should head out to the obelisk at the center of the square and read this. But let me guess—it's 95 degrees outside, right? OK, find a shady spot under one of these stone sequoias. If the pigeons have left a clean spot, sit on it.*

St. Peter's Square

St. Peter's Square, with its ring of columns, symbolizes the arms of the church welcoming everyone—believers and non-believers—with its motherly embrace. It was designed a century after Michelangelo by the Baroque architect Gian Lorenzo Bernini, who did much of the work that we'll see inside. Numbers first: 284 columns, 56 feet high, in stern Doric style. Topping them are Bernini's 140 favorite saints, each 10 feet tall. The "square" itself is actually elliptical, 660 by 500 feet (roughly the same dimensions as the Colosseum). Though large, it's designed like a saucer, a little higher around the edges, so that even when full of crowds (as it often is), it allows those on the periphery to see above the throngs.

The **obelisk** in the center is 90 feet of solid granite weighing more than 300 tons. It once stood about 100 yards from its current location, in the center of the circus course (to the left of where St. Peter's is today). Think for a second about how much history this monument has seen. Originally erected in Egypt more than 2,000 years ago, it witnessed the fall of the pharaohs to the Greeks and then to the Romans. Then the emperor Caligula moved it to imperial Rome, where it stood impassively watching the slaughter of Christians at the racecourse and the torture of Protestants by the Inquisition (in the yellow-and-rust building just outside the square, to the left of the church). Today, it watches over the church, a reminder that each civilization builds on the previous ones. The puny cross on top reminds us that Christian culture has cast but a thin veneer over our pagan origins.

• *Now venture out across the burning desert to the obelisk, which provides a narrow sliver of shade.*

As you face the church, the gray building to the right at two

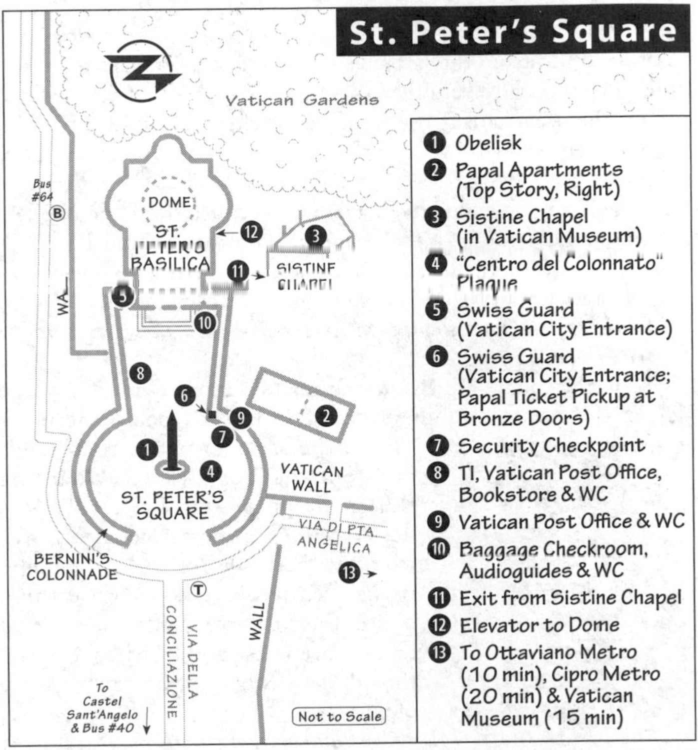
St. Peter's Square
Vatican Gardens
Bus #64
B
DOME
ST.
BASILICA
12
3
11
5
10
WALL
8
6
9
2
7
1
4
VATICAN WALL
ST. PETER'S SQUARE
VIA DI PTA. ANGELICA
13
BERNINI'S COLONNADE
T
WALL
VIA DELLA CONCILIAZIONE
To Castel Sant'Angelo & Bus #40
Not to Scale
1 Obelisk
2 Papal Apartments (Top Story, Right)
3 Sistine Chapel (in Vatican Museum)
4 "Centro del Colonnato" Plaque
5 Swiss Guard (Vatican City Entrance)
6 Swiss Guard (Vatican City Entrance; Papal Ticket Pickup at Bronze Doors)
7 Security Checkpoint
8 TI, Vatican Post Office, Bookstore & WC
9 Vatican Post Office & WC
10 Baggage Checkroom, Audioguides & WC
11 Exit from Sistine Chapel
12 Elevator to Dome
13 To Ottaviano Metro (10 min), Cipro Metro (20 min) & Vatican Museum (15 min)

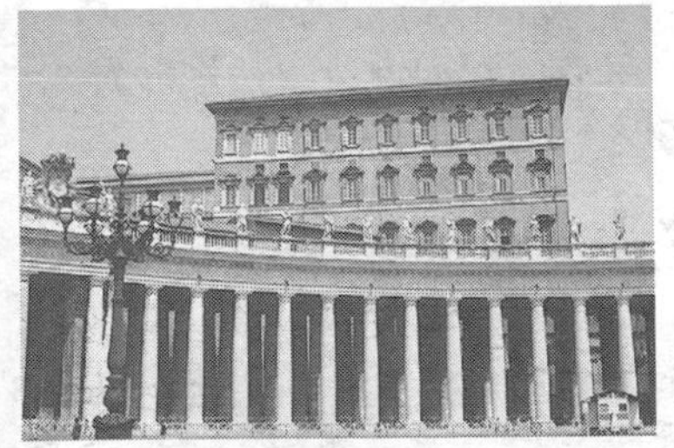

o'clock, rising up behind Bernini's colonnade, is the **pope's abode.** The last window on the right of the top floor is his bedroom. To the left of that window is his study window, where he appears occasionally to greet the masses. If you come to the square at night as a Poping Tom, you might see the light on—the pope burns much midnight oil.

On more formal occasions (which you may have seen on TV), the pope appears from the church itself, on the small balcony above the central door.

The Sistine Chapel is just to the right of the facade—the small gray-brown building with the triangular roof,

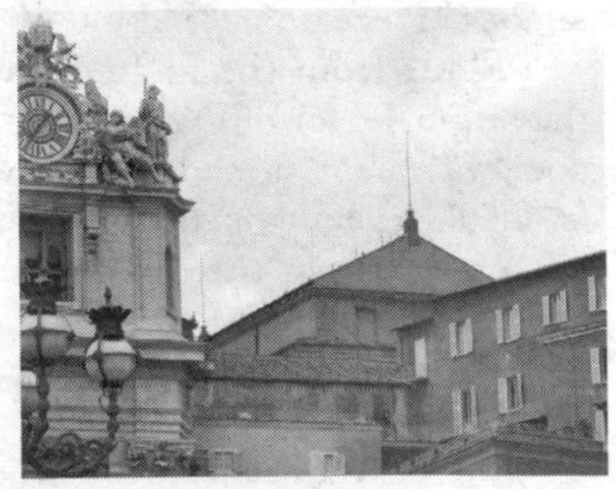

topped by an antenna. The tiny chimney—the pimple along the roofline midway up the left side—is where the famous smoke signals announce the election of each new pope (an extension is added on for the occasion). If the smoke is black, a two-thirds majority hasn't been reached. White smoke means a new pope has been selected.

Walk to the right, five pavement plaques from the obelisk, to one marked *Centro del Colonnato*. From here, all of Bernini's columns on the right side line up. The curved Baroque square still pays its respects to Renaissance mathematical symmetry.

• *Climb the gradually sloping pavement past crowd barriers and the security checkpoint.*

On the square are two entrances to Vatican City: one to the left of the facade, and one to the right in the crook of Bernini's "arm" (the same entrance that hands out pope-viewing tickets). Guarding this small but powerful country's border crossing are the mercenary guards from Switzerland. You have to wonder if they really know how to use those pikes. Their colorful uniforms are said to have been designed by Michelangelo, though he was not known for his sense of humor.

• *Continue up, passing the huge statues of St. Paul (with his two-edged sword) and St. Peter (with his bushy hair and keys). Along the way, you'll pass by the dress-code enforcers and a gaggle of ticked-off tourists in shorts. Enter the atrium (entrance hall) of the church.*

The Basilica

The Atrium

The atrium is itself bigger than most churches. The huge white columns on the portico date from the first church (fourth century). Five famous bronze doors lead into the church.

Made from the melted-down bronze of the original door of Old St. Peter's, the central door was the first Renaissance work in Rome (c. 1450). It's only opened on special occasions. The panels (from the top down) feature Jesus and Mary, Paul and Peter, and (at the bottom) how each was martyred: Paul decapitated, Peter crucified upside down.

The far-right entrance is the **Holy Door,**

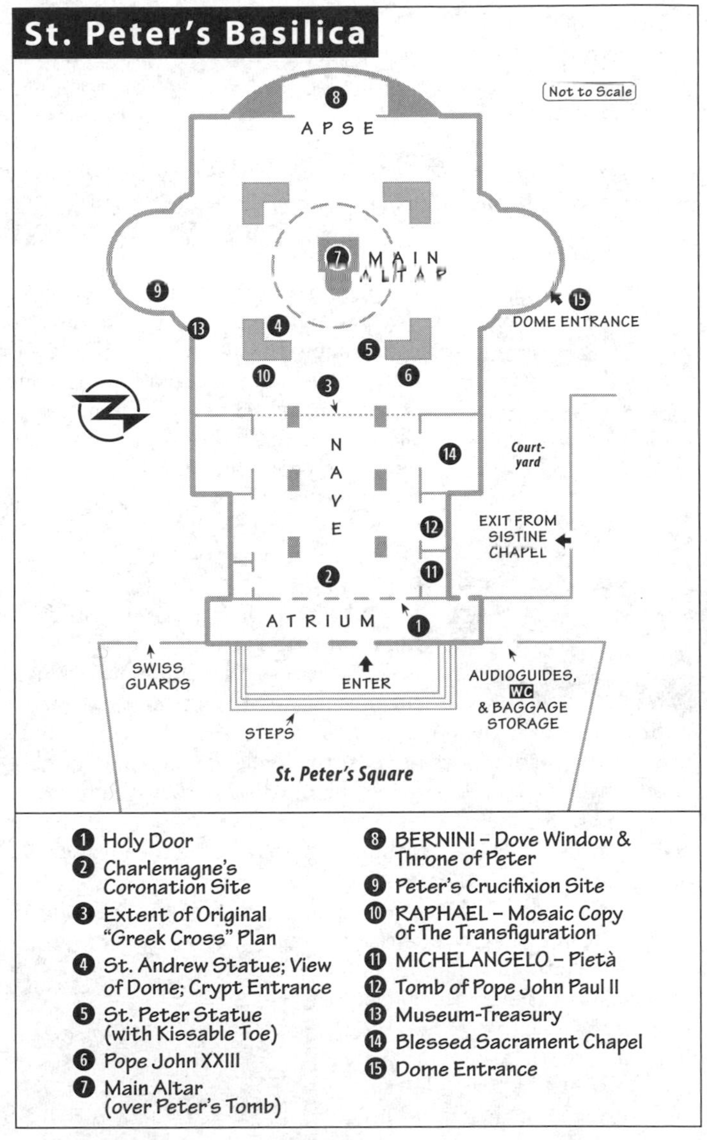

opened only during Holy Years. On Christmas Eve every 25 years, the pope knocks three times with a silver hammer and the door opens, welcoming pilgrims to pass through. After Pope John Paul II opened the door on Christmas Eve, 1999, he bricked it up again with a ceremonial trowel a year later to wait another 24 years. (A plaque above the door fudges a bit for effect: It says that Pope "IOANNES PAULUS II" opened the door in the year

"MM"—2000—and closed it in "MMI.") On the door itself, note the crucified Jesus and his shiny knees, polished by pious pilgrims who touch them for a blessing.

• *Now for one of Europe's great "wow" experiences. Enter the church. Gape for a while. But don't gape at Michelangelo's famous* Pietà *(on the right). I'll cover it later on the tour. I'll wait for you at the round maroon pavement stone on the floor near the central doorway.*

The Church

This church is appropriately huge. Size before beauty: The golden window at the far end is two football fields away. The dove in the window has the wingspan of a 747 (OK, maybe not quite, but it *is* big). The church covers six acres. The babies at the base of the pillars along the main hall (the nave) are adult-size. The lettering in the gold band along the top of the pillars is seven feet high. Really. The church has a capacity of 60,000 standing worshippers (or 1,200 tour groups).

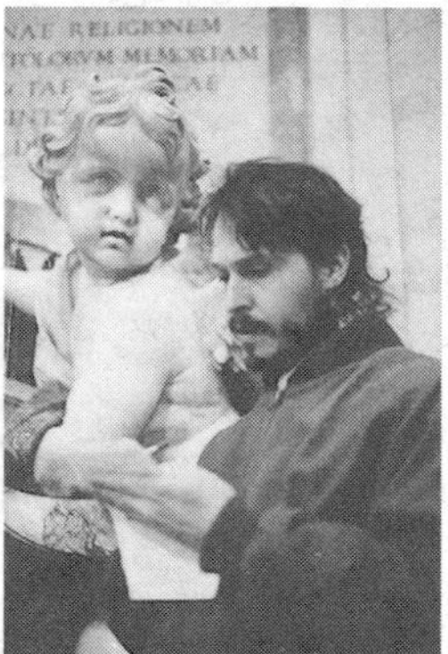

The church is huge and it feels huge, but everything is designed to make it seem smaller and more intimate than it really is. For example, the statue of St. Teresa near the bottom of the first pillar on the right is 15 feet tall. The statue above her near the top looks the same size, but is actually six feet taller, giving the impression that it's not so far away. Similarly, the fancy bronze canopy over the altar at the far end is as tall as a seven-story building. That makes the great height of the dome seem smaller.

Looking down the nave, we get a sense of the splendor of ancient Rome that was carried on by the Catholic Church. The floor plan is based on the ancient Roman basilica, or law-court building, with a central aisle (nave) flanked by two side aisles. In fact, many of the stones used to build St. Peter's were scavenged from the ruined law courts of ancient Rome.

On the floor near the central doorway is a round slab of **porphyry stone** in the maroon color of ancient Roman officials. This is the spot where, on Christmas night in A.D. 800, the French king Charlemagne was crowned Holy Roman Emperor. Even in the Dark Ages, when Rome was virtually abandoned and visitors

From Pope to Pope

When a pope dies, the tiny, peaceful Vatican stirs from its timeless slumber and becomes headline news. Millions of people converge on Vatican City, and hundreds of millions around the world watch anxiously on TV.

The deceased pope's body is displayed in state in front of the main altar in St. Peter's Basilica. Thousands of pilgrims line up down Via della Conciliazione, waiting for one last look at their pope. On the day of the funeral, hundreds of thousands of mourners, dignitaries, and security personnel gather in St. Peter's Square. The pope's coffin is carried out to the square, where a eulogy is given.

Most popes are laid to rest in the crypt below St. Peter's Basilica, near the tomb of St. Peter and among shrines to many other popes. Especially popular popes—such as John Paul II or John XXIII—may eventually find a place upstairs, inside St. Peter's itself.

While the previous pope is being laid to rest, cardinals representing Catholics around the globe descend on Rome to elect a new pope. Once they've assembled, the 100-plus cardinals, dressed in crimson, are stripped of their mobile phones, given a vow of secrecy, and locked inside the Sistine Chapel. This begins the "conclave" (from Latin *cum clave,* with key). As they cast votes with paper ballots, the used ballots are burned in a stove temporarily set up inside the Sistine Chapel. The smoke rises up and out the tiny chimney, visible from St. Peter's Square. Black smoke means they haven't yet agreed on a new pope.

Finally, the anxious crowd in St. Peter's Square looks up to see a puff of white smoke emerging from the Sistine Chapel. The bells in St. Peter's clock towers ring out gloriously (a new tradition) confirming that, indeed, a pope has been elected. The crowd erupts in cheers, and Romans watching on their TVs hail taxis to hurry to the square.

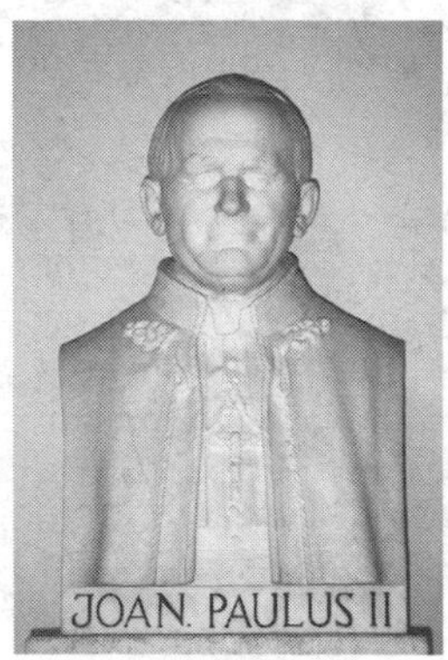

On the balcony of St. Peter's facade, the newly-elected pope steps up and raises his hands, as thousands chant *"Viva il Papa."* A cardinal introduces him to the crowd, announcing his newly-chosen name. "Brothers and sisters," the cardinal says in several languages, *"Habemus Papam."* "We have a pope."

ST. PETER'S BASILICA

reported that the city had more thieves and wolves than decent people, its imperial legacy made it a fitting place to symbolically establish a briefly united Europe.

St. Peter's was very expensive to build and decorate. The popes financed it by selling "indulgences," allowing the rich to buy forgiveness for their sins from the Church. This kind of corruption inspired an obscure German monk named Martin Luther to rebel and start the Protestant Reformation.

The ornate, Baroque-style interior decoration—a riot of marble, gold, stucco, mosaics, columns of stone, and pillars of light—was part of the Church's "Counter" Reformation. Baroque art and architecture served as cheery propaganda, impressing followers with the authority of the Church and giving them a glimpse of the heaven that awaited the faithful.

• *Now, walk straight up the center of the nave toward the altar.*

"Michelangelo's Church"—The Greek Cross

The plaques on the floor show where other, smaller churches of the world would end if they were placed inside St. Peter's: St. Paul's Cathedral in London (Londinense), Florence's Duomo, and so on.

You'll also walk over circular golden grates. Stop at the second one (at the third pillar from the entrance). Look back at the entrance and realize that if Michelangelo had had his way, this whole long section of the church wouldn't exist. The nave was extended after his death.

Michelangelo was 71 years old when the pope persuaded him to take over the church project and cap it with a dome. He agreed, intending to put the dome over Donato Bramante's original "Greek Cross" floor plan, with four equal arms. In optimistic Renaissance times, this symmetrical arrangement symbolized perfection—the orderliness of the created world and the goodness of man (who was created in God's image). But Michelangelo was a Renaissance Man in Counter-Reformation times. The Church, struggling against Protestants and its own corruption, opted for a plan designed to impress the world with its grandeur—the Latin cross of the Crucifixion, with its nave extended to accommodate the grand religious spectacles of the Baroque period.

• *Continue toward the altar, entering "Michelangelo's Church." Park yourself in front of the statue of St. Andrew to the left of the altar, the guy holding an X-shaped cross. Like Andrew, gaze up into the dome,*

and also like him, gasp. (Never stifle a gasp.)

Note: The entrance to the crypt is usually down the stairs beside the statue of St. Andrew. Save the crypt for later, though, as it exits outside the basilica (see the end of this tour for more details).

The Dome

The dome soars higher than a football field on end, 448 feet from the floor of the cathedral to the top of the lantern. It glows with light from its windows, the blue and gold mosaics creating a cool, solemn atmosphere. In this majestic vision of heaven (not painted by Michelangelo), we see (above the windows) Jesus, Mary, and a ring of saints, more rings of angels above them, and, way up in the ozone, God the Father (a blur of blue and red, unless you have binoculars).

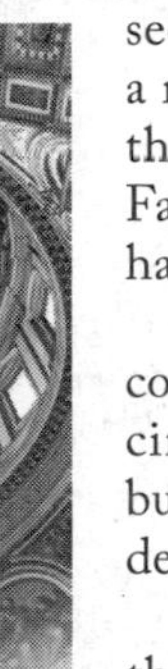

When Michelangelo died (1564), he'd completed only the drum of the dome—the circular base up as far as the windows—but the next architects were guided by his designs.

Listen to the hum of visitors echoing through St. Peter's and reflect on our place in the cosmos: half animal, half angel, stretched between heaven and earth, born to live only a short while, a bubble of foam on a great cresting wave of humanity.

• *But I digress.*

Peter's Remains

The base of the dome is ringed with a gold banner telling us in massive blue letters why this church is so important. According to Catholics, Peter was selected by Jesus to head the church. The banner in Latin quotes from the Bible where Jesus says to him, "You are Peter *(Tu es Petrus)* and upon this rock I will build my church, and to you I will give the keys of the kingdom of heaven" (Matthew 16:18). (Every quote from Jesus to Peter found in the Bible is written out in seven-foot-tall

Peter, the "Fisher of Men"

According to the Bible, Peter was a fisherman who was chosen by Christ to catch sinners instead. This "fisher of men" had human weaknesses that have endeared him to Christians. He was the disciple who tried to walk on water—but failed. In another incident, he impetuously cut off a man's ear when soldiers came to arrest Jesus. And he even denied knowing Christ, to save his own skin. But Jesus chose him anyway and gave him his nickname—Rock (in Latin: *Petrus*).

Legends say that Peter came to the wicked city of Rome after Jesus' death to spread the gospel of love. He may have been imprisoned in the Mamertine Prison near the Roman Forum (see page 49), and other stories claim he had a vision of Christ along the Appian Way (see page 310). Eventually, Peter's preaching offended the Nero administration. Christ's fisherman was arrested, crucified upside down, and buried here, where St. Peter's now stands.

letters that continue around the entire church.)

Peter was the first bishop of Rome. His prestige and that of the city itself made this bishopric more illustrious than all others, and Peter's authority has supposedly passed in an unbroken chain to each succeeding bishop of Rome—that is, the 250-odd popes that followed.

Under the dome, under the bronze canopy, under the altar, some 23 feet under the marble floor, rest the bones of St. Peter, the "rock" upon which this particular church was built. You can't see the tomb, but go to the railing and look down into the small, lighted niche below the altar with a box containing bishops' shawls—a symbol of how Peter's authority spread to the other churches. Peter's tomb (not visible) is just below this box.

Are they really the bones of Jesus' apostle? According to a papal pronouncement: definitely maybe. The traditional site of his tomb was sealed up when Old St. Peter's was built on it in A.D. 326, and it remained sealed until 1940, when it was opened for archaeological study. Bones were found, dated from the first century, of a robust man who died in old age. His body was wrapped in expensive cloth. A third-century tag artist had graffitied a wall near the tomb with "Peter is here," indicating that early visitors thought this was Peter's tomb. Does that mean it's really Peter? Who am I to disagree with the pope? Definitely maybe.

If you line up the cross on the altar with the dove in the window, you'll notice that the niche below the cross is just off-center compared with the rest of the church. Why? Because Michelangelo built the church around the traditional location of the tomb, not the actual location—about two feet away—discovered by modern archaeology.

Back in the nave sits a bronze **statue of Peter** under a canopy. This is one of a handful of pieces of art that were in the earlier church. In one hand he holds the keys, the symbol of the authority given him by Christ, while with the other hand he blesses us. He's wearing the toga of a Roman senator. It may be that the original statue was of a senator and that the bushy head and keys were added later to make it Peter. His big right toe has been worn smooth by the lips of pilgrims and foot-fetishists. Stand in line and kiss it, or, to avoid foot-and-mouth disease, touch your hand to your lips, then rub the toe. This is simply an act of reverence with no legend attached, though you can make one up if you like.

• *Circle to the right around the statue of Peter to find another popular stop among pilgrims: the lighted glass niche with the red-robed body of...*

Pope John XXIII

Pope John XXIII, whose papacy lasted from 1958 to 1963, is nicknamed "the good pope." He is best known for initiating the landmark Vatican II Council (1962-1965) that instituted major reforms, bringing the Church into the modern age. The Council allowed Mass to be conducted in the vernacular rather than in Latin. Lay people were invited to participate more in services, Church leadership underwent some healthy self-criticism, and a spirit of ecumenism flourished. Pope John was a populist, referring to people as "brothers and sisters"...a phrase popular today among popes. In 2000, during the beatification process (a stop on the way to sainthood), Church authorities checked his body, and it was surprisingly fresh. So they moved it upstairs, put it behind glass, and now old Catholics who remember him fondly enjoy another stop on their St. Peter's visit.

We'll visit the tomb of another beloved pope—the recently beatified John Paul II—near the end of this tour.

The Main Altar

The main altar beneath the dome and canopy (the white marble slab with cross and candlesticks) is used only when the pope himself says Mass. He sometimes conducts the Sunday morning service when he's in town, a sight worth seeing. I must admit, though, it's a little strange being frisked for weapons at the door to the

Benedict XVI

When Josef Ratzinger became the 265th pope, he introduced himself as "a simple, humble worker in the vineyard of the Lord." But the man has a complex history, a reputation for intellectual brilliance, a flair for the piano, and a penchant for controversy for his unbending devotion to traditional Catholic doctrine.

Born in small-town Bavaria in 1927, he lived under Nazi rule as many Germans did—outwardly obeying leaders while inwardly conflicted. Like all 14-year-old boys, he joined the Hitler Youth and, like most German men, was drafted into the army. During World War II, he trained to spray flak from anti-aircraft guns, saw Jews transported to death camps, and, like many Germans in the final days of the war, deserted his post.

After the war, he completed his studies in theology and became a rising voice of liberal Catholicism, serving as an advisor at the Second Vatican Council (1962-1965). But after the May 1968 student revolts rocked Europe's Establishment, he became increasingly convinced that Church tradition was needed to offset the growing chaos of the world.

holiest place in Christendom.

The tiny altar would be lost in this enormous church if it weren't for Gian Lorenzo Bernini's seven-story bronze canopy (God's "four-poster bed"), which "extends" the altar upward and reduces the perceived distance between floor and ceiling. The corkscrew columns echo the marble ones that surrounded the altar/tomb in Old St. Peter's. Some of the bronze used here was taken and melted down from the ancient Pantheon. On the marble base of the columns are three bees on a shield, the symbol of the Barberini family, who commissioned the work and ordered the raid on the Pantheon. As the saying went, "What the barbarians didn't do, the Barberini did."

Starting from the column to the left of the altar, walk clockwise around the canopy. Notice the female faces on the marble

Pope John Paul II appointed him to several positions, and Ratzinger became the pope's closest advisor and good friend. Every Friday afternoon for two decades, they met for lunch, intellectual sparring, and friendly conversation.

Under John Paul II, Ratzinger served as the "enforcer" of Church doctrine, earning the nickname "God's Rottweiler." He spoke out against ordaining women, chastised Latin American priests for fomenting class warfare (Liberation theology), reassigned bishops who were soft on homosexuality, reaffirmed opposition to birth control, and wrote thoughtful papers challenging the secular world's moral relativism. He also punished pedophile priests, though critics charged him with being too focused on preserving the Church's image. In 2010, he was again criticized, now as pope, for not dealing forcefully enough with sex abusers.

Ratzinger chose the name of "Benedict" to recall both Pope Benedict XV (who tried to bring Europeans together after World War I) and the original St. Benedict (c. 480-543), the monk who symbolizes Europe's Christian roots. A true pan-European who speaks many languages, Ratzinger heads a Church that thrives everywhere except Europe, which is becoming increasingly secular (with the notable exception of an increasing Muslim population). Benedict XVI has continued John Paul II's two priorities: defending Catholic doctrine in a changing world and building bridges with fellow Christians.

bases, about eye level above the bees. Someone in the Barberini family was pregnant during the making of the canopy, so Bernini put the various stages of childbirth on the bases. Continue clockwise to the last base to see how it came out.

Bernini (1598-1680), the Michelangelo of the Baroque era, is the man most responsible for the interior decoration of the church. The altar area was his masterpiece, a "theater" for holy spectacles. Bernini did: 1) the bronze canopy; 2) the dove window in the apse, surrounded by bronze work and statues; 3) the massive statue of lance-bearing St. Longinus ("The hills are alive..."), which became the model for the other three statues in the niches around the main altar; 4) much of the marble floor decoration; and 5) the balconies above the four statues, incorporating some of the actual corkscrew columns from Old St. Peter's, said to have been looted by the Romans from the Temple of Herod (called "Solomon's Temple") in Jerusalem. Bernini, the father of Baroque, gave an impressive unity to an amazing variety of pillars, windows, statues, chapels, and aisles.

• *Approach the apse, the front area with the golden dove window.*

The Apse

Bernini's **dove window** shines above the smaller front altar used for everyday services. The Holy Spirit, in the form of a six-foot-high dove, pours sunlight onto the faithful through the alabaster windows, turning into artificial rays of gold and reflecting off swirling gold clouds, angels, and winged babies. During a service, real sunlight passes through real clouds of incense, mingling with Bernini's sculpture. This is the epitome of Baroque—an ornate, mixed-media work designed to overwhelm the viewer.

Beneath the dove is the centerpiece of this structure, the so-called Throne of St. Peter, an oak chair built in medieval times for a king. Subsequently, it was encrusted with tradition and encased in bronze by Bernini as a symbol of papal authority. Statues of four early Church Fathers support the chair, a symbol of how bishops should support the pope in troubled times—times like the Counter-Reformation.

Remember that St. Peter's is a church, not a museum. In the apse, Mass is said daily for pilgrims, tourists, and Roman citizens alike (for Mass times, see "Hours" on page 182). Wooden confessional booths are available in the north transept (to the right of the main altar) for Catholics to tell their sins to a listening ear and receive forgiveness and peace of mind (daily, usually mornings and late afternoons—see website). The faithful renew their faith, and the faithless gain inspiration. Look at the light streaming through the windows, turn and gaze up into the dome, and quietly contemplate your deity (or lack thereof).

• *To the left of the main altar is the south transept. It may be roped off for worship, but anyone can step past the guard if you're there "for prayer." At the far end, left side, find the dark "painting" of St. Peter crucified upside down.*

South Transept—Peter's Crucifixion Site

This marks the exact spot (according to tradition) where Peter was killed 1,900 years ago. Peter had come to the world's greatest city to preach Jesus' message of love to the pagan, often hostile Romans. During the reign of Emperor Nero, he was arrested and brought to Nero's Circus so all of Rome could witness his execution. When

Bernini Blitz

Nowhere is there such a conglomeration of works by the flamboyant genius who remade this church—and the city—in the Baroque style. Here's your scavenger-hunt list. You have 20 minutes. Go!

1. St. Peter's Square: design and statues
2. Constantine equestrian relief (right end of atrium)
3. Decoration (stucco, gold leaf, marble, etc.) of side aisles (flanking the nave)
4. Tabernacle (the temple-like receptacle) inside Blessed Sacrament Chapel
5. Much of the marble floor throughout church
6. Bronze canopy *(baldacchino)* over the altar
7. St. Longinus statue (holding a lance) near main altar
8. Balconies (above each of the four statues ringing the main altar) with corkscrew columns
9. Dove window, bronze sunburst, angels, "Throne," and Church Fathers (in the apse)
10. Tomb of Pope Urban VIII (far end of the apse, right side)
11. Tomb of Pope Alexander VII (between the apse and the left transept, over a doorway, with the gold skeleton smothered in jasper poured like maple syrup)

Bizarre...Baroque...Bernini.

the authorities told Peter he was to be crucified just like his Lord, Peter said essentially, "I'm not worthy" and insisted they nail him on the cross upside down.

The Romans were actually quite tolerant of other religions, but they required their conquered peoples to worship the Roman emperor as a god. For most religions, this was no problem, but monotheistic Christians refused to worship the emperor even when they were burned alive, crucified, or thrown to the lions. Their bravery, optimism in suffering, and message of love struck a chord among slaves and members of the lower classes. The religion started by a poor carpenter grew, despite occasional pogroms (persecution of minorities) by fanatical emperors. In three short centuries, Christianity went from a small Jewish sect in Jerusalem to the official religion of the world's greatest empire.

This and all the other "paintings" in the church are actually mosaic copies made from thousands of colored chips the size of your little fingernail. Smoke and humidity would damage real paintings. Around the corner on the right (heading back toward the central nave), pause at the copy of Raphael's huge "painting" (mosaic) of ***The Transfiguration,*** especially if you won't be seeing the original in the Vatican Museum.

• *Back near the entrance of the church, in the far corner, behind bullet-proof glass, is the sculpture everyone has come to see, the...*

Pietà

Michelangelo was 24 years old when he completed this *Pietà* (pee-ay-TAH) of Mary with the body of Christ taken from the cross. It was Michelangelo's first major commission (by the French ambassador to the Vatican), done for Holy Year 1500.

Pietà means "pity." Michelangelo, with his total mastery of the real world, captures the sadness of the moment. Mary cradles her crucified son in her lap. Christ's lifeless right arm drooping down lets us know how heavy this corpse is. His smooth skin is accented by the rough folds of Mary's robe. Mary tilts her head down, looking at her dead son with sad tenderness. Her left hand turns upward, asking, "How could they do this to you?"

Michelangelo didn't think of sculpting as creating a figure, but as simply freeing the God-made figure from the prison of marble around it. He'd attack a project like this with an inspired passion, chipping away to find what God put inside.

The bunched-up shoulder and rigor-mortis legs show that Michelangelo learned well from his studies of cadavers. But realistic as this work is, its true power lies in the subtle "unreal" features. Life-size Christ looks childlike compared with larger-than-life Mary. Unnoticed at first, this accentuates the subconscious impression of Mary enfolding Jesus in her maternal love. Mary—the mother of a 33-year-old man—looks like a teenager, emphasizing how Mary was the eternally youthful "handmaiden" of the Lord, always serving him, even at this moment of supreme sacrifice. She accepts God's will, even if it means giving up her son.

The statue is a solid pyramid of maternal tenderness. Yet

within this, Christ's body tilts diagonally down to the right and Mary's hem flows with it. Subconsciously, we feel the weight of this dead God sliding from her lap to the ground.

At 11:30 on May 23, 1972, a madman with a hammer entered St. Peter's and began hacking away at the *Pietà*. The damage was repaired, but that's why there's now a shield of bulletproof glass in front of the sculpture.

This is Michelangelo's only signed work. The story goes that he overheard some pilgrims praising his finished *Pietà*, but attributing it to a second-rate sculptor from a lesser city. He was so enraged that he grabbed his chisel and chipped "Michelangelo Buonarroti of Florence did this" in the ribbon running down Mary's chest.

On your right (covered in gray concrete with a gold cross) is the inside of the Holy Door. It won't be opened until Christmas Eve, 2024, the dawn of the next Jubilee Year. If there's a prayer inside you, ask that St. Peter's will no longer need security checks or bulletproof glass when this door is next opened.

• *In the chapel to the left is the...*

Tomb of Pope John Paul II

Originally located in the crypt beneath the church, the tomb of John Paul II was moved to the Chapel of San Sebastian in 2011, after he was beatified by Pope Benedict XVI. Beatification, a step on the road to sainthood, means that John Paul is considered "blessed" and has had one miracle attributed to him (he needs one more to become a saint).

John Paul II (1920-2005) was one of the most beloved popes of recent times. During his papacy (1978-2005), he was the highly visible "face" of the Catholic Church as it labored to stay relevant in an increasingly secular world. The first non-Italian pope in four centuries, he traveled widely. He was the first pope to visit a mosque and a synagogue. He oversaw the fall of communism in his native Poland. He survived an assassination attempt, and he publicly endured his slow decline from Parkinson's disease with great stoicism.

When John Paul II died in 2005, hundreds of thousands lined up outside the church, waiting up to 24 hours to pay their respects. At his funeral in St. Peter's Square, the crowd began chanting "*Santo subito, santo subito*!" insisting he be made a saint *(santo)* right now *(subito)*. By Vatican standards, the honorific process is moving at light speed.

Pope Benedict XVI celebrated the beatification Mass for John Paul II on May 1, 2011, while hundreds of thousands of faithful crowded into the church and St. Peter's Square. The tomb has no monument—just a simple stone slab with the inscription *Beatus*

Ioannes Paulus PP. II (1920-2005). John Paul II lies beneath a painting of the steadfast St. Sebastian—the martyr who calmly suffered the slings and arrows of outrageous Romans. Sebastian was John Paul's favorite saint. There's also a plaque in the floor on the opposite side of the church honoring the man. Of 250-plus popes, two have been given the title "Great." That elite group may soon grow by 50 percent, as there's talk of calling him "John Paul the Great."

The Rest of the Church

The Crypt (a.k.a. Grotte or Tombe)

Visitors can go down to the foundations of Old St. Peter's, containing tombs of popes and memorial chapels. The crypt entrance is usually beside the statue of St. Andrew, to the left of the main altar. Stairs lead you down to the floor level of the previous church, where you'll pass the sepulcher of Peter. This lighted niche with an icon is not Peter's actual tomb, but part of a shrine that stands atop Peter's tomb. Nearby is the chapel where Pope John Paul II was buried before being moved upstairs in 2011. Next are the tombs of past popes, including the traditionalist Paul VI (1897-1978), who suffered reluctantly through the church's modernization. Finally, you can see a few column fragments from Old St. Peter's (a.k.a. "Basilica Costantiniana"). Continue your one-way visit until it spills you out, usually near the checkroom.

The walk through the crypt is free and quick (15 minutes)—but you won't see St. Peter's original grave unless you take a Scavi "Excavations" tour (see "Tours" on page 183).

Museum-Treasury (Museo-Tesoro)

The museum, located on the left side of the nave near the altar, contains an original corkscrew column from Old St. Peter's, the room-size tomb of Sixtus IV by Antonio Pollaiuolo, a big pair of Roman pincers used to torture Christians, and assorted jewels, papal robes, and golden reliquaries—a marked contrast to the poverty of early Christians.

Blessed Sacrament Chapel (Capella di Santissimo Sacramento)

You're welcome to step through the metalwork gates into this oasis of peace reserved for prayer and meditation. It's located on the right-hand side of the church, about midway to the altar.

Up to the Dome (Cupola)

A good way to finish a visit to St. Peter's is to go up to the dome for the best view of Rome anywhere. The entrance to the dome is along the right side of the church, but the line begins to form out front, at the church's right door (as you face the church).

There are two levels: the rooftop of the church and the very top of the dome. Climb (for €6) or take an elevator (€7) to the first level, on the church roof just above the facade. From the roof, you have a commanding view of St. Peter's Square, the statues on the colonnade, Rome across the Tiber in front of you, and the dome itself—almost terrifying in its nearness—looming behind you.

From here, you can also go inside to the gallery ringing the interior of the dome, where you can look down inside the church. Notice the dusty top of Bernini's seven-story-tall canopy far below. Study the mosaics up close—and those huge letters! It's worth the elevator ride for this view alone.

From this level, if you're energetic, continue all the way up to the top of the dome. The staircase actually winds between the outer shell and the inner one. It's a sweaty, crowded, claustrophobic 15-minute, 323-step climb, but worth it. The view from the summit is great, the fresh air even better. Admire the arms of Bernini's colonnade encircling St. Peter's Square. Find the big, white Victor Emmanuel Monument, with the two statues on top; and the Pantheon, with its large, light, shallow dome. The large rectangular building to the left of the obelisk is the Vatican Museum, stuffed with art. Survey the Vatican grounds, with its mini-train system and lush gardens. Look down into the square on the tiny pilgrims buzzing like electrons around the nucleus of Catholicism.

VATICAN MUSEUM TOUR

Musei Vaticani

The glories of the ancient world displayed in a lavish papal palace, decorated by the likes of Michelangelo and Raphael...the Musei Vaticani. A conglomerate of many submuseums, the Vatican Museum holds some of the greatest art anywhere. Unfortunately, many tourists see these collections only as an obstacle between them and the grand finale, the Sistine Chapel. True, this huge, confusing, and crowded megamuseum can be a jungle—but with this book as your vine, you should swing through with ease, enjoying the highlights and getting to the Sistine just before you collapse.

With the Fall of Rome (A.D. 476), the Catholic (or "universal") Church became the great preserver of civilization, collecting artifacts from cultures dead and dying. Renaissance popes (15th and 16th centuries) collected most of what we'll see, using it as furniture to decorate their palace (today's museum). Combining the classical and Christian worlds, they found the divine in the creations of man.

We'll concentrate on classical sculpture and Renaissance painting. But along the way (and there's a lot of along-the-way here), we'll stop to leaf through a few yellowed pages from this 5,000-year-old scrapbook of humankind.

The always crowded museum now has an online reservation system and a website with up-to-date hours and information. Plan ahead for your visit at http://mv.vatican.va. For more on Vatican City, the small, independent country where this museum is located, see page 63.

Orientation

Cost: €15 plus optional €4 reservation fee, free on the last Sun of each month (when it's very crowded).

Hours: Mon-Sat 9:00-18:00, last entry at 16:00 (though the official closing time is 18:00, the staff starts ushering you out at 17:30). Closed Sun, except last Sun of the month, when it's open 9:00-14:00, last entry at 12:30. May be open Fri nights May-July and Sept-Oct 19:00-23:00 (last entry at 21:30) by online reservation only—check the website (click on "Vatican Museums Under the Stars"; note that during evening visits, parts of the museum—including the Pinacoteca—are often closed). Those with reservations can enter the museum as early as 8:00, before the ticket-buying crowds.

The museum is closed on many holidays (mainly religious ones), including, for 2013: Jan 1 (New Year's), Jan 6 (Epiphany), Feb 11 (Vatican City established), March 19 (St. Joseph), April 1 (Easter Monday), May 1 (Labor Day), June 29 (Sts. Peter and Paul), Aug 15 plus either Aug 14 or 16—it varies year to year (Assumption of the Virgin), Nov 1 (All Saints' Day), Dec 8 (Immaculate Conception), and Dec 25 and 26 (Christmas). Because changes in hours (which are notoriously irregular) and other holiday closures may occur, always check the current hours and calendar at http://mv.vatican.va.

Individual rooms may close at odd hours, especially in the afternoon. The rooms described here are usually open.

Reservations: Bypass the long ticket lines by reserving an entry time online at http://mv.vatican.va. It costs €19 (€15 ticket plus €4 booking fee, pay with credit card). It's easy. You choose your day and time, they email you a confirmation immediately, and you print out the voucher with its reservation bar code. At the Vatican Museum, bypass the ticket-buying line and queue up at the "Entrance with Reservations" line (to the right). Show your voucher to the guard, who will scan it and let you in. Once inside the museum, go to a ticket window *(a cassa)*, either in the lobby or upstairs, present your voucher and ID, and they'll issue your ticket.

When to Go: The museum is generally hot and crowded, with waits of up to two hours to buy tickets (figure about a 10-minute wait for every 100 yards in line). The worst days are Saturdays, the last Sunday of the month (when it's free), Mondays, rainy days, and any day before or after a holiday closure. Mornings are most crowded. To see the Sistine Chapel with fewer crowds, visit at the end of the day.

Avoiding Lines: The best way to skip the long lines is to **reserve tickets** in advance (described on previous page). If you book a **guided tour** (see next page), you can approach the guard with your voucher and go right in. If you book with a private tour company, you may still have a short wait at crowded times.

You can often buy **same-day, skip-the-line tickets** through the TI in St. Peter's Square (to the left, as you face the basilica). You pay the same price (€15 ticket plus €4 reservation fee) that you would online. If the TI doesn't have tickets, you could try the tour company called Roma Cristiana, which sells higher-priced, same-day tickets from their kiosk at St. Peter's Square (€15 ticket plus €11 booking fee, entrances almost hourly, tel. 06-6980-6380, www.operaromanapellegrinaggi.org).

If you don't have a reservation, **try arriving after 14:00,** when crowds subside somewhat. Another good time is during the papal audience, on Wednesday at 10:30, when many tourists are at St. Peter's Basilica.

Make sure you get in the right line. Generally, individuals without tickets line up against the Vatican City wall (to the left of the entrance as you face it), and reservation holders (both individuals and groups) enter on the right.

Dress Code: Modest dress is required (no shorts, above-knee skirts, or bare shoulders). This dress code is strictly enforced here, at St. Peter's Basilica, and throughout Vatican City.

Getting There: The Ottaviano Metro stop is a 10-minute walk from the entrance. Bus #49 from Piazza Cavour stops right at the entrance. Bus #23 from Trastevere hugs the west bank of the Tiber and stops on Via Leone IV, just downhill from the entrance. Bus #492 heads from the city center past Piazza Risorgimento and the Vatican walls, and also stops on Via Leone IV. Bus #64 stops on the other side of St. Peter's Square, a 15- to 20-minute walk (facing the church from the obelisk, take a right through the colonnade and follow the Vatican Wall). Taxis are reasonable (hop in and say, "moo-ZAY-ee vah-tee-KAH-nee").

Information: As you enter the main lobby of the museum, an info desk is to your left, and TV screens list what rooms are open or closed. Bookstores are scattered throughout the museum. Some exhibits have English explanations. Tel. 06-6988-3860 or 06-6988-1662. The Vatican website (http://mv.vatican.va) allows you to reserve an entry time, sign up for a tour, get general information, and see what days the museum is closed. To prepare for your Sistine Chapel visit, you can virtually tour it online before your trip at http://www.vatican.va/various/cappelle/sistina_vr/index.html.

Tours: A €7 **audioguide** is available at the top of the spiral ramp/escalator (ID required). If you rent an audioguide, you lose the option of taking the shortcut from the Sistine Chapel to St. Peter's (described later, under "Museum Strategies"), since audioguides must be returned to the museum entrance/exit.

You can download the Sistine Chapel portion of this chapter as a free Rick Steves **audio tour** (see page 27).

The Vatican offers **English tours** that are easy to book online (€31, includes admission, http://mv.vatican.va). As with individual ticket reservations, present your confirmation voucher to a guard to the right of the entrance; then, once inside, go to the Guided Tours desk (in the lobby, up a few stairs).

Both **private tour** companies and private guides offer English tours of the museum, usually allowing you to skip the long ticket-buying line. For a listing of several companies, see page 39.

Length of This Tour: Until you expire, the museum closes, or 2.5 hours, whichever comes first.

With Limited Time: See the octagonal courtyard *(Laocoön),* then follow the crowd flow directly to the Sistine Chapel, sightseeing along the way. Skip the Etruscan Wing and the Pinacoteca. From the Sistine Chapel, head straight to St. Peter's via the shortcut, if open (see "Museum Strategies," below).

Security and Baggage Check: To enter the museum, you pass through a metal detector (no pocket knives allowed). The baggage check (to the right after security) takes only bigger bags; you'll need to carry your day bag with you.

Services: The post office, with stamps that make collectors drool, is upstairs. WCs are mainly at the entrance/exit, plus a few scattered within the collection.

Museum Strategies: The museum has two exits, and you'll want to decide which you'll take before you enter. The **main exit** is right near the entrance. Use this one if you want to rent an audioguide (which you must return at the entrance) or if you plan on following this self-guided tour exactly as laid out, visiting the Pinacoteca at the end.

The other exit is a handy (but sometimes closed) **shortcut** that leads from the Sistine Chapel directly to St. Peter's Basilica (spilling out alongside the church; see map on page 211). This route saves you a 30-minute walk (15 minutes back to the Vatican Museum entry/exit, then 15 minutes to St.

Peter's) and lets you avoid the often-long security line at the basilica's main entrance. If you take this route, you'll have to forgo an audioguide and skip the Pinacoteca (or tour it earlier). Officially, this exit is for Vatican guides and their groups only. However, it's often open to anyone (depending on how crowded the chapel is and how the guards feel). It's worth a shot (try blending in with a group that's leaving), but be prepared for the possibility that you won't get through.

Photography: No photos are allowed in the Sistine Chapel. Elsewhere in the museum, photos without a flash are permitted.

Cuisine Art: A self-service cafeteria is inside, near the Pinacoteca. Smaller cafés are in the outdoor Cortile della Pigna and near the Sistine Chapel. All offer mediocre food at high prices. Cheaper choices outside the museum include the great Mercato Trionfale produce market on Via Andrea Doria, three blocks north of the entrance (head across the street, down the stairs, and continue straight). Inexpensive *pizza rustica* shops selling pizza by the slice line Viale Giulio Cesare and Via Candia, and good restaurants are nearby (see page 371).

Starring: World history, a pope's palace, Michelangelo, Raphael, *Laocoön,* the Greek masters, and their Roman copyists.

The Tour Begins

This heavyweight museum is shaped like a barbell—two buildings connected by a long hall. The entrance building covers the ancient world (Egypt, Greece, Rome). The one at the far end covers its "rebirth" in the Renaissance (including the Sistine Chapel). The halls there and back are a mix of old and new. Move quickly—don't burn out before the Sistine Chapel, near the end of this tour—and see how each civilization borrows from and builds on the previous one.

• *Leave Italy by entering the doors.*

Once you clear the security checkpoint, exchange your printed voucher (on ground floor) or buy your ticket (upstairs). Punch the

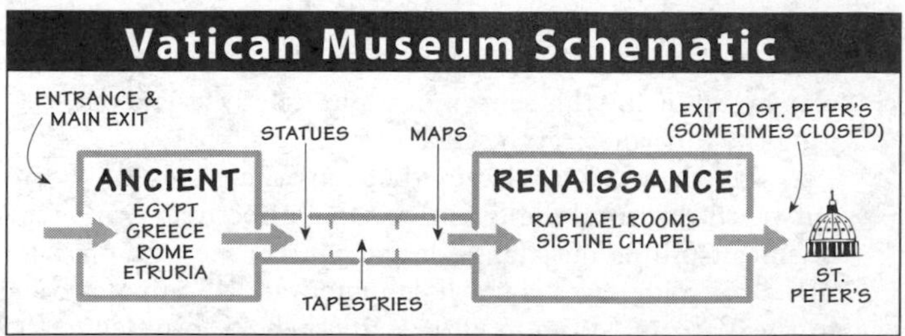

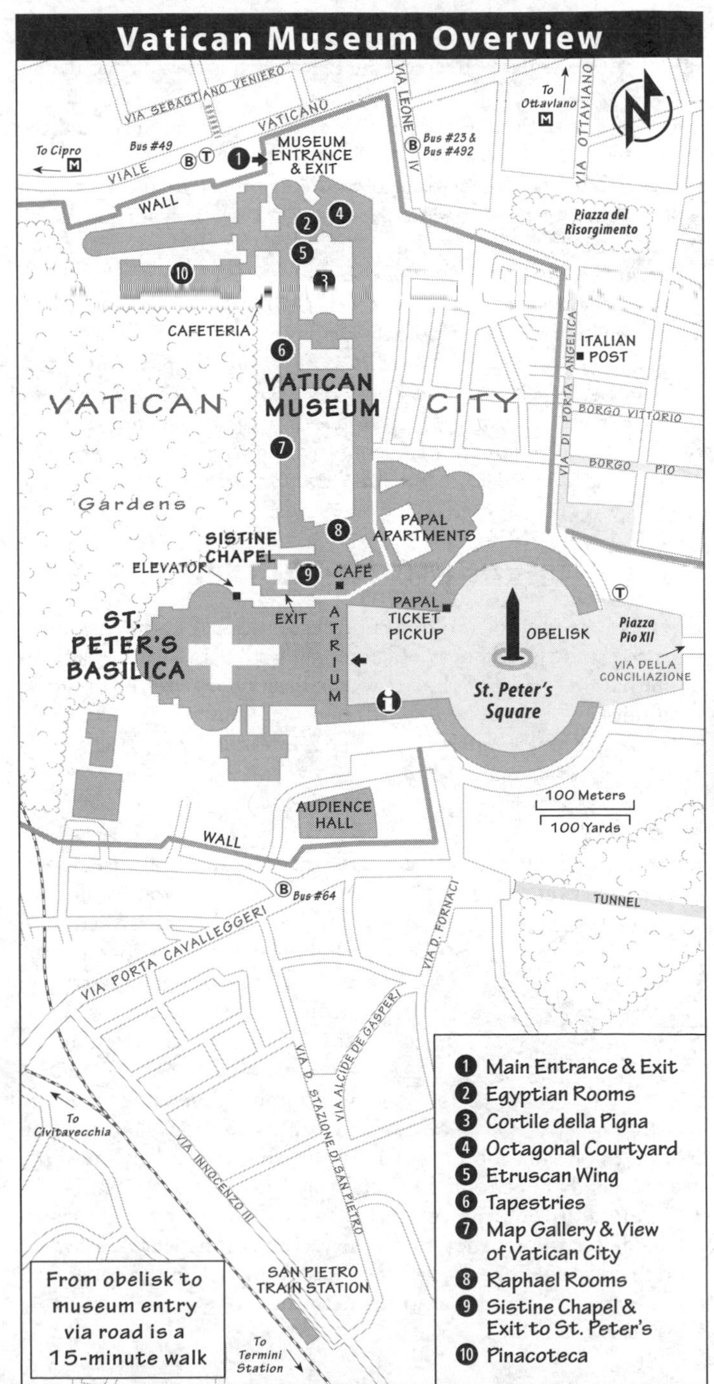
Vatican Museum Overview
VIA SEBASTIANO VENIERO
VIALE VATICANO
VIA LEONE IV
VIA OTTAVIANO
To Ottaviano
To Cipro
Bus #49
MUSEUM ENTRANCE & EXIT
Bus #23 & Bus #492
WALL
Piazza del Risorgimento
CAFETERIA
ITALIAN POST
VATICAN
VATICAN MUSEUM
CITY
VIA DI PORTA ANGELICA
BORGO VITTORIO
BORGO PIO
Gardens
PAPAL APARTMENTS
SISTINE CHAPEL
ELEVATOR
CAFE
EXIT
PAPAL TICKET PICKUP
OBELISK
Piazza Pio XII
ST. PETER'S BASILICA
ATRIUM
VIA DELLA CONCILIAZIONE
St. Peter's Square
100 Meters
100 Yards
AUDIENCE HALL
WALL
Bus #64
TUNNEL
VIA PORTA CAVALLEGGERI
VIA D. FORNACI
VIA ALCIDE DE GASPERI
VIA D. STAZIONE DI SAN PIETRO
To Civitavecchia
VIA INNOCENZO III
SAN PIETRO TRAIN STATION
To Termini Station
From obelisk to museum entry via road is a 15-minute walk
1 Main Entrance & Exit
2 Egyptian Rooms
3 Cortile della Pigna
4 Octagonal Courtyard
5 Etruscan Wing
6 Tapestries
7 Map Gallery & View of Vatican City
8 Raphael Rooms
9 Sistine Chapel & Exit to St. Peter's
10 Pinacoteca
VATICAN MUSEUM

ticket in the turnstiles, then take the long escalator or spiral ramp up, up, up to a glass-covered courtyard with a view of St. Peter's dome.

Pause at the courtyard: To your right is the cafeteria and the Pinacoteca painting gallery (consider touring the Pinacoteca now if you plan to take the Sistine-to-St. Peter's shortcut at the end; for a description of the Pinacoteca, see page 238). To your left is the beginning of our tour.

• *To start our tour, go left, then take another left up a flight of stairs to reach the first-floor Egyptian Rooms (Museo Egizio) on your right. Don't stop until you find your mummy.*

Note: Occasionally, the stairs up to Egypt are closed off, and crowds are routed through a spacious open-air courtyard, the Cortile della Pigna (see map on previous page). Just keep following the masses until you reach the Apollo Belvedere *and* Laocoön *figures. Tour the museum from there to the "Sarcophagi," where you'll find the entrance to the Egyptian rooms.*

Egypt (3000-1000 B.C.)

Egyptian art was for religion, not decoration. A statue or painting preserved the likeness of someone, giving him or her a form of eternal life. Most of the art was for tombs, where they put the mummies.

• *Pass beyond the imitation Egyptian pillars to the left of the case in the center of the room, and you'll find...*

Mummies

This woman died three millennia ago. Her corpse was disemboweled, and her organs were placed in a jar like those you see nearby.

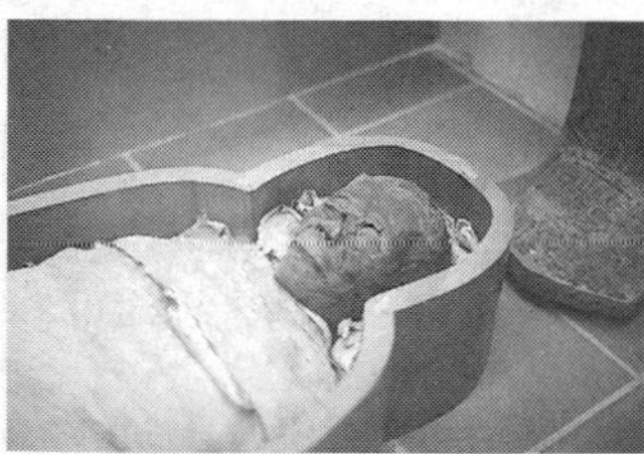

Then the body was refilled with pitch, dried with natron (a natural sodium carbonate), wrapped in linen, and placed in a wood coffin, which went inside a stone coffin, which was placed in a tomb. (Remember that the pyramids were just big tombs.) Notice the henna job on her hair—in the next life, your spirit needed a body to be rooted to...and you wanted to look your best.

Painted inside the coffin lid is a list of what the deceased "packed" for the journey to eternity. The coffins were decorated with magical spells to protect the body from evil and to act as crib notes for the confused soul in the netherworld.

• *In the next room are...*

Egyptian Statues

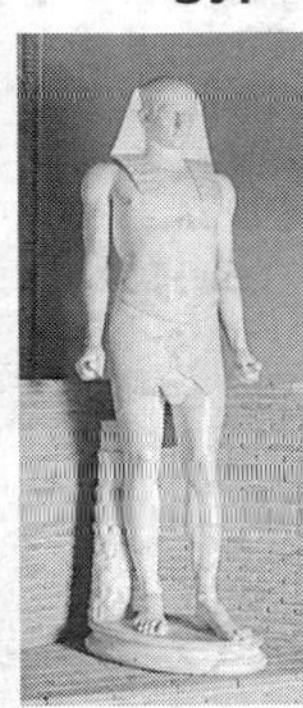

Egyptian statues walk awkwardly, as if they're carrying heavy buckets, with arms straight down at their sides. Even these Roman reproductions (made for Hadrian's Villa) are stiff, two-dimensional, and schematic—the art is only realistic enough to get the job done. In Egyptian belief, a statue like this could be a stable refuge for the wandering soul of a dead person. Each was made according to an established set of proportions. Little changed over the centuries—these statues had a function, and they worked.

• *Walk through the next small room and into the curved hallway, and look for...*

Various Egyptian Gods as Animals

Before technology made humans top dogs on earth, it was easier to appreciate our fellow creatures. Egyptians saw the superiority of animals and worshipped them as incarnations of the gods. Wander through a pet store of Egyptian animal gods. Find Anubis, a jackal in a toga. In the curved room, find the lioness, the fierce goddess Sekhmet. The clever baboon is the god of wisdom, Thoth. At the end of the curved hall on your right is Bes (the small white marble statue), the patron of pregnant women (and beer-bellied men).

• *Continue to room VIII (the third room), pausing at the glass case, which contains brown clay tablets.*

Sumerian Writing

Even before Egypt, civilizations flourished in the Middle East. The Sumerian culture in Mesopotamia (the ancestors of the ancient Babylonians and of today's Iraqis) invented writing in about 3000 B.C. People wrote on clay tablets by pressing into the wet clay with a wedge-shaped (cuneiform) pen. The Sumerians also rolled cylinder seals into soft clay to make an impression that authenticated documents and marked property.

• *Pass through the next room, and then turn left, to a balcony with a view of Rome through the window. Then enter the octagonal courtyard.*

Sculpture—Greece and Rome (500 B.C.–A.D. 500)

This palace wouldn't be here, this sculpture wouldn't be here, and our lives would likely be quite different if it weren't for a few thousand Greeks in a small city about 450 years before Christ. Athens set the tone for the rest of the West. Democracy, theater, economics, literature, and art all flourished in Athens during a 50-year "Golden Age." Greek culture was then appropriated by Rome, and revived again 1,500 years later, during the Renaissance. The Renaissance popes built and decorated these papal palaces, re-creating the glory of the classical world.

Apollo Belvedere

Apollo, the god of the sun and of music, is hunting. He's been running through the woods, and now he spots his prey. Keeping his eye on the animal, he slows down and prepares to put a (missing) arrow into his (missing) bow. The optimistic Greeks conceived of their gods in human form...and buck naked.

This Apollo is a Roman copy (fourth century B.C.) of a Hellenistic original that followed the style of the great Greek sculptor Praxiteles. It fully captures the beauty of the human form. The anatomy is perfect, his pose is natural. Instead of standing at attention, face-forward with his arms at his sides (Egyptian-style), Apollo is on the move, coming to rest with his weight on one leg.

The Greeks loved balance. A well-rounded man was both a thinker and an athlete, a poet and a warrior. In art, the *Apollo Belvedere* balances several opposites. He's moving, but not out of control. Apollo eyes his target, but hasn't attacked yet. He's realistic, but with idealized, godlike features. And the smoothness of his muscles is balanced by the rough folds of his cloak. The only sour note: his left hand, added in modern times. Could we try a size smaller?

During the Renaissance, when this Roman copy was discovered, it was considered the most perfect work of art in the world. The handsome face, eternal youth, and body that seems to float just above the pedestal made *Apollo Belvedere* seem superhuman, divine, and godlike, even for devout Christians.

• *In the neighboring niche to the right, a bearded old Roman river god lounges in the shade. This pose inspired Michelangelo's* Adam, *in the Sistine Chapel (coming soon). While there are a few fancy bathtubs in this courtyard, most of the carved boxes you see are sarcophagi—Roman*

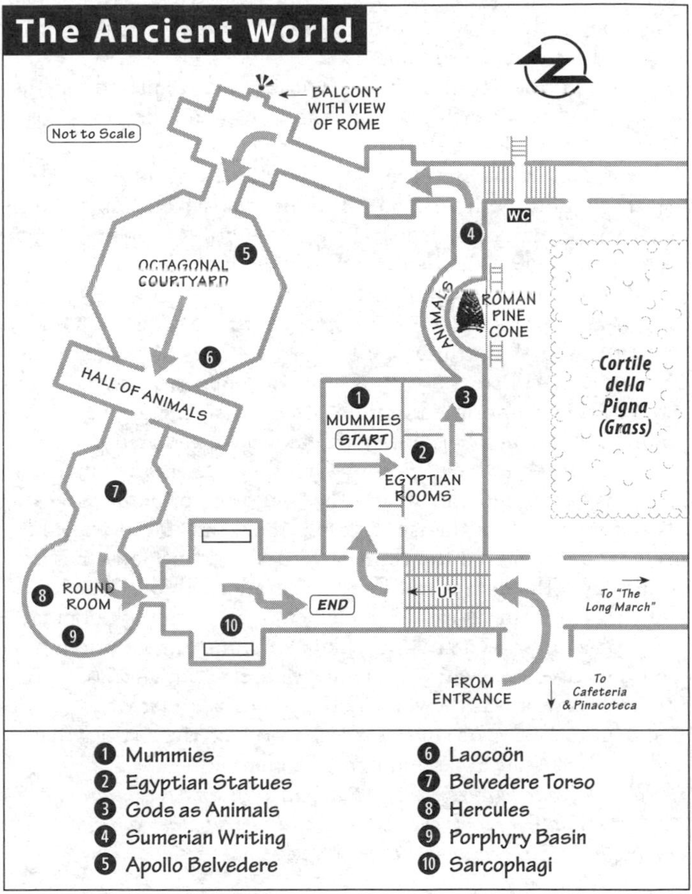

The Ancient World

Not to Scale

BALCONY WITH VIEW OF ROME

OCTAGONAL COURTYARD

HALL OF ANIMALS

ROUND ROOM

MUMMIES START

EGYPTIAN ROOMS

ANIMALS

ROMAN PINE CONE

WC

Cortile della Pigna (Grass)

UP

END

To "The Long March"

FROM ENTRANCE

To Cafeteria & Pinacoteca

1. Mummies
2. Egyptian Statues
3. Gods as Animals
4. Sumerian Writing
5. Apollo Belvedere
6. Laocoön
7. Belvedere Torso
8. Hercules
9. Porphyry Basin
10. Sarcophagi

coffins and relic holders, carved with the deceased's epitaph in picture form.

Laocoön

Laocoön (lay-AWK-oh-wahn), the high priest of Troy, warned his fellow Trojans: "Beware of Greeks bearing gifts." The attacking Greeks had brought the Trojan Horse to the gates as a ploy to get inside the city walls, and Laocoön tried to warn his people not to bring it inside. But the gods wanted the Greeks to win, so they sent huge snakes to crush Laocoön and his two sons to death. We see them at the height of their terror, when they realize that, no matter how hard they struggle, they—and their entire race—are doomed.

The figures (carved from four blocks of marble pieced together seamlessly) are powerful, not light and graceful. The poses are as twisted as possible, accentuating every rippling muscle and bulging vein. Follow the line of motion from Laocoön's left foot, up his leg, through his body, and out his right arm (which some historians used to think extended straight out—until the elbow was dug up early in the 1900s). Goethe would stand here and blink his eyes rapidly, watching the statue flicker to life.

Laocoön was sculpted some four centuries after the Golden Age (fifth-fourth centuries B.C.), after the scales of "balance" had been tipped. Whereas *Apollo* is a balance between stillness and motion, this is unbridled motion. *Apollo* is serene, graceful, and godlike, while *Laocoön* is powerful, emotional, and gritty.

Laocoön—the most famous Greek statue in ancient Rome and considered "superior to all other sculpture or painting"—was lost for more than a thousand years. Then, in 1506, it was unexpectedly unearthed in the ruins of Nero's Golden House near the Colosseum. The discovery caused a sensation. They cleaned it off and paraded it through the streets before an awestruck populace. No one had ever seen anything like its motion and emotion, having been raised on a white-bread diet of pretty-boy *Apollo*s. One of those who saw it was the young Michelangelo, and it was a revelation to him. Two years later, he started work on the Sistine Chapel, and the Renaissance was about to take another turn.

• *Leave the courtyard to the right of* Laocoön *and swing around the Hall of Animals, a jungle of beasts real and surreal. Then continue to the limbless torso in the middle of the next large hall.*

Belvedere Torso

My experience with sculpting statues ends with snowmen. But standing face-to-face with this hunk of shaped rock makes you appreciate the sheer physical labor involved in chipping a figure out of solid stone. It takes great strength but, at the same time, great delicacy.

This is all that remains of an ancient statue of Hercules seated on a lion skin. Michelangelo loved this old rock. He knew that he was the best sculptor of his day. The ancients were his only peers—and his rivals. He'd caress this statue lovingly and tell people, "I am the pupil of the Torso." To him, it contained all the beauty of classical sculpture. But it's not beautiful. Compared with the pure grace of the *Apollo,* it's downright ugly.

But Michelangelo, an ugly man himself, was looking for a new kind of beauty—not the beauty of idealized gods, but the innate beauty of every person, even so-called ugly ones. With its knotty lumps of muscle, the Torso has a brute power and a distinct personality despite—or because of—its rough edges. Remember this Torso, because we'll see it again later on.

• *Enter the next, domed room.*

Round Room

This room, modeled on the Pantheon interior, gives some idea of Roman grandeur. Romans took Greek ideas and made them bigger, like the big bronze statue of Hercules with his club, found near the Theater of Pompey (by modern-day Campo de' Fiori). The mosaic floor once decorated the bottom of a pool in an ancient Roman bath. The enormous Roman basin/hot tub/birdbath/vase decorated Nero's place. It was made of a single block of purple porphyry marble stone imported from Egypt. Purple was a rare, royal, expensive, and prestigious color in pre-Crayola days. This particular variety, called "imperial porphyry," came from a single mountain in Egypt, and was the stone of emperors...and then of popes. Now that source is quarried out, and the only "imperial porphyry" available to anyone has been recycled.

• *Enter the next room.*

Sarcophagi

These two large porphyry marble coffins were made (though not used) for the Roman emperor Constantine's mother (Helena, on left) and daughter (Constanza, on right). Helena's coffin depicts a battle game showing dying victims in their barbarian dress. Constanza's is decorated with a mix of Christian and pagan themes. Helena and Constanza were Christians—and therefore outlaws—until Constantine made Christianity legal in A.D. 313, and they became saints. Both sarcophagi were quarried and worked in Egypt. The technique for working this extremely hard stone (a special tempering of metal was required) was lost after this, and porphyry marble was not

chiseled again until Renaissance times in Florence.

• *See how we've come full circle in this building—the Egyptian Rooms are ahead on your left. Go upstairs and prepare for the Long March down the hall lined with statues, toward the Sistine Chapel and Raphael Rooms.*

Overachievers may first choose to pop into the Etruscan wing—labeled Museo Gregoriano Etrusco*—located a few steps up from the Long March level. (Others have permission to save their aesthetic energy for the Sistine.)*

The Etruscans (800-300 B.C.)

Room I

The chariot is from 550 B.C., when crude Romans were ruled by their more civilized neighbors to the north—the Etruscans. (The wooden portions are a reconstruction.) Imagine the chariot racing around the dirt track of the Circus Maximus, through the marshy valley of the newly drained Forum, or up Capitoline Hill to the Temple of Jupiter—all originally built by Rome's Etruscan kings.

Room II

The golden breastplate (*Pectoral*, 650 B.C., immediately to the right), decorated with tiny winged figures and animals, shows off the sophistication of the Etruscans. Though unwarlike and politically decentralized, these people were able to "conquer" all of central Italy around 650 B.C. through trade, offering tempting metalwork goods like this.

The Etruscan vases done in the Greek style remind us of the other great pre-Roman power—the Greek colonists who settled in southern Italy (Magna Graecia). The Etruscans traded with the Greeks, adopting their fashions. Rome, cradled between the two, grew up learning from both cultures.

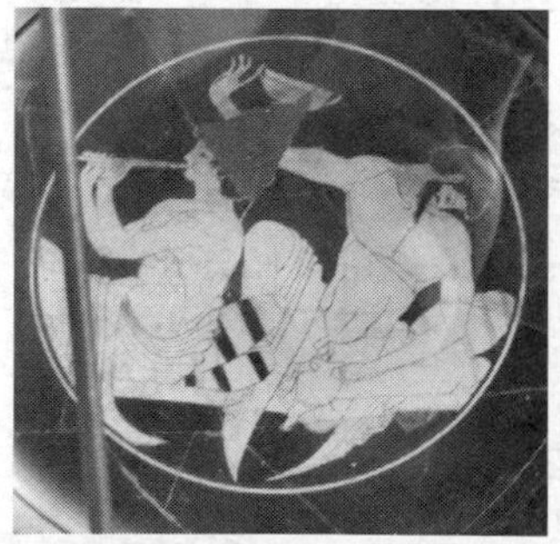

A Greek-style bowl (far corner of the room) depicting a man and woman in bed together would have scandalized early Roman farmers. He's peeing in a chamberpot, she's blowing a flute. Etruscan art often showed husbands and wives at ease together, giving them a reputation among the Romans as immoral, flute-playing degenerates.

Room III

This bronze warrior (late fifth century B.C.), whose helmet was sawed off by lightning, has a rare inscription that's readable (on armor below the navel). It probably refers to the statue's former owner: "Aha! Trutitis gave [this] as [a] gift." Archaeologists understand the Etruscans' Greek-style alphabet and some individual words, but they've yet to fully crack the code. As you look around at beautiful bronze pitchers, candlesticks, shields, and urns, ponder yet another of Etruria's unsolved mysteries—no one is sure where these sophisticated people came from.

Room IV

Most of our knowledge of the Etruscans is from sarcophagi and art in Etruscan tombs. Their funeral art is solemn, but hardly morbid—check out the sarcopha-guy with the bulging belly, enjoying a banquet for all eternity.

The Etruscans' origins are obscure, but their legacy is clear. In 509 B.C., the Etruscan king's son raped a Roman noblewoman. The king was thrown out, the republic was declared, Etruscan cities were conquered by Rome's legions, and their culture was swallowed up in Roman expansion. By Julius Caesar's time, the few remaining ethnic Etruscans were reduced to serving their masters as flute players, goldsmiths, surgeons, and street-corner preachers, like the one that Caesar brushed aside when he called out, "Beware the Ides of March..."

• *Browse the remaining dozen rooms of the Etruscan Wing, or backtrack to the long hall (the Gallery of the Candelabra) leading to the Sistine Chapel and Raphael Rooms.*

The Long March—Sculpture, Tapestries, Maps, and Views

This quarter-mile walk gives you a sense of the scale that Renaissance popes built on. Remember, this building was originally a series of papal palaces. The popes loved beautiful things—statues, urns, marble floors, friezes, stuccoed ceilings—and, as heirs of imperial Rome, they felt they deserved such luxury. The

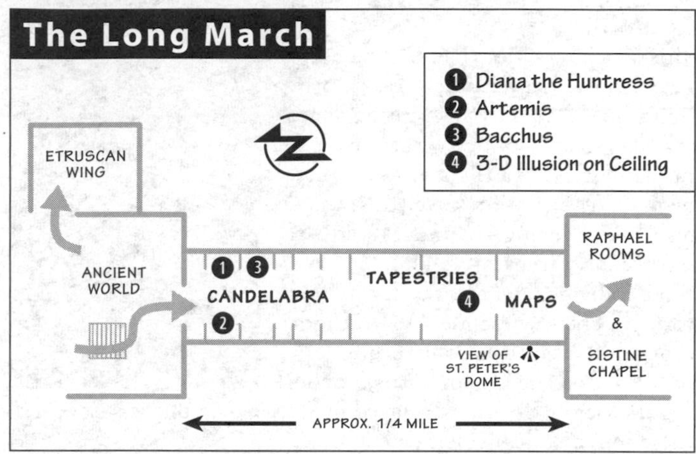

palaces and art represent both the peak and the decline of the Catholic Church in Europe. It was extravagant spending like this that inspired Martin Luther to rebel, starting the Protestant Reformation.

Gallery of the Candelabra: Classical Sculpture

In the second "room" of the long hall, stop at the statue of Diana the Huntress on the left. Here, the virgin goddess goes hunting. Roman hunters would pray and give offerings to statues like this to get divine help in their search for food.

Farmers might pray to another version of the same goddess, in her guise as Artemis, on the opposite wall. This billion-breasted beauty stood for fertility. "Boobs or bulls' balls?" Some historians say that bulls were sacrificed and castrated, with the testicles draped over the statues as symbols of fertility.

• *Shuffle along to the next "room." On the left is Bacchus, with a baby on his shoulders.*

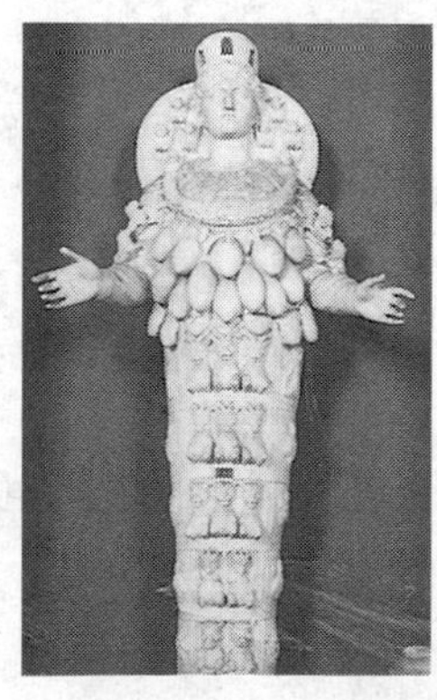

Fig Leaves

Why do the statues have fig leaves? Like Bacchus, many of these statues originally looked much different than they do now. First off, they were painted, often in gaudy colors. Bacchus may have had brown hair, rosy cheeks, purple grapes, and a leopard-skin sidekick at his feet. Even the *Apollo Belvedere,* whose cool gray tones we now admire as "classic Greek austerity," may have had a paisley pink cloak for all we know. Also, many statues had glass eyes like Bacchus.

And the fig leaves? Those came from the years 1550 to 1800, when the Church decided that certain parts of the human anatomy were obscene. (Why not the feet?) Perhaps Church leaders associated these full-frontal statues with the outbreak of Renaissance humanism that reduced their power in Europe. Whatever the cause, they reacted by covering classical crotches with plaster fig leaves, the same leaves Adam and Eve had used when the concept of "privates" was invented.

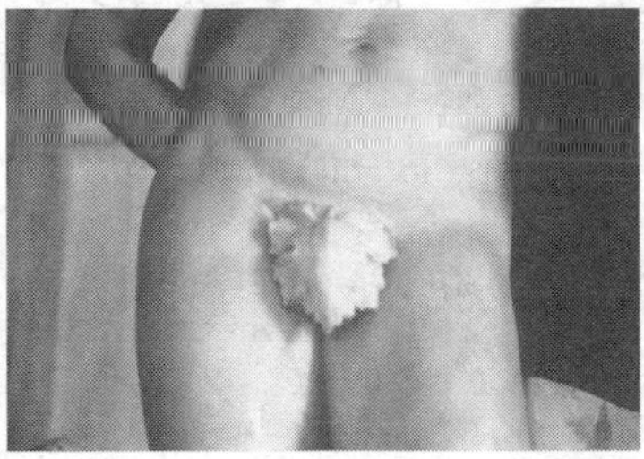

Note: The leaves could be removed at any time if the museum officials were so motivated. There are suggestion boxes around the museum. Whenever I see a fig leaf, I get the urge to pick-it. We could start an organ-ized campaign...

• *Cover your eyes in case they forgot a fig leaf or two, and continue to the...*

Tapestries

Along the left wall are tapestries designed by Raphael's workshop and made in Brussels. They show scenes from the life of Christ: Baby Jesus in the manger, being adored by shepherds, and presented in the temple. The Resurrection tapestry, with Jesus coming out of the tomb, is curiously interactive...as you walk, Jesus' eyes, feet, knee, and even the stone square follow you across the room. Next to it, *The Supper at Emmaus* (with Jesus sitting at a table) seems equally flexible.

Check out the beautiful sculpted reliefs on the ceiling. Admire the workmanship of this relief, then realize that it's not a relief at all—it's painted on a flat surface! Illusions like this were proof that painters had mastered the 3-D realism of ancient statues.

Map Gallery and View of Vatican City

This gallery still feels like a pope's palace. The crusted ceiling of colorful stucco and paint is pure papal splendor. The 16th-century maps on the walls show the regions of Italy. Popes could take visitors on a tour of Italy, from the toe (entrance end) to the Alps (far end), with east Italy on the right wall, west on the left. The scenes on the ceiling portray exciting moments in Church history in each of those regions.

The windows give you your best look at the tiny country of Vatican City, formed in 1929. It has its own radio station, as you see from the tower on the hill. What you see here is pretty much all there is—these gardens, the palaces you're in, and St. Peter's (for more on Vatican City, see sidebar on page 184).

If you have the chance to lean out and look left, you'll see the dome of St. Peter's the way Michelangelo would have liked you to see it—without the bulky Baroque facade.

At the far end, maps show Italy's four ports of entry (including Venice). Also look for maps of Antique Italy (names in Latin, Roman political boundaries in gold) and New Italy.

• Exit the map room, and take a breather in the next small tapestry hall before turning left into the crowded rooms that lead to the Raphael Rooms. From here, tired visitors can skip the Raphael Rooms and make a beeline to the Sistine Chapel by going straight ahead (unless this route is roped off). But our tour turns left into the Raphael Rooms.

Renaissance Art

Raphael Rooms: Papal Wallpaper

We've seen art from the ancient world; now we'll see its rebirth in the Renaissance. We're entering the living quarters of the great Renaissance popes—where they slept, worked, and worshipped. The rooms reflect the grandeur of their position. They hired the best artists—mostly from Florence—to paint the walls and ceilings, combining classical and Christian motifs.

Entering, you'll immediately see a huge (non-Raphael) 19th-century painting that depicts the Polish King Jan III Sobieski liberating Vienna from the Ottomans in

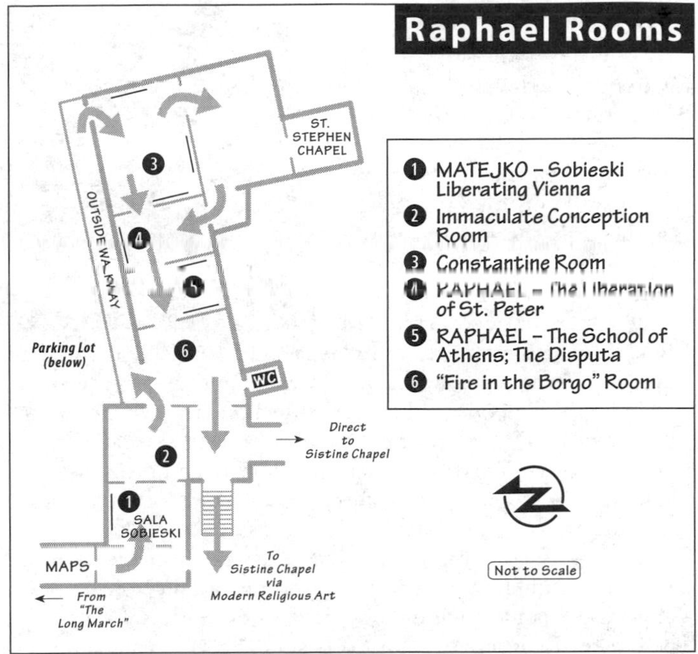

1683, finally tipping the tide in favor of a Christian Europe. See the Muslim tents on the left and the spires of Christian Vienna on the right.

The second room's paintings celebrate the doctrine of the Immaculate Conception, establishing that Mary herself was conceived free from original sin. This medieval idea wasn't actually made dogma until a century ago. The largest fresco shows how the inspiration came straight from heaven (upper left) in a thin ray of light directly to the pope.

• *Next, you'll pass along an outside walkway that overlooks a courtyard (is that the pope's Fiat?), finally ending up in the first of the Raphael Rooms, the...*

Constantine Room

These frescoes, painted between 1517 and 1524 (finished after Raphael's death by his assistants, notably Giulio Romano), celebrate the passing of the baton from one culture to the next. Remember, Rome was a pagan empire persecuting a new cult from the East—Christianity.

Then, on the night of October 27, A.D. 312 (left wall), as General Constantine (in gold, with crown) was preparing his troops for a coup d'état, he looked up and saw something strange. A cross appeared in the sky with the words, "You will conquer in this sign."

The next day (long wall), his troops raged victoriously into battle with the Christian cross atop their Roman eagle banners. There's Constantine in the center with a smile on his face, slashing through the enemy, while God's warrior angels ride shotgun overhead.

Constantine even stripped (right wall) and knelt before the pope to be baptized a Christian (some say). As emperor, he legalized Christianity and worked hand in hand with the pope, although the document in which he supposedly "gave" Rome to the pope (window wall) was later shown to be a forgery. When Rome fell, its glory lived on through the Dark Ages in the pomp, pageantry, and learning of the Catholic Church.

Look at the ceiling painting. A classical statue is knocked backward, crumbling before the overpowering force of the cross. Whoa! Christianity triumphs over pagan Rome. (This was painted, I believe, by Raphael's surrealist colleague, Salvadorus Dalio.)

• *While viewing these frescoes, ponder the life and times of...*

Raphael

Raphael was only 25 when Pope Julius II invited him, in 1508, to paint the walls of his personal living quarters. Julius was so impressed by Raphael's talent that he had the work of earlier masters scraped off and gave Raphael free rein to paint what he wanted.

Raphael lived a charmed life. He was handsome and sophisticated, and soon became Julius' favorite. He painted masterpieces effortlessly. In a different decade, he might have been thrown out of the Church as a great sinner, but his love affairs and devil-may-care personality seemed to epitomize the optimistic pagan spirit of the Renaissance. His works are graceful but never lightweight or frilly—they're strong, balanced, and harmonious in the best Renaissance tradition. When he died young in 1520, the High Renaissance died with him.

• *Continue on. In the next room you'll reach a room with frescoes arching over the windows (Room of Heliodorus, 1512–1514). Block the sunlight with your hand to see...*

The Liberation of St. Peter

Peter, Jesus' right-hand man, was thrown into prison in Jerusalem for his beliefs. In the middle of the night, an angel appeared and

rescued him from the sleeping guards (Acts 12:5-12). The chains miraculously fell away (and were later brought to the St. Peter-in-Chains Church in Rome), and the angel led him to safety (right), while the guards took hell from their captain (left). This little "play" is neatly divided into three separate acts that make a balanced composition.

Raphael makes the miraculous event even more dramatic with the use of four kinds of light illuminating the dark cell—half-moonlight, the captain's torch, the radiant angel, and the natural light spilling through the museum's window. Raphael's mastery of realism, rich colors, and sense of drama made him understandably famous.

Find Pope Julius II (who also commissioned Michelangelo to do the Sistine ceiling) in the role of Peter in *The Liberation,* and as the bearded and kneeling pope in *The Mass of Bolsena* (opposite wall).

• *Enter the next room (Room of the Segnatura, 1508-1511). Here in the pope's private study, Raphael painted...*

The School of Athens

In both style and subject matter, this fresco sums up the spirit of the Renaissance, which was not only the rebirth of classical art, but a rebirth of learning, discovery, and the optimistic spirit that man is a rational creature. Raphael pays respect to the great thinkers and scientists of ancient Greece, gathering them together at one time in a mythical school setting.

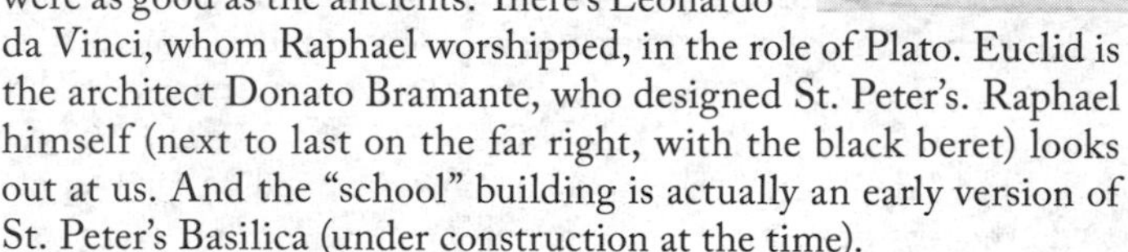

In the center are Plato and Aristotle, the two greatest Greeks. Plato points up, indicating his philosophy that mathematics and pure ideas are the source of truth, while Aristotle points down, showing preference for hands-on study of the material world. There's their master, Socrates (midway to the left, in green), ticking off arguments on his fingers. And in the foreground at right, bald Euclid bends over a slate to demonstrate a geometrical formula.

Raphael shows that Renaissance thinkers were as good as the ancients. There's Leonardo da Vinci, whom Raphael worshipped, in the role of Plato. Euclid is the architect Donato Bramante, who designed St. Peter's. Raphael himself (next to last on the far right, with the black beret) looks out at us. And the "school" building is actually an early version of St. Peter's Basilica (under construction at the time).

Raphael balances everything symmetrically—thinkers to the left, scientists to the right, with Plato and Aristotle dead center—showing the geometrical order found in the world. Look at the square floor tiles in the foreground. If you laid a ruler over them and extended the line upward, it would run right to the center of the picture. Similarly, the tops of the columns all point down to the middle. All the lines of sight draw our attention to Plato and Aristotle, and to the small arch over their heads—a halo over these two secular saints in the divine pursuit of knowledge.

While Raphael was painting this room, Michelangelo was at work down the hall in the Sistine Chapel. Raphael had just finished *The School of Athens* when he got a look at Michelangelo's powerful figures and dramatic scenes. He was astonished. From this point on, Raphael began to beef up his delicate, graceful style to a more heroic level. He returned to *The School of Athens* and added one more figure to the scene—Michelangelo, the brooding, melancholy figure in front, leaning on a block of marble.

• *On the opposite wall is...*

The Disputa

As if to underline the new attitude that pre-Christian philosophy and Church thinking could coexist, Raphael painted *The Disputa* facing *The School of Athens*. Christ and the saints in heaven are overseeing a discussion of the Eucharist (the communion wafer) by

mortals below. The classical-looking character in blue and gold looks out as if to say, "The pagans had their *School of Athens*, but we Christians (pointing up) have the School of Heaven." These rooms were the papal library, so themes featuring learning, knowledge, and debate were appropriate.

In Catholic terms, the communion wafer miraculously becomes the body of Christ when it's consecrated by a priest, bringing a little bit of heaven into the material world. Raphael's painting also connects heaven and earth, with descending circles: Jesus in a halo floats above a circle surrounding the dove of the Holy Spirit, which radiates down toward the round communion wafer on the altar. Balance and symmetry reign, from the angel trios in the upper corners to the books littering the floor. Find Dante wearing his poet's laureate in the lower right. (Hint: He's the guy on your €2 coin, modeled after this detail of *The Disputa*.)

Moving along, the last Raphael Room (called the "Fire in the Borgo" Room, 1514-1517) shows work done mostly by Raphael's students, who were influenced by the bulging muscles and bodybuilder poses of Michelangelo.

• *Pause here—WCs are nearby. Next stop, the Sistine Chapel, just a five-minute walk away. Exit the final Raphael Room through a passageway, bear right, and go down the stairs. At the foot of the stairs you'll find several quiet rooms with benches. Have a seat and read ahead before entering the hectic Sistine Chapel.*

When you're ready to tackle the Sistine, stroll through the impressive Modern Religious Art collection, following signs to the chapel.

The Sistine Chapel

The Sistine Chapel contains Michelangelo's ceiling and his huge *The Last Judgment*. The Sistine is the personal chapel of the pope and the place where new popes are elected. (The small, old-fashioned stove that burns pope-vote ballots—which sends out

The Sistine Schematic

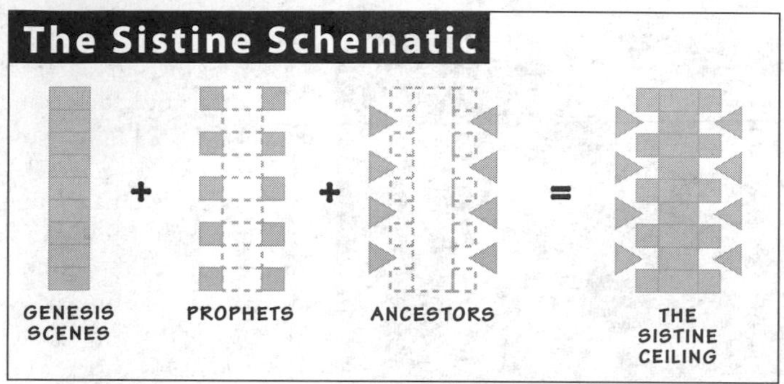

puffs of telltale smoke—is placed near today's shortcut exit.)

When Pope Julius II asked Michelangelo to take on this important project, he said, "No, *grazie*." Michelangelo insisted he was a sculptor, not a painter. The Sistine ceiling was a vast undertaking, and he didn't want to do a half-vast job. But the pope pleaded, bribed, and threatened until Michelangelo finally consented, on the condition that he be able to do it all his own way.

Julius had asked for only 12 apostles along the sides of the ceiling, but Michelangelo had a grander vision—the entire history of the world until Jesus. He spent the next four years (1508-1512) craning his neck on scaffolding six stories up, covering the ceiling with frescoes of biblical scenes.

In sheer physical terms, it's an astonishing achievement: 5,900 square feet, with the vast majority done by his own hand. (Raphael only designed most of his rooms, letting assistants do the grunt work.)

First, he had to design and erect the scaffolding. Any materials had to be hauled up on pulleys. Then, a section of ceiling would be plastered. With fresco—painting on wet plaster—if you don't get it right the first time, you have to scrape the whole thing off and start over. And if you've ever struggled with a ceiling light fixture or worked underneath a car for even five minutes, you know how heavy your arms get. The physical effort, the paint dripping in his eyes, the creative drain, and the mental stress from a pushy

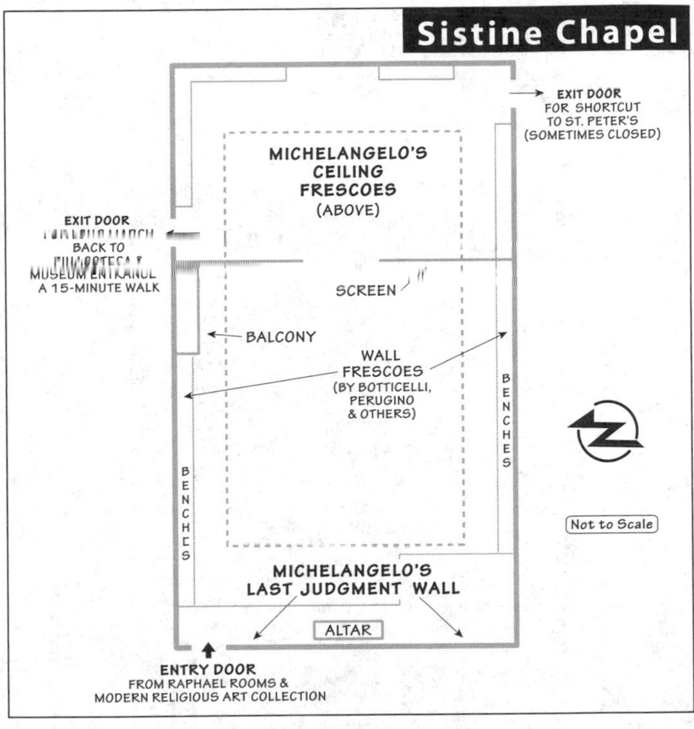

pope combined to almost kill Michelangelo.

But when the ceiling was finished and revealed to the public, it simply blew 'em away. Like the *Laocoön* statue discovered six years earlier, it was unlike anything seen before. It both caps the Renaissance and turns it in a new direction. In perfect Renaissance spirit, it mixes Old Testament prophets with classical figures. But the style is more dramatic, shocking, and emotional than the balanced Renaissance works before it. This is a very personal work—the Gospel according to Michelangelo—but its themes and subject matter are universal. Many art scholars contend that the Sistine ceiling is the single greatest work of art by any one human being.

The Sistine Ceiling: Understanding What You're Standing Under

The ceiling shows the history of the world before the birth of Jesus. We see God creating the world, creating man and woman, destroying the earth by flood, and so on. God himself, in his purple robe, actually appears in the first five scenes. Along the sides (where the ceiling starts to curve), we see the Old Testament prophets and pagan Greek prophetesses who foretold the coming of Christ. Dividing these scenes and figures are fake niches (a painted 3-D

The Sistine Ceiling

WALL

DAVID & GOLIATH | ZACHARIAH | JUDITH & HOLOFERNES

JOEL | DRUNKENESS OF NOAH | DELPHICA

ZOROBABEL | THE FLOOD | JOSIAH

ERYTHRAEA | SACRIFICE OF NOAH | ISAIAH

OZIAS | TEMPTATION AND EXPULSION | EZEKIAS

EZEKIEL | CREATION OF EVE | CUMAEA

ROBOAM | CREATION OF ADAM | ASA

PERSICA | SEPARATION OF LAND FROM WATER | DANIEL

SALMON | CREATION OF SUN, MOON & PLANETS | JESSE

JEREMIAH | SEPARATION OF LIGHT FROM DARKNESS | LIBICA

DEATH OF HAMAN | JONAH | BRAZEN SERPENT

WALL (left) — WALL (right)

See photo on facing page

LAST JUDGMENT WALL

ENTRY DOOR → FROM RAPHAEL ROOMS & MODERN RELIGIOUS ART...

☆ TO USE THIS DIAGRAM: FACE THE LAST JUDGMENT & HOLD THE BOOK UP TO THE CEILING.

illusion) decorated with nude statue-like figures with symbolic meaning.

The key is to see three simple divisions in the tangle of bodies:

1. The central spine of nine rectangular biblical scenes;
2. The line of prophets on either side; and
3. The triangles between the prophets showing the ancestors of Christ.

• *Ready? Within the chapel, grab a seat along the side (when there's room—people come and go). Face the altar with the big* Last Judgment *on the wall (more on that later). Now look up to the ceiling and find the central panel of...*

The Creation of Adam

God and man take center stage in this Renaissance version of creation. Adam, newly formed in the image of God, lounges dreamily in perfect naked innocence. God, with his entourage, swoops in with a swirl of activity (which—with a little imagination—looks like a cross-section of a human brain... quite a strong humanist statement). Their reaching hands are the center of this work. Adam's is limp and passive; God's is strong and forceful, his finger twitching upward with energy. Here is the very moment of creation, as God passes the spark of life to man, the crowning work of his creation.

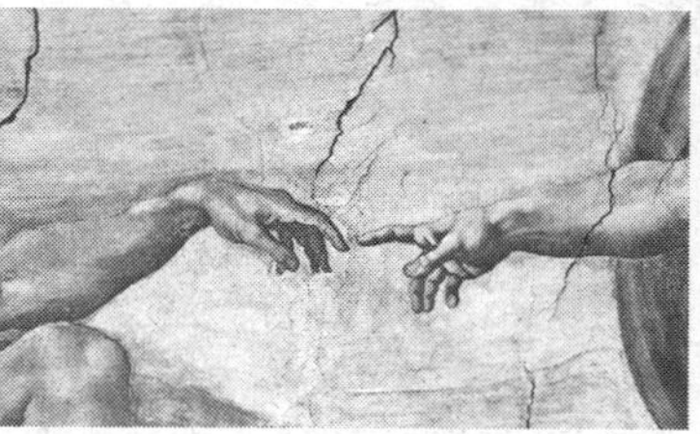

This is the spirit of the Renaissance. God is not a terrifying giant reaching down to puny and helpless man from way on high. Here they are on an equal plane, divided only by the diagonal bit of sky. God's billowing robe and the patch of green upon which Adam is lying balance each other. They are like two pieces of a jigsaw puzzle, or two long-separated continents, or like the yin and yang symbols finally coming together—uniting, complementing each other, creating wholeness. God and man work together in the divine process of creation.

• *This celebration of man permeates the ceiling. Notice the Adonises-come-to-life on the pedestals that divide the central panels. And then came woman.*

The Garden of Eden

In one panel, we see two scenes from the Garden of Eden: *Temptation* and *Expulsion*. On the left is the leafy garden of paradise where Adam and Eve lie around blissfully. But the devil comes along—a serpent with a woman's torso—and winds around the forbidden Tree of Knowledge. The temptation to gain new knowl-

edge is too great for these Renaissance people. They eat the forbidden fruit.

At right, a sword-wielding angel drives them from Paradise into the barren plains. They're grieving, but they're far from helpless. Adam's body is thick and sturdy, and we know they'll survive in the cruel world. Adam firmly gestures to the angel, like he's saying, "All right, already! We're going!"

The Nine Scenes from Genesis

Take some time with these central scenes to understand the story that the ceiling tells. They run in sequence, starting at the front:

1. God, in purple, divides the light from darkness.
2. God creates the sun (burning orange) and the moon (pale white, to the right). Oops, I guess there's another moon.
3. God bursts toward us to separate the land and water.
4. God creates Adam.
5. God creates Eve, who dives into existence out of Adam's side.
6. Adam and Eve are tempted, then expelled, from the Garden of Eden.
7. Noah kills a ram and stokes the altar fires to make a sacrifice to God.
8. The great flood, sent by God, destroys the wicked, who desperately head for higher ground. In the distance, the Ark carries Noah's family to safety. (The blank spot dates to 1793, when a nearby gunpowder depot exploded, shaking the building.)
9. Noah's sons see their drunken father. (Perhaps Michelangelo chose to end his work with this scene as a reminder that even the best of men are fallible.)

Prophets

You'll notice that the figures at the far end of the chapel are a bit smaller than those over *The Last Judgment*.

Michelangelo started at the far end, with the Noah scenes. By 1510, he'd finished the first half of the ceiling. When they took the scaffolding down and could finally see what he'd been working on for two years, everyone was awestruck—except Michelangelo. As powerful as his figures are, from the floor they didn't look dramatic enough for Michelangelo. For the other half, he pulled out all the stops.

Compare the Noah scenes (far end) with their many small figures to the huge images of God at the other end. Similarly, Isaiah (near the lattice screen, marked "Esaias") is stately and balanced, while Jeremiah ("Hieremias," in the corner by *The Last Judgment*) is a dark, brooding figure. This prophet who witnessed the destruction of Israel slumps his chin in his hand and ponders the fate of his people. Like the difference between the stately *Apollo Belvedere* and the excited *Laocoön*, Michelangelo added a new emotional dimension to Renaissance painting.

The Last Judgment

When Michelangelo returned to paint the altar wall 23 years later (1535), the mood of Europe—and of Michelangelo—was

completely different. The Protestant Reformation had forced the Catholic Church to clamp down on free thought, and religious wars raged. Rome had recently been pillaged by roving bands of mercenaries. The Renaissance spirit of optimism was fading. Michelangelo himself had begun to question the innate goodness of mankind.

It's Judgment Day, and Christ—the powerful figure in the center, raising his arm to spank the wicked—has come to find out who's naughty and who's nice. Beneath him, a band of angels blows its trumpets Dizzy Gillespie-style, giving a wake-up call to the

The Cleaning Project

The ceiling and *The Last Judgment* were cleaned in the 1980s and 1990s, removing centuries of preservatives, dirt, and soot from candles, oil lamps, and the annual Papal Barbecue (just kidding). The bright, bright colors that emerged are a bit shocking, forcing many art experts to reevaluate Michelangelo's style. Notice the very dark patches left in the corner above *The Last Judgment,* and imagine how dreary and dark it was before the cleaning.

sleeping dead. The dead at lower left leave their graves and prepare to be judged. The righteous, on Christ's right hand (the left side of the picture), are carried up to the glories of heaven. The wicked on the other side are hurled down to hell, where demons wait to torture them. Charon, from the underworld of Greek mythology, waits below to ferry the souls of the damned to hell.

It's a grim picture. No one, but no one, is smiling. Even many of the righteous being resurrected (lower left) are either skeletons or cadavers with ghastly skin. The angels have to play tug-of-war with subterranean monsters to drag them from their graves.

Over in hell, the wicked are tortured by gleeful demons. One of the damned (to the right of the trumpeting angels) has an utterly lost expression, as if saying, "Why did I cheat on my wife?!" Two demons grab him around the ankles to pull him down to the bowels of hell, condemned to an eternity of constipation.

But it's the terrifying figure of Christ that dominates this scene. He raises his arm to smite the wicked, sending a ripple of fear through everyone. Even the saints around him—even Mary beneath his arm (whose interceding days are clearly over)—shrink back in terror from this uncharacteristic outburst from loving Jesus. His expression is completely closed, and he turns his head, refusing to even listen to the whining alibis of the damned. Look at Christ's twisting upper body. If this muscular figure looks familiar to you, it's because you've seen it before—the Belvedere Torso.

When *The Last Judgment* was unveiled to the public in 1541, it caused a sensation. The pope is said to have dropped to his knees and cried, "Lord, charge me not with my sins when thou shalt come on the Day of Judgment."

And it changed the course of art. The complex composition,

with more than 300 figures swirling around the figure of Christ, went far beyond traditional Renaissance balance. The twisted figures shown from every imaginable angle challenged other painters to try and top this master of 3-D illusion. And the sheer terror and drama of the scene was a striking contrast to the placid optimism of, say, Raphael's *School of Athens*. Michelangelo had Baroque-en all the rules of the Renaissance, signaling a new era of art.

With the Renaissance fading, the fleshy figures in *The Last Judgment* aroused murmurs of discontent from Church authorities. Michelangelo rebelled by painting his chief critic into the scene—in hell. He's the jackassed demon in the bottom-right corner, wrapped in a snake. Look at how Michelangelo covered his privates. Sweet revenge.

(After Michelangelo's death, prudish Church authorities painted the wisps of clothing that we see today.)

Now move up close. Study the details of the lower part of the painting from right to left. Charon, with Dr. Spock ears and a Dalí moustache, paddles the damned in a boat full of human turbulence. Look more closely at the J-Day band. Are they reading music, or is it the Judgment Day tally? Before the piece was cleaned, these details were lost in murk.

The Last Judgment marks the end of Renaissance optimism epitomized in *The Creation of Adam,* with its innocence and exaltation of man. There, he was the wakening man-child of a fatherly God. Here, man cowers in fear and unworthiness before a terrifying, wrathful deity.

Michelangelo himself must have wondered how he would be judged—had he used his God-given talents wisely? Look at St. Bartholomew, the bald, bearded guy at Christ's left foot (our right). In the flayed skin he's holding is a barely recognizable face—the twisted self-portrait of a self-questioning Michelangelo.

• *There are two exits from the Sistine Chapel.*

1. To return to the main entrance/exit, leave the Sistine through the side door next to the screen. You'll soon find yourself facing ***The Long March back*** *to the museum's entrance (about 15 minutes away) and the Pinacoteca. Along this corridor (located one floor below the long corridor that you walked to get here), you'll see some of the wealth amassed by the popes, mostly gifts from royalty. Find your hometown on the 1529 map of the world—look in the land labeled "Terra Incognita." The elaborately decorated library that branches off to the right contains rare manuscripts. The corridor eventually spills back outside. Follow signs to the Pinacoteca, where our tour picks up below.*

2. To take the ***shortcut directly to St. Peter's Basilica*** *(see "Museum Strategies," page 209), you'll exit at the far-right corner of the Sistine Chapel (with your back to the altar). This route saves you a 30-minute walk and the wait in the St. Peter's security line, but you can't get back to the main entrance/exit or the Pinacoteca. Though this corner door is likely labeled "Exit for private tour groups only," you can usually just slide through with the crowds (or protest that your group has left you behind). If this exit is closed (which can happen without notice), hang out in the Sistine Chapel for a few more minutes—it'll likely reopen shortly.*

Pinacoteca

Like Lou Gehrig batting behind Babe Ruth, the Pinacoteca (Painting Gallery) has to follow the mighty Sistine & Co. But after the Vatican's artistic feast, this little collection of paintings is a delicious 15-minute after-dinner mint.

See this gallery of paintings as you'd view a time-lapse blossoming of a flower, walking through the evolution of painting from medieval to Baroque with just a few stops.

• *Enter, passing a model of Michelangelo's* Pietà *(offering a handy close-up look), and stroll up to room IV.*

Melozzo da Forlì—Musician Angels (1470s)

Removed from the apse of a Roman church, this playful series of frescoes shows the delicate grace and nobility of Italy during the time known fondly as the Quattrocento (1400s). Notice the detail in the serene faces; the soothing primary colors; the bright and even light; and the classical purity given these religious figures. Rock on.

• *Walk on to the end room (room VIII), where precious Raphael-designed tapestries that once hung in the Sistine Chapel now surround the highlight of this collection. They've turned on the dark to let Raphael's* Transfiguration *shine. Take a seat.*

Raphael—*The Transfiguration* (1516-1520)

Christ floats above a stumpy mountaintop, visited in a vision by the prophets Moses and Elijah. Peter, James, and John, who wanted visual proof that Jesus was Lord, cower in awe under their savior, "transfigured before them, his face

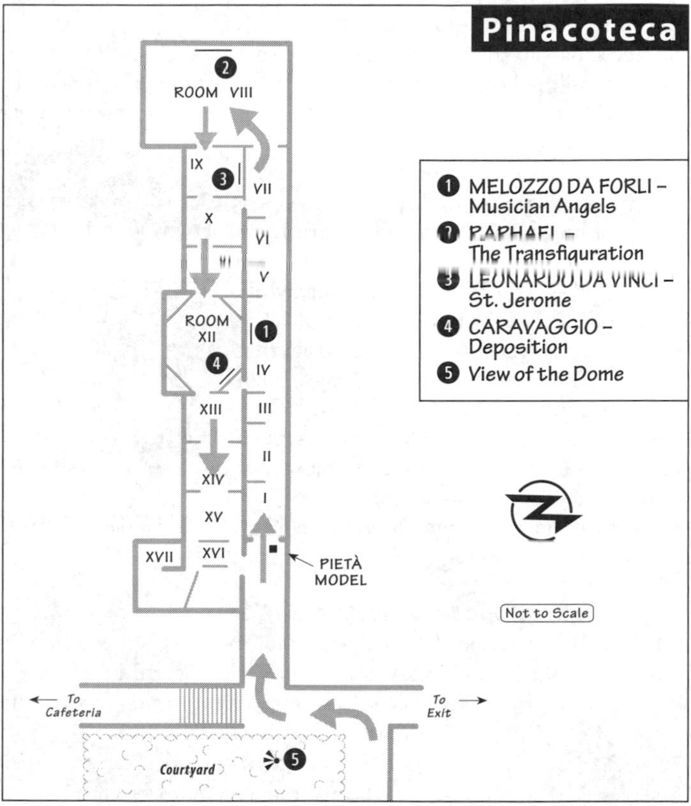

Pinacoteca

1. MELOZZO DA FORLI – Musician Angels
2. RAPHAEL – The Transfiguration
3. LEONARDO DA VINCI – St. Jerome
4. CARAVAGGIO – Deposition
5. View of the Dome

ROOM VIII, IX, X, XI, ROOM XII, XIII, XIV, XV, XVI, XVII, VII, VI, V, IV, III, II, I

PIETÀ MODEL

To Cafeteria

To Exit

Courtyard

Not to Scale

shining as the sun, his raiment white as light" (as described by the evangelist Matthew—who can be seen taking notes in the painting's lower left).

Raphael composes the scene in three descending tiers: Christ, the holiest, is on top, then Peter-James-John, and finally, the nine remaining apostles surround a boy possessed by demons. They direct him and his mother to Jesus for healing.

Raphael died in 1520, leaving this final work to be finished by his pupils. The last thing Raphael painted was the beatific face of Jesus, perhaps the most beautiful Christ in existence. When Raphael was buried (in the Pantheon, at age 37), this work accompanied the funeral.

• *Heading back down the parallel corridor, stop in room IX at the brown, unfinished work by Leonardo.*

Leonardo da Vinci—*St. Jerome* (c. 1482)

Jerome squats in the rocky desert. He's spent too much time alone, fasting and meditating on his sins. His soulful face is echoed by his friend, the roaring lion.

This unfinished work gives us a glimpse behind the scenes at Leonardo's technique. Even in the brown undercoating, we see the psychological power of Leonardo's genius. Jerome's emaciated body on the rocks expresses his intense penitence, while his pleading eyes hold a glimmer of hope for divine forgiveness. Leonardo wrote that a good painter must paint two things: "man and the movements of his spirit." (The patchwork effect is due to Jerome's head having been cut out and used as the seat of a stool in a shoemaker's shop.)

• *Roll on through the sappy sweetness of the Mannerist rooms into the gritty realism of Caravaggio (room XII).*

Caravaggio—*Deposition* (c. 1600-1604)

Christ is being buried. In the dark tomb, the faces of his followers emerge, lit by a harsh light. Christ's body has a deathlike color. We see Christ's dirty toes and Nicodemus' wrinkled, sunburned face.

Caravaggio was the first painter to intentionally shock his viewers. By exaggerating the contrast between light and dark, shining a brutal third-degree-interrogation light on his subjects, and using everyday models in sacred scenes, he takes a huge leap away from the Raphael-pretty past and into the "expressive realism" of the modern world.

A tangle of grief looms in the darkness as Christ's heavy, dead body nearly pulls the whole group with him from the cross into the tomb. After this museum, I know how he feels.

• *Walk through the rest of the gallery's canvas history of art, enjoy one last view of the Vatican grounds and Michelangelo's dome, then follow the grand spiral staircase down. Go in peace.*

BORGHESE GALLERY TOUR

Museo e Galleria Borghese

More than just a great museum, the Borghese Gallery is a beautiful villa set in the greenery of surrounding gardens. You get to see art commissioned by the luxury-loving Borghese family displayed in the very rooms for which it was created. Frescoes, marble, stucco, and interior design enhance the masterpieces. This is a place where—regardless of whether you learn a darn thing—you can sit back and enjoy the sheer beauty of the palace and its art.

Orientation

Cost: €12.50; drops to €8.50 when there's no temporary exhibit, both prices include basic €2 reservation fee (see "Reservations" below). Credit cards are accepted.

Hours: Tue-Sun 9:00-19:00, closed Mon, ticket office closes one hour before museum.

Reservations: Reservations are mandatory and simple to get. It's easiest by booking online (www.ticketeria.it, €1 extra booking fee, user-friendly website). You can also reserve by telephone (tel. 06-32810, press 2 for English, pay for tickets on arrival). Call during Italian office hours: Mon-Fri 9:00-18:00, Sat 9:00-13:00, office closed Sat in Aug and Sun year-round.

Every two hours, 360 people are allowed to enter the museum. Entry times are 9:00, 11:00, 13:00, 15:00, and 17:00. Reserve a *minimum* of several days in advance for a weekday visit, and at least a week ahead for weekends. Reservations are tightest at 11:00 and 15:00, on Tuesdays, and on weekends. For off-season weekdays (but not weekends), your chances of getting a same-day reservation are fairly high if you're flexible about the entry time (but you must go in person—you can't call to reserve same-day tickets).

After you reserve a day and time, you'll get a claim number. Be at the Borghese Gallery 30 minutes before your appointed time to pick up your ticket in the lobby on the lower level. Punctuality is critical (arriving late can mean forfeiting your reservation). You can try skipping the ticket pickup line by paying with a credit card at one of the computer kiosks (but they don't always work).

You can use a Roma Pass for entry, but you still need to make a reservation (by phone only—not online; specify that you have the Roma Pass). If you don't have a reservation, try arriving near the top of the hour, when the museum sells unclaimed tickets to those standing by. Generally, out of 360 reservations, a few will fail to show (but more than a few may be waiting to grab them). You're most likely to land a stand-by ticket at 9:00.

Getting There: The museum is set idyllically but inconveniently in the vast Villa Borghese Gardens. To avoid missing your appointment, allow yourself plenty of time to find the place. A taxi drops you 100 yards from the museum. Your destination is the Galleria Borghese (gah-leh-REE-ah bor-GAY-zay). Be sure *not* to tell the cabbie "Villa Borghese"—which is the park, not the museum.

Bus #910 goes from Termini train station to the Via Pinciana stop (a few steps from the villa). Coming from Campo de' Fiori or Via del Corso (at Via Minghetti), bus #116 drops you off at the southern edge of the park. From Largo Argentina, bus #63 takes you to the US Embassy on Via Veneto; walk uphill on Via Veneto to the southern edge of the park.

By Metro, from the Barberini Metro stop, walk 10 minutes up Via Veneto, enter the park, and turn right, following signs another 10 minutes to the Borghese Gallery.

Information: Tel. 06-32810 or 06-841-3979, www.galleriaborghese.it. For info on the park or Rome sights in general, try the nearby park TI (sporadically open; facing Borghese Gallery, turn left, walk 30 yards down, turn right toward the gate and find the poorly signed TI immediately on the left).

Tours: Guided English tours are offered at 9:10 and 11:10 (€6.50; may also be offered on busy weekends at 13:10 and 15:10). You can't book a tour when you make your museum reservation—sign up as soon as you arrive. Or consider the excellent 1.5-

hour audioguide tour (€5).

Length of This Tour: Two hours is all you get...and you'll want every minute.

With Limited Time: Focus on the ground-floor sculptures, especially Bernini.

Museum Strategy: Visits are strictly limited to two hours. Budget most of your time for the more interesting ground floor, but set aside 30 minutes for the paintings of the Pinacoteca upstairs (highlights are marked by the audioguide icons). Avoid the crowds by seeing the Pinacoteca first. The fine bookshop and cafeteria are best visited outside your two-hour entry window (the bookshop closes 30 minutes before the gallery).

Cloakroom: Baggage check is free, mandatory, and strictly enforced. Even small purses must be checked. The checkroom does not take coats.

Photography: No photos allowed; you must check your camera.

Cuisine Art: A café is on-site. A picnic-friendly park with benches is just in front of the museum (you can check your picnic with your bags, and feast after your visit).

Starring: Sculptures by Bernini and Canova; paintings by Caravaggio, Raphael, and Titian; and the elegant villa itself.

The Tour Begins

Exterior

As you visit this palace-in-a-garden, consider its purpose. Cardinal Scipione Borghese (1576-1633) wanted to create a place just outside the city where he could showcase his fine art while wining and dining the VIPs of his age. He had the villa built, collected ancient works, and hired the best artists of his day. In pursuing the optimistic spirit of the Renaissance, they invented Baroque.

The cardinal was controversial because he was not religious. But as nepotism was routine in the 17th century, just being a nephew of the pope was justification enough to be made a cardinal. And the power of a cardinal could be parlayed into great wealth, still on incredible display here in the gallery.

Main Entry Hall

The first room that guests saw upon entry was a "theater of the arts"—a multimedia and multi-era extravaganza of art treasures. Baroque frescoes on the ceiling, Greek statues along the walls, and ancient Roman mosaics on the floor capture the essence of the collection—a gathering of beautiful objects from every age and culture inside a lavish 17th-century villa.

Five second- and third-century mosaics from a private Roman villa adorn the floor with colorful, festive scenes of slaughter.

Gladiators—as famous in their day as the sports heroes of our age—fight animals and each other with swords, whips, and tridents. The Greek letter Θ marks the dead. Notice some of the gladiators' pro-wrestler nicknames: "Cupid(-o)," "Serpent(-ius)," "Licentious(-us)." On the far left a scene shows how "Alumnusvic" killed "Mazicinus" and left him lying upside down in a pool of blood.

High up on the wall is a thrilling first-century Greek sculpture of a horse falling. The Renaissance-era rider was added by Pietro Bernini, father of the famous Gian Lorenzo Bernini.

Room I

Antonio Canova—*Pauline Borghese as Venus* (*Paolina Borghese come Venere,* 1808)

Napoleon's sister went the full monty for the sculptor Canova, scandalizing Europe. ("How could you have done such a thing?!" she was asked. She replied, "The room wasn't cold.") With the famous nose of her conqueror brother, she strikes the pose of Venus as conqueror of men's hearts. Her relaxed afterglow and slight smirk say she's already had her man. The light dent she puts in the mattress makes this goddess human.

Notice the contrasting textures that Canova (1757-1822) gets out of the pure white marble: the rumpled sheet versus her smooth skin, the satiny-smooth pillows and mattress versus the creases in them, her porcelain skin versus the hint of a love handle. Canova polished and waxed the marble until it looked as soft and pliable as cloth.

The mythological pose, the Roman couch, the ancient hairdo, and the calm harmony make Pauline the epitome of the Neoclassical style.

Room II

Gian Lorenzo Bernini—*David* (1624)

Duck! David twists around to put a big rock in his sling. He purses his lips, knits his brow, and winds his body like a spring as his eyes lock onto the target—Goliath, who's somewhere behind us, putting us right in the line of fire.

The face of David is a self-portrait of the 25-year-old Bernini (1598-1680). Looking

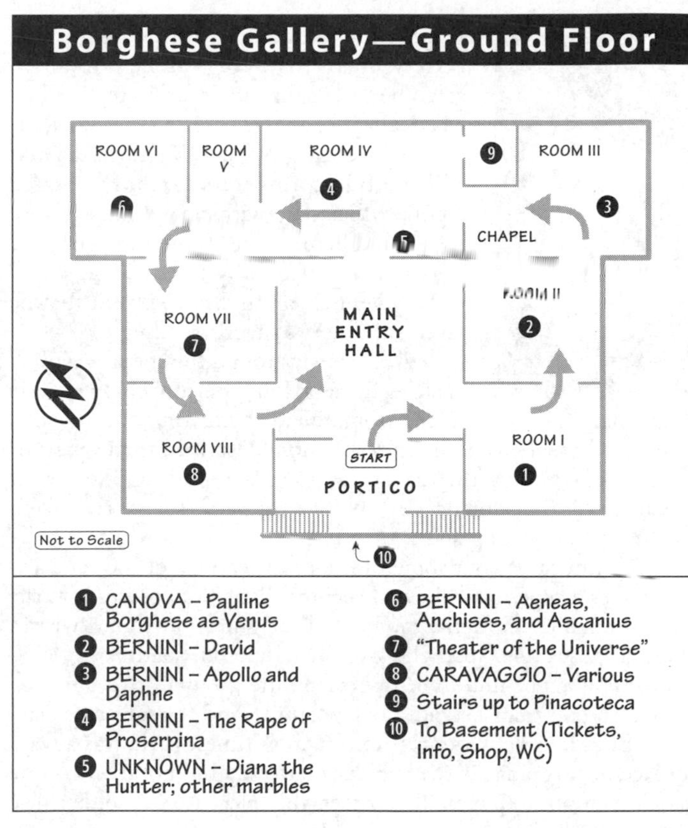

ready to take on the world, David is charged with the same fighting energy that fueled the missionaries and conquistadors of the Counter-Reformation.

Compared with Michelangelo's *David,* this is unvarnished realism—an unbalanced pose, bulging veins, unflattering face, and armpit hair. Michelangelo's *David* thinks, whereas Bernini's acts—with lips pursed, eyes concentrating, and sling stretched. Bernini slays the pretty-boy *David*s of the Renaissance and prepares to invent Baroque.

Flanking David are two ancient sarcophagi carved with scenes from the *Labors of Hercules* (A.D. 160; find Hercules with his club). The twisting bodybuilders' poses were the Hellenistic inspiration for Bernini's Baroque. The painting behind them, by a follower of Caravaggio, shows a triumphant David with the giant's head.

Room III

Bernini—*Apollo and Daphne* (*Apollo e Dafne*, 1625)

Apollo—made stupid by Cupid's arrow of love—chases after

Daphne, who has been turned off by the "arrow of disgust." Just as he's about to catch her, she calls to her father to save her. Magically, her fingers begin to sprout leaves, her toes become roots, her skin turns to bark, and she transforms into a tree. Frustrated Apollo will end up with a handful of leaves.

Stand behind the statue to experience it as Bernini originally intended. It's only when you circle around to the front that he reveals the story's surprise ending.

Walk slowly around the statue. Apollo's back leg defies gravity. Bernini chipped away more than half of the block of marble, leaving airy, open spaces. The statue spent two years in restoration (described to me as similar to dental work). The marble leaves at the top ring like crystal when struck (but don't try it). Notice the same scene, colorized, painted on the ceiling above.

Bernini carves out some of the chief features of Baroque art. He makes a supernatural event seem realistic. He freezes it at the most dramatic, emotional moment. The figures move and twist in unusual poses. He turns the wind machine on, sending Apollo's cape billowing behind him. It's a sculpture group of two, forming a scene, rather than a stand-alone portrait. And the subject is classical. Even in strict Counter-Reformation times, there was always a place for groping, if the subject matter had a moral—this one taught you not to pursue fleeting earthly pleasures. And, besides, Bernini tends to show a lot of skin, but no genitals.

The cardinal's private chapel (between rooms III and IV) is the only even vaguely religious room in the palace. It's relatively humble, a reminder that the cardinal probably didn't usually stop in here for much longer than tourists do today.

Room IV

Bernini—*The Rape of Proserpina* (*Il Ratto di Proserpina*, 1622)

Pluto, King of the Underworld, strides into his realm and shows off his catch—the beautiful daughter of the earth goddess Ceres. His three-headed guard dog, Cerberus (who guards the gates of hell), barks triumphantly. Pluto is squat, thick, and uncouth, with knotted muscles and untrimmed beard. He's trying not to hurt Proserpina, but she pushes her divine molester away and twists to call out for help. Tears roll down her cheeks. She wishes she could turn into a tree.

Bernini was the master of marble. With this work, at the age of 24, he had discovered his Baroque niche. While Renaissance works were designed to be seen from the front, Baroque is theater-in-the-round—full of action, designed to be experienced as you walk around it. Look how Pluto's fingers dig into her frantic body as if it was real flesh. Bernini picked out this Carrara marble, knowing that its relative suppleness and ivory hue would lend itself to a fleshy statue.

• *In a niche over Pluto's right shoulder, find...*

Artist Unknown—Diana the Hunter *(Artemide)*

The goddess has been running through the forest. Now she's spotted her prey, and slows down, preparing to string her (missing) bow with an arrow. Or is she smoking a (missing) cigarette? Scholars debate it.

The statues in the niches are classical originals. Diana the Hunter is a rare Greek original, with every limb and finger intact, from the second century B.C. The traditional *contrapposto* pose (weight on one leg) and idealized grace were an inspiration for artists such as Canova, who grew tired of Bernini's Baroque bombast.

The Marbles in Room IV

The many ancient Roman statues and portrait busts of Roman emperors in this room were intended as a reminder that the pope was essentially a king, the successor to ancient Roman rulers of the past. (Until around 1800, popes held vast political—and even military—power.)

Appreciate the beauty of the different types of marble in the room: Bernini's ivory Carrara, Diana's translucent white, purple porphyry emperors and the granite-like columns supporting them, wood-grained pilasters on the walls, and the various colors on the floor—green, red, gray, lavender, and yellow, some grainy, some "marbled" like a steak. Some of the world's most beautiful and durable things have been made from the shells of sea creatures layered in sediment, fossilized into limestone, then baked and crystallized by the pressure of the earth—marble.

Room VI

Bernini—*Aeneas, Anchises, and Ascanius* (1618-1619)

Aeneas' home in Troy is in flames, and he escapes with the three most important things: his family (elderly father Anchises on his shoulder, baby boy Ascanius at his leg), his household gods (the statues in Dad's hands), and the Eternal Flame (carried by son). They're all in shock, lost in thought, facing an uncertain future. Aeneas isn't even looking where he's going; he just puts one foot in front of the other. Little do they know that eventually they'll wind up in Italy, where—according to legend—Aeneas will found the city of Rome and house the flame in the Temple of Vesta.

Bernini was just 20 when he started this, his first major work for Cardinal Borghese. He was probably helped by his dad, who nurtured the child prodigy much like Leopold mentored Mozart, but without the rivalry. Bernini's portrayal of human flesh—from baby fat to middle-aged muscle to sagging decrepitude—is astonishing. Still, the flat-footed statue just stands there—it lacks the Baroque energy of his more mature work. More lively are the reliefs up at the ceiling, with their dancing, light-footed soldiers with do-si-do shields.

Room VII

The "Theater of the Universe"

The room's decor sums up the eclectic nature of the villa. There are Greek statues and Roman mosaics. There are fake "Egyptian" sphinxes and hieroglyphs (perfectly symmetrical, in good Neoclassical style). Look out the window past the sculpted gardens at the mesh domes of the aviary, once filled with exotic birds. Cardinal Borghese's vision was to make a place where art, history, music, nature, and science from every place and time would come together in "a theater of the universe."

Room VIII

Caravaggio

This room holds the greatest collection of Caravaggio paintings anywhere. Michelangelo Merisi (1571-1610), nicknamed Caravaggio after his hometown (near Milan), brought Christian saints down to earth with gritty realism. In each of these paintings you see the Baroque innovator Caravaggio's unique style: His saints are balding and wrinkled. His Bacchus (a self-portrait) is pale and puffy-faced. David sticks Goliath's severed head (a self-portrait of the artist) right in your face. The Madonnas scarcely glow. The boy Jesus is buck naked. Ordinary people were his models. People emerge from a dark background, lit by a harsh, unflattering light, which highlights part of the figure, leaving the rest in deep shadows. Caravaggio's straightforwardness can be a refreshing change in a museum full of (sometimes overly) refined beauty.

The painting *Madonna dei Palafrenieri* (1605) was removed

Gian Lorenzo Bernini
(1598-1680)

A Renaissance Man in Counter-Reformation times, Bernini almost personally invented the Baroque style, transforming the city of Rome. If you're visiting Rome, you will see Bernini's work, guaranteed.

Bernini was a child prodigy in his father's sculpting studio, growing up among Europe's rich and powerful. His flamboyant personality endeared him to his cultured employers—the popes in Rome, Louis XIV in France, and Charles I in England. He was extremely prolific, working fast and utilizing an army of assistants.

Despite the fleshiness and sensuality of his works, Bernini was a religious man, seeing his creativity as an extension of God's. In stark contrast to the Protestant world's sobriety, Bernini shamelessly embraced pagan myths and nude goddesses, declaring them all part of the "catholic"—that is, universal—Church.

Bernini, a master of multimedia, was a...

- Sculptor (Borghese Gallery and *St. Teresa in Ecstasy,* pictured above and described on page 77)
- Architect (elements of St. Peter's—see "Bernini Blitz," page 201, and the Church of Sant'Andrea al Quirinale)
- Painter (Borghese Gallery)
- Interior decorator (the *baldacchino* canopy and other works in St. Peter's)
- Civic engineer (he laid out St. Peter's Square, and he designed and renovated Rome's fountains in Piazza Navona, Piazza Barberini, Piazza di Spagna, and more).

Even works done by other artists a century later (such as the Trevi Fountain) can be traced indirectly to Bernini, the man who invented Baroque, the "look" of Rome for the next two centuries.

from St. Peter's for its lack of decorum. Jesus and Mary step on the snake of evil (that is, Protestantism). The pope had no problem with that...but the face of Mary is the face of Rome's most famous prostitute of the day. Cardinal Borghese didn't care; he bought the painting and hung it here.

David with the Head of Goliath (1609-1610) was painted after Caravaggio killed a man and was forced to flee Rome. By portraying himself as Goliath, he symbolically gives his head to the pope as a request for forgiveness. The pope accepted, but Caravaggio died of yellow fever on his way home.

• *To reach the Pinacoteca, head through the main entry hall back to room IV, find the entry to the staircase in the far-right corner, and spiral up to the...*

Pinacoteca (Painting Gallery)

You must visit the Pinacoteca within the two-hour window of time printed on your Borghese Gallery ticket. Most visitors wait until the last half-hour to see the Pinacoteca, so that's when it's most crowded (and the ground floor is less crowded). If you see the paintings first, remember to save most of your two-hour visit for the ground-floor sculptures.

• *Along the long wall of room XIV, you'll find the following statues and paintings by Bernini. First, find the two identical white busts set on columns.*

Room XIV

Two Bernini Busts of Cardinal Borghese (1632)

Say *grazie* to the man who built this villa, assembled the collection, and hired Bernini to sculpt masterpieces. The cardinal is caught turning as though to greet someone at a party. There's a twinkle in his eye, and he opens his mouth to make a witty comment. This man of the cloth was, in fact, a sophisticated hedonist.

Notice that there are two identical versions of this bust. The first one started cracking along the forehead (visible) just as Bernini was finishing it. *No problema*—Bernini whipped out a replacement in just three days.

• *On the left wall above the middle table, find these paintings...*

Two Bernini Self-Portraits (*Autoritratto Giovanile*, 1623, and *Autoritratto in età Matura*, 1630-1635)

Bernini was a master of many media, including painting. The younger Bernini (age 25) looks out a bit hesitantly, as if he's still finding his way in high-class society. His jet-black eyes came from his southern Italian mother who, it's said, also gave him his passionate personality.

In his next self-portrait (roughly age 35), with a few masterpieces under his belt, Bernini shows himself with more confidence and facial hair—the dashing, vibrant man who would rebuild Rome in Baroque style, from St. Peter's Square to the fountains that dot the piazzas.

• *On the table below, find the smaller...*

Bust of Pope Paul V (1618)

The cardinal's uncle was a more sober man, but he was also a patron of the arts with a good eye for talent who hired Bernini's father. When Pope Paul V saw sketches made by little Gian Lorenzo, he announced, "This boy will be the Michelangelo of his age."

• *To the right of the Borghese busts, find a small statue of...*

The Goat Amalthea with the Child Jupiter and a Faun (1615)

Bernini was barely 17 years old when he did this. That's about the age when I mastered how to make a Play-Doh snake.

• *Room IX is back near the top of the staircase you ascended to get here.*

Room IX

Raphael (Raffaello Sanzio)—*Deposition* (*Deposizione,* 1507)

Jesus is being taken from the cross. The men support him while the women support Mary (in purple), who has fainted. Mary Magdalene rushes up to take Christ's hand. The woman who commissioned the painting had recently lost her son. She wanted to show the death of a son and the grief of a mother. We see two different faces of grief—mother Mary faints at the horror, while Mary Magdalene still can't quite believe he's gone.

In true Renaissance style, Raphael (1483-1520) orders the scene with geometrical perfection. The curve of Jesus' body is echoed by the swirl of Mary Magdalene's hair, and then by the curve of Calvary Hill, where Christ met his fate.

Room X

Correggio—*Danae* (c. 1531)

Cupid strips Danae as she spreads her legs, most unladylike, to receive a trickle of gold from the smudgy cloud overhead—this was Zeus' idea of intercourse with a human. The sheets are rumpled, and Danae looks right where the action is with a smile on her face. It's hard to believe that a supposedly religious family would display such an erotic work. But the Borgheses felt that the Church was truly

"catholic" (universal) and that all forms of human expression—including physical passion—glorified God.

• *Backtrack through the room with the two cardinal busts, then turn left and travel to the farthest room.*

Room XX

Titian (Tiziano Vecellio)—*Sacred and Profane Love* (*Amor Sacro e Amor Profano,* c. 1515)

While you might guess that the naked woman on the right embodies profane love, that's actually represented by the material girl on the left—with her box of treasures, fortified castle, and dark, claustrophobic landscape. Sacred love is represented by the naked woman who has nothing to hide and enjoys open spaces filled with light, life, a church in the distance, and even a couple of lovers in the field.

The clothed woman at left has recently married, and she cradles a vase filled with jewels representing the riches of earthly love. Her naked twin on the right holds the burning flame of eternal, heavenly love. Baby Cupid, between them, playfully stirs the waters.

Symbolically, the steeple on the right points up to the love of heaven, while on the left, soldiers prepare to "storm the castle" of the new bride. Miss Heavenly Love looks jealous.

This exquisite painting expresses the spirit of the Renaissance—that earth and heaven are two sides of the same coin. And here in the Borghese Gallery, that love of earthly beauty can be spiritually uplifting—as long as you feel it within two hours.

NATIONAL MUSEUM OF ROME TOUR

Museo Nazionale Romano / Palazzo Massimo

Rome lasted a thousand years...and so do most Roman history courses. But if you want a breezy overview of this fascinating society, there's no better place than the National Museum of Rome.

Rome took Greek culture and wrote it in capital letters. Thanks to this lack of originality, ancient Greek statues were preserved for our enjoyment today. But the Romans also pioneered a totally new form of art—sculpting painfully realistic portraits of emperors and important citizens.

Think of this museum as a walk back in time. As you gaze at the same statues that the Romans swooned over, the history of Rome comes alive—from Julius Caesar's murder to Caligula's incest to Vespasian's Colosseum to the coming of Christianity.

Orientation

Cost: €10 combo-ticket valid for three days, includes entry into three lesser National Museum branches: the nearby Museum of the Bath (lackluster ancient inscriptions), Palazzo Altemps (so-so sculptures), and Crypta Balbi (medieval art). Price drops to €7 without mandatory special exhibits.

Hours: Tue-Sun 9:00-19:45, closed Mon, last entry 45 minutes before closing.

When to Go: The museum is never crowded. Since it has a convenient and free bag check (even for backpacks and suitcases), consider a visit en route from the train station.

Getting There: The museum is in Palazzo Massimo, situated between Piazza della Repubblica (Metro: Repubblica) and Termini Station (Metro: Termini). It's a few minutes' walk from either Metro stop. As you leave Termini, it's the sandstone-brick building on your left. Enter at the far end, at

Largo di Villa Peretti.
Information: Tel. 06-3996-7700, http://archeoroma.beniculturali.it/en.
Audioguide: €5 (3 hours).
Length of This Tour: Allow two hours.
With Limited Time: Do the ground floor and the first floor as far as the Discus Thrower.
Photography: Photos allowed without flash.
Starring: Roman emperor busts, the Discus Thrower, original Greek statues, and fine Roman copies.

The Tour Begins

Overview

The Palazzo Massimo is the permanent home of major Greek and Roman statues that were formerly scattered in other national museums around town.

The museum is rectangular, with rooms and hallways built around a central courtyard. The ground-floor displays follow Rome's history as it changes from a democratic republic to a dictatorial empire. The first-floor exhibits take Rome from its peak through its slow decline. The second floor houses rare frescoes and fine mosaics, and the basement presents coins and everyday objects. As you tour this museum, note that in Italian, "room" is *sala* and "hall" is *galleria*.

Ground Floor—From Senators to Caesars

• *Buy your ticket and pass through the turnstile, where you'll find...*

Minerva

It's big, it's gaudy, it's a weird goddess from a pagan cult. Welcome to the Roman world. The statue is also a good reminder that all the statues in this museum—now missing limbs, scarred by erosion, or weathered down to bare stone—were once whole, and painted to look as lifelike as possible.

• *Turning to the right, you'll find Gallery I; this hallway is lined with portrait busts.*

Gallery I—Portrait Heads from the Republic (500-1 B.C.)

Stare into the eyes of these stern, hardy, no-nonsense farmer-stock people who founded Rome. The wrinkles and crags of these origi-

National Museum—Ground Floor

ROOM III
ROOM II
ROOM I
STAIRS
ELEV.
BAGGAGE CHECK
WC
GALLERY I
STEPS
TICKETS
ENTRY
ROOM IV
GALLERY II
ROOM V
Open air Courtyard
VIA VIMINALE
GALLERY III
ROOM VI
ROOM VII
ROOM VIII
STAIRS UP TO FIRST FLOOR
To Termini Train Station
To Piazza Repubblica

1. Minerva
2. Portrait Heads
3. Julius Caesar (?)
4. Augustus as Pontifex Maximus
5. Livia
6. Tiberius
7. Caligula
8. Alexander the Great
9. Socrates
10. Dying Niobid
11. The Boxer at Rest & Hellenistic Prince

nal "ugly republicans" tell the story of Rome's roots as a small agricultural tribe, fighting for survival with neighboring bands.

These faces are brutally realistic, unlike more idealized Greek statues. Romans honored their ancestors and worthy citizens in the "family" *(gens)* of Rome. They wanted lifelike statues to remember them by, and to instruct the young with their air of moral rectitude.

In its first 500 years, Rome was a republic ruled by a Senate of wealthy landowners. But as Rome expanded throughout Italy, and the economy shifted from farming to booty, changes became necessary.

• *Enter room I (sala I). Along the wall between the doorways, find the portrait bust that may (or may not) be Julius Caesar.*

Room I

Julius Caesar(?) (labeled *Rilievo con ritratto di uomo anziano*)

Some scholars have identified this bust as representing Rome's most famous citizen (while others disagree).

Julius Caesar (c. 100-44 B.C.)—with

his prominent brow, high cheekbones, and male-pattern baldness with the forward comb-over—changed Rome forever.

When this charismatic general swept onto the scene, Rome was in chaos. Rich landowners were fighting middle-class plebs, who wanted their slice of the plunder. Slaves such as Spartacus were picking up hoes and hacking up masters. And renegade generals—the new providers of wealth and security in an economy of plunder—were becoming dictators. (Notice the **life-size statue** with a shaved-off head, of an unknown but obviously once-renowned general.)

Caesar was a people's favorite. He conquered Gaul (France), then sacked Egypt, then impregnated Cleopatra. He defeated rivals and made them his allies. He gave great speeches. Chicks dug him.

With the army at his back and the people in awe, he took the reins of government, instituted sweeping changes, made himself the center of power...and antagonized the Senate.

A band of republican assassins surrounded him in a Senate meeting. He called out for help as one by one they stepped up to take turns stabbing him. The senators sat and watched in silence. One of the killers was his adopted son, Brutus, and Caesar—astonished that even he joined in—died saying, *"Et tu, Brute?"*

• *At the end of Gallery I, turn left and enter the large glassed-in room V, with a life-size statue of Augustus.*

Room V—Augustus

Augustus as Pontifex Maximus *(Augusto Pontefice Massimo)*

Julius Caesar died, but his family name, his politics, and his flamboyance lived on. Julius had adopted his grandnephew, Octavian, who united Rome's warring factions and took the name and title "Augustus," meaning "venerable" or "protected by the gods."

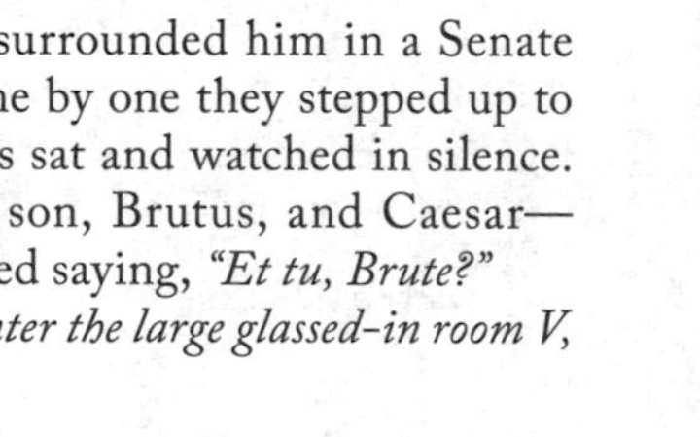

Here, Emperor Augustus has taken off his armor and laurel-leaf crown, donning the simple hooded robes of a priest. He's retiring to a desk job after a lifetime of fighting to reunite Rome. He killed Brutus and eliminated his rivals, Mark Antony and Cleopatra. For the first time in almost a century of fighting, one general reigned supreme. Augustus became the first of the emperors who would rule Rome for the next 500 years.

In fact, Augustus was a down-to-earth man who lived simply, worked hard, read books, listened to underlings, and tried to restore traditional Roman values after the turbulence of Julius

Caesar's time. He outwardly praised the Senate, while actually reducing it to a rubber-stamp body. Augustus' reign marked the start of 200 years of peace and prosperity, the Pax Romana.

See if the statue matches this description of Augustus by a contemporary, the historian Suetonius: "He was unusually handsome. His expression was calm and mild. He had clear, bright eyes, in which was a kind of divine power. His hair was slightly curly and somewhat golden." Any variations were made by sculptors who idealized features to make him almost godlike.

Augustus proclaimed himself a god—not arrogantly or blasphemously, as Caligula later did, but as the honored "father" of the "family" of Rome. As the empire expanded, the vanquished had to worship statues like this one as a show of loyalty.

• *Cross the hallway into room IV. Near the doorway, find the bust of the empress Livia.*

Room IV—Rome's First Emperors (c. 50 B.C.-A.D. 68)

Julius Caesar's descendants—the Julio-Claudian family—ruled Rome for a century after his death, turning the family surname "Caesar" into a title.

Livia

Augustus' wife, Livia, was a major power behind the throne. Her stern, thin-lipped gaze withered rivals at court. Her hairstyle—bunched up in a peak, braided down the center, and tied in back—became the rage throughout the empire, as her face appeared everywhere, from statues to coins. Notice that by the next generation, a simpler bun was chic (Antonia Minore, Livia's daughter-in-law, next to Livia). And by the following generation, the trend was tight curls. Empresses dictated fashion the way emperors dictated policy.

Livia bore Augustus no sons. She lobbied hard for Tiberius, her own son by a first marriage, to succeed as emperor. Augustus didn't like him, but Livia was persuasive. He relented, ate some bad figs, and died—the gossip was that Livia poisoned him to seal the bargain. The pattern of succession was established—adopt a son from within the extended family—and Tiberius was proclaimed emperor. (The fine frescoed walls of Livia's Anzio villa are upstairs on the second floor.)

• *In the corner of the room, find the well-worn bust of...*

Tiberius (*Tiberio,* ruled A.D. 14-37)

Scholars speculate that acne may have soured Tiberius to the world (but this statue is pocked by erosion). Shy and sullen but diligent, he worked hard to be the easygoing leader that Augustus had been. Early on, he was wise and patient, but he suffered personal setbacks. Politics forced him to divorce his only beloved and marry a slut. His favorite brother died, then his son. Embittered, he let subordinates run things and retired to Capri, where he built a villa with underground dungeons. There he hosted orgies of sex, drugs, torture, really loud music, and execution. At his side was his young grandnephew, whom he adopted as the next emperor.

• *To your right, in the glass case, is the small bust of...*

Caligula (*Caligola,* ruled A.D. 37-41)

This emperor had sex with his sisters, tortured his enemies, made off with friends' wives during dinner parties and then returned to rate their performance in bed, crucified Christians, took cuts in line at the Vatican Museum, and ordered men to kneel before him as a god. Caligula has become the archetype of a man with enough power to act out his basest fantasies.

Politically, he squandered Rome's money, then taxed and extorted from the citizens. Perhaps he was made mad by illness, perhaps he was the victim of vindictive historians, but still, no one mourned when assassins ambushed him and ran a sword through his privates. Rome was tiring of this family dynasty's dysfunction.

• *Continue down Gallery II and turn left. Busts line Gallery III. Find Alexander the Great (outside room VI) and Socrates (farther down the hall, outside room VIII).*

Gallery III—Rome's Greek Mentors

Rome's legions easily conquered the less-organized but more-cultured Greek civilization that had dominated the Mediterranean for centuries. Romans adopted Greek gods, art styles, and fashions, and sophisticates sprinkled their conversation with Greek phrases.

Alexander the Great *(Alessandro Magno)*

Alexander the Great (356-323 B.C.) single-handedly created a Greek-speaking empire by conquering, in just a few short years, lands from Greece to Egypt to Persia. Later, when the Romans conquered Greece (c. 200 B.C.), they inherited this pre-existing

collection of cultured Greek cities ringing the Mediterranean.

Alexander's handsome statues set the standard for those of later Roman emperors. His features were chiseled and youthful, and this statue was adorned with pompous decorations, like a golden sunburst aura (fitted into the holes). The greatest man of his day, he ruled the known world by the age of 30.

Alexander's teacher was none other than the philosopher Aristotle. Aristotle's teacher was Plato, whose mentor was...

Socrates *(Socrate)*

This nonconformist critic of complacent thinking is the father of philosophy. The Greeks were an intellectual, introspective, sensitive, and artistic people. The Romans were practical, no-nonsense soldiers, salesmen, and bureaucrats. Many a Greek slave was more cultured than his master, reduced to the role of warning his boss not to wear a plaid toga with a polka-dot robe.

• *Backtrack and enter room VI.*

Room VI—Greek Beauty in Originals and Copies

Dying Niobid (*Niobide Morente,* 440 B.C.)

The Romans were astonished by the beauty of Greek statues. The smooth skin of this Niobid (the term for any child of the goddess Niobe) contrasts with the rough folds of her clothing. She twists naturally around an axis running straight up and down. This woman looks like a classical goddess awakening from a beautiful dream, but...

Circle around back. The hole bored in her back, right in that itchy place you can't quite reach, once held a golden arrow. The woman has been shot by Artemis, goddess of hunting, because her mother dared to boast to the gods about her kids. The Niobid reaches back in vain, trying to remove the arrow before it drains her of life.

Romans ate this stuff up: the sensual beauty, the underplayed pathos, the very Greekness of it. They crated up centuries-old statues like this and brought them home to their gardens and palaces. Soon there weren't enough old statues to meet the demand. Crafty Greeks began cranking out knockoffs of Greek originals for mass consumption. Rooms VII and VIII contain both originals (like Niobid) and copies—some of extremely high quality, others resembling cheesy fake *David*s in a garden store. Appreciate the beauty of the world's rare, surviving Greek originals.

Rome conquered Greece, but culturally the Greeks conquered the Romans.

• *Move next door to see...*

Room VII—Hellenistic and Classical Bronzes

The Boxer at Rest (*Pugilatore,* first century B.C.)

An exhausted boxer sits between rounds and gasps for air. Check out the brass knuckles-type Roman boxing gloves. Textbook Hellenistic, this pugilist is realistic and full of emotion. His face is scarred, his back muscles are knotted, and he's got cauliflower ears. He's losing.

Slumped over, he turns with a questioning look ("Why am I losing again?"), and eyes that once held glass now make him look empty indeed. "I coulda been a contender."

Hellenistic Prince (*Principe Elenistico*)

Back then, everyone wanted to be like Alexander the Great. This restored bronze statue—naked and leaning on a spear—shows a prince (probably Attalus II of Pergamon) in the style of a famous statue of his hero from the second century B.C.

• *We've covered Rome's first 500 years. At the end of the hall are the stairs up to the first floor.*

First Floor—Rome's Peak and Slow Fall

As we saw, Augustus' family did not always rule wisely. Under Nero (ruled A.D. 54-68), the debauchery, violence, and paranoia typical of the Julio-Claudians festered to a head. When the city burned in the great fire of 64, the Romans suspected Nero of torching it himself to clear land for his enormous luxury palace.

Enough. Facing a death sentence, Nero committed suicide

National Museum—First Floor

ROOM VIII, ROOM IX, ROOM X, ROOM XI, ROOM XII, ROOM VII, ROOM VI, ROOM V, ROOM I, ROOM II, ROOM XIII, ROOM XIV, GALLERY II, Open Courtyard Below, STAIRS FROM GROUND FLOOR

1. Vespasian
2. Domitian
3. Domitia
4. Nerva
5. Trajan
6. Hadrian
7. Aphrodite Crouching
8. The Discus Thrower
9. Apollo
10. Septimius Severus
11. Caracalla
12. Sarcophagus with Processional Scene
13. Christ Teaching

with the help of a servant. An outsider was brought in to rule—Vespasian, from the Flavian family.

• *At the top of the stairs, enter room I and then move into the hallway on the left. To your left is...*

The Flavian Family

Vespasian (*Vespasianus,* ruled A.D. 69-79)

Balding and wrinkled, with a big head, a double chin, and a shy smile, Vespasian was a common man. The son of a tax collector, he rose through the military ranks with a reputation as a competent drudge. As emperor, he restored integrity, raised taxes, started the Colosseum, and suppressed the Jewish rebellion in Palestine.

Domitian (*Domitianus,* ruled A.D. 81-96)

Vespasian's son, Domitian, used his father's tax revenues to construct the massive Imperial Palace on Palatine Hill, home to emperors for the next three centuries. Shown with his lips curled in a sneer, he was a moralistic prude who executed several Vestal ex-Virgins, while in private he took one mistress after another. Until...

Domitia

...his stern wife found out and hired a servant to stab him in the groin. Domitia's hairstyle is a far cry from the "Livia" cut, with a high crown of tight curls.

Nerva (ruled A.D. 96-98)

Nerva realized that the Flavian dynasty was no better than its predecessors. Old and childless, he made a bold, far-sighted move—he adopted a son from outside of Rome's corrupting influence.

• *Go back to room I and head straight to room II, where you'll find Trajan on the left wall.*

Room II—A Cosmopolitan Culture

Trajan (*Traianus-Hercules,* ruled A.D. 98-117)

Born in Spain, this conquering hero pushed Rome's borders to their greatest extent, creating a truly worldwide empire. The spoils of three continents funneled into a city of a million-plus people. Trajan could dress up in a lion's skin, presenting himself as a "new Hercules," and no one found it funny. Romans felt a spirit of Manifest Destiny: "The gods desire that the City of Rome shall be the capital of all the countries of the world" (Livy).

• *On the opposite wall is...*

Hadrian (*Hadrianus,* ruled A.D. 117-138)

Hadrian was a fully cosmopolitan man. His beard—the first we've seen—shows his taste for foreign things; he poses like the Greek philosopher he imagined himself to be.

Hadrian was a voracious tourist, personally visiting almost every corner of the vast empire, from Britain (where he built Hadrian's Wall) to Egypt (where he sailed the Nile), from Jerusalem (where he suppressed another Jewish revolt) to Athens (where he soaked up classical culture). He scaled Sicily's Mount Etna just to see what made a volcano tick. Back home, he beautified Rome with the Pantheon and his villa at

Tivoli, a microcosm of places he'd visited.

Hadrian is flanked here by the two loves of his life. His wife, **Sabina** (left), with modest hairstyle and scarf, kept the home fires burning for her traveling husband. Hadrian was 50 years old when he became captivated by a teenage boy named **Antinous** (right), with his curly hair and full, sensual lips. Together they traveled the Nile, where Antinous drowned. Hadrian wept. Statues of Antinous subsequently went up throughout the Empire, much to the embarrassment of the stoic Romans.

Hadrian spent his last years at his lavish villa outside Rome, surrounded by buildings and souvenirs that reminded him of his traveling days (see Tivoli Day Trip chapter).

• *Backtrack through room I and turn right, down the hall that leads into the large room V.*

Rooms V and VI—Rome's Grandeur

Pause at Rome's peak to admire the things the Romans found beautiful. Imagine these statues as they originally stood—in the pleasure gardens of the Roman rich, surrounded by greenery with the splashing sound of fountains, all painted in bright, lifelike colors. Though executed by Romans, the themes are mostly Greek, with godlike humans and human-looking gods.

• *At the beginning of room V is...*

Aphrodite Crouching *(Afrodite al bagno accovacciata)*

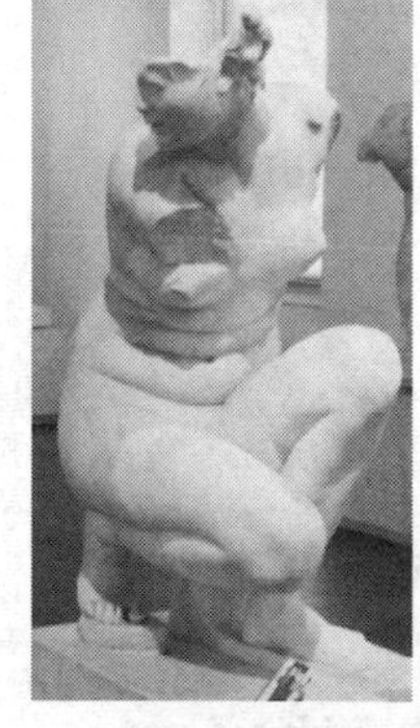

The goddess of beauty crouches while bathing, then turns to admire herself. This sets her whole body in motion—one thigh goes down, the other up; her head turns clockwise while her body goes in reverse—yet she's perfectly still. The crouch creates a series of symmetrical love handles, molded by the sculptor into the marble-like wax. Hadrian had good taste—he ordered a copy of this Greek classic for his bathroom.

• *At the far end of the room, pass into room VI, with...*

The Discus Thrower *(Discobolo)*

An athlete winds up, about to unleash his pent-up energy and hurl the discus. The sculptor has frozen the moment for us so that we can examine the inner workings of the wonder called Man. The perfect pecs and washboard abs make this human godlike. Geometrically, you could draw a perfect circle around him, with his hipbone at the center. He's natural yet ideal, twisting yet balanced, moving while at rest. For the Greeks, the universe was a rational place, and the human body was the perfect embodiment of the order found in nature.

This statue is the best-preserved Roman copy (not one member is missing—I checked) of the original Greek work by Myron (450 B.C.). (The subtle nubs on his head were aids for a measuring device used when making copies.) Statues of athletes like this commonly stood in the baths, where Romans cultivated healthy bodies, minds, and social skills, hoping to lead well-rounded lives. The Discus Thrower, with his geometrical perfection and godlike air, sums up all that is best in the classical world.

• *Continue into the center of room VII.*

Room VII

Apollo *(Apollo del Tevere)*

The god of light appears as a slender youth, not as some burly, powerful, autocratic god. He stands *contrapposto*—originally he was leaning against the tree—in a relaxed and very human way. His curled hair is tied with a headband, strands tumbling down his neck. His muscles and skin are smooth. (The rusty stains come from the centuries the statue spent submerged in the Tiber.) Apollo is in a reflective mood, and the serenity and intelligence in his face show off classical Greece as a nation of thinkers.

• *Exit room VII at the far end on the left. Then turn right into room XIII and look to the right to find the bust of Septimius Severus.*

Room XIII—Beginning of the End

Septimius Severus (ruled A.D. 193-211)

Rome's sprawling empire was starting to unravel, and it took a disciplined emperor-warrior like this African to keep it together. Severus' victories on the frontier earned him a grand triumphal arch in the Forum, but here he seems to be rolling his eyes at the chaos growing around him.

• *Near Severus is his son...*

Caracalla (ruled A.D. 211-217)

The stubbly beard, cruel frown, and glaring eyes tell us that Severus' son was bad news. He murdered his little brother to seize power, then proceeded to massacre thousands of loyal citizens on a whim. The army came to distrust rulers whose personal agenda got in their way, and Caracalla was stabbed in the back by a man whose brother had just been executed. Rome's long slide had begun.

Room XIV—The Fall

There are a lot of serious faces in this room. People who grew up in the lap of luxury and security were witnessing the unthinkable—the disintegration of a thousand years of tradition. Rome never recovered from the chaos of the third century. Disease, corruption, revolts from within, and "barbarians" pecking away at the borders were body blows that sapped Rome's strength.

• *Immediately after entering this long room, find the...*

Sarcophagus with Processional Scene (*Sarcofago con Corteo,* A.D. 270)

A parade of dignitaries, accompanying a new Roman leader, marches up Capitoline Hill. They huddle together, their backs to the wall, looking around suspiciously for assassins. Their faces reflect the fear of the age.

By the third century, the Roman army could virtually hand-pick an emperor to be their front man. At one point, the office of emperor was literally auctioned to the highest bidder. In the space of 40 years, 15 different emperors were saluted, then murdered, at the whims of soldiers of fortune.

Rome would stagger on for another 200 years, but the glory of old Rome was gone. The city was becoming a den of thugs, thieves, prostitutes, barbarians...and Christians.

• *Farther along, on the right-hand wall, find the small...*

Christ Teaching (*Cristo Docente,* A.D. 350)

Christ sits like a Roman senator—in a toga, holding a scroll,

dispensing wisdom like the law of the land. The statuette comes from those delirious days when formerly persecuted Christians could now "come out" and worship in public. Emperor Constantine (ruled A.D. 306-337) legalized Christianity, and within two generations it was Rome's official religion.

Whether Christianity invigorated or ruined Rome is debated, but the fall was inevitable. Rome's once-great legions backpedaled, until even the city itself was raped and plundered by foreigners (410). In 476, the last emperor sold his title for a comfy pension plan, "Rome" became just another dirty city with a big history, and the artistic masterpieces now in this museum were buried under rubble.

The Rest of the Museum

• *For extra credit, consider exploring two more parts of the National Museum.*

Second Floor

This floor contains frescoes and mosaics that once decorated the walls and floors of Roman villas. They're remarkably realistic and unstuffy, featuring everyday people, animals, flowery patterns, and geometrical designs. The **Villa Farnesina frescoes**—in black, red, yellow, and blue—are mostly architectural designs, with fake columns, friezes, and garlands. The **Villa di Livia frescoes,** owned by the wily wife of Augustus, immerse you in a leafy green garden full of birds and fruit trees, symbolizing the gods.

Basement (Floor -2)

The **"Luxury in Rome"** rooms give a peek into the lives of Rome's well-to-do citizens, featuring fine jewelry, common everyday objects, and an eight-year-old girl's mummy.

Next, enter the **coin collection.** Find your favorite emperor or empress on the coins by using remote-controlled magnifying glasses: Julius Caesar (case 8, #41-44), Augustus (case 8, #65-69, and case 9, #1-38), Augustus' system of denars (case 10), Tiberius (case 10, #1-16), Caligula (case 10, #17-28), and Nero (case 11,

#2-33). Evaluate Roman life by studying how Diocletian tweaked the gold standard (glass case 21). In A.D. 300, one denar bought one egg. The rest of the displays trace Europe's money from denars to euros. The final exhibit (case 59) features a monetary unit that is now history—the Italian lira.

BATHS OF DIOCLETIAN TOUR

Terme di Diocleziano

Of all the marvelous structures built by the Romans, their public baths were arguably the grandest, and the Baths of Diocletian were the granddaddy of them all. Sprawling over 30 acres—roughly five times the size of the Colosseum—these baths could cleanse 3,000 Romans at once. Today, tourists can visit one grand section of the baths. It's now the **Church of Santa Maria degli Angeli,** housed in the former main hall of the baths, an impressive remnant of the ancient complex.

Energetic architecture wonks can walk the perimeter of the baths: from Via Torino to Piazza dei Cinquecento to Via Volturno to Via XX Settembre. Note that nearby Museum of the Bath (Museo Nazionale Romano Terme di Diocleziano), despite the name, has nothing to with the ancient baths.

Orientation

Cost and Hours: Free, Mon-Sat 7:00-18:30, Sun 7:00-19:30.

Getting There: The entrance is on Piazza della Repubblica (Metro: Repubblica).

Length of This Tour: Allow 30 minutes.

The Tour Begins

Santa Maria degli Angeli

• *Start your tour standing outside the church.*

Exterior—The Baths' Caldarium

The curved brick facade of today's church was once part of the *caldarium,* or steam room of the ancient baths. Romans loved to sweat out last night's indulgences. After entering the main lobby (located

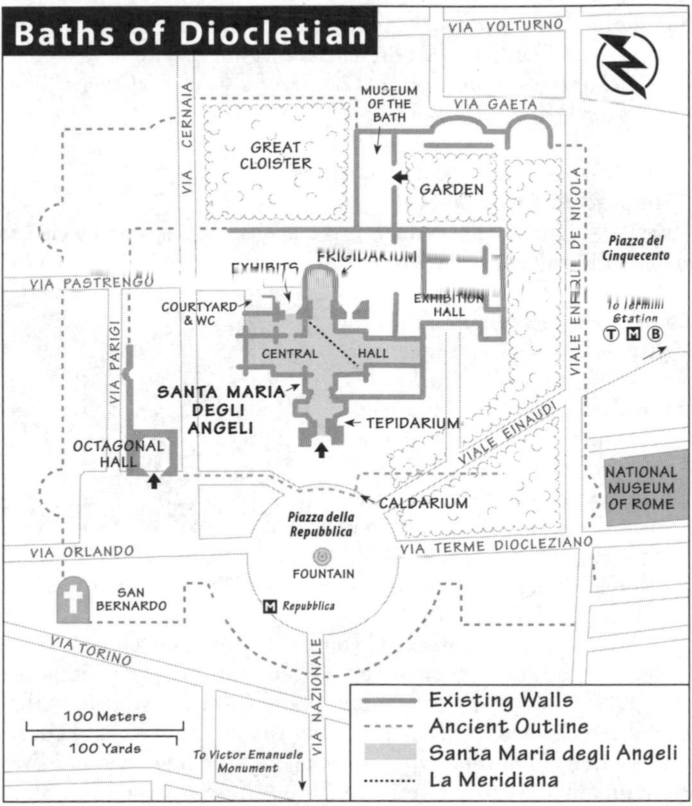

Baths of Diocletian

VIA VOLTURNO
MUSEUM OF THE BATH
VIA GAETA
VIA CERNAIA
GREAT CLOISTER
GARDEN
VIALE ENRICO DE NICOLA
Piazza del Cinquecento
FRIGIDARIUM
EXHIBITS
VIA PASTRENGO
COURTYARD & WC
EXHIBITION HALL
To Termini Station
CENTRAL HALL
VIA PARIGI
SANTA MARIA DEGLI ANGELI
TEPIDARIUM
VIALE EINAUDI
OCTAGONAL HALL
NATIONAL MUSEUM OF ROME
CALDARIUM
Piazza della Repubblica
VIA ORLANDO
VIA TERME DIOCLEZIANO
FOUNTAIN
SAN BERNARDO
Repubblica
VIA TORINO
VIA NAZIONALE
100 Meters
100 Yards
To Victor Emanuele Monument
Existing Walls
Ancient Outline
Santa Maria degli Angeli
La Meridiana

where Piazza della Repubblica is today), they'd strip in the locker rooms, then enter the steam room. The *caldarium* had wood furnaces under the raised floors. Stoked by slaves, these furnaces were used to heat the floors and hot tubs. The low ceiling helped keep the room steamy.

From the *caldarium,* the Romans moved into the next room, and so should you.

• *From noisy Piazza della Repubblica, step into the vast and cool church built upon the remains of a vast and steamy Roman bath complex.*

The Church's Entry Hall—The Baths' Tepidarium

This round domed room with an oculus (open skylight, now with modern stained glass) was once the *tepidarium*—the cooling-off room of the baths, where medium, "tepid" temperatures were maintained. This is where masseuses would rub you down and scrape you off with a stick (Romans didn't use soap).

• *In ancient times, Romans would have continued on to the central area of the baths. You'll continue to...*

The Church's Large Transept—The Baths' Central Hall

This hall retains the grandeur of the ancient baths. It's the size of a football field and seven stories high—once even higher, since the original ancient floor was about 15 feet below its present level. The ceiling's crisscross arches were an architectural feat unmatched for a thousand years. The eight red granite columns are original, from ancient Rome—stand next to one and feel its five-foot girth. (Only the eight in the transept proper are original. The others are made of plastered-over brick.) In Roman times, this hall was covered with mosaics, marble, and gold, and lined with statues.

From here, Romans could continue (through what is now the apse, near the altar) into an open-air courtyard to take a dip in the vast 32,000-square-foot swimming pool (in the *frigidarium*) that paralleled this huge hall. Many other rooms, gardens, and courtyards extended beyond what we see here. The huge complex was built in only 10 years (around A.D. 300)—amazing when you think of the centuries it took builders of puny medieval cathedrals, such as Paris' Notre-Dame.

Mentally undress your fellow tourists and churchgoers, and imagine hundreds of naked or toga-clad Romans wrestling, doing jumping jacks, singing in the baths, networking, or just milling about.

The baths were more than washrooms. They were health clubs with exercising areas, equipment, and swimming pools. They had gardens for socializing. Libraries, shops, bars, fast-food vendors, pedicurists, depilatories, and brothels catered to every Roman need. Most important, perhaps, the baths offered a spacious, cool-in-summer/warm-in-winter place for Romans to get out of their stuffy apartments and schmooze or simply hang out.

Admission was virtually free, requiring only the smallest coin. Baths were open to men and women—and during Nero's reign, coed bathing was popular—but generally there were either separate rooms or separate entry times. Most Romans went daily.

The church we see today was (at least partly) designed by

Michelangelo (1561), who used the baths' main hall as the nave. Later, when Piazza della Repubblica became an important Roman intersection, another architect renovated the church. To allow people to enter from the grand new piazza, he spun it 90 degrees, turning Michelangelo's nave into a long transept.

• *Embedded in the floor of the right transept (roped off) is a brass rod called...*

La Meridiana (1702)

This is a meridian, pointing due north. It acts as a sundial. As the sun arcs across the southern sky, a ray of light beams into the church through a tiny hole high in the wall and a cut in the cornice of the right transept. (To find the hole, follow the rod to the right to the wall and look up 65 feet.) The sunbeam sweeps across the church floor, crossing the meridian rod at exactly noon. (Allow for variances due to Daylight Saving Time and the approximate time zones of Greenwich Mean Time.)

This celestial clock is also a calendar. In summer, when the sun is high overhead, the sunbeam strikes the southern end of the rod. With each passing day, the sun travels up the rod (toward the apse), passing through the signs of the zodiac (the 28-day months of the moon's phases) marked alongside the rod. Many of the meridian's markings were intended for its other use, charting the movement of the stars. However, the tiny window that once let in light from the North Star (originally above the archway of the entrance to the apse) has been filled in.

Find some key dates in the Christian calendar, particularly the spring equinox and Easter (near Aries the Ram). Most Christians agree that Easter is the first Sunday after the first full moon after the vernal equinox (established with the Nicene Creed, A.D. 325). It took large meridians like this to measure the sun's movements accurately enough to predict Easter and other holidays years in advance.

La Meridiana was Rome's official city timekeeper until 1846, when it was replaced by the cannon atop Gianicolo Hill (which is still fired every day at exactly noon).

In the left transept (opposite end), you'll find a monumental organ built for the Jubilee Year of 2000. Free concerts are held regularly; check the schedule posted near the organ.

• *Step into the Sacrestia, the small room to the left of the main altar, which now houses...*

Exhibits

Temporary exhibits often illuminate the church's rich architectural history. Admire both the immensity and height of the ancient Roman brickwork in this room. Step outside into the courtyard and re-create the grand architecture. Notice the *exedra* (semicircular recess in a wall or building)—a motif Romans used for decoration and as a kind of stage for philosophers and orators. See the niches that once housed statues, the rectangular holes that could be used to hold wood-beam scaffolding, and the small pockmarks where iron pegs once secured the marble paneling.

Large building projects like this were political security: They provided employment and fed the masses. Diocletian (ruled A.D. 285-305) struggled with a system to rule his unwieldy empire. He broke it into zones ruled by four "tetrarchs." During Diocletian's "tetrarchs" period, architecture and art were grandiose, but almost a caricature of greatness—meant to proclaim to Romans that their city was still the power it had once been.

The baths were one of the last great structures built before Rome's 200-year fall. They functioned until A.D. 537, when barbarians cut the city's aqueducts, plunging Rome into a thousand years of poverty, darkness, and B.O.

• *There's a* WC (€0.50) *and tiny shop nearby. When you're ready to leave, exit where you entered. If you're feeling lucky, turn right and walk 100 yards to the entrance of the restored (but rarely open)...*

Octagonal Hall (Aula Ottagona)

This octagonal building, capped by a dome with a hole in the top, may have served as a cool room *(frigidarium)*, with small pools of cold water for plunging into. Or, because of its many doors, it may simply have been a large intersection, connecting other parts of the baths. Originally, the floor was 25 feet lower—as you can see through the glass-covered hole in the floor. The graceful iron grid overhead supported the canopy of a 1928 planetarium. Today, the hall is used for temporary exhibits and events.

Piazza della Repubblica

The piazza, shaped like an *exedra* (curved recess), echoes the wall of a stadium adjoining the original baths. It was called Piazza Esedra until Italian unification (and is still called that by many Romans). The thundering Via Nazionale starts at what was an ancient door. Look down it (past the erotic nymphs of the Naiad fountain) to the Victor Emmanuel Monument. The Art Nouveau fountain of the four water nymphs created quite a stir when unveiled in 1911. The nymphs were modeled after a set of twins, who kept coming to visit as late as the 1960s to remind themselves of their nubile youth. Here at the site of the ancient Thermae, the statues bathe eternally.

PILGRIM'S ROME TOUR

Pilgrimage Churches

Rome is the "capital" of the world's 1.1 billion Catholics. In Rome, you'll rub elbows with religious pilgrims from around the world—Nigerian nuns, Bulgarian theology students, extended Mexican families, and everyday Catholics returning to their religious roots.

The pilgrim industry helped shape Rome after the fall of the empire. Ancient Rome's population peaked at about 1.2 million. After Rome fell in A.D. 476, barbarians cut off the water supply by breaking the aqueducts, Romans fled the city, and the mouth of the Tiber River filled with silt and became a swamp.

During the Dark Ages, mosquitoes ruled over a pathetic village of 50,000...bad news for pilgrims, bad news for the papacy. Back then, the Catholic Church was the Christian Church. Centuries later, during the Renaissance, popes sought to project an image of prestige and authority. The Church revitalized the city, creating a place fit for pilgrimages. Owners of hotels and restaurants cheered.

In 1587, Pope Sixtus V reconnected aqueducts and built long, straight boulevards connecting the great churches and pilgrimage sites. Obelisks were moved to serve as markers. As you explore the city, think like a pilgrim. Look down long roads and you'll see either a grand church or an obelisk (from which you'll see a grand church).

Orientation

Church of San Giovanni in Laterano: Free, daily 7:00-18:30, €5 audioguide available at info desk inside (ID required), includes entry to the cloister. The **Holy Stairs** (Scala Santa), in a building across the street from the church, are free and open daily (April-Sept 6:15-12:00 & 15:30-18:45, Oct-March

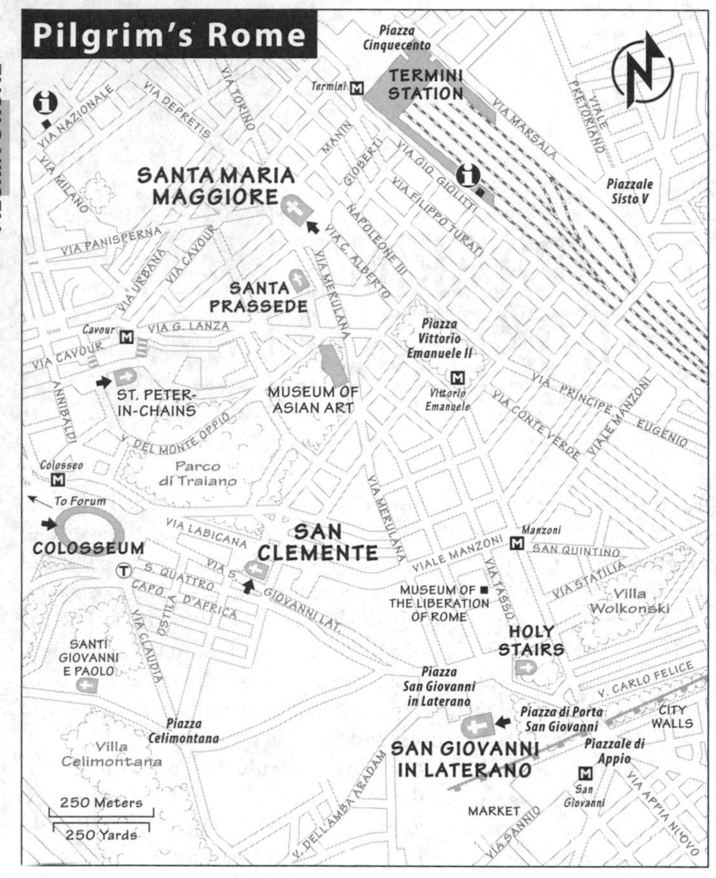

6:15-12:00 & 15:00-18:15).

Church of Santa Maria Maggiore: Free, daily 7:00-19:00, skip the €5 audioguide and €4 museum.

Church of Santa Prassede: Free, bring €0.50 and €1 coins for lights, daily 7:00-12:00 & 16:00-18:30.

Church of San Clemente: Upper church—free, lower church—€5, both open Mon-Sat 9:00-12:30 & 15:00-18:00, Sun 12:00-18:00, last entry for lower church 20 minutes before closing.

Dress Code: Modest dress is recommended.

Getting There: Metro line A stops at Piazza di San Giovanni in Laterano (where this tour begins) and Piazza Vittorio Emanuele II (near the Church of Santa Maria Maggiore and Church of Santa Prassede). Bus #87 runs from Largo Argentina to Piazza Venezia to the Colosseum to the Church of San Clemente to the Church of San Giovanni in Laterano. Bus #85 does the same route but skips Largo Argentina.

With Limited Time: San Giovanni in Laterano (with its Holy Stairs) and Santa Maria Maggiore (with nearby Santa Prassede) are easiest to reach by Metro.

Photography: Generally, photos without flash are allowed in Rome's churches. On this tour, however, no photos are allowed in San Clemente.

The Tour Begins

Overview

Pilgrims to Rome try to visit four great basilicas: St. Peter's Basilica, of course (see tour in this book), St. Paul's Outside the Walls (see page 89), San Giovanni in Laterano, and Santa Maria Maggiore. The last two are covered in this chapter, as well as two other "honorable mentions": For the best Byzantine-style mosaics in Rome, visit the Church of Santa Prassede (near Santa Maria Maggiore). And the fascinating and central San Clemente is not far from San Giovanni in Laterano.

San Giovanni in Laterano

Imagine the jubilation when this church—the first Christian church in the city of Rome—was opened in about A.D. 318. Christians could finally "come out" and worship openly without fear of reprisal. (Still, most Romans were pagan, so this first great church was tucked away from the center of things, near the city wall.) After that glorious beginning, the church served as the center of Catholicism and the home of the popes until the Renaissance renovation of St. Peter's. Until 1870, all popes were "crowned" here. Even today, it's the home church of the Bishop of Rome—the pope.

• *The church is located on Piazza di San Giovanni in Laterano (Metro: San Giovanni). From the Metro station, go through the old city walls and look left. The **Via Sannio market**, selling clothing and some handicrafts every morning except Sunday, is a block south of the church.*

Exterior

The massive facade is 18th-century, with Christ triumphant on the top. The blocky peach-colored building adjacent on the right is the Lateran Palace, standing on the site of the old Papal Palace—residence of popes until about 1300. Across the street to your

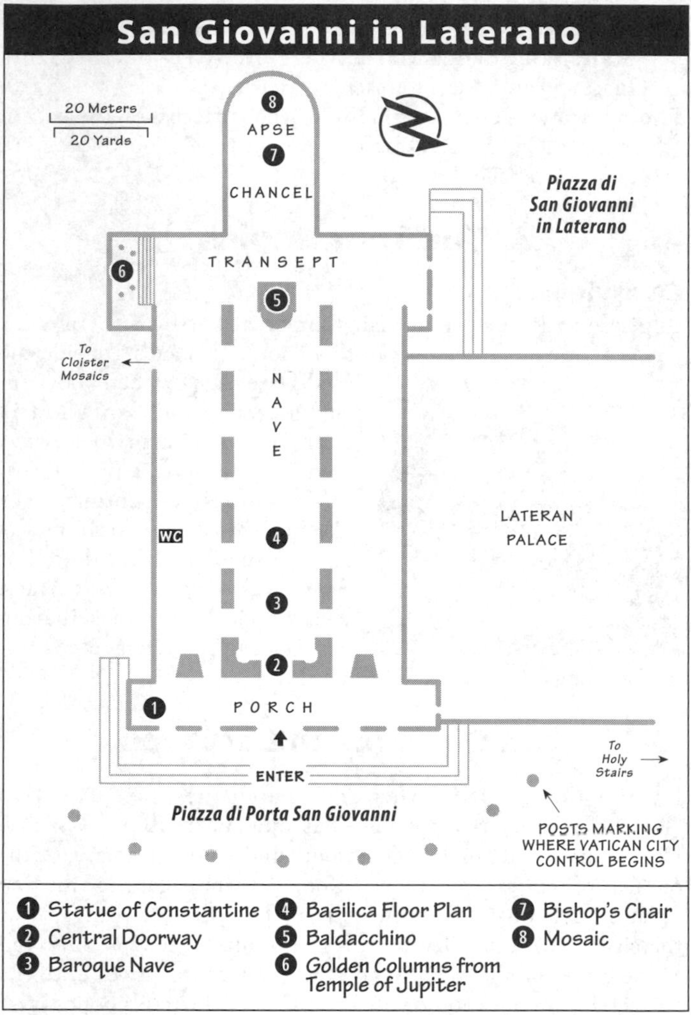

San Giovanni in Laterano

20 Meters
20 Yards
APSE
CHANCEL
TRANSEPT
NAVE
PORCH
ENTER
To Cloister Mosaics
WC
LATERAN PALACE
Piazza di San Giovanni in Laterano
Piazza di Porta San Giovanni
To Holy Stairs
POSTS MARKING WHERE VATICAN CITY CONTROL BEGINS

1. Statue of Constantine
2. Central Doorway
3. Baroque Nave
4. Basilica Floor Plan
5. Baldacchino
6. Golden Columns from Temple of Jupiter
7. Bishop's Chair
8. Mosaic

right are the pope's private chapel and the Holy Stairs (Scala Santa), popular with pilgrims (we'll see the stairs later). To the left is a well-preserved chunk of the ancient Roman wall. Pass the three-foot-high granite posts surrounding the church to leave Italy and enter the Vatican State—carabinieri must leave their guns at the door.

• *Step inside the portico and look left.*

❶ Statue of Constantine

It's October 28, A.D. 312, and Constantine—sword tucked under his arm and leaning confidently on a (missing) spear—has conquered Maxentius and liberated Rome. Constantine marched to this spot where his enemy's personal bodyguards lived, trashed their pagan idols, and dedicated the place to the god who gave him his victory—Christ. The holes in Constantine's head once held a golden halo-like crown for the emperor who legalized Christianity. In the relief above the statue, you'll see a beheaded John the Baptist.

At the other end of the portico is the Vatican History Museum (€5). It's worthwhile only if: it's the top of the hour (when visitors are admitted), and you like old paintings by no-name artists.

• *In the portico, take a look at the...*

❷ Central Doorway

These tall green bronze doors, with their floral designs and acorn studs, are the original doors from ancient Rome's Senate House (Curia) in the Forum. The Church moved these here in the 1650s to remind people that, from now on, the Church was Europe's lawmaker. The star borders were added to make these big doors bigger. Imagine, those cool little acorns date to the third century.

• *Now go inside the main part of the church. Stand in the back of the nave.*

❸ Baroque Nave

Very little survives from the original church—most of what you see was built after 1600. In preparation for the 1650 Jubilee, Pope Innocent X commissioned architect Francesco Borromini (rival to Bernini) to remake the interior. He redesigned the basilica in the Baroque style, reorganizing the nave, and adding the huge statues of the apostles (stepping out of niches to symbolically bring celestial Jerusalem to our world). The relief panels above the statues depict parallel events from the Old Testament (on the left) and New Testament (on the right). For instance, in the very back you'll see two resurrections: Jonah escaping the whale and Jesus escaping death. Only the ceiling (which should have been a white vault) breaks from the Baroque style—it's Renaissance, and the pope wanted it to stay.

❹ Basilica Floor Plan

San Giovanni was the first public church in Rome and the model for all later churches, including St. Peter's. The floor plan—a large central hall (nave) flanked by two side aisles—was based on the ancient Roman basilica (law courts) floor plan. These buildings were big enough to accommodate the large Christian congregations. Note that Roman basilicas came with two apses. You came in through the main entrance, which was designed to stress the authority of the place by slightly overwhelming and intimidating those who entered. When the design was adapted for use as a church, a grand and welcoming entry (the west portal) replaced one of the apses. Upon entering, the worshipper could take in the entire space instantly, and the rows of columns welcomed him to proceed to the altar.

• *The canopy over the altar is called the...*

❺ *Baldacchino*

In the upper cage are two silver statues of Sts. Peter (with keys) and Paul (sword), which contain pieces of their...heads.

The gossip buzzing among Rome's amateur archaeologists is that the Vatican tested DNA from Peter's head (located here) and from his body (located at St. Peter's)...and they didn't match.

• *Standing in the left transept are the...*

❻ Golden Columns from Temple of Jupiter

Tradition says that these gilded bronze columns once stood in pagan Rome's holiest spot—the Temple of Jupiter, dedicated to the King of all gods, on the summit of Capitoline Hill (c. 50 B.C.). Now they support a triangular pediment inhabited by a bearded, Jupiter-like God the Father.

• *In the apse, you'll find the...*

❼ Bishop's Chair

The chair (called a "cathedra") reminds visitors that this is the cathedral of Rome...and the pope himself is the bishop who sits here. Once elected, the new pope must actually sit in this chair to officially become the pope. The ceremonial sitting usually happens within one month of election—Pope Benedict XVI took his seat on May 3, 2005.

• *Under the semicircular dome of the apse, take a close look at the...*

❽ Mosaic

The original design dates from about 450 (although it was made in the 13th century and heavily restored in the 19th century). Pop in a coin for light. You'll see a cross, animals, plants, and the River Jordan running along the base. Mosaic, of course, was an ancient Roman specialty adapted by medieval Christians. The head of Christ (above the cross) must have been a glorious sight to early worshippers. It was one of the first legal images of Christ ever seen in formerly pagan Rome.

• *Fans of Cosmatesque marble-inlay floor (c. 1100–1300) may want to visit the cloister (€5, includes audioguide, daily 9:00–18:00, last entry 30 minutes before closing, enter near left transept).*

The Holy Stairs are outside the church in a building across the street. To get there, exit the church, turn left, and cross the street to the nondescript building that houses the...

Holy Stairs (Scala Santa)

In 326, Emperor Constantine's mother (Sta. Helena) brought home the 28 marble steps of Pontius Pilate's residence in Jerusalem. Jesus climbed these steps on the day he was sentenced to death. Each day, hundreds of faithful penitents climb these steps on their knees reciting a litany of prayers.

Covered with walnut wood with small glass-covered holes showing stains from Jesus' blood, the steps lead to the "Holy of Holies" (Sancta Sanctorum), the private chapel of the popes in the Middle Ages. With its world-class relics, this chapel was considered the holiest place on earth. The relics were moved to the Vatican in 1905, and the chapel is open only a few hours a week.

You can climb the tourist staircases along the sides, look inside the "Holy of Holies" through the grated windows, and buy a souvenir at the gift shop. Or you're welcome to actually climb the stairs on your knees (pick up the €2.50 booklet at the gift shop that gives the proper prayer for each of the 28 steps). If you've done a lot of praying in your life, but never accompanied your prayers with a little pain—actually a lot of pain—give this a try.

On September 20, 1870, as nationalist forces unifying Italy took Rome and ended the pope's temporal power, Pope Pius IX left his Quirinal Palace home for the last time. He stopped here to climb the steps, pray in his chapel, and bless his supporters from the top of the steps. Then he fled to the Vatican, where he spent the rest of his days.

Santa Maria Maggiore

The basilica of Santa Maria celebrates Holy Mary, the mother of Jesus. One of Rome's oldest and best-preserved churches, it was built (A.D. 432) while Rome was falling around it. The city had been sacked by Visigoths (410), and the emperors were about to check out (476). Increasingly, popes stepped in to fill the vacuum of leadership. The fifth-century mosaics give the church the feel of the early-Christian community. The general ambience of the church really takes you back to ancient times.

• *The church is at Piazza Santa Maria Maggiore (Metro: Termini or Vittorio Emanuele).*

Exterior

Mary's column originally stood in the Forum's Basilica of Constantine. The fifth-century church built in her honor proclaims she was indeed the Mother of God—a fact disputed by hair-splitting theologians of the day. When you step inside the church, you'll be exiting Italy and entering the Vatican—the Maggiore indicates that this church, a Vatican possession, was much more important than other churches dedicated to the Virgin Mary.

Interior

Despite the Renaissance ceiling and Baroque crusting, you still feel like you're walking into an early Christian church. The stately rows of columns, the simple basilica layout, the cheery colors, the spacious nave—it's easy to imagine worshipers finding an oasis of peace here as the Roman Empire crashed around them. (The 15th-century coffered ceiling is gilded with gold—perhaps brought back from America by Columbus.)

• *In the center of the church is the main altar, under a purple and gold canopy. Underneath the altar, in a lighted niche, are...*

❶ Manger Fragments

A kneeling Pope Pius IX (who established the dogma of the Immaculate Conception in the 19th century) prays before a glass case with an urn that contains several pieces of wood, bound by iron—these pieces are said to be from Jesus' crib. The church, dedicated to Mary's motherhood, displays these relics as physical evidence

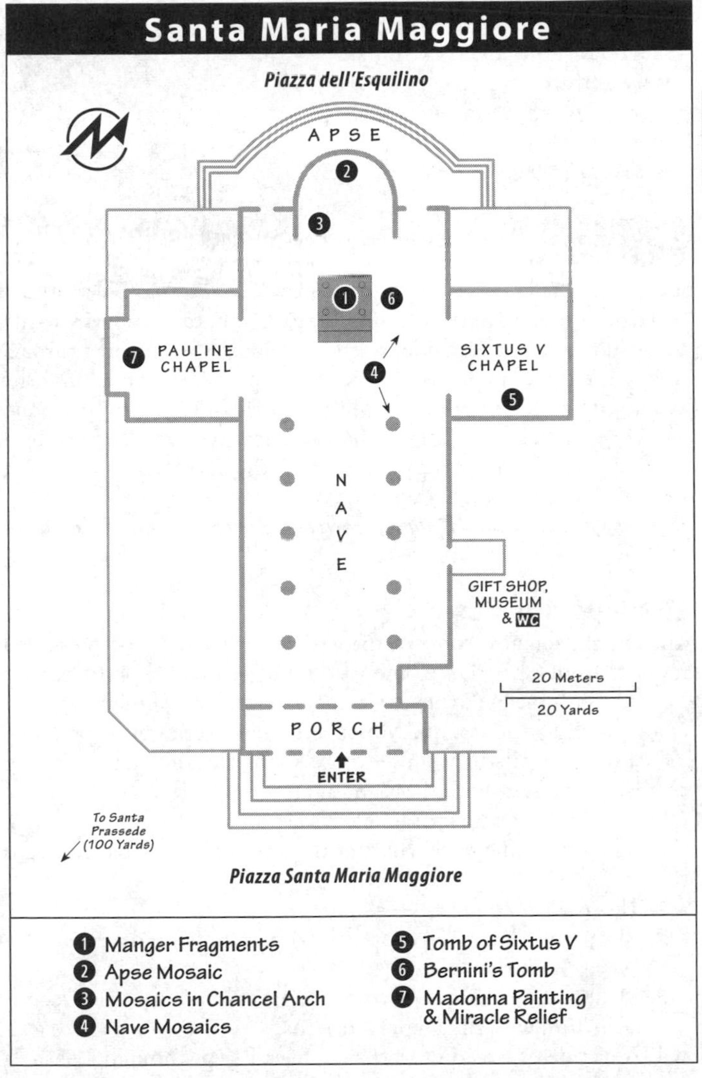

that Mary was indeed the mother of Christ. (The church is also built on the site of a former pagan temple dedicated to Rome's mother goddess, Juno.) Is the manger the real thing? Look into the eyes of pilgrims who visit.

• *In the apse, topped with a semicircular dome, find the...*

❷ Apse Mosaic

This 13th-century mosaic shows Mary being crowned by Jesus, both on the same throne. They float in a bubble representing heaven, borne aloft by angels. By the Middle Ages, Mary's cult status was secure.

• *Up in the arch that frames the outside of the apse, you'll find some of the church's oldest mosaics.*

❸ Mosaics in Chancel Arch

Colorful panels tell Mary's story in fifth-century Roman terms. Haloed senator-saints in white togas (top panel on left side) attend to Mary, who sits on a throne, dressed in gold and crowned like an empress. The angel Gabriel swoops down to announce to Mary that she'll conceive Jesus, and the Dove of the Holy Spirit follows. Below (the panel in the bottom-left corner) are sheep representing the apostles, entering the city of Jerusalem ("HIERVSALVM").

• *On the right side of the nave, starting near the altar, take a look at the...*

❹ Nave Mosaics

The church contains some of the world's oldest and best-preserved mosaics from Christian Rome. If the floodlights are on (it doesn't hurt to ask someone), those with good eyesight or binoculars will enjoy watching the story of Moses unfold in a series of surprisingly colorful and realistic scenes—more sophisticated than anything that would be seen for a thousand years.

The small, square mosaic panels are above all the columns, on the right side of the nave. Start at the altar and work back toward the entry.

1. This is a later painting—skip it.
2. Pharaoh's daughter (upper left) and her maids take baby Moses from the Nile.
3. Moses (lower half of panel) sees a burning bush that reconnects him with his Hebrew origins.
4. A parade of Israelites (left side) flees Egypt through a path in the Red Sea, while Pharaoh's troops drown.
5. Moses leads them across the Sinai desert (upper half), and God provides for them with a flock of quail (lower half).
6. Moses (upper half) sticks his magic rod in a river to desalinate it.
7. The Israelites battle their enemies while Moses commands from a hillside.
8. Skip it.
9. Moses (upper left) brings the Ten Commandments, then goes with Joshua (upper right) to lie down and die.

10. Joshua crosses the (rather puny) Jordan River...
11. ...and attacks Jericho...
12. ...and then the walls come a-tumblin' down.

• *If the gate is open, enter the chapel in the right transept (otherwise skip ahead to Bernini's Tomb). On the right wall of the chapel is a statue of a praying pope, atop the...*

❺ Tomb of Sixtus V

The Rome we see today is due largely to Pope Sixtus V (or was it Fiftus VI?). This energetic pope (1585-1590) leveled shoddy medieval Rome and erected grand churches connected by long, broad boulevards spiked with obelisks as focal points (such as the obelisk in Piazza dell'Esquilino behind Santa Maria Maggiore). The city of Rome has 13 Egyptian obelisks—all of Egypt has only 5. The white carved-marble relief panels (especially the one in the upper right) show some of the obelisks and buildings he commissioned.

• *Walk back toward the main altar. On a step between two pillars, you'll find an inscription on the ground marking...*

❻ Bernini's Tomb

The plaque reads, *"Ioannes Laurentivs Bernini"*—Gian Lorenzo Bernini (1598-1680)—"who brought honor to art and the city, here humbly rests." Next to it is another plaque to the *"Familia Bernini."* It's certainly humble...a simple memorial for the man who grew up in this neighborhood, then went on to remake Rome in the ornate Baroque style. (For more on Bernini, see page 249.)

• *In the left transept, over the altar, you'll see a...*

❼ Madonna Painting and Miracle Relief

The altar, a geologist's delight, is adorned with jasper, agate, amethyst, lapis lazuli, and gold angels. Amid it all is a simple icon of the lady this church is dedicated to: Mary.

Above the painting is a bronze relief panel showing a pope, with amazed bystanders, shoveling snow. One hot August night in the year 432, Mary appeared to Pope Liberius in a dream, telling him: "Build me a church where the snow falls." The next morning, they discovered a small patch of snow here on Esquiline Hill—on August 5—and this church, dedicated to Santa Maria, was begun.

• *After looking around Santa Maria Maggiore, fans of mosaics, Byzantines, and the offbeat should consider a visit to the nearby Church of Santa Prassede, about 100 yards away.*

Exiting Santa Maria Maggiore, walk away from the church and cross the street to the right of Mary on her column, then turn right down the small street Via S. Giovanni Gualberto.

Santa Prassede

The mosaics at the Church of Santa Prassede, from A.D. 822, are the best Byzantine-style mosaics in Rome. The Byzantine Empire, with its capital in Constantinople (modern Istanbul), was the eastern half of the Roman Empire. Unlike the western half, it didn't "fall," and its inhabitants remained Christian, Greek-speaking, and cultured for a thousand years while their distant cousins in Italy were fumbling for the light switch in the Dark Ages. Byzantine craftsmen preserved the techniques of ancient Roman mosaicists (who decorated floors and walls of villas and public buildings), then re-infused this learning into Rome during the city's darkest era. Take the time to let your eyes adjust, and appreciate the Byzantine glory glowing out of the dark church.

Bring €0.50 and €1 coins to buy floodlighting. (While €1 feels like a lot for five minutes of light, consider it a donation to maintain the church and treat all those visiting to the full sparkle of the mosaics.) Popping a coin into the box in the Chapel of St. Zeno (described below) saves you a trip to Ravenna.

• *The best mosaics are in the apse (behind the main altar) and in the small Chapel of St. Zeno along the right (north) side of the nave.*

Apse Mosaics

On a blue background is Christ, standing in a rainbow-colored river, flanked by saints. Christ has commanded Peter (to our right of Christ, with white hair and beard) to spread the Good News to all the world. Beneath Christ, 12 symbolic sheep leave Jerusalem's city gates to preach to the world. Peter came here to the world's biggest city to preach love...and was met with a hostile environment. He turns his palm up in a plea for help. Persecuted Peter was taken in by a hospitable woman named Pudentia (next to him) and her sister, Praxedes (to the left of Christ, between two other saints), whose house was located on this spot. (The church is named for Praxedes.)

The saint on the far left (with the square halo, indicating he was alive at the time this was made) is Pope Paschal I, who built the church in the 800s in memory of these early sisters, hiring the best craftsmen in the known world to do the mosaics.

Chapel of St. Zeno

The ceiling is gold, representing the Byzantine heaven. An icon-like Christ emerges from the background, supported by winged angels in white. On the walls are saints walking among patches of flowers. In the altar niche, Mary and the child Jesus are flanked by the sisters Praxedes and Pudentia. On the side wall, the woman with the square blue halo is Theodora, the mom of the pope who built this.

The chapel, covered completely with mosaics, may be underwhelming to our modern eyes, but in the darkness of Rome's medieval era, it was known as the "Garden of Paradise."

San Clemente

Here, like nowhere else, you'll enjoy the layers of Rome—a 12th-century basilica sits atop a fourth-century Christian basilica, which sits atop a second-century Mithraic Temple and some even earlier Roman buildings.

• *The church is on Via di San Giovanni in Laterano (Metro: Colosseo). Bus #85 or #87 connects San Clemente and San Giovanni in Laterano, saving a 10-minute walk.*

Upper Church—12th Century

The church (at today's ground level) is dedicated to the fourth pope, Clement, who shepherded the small Christian community when the religion was, at best, tolerated, and at worst, a capital offense. Clement himself was martyred by drowning in about A.D. 100—tied to an anchor by angry Romans and tossed overboard. You'll see his symbol, the anchor, around the church. The painting on the ceiling shows Clement being carried aloft to heaven.

While today's main entry is on the side, the original entry was through the courtyard in back, a kind of defensive atrium common in medieval times. To reach the original entry, enter the church through today's main entrance, walk diagonally toward the right, and exit again into this courtyard. Turn around and face the original entry. (This courtyard is inviting for a cool quiet break, as I imagine it was for a visiting medieval pilgrim.)

Back inside the church, step up to the carved marble choir—an enclosure in the middle of the church (Schola Cantorum) where the cantors sat. About 1,200 years ago, it stood in the old church beneath us, before that church was looted and destroyed by invading Normans.

In the apse (behind the altar), study the fine 12th-century mosaics. The delicate Crucifixion—with Christ sharing the cross with a dozen apostles as doves—is engulfed by a Tree of Life richly inhabited by deer, birds, and saints. The message is clear: All life springs from God in Christ. Above it all, a triumphant Christ, one hand on the Bible, blesses the congregation.

St. Catherine Chapel

The chapel near the side (tourists') entrance—considered one of the first great Renaissance masterpieces—is dedicated to St. Catherine of Alexandria, a noblewoman martyred for her defense of persecuted Christians. The fresco on the left wall—which shows an early Renaissance three-dimensional representation of space—is by the Florentine master Masolino (1428), perhaps aided by his young assistant, Masaccio. Studying the left wall, working from left to right, you can follow her story:

1. Catherine (lower-left panel), in black, confronts an assembly of the pagan Emperor Maxentius and his counselors. She bravely ticks off arguments on her fingers why Christianity should be legalized. Her powerful delivery silences the crowd.
2. Under the rotunda of a pagan temple (above, on the upper-left panel), Catherine, in blue, points up at a statue and tells a crowd of pagans, "Your gods are puny compared to mine."

3. Catherine, in blue (upper-right panel, left side), is thrown in prison, where she's visited by the emperor's wife (in green). Catherine converts her.
4. Emperor Maxentius, enraged, orders his own wife killed. The executioner (upper panel, right side), standing next to the empress' decapitated corpse, impassively sheathes his sword.
5. In the best-known scene (the middle panel on the bottom), Maxentius, in black, looks down from a balcony and condemns Catherine (in black) to be torn apart between two large, spiked wheels turned by executioners. But suddenly, an angel swoops in with a sword to cut her loose.
6. Catherine is eventually martyred (lower-right panel). Now dressed in green, she kneels before the executioner, who raises his sword to finish the job.

7. Finally, on the top of holy Mount Sinai (lower-right panel, upper-right side), two angels bear Catherine's body to its final resting place.

Taking a few steps back, look up at the arch that frames the chapel, topped by the delightful Annunciation fresco (top of the arch) by Masolino. Also notice the big St. Christopher, patron saint of travelers (left pillar), with 500-year-old graffiti scratched in by pilgrims.

Lower Church—Fourth Century

Buy a €5 ticket in the bookshop, and descend 1,700 years to the time when Christians were razzed on their way to church by pagan neighbors. The first room you enter was the original atrium (entry hall)—the nave extends to the right. (Everything you'll visit from here on was buried until the 19th century.)

• *On the flippable stone in the atrium, look for the...*

Pagan Inscription

This two-sided recycled marble burial slab—one side (with leafy decorations) for a Christian, the other for a pagan (you can turn it)—shows how the two Romes lived side by side in the fourth century.

• *In the nave, five yards before the altar, on the left wall, look for the...*

Fresco of St. Clement and Sisinnius

Clement (center) holds a secret Mass for early Christians back when it was a capital crime. Theodora, a prominent Roman (in yellow, to the right), is one of the undercover faithful. Her pagan husband, Sisinnius, has come to retrieve and punish her when—zap!—he's struck blind and has to be led away (right side).

But Sisinnius is still unconvinced. When Clement cures his blindness, Sisinnius (very faded, lower panel, far right) orders two servants to drag Clement off to the authorities. But through a miraculous intervention, the servants mistake a column for Clement (see the shadowy black log) and drag that out of the house instead. The inscription (crossword-style on right, waist-high, very faded) is famous among Italians because it's one of the earliest examples of the transition from Latin to Italian. Sisinnius encourages his servants by yelling *"Fili dele pute, traite!"* ("You sons of bitches, pull!")

• *In the far-left corner of the lower church (in the room behind the fresco you just saw), near the staircase leading down, is the...*

Presumed Burial Place of St. Cyril

Cyril, who died in A.D. 869 (see the modern, icon-like mosaic of him), was an inveterate traveler who spread Christianity to the

Slavic lands and Russia—today's Russian Orthodox faithful. Along the way, he introduced the Cyrillic alphabet still used by Russians and many other Slavs.

Temple of Mithras (Mithreum)—Second Century

Now descend (through a door immediately to the right of the altar and down steps) farther to the dark, dank Mithraic Temple (Mithreum). Nowhere in Rome is there a better place to experience this weird cult.

• *The barred room to the left is the...*

Worship Hall

Worshippers of Mithras—men only—reclined on the benches on either side of the room. At the far end is a small statue of the god Mithras, in a billowing cape. In the center sits an altar carved with a relief showing Mithras fighting with a bull that contains all life. A scorpion, a dog, and a snake try to stop Mithras, but he wins, running his sword through the bull. The blood spills out, bringing life to the world.

Mithras' fans gathered here, in this tiny microcosm of the universe (the ceiling was decorated with stars), to celebrate the victory with a ritual meal. Every spring, Mithras brought new life again, and so they ritually kept track of the seasons—the four square shafts in the corners of the ceiling represent the seasons, the seven round ones were the great constellations. Initiates went through hazing rituals representing the darkness of this world, then emerged into the light-filled world brought by Mithras.

Rome's official pagan religion had no real spiritual content and did not offer any concept of salvation. As the empire slowly crumbled, people turned more and more to Eastern religions (including Christianity), in search of answers and comfort. The cult of Mithras, stressing loyalty and based on the tenuousness of life, was popular among soldiers. Part of its uniqueness and popularity (in this very class-conscious society) was due to its belief that all were equal before God. It dates back to the time of Alexander the Great, who brought it from Persia. In

67 B.C., soldiers who had survived the bloody conquest of Asia Minor returned to Rome swearing by Mithras. When Christians gained power, they banished the worship of Mithras.

Facing the barred room are two Corinthian columns supporting three arches of the temple's entryway, decorated with a fine stucco coffered ceiling. At the far end of the hallway, another barred door marks the equivalent of a Mithraic Sunday school room. Peeking inside, see a faded fresco of bearded Mithras (right wall) and seven niches carved into the walls representing the seven stages a novice had to go through. Exit signs direct you down. You'll pass a very narrow ancient alleyway separating Roman walls barely three feet across. Step into this and imagine the first Western city to reach one million. Forget the two churches above you, and imagine standing on this exact spot and looking up at the sky 2,000 years ago. Now climb back through the centuries to today's street level.

TRASTEVERE WALK

From the Tiber to the Church of Santa Maria in Trastevere

Trastevere—the colorful neighborhood across the river from downtown—is *the* place to immerse yourself in the crustier side of Rome. This half-mile walk is designed to train your eye to see Rome more intimately. In Trastevere (trahs-TAY-veh-ray), you'll discover a secret, hidden city of heroic young martyrs, lovers kissing on Vespas, party-loving Renaissance bankers, and feisty "Trasteverini"—old-timers who pride themselves on never setting foot on the opposite bank of the Tiber River.

Orientation

Length of This Walk: Allow 1.5 hours.

With Limited Time: Take a taxi directly to Santa Maria in Trastevere. You'll still capture plenty of ambience.

When to Go: This walk can work well at any time of day. Mornings are cool and relatively quiet. Note that many churches are closed at midday, and Villa Farnesina closes at 14:00 Tue-Fri (and is closed on Sun). Strolling through Trastevere at dusk is especially atmospheric. Consider combining this walk with a meal or as a prelude to my Heart of Rome Walk (see page 96).

Getting There: Trastevere is on the west side of the Tiber River, south of Vatican City and across the river from the Forum and Capitoline Hill area. To get there by foot from Capitoline Hill, cross the Tiber using the bridges linked to Isola Tiberna: the Ponte Fabricio and Ponte Cestio. You can also reach Trastevere on tram #8 from Largo Argentina, or on express bus #H from Termini train station and Via Nazionale; if taking either of these, get off at Piazza Belli, just after crossing the Tiber. From the Vatican (Piazza

Risorgimento), take bus #23 or #271.

Church of Santa Cecilia: Free, Mon-Sat 9:30-12:30 & 16:00-18:30, Sun 16:00-18:30; crypt-€2.50, same hours as church; loft with frescoes-€2.50, Mon-Sat 10:00-12:30, closed Sun.

Church of Santa Maria in Trastevere: Free, daily 7:30-21:00.

Villa Farnesina: €5, Tue-Fri 9:00-14:00, Mon and Sat 9:00-17:00, closed Sun.

Audio Tour: You can download this chapter as a free Rick Steves audio tour (see page 27).

Eateries: Several recommended restaurants are on the map and described in the Eating in Rome chapter (see page 356).

The Walk Begins

• *Start halfway across the Ponte Cestio (Cestius Bridge)—called the "Ponte Fabricio" on the east side of the river—which connects Isola Tiberina ("Island in the Tiber") to Trastevere.*

Isola Tiberina and the Tiber River

Rome got its start 3,000 years ago along the Tiber River at this point. This was as far upstream as big boats could sail and the first place the river could be crossed by bridge. As a center of river trade, Rome connected the interior of the Italian peninsula with the Mediterranean. The area below you would have been bustling in ancient times. Look down and imagine small ports, water mills, ramshackle boats, and platforms for fishing.

The **island** itself was once the site of a temple dedicated to Asclepius, the god of medicine. Ancient Romans who were ill spent the night here and left little statues of their healed body parts (feet, livers, hearts...) as thank-you notes. This tradition survives: Today, throughout Italy, Catholic altars are often encrusted with votive offerings, symbolizing gratitude for answered prayers. During plagues and epidemics, the sick were isolated on the island. These days, the island's largest building is the Fatebenefratelli, the public hospital favored by Roman women for childbirth. The island's reputation for medical care lives on.

The high point of the **bridge** (upon which you're probably leaning) is an ancient stone with a faded inscription dating from about A.D. 370, when this then-400-year-old bridge was rebuilt. The eroding plaque is stapled into the balustrade like a piece of recycled scrap. Run your fingers over the word "Caesar" (top line,

just right of center). This part of the Tiber River flooded frequently, which devalued the land on the north bank; in time it would become the site of the Jewish ghetto (started in the 16th century, but now long gone, though Rome's synagogue remains—✪ see the Jewish Ghetto Walk chapter).

In the 1870s, the Romans removed the threat of flooding by practically walling off the Tiber, building the tall, anonymous embankments that continue to isolate the river from the city today.

• *Head south to leave the bridge. If open, the green riverside Sora Mirella kiosk on the right (run by Mirella's son, Stefano) is the most famous vendor of Rome's summer refresher called a* grattachecca *(pronounced*

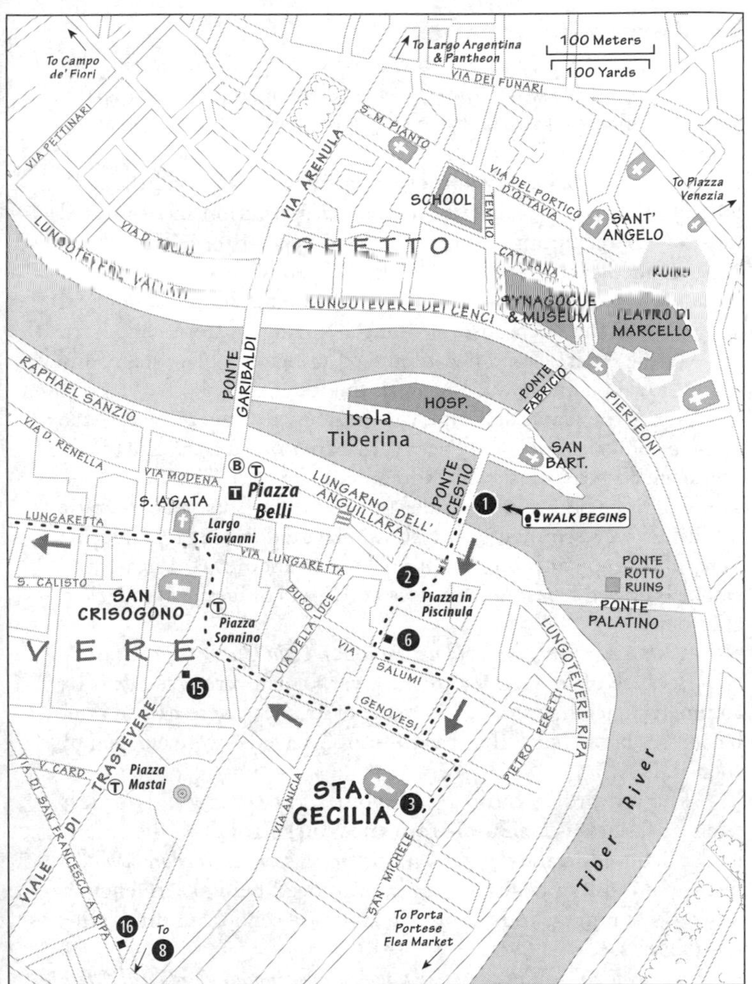

grah-tah-kek-kah, €4), a concoction of shaved ice with fruit-flavored syrup and chopped fruit (similar to an American granita). Cross the street and go down the steps into the car-filled piazza.

Piazza in Piscinula

This square is famous for its church bell tower (the cute little thing directly across from the bridge); dating from 1069, it's the oldest working one in the city. Study the brown building on the riverside and spot faint traces of Renaissance decoration. Today's earth-tone shades of the city echo this original Roman brown.

• *Facing the tower, exit the square from the far-right corner, opposite where you entered, going uphill on Via dell'Arco de' Tolomei.*

Trastevere Back Lanes

Look up and directly ahead to the top of the hill to see the elegantly restored, freshly painted **tower** sandwiched between apartments. In medieval times, the city skyline had 300 of these towers (about 50 survive). Each noble family competed for the tallest one until, in about 1250, city authorities got fed up and had them all lopped off. Later—mainly Baroque—construction incorporated most of the remaining "stumps," and you can still see these remnants of medieval Rome all over the old center. Incorporating old structures into new ones was always considered more economical and practical than demolishing and starting again from scratch. In the Middle Ages, Rome had regressed to being a big village; any idea of town planning was lost until the Renaissance.

Notice the plants spilling over the many rooftop terraces—the Roman equivalent of a leafy backyard. An *attico con terrazzo* (penthouse with a terrace) is every Roman's dream.

Continue on, walking under the low arch. Lots of aristocratic buildings were connected by these elevated passages. Imagine herds of sheep shuffling through here in medieval times while smoke billowed from the windows and doors of homes that lacked chimneys.

• *Turn left and walk along Via dei Salumi ("Cold Cuts Street").*

Because of its vicinity to the river, Trastevere was always a commercial neighborhood, and many of its alleys were named after businesses based here. The streets—rarely paved—were clogged by shop stalls.

The red-brown building on your right (pretty ugly unless you're a fascist) is a **school from the Mussolini era.** The fascist leader believed in the classical motto *mens sana in corpore sano* ("a healthy mind in a healthy body"), and loved being seen fencing, boxing, swimming, and riding. He endowed school buildings with lots of gyms.

• *After passing the school, turn right again, heading up Vicolo dell'Atleta ("Alley of the Athlete").*

Check out the latest fashions in underwear hanging out to dry. Apartments in Rome tend to be quite small, and electricity is more expensive than in the US, so few have clothes dryers.

Strolling here, you'll understand why the Italian language has no word for "privacy" (they use our word and roll the *r*). Reading a letter on the Metro attracts a crowd. If someone has a fight (or a particularly good orgasm), the entire neighborhood knows. Young lovers with no place to go are adept at riding *motorini*...while parked.

All around, ancient fragments are recycled ingloriously into medieval buildings. Halfway down the alley on the right is a restaurant that, a thousand years ago, was a **synagogue.** Find the Hebrew faintly inscribed on the base of the columns of the exposed brick structure. A large part of Rome's Jewish community, the most ancient outside Palestine, lived in Trastevere until the popes moved them into the ghetto on the other side of the river in the 1500s.

• *Continue, turning left on Via dei Genovesi, then right on Via di Sta. Cecilia to reach Piazza di Santa Cecilia. Enter the convent courtyard of the church, sit by the fountain, and take a moment to enjoy the peace and quiet.*

Church of Santa Cecilia

Trastevere had early Christian churches like Santa Cecilia because, in the second and third centuries, a large community of foreigners lived here. Early Christians from Greece and Judaea introduced their cultures and religions to the neighborhood.

Notice the church's eclectic exterior. Its mismatched columns were recycled from pagan temples. The typical medieval bell tower sports an 18th-century facade. This church, dedicated to Cecilia, patron saint of musicians and singers, is popular for weddings. Of Rome's 40 medieval churches, many have two-year waiting lists for weekend weddings. While most young Roman couples favor the more sober elegance of medieval churches over Baroque (usually dismissed as *troppo pesante*—"too heavy"), the typical Italian wedding gowns are far from understated.

A Christian convert from a wealthy family in a time of persecution, Cecilia revealed her faith to her pagan husband on their wedding night and told him of her aspiration to remain chaste (uh-oh...). An angel appeared to reason with the frustrated groom. Once converted, he devoted himself to carrying out Christian burials in the catacombs, until he himself was killed. Cecilia was soon condemned as well. The Romans, who tried unsuccessfully for three days to suffocate her with steam in her bath to make it appear accidental, finally lost patience and beheaded her. Cecilia bequeathed her house to the neighborhood community, and this spot has been a place of worship ever since.

In the days when Christianity was illegal, wealthy converts hosted Mass for the local community in their homes. When Christians were finally allowed to build churches, they often did so on the sites of these homes for the sake of continuity. While this site was a place of worship during and after Cecilia's lifetime, what we see today was built in the early ninth century and extensively

Soccer: The National Obsession

One of Rome's most local "sights" is a soccer match. Winston Churchill said that Italians lose wars like soccer matches and soccer matches like wars. Soccer *(calcio)* is the national obsession: Everyone, regardless of age or social class, is an expert, quick with an opinion on a coach's lousy decision or a referee's unprofessional conduct. Fans love to insult officials: A favorite is *"arbitro cornuto!"*—the referee is a cuckold (i.e., his wife sleeps around). The country's obsession turned into jubilation on July 9, 2006, when Italy won the World Cup, and Rome—along with every other city, town, and village in Italy—went crazy with joy.

Rome has a special passion for soccer. It has two teams, Roma (representing the city) and Lazio (the region), and the rivalry is fanatic. When Romans are introduced, they ask each other, *"Laziale o romanista?"* The answer can compromise a relationship. Both Roma (jersey: yellow and red; symbol: she-wolf) and Lazio (jersey: light blue and white; symbol: imperial eagle) claim to be truly Roman. Lazio is older (founded in 1900), but Roma has more supporters. Lazio is supposed to be more upper-class, Roma more popular, but the social division is blurred.

restored in the eighteenth century.

Enter the church. Find the **statue of Sta. Cecilia** by Stefano Maderno (in the case below the altar). During the Catholic Counter-Reformation, art charged with great emotional impact was used to enhance faith. The new appetite for relics led to a search for Cecilia's remains. When her tomb was opened, Maderno was present and claimed, along with other bystanders, to have seen her body perfectly preserved for an unforgettable instant before it turned to dust. He created this touching statue from his memory of that scene. Cecilia lies with her face turned and hidden, the violence of her death suggested only by the gash in her neck, the position of her fingers indicating the oneness of the Trinity. (Like Italians today, she counted starting with her thumb.)

The **canopy** above the altar, dating from the 1200s, represents an innovative fusion of Roman and French Gothic architecture and sculpture, showing that the artist (Arnolfo di Cambio) knew his classics and had also been to Paris.

The **mosaic** in the apse dates from the ninth century. Pope Paschal (on the left), who built the church, holds a little model of

The most eagerly awaited sporting event of the year is the derby, when the two teams fight it out at the Olympic Stadium (Stadio Olimpico). All of Italy acknowledges that team spirit is most fervent in Rome. Fans prepare months in advance, and on the day of the match they fill the entire stadium with team colors, flags, banners, and smoke candles.

Witty slogans on banners work like dialogues: A Roma banner proclaimed, "Roma: Only the sky is higher than you." The Lazio banner replied, "In fact, the sky is blue and white" (like its team colors). The exchange revealed that there had been a Lazio informer on the Roma side, which traumatized Roma fans for weeks. Tourists go to a match more for the action in the stands than the action on the field—for some, it's the most Roman of all experiences.

Both teams call the Olympic Stadium home, so you can catch a game most weekends from September to May (Metro line A to Flaminio, then catch tram #2 to the end of the line, Piazza Mancini, and cross the bridge to the stadium). If you're coming from Termini train station, take bus #910; from the Vatican, take bus #32 from Piazza Risorgimento. It's best to buy tickets in advance at www.listicket.it or in town at a team store.

it in his hands. His square halo (the "halo of the living") signifies that he was alive when the mosaic was made.

If you visit mid-morning, you have two options before leaving: You can go downstairs to see the crypt or head upstairs to the loft to view some fancy frescoes.

The **crypt** contains the scant ancient remains of a complex of ancient buildings, including Cecilia's house. The house is pretty bare, but it does have some early Christian iconography, original mosaic floors, and grain storage bins (€2.50, same hours as church, follow sign to *crypt*).

The **loft,** where cloistered nuns would view the Mass while hidden behind a screen, contains a fragmentary but extraordinary Last Judgment fresco painted by Pietro Cavallini, a contemporary of Giotto (c. 1300). Scholars debate who influenced whom: Giotto or Cavallini. But there's no debate that the art here shows cutting-edge realism in the expressive faces of the apostles who sit believably in their chairs (€2.50; Mon-Sat 10:00-12:30, closed Sun; ring the bell on the left side of the facade). If you're here at 18:00 on a Saturday, you're welcome to read the Lectio Divina with the nuns.

• *Leaving the church, backtrack left, and take the first left onto Via de Genovesi. To pop into the last traditional cookie bakery in the area, detour right at Via della Luce and walk half a block to #21, where you'll find* ***Biscottificio Artigiano.*** *Here, in the face of modern efficiency, humble Stefania Innocenti courageously strives to keep the tradition of seasonal cookies alive in Rome. Return to Via de Genovesi, and hike straight ahead to where it meets a busy street.*

Viale di Trastevere to Piazza di Santa Maria

The wide, modern boulevard called Viale di Trastevere bisects Trastevere, which was otherwise spared most of the demolishing and rebuilding suffered by other traditional neighborhoods when Rome became the capital of united Italy in 1870. Cross to the other side of Viale di Trastevere and turn right, then left into Largo San Giovanni de Matha. Pass by the textbook Baroque facade of the faded yellow church and continue to Via della Lungaretta. You'll notice a change in atmosphere—the quiet, mystical charm of the first part of your walk has given way to livelier, more colorful, more touristy (and higher-rent) surroundings. Look up. Now, along with underwear...you see art. Walk to the big square and sit down on the fountain steps.

Piazza di Santa Maria in Trastevere

You're in the heart of the neighborhood. Piazza di Santa Maria is the district's most important meeting place. With its broad and inviting steps, the 17th-century fountain was actually designed to be the "sofa" of the neighborhood. During major soccer games, a large screen is set up here so that everybody can share in the tension and excitement. At other times, children gather here with a ball and improvise matches of their own. For more on soccer, see the sidebar.

• *Dominating the square is the...*

Church of Santa Maria in Trastevere

One of Rome's oldest church sites, this building stands where early Christians worshipped illegally in a home until the year 313. It was made a basilica—probably the first church in Rome dedicated to the Virgin Mary—in the fourth century, when Christianity was legalized. The tower survives from the 12th century, when the entire church was rebuilt. The portico (covered area just outside the door) is decorated with ancient fragments (some from the earlier church). Filled with early Christian symbolism such as the dove and olive branch, many of these stones were lids to burial niches from catacombs. Notice how early Christians prayed as evangelical Christians do today.

Step inside. Immediately to the left of the entry, a **plaque** on the wall is dedicated to "Olea Sancta." The "holy oil" was actually a small petroleum deposit discovered here in 30 B.C. This black liquid was almost magical in its ability to power lamps and was incorporated into the lore of this church.

Grab a pew. Most of what you see dates from around the 12th century, although the granite columns are from ancient Roman buildings. Later architects tried hard to match them, but notice how the shorter columns have taller bases and how the capitals are mismatched. (Some have tiny pagan heads of Egyptian gods.) The ancient basilica floor plan (and ambience) survives. The intricate coffered ceiling has an unusual image of Mary painted on copper at the center.

Step up behind the main **altar** (left side) for a closer look at the fine mosaic work. Pop a coin in the box for light. The central scene is one of the few surviving examples of an early medieval mosaic (8th–10th century) in Rome. It's rich in symbolism. Christ is flanked by the first two popes. Notice the stature Mary is given. Tour guides claim this is the first mosaic to show her at the throne with Jesus in heaven. He has his arm around his mother as if introducing her to us. Sitting below Jesus, Mary, and the popes is the throne-like chair of the bishop, giving legitimacy to the Church leadership. The flock of sheep is not just any flock—it represents Jesus in the middle (marked by a halo with a cross in it) and the 12 apostles.

The more "modern" mosaic panels show scenes from the life of Mary. These mosaics from the late 1300s (by Cavallini) are impressively realistic and expressive, yet predate the Renaissance by a hundred years. The first of six panels (to the left of the curved apse) shows the birth of Mary. A servant in the corner checks the temperature of the water with her hand before she bathes the baby, introducing an element of tenderness that breaks the abstract rigidity of medieval art. Next comes the angel announcing Jesus' coming to Mary, Jesus' birth, the adoration of the Magi, the presentation of Jesus in the temple, and Mary's eternal sleep (not death). The gold mosaic backgrounds show buildings that, while still unrealistic, are a good step toward accurate 3-D representation.

The incredibly expensive 13th-century **floor** is a fine example of Cosmati mosaic work—a style of mosaic featuring intricate geometric shapes (in this case, made with marble scavenged from Roman ruins).

As you leave, spend a moment with **St. Anthony** (in the back corner, opposite the entry). He was a favorite of the poor and is inundated with prayer requests on scraps of paper. The Community of St. Egidio operates from this church. They feed the local poor and care for young drug addicts. Each Christmas they take out all the pews, move in tables and chairs, and put on a huge dinner for those in need.

Tour Over

From here, enjoy simply exploring Rome's most colorful district. Saunter around the streets to the left of the church as you leave. The farther you venture from the square, the less touristy and more rustic the neighborhood becomes. Wandering the back lanes and pondering the earthy enthusiasm people seem to have for life here, I can imagine that bygone day when proud Trastevere locals would brag that they never crossed the river.

• *To cap off your Trastevere stroll with one more sight, consider visiting* ***Villa Farnesina,*** *a Renaissance villa decorated by Raphael (see page 81 for a self-guided tour). To get there, face the Church of Santa Maria in Trastevere and leave the piazza by walking along the right side of the church, following Via della Paglia to Piazza di S. Egidio. Exit the piazza near the church and you'll be on Via della Scala. Follow through the Porta Settimiana, where the street changes names to Via della Lungara. On your right, you'll pass John Cabot University. Look for a white arch that reads Accademia dei Lincei. The villa is through this gate at #230.*

If you're in the mood to extend this walk, head to the river, cross the pedestrian bridge, Ponte Sisto, and make your way to Campo de' Fiori, where the ***Heart of Rome Walk*** *begins (see that chapter for details).*

JEWISH GHETTO WALK

North Bank of the Tiber

For centuries, Rome's Jewish ghetto has been the site of both relentless persecution and the undying pride and solidarity of a tight-knit community. Built in 1555 on the banks of a frequently flooded bend of the Tiber River, the ghetto was the forced home of the Roman Jewish population for more than 300 years, between the Counter-Reformation (16th century) and Italian unification (1870). Though most of the old ghetto has been torn down, you can still find a few reminders of the Roman Jews' storied past and lively present.

Orientation

Length of This Walk: Allow one hour.

When to Go: If you want to visit the synagogue and museum, avoid this walk on a Saturday, when they're closed.

Getting There: The Jewish ghetto was—and Rome's main synagogue still is—on the east bank of the Tiber, near the Isola Tiberina ("Island in the Tiber") and the ancient ruins of the Theater of Marcellus (Teatro di Marcello). It's a three-minute walk from Largo Argentina.

Synagogue and Jewish Museum: €10 ticket includes both; mid-June-mid-Sept Sun-Thu 10:00-19:00, Fri 10:00-16:00, closed Sat; mid-Sept-mid-June Sun-Thu 10:00-17:00, Fri 9:00-14:00, closed Sat; last entry 45 minutes before closing; on Lungotevere dei Cenci, tel. 06-6840-0661, www.museoebraico.roma.it. Modest dress is required. The only way to visit the synagogue (if you're not there for a prayer service) is with an hourly **tour** (included in admission, English tours usually at :15 past the hour, 30 minutes, check schedule at ticket counter).

Tours: The museum conducts walking tours of the Jewish Ghetto at least once a day Sun-Fri (€8, usually at 13:15, no tours on Sat). Ask for the schedule at the museum entry and sign up at least 30 minutes before the tour departure time (minimum of three required).

Local guide Micaela Pavoncello is uniquely equipped to guide visitors through the neighborhood that her family has lived in since ancient Roman times (€130/2 hours, ask for Ghetto Tour, tel. 328-863-8128, www.jewishroma.com, info@jewishroma.com).

You can also download this chapter as a free Rick Steves **audio tour** (see page 27).

Eateries: One of the stops near the end of this tour is at a Jewish bakery. Recommended **Sora Margherita,** offering traditional Roman and Jewish fare, hides without a sign on a square a block from the end of this tour (closed Sun, also closed Sat in June-July, closed all of Aug, Piazza delle Cinque Scole 30; see page 359).

History

Today, of Italy's 35,000 Jews, nearly half call Rome home. Jews here have a uniquely Roman style of worship and even preserve remnants of their own Judaic-Roman dialect. That's because, unlike most of the world's Jewish people, Roman Jews are neither Sephardic (descended from Spain) nor Ashkenazi (descended from Eastern Europe). Italy's Jews came directly from the Holy Land before the Diaspora, first arriving in Rome in the second century B.C. as esteemed envoys (hoping to establish business ties) and then, after Rome invaded Judaea in the first century A.D., as POWs sold into slavery. These first Jews lived, like other foreigners, outside the city—across the river, in Trastevere.

The Romans favored the Jews because they were well-networked throughout the empire, they didn't push their religion on others, and most important, they paid their taxes. But with the fall of the Roman Empire, the status of Jews declined. As Christianity enveloped Rome, the state denied Jews their full rights as citizens, and once the pope became literally the king of Rome, the Church enforced laws that limited the spread of the Jewish faith (e.g., no proselytizing, no new synagogues, no intermarriage). The severity of these laws varied from pope to pope. Through most of the Middle Ages, the standing of Rome's Jews

In the Ghetto

The word "ghetto" is Italian, first used in Venice in the 1600s to describe the part of town where Jews lived—near the copper foundry (*geto* was the word for foundry). Initially the term meant only Jewish neighborhoods, but as the word spread through Europe and beyond, it was used generically to mean any neighborhood where a single ethnic group is segregated.

fluctuated, but for the most part they prospered and were often held in high regard as physicians, businessmen, and confidants of popes. The community in Trastevere was even allowed to spill across to the opposite bank of the Tiber.

Then, in 1492, Spain expelled its Jews, with similar removals following in other European countries. Rome's Jewish population doubled, swelling with refugees. By the 1500s, the Catholic Counter-Reformation—begun to combat rising Protestantism—turned its attention to anything deemed a "heresy" or simply not Catholic, including Judaism. In 1555, Pope Paul IV forcibly moved all of Rome's Jews into the undesirable flood zone inside a bend of the Tiber River, creating a ghetto of some 4,000 Jews packed into a miserable seven acres of mucky land. There they lived—in cramped conditions, behind a wall, with a curfew—for three centuries. They could go out by day, but had to return before the gates were locked at night. Jews were forced to wear yellow scarves and caps, and were prohibited from owning property or holding good jobs. During Carnevale (Mardi Gras), they were forced to parade down Via del Corso while Christians lined the streets and shouted insults. Through this long stretch of oppression, the synagogue was the only place Jews could feel respected and dignified. It's no wonder such loving attention was given to the Jewish tools of worship.

Rome's Jews enjoyed a little boost in freedom when Napoleon occupied the city (1805-1814) and after the ghetto walls were torn down in 1848. But it was only after Italian unification in 1870—when a secular government replaced the religious rule of the Vatican—that the ghetto's inhabitants were granted full rights and citizenship. When Rome became the country's capital, the city—ashamed of its shoddy Jewish quarter—destroyed the old ghetto and modernized the district, giving it the street plan we see today.

Then came the rise of fascism. Even though Mussolini wasn't rabidly anti-Semitic, he instituted a slew of anti-Jewish laws as he allied himself more strongly with Hitler. When Mussolini was deposed and the Nazis occupied Rome late in the war, the ghetto community was suddenly in even greater danger. Of the 13,000 ghetto dwellers, 2,000 were sent off to concentration camps. Only

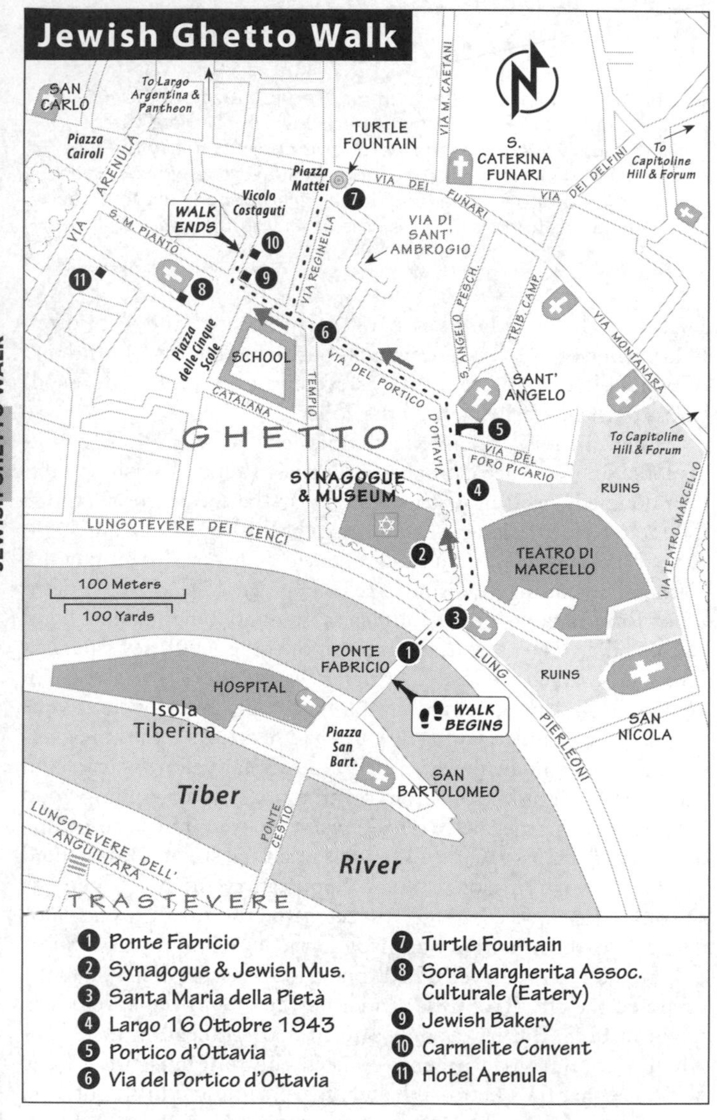

a handful came back.

A measure of healing and reconciliation came with Pope John Paul II, who took a special interest in fostering relations with the Jewish community. It was John Paul II who finally acknowledged that the Church should have intervened more forcefully to defend the Jews during the Holocaust. He was also the first pope in history to enter a synagogue (here in this neighborhood in 1986—described later on this walk). In his last letter, John Paul

II thanked Rome's emeritus rabbi for allowing him to initiate this long overdue Catholic-Jewish rapprochement. In 2010, Pope Benedict followed up with a visit here, where he also condemned the persecutions of the past.

The Walk Begins

• *Start at the north end of Ponte Fabricio, which connects central Rome with the Isola Tiberina and the neighborhood of Trastevere. You'll see the big synagogue with its square dome. The former ghetto consists of the synagogue and the several blocks behind it.*

Ponte Fabricio

Ponte Fabricio is nicknamed Ponte Quattro Capi ("Bridge of the Four Heads") for its statues of the two-faced pagan god Janus. In ancient times, it was called Pons Judaeorum ("Jews' Bridge") because foreigners, immigrants, and Jews—who weren't allowed to live in central Rome—would commute across this bridge to get into town. Some 30,000 Jews once lived in a thriving community in Trastevere. Look down at the river. The embankment was only built in the late 19th century. Before then, this was the worst flood zone along the Roman riverbank—just right for a ghetto for the politically powerless.

• *With your back to the river, at your left is the...*

Synagogue (Sinagoga) and Jewish Museum (Museo Ebraico)

In the 16th century, when Pope Paul IV forced the Jews to reside within a walled ghetto, the center was this synagogue. When Rome became the capital of the newly unified Italy in 1870, Jews regained their civil rights and were free to live anywhere in the city. The ghetto was essentially demolished, replaced with the modern blocks you see today.

The Jews were initially offered better real estate for their synagogue, but chose instead to rebuild here, on the original site. This new "Synagogue of Emancipation" was built in a remarkable three years (completed 1904) with the enthusiastic support of the entire Roman community. This is where Pope John Paul II made his historic visit in 1986.

Enter the synagogue via the main door on the riverside. The admission price includes the museum entrance and a guided synagogue visit.

Inside the **synagogue,** take in the impressive dome, which is square to distinguish it from a Christian church. Ponder the inside of the dome, painted with the colors of the rainbow—symbolic of God's promise to Noah that there would be no more floods. The stars on the ceiling recall God's pledge that Abraham's descendants would flourish and be as many as the stars in the sky. Architects designed the structure in the Art Nouveau style with a dash of Tiffany. The sandy color tones are a reminder of the community's desert heritage.

The **museum** shows off historically significant artifacts described in English. You'll see second-century B.C. reliefs with Jewish symbols, finely worked Judaica (religious items), and other relics of the Jewish past. As the Jews were not allowed to be craftsmen during the ghetto period, they had to commission many of the pieces you'll see from some of the finest Christian artists of that time—the same artists working for the kings and aristocracy of Europe—making these items historically and artistically significant. The museum also shows a film in English about the Nazi occupation of Rome.

Back outside, you may notice security measures around the synagogue: heavy concrete planter boxes (that double as car-bomb barriers), policemen in kiosks, and video cameras on the fences.

• *Look for the beige church across from the Ponte Fabricio...*

Santa Maria della Pietà (a.k.a. San Gregorio)

When the ghetto was a walled-in town, Catholics built churches at each gate to try and spread their faith to the Jews. Notice the Hebrew script under the crucifix. It quotes the Jewish prophet Isaiah—"All day long, I have stretched out my hands to a disobedient and faithless nation that has lost its way" (Isaiah 65:2)—but misuses the quote to give it an anti-Semitic twist.

• *Walk away from the river behind the synagogue toward the ancient Roman ruins. The small square in front of the ruins is called...*

Largo 16 Ottobre 1943

This square is named for the day when Nazi trucks parked here and threatened to take the Jews to concentration camps unless the community came up with 50 kilos (110 pounds) of gold in 24 hours. Everyone, including non-Jewish Romans, tossed in their precious gold, and the demand was met. The Nazis took the gold—and later, they took the Jews as well.

• *The big ancient ruin is the...*

Portico d'Ottavia

This monumental gateway—with columns supporting a triangular pediment—was built by soon-to-be-emperor Augustus. Once flanked by temples and libraries, the passageway served as a kind of cultural center. After Rome's fall, the portico housed a thriving fish market. In the eighth century, the ruins of the portico were incorporated into the Church of Sant'Angelo in Pescheria. For centuries, this Christian church was packed every Saturday with Jews—forced by decree to listen to Christian sermons. Notice the faded bits of Christian fresco on the arch. Locals love to tell of the poor old woman who refused to sell her land and now owns this priceless bit of real estate that includes the ancient arch (at #25 under the arch).

To the left is the main drag of today's ghetto. We'll head there soon, but first go to the bridge on your right to look down at the level of the street in Roman times. Just past the bridge, the former oratory is now a wedding-registry shop. (If it's open, pop in and see who's getting married when and admire their choice of table setting.) From the bridge, you get a fine view of Teatro di Marcello (which predates the Colosseum). Beyond it is the tree-capped Capitoline Hill.

• *Now walk around the arch to the ghetto's main street...*

Via del Portico d'Ottavia

This main drag is a fine place to get a taste of yesterday's ghetto and today's Rome. From the start (near the Roman arch), look down the street. On the left is a new building from 1911. On the right, in the distance, is the only surviving line of old ghetto building fronts. Imagine today's street as it was then: much narrower (as it is at the far end today). Walking down the street, notice kosher restaurants proudly serving *carciofi* (artichokes, which only Jewish grandmothers can cook properly) and shops of fine, locally produced Judaica. You might see posters for community events, a few men wearing yarmulkes, and political graffiti, both pro- and anti-Israel. The Palestine Liberation Organization attacked this area in 1982, and a police presence still lingers.

After a block, you reach the center of the district. Look right, down Via di Sant'Ambrogio, to see an old surviving street. Looking down this lane, imagine the dense population, flood muck, and squalor of the past. The pedestrianized square ahead is where older folks hang out together and shoot the breeze, sometimes even bringing their favorite chairs from home. Though the Jewish community has long since dispersed all over Rome, most Roman Jews continue to spend time in this neighborhood to enjoy the strong feeling of community that survives. The big yellow building (on the left) houses the Jewish school.

This neighborhood has become trendy recently, and apartment prices are now beyond the means of most members of the Jewish community. Ironically, only the richest Jews could afford to relocate after 1870—and because the poor had to stay, their descendants have enjoyed healthy real-estate appreciation.

At #7, there's a gallery that generally features modern Israeli artists. At its door is a mezuzah (prayer capsule)—residents touch it as they come and go to recall their Jewish creed.

Opposite the big school, take a one-block detour down Via della Reginella. At #28, notice where the six-floor buildings end and more elegant and spacious (but no taller) three-floor buildings begin...marking the end of the ghetto. In the square (Piazza Mattei) at the end of the lane is a fun **fountain**—an old Mannerist work, later embellished with turtles by Bernini. It's said that Bernini cared about the Jews and honored them with the symbol of a turtle—an ancient creature that carries all its belongings on its back.

Returning to the main drag (Via del Portico d'Ottavia), continue to Bar Toto, where you'll see a slot in the wall—a ghetto-era charity box for orphans that still accepts donations for worthy causes. The ancient relief above the box marks the home of a big shot who, at the start of the Renaissance age (before the ghetto's establishment in 1555), plugged this chunk of ancient Rome into his facade for prestige. A bit farther down (at #1), another bit of ancient marble depicts a lion attacking a gazelle. Notice the big stone inset with a Latin inscription dated "MMCCXX." Yes, that's 2220, and no, it's not from the future. It marks the years since the birth of Rome in 753 B.C.—meaning it was carved in A.D. 1467.

At the next intersection (Piazza Costaguti), stand in the white decorative square in the cobbles. The recommended **Sora Margherita Associazione Culturale,** a restaurant with no sign, is located on the car-filled square—Piazza delle Cinque Scole—30 yards to the left, at #30 (described on page 359). On your right is a traditional Jewish bakery. Go inside to check out the braided challah bread, cheesecakes, almond paste-filled macaroons, and "Jewish pizzas" *(pizza Ebraica)*—like little €2 fruitcakes, but better tasting. Just beyond that, the curving, white-columned structure is part of a former **Carmelite convent.** Imagine the outrage of the Jewish community when the Church built a convent and a Catholic school here in the ghetto to preach to their children, and forced locals to attend Mass.

Pop into the tunnel-like alleyway next to it, and—in the evocative little courtyard—imagine the tight conditions of thousands of Jews living in this small seven-acre area. Then head back to the main square and consider how times are much better today.

ANCIENT APPIAN WAY TOUR

Via Appia Antica

The wonder of its day, Appian Way was the largest, widest, fastest road ever, called the "Queen of Roads." Built in 312 B.C. and named after Appius Claudius Caecus (a Roman official), it connected Rome with Capua (near Naples), running in a straight line for much of the way, ignoring the natural contour of the land. Eventually, this most important of Roman roads stretched 430 miles to the port of Brindisi—the gateway to the East—where boats sailed for Greece and Egypt. Twenty-nine such roads fanned out from Rome. Just as Hitler built the Autobahn system in anticipation of empire maintenance, the expansion-minded Roman government realized the military and political value of a good road system.

Hollywood created the famous image of Appian Way lined with the crucified bodies of Spartacus and his gang of slave rebels. This image is only partially accurate—Spartacus was killed in battle after a two-year conflict. But historians do believe that after his defeat in 71 B.C., 6,000 slaves from the revolt were crucified on crosses spaced about 30 yards apart along the length of Appian Way—a distance of over 100 miles. Their bodies were left to hang for several months as a warning to other slaves. Imagine the eerie welcome this provided visitors arriving in Rome.

When the Christian faith permeated Rome, Appian Way became a popular underground burial place for Christians. It later entered Romantic lore (though untrue) as a place where Christians hid from persecution. Today the road and the landscape around it are preserved as a cultural park.

For the tourist, the ancient Appian Way offers three attractions: the road itself, with its ruined monuments; the two major Christian catacombs open to visitors; and the peaceful atmosphere, which provides a respite from the city. Be aware, however, that the road today is busy with traffic—and actually quite treacherous in spots. I recommend following this tour's route, which lets you avoid the worst of the traffic, making the area a pleasant place for strolling or biking.

Orientation

Length of This Tour: Budget five hours to get to and from Appian Way, walk or bike the stretch of sights, and visit one of the catacombs.

When to Go: Visit in the morning or late afternoon, since many of the sights—including the Catacombs of San Callisto—shut down from 12:00 to 14:00. All the recommended sights are open on Tuesday, Thursday, Friday, and Saturday. On Monday, several sights are closed, including Tomb of Cecilia Metella, Circus and Villa of Maxentius, and San Sebastiano Gate and Museum of the Walls. On Wednesday, Catacombs of San Callisto and the pedestrian path through the park are closed. On Sunday, the Catacombs of San Sebastiano are closed; however, Appian Way is closed to car traffic, making it a great day for walking or biking (although the old stones can be bumpy).

Getting There: Bus #660 drops you off right where our tour starts, at Tomb of Cecilia Metella. In Rome, take Metro line A to the Colli Albani stop, where you catch bus #660 (2/hour, along Via Appia Nuova) and ride 10 minutes to the last stop—Cecilia Metella/Via Appia Antica (at the intersection of Via Cecilia Metella and Via Appia Antica). As it can be frustrating to buy a bus ticket on Appian Way, have one in hand for your return trip.

A **taxi** will get you from Rome to Tomb of Cecilia Metella for about €20. However, to return by taxi, you'll have to phone for one; there are no taxi stands on Appian Way (or just take handy bus #118 back to Rome).

Bus #118 gets you to the sights on the northern part of Appian Way, if you want to visit just a few sights without following the exact tour route outlined here. In Rome, catch #118 from either the Piramide or Circo Massimo Metro stops; going away from the city center, it stops at San Sebastiano Gate, Domine Quo Vadis Church, Catacombs of San Callisto, and Catacombs of San Sebastiano. Although bus #118 does not stop at Tomb of Cecilia Metella, the tomb is only 500 yards away from the San Sebastiano bus stop. Going back to Rome, bus #118 takes a somewhat different route (skipping Catacombs of San Sebastiano); catch this northbound bus just up the road at Catacombs of San Callisto.

Sebastiano vs. Callisto

Which of the two catacombs is the best? They're actually quite similar. Both include a half-hour tour, where you go underground to see the niches where early Christians were buried (but no bones). Both have some faded frescoes and graffiti with Christian symbols. Both have small chapels and a few memorial statues. Most people pick one catacomb to visit, and either will fit the bill. I lean slightly in favor of San Callisto, but only because of its historical importance, not because it's inherently more interesting.

(Note that the **Catacombs of Priscilla**—more intimate and less crowded than these two more famous ones—can be found at the other end of town, northeast of the Villa Borghese Gardens; see page 73.)

Bus #218 goes from San Giovanni in Laterano to Domine Quo Vadis Church and the west entrance of Catacombs of San Callisto, but isn't that useful for other Appian Way sights.

The handy, but much more expensive, **Archeobus** runs from Termini train station to the major Appian Way sights (see page 42, under "Tours"). It stops at all the key attractions—you can hop off, tour the sights, and pick up a later bus (officially runs twice hourly, but service can be spotty).

Getting Back: No matter how you arrive at Appian Way, **bus #118** is the easiest and cheapest way to return to Rome (get off at the end of the line, the Piramide Metro stop).

Information: The **Via Appia Antica TI** near Domine Quo Vadis Church gives out maps and information on the entire park, which stretches east and south of the visit outlined here (daily April-Oct 9:30-17:30, Nov-March 9:30-16:30, rents bikes, Via Appia Antica 58/60, tel. 06-513-5316, www.parcoappiaantica.it, general info at http://archeoroma.beniculturali.it/en). The Archeobus map shows everything clearly. **Capo di Bove** has a small info center with a good €4 map/guide, active excavations, and a relaxing garden (Mon-Sat 10:00-16:00, Sun 10:00-18:00, great place for discreet picnic, clean WCs, Via Appia Antica 222, tel. 06-3996-7700); it's 100 yards uphill from Appia Antica Caffè, which also has maps (described next). For in-depth background on Catacombs of San Callisto, see www.catacombe.roma.it.

Tomb of Cecilia Metella: €6, includes entry to the Baths of Caracalla and Villa dei Quintili, April-Sept Tue-Sun 9:00-19:00, closes earlier Oct-March, closed Mon year-round, last entry one hour before closing, tel. 06-3996-7700.

Circus and Villa of Maxentius: €4, Tue-Sun 9:00-13:30, closed

Mon, last entry 30 minutes before closing, tel. 06-780-1324.

Catacombs of San Sebastiano: €8, includes 35-minute tour, 2/hour; Mon-Sat 10:00-17:00, closed Sun and mid-Nov-mid-Dec, last entry 30 minutes before closing.

Catacombs of San Callisto: €8, includes 30-minute tour, at least 2/hour; Thu-Tue 9:00-12:00 & 14:00-17:00, closed Wed and Feb.

Domine Quo Vadis Church: Free, daily 8:00-19:30 (until 18:30 off-season), tel. 06-512-0441.

San Sebastiano Gate and Museum of the Walls: €4, Tue-Sun 9:00-14:00, closed Mon, last entry 30 minutes before closing, tel. 06-7047-5284.

Bike Rental: The best day for biking is Sunday, when Appian Way is closed to traffic. Take bus #660 to the last stop (Cecilia Metella/Via Appia Antica), and you'll find **Appia Antica Caffè,** where you can rent a bike (€3.50/hour, €12/4 hours, 10 percent discount on bikes and food with this book, handy €1 map, daily 9:00-sunset, at corner of Appian Way and Via Cecilia Metella, near Tomb of Cecilia Metella at Via Appia Antica 175, mobile 338-3465-440, www.appiaanticacaffe.it). You can also rent a bike from the **Via Appia Antica TI** (€3/hour, €15/day; see "Information," above). If you don't mind heavy traffic, you could even bike from the Colosseum or Santa Maria Maggiore out past the wall and down Appian Way. For bike rental in the city center, see "By Bike," on page 38.

Services: Free WCs are at the San Sebastiano and San Callisto catacombs and at Capo di Bove, and WCs for paying customers are at the Tomb of Cecilia Metella and the Appia Antica Caffè. There are several water fountains along the way to refill water bottles.

Eating: Appia Antica Caffè (see "Bike Rental," earlier) makes big salads and abundant sandwiches and has a shaded, restful seating area in back. Or go 50 yards uphill (south) from the café to buy food at a hole-in-the-wall *alimentari* (market), perfect for assembling a picnic (Mon-Sat 7:00-14:00 & 15:00-20:00, Sun 9:00-15:00). Great picnic spots are just a half-mile farther uphill (south) from here. Several pricey restaurants are along the stretch between the Tomb of Cecilia Metella and the Catacombs of San Sebastiano (which normally has a sandwich-and-drinks cart).

Starring: An old road, crumbling tombs, and underground Christian cemeteries.

Overview

Our tour begins near the Tomb of Cecilia Metella, at the far (southern) end of the sightseeing highlights, and works northward—mostly downhill—to Domine Quo Vadis Church, toward the center of Rome. We'll arrive by bus #660 or taxi, walk a mile-and-a-half along Appian Way, and return to Rome on bus #118. Or take the Archeobus, hopping on and off at key stops.

Sightseers share the road with speeding drivers talking on mobile phones (except on traffic-free Sundays), but there's really only one bad stretch—between the Catacombs of San Sebastiano and Domine Quo Vadis Church. We'll avoid that traffic by taking a pedestrian path through a quiet park that parallels the busy road (except on Wednesdays, when the path is closed).

The Tour Begins

• *From the café near the Tomb of Cecilia Metella, head downhill 100 yards, where you walk (or rattle your bike) over a stretch of the...*

Original Paved Road

Huge basalt stones formed the sturdy base of a road 14 feet across. In its heyday, a central strip accommodated animal-powered vehicles, and elevated sidewalks served pedestrians. The first section (near Rome) was perfectly straight and lined with tombs and funerary monuments.

Nearby (to the right of the entrance to the Tomb of Cecilia Metella) is the original **mile marker III,** one of more than 400 such stones that counted the distance from Rome to Brindisi. Emperors knew that a fine network of roads was key to expanding and administering the empire. This road, from c. 312 B.C., kicks off the expansion period.

• *You can't miss (on the right side) the...*

Tomb of Cecilia Metella (Mausoleo di Cecilia Metella)

This massive cylindrical tomb, one of the best preserved of the many tombs of prominent Romans that line the road, was built in the time of Augustus (c. 30 B.C.) for the daughter-in-law of Crassus, Rome's richest man. Faced with white travertine and situated on the crest of a hill, the tomb was an imposing sight. This grand tomb in the suburbs rivaled Augustus' own round mausoleum in the city center (near the Ara Pacis, see page 75).

Since no one was allowed to be buried inside the city walls,

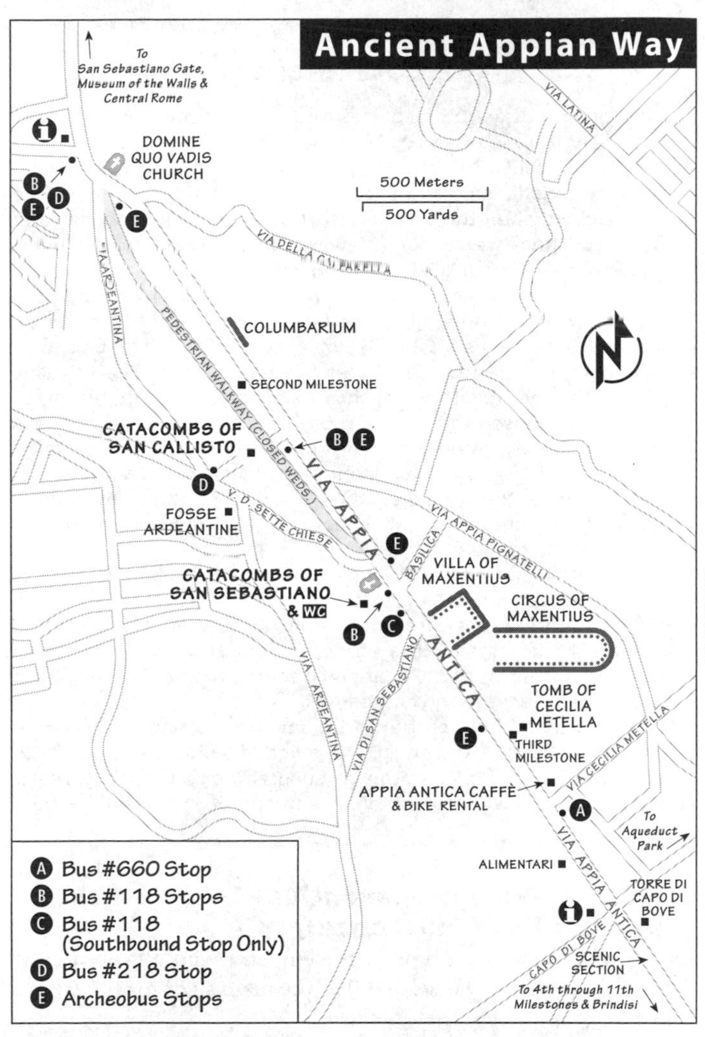

Appian Way was a popular place to have a tomb where everyone could see and admire it. Later, Christians were buried here, though not in tombs (they preferred to be buried underground). Picture a funeral procession passing under the pines and cypresses, past a long line of pyramids, private mini-temples, altars, and tombs.

If you pay to go inside, you'll see the tomb's hollow interior; a few statues of deceased Romans that once adorned tombs; and a former paving-stone quarry with a preserved wagon-wheel groove. • *About 200 yards farther downhill from the tomb (on the right) are the ruins of the...*

Catacombs

The catacombs are burial places for (mostly) Christians who died in ancient Roman times. By law, no one was allowed to be buried within the walls of Rome. While pagan Romans were into cremation, Christians preferred to be buried (so that they could be resurrected when the time came). But land was expensive, and most Christians were poor. A few wealthy, landowning Christians allowed their properties to be used as burial places.

The 40 or so known catacombs are scattered outside the ancient walls of Rome. From the first through the fifth centuries, Christians dug an estimated 375 miles of tomb-lined tunnels, with networks of galleries as many as five layers deep. The volcanic tuff that Rome sits atop—which is soft and easy to cut, but hardens when exposed to air—was perfect for the job. The Christians burrowed many layers deep for two reasons: to get more mileage out of the donated land, and to be near martyrs and saints already buried there. Bodies were wrapped in linen (like Christ's). Since they figured the Second Coming was imminent, there was no interest in embalming the body.

When Emperor Constantine legalized Christianity in A.D. 313, Christians had a new, interesting problem: There would be no more recently persecuted martyrs to bind them together and inspire them. Instead, the early martyrs and popes assumed more importance, and Christians began making pilgrimages to their burial places in the catacombs.

In the 800s, when barbarian invaders started ransacking the tombs, Christians moved the relics of saints and martyrs to the safety of churches in the city center. For a thousand years, the catacombs were forgotten. In early modern times, they were

Circus and Villa of Maxentius (Circo e Villa di Massenzio)

This was the suburban home of the emperor who was eventually defeated by Constantine in A.D. 312. The main sight to see here is a whole lot of nothing—that is, the expansive stretch of open space contained by this huge former chariot race track. You can see essentially all of it for free from the road. If you pay the admission, you can walk between the entrance towers to the long central spine, and imagine chariots racing around it while 10,000 fans cheered. Maxentius watched from the building rising up above the bleachers, where the chariots made their hairiest turn. At the far end of the 260-yard track is the triumphal arch under which the

excavated and became part of the Romantic Age's Grand Tour of Europe.

When abandoned plates and utensils from ritual meals were found, 18th- and 19th-century Romantics guessed that persecuted Christians hid out in these candlelit galleries. The popularity of this legend grew, even though it was untrue: By the second century, more than a million people lived in Rome, and the 10,000 early Christians didn't need to camp out in the catacombs. They hid in plain view, melting into obscurity within the city itself.

The underground tunnels, while empty of bones, are rich in early Christian symbolism, which functioned as a secret language. The dove represented the soul. You'll see it quenching its thirst (worshipping), with an olive branch (at rest), or happily perched (in paradise). Peacocks, known for their purportedly

"incorruptible flesh," embodied immortality. The shepherd with a lamb on his shoulders was the "good shepherd," the first portrayal of Christ as a kindly leader of his flock. The fish was used because the first letters of these words—"Jesus Christ, Son of God, Savior"—spelled "fish" in Greek. And the anchor is a cross in disguise. A second-century bishop had written on his tomb, "All who understand these things, pray for me." You'll see pictures of people praying with their hands raised—the custom at the time.

winner rode to receive his reward.

Also, just down Appian Way from this circus is a square wall of ruins enclosing a modern building. Behind that modern building, you can glimpse the circular mausoleum of Maxentius' son, Romulus.

• *About 300 yards farther down the road (on the left) are the...*

▲▲Catacombs of San Sebastiano

This underground cemetery is named for the Christian soldier who was tied to a column and shot through with arrows because of his faith—a subject depicted by many artists through history. A guide takes you below ground to see burial niches, frescoes, and graffiti. It's said that the bodies of Peter and Paul were kept here for a while in the third century.

Besides the catacombs, the site also has a basilica (free) containing various relics. In the first chapel to the left are St. Sebastian's supposed remains, marked with a statue of an arrow-pierced

corpse. On the opposite side of the nave, a chapel displays an arrow he was shot with, a section of the column he was tied to, and a couple of footprints from the Domine Quo Vadis legend (see below). Nearby stands a curly-haired bust of *The Savior (Il Salvatore)* by Bernini.

• *The stretch of Appian Way past the Catacombs of San Sebastiano is the least interesting and most crowded (even dangerous). Avoid it by taking the pedestrian and bike path (open daily except Wed), which begins just past the Catacombs of San Sebastiano, at the intersection with Via delle Sette Chiese. To reach the path, go through the arch at #126. The quiet path parallels Appian Way and takes you directly to the Catacombs of San Callisto. On Wednesdays, when the gate is closed, you'll have to stay straight on Via Appia Antica, being careful of traffic.*

▲▲Catacombs of San Callisto

These are my favorite catacombs, named for the cemetery's first caretaker, St. Callixtus. This was the official cemetery for Rome's early Christians and the burial place of nine third-century popes, other bishops of Rome, and various martyrs. The most famous martyr was Sta. Cecilia, patron saint of music, a Roman noble who was killed for converting to Christianity. Her tomb is marked with a copy of a famous Maderno statue. (For more on Cecilia and the statue, ✪ see the Trastevere Walk chapter.)

Buy your ticket and wait for your language to be called. They move lots of people quickly. If one group seems ridiculously large (more than 50 people), wait for the next tour in English.

• *After you visit the catacombs, an optional detour brings you to the evocative* ***Fosse Ardeantine,*** *a memorial tomb to 335 Italians gunned down by Nazis during World War II to avenge a bomb attack in Rome that killed 32 German soldiers. With your back to the San Callisto ticket booth, go right, walk downhill through the gate (where you can also catch bus #218 back to San Giovanni), and follow signs to* Fosse Ardeantine*—about a five-minute walk (Mon-Fri 8:15-15:00, Sat-Sun 8:15-16:30, tel. 06-513-6742).*

Back at the catacombs, continue north (downhill) another three-quarters of a mile, where the pedestrian path spills out at a busy three-way intersection. There you'll find the small...

Domine Quo Vadis Church

The tiny ninth-century church (redone in the 17th) was built on the spot where Peter, while fleeing the city to escape Nero's persecution, saw a vision of Christ. Peter asked Jesus, "Lord, where are you

going?" ("*Domine quo vadis?*" in Latin), to which Christ replied, "I am going to Rome to be crucified again." This miraculous sign gave Peter faith and courage and caused him to return to Rome. Inside the nave of the church, stumble over the stone marked with the supposed footprints of Jesus. You'll see a fresco of Peter with keys on the left wall and one of Jesus on the right. A bust depicts Nobel Prize-winning Polish author Henryk Sienkiewicz, who wrote a historical novel that was the basis for the 1951 Hollywood movie *Quo Vadis.*

• *The tour is over. "Quo vadis, pilgrim?"*

To return to central Rome, it's another two miles north along a busy stretch of road, not recommended on foot or bike. Instead, catch bus #118 from the bus stop about 75 yards past Domine Quo Vadis Church (across from the TI). Bus #118 makes several interesting stops (see below) on its way to the Piramide Metro stop. (Note that another bus, the #218, also goes from here to San Giovanni in Laterano.)

For those with more energy, there's more to see, especially if you're renting a bike and want to just get away from it all.

Other Sights on or near Appian Way

Consider these diversions if you have the time and interest.

More of Appian Way: Heading south (away from downtown Rome), past the Tomb of Cecilia Metella, you'll find the best-preserved part of Appian Way—quieter, less touristed, and lined with cypresses, pines, and crumbling tombs. It's all downhill after the first few hundred yards. On a bike, you'll travel over lots of rough paving stones (or dirt sidewalks) for about 30 minutes to reach a big pyramid-shaped ruin on its tiny base, and then five minutes more to the back side of Villa dei Quintili. Usually, you can't enter the villa from here, but you can admire the semicircular nymphaeum, or fake grotto. Enjoy a picnic, then turn around and pedal up that long hill to return your bike.

Aqueduct Park (Parco degli Acquedotti): Rome's mighty aqueducts kept water flowing into the thriving and thirsty ancient city of one million. (They also eventually provided a handy Achilles' heel for invading barbarians: Simply break an arch in the aqueduct, and life becomes very tough within the city walls.) This sprawling, evocative park may seem miles from anywhere, but it's a snap to reach by Metro. The green space is a favorite these days with Roman joggers, picnickers, and anyone looking for a break from the big city. If you're coming straight from Rome, take Metro line A to Giulio Agricola. If coming from Appian Way, start at Appia Antica Caffè (near Tomb of Cecilia Metella), take bus #660 to the Colli Albani Metro station, and catch the Metro to Giulio Agricola.

As you exit the Giulio Agricola Metro stop, follow signs for *Viale Giulio Agricola*. This street has trees in its median strip and ends at a modern church several blocks away. Head for the church, passing a number of cafés and grocery stores (good for picnic fare). To the right of the church, enter the park and pass through the squat brick arches of the first aqueduct (actually two aqueducts—the 16th-century Acqua Felice, piggybacked on top of the Acqua Marcia from the second century B.C.). Continue across the field and up the small hill where you'll see fragments of the more impressive Acqua Claudia (first century A.D.). Follow the path to the left for about 10 minutes; you'll come to the best preserved section, which stretches into the distance and makes for an easy walk. Loop back to the church and Metro when you're done. If you're not afraid of traffic, you could bike from Appian Way to the Aqueduct Park (takes about an hour; get directions when you rent your bike).

Sights on Bus #118 Route Back to Rome: On the way back, about a half-mile from Domine Quo Vadis Church, the bus stops alongside Rome's ancient city wall. The **San Sebastiano Gate and Museum of the Walls** offers an interesting look at Roman defense and a chance to scramble along a stretch of the ramparts. The Aurelian Walls (c. A.D. 270) were built in five years because of threat of invasions. At 12 miles around, it was the biggest building project ever undertaken within the city of Rome.

A few minutes farther on, bus #118 stops near the **Baths of Caracalla.** Next, it makes a stop at the east end of the **Circus Maximus** (the Circo Massimo Metro stop is nearby). The bus terminates at **Piramide,** which has several interesting sights clustered around the Metro station (see page 85). From Piramide, catch the Metro home.

SLEEPING IN ROME

For hassle-free efficiency, I favor accommodations and restaurants handy to your sightseeing activities. Rather than list hotels scattered throughout Rome, I describe my favorite neighborhoods and recommend the best accommodation values in each, from hotels with all of the comforts to less-expensive hostels and convents.

A major feature of this book is its extensive listing of good-value rooms—especially in Rome, where hotels are generally pricey, the cheaper hotels can be depressing, and the TI isn't allowed to give opinions on quality. I like places that are clean, central, relatively quiet at night, reasonably priced, friendly, small enough to have a hands-on owner and stable staff, run with a respect for Italian traditions, and not listed in other guidebooks. (In Rome, for me, six out of these eight criteria means it's a keeper.) I'm more impressed by a handy location and a fun-loving philosophy than flat-screen TVs and shoeshine machines.

Book your accommodations well in advance if you'll be traveling during busy times. See page 491 for a list of major holidays and festivals in Rome; for tips on making reservations, see page 324.

Rates and Deals

I've described my recommended accommodations using a Sleep Code (see sidebar). Prices listed are for one-night stays in peak season, and assume you're booking directly (not through a TI or online hotel-booking engine). Using an online booking service costs the hotel about 20 percent and logically closes the door on special deals. Book direct.

While most taxes are included in the price, a tax of €2-3/person per night is added to all hotel bills, and must be paid in cash. The only exemptions are for hostelers and children under the age of two.

These days, many hotels change prices from day to day according to demand. Given the economic downturn, hoteliers are often willing and eager to make a deal. I'd suggest emailing several hotels to ask for their best price. Comparison-shop and make your choice.

As you look over the listings, you'll notice that some accommodations promise special prices to my readers who book direct (without using a room-finding service or hotel-booking website, which take a commission). To get these rates, you must mention this book when you reserve, and then show the book upon arrival. Rick Steves discounts apply to readers with ebooks as well as printed books.

In general, prices can soften if you do any of the following: offer to pay cash, stay at least three nights, or mention this book. You can also try asking for a cheaper room or a discount, or offer to skip breakfast.

Haggle if you arrive late in the day during off-season (roughly mid-July through August and November through mid-March). It's common for hotels in Rome to lower their prices 10-50 percent in the off-season, although prices at hostels and the cheaper hotels won't fluctuate much. Room rates are lowest in sweltering August.

Types of Accommodations

Hotels

Double rooms listed in this book range from about €65 (very simple, toilet and shower down the hall) to €400 (maximum plumbing and more), with most clustering around €150 (with private bathrooms). I've favored these pricier options, because intense Rome is easier to enjoy with a welcoming oasis to call home.

Solo travelers find that the cost of a *camera singola* is often only 25 percent less than a *camera doppia*. Three or four people can save money by requesting one big room. (If a Db is €110, a Qb would be about €150.) Most listed hotels have rooms for anywhere from one to five people. If there's room for an extra cot, they'll cram it in for you (charging you around €25). English works in all but the cheapest places.

Traffic in Rome roars. Thanks to double-paned windows and air-conditioning, night noise is not the problem it once was. Even so, light sleepers who ask for a *tranquillo* room will likely get a room in the back...and sleep better. Once you actually see your room, consider the potential problem of night noise. If necessary, don't hesitate to ask for a quieter room.

Nearly all places offer private bathrooms. Generally rooms with a bath or shower also have a toilet and a bidet (which Italians use for quick sponge baths). The cord over the tub or shower is not

Chill Out

All but the cheapest hotels have air-conditioning. Because Europeans are generally careful with energy use, you'll find government-enforced limits on air-conditioning and heating. There's a one-month period each spring and fall when neither is allowed. Air-conditioning sometimes costs an extra per-day charge, is worth seeking out in summer (though it may be on only at certain times of the day), and is rarely available from fall through spring. Conveniently, many business-class hotels drop their prices in July and August, just when the air conditioned comfort they offer is most important.

Most hotel rooms with air-conditioners come with a control stick (like a TV remote) that generally has the same symbols and features: fan icon (click to toggle through wind power, from light to gale); louver icon (choose steady airflow or waves); snowflake and sunshine icons (cold air or heat, depending on season); clock ("O" setting: run x hours before turning off; "I" setting: wait x hours to start); and the temperature control (21 degrees Celsius is comfortable).

a clothesline. You pull it when you've fallen and can't get up.

Double beds are called *matrimoniale,* even though hotels aren't interested in your marital status. Twins are *due letti singoli.*

When you check in, the receptionist will normally ask for your passport and keep it for a couple of hours. Hotels are legally required to register each guest with the police. Relax. Americans are notorious for making this chore more difficult than it needs to be.

Assume that breakfast is included in the prices I've listed, unless otherwise noted. If breakfast is included but optional, you may want to skip it. While convenient, it's usually expensive—€5-8 for a simple continental buffet with ham, cheese, yogurt, and unlimited *caffè latte.* A picnic in your room followed by a coffee at the corner café can be lots cheaper.

More pillows and blankets are usually in the closet or available on request. In Italy, towels and linen aren't always replaced every day. Hang your towel up to dry. Some hotels use lightweight "waffle" or very thin tablecloth-type towels; these take less water and electricity to launder and are preferred by many Italians.

Most hotel rooms have a TV and telephone, and Internet access (usually Wi-Fi) is common. Simpler places rarely have a phone. Pricier hotels usually come with a small stocked fridge called a *frigo bar* (FREE-goh bar; pay for what you use).

Almost no hotels have parking, but nearly all have a line on spots in a nearby garage (about €24/day).

If you arrive on an early flight or an overnight train, your room

Making Reservations

Given the quality of the accommodations I've found for this book, I'd recommend that you reserve your rooms several weeks advance—or as soon as you've pinned down your travel dates—particularly if you'll be traveling during peak season. Note that some national holidays jam things up and merit your making reservations far in advance (see "Holidays and Festivals" on page 491).

Requesting a Reservation: It's usually easiest to book your room through the hotel's website; many have a reservation-request form built right in. Just type in your preferred dates and the website will automatically display a list of available rooms and prices. Simpler websites will generate an email to the hotelier with your request. If there's no reservation form, or for complicated requests, send an email. Other options include calling (see "Phoning" below, and be mindful of time zones) or faxing. Most recommended hotels are accustomed to guests who speak only English.

The hotelier wants to know these key pieces of information about your stay (also included in the sample request form in the appendix):

- number and type of rooms
- number of nights
- date of arrival
- date of departure
- any special needs (e.g., bathroom in the room or down the hall, twin beds vs. double bed, air-conditioning, quiet, view, ground floor, etc.)

When you request a room, use the European style for writing dates: day/month/year. For example, for a two-night stay in July of 2013, I would request: "1 double room for 2 nights, arrive 16/07/13, depart 18/07/13." Consider carefully how long you'll stay; don't just assume you can tack on extra days once you arrive. Make sure you mention any discounts—for Rick Steves readers or otherwise—when you make the reservation.

If you don't get a response to your email, it usually means the hotel is already fully booked—but try sending the message again or call to follow up.

Confirming a Reservation: Most places will request your credit-card number to hold the room. To confirm a room using a hotel's secure online reservation form, enter your contact information and credit-card number; the hotel will email a confirmation. For the best rates, be sure to use the hotel's official site and not a booking agency's site.

If you sent an email to request a reservation, the hotel will reply with its room availability and rates. This is not a confirmation. You must email back to say that you want the room at the given rate. While you can email your credit-card information (I do), it's safer to share that confidential info via phone call, fax, two emails (splitting your number between them), or the hotel's secure online reservation form.

Canceling a Reservation: If you must cancel your reservation, it's courteous to do so with as much advance notice as possible—at least three days. Simply make a quick phone call or send an email. Family-run places lose money if they turn away customers while holding a room for someone who doesn't show up. Understandably, many hoteliers bill no-shows for one night.

Cancellation policies can be strict: For example, you might lose a deposit if you cancel within two weeks of your reserved stay, or you might be billed for the entire visit if you leave early. Internet deals may require prepayment, with no refunds for cancellations. Ask about cancellation policies before you book.

If canceling via email, request confirmation that your cancellation was received to avoid being billed.

Reconfirming Your Reservation: Always call to reconfirm your room reservation a few days in advance. Smaller hotels and B&Bs appreciate knowing your time of arrival. If you'll be arriving late (after 17:00), let them know. On the small chance that a hotel loses track of your reservation, bring along a hard copy of their confirmation.

Reserving Rooms as You Travel: You can make reservations as you travel, calling hotels a few days to a week before your arrival. If everything's full, don't despair. Call a day or two in advance and fill a cancellation. If you'd rather travel without any reservations at all, you'll have greater success snaring rooms if you arrive at your destination early in the day. When you anticipate crowds (weekends are worst), call hotels at about 9:00 or 10:00 on the day you plan to arrive, when the hotel clerk knows who'll be checking out and just which rooms will be available. If you encounter a language barrier, ask the fluent receptionist at your current hotel to call for you.

Phoning: To call Italy from the US or Canada, dial 011-39 and then the local number. (The 011 is our international access code, and 39 is Italy's country code.) If you're calling Italy from another European country, dial 00-39-local number. (The 00 is Europe's international access code.) To call a Rome hotel from anywhere in Italy (including Rome), simply dial the local number. For more tips on calling, see page 462.

probably won't be ready first thing in the morning. You should be able to safely check your bag at the hotel and dive right into sightseeing.

Hoteliers can be a great help and source of advice. Most know their city well and can assist you with everything from public transit and airport connections to finding a good restaurant, the nearest launderette, or an Internet café. But even at the best places, mechanical breakdowns occur: Air-conditioning malfunctions, sinks leak, hot water turns cold, and toilets gurgle and smell. Report your concerns clearly and calmly at the front desk. For more complicated problems, don't expect instant results.

To guard against theft in your room, keep valuables out of sight. Some rooms come with a safe, and other hotels have safes at the front desk. Use them if you're concerned.

Checkout can pose problems if surprise charges pop up on your bill. If you settle your bill the afternoon before you leave, you'll have time to discuss and address any points of contention (before 19:00, when the night shift usually arrives).

Above all, keep a positive attitude. Remember, you're on vacation. If your hotel is a disappointment, spend more time out enjoying the city you came to see.

Bed-and-Breakfasts (B&Bs)

B&Bs offer double the cultural intimacy for a good deal less than most hotel rooms. Roman B&Bs are small—most have no more than three rooms, and the owner generally lives on-site. (Be aware that small hotels sometimes erroneously use the term "B&B.") You'll pay in cash rather than by credit card. Expect few services and no amenities such as public lounges, in-room phones, private bathrooms, and daily bed-sheet changes (though the basics, such as sheets and towels, are provided). After picking up your keys, you can come and go as you wish. When reserving, confirm what kind of breakfast is included—some less-expensive B&Bs simply give you a voucher for a pastry and coffee at a nearby bar.

Doubles with breakfast start at around €65, with prices increasing along with the number of amenities. Because of my large volume of readers and the small size of Roman B&Bs, it isn't practical to include many B&B listings here. To find a B&B in Rome, start your search with a website such as www.bedandbreakfast.com or www.b-b.rm.it. You'll get better prices, however, by booking directly with the B&B. Some websites connect you directly with the B&B owner, including www.wheninromebandb.com and www.gulliverslodge.com (see listing on page 333).

Many B&Bs come with thin walls and doors that can make for a noisy night. If you're a light sleeper, bring earplugs. And please be quiet in the halls and in your rooms at night (talk softly, and keep the TV volume low)...those of us getting up early will thank you for it.

Convents

Although I list just a few, Rome has many convents that rent out rooms. See the Church of Santa Susanna's website for a list (www.santasusanna.org, select "Coming to Rome"). At convents, the beds are twins and English is often in short supply, but the price is right.

Consider these nun-run places, all listed in this chapter: the expensive but divine **Casa di Santa Brigida** (near Campo de' Fiori), **Suore di Santa Elisabetta** (near Santa Maria Maggiore), **Casa Sant'Anna** (near the Colosseum), **Casa Il Rosario** (near Piazza Venezia), and **Casa per Ferie Santa Maria alle Fornaci** (near the Vatican).

Hostels

You'll pay about €25 per bed to stay at a hostel. Travelers of any age are welcome if they don't mind dorm-style accommodations and meeting other travelers. Most hostels offer kitchen facilities, Internet access, Wi-Fi, and a self-service laundry. **Independent hostels** tend to be easygoing, colorful, and informal (no membership required); see www.hostelz.com, www.hostelseurope.com, www.hostels.com, and www.hostelworld.com. **Official hostels** are part of Hostelling International and share an online booking site (www.hihostels.com); they require that you either have a membership card or pay extra per night.

If going the hostel route, consider the ones I list in this chapter (within a 10-minute walk of Termini train station), or check www.backpackers.it for more listings.

Apartments

Many locals rent out their apartments in downtown Rome, a great value for families or multiple couples traveling together. Rentals are generally by the week, with prices around €120 per day. Apartments typically offer a couple of bedrooms, a sitting area, and a teensy *cucinetta* (kitchenette), usually stocked with dishes and flatware. After you check in, you're basically on your own. While you won't have a doorman to carry your bags or a maid to clean your room each day, you will get an inside peek at a Roman home, and you can save lots of money—especially if you take advantage of the cooking facilities—with no loss of comfort. Most places are rented through booking agencies, the TI, or websites. Browse through www.homeaway.com, www.vrbo.com, and www.wantedinrome.com.

Sleep Code

(€1 = about $1.40)

Price Rankings

To help you easily sort through these listings, I've divided the accommodations into three categories based on the price for a double room with bath during high season:

$$$ Higher Priced—Most rooms €180 or more.
$$ Moderately Priced—Most rooms between €130-180.
$ Lower Priced—Most rooms €130 or less.

I always rate hostels as $, whether or not they have double rooms, because they have the cheapest beds in town. Prices can change without notice; verify the hotel's current rates online or by email.

Abbreviations

To give maximum information in a minimum of space, I use the following code to describe accommodations. Prices listed are per room, not per person. When a price range is given for a type of room (such as double rooms listing for €100-150), it means the price fluctuates with the season, size of room, or length of stay; expect to pay the upper end for peak-season stays.

S = Single room (or price for one person in a double).
D = Double or Twin room. "Double beds" are often two twins sheeted together and are usually big enough for nonromantic couples.
T = Triple (generally a double bed with a single).
Q = Quad (usually two double beds; adding an extra child's bed to a T is usually cheaper).
b = Private bathroom with toilet and shower or tub.
s = Private shower or tub only (toilet is down the hall).

According to this code, a couple staying at a "Db-€140" hotel would pay a total of €140 (about $195) per night for a double room with a private bathroom. Unless otherwise noted, breakfast is included, hotel staff speaks basic English, and credit cards are accepted.

Rome charges a hotel tax of €2-3 per person, per night. This tax is typically not included in the prices I've listed here.

If I mention "Internet access" in a listing, there's a public terminal in the lobby for guests to use. If I specify "Wi-Fi," you can generally access it in public areas and often (though not always) in your room.

Steve and Linda of **The Beehive** run a booking service for private rooms and apartments in the old centers of Rome, Florence, and Venice; rates start at €30 per person (see listing on page 334, www.cross-pollinate.com). Frederick and Mayra of **Tournights** run a similar apartment-finding service in Rome and Florence (www.tournights.com).

Accommodations

Near Termini Train Station

While not as atmospheric as other areas of Rome, the hotels near Termini train station are less expensive, and public-transportation options link these places easily with the entire city. The city's two Metro lines intersect at the station, and most buses leave from here. Piazza Venezia is a 20-minute walk down Via Nazionale.

West of the Station

Most of these hotels are on or near Via Firenze, a safe, handy, central, and relatively quiet street that's a 10-minute walk from Termini train station and the airport train, and two blocks beyond Piazza della Repubblica. The Defense Ministry is nearby, so you've got heavily armed guards watching over you all night.

The neighborhood is well-connected by public transportation (with the Repubblica Metro stop nearby). Virtually all the city buses that rumble down Via Nazionale (#64, #70, #115, #640, #492, and the #40 express) take you to Piazza Venezia (Forum) and Largo Argentina (Pantheon). From Largo Argentina, bus #64 (jammed with people and thieves), the #40 express bus, and bus #492 continue to the Vatican. Or, at Largo Argentina, you can transfer to electric trolley #8 to Trastevere (get off at first stop after crossing the river).

To stock your closet pantry, pop over to **Despar Supermarket** (daily 8:00-21:00, Via Nazionale 213, at the corner of Via Venezia). A 24-hour **pharmacy** near the recommended hotels is Farmacia Piram (Via Nazionale 228, tel. 06-488-4437).

$$$ Residenza Cellini feels like the guest wing of a gorgeous Neoclassical palace. It offers 11 rooms, "ortho/anti-allergy beds," four-star comforts and service, and a breezy breakfast terrace (Db-€190, larger Db-€210, extra bed-€25, prices good through 2013 with this book and cash, air-con, elevator, Internet access and Wi-Fi, Via Modena 5, tel. 06-4782-5204, fax 06-4788-1806, www.residenzacellini.it, residenzacellini@tin.it, Barbara, Gaetano, and Donato).

$$$ Hotel Modigliani, a delightful 23-room place, is energetically run in a clean, bright, minimalist yet in-love-with-life style that its artist namesake would appreciate. It has a vast and

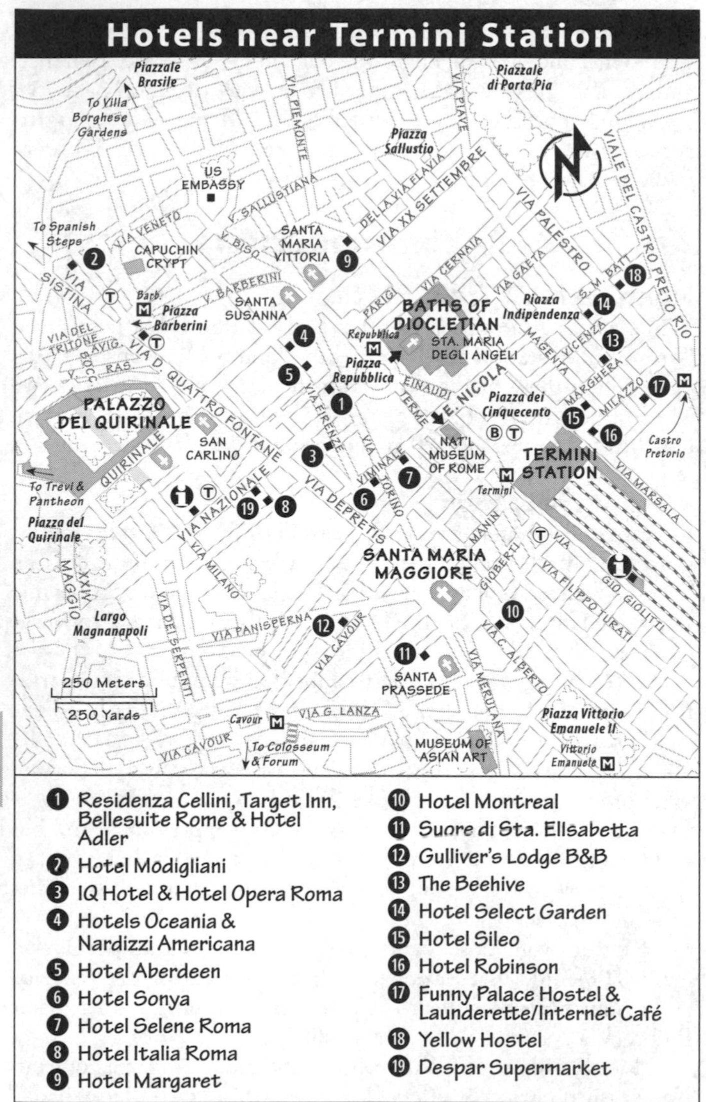

plush lounge, a garden, and a newsletter introducing you to each of the staff (Db-€195, but check website for deals and ask for a 10 percent Rick Steves discount; air-con, Wi-Fi; northwest of Via Firenze—from Tritone Fountain on Piazza Barberini, go 2 blocks up Via della Purificazione to #42; tel. 06-4281-5226, www.hotelmodigliani.com, info@hotelmodigliani.com, Giulia and Marco).

$$$ IQ Hotel, facing the Opera House, opened in 2010 and feels almost Scandinavian in its efficiency, without a hint of the

Old World. Its 88 rooms are fresh and spacious, the roof garden comes with a swing set, and vending machines dispense bottles of wine (Db-€100-220 depending on room size and season—likely €200 in peak season, €40 extra for 3rd and 4th person, 10 percent discount off best web price for Rick Steves readers—must book direct and request at time of booking, breakfast-€10, air-con, elevator, Internet access and Wi-Fi, cheap self-service laundry, gym, Via Firenze 8, tel. 06-4880-0165, fax 06-4893-0442, www.iqhotelroma.it, info@iqhotelroma.it, manager Diego).

$$ Hotel Oceania is a peaceful slice of air-conditioned heaven. This 24-room manor house-type hotel is spacious and quiet, with tastefully decorated rooms. Stefano runs a fine staff, serves wonderful coffee, provides lots of thoughtful extra touches, and works hard to maintain a caring family atmosphere (Sb-€135, Db-€168, Tb-€198, Qb-€220, these prices good through 2013 with this book, 5 percent less with cash, deep discounts summer and winter, roof terrace, family suite, Internet access and Wi-Fi, videos in the TV lounge, Via Firenze 38, third floor, tel. 06-482-4696, fax 06-488-5586, www.hoteloceania.it, info@hoteloceania.it; Anna and Radu round out the staff).

$$ Hotel Aberdeen, which perfectly combines high quality and friendliness, is warmly run by Annamaria, with support from sister Laura and cousin Cinzia, and staff members Mariano and Costel. The 37 comfy, modern rooms are a good value (Sb-€102, Db-€170, Tb-€180, Qb-€200, for these rates—or better—book direct via email or use the "Rick Steves reader reservations" link on their website, much cheaper rates off-season, air-con, Internet access and Wi-Fi, Via Firenze 48, tel. 06-482-3920, fax 06-482-1092, www.hotelaberdeen.it, info@hotelaberdeen.it).

$$ Hotel Opera Roma, with contemporary furnishings and marble accents, boasts 15 spacious, modern, and thoughtfully appointed rooms. It's quiet and just a stone's throw from the Opera House (Db-€165, Tb-€190, these prices good through 2013 with this book, 5 percent less with cash, air-con, elevator, Internet access and loaner laptop on request, Via Firenze 11, tel. 06-487-1787, www.hoteloperaroma.com, info@hoteloperaroma.com, Rezza, Litu, and Federica).

$$ Hotel Sonya offers 34 well-equipped rooms, a hearty breakfast, a central location, and decent prices (Sb-€90, Db-€150, Tb-€165, Qb-€185, Quint/b-€200, 5 percent discount with this book and cash, air-con, elevator, loaner laptops in room and Wi-Fi, faces the Opera House at Via Viminale 58, Metro: Repubblica or Termini, tel. 06-481-9911, fax 06-488-5678, www.hotelsonya.it, info@hotelsonya.it, Francesca and Ivan).

$$ Hotel Selene Roma spreads its 40 rooms out on a few floors of a big palazzo. With elegant furnishings and room to breathe, it's a fine value (Db-€150, Tb-€165, email direct for 10 percent discount, air-con, elevator, Wi-Fi, Via del Viminale 8, tel. 06-474-4781, www.hotelseleneroma.it, reception@hotelselene roma.it).

$$ Bellesuite Rome offers six bright, modern rooms with all the comforts in a quiet building (Db-€150, Tb-€190, Qb-€215, air-con, elevator, Wi-Fi, Via Modena 5, tel. 06-9521-3049, www.belle suiterome.com, mail@bellesuiterome.com).

$$ Target Inn is a sleek, practical-but-forgettable six-room place next to Residenza Cellini (listed earlier). It's owned by the same people who run the recommended Target Restaurant nearby (Db-€150, air-con, elevator, Wi-Fi, Via Modena 5, tel. 06-474-5399, www.targetinn.com, info@targetinn.com).

$ Hotel Adler evokes a more genteel age of travel, with a small garden patio and eight basic rooms on a wide and elegant hall (Db-€125, Tb-€165, Qb-€190, Quint/b-€210, 5 percent off these prices with this book, additional 5 percent discount if you pay cash, air-con, elevator, Internet access and Wi-Fi, Via Modena 5, second floor, tel. 06-484-466, fax 06-488-0940, www.hotel adler-roma.com, info@hoteladler-roma.com).

$ Hotel Nardizzi Americana, with 33 decent rooms and a delightful rooftop terrace, is another solid value (Sb-€95, Db-€125, Tb-€155, Qb-€175; to get the best rates, check their "Rick Steves readers reservations" link along with the rest of their website; additional 10 percent off any price with cash, air-con, elevator, Internet access and Wi-Fi, Via Firenze 38, fourth floor, tel. 06-488-0035, fax 06-488-0368, www.hotelnardizzi.it, info@hotelnardizzi.it; friendly Stefano, Fabrizio, Mario, and Giancarlo).

$ Hotel Italia Roma, in a busy and handy locale, is located safely on a quiet street next to the Ministry of the Interior. Thoughtfully run by Andrea, Sabrina, Abdul, and Gabriel, it has 35 modest but comfortable rooms (Sb-€90, Db-€130, Tb-€180, Qb-€200, 30 percent cheaper July-Aug, air-con-€10 extra per day, elevator, Internet access and Wi-Fi, Via Venezia 18, just off Via Nazionale, Metro: Repubblica, tel. 06-482-8355, fax 06-474-5550, www.hotel italiaroma.it, info@hotelitaliaroma.it). The four "residenza" rooms upstairs on the third floor are newer and a bit more expensive. They also have eight similar annex rooms across the street.

$ Hotel Margaret fills its walls with Impressionist prints and offers 12 decent rooms at a fair price (Db-€110, Tb-€150, Qb-€170, mention this book for best rates, air-con, elevator, Wi-Fi, north of Piazza Repubblica at Via Antonio Salandra 6, fourth floor, tel. 06-482-4285, fax 06-482-4277, www.hotelmargaret.net, info@hotelmargaret.net, Emanuela).

Southwest of the Station

These good-value places cluster around the basilica of Santa Maria Maggiore, on the edge of Rome's international district.

$ Hotel Montreal is a basic three-star place with 27 small rooms on a big street a block southeast of Santa Maria Maggiore (Sb-€90, Db-€110, Tb-€135, may be less if you email direct and ask for a Rick Steves discount, air-con, elevator, Internet access and Wi-Fi, small garden terrace, good security, Via Carlo Alberto 4, 1 block from Metro: Vittorio Emanuele, 3 blocks from Termini train station, tel. 06-445-7797, fax 06-446-5522, www.hotelmontrealroma.com, info@hotelmontrealroma.com, Pasquale).

$ Suore di Santa Elisabetta is a heavenly Polish-run convent with a serene garden and 70 beds in tidy twin-bedded (only) rooms. Often booked long in advance, with such tranquility it's a super value (S-€40, Sb-€48, D-€66, Db-€85, Tb-€106, Qb-€128, Quint/b-€142, no air-con, elevator serves top floors only, fine view roof terrace and breakfast hall, 23:00 curfew, a block southwest of Santa Maria Maggiore at Via dell'Olmata 9, Metro: Termini or Vittorio Emanuele, tel. 06-488-8271, fax 06-488-4066, www.csse-roma.eu, ist.it.s.elisabetta@libero.it).

$ Gulliver's Lodge B&B has four fun, colorful rooms on the ground floor of a large, secure building. While on a busy street, the rooms are quiet. Although the public spaces are few, in-room extras like DVD players (and DVDs, including my Italy shows) make it a fine home base (Db-€120, Tb-€135, mention the book for these prices, cash only, air-con, Internet access and Wi-Fi, a 15-minute walk southwest of Termini train station at Via Cavour 101, Metro: Cavour, tel. 06-9727-3787, www.gulliverslodge.com, info@gulliverslodge.com, Sara and Mary).

Sleeping Cheaply, Northeast of Termini Train Station

The cheapest beds in town are northeast of Termini train station (Metro: Termini). Some travelers feel this area is weird and spooky after dark, but these hotels feel plenty safe. With your back to the train tracks, turn right and walk two blocks out of the station. **Splashnet** launderette/Internet café is handy (€8 full-serve wash and dry, Internet access-€1.50/hour, €2 luggage storage per day—or free if you wash and go online, daily 8:30-23:00, just off Via Milazzo at Via Varese 33, tel. 06-4470-3523).

$ The Beehive gives vagabonds—old and young—a cheap, clean, and comfy home in Rome, thoughtfully and creatively run by Steve and Linda, a friendly American couple, and their hard-working staff. They offer six great-value artsy-mod double rooms (D-€80, T-€105) and an eight-bed dorm (€30 bunks). Their nearby annex, The Sweets, has similar style and several rooms with private baths (Sb-€60, Db-€100, air-con-€10, Internet access and Wi-Fi, private garden terrace, 2 blocks from Termini train station at Via Marghera 8, tel. 06-4470-4553, www.the-beehive.com, info@the-beehive.com). They're also a good resource for apartments across the city (www.cross-pollinate.com).

$ Hotel Select Garden, a modern and comfortable 21-room hotel run by the cheery Picca family, boasts lively modern art adorning the walls and a beautiful lemon-tree garden. It's a safe, tranquil, and welcoming refuge just a couple of blocks from the train station (Sb-€95, Db-€120, Tb-€140, these prices good through 2013 with this book, air-con, Wi-Fi, Via V. Bachelet 6, tel. 06-445-6383, fax 06-444-1086, www.hotelselectgarden.com, info@hotelselectgarden.com, Armando).

$ Hotel Sileo, with shiny chandeliers in dim rooms, is a homely little place renting 10 basic rooms (Db-€75, Tb-€90, air-con, elevator, Wi-Fi, Via Magenta 39, fourth floor, tel. & fax 06-445-0246, www.hotelsileo.com, info@hotelsileo.com). Friendly Alessandro and Maria Savioli don't speak English, but daughter Anna does.

$ Hotel Robinson is just a few steps from the station, but tucked away from the commotion. Set on an interior courtyard, it has 20 simple rooms that are a fine value (Sb-€65, Db-€85, Tb-€120, mention this book for these rates and a small breakfast, air-con-€10, Wi-Fi, Via Milazzo 3, tel. 06-491-423, fax 06-8968-5644, www.hotelrobinsonrome.com, info@hotelrobinsonrome.com).

$ Funny Palace Hostel, adjacent to Splashnet and run by its entrepreneurial owner Mabri, rents dorm beds in quiet four-person rooms and 18 stark-but-clean private rooms (dorm beds-€25, Db-€100, cash only, reception in the launderette—described earlier, Via Varese 33/31, tel. 06-4470-3523, www.hostelfunny.com).

$ Yellow Hostel rents 130 beds in 4-, 6-, and 12-bed coed dorms to 18- through 39-year-olds only (they also have 11 private rooms). Hip yet sane, it's well-run with fine facilities, including lockers. There's no curfew, and its café/late-night bar is next door (€18-35/bed depending on plumbing, size, and season; reserve via email—no telephone reservations accepted, Wi-Fi and iPad rental available, 6 blocks from station, just past Via Vicenza at Via Palestro 40/44, tel. 06-493-82682, www.yellowhostel.com).

Near Ancient Rome

Stretching from the Colosseum to Piazza Venezia, this area is central. Sightseers are a short walk from the Colosseum, Roman Forum, and Trajan's Column.

Near the Colosseum

$$$ Hotel Lancelot is a comfortable yet elegant refuge—a 60-room hotel with the ambience of a B&B. It's quiet and safe, with a shady courtyard, restaurant, bar, and tiny communal sixth-floor terrace. It's well-run by Faris and Lubna Khan, who serve a good €25 dinner—a chance to connect with your hotel neighbors and the staff. No wonder it's popular with returning guests (Sb-€126, Db-€194, Tb-€224, Qb-€264, €20 extra for sixth-floor terrace room with a Colosseum view, 5 percent off these rates with this book, air-con, elevator, wheelchair-accessible, Wi-Fi, parking-€10/day, 10-minute walk behind Colosseum near San Clemente Church at Via Capo d'Africa 47, tel. 06-7045-0615, fax 06-7045-0640, www.lancelothotel.com, info@lancelothotel.com). Faris and Lubna speak the Queen's English.

$$ Hotel Paba has seven fresh rooms, chocolate-box-tidy and lovingly cared for by Alberta Castelli. Though it overlooks busy Via Cavour just two blocks from the Colosseum, it's quiet enough (Db-€135, extra bed-€40, 5 percent cash discount, big beds, breakfast served in room, air-con, elevator, Wi-Fi, Via Cavour 266, Metro: Cavour, tel. 06-4782-4902, fax 06-4788-1225, www.hotelpaba.com, info@hotelpaba.com).

$$ Nicolas Inn Bed & Breakfast, a delightful little four-room place with thoughtful touches, is spacious and bright. It's run by François and American expat Melissa, who make you feel like you have caring friends in Rome (Db-€150-170, 10 percent Rick Steves discount with this book, cash only, included breakfast served at neighboring bar, air-con, Wi-Fi, Via Cavour 295, tel. 06-9761-8483, www.nicolasinn.com, info@nicolasinn.com).

$ Hotel Pensione Rosetta, homey and family-run, rents 18 rooms. It's pretty minimal, with no lounge and no breakfast, but has a good location and reasonable prices (Sb-€70, Db-€95, Tb-€110, air-con, Wi-Fi, Via Cavour 295, tel. 06-478-23069, www.rosettahotel.com, info@rosettahotel.com, Antonietta and Francesca).

$ Casa Sant'Anna, while stern and sterile, is still a welcoming and cozy convent that rents 60 rooms to travelers. Built for Russian and Brazilian pilgrims, it's well-run and situated on a characteristic square near a Metro stop and the Roman Forum (Sb-€50, Db-€80, dinner-€20, Piazza della Madonna dei Monti 3, Metro: Cavour, tel. 06-485-778, www.casasantanna.it, info@casasantanna.it).

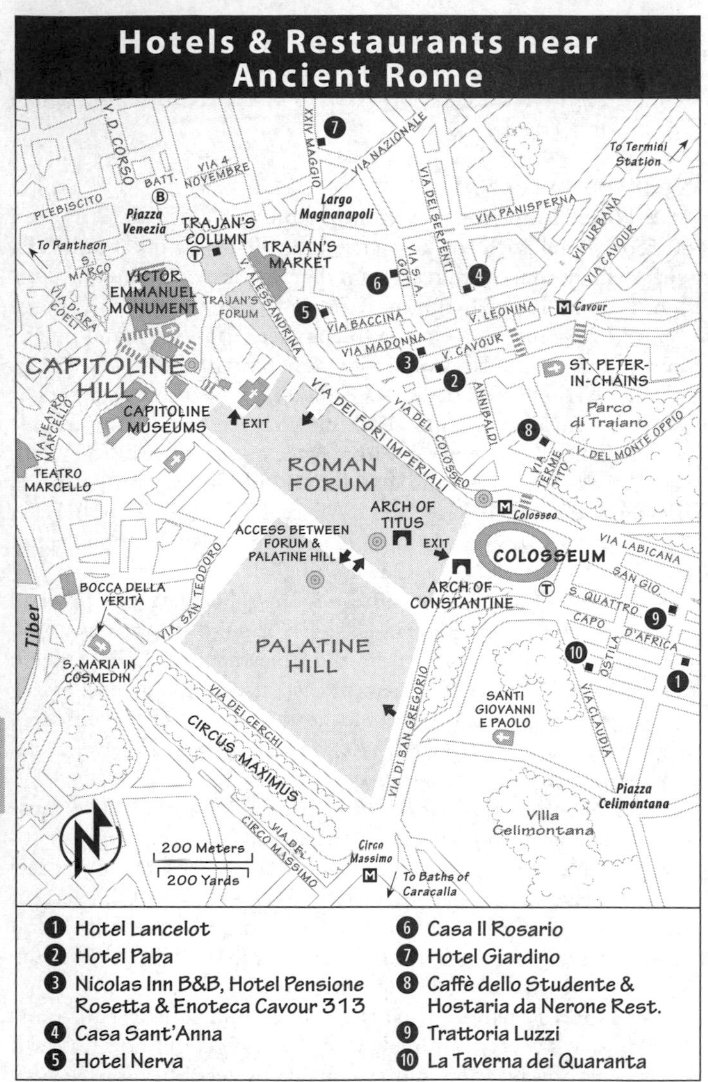

Near Piazza Venezia

$$$ Hotel Nerva is a three-star slice of tranquility with 19 small, overpriced (but often discounted) rooms on a surprisingly quiet back street just steps away from the Roman Forum (Sb-€130, Db-€190, extra bed-€40, ask for Rick Steves discount, rates very soft—especially off-season, air-con, elevator, Wi-Fi, Via Tor de' Conti 3, tel. 06-678-1835, fax 06-6992-2204, www.hotelnerva.com, info@hotelnerva.com, Antonio, Paolo, Anna).

$ Casa Il Rosario is a peaceful, well-run Dominican convent renting 40 rooms with monastic simplicity to both pilgrims and tourists in a good neighborhood (reserve several months in advance, S-€42, Sb-€56, Db-€94, Tb-€120, single beds only, fans, free Internet access, roof-terrace picnics welcome, 23:00 curfew, midway between Quirinale and Colosseum near bottom of Via Nazionale at Via Sant'Agata dei Goti 10, bus #40 or #170 from Termini, tel. 06-679-2346, fax 06-6994-1106, irodopre@tin.it).

$ Hotel Giardino offers 11 basic rooms in a central location three blocks northeast of Piazza Venezia. With a tiny central lobby and a small breakfast room, it suits travelers who prize location over big-hotel amenities (Sb-€85, Db-€130, one smaller Db for 15 percent less, these prices with cash and this book, air-con, Wi-Fi, effective double-paned windows, on a busy street off Piazza di Quirinale at Via XXIV Maggio 51, tel. 06-679-4584, fax 06-8928-1175, www.hotel-giardino-roma.com, info@hotel-giardino-roma.com, helpful Gianluca).

In the Pantheon Neighborhood

Winding, narrow lanes filled with foot traffic and lined with boutique shops and tiny trattorias...this is village Rome at its best. The atmosphere isn't cheap, but this is where you want to be—especially at night, when Romans and tourists gather in the floodlit piazzas for the evening stroll, the *passeggiata*.

Near Campo de' Fiori

You'll pay a premium (and endure a little extra night noise) to stay in the old center. But each of these places is romantically set deep in the tangled back streets near the idyllic Campo de' Fiori and, for many, worth the extra money.

$$$ Casa di Santa Brigida overlooks the elegant Piazza Farnese. With soft-spoken sisters gliding down polished hallways and pearly gates instead of doors, this lavish 20-room convent makes exhaust-stained Roman tourists feel like they've died and gone to heaven. If you don't need a double bed or a TV in your room, it's worth the splurge—especially if you luxuriate in its ample public spaces or on its lovely roof terrace (Sb-€120, twin Db-€200, book well in advance, air-con, elevator, Internet access and Wi-Fi, tasty €25 dinners, roof garden, plush library, Monserrato 54, tel. 06-6889-2596, fax 06-6889-1573, piazzafarnese@brigidine.org, many of the sisters are from India and speak English—pray you get to work with wonderful sister Gertrude).

$$$ Relais Teatro Argentina, a six-room gem, is steeped in tasteful old-Rome elegance, but has all the modern comforts. It's cozy and quiet like a B&B and couldn't be more centrally located

(Db-€210, Tb-€240, discounts for cash and for stays of 3 days or more, air-con, no elevator, 3 flights of stairs, Internet access and Wi-Fi, Via del Sudario 35, tel. 06-9893-1617, www.relaisteatroargentina.com, info@relaisteatroargentina.com, Carlotta).

$$ Hotel Smeraldo, with 50 rooms, is strictly run, clean, and a reasonable deal (Sb-€110, Db-€140, Tb-€170, buffet breakfast free with this book in 2013, air-con, elevator, Internet access and Wi-Fi, flowery roof terrace, midway between Campo de' Fiori and Largo Argentina at Vicolo dei Chiodaroli 9, tel. 06-687-5929, fax 06-6880-5495, www.smeraldoroma.com, info@smeraldoroma.com, Massimo and Walter). Their **Dipendenza Smeraldo,** 10 yards around the corner at Via dei Chiavari 32, has 16 similar rooms (same price and free breakfast, same reception and contact info).

In the Jewish Ghetto

$$ Hotel Arenula, with 50 decent rooms, is the only hotel in Rome's old Jewish ghetto. Though it has the ambience of a gym and attracts lots of students, it is in the thick of old Rome (Sb-€75-98, Db-€133, 5 percent off with this book in high season of 2013, extra bed-€21, air-con, no elevator, Wi-Fi, opposite the fountain in the park on Via Arenula at Via Santa Maria de' Calderari 47, tel. 06-687-9454, fax 06-689-6188, www.hotelarenula.com, info@hotelarenula.com).

Close to the Pantheon

These places are buried in the pedestrian-friendly heart of ancient Rome, each within about a five-minute walk of the Pantheon. You'll pay more here—but you'll save time and money by being exactly where you want to be for your early and late wandering.

$$$ Hotel Nazionale, a four-star landmark, is a 16th-century palace that shares a well-policed square with the Parliament building. Its 100 rooms are accentuated by lush public spaces, fancy bars, a uniformed staff, and a marble-floored restaurant. It's a big, stuffy hotel with a revolving front door, but it's a worthy splurge if you want security, comfort, and the heart of Rome at your doorstep (Sb-€220, Db-€350, giant deluxe Db-€480, extra person-€70, check online for summer and weekend discounts—you'll typically save 30 percent off their sky-high rack rates, air-con, elevator, Wi-Fi, Piazza Montecitorio 131, tel. 06-695-001, fax 06-678-6677, www.hotelnazionale.it, info@hotelnazionale.it).

$$$ Albergo Santa Chiara, in the old center, is big, solid, and hotelesque. Flavia, Silvio, and their fine staff offer marbled elegance (but basic furniture) and all the hotel services. Its ample public lounges are dressy and professional, and its 99 rooms are quiet and spacious (Sb-€138, Db-€190, Db-€215 April-June and Oct, Tb-€262, check website for discounts, book online direct and request special Rick Steves rates, elevator, air-con, Wi-Fi, behind Pantheon at Via di Santa Chiara 21, tel. 06-687-2979, fax 06-687-3144, www.albergosantachiara.com, info@albergosantachiara.com).

$$$ Hotel Portoghesi is a classic hotel with 28 rooms in the medieval heart of Rome. It's peaceful, quiet, and calmly run, and comes with a delightful roof terrace—though you pay for the location (Sb-€130-160, Db-€160-200, price range reflects low and high season, breakfast on roof, air-con, elevator, Wi-Fi, Via dei Portoghesi 1, tel. 06-686-4231, fax 06-687-6976, www.hotelportoghesiroma.it, info@hotelportoghesiroma.it).

$$$ Hotel Due Torri, hiding out on a tiny quiet street, is beautifully located. It feels professional yet homey, with an accommodating staff, generous public spaces, and 26 small rooms. While the location and lounge are great, the rooms are overpriced (Sb-€125, Db-€195, family apartment-€240 for 3 and €260 for 4, check website for frequent discounts, air-con, elevator, Wi-Fi, a block off Via della Scrofa at Vicolo del Leonetto 23, tel. 06-6880-6956, fax 06-686-5442, www.hotelduetorriroma.com, info@hoteldue torriroma.com, Cinzia).

In Trastevere

Colorful and genuine in a gritty sort of way, Trastevere is a treat for travelers looking for a less touristy and more bohemian atmosphere. Choices are few here, but by trekking across the Tiber, you can have the experience of being comfortably immersed in old Rome. To locate the following places, see the map on page 292.

$$$ Hotel Santa Maria sits like a lazy hacienda in the midst of Trastevere. Surrounded by a medieval skyline, you'll feel as if you're on some romantic stage set. Its 20 small but well-equipped, air-conditioned rooms—former cells in a cloister—are all on the ground floor, as are a few suites for up to six people. The rooms circle a gravelly courtyard of orange trees and stay-awhile patio furniture (Db-€180, Tb-€220; prices good through 2013 with this book, cash, and minimum stay of three nights; family rooms, free loaner bikes, Internet access and Wi-Fi, face church on Piazza Maria Trastevere and go right down Via della Fonte d'Olio 50 yards to Vicolo del Piede 2, tel. 06-589-4626, fax 06-589-4815, www.hotelsantamaria.info, info@hotelsanta maria.info). Some rooms come with family-friendly fold-down bunks for €30 extra per person. Their freshly renovated six-room **Residenza Santa Maria** is a couple of blocks away (same prices and contact info).

$$$ Residenza Arco dei Tolomei is your most poetic Trastevere experience imaginable, with six small, unique, antique-filled rooms boasting fragrant balconies. With its quiet and elegant setting, you can pretend you're visiting aristocratic relatives (Db-€200, discounts for cash and for stays of three days or more, reserve well in advance, Internet access and Wi-Fi, from Piazza Piscinula a block up Via dell'Arco de' Tolomei at #27, tel. 06-5832-0819, fax 06-6456-1375, www.bbarcodeitolomei.com, info@bb arcodeitolomei.com; Marco, Gianna Paola, and dog Pixel).

$$ Casa San Giuseppe is down a characteristic laundry-strewn lane with a sunny roof terrace and views of Aurelian Walls. While convent-owned, it's a secular place renting 29 plain but peaceful, spacious, and spotless rooms (Sb-€115, Db-€155, Tb-€185, Qb-€215, garden-facing rooms are quiet, air-con, elevator, Internet access, parking-€15, just north of Piazza Trilussa at Vicolo Moroni 22, tel. 06-5833-3490, fax 06-5833-5754, www.casasangiuseppe.it, info@casasangiuseppe.it, Andrea).

$$ Arco del Lauro B&B rents six white, minimalist rooms in a good location. Facing a courtyard (no views but little noise), the friendly welcome and good value make up for the lack of public spaces (Db-€135, Qb-€185, prices good if booked direct, cash only, includes breakfast served in a café, air-con, Internet access and Wi-Fi, from Piazza Piscinula a block up Via dell'Arco de' Tolomei at #29, tel. 06-9784-0350, mobile 346-244-3212, fax 06-9725-6541, www.arcodellauro.it, info@arcodellauro.it, Lorenza and Daniela).

$$ Hotel San Francesco, big and blocky yet welcoming, stands like a practical and efficient oasis at the edge of all the Trastevere action. Renting 24 trim rooms in this authentic district, it comes with an inviting roof terrace and a helpful staff. Handy trams to Largo Argentina are just a block away (Db-€90-180, prices vary wildly, email direct and mention this book for best rates, air-con, elevator, Wi-Fi, Via Jacopa de' Settesoli 7, tel. 06-5830-0051, www.hotelsanfrancesco.net, info@hotelsanfrancesco.net).

Near Vatican City

Sleeping near the Vatican is expensive, but some enjoy calling this more relaxed, residential neighborhood home. Even though it's handy to the Vatican (when the rapture hits, you're right there), everything else is a long way away. Fortunately, it's well-served by public transit—use the Metro (line A) and bus (ask your hotel for the most convenient routes) to easily connect with the center.

$$$ Hotel Alimandi Vaticano, facing the Vatican Museum, is beautifully designed. Run by the Alimandi family (Enrico, Irene, and Germano), it features four stars, 24 spacious rooms, and all the modern comforts you can imagine (Sb-€170, standard Db-€170-200, big Db with 2 double beds-€240-260, Tb-€230-260, 5 percent less with cash, air-con, elevator, Internet access and Wi-Fi, Viale Vaticano 99, Metro: Ottaviano, tel. 06-397-45562, fax 06-397-30132, www.alimandivaticanohotel.com, alimandivaticano@alimandi.com).

$$ Hotel Alimandi Tunisi is a good value, run by other members of the friendly and entrepreneurial Alimandi family—Paolo, Luigi, Marta, and Barbara. They have 27 modest but comfortable rooms and vast public spaces, including a piano lounge, pool table, and rooftop terrace where the grand buffet breakfast is served (Sb-€90, Db-€130-175, 5 percent less with cash, elevator, air-con, Internet access and Wi-Fi, down the stairs directly in front of Vatican Museum, Via Tunisi 8, Metro: Ottaviano, tel. 06-3972-3941, fax 06-3972-3943, www.alimanditunisi.com, alimandi@tin.it).

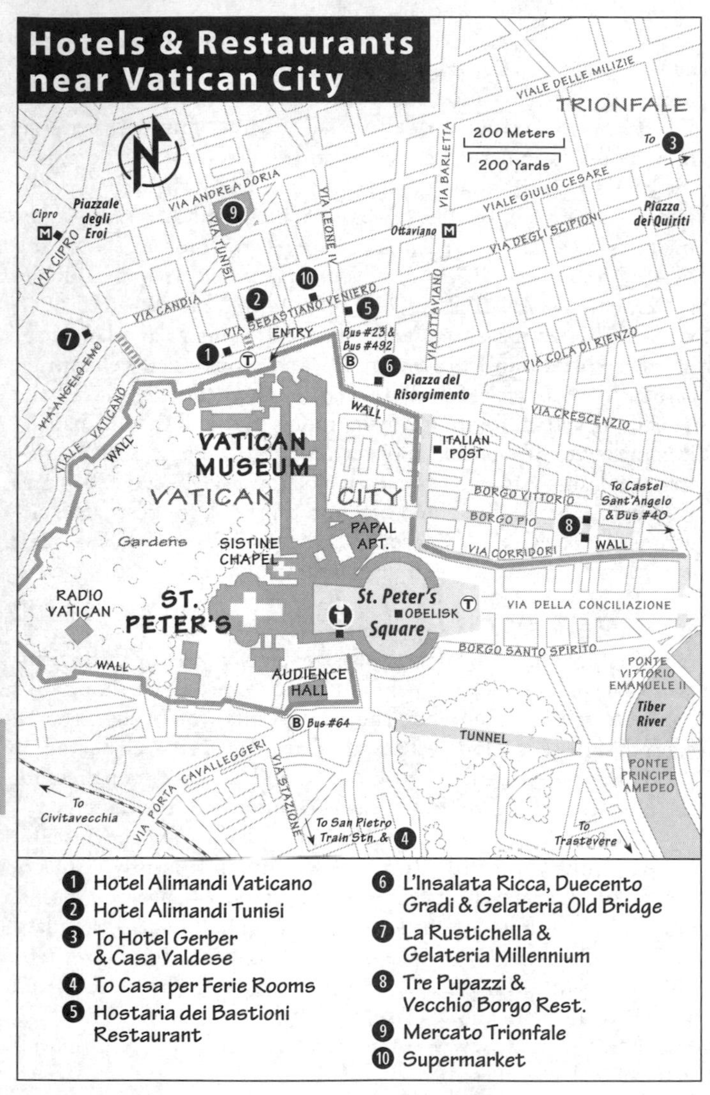

$$ Hotel Gerber, set in a quiet residential area, is family-run with 27 well-polished, businesslike rooms (Sb-€140, Db-€180, Tb-€200, Qb-€220, 10 percent high-season discount and 15 percent low-season discount off these prices with this book in 2013 when you book direct, air-con, elevator, Wi-Fi, leafy terrace; from Lepanto Metro station, go one block down Via M. Colonna and turn right to Via degli Scipioni 241; tel. 06-321-6485, fax 06-321-7048, www.hotelgerber.it, info@hotelgerber.it; Peter, Simonetta, and friendly dog Kira).

$ Casa Valdese is an efficient, well-managed, church-run hotel that's popular with Germans. Its 33 big, quiet rooms are located just over the Tiber River and near the Vatican. It feels safe if a bit institutional, with the bonus of two breezy, communal roof terraces with incredible views (two external Sb-€58, Db-€130, Tb-€180, Qb-€210, discounts for 3-night stays, air-con, Internet access and Wi-Fi; from Lepanto Metro station, go one block down Via M. Colonna, turn left on Via degli Scipioni, then continue for a block to the intersection with Via Alessandro Farnese 18; tel. 06-321-5362, fax 06-321-1843, www.casavaldeseroma.it, reception@casavaldeseroma.it, Matteo).

$ Casa per Ferie Santa Maria alle Fornaci is simple and efficient, housing pilgrims and secular tourists just a short walk south of the Vatican in 54 identical, stark, utilitarian, mostly twin-bedded rooms. Reserve at least three months in advance (Sb-€70, Db-€100, Tb-€135, air-con, elevator; take bus #64 from Termini train station to San Pietro train station, then walk 100 yards north along Via della Stazione di San Pietro to Piazza Santa Maria alle Fornaci 27; tel. 06-393-67632, fax 06-393-66795, www.trinitaridematha.it, cffornaci@tin.it, Carmine).

EATING IN ROME

The Italians are masters of the art of fine living. That means eating...long and well. Lengthy, multi-course lunches and dinners and endless hours sitting in outdoor cafés are the norm. Americans eat on their way to an evening event and complain if the check is slow in coming. For Italians, the meal is an end in itself, and only rude waiters rush you. When you want the bill, mime-scribble on your raised palm or ask for it: *"Il conto?"* You may have to ask for it more than once. To save time, you could ask for the check when you receive the last item you order.

Even those of us who liked dorm food will find that the cafés, cuisine, and wines become a highlight of our Italian adventure. Trust me: This is sightseeing for your palate, and even if the rest of you is sleeping in cheap hotels, your taste buds will relish an occasional first-class splurge. You can eat well without going broke. But be careful: You're just as likely to blow a small fortune on a disappointing meal as you are to dine wonderfully for €25.

Restaurants

When restaurant-hunting, choose places filled with locals, not the place with the big neon signs boasting, "We speak English and accept credit cards." Restaurants parked on famous squares generally serve bad food at high prices to tourists. Locals eat better at lower-rent locales. Family-run places operate without hired help and can offer cheaper meals.

Good restaurants don't open for dinner before 19:00. Restaurants in Rome seem touristy in the early evening because tourists generally eat early, and Romans often eat late. Dinnertime is generally 20:00 to 22:00, and in restaurants it is a multi-course affair.

If you're traveling solo, be aware that dining in the evening

Tipping

In Italy, the service charge *(servizio)* is usually built into your bill's grand total in one of two ways. If the menu states *servizio incluso* (or nothing at all), the listed prices already include service. If the menu states *servizio non incluso,* or *servizio* with a specific percentage, a fixed percentage (usually 10-15 percent of the total) will be added as a line item to the bottom of the bill. In either case, the total you pay already includes a basic tip. Some Italians don't tip beyond this, but if you're pleased with the service, round up the bill by a euro or two per person. If you pay your bill with a credit card, it's best to tip in cash—leave it on the table or hand it directly to your server. If you order your food at a counter, don't tip.

can be frustrating here. People eating dinner alone are often passed over, and not seated as quickly as couples—or may be seated at the worst table in the place. Fortunately, this practice is less common at breakfast and lunch, when restaurants are more accustomed to serving single diners.

Before you sit down, look at a menu to see what extra charges a restaurant adds on. As elsewhere in Italy, many (but not all) restaurants in Rome add a cover charge *(coperto)* of €1-2 per person to your bill. Sometimes this is phrased as "bread and cover" *(pane e coperto).* It's not negotiable, even if you don't eat the bread. Think of it as covering the cost of using the table for as long as you like. (Italians like to linger, and most restaurants don't depend on turning the table over multiple times in an evening.) Restaurants with a separate service charge, however, are in the minority (the charge is usually 10-12 percent). Places with both a cover *and* a service charge are best avoided (the restaurant is counting on a nonlocal clientele that can't gauge a value), as are places that advertise "no cover, no service charge" (they're likely raising their prices to compensate). Tip by rounding the bill up, the equivalent of €1-2 per person.

You can save a lot by getting fixed-priced meals, which are frequently exempt from cover and service charges. However, the cheapest ones tend to be bland and heavy, pairing a very basic pasta with reheated schnitzel and roast meats (usually around €15-20, often called *menù turistico,* or sometimes, usually falsely, *menù del giorno*—menu of the day). It's worth paying more for an inventive fixed-price meal that shows off the chef's creativity. While fixed-price meals can be easy and convenient, galloping gourmets order à la carte with the help of a menu translator. (*Rick Steves' Italian Phrase Book & Dictionary* has a menu decoder with enough phrases for intermediate eaters.) When going to an especially good restaurant with an approachable staff, my favorite strategy is to simply say, "Make me happy" (in this case, it's just fine to set a price limit).

A full meal consists of an appetizer (antipasto, €4-6), a first course (*primo piatto,* pasta or soup, generally €5-12), and a second course (*secondo piatto,* an expensive meat or fish dish, typically €6-15). Vegetables *(contorni, verdure)* rarely come with the *secondo* and cost extra (€4-6) as a side dish (an ample size for two people).

The euros can add up in a hurry. Light and budget eaters get a *primo piatto* each and share an antipasto. (Italians admit that the *secondo* is the least interesting aspect of their cuisine.) Another good option is sharing an array of *antipasti*—either several specific dishes or a plate of mixed delights assembled from a buffet. When Americans hear "buffet," we think it's a pile-the-plate-high, go-back-for-more, all-you-can-eat deal; but in Italy, an *antipasti* buffet is designed and priced as an appetizer—locals visit it once, taking a moderate amount. Watch others and imitate.

Some special dishes come in large quantities meant for two people; the shorthand way of showing this on a menu is "X2" (meaning "for two people"). The price listed generally indicates the cost per person.

Note that steak and seafood are often sold by weight (priced by the kilo—1,000 grams, or just more than 2 pounds; or by the *etto*—100 grams). The letters "s.q." mean according to quantity. Fish is usually served whole with the head and tail; you can't just get half a fish or a filet unless it already comes prepared as just a filet (*filetto,* sometimes *trancio*—slice, as in tuna or swordfish). However, you can ask your waiter to select a smaller fish for you. Somctimes, especially for steak, restaurants require a minimum order of four or five *etti*. Beware, or be shell-shocked by €50 entrées. Make sure you're really clear on the price before ordering.

Wine Bars *(Enoteche)*

An *enoteca* is a popular, fast, and inexpensive option for lunch. Surrounded by the office crowd, you can get a salad, plate of meats and cheeses, and a glass of good wine (see blackboards for the day's selection and price per glass). The area around the Pantheon and Piazza Parlamento (popular with politicians and bureaucrats) has plenty of *enoteche* handy for a sightseeing lunch break or evening destination. For more on wines, see page 354.

Bars/Cafés

Italian "bars" are not taverns but cafés. These neighborhood hang-outs serve coffee, mini-pizzas, sandwiches, and drinks from the cooler. Many dish up plates of fried cheese and vegetables from under the glass counter, ready to reheat. This budget choice is the

Italian equivalent of English pub grub.

For quick meals, bars usually have trays of cheap, ready-made sandwiches (*panini* or *tramezzini*). Some kinds are delightful grilled. To save time for sightseeing and room for dinner, consider a ham-and-cheese *panino* for lunch at a bar (called *toast;* have it grilled twice if you want it really hot). To get food "to go," say, *"Da portar via"* (for the road). All bars have a WC *(toilette, bagno)* in the back, and customers—and the discreet public—can use it.

Bars serve great drinks: hot, cold, sweet, caffeinated, or alcoholic. Chilled bottled water, still *(naturale)* or carbonated *(frizzante),* is sold cheap to go.

Coffee: Coffee is as important as wine in Rome, and Italian coffee is some of the world's best. If you ask for *"un caffè,"* you'll get espresso. If you ask for a latte, you'll get just that—a glass of hot milk. Cappuccino is served to locals before noon and to tourists any time of day. (To an Italian, cappuccino is a breakfast drink and a travesty after eating anything with tomatoes.) Italians like their coffee only warm. To get it hot, request *"Molto caldo"* (MOHL-toh KAHL-doh; very hot) or *"Più caldo, per favore"* (pew KAHL-doh pehr fah-VOH-ray; hotter, please).

Romans like iced coffee in the summer. It's slightly diluted, sugared espresso, called *caffè freddo;* to get it with ice, say *"con ghiaccio"* (kohn ghee-AH-choh, with a hard *g*). *Cappuccino freddo* is cold cappuccino served in a tall glass.

Experiment with a few of the hot options:

- Cappuccino: Espresso with foamed milk on top
- *Caffè latte:* Tall glass with espresso and hot milk mixed, no foam
- *Caffè hag:* Instant decaf (you can order decaffeinated versions of any coffee drink—ask for it *decaffeinato*)
- *Caffè macchiato* (mah-kee-AH-toh): Espresso with only a little milk
- *Caffè americano:* Espresso diluted with water
- *Caffè corretto:* Espresso with a shot of liqueur

Juice: *Spremuta* means freshly squeezed as far as *succo* (fruit juice) is concerned; it's usually orange juice, and February through April it's almost always made from blood oranges. (Note: *Spumante* means sparkling wine.)

Beer: Beer on tap is *alla spina*. Get it *piccola* (33 cl, 11 oz), *media* (50 cl, about a pint), or *grande* (a liter, about 2 pints).

Wine: To order a glass (*bicchiere;* bee-kee-AY-ree) of red *(rosso)* or white *(bianco)* wine, say, *"Un bicchiere di vino rosso/bianco." Corposo* means full-bodied. House wine *(vino della casa)* often comes in a quarter-liter carafe (8.5 oz, *un quarto*), half-liter pitcher (17 oz, *un mezzo*), or one-liter pitcher (34 oz, *un litro*). For more on wine, see page 354.

Other Drinks: A common *digestivo* in Rome is an *amaro,* which means "bitter." These alcoholic brews are sometimes homemade by restaurants from a secret combination of herbs to aid digestion. Popular commercial brands are Fernet Branca and Montenegro. If your tastes run sweeter, try an anise-flavored liqueur called Sambuca, served *con moscha* (with three "flies"—coffee beans).

Prices: You'll notice a two- or three-tiered price system. It's cheapest to drink a cup of coffee while standing at the bar; you'll pay more for that same cup to sit at an indoor table, and often still more at an outdoor table. If you're on a budget, don't sit without first checking out the financial consequences. Ask, "Same price if I sit or stand?" by saying, *"Costa uguale al tavolo o al banco?"* (KOH-stah oo-GWAH-lay ahl TAH-voh-loh oh ahl BAHN-koh?). A cup of coffee at any bar generally costs only a euro if you stand. While coffee may cost €5 at a table, you can stand at the fanciest place in town and sip your coffee at the bar for the same price as at a simple café.

Budget Options

Rome offers many budget options for hungry travelers. Stop by a *rosticceria* for great cooked deli food. Self-service cafeterias (called "free flow" in Italian) offer the basics without add-on charges.

Pizza, readily available, is inexpensive. Key pizza vocabulary: *capricciosa* (generally ham, mushrooms, olives, and artichokes), *funghi* (mushrooms), *marinara* (tomato sauce, oregano, garlic, no cheese), *quattro formaggi* (four different cheeses), and *quattro stagioni* (different toppings on each of the four quarters, for those who can't choose just one menu item). If you ask for *peperoni* on your pizza, you'll get green or red peppers, not sausage. Kids like the simple *margherita* (cheese with tomato sauce) or *diavola* (the closest thing in Italy to American pepperoni). At take-out shops, pizza is sold either by the slice *(pizza a taglio)* or by the weight *(pizza rustica;* 100 grams, or *un etto,* is a cheap snack; 200 grams, or *due etti,* makes a light meal).

For a fast, cheap, and healthy lunch, find a *tavola calda* ("hot table") bar with a buffet spread of meat and vegetables, and ask for a mixed plate of vegetables with a hunk of mozzarella *(piatto misto di verdure con mozzarella).* Don't be limited by what you can see. If you'd like a salad with a slice of cantaloupe and a hunk of cheese, they'll whip that up for you in a snap. Belly up to the bar, and with a

Ordering Food at *Tavola Caldas*

plate of mixed veggies	*piatto misto di verdure*	pee-AH-toh MEES-toh dee vehr-DOO-ray
"Heated, please."	*"Scaldare, per favore."*	skahl-DAH-ray, pehr fah-VOH-ray
"A taste, please."	*"Un assaggio, per favore."*	oon ah-SAH-joh, pehr fah-VOH-ray
artichoke	*carciofi*	kar-CHOH-fee
asparagus	*asparagi*	ah-spah-RAH-jee
beans	*fagioli*	fah-JOH-lee
breadsticks	*grissini*	gree-SEE-nee
broccoli	*broccoli*	BROH-koh-lee
cantaloupe	*melone*	may-LOH-nay
carrots	*carote*	kah-ROT-ay
green beans	*fagiolini*	fah-joh-LEE-nee
ham	*prosciutto*	proh-SHOO-toh
mushrooms	*funghi*	FOONG-ghee
potatoes	*patate*	pah-TAH-tay
rice	*riso*	REE-zoh
spinach	*spinaci*	speen-AH-chee
tomatoes	*pomodori*	poh-moh-DOH-ree
zucchini	*zucchine*	zoo-KEE-nay

(Excerpted from *Rick Steves' Italian Phrase Book & Dictionary*)

pointing finger and key words in the chart in this chapter, you can get a fine mixed plate of vegetables. If something's a mystery, ask for a small taste (*un assaggio;* oon ah-SAH-joh).

Many places sell sandwiches of rustic bread and roasted pork with herbs (look for *porchetta,* por-KET-ah).

You might see *döner kebab* places selling slow-roasted meat, or falafel and salad fixings wrapped in pita bread, offering a cheap break from Italian food.

Beware of cheap eateries sporting big color photos of pizza and piles of different pastas. They have no kitchens and simply microwave disgusting prepackaged food. Unless you like lasagna with ice in the center, avoid these.

Picnics

In Rome, picnicking saves lots of euros and is a great way to sample regional specialties. In the process of assembling your meal, you get to deal with the Romans in the market scene. For a

Eating with the Seasons

Italian cooks love to serve you fresh produce and seafood at its tastiest. If you must have porcini mushrooms outside of October and November, they'll be frozen. To get the freshest veggies at a fine restaurant, request *"Un piatto di verdure della stagioni, per favore"* ("A plate of veggies in season, please").

Here are a few examples of what's fresh when:

April-May:	Calamari, green beans, asparagus, artichokes, and zucchini flowers
April-May and Sept-Oct:	Black truffles
May-June:	Mussels, asparagus, zucchini, cantaloupe, and strawberries
May-Aug:	Eggplant
Oct-Nov:	Mushrooms, white truffles, and chestnuts
Fresh year-round:	Clams and meats

colorful experience, gather your ingredients in the morning at one of Rome's open-air produce markets (see the Shopping in Rome chapter); you'll probably visit several small stores or market stalls to put together a complete meal, and many close around noon.

While it's fun to visit the small specialty shops, an *alimentari* is your one-stop corner grocery store. A *supermercato* gives you more efficiency with less color for less cost. At busier supermarkets, you'll need to take a number for deli service. You'll find handy late-night supermarkets near the Pantheon (Via Giustiniani), Spanish Steps (Via Vittoria), Trevi Fountain (Via del Bufalo), and Campo de' Fiori (Via di Monte della Farina). Many *alimentari* and even supermarkets will gladly make you a fresh sandwich, charging you only for the weight of what you take and the piece of bread. And *rosticcerie* sell cheap food to go—you'll find options such as lasagna, rotisserie chicken, and sides like roasted potatoes and spinach.

Juice-lovers can get a liter of O.J. for the price of a Coke or coffee. Look for "100% *succo*" (juice) on the label. Hang on to the half-liter mineral-water bottles (sold everywhere for about €1). Buy juice in cheap liter boxes, then drink some and store the extra in your water bottle. Tap water—*acqua del rubinetto*—is fine; like the Romans do, I refill my water bottle from the public taps found all over the city (often near fountains).

Picnics can be an adventure in high cuisine. Be daring. Try the fresh mozzarella, *presto* pesto, shriveled olives, and any regional specialties the locals are excited about. Shopkeepers are happy to sell small quantities of produce. They seem to enjoy giving you a taste *(un assaggio)*. It is customary to let the merchant choose the produce for you. Say *"Per oggi"* (pehr OH-jee; "For today,") and he or she will grab you something ready to eat, weigh it, and make the sale. A typical picnic for two might be fresh rolls, 100 grams of meat (*un etto* = 100 grams = about a quarter pound), 100 grams of cheese, two tomatoes, three carrots, two apples, yogurt, and a liter box of juice. Total cost: about €10.

Rome discourages people from picnicking or drinking at historic monuments (such as on the Spanish Steps) in the old center. Technically violators can be fined, though it rarely happens. You'll be fine if you eat *with* a view rather than *on* the view.

Roman Cuisine

In ancient times, the dinner party was the center of Roman social life. It was a luxurious affair, set in the *triclinium* (formal dining room). Guest lists were small (3-9 people), and the select few reclined on couches during the exotic multi-course meal. Today the couches are gone, and the fare may not include jellyfish, boiled tree fungi, or flamingo, but the *cucina Romana* influence remains. It's fair to say that while French cuisine makes an art of the preparation, Italian (and Roman) cuisine is simpler and all about the ingredients.

Roman meals are still lengthy social occasions. Simple, fresh, seasonal ingredients dominate the dishes. The *cucina* is robust, strongly flavored, and unpretentious—much like the people who've created it over the centuries. It is said that Roman cooking didn't come out of emperors' or popes' kitchens, but from the *cucina povera*—the home cooking of the common people. This may explain the Romans' fondness for meats known as the *quinto quarto* ("fifth quarter"), such as tripe, tail, brain, and pigs' feet, as well as their interest in natural preservatives like chili peppers and garlic.

Rome belongs to the warm, southern region of Lazio, which produces a rich variety of flavorful vegetables and fruit that are the envy of American supermarkets. Rome's proximity to the Mediterranean also allows for a great variety of seafood (especially on Fridays) that can be pricey if you're dining out.

Today, eating like a Roman means stopping at the neighborhood bar each morning for a pastry and coffee (usually cappuccino or espresso). Lunch (between 13:00 and 15:00) is traditionally the largest meal of the day, eaten at home, although work habits have changed this for many people who don't want to spend time commuting. Instead, they grab a quick meal in a *tavola calda* (cafeteria) buffet or a *panino* or *tramezzino* (sandwich).

When it's hot outside, a shaved-ice-with-fruit-syrup concoction called a *grattachecca* (grah-tah-KEK-kah) cools you down fast. The vendors at the little booths scrape shavings off ice blocks and then flavor them with syrups. Try the combo-flavors such as *limoncocco*—lemon and coconut syrups with fresh chunks of coconut.

Specialties you may find on a menu include the following:

Antipasti (Appetizers)

Antipasto misto: A plate of marinated or grilled vegetables (eggplant, artichokes, peppers, mushrooms), cured meats, cheeses, or seafood (anchovies, octopus).

Bruschetta: Toasted bread brushed with olive oil and garlic, topped with chopped tomatoes, mushrooms, or whatever else sounds good.

Fritti: Little fried snacks that have been either battered or breaded—often olives stuffed with meat, potato croquettes, and mozzarella cheese. Other classic *fritti* are *supplí* (oval-shaped rice balls with tomato sauce and mozzarella) and *fiori di zucca* (squash blossoms filled with mozzarella and anchovies).

Prosciutto e melone: Thin slices of ham wrapped around pieces of cantaloupe.

Salumi: Cured meat, usually pork. Salami is one kind of *salume;* prosciutto and pancetta are two more.

Primi Piatti (First Courses)

Spaghetti alla carbonara: Any type of pasta with a sauce made from beaten eggs, fried pancetta (similar to bacon) or *guanciale* (cured pork cheek), cheese (*pecorino romano* or *parmigiano reggiano*), and black pepper.

Bucatini all'amatriciana: Thin pasta tubes with a sauce of tomatoes, onion, pancetta, and pecorino cheese on top.

Gnocchi alla romana: Small dumpling-like disks made from semolina, instead of potato, and baked with butter and cheese.

Penne all'arrabbiata: "Angry quills"—quill-shaped pasta topped with a spicy tomato sauce of chili peppers *(pepperoncini)* and garlic.

Rigatoni con la pajata: Medium-size wide pasta tubes topped with a stew of milk-fed calf intestines.

Stracciatella alla romana: Meat broth with whipped eggs, topped with parmesan cheese.

Spaghetti alle vongole veraci: Small clams in the shell sautéed with white wine and herbs, served over pasta.

Secondi Piatti (Second Courses)

Saltimbocca alla romana: "Jump-in-the-mouth"—thinly sliced veal layered with prosciutto and sage, then lightly fried.

Abbacchio alla scottadito: Baby lamb chops grilled and eaten as finger food.

Trippa alla romana: Tripe braised with onions, carrots, and mint.

Coda alla vaccinara: Oxtail braised with garlic, wine, tomato, and celery.

Involtini al sugo: Veal cutlets rolled with prosciutto, celery, and cheese in a tomato sauce.

Anguillette in umido: Stewed baby eels from nearby Lake Bracciano.

Filetti di baccalà: Salted cod fried in a batter (like "fish and chips" minus the chips).

Contorni (Side Dishes)

Sometimes the second course is not served with a vegetable, and you may want to order a side dish separately. If you get a salad, note that olive oil and wine vinegar are the only dressings.

Carciofi alla giudia: Small artichokes flattened and fried.

Fave al guanciale: Fava beans simmered with *guanciale* (cured pork cheek) and onion.

Misticanza: Mixed green salad of arugula *(rucola)* and curly endive *(puntarelle)* with anchovies.

Dolci (Desserts)

Dessert can be a seasonal fruit, such as *fragole* (strawberries) or *pesche* (peaches), or even cheese, such as *pecorino romano* (made from ewe's milk) or *caciotta romana* (made from a combination of ewe's and cow's milk).

Crostata di ricotta: A cheesecake-like dessert with ricotta, Marsala wine, cinnamon, and bits of chocolate.

Bignè: Cream puff-like pastries filled with *zabaglione* (egg yolks, sugar, and Marsala wine).

Tartufo: Rich dark-chocolate gelato ball with a cherry inside. ***Con***

Wine Labels and Lingo

The ancient Greeks who colonized Italy more than 2,000 years ago called it *"Oenotria"*—land of the grape. Little has changed over the centuries. Ideal conditions for grapes (warm climate, well-draining soil, and an abundance of hillsides) make the Italian peninsula a paradise for grape-growers, winemakers, and wine drinkers. Italy makes and consumes more wine per capita than any other country.

In almost every part of Italy you'll find wine varieties designed to go with the regional cuisine. Choosing a wine can be intimidating, but the Italian government tries to help you choose something decent, even if you're clueless. In general, wines are designated by one of four categories:

Vino da Tavola (table wine) is the lowest grade. It's inexpensive, but Italy's wines are so good that, for many people, a basic *vino da tavola* is just fine with a meal. Many restaurants, even modest ones, take pride in their house wine *(vino della casa),* bottling their own or working with wineries.

Denominazione di Origine Controllata (DOC), a cut above table wine, is usually cheap, but can be surprisingly good. Hundreds of wines have earned the DOC designation, and you'll see them all over Italy.

Denominazione di Origine Controllata e Guarantita (DOCG) is the highest grade, and can be identified by the pink or green label on the neck and the scary price tag on the shelf. Only a limited number of wines in Italy can be called DOCG. They're generally a good bet if you want a quality wine, but you don't know anything else about the winemaker. (*Riserva* is a DOC or

panna gets you whipped cream on top.

Gelato: Rather than order dessert in a restaurant, I like to stroll with a cup or cone of gelato picked up at one of Rome's popular *gelaterie.*

Top Local Wines

Although Lazio is not the most notable wine region in Italy, it produces several pleasant white wines and a few reds.

Frascati: An inexpensive dry white made from Trebbiano and Malvasia grapes. This is probably the best-known wine of the region.

DOCG wine matured for a longer, more specific time.)

Indicazione Geographica Tipica (IGT) is a broad group of wines that range from basic to some of Italy's best. It includes the "Super Tuscans"—wines that don't follow the strict "recipe" required for DOC or DOCG status, but that give local vintners more opportunity to be creative. Super Tuscans are made from a mix of international grapes (such as Cabernet Sauvignon) grown in Tuscany and aged in small oak barrels for only two years. The result is a lively full-bodied wine that dances all over your head... and is worth the steep price for aficionados.

Visit an *enoteca* (wine bar) and sample these wines side by side to figure out what you like—and what suits your pocketbook.

Words to Live by, or...How to Describe Wine in Italian

As you can see from many of the words listed below, adding a vowel to the English word often gets you close to the Italian one. Have some fun, gesture like a local, and you'll have no problems speaking the language of the *enoteca. Salute!*

dry	*secco*	SAY-koh
sweet	*dolce*	DOHL-chay
earthy	*terroso*	tay-ROH-zoh
tannic	*tannico*	TAH-nee-koh
young	*giovane*	joh-VAH-nay
mature	*maturo*	mah-TOO-roh
sparkling	*spumante*	spoo-MAHN-tay
fruity	*fruttoso*	froo-TOH-zoh
full-bodied	*corposo*	kor-POH-zoh
elegant	*elegante*	ay-lay-GAHN-tay

Castelli Romani: Also made from Trebbiano grapes, from the hills just south of Rome. This wine is similar to **Marino, Colli Albani,** and **Velletri,** which are all light and fairly dry.

Torre Ercolana: Known as Lazio's finest red. This dense wine is made from the regional Cesanese grape, as well as Cabernet and Merlot. Produced in small quantities, it must be aged for at least five years.

Restaurants

I've listed a number of restaurants I enjoy. While most are in quaint and therefore pricey and touristy areas (Piazza Navona, the Pantheon neighborhood, Campo de' Fiori, and Trastevere), many are tucked away just off the tourist crush.

I'm impressed by how small the price difference can be between a mediocre Roman restaurant and a fine one. You can pay about 20 percent more for double the quality. If I had $90 for three meals in Rome, I'd spend $50 for one and $20 each for the other two, rather than $30 on all three. For splurge meals, I'd consider Gabriello, Fortunato, and Taverna Trilussa (in that order).

Rome's fabled nightspots (most notably Piazza Navona, near the Pantheon, and Campo de' Fiori) are lined with the outdoor tables of touristy restaurants with enticing menus and formal-vested waiters. The atmosphere is super-romantic: I, too, like the idea of dining under floodlit monuments, amid a constantly flowing parade of people. But you'll likely be surrounded by tourists, and noisy English-speakers can kill the ambience of the spot...leaving you with just a forgettable and overpriced meal. Restaurants in these areas are notorious for surprise charges, forgettable food, microwaved ravioli, and bad service.

I enjoy the view by savoring just a drink or dessert on a famous square, but I dine with locals on nearby low-rent streets, where the proprietor needs to serve a good-value meal and nurture a local following to stay in business. If you're set on eating—or just drinking and snacking—on a famous piazza, you don't need a guidebook listing to choose a spot; enjoy the ritual of slowly circling the square, observing both the food and the people eating it, and sit where the view and menu appeal to you.

In Trastevere

Colorful Trastevere is now pretty touristy. Still, Romans join the tourists to eat on the rustic side of the Tiber River. Start at the central square, Piazza di Santa Maria. This is where the tourists dine, while others wander the back streets in search of mom-and-pop places with barely a menu. My recommendations are within a few minutes' walk of each other (between Piazza di Santa Maria in Trastevere and Ponte Sisto; see map on page 292).

Taverna Trilussa is your best bet for dining well in Trastevere. Brothers Massimo and Maurizio offer quality and value without pretense. With a proud 100-year-old tradition, this place has the right mix of style and informality. The service is fun-loving (they're happy to let you split plates into smaller portions to enjoy a family-style meal), yet professional. The menu celebrates local classics and seasonal specials, and comes with a big wine selection. The spacious dining hall is strewn with eclectic Roman souvenirs. For those who'd rather eat outdoors, Trilussa has an actual terrace rather than just tables jumbled together on the sidewalk (€15 pastas, €20 *secondi,* Mon-Sat from 19:30 for dinner, closed Sun, reservations very smart, Via del Politeama 23, tel. 06-581-8918).

Resources for Foodies

For those looking to take their Roman culinary endeavors seriously, there's no shortage of in-depth advice. Books and blogs on Roman cuisine abound, and several local companies run food- and wine-themed tours. Here is a sampling:

* David Downie's 2009 book ***Food Wine Rome*** has extensive listings of traditional eateries of every stripe, as well as background on Rome's culinary traditions.
* Katie Parla's website, **www.parlafood.com,** has all the latest on the Roman food scene. She also offers private food-oriented tours and tastings.
* **Rome for Foodies,** Parla's excellent smartphone app, transfers her advice into an easy-to-use, searchable format (and once it's on your device, it doesn't require an Internet connection).
* **Eating Italy Food Tours** leads fun and insightful walks almost daily through Rome's colorful Testaccio neighborhood, interspersing history, tradition, and local food culture while giving you a great glimpse into daily life in a less-seen side of the city (www.eatingitalyfoodtours.com).
* **Vino Roma** offers several walks, as well as an informal, nightly wine-tasting class (www.vinoroma.com).

Buon appetito, e salute!

Trattoria da Lucia lets you enjoy simple, traditional food at a good price. It's your basic old-school, Trastevere dining experience, and has been family-run since World War II. You'll meet four generations of the family, including Giuliano and Renato, their uncle Ennio, and Ennio's mom—pictured on the menu in the 1950s. The family specialty is *spaghetti alla Gricia,* with pancetta (€9 pastas, €11 *secondi,* Tue-Sun 12:30-15:00 & 19:30-23:00, closed Mon, cash only, evocative outdoor or comfy indoor seating—but avoid back room, just off Via del Mattonato at Vicolo del Mattonato 2, tel. 06-580-3601).

Trattoria da Olindo takes homey to extremes. You really feel like you dropped in on a family that cooks for the neighborhood to supplement their income. Don't expect any smiles here (€8 pastas, €10 *secondi,* Mon-Sat dinner served 20:00-22:30, closed Sun, cash only, indoor and funky outdoor seating, on the corner of Vicolo della Scala and Via del Mattonato at #8, tel. 06-581-8835).

Dar Poeta Pizzeria, tucked in a back alley and a hit with local students, cranks out some of the best wood-fired pizza I've had in Rome. It's run by three friends—Marco, Paolo, and another Marco—who welcome you into the informal restaurant beneath exposed brick arches. If you're in a spicy mood, order *lingua di fuoco* (tongue of fire). If you're extra hungry, pay an extra euro for *pizza alto* (thicker crust). Choose between their classic, cramped interior and lively tables outside on the cobblestones. Their chocolate dessert calzone is a favorite (€6-9 pizzas, daily 12:00-24:00, Vicolo del Bologna 45, tel. 06-588-0516).

Osteria Ponte Sisto da Oliviero, small and Mediterranean, specializes in traditional Roman cuisine, but has frequent Neapolitan specials as well. Just outside the tourist zone, it caters mostly to Romans and offers beautiful desserts and a fine value (€9 pastas, €12 *secondi*, Thu-Tue 12:30-15:30 & 19:30-24:00, closed Wed, Via Ponte Sisto 80, tel. 06-588-3411, reservations smart, Oliviero). If you're coming from the city center, cross Ponte Sisto (pedestrian bridge), continue across the little square (Piazza Trilussa), and you'll see it on the right.

Ristorante Checco er Carettiere is a big, family-run place that's been a Trastevere fixture for four generations—as the photos on the wall attest. With white tablecloths, well-presented food, and dressy local diners, this is a popular place for a special meal in Trastevere. While it's overpriced, you'll eat well amid lots of fun commotion (€18 pastas, €22 *secondi,* daily 12:30-15:00 & 19:30-23:15, Via Benedetta 10, tel. 06-580-0985). Their *osteria* next door (at #13) shares the same kitchen and offers less ambience, lower prices, and a more basic menu (€11 pastas, €15 *secondi*). Many Romans consider their *gelateria* (next door at #7) to be among the best on this side of the river.

Pizzeria "Ai Marmi" is a bright and noisy festival of pizza, where the oven and pizza-assembly line are surrounded by marble-slab tables (hence the nickname "the Morgue"). It's a classic Roman scene, whether you enjoy the chaos inside or sit at a sidewalk table, with famously good €8 pizzas and very tight seating. Expect a long line between 20:00 and 22:00 (Thu-Tue 19:00-24:00, closed Wed, cash only, tram #8 from Largo Argentina to first stop over bridge, just beyond Piazza Sonnino at Viale di Trastevere 53, tel. 06-580-0919).

Cantina Paradiso Wine and Cocktail Bar, a block over Viale di Trastevere from the touristy action, has a funky romantic charm. During happy hour (18:00-21:00), the €8 drinks come with a well-made little buffet that can turn into a cheap, light dinner (€8 pastas, daily 12:00-24:00, Via San Francesco a Ripa 73, tel. 06-589-9799, Weronika).

And for Dessert: **Gelateria alla Checco er Carettiere,** run by and next door to the famous, recommended restaurant of the same name, is many locals' favorite spot for gelato in Trastevere (daily 12:00-24:00, Via Benedetta 7).

In the Jewish Ghetto

The Jewish Ghetto sits just across the river from Trastevere (see map on page 304).

Sora Margherita, hiding without a sign on a cluttered square, has been a rustic neighborhood favorite since 1927. Amid a picturesque commotion, families chow down on old-time Roman and Jewish dishes for a decent price. It's technically not a real restaurant (it avoids red tape by officially registering itself an *associazione culturale*)—you can even sign a card to join the "cultural association" (don't worry, membership has no obligations except that you enjoy your meal). The menu's crude term for the fettuccini gives you some idea of the mood of this place: *nazzica culo* ("shaky ass"—what happens while it's made). Reservations are almost always necessary (€10 pastas, €12 *secondi*; Sept-May Mon-Sat 12:30-15:00, dinner seatings on Mon, Wed, Fri, and Sat at 20:00 and 21:30, closed Sun; June-July same hours except closed Sat, closed in Aug, just south of Via del Portico d'Ottavia at Piazza delle Cinque Scole 30—look for the red curtain, tel. 06-687-4216).

In the Pantheon Neighborhood

For the restaurants in this central area, I've listed them based on which landmark they're closest to: Campo de' Fiori, Piazza Navona, the Trevi Fountain, or the Pantheon itself.

On and near Campo de' Fiori

While it is touristy, Campo de' Fiori offers a sublimely romantic setting. And, since it's so close to the heart of the Roman people, it remains popular with locals, even though its restaurants offer greater atmosphere than food value. The square is lined with popular and interesting bars, pizzerias, and small restaurants—all great for people-watching over a glass of wine. Later at night it's taken over by a younger clubbing crowd.

Osteria da Giovanni ar Galletto is nearby, on the more elegant and peaceful Piazza Farnese. Angelo entertains an upscale Roman clientele and has magical outdoor seating. Regrettably, service can be horrible, you need to double-check the bill, and single diners aren't treated very well. Still, if you're in no hurry and ready to savor my favorite al fresco setting in Rome (while humoring the waiters), this can be a good bet (€12 pastas, €15-20 *secondi,* Mon-Sat 12:15-15:00 & 19:30-23:00, closed Sun, reservations smart for outdoor seating, tucked in corner of Piazza Farnese at #104, tel. 06-686-1714).

Osteria Enoteca al Bric is a mod bistro run by helpful Roberto and Barbara, who love to cook, serve fine wine, and listen to jazz. Wine-case lids decorate the wall like happy memories. They offer a fun, €22 happy-hour deal for two from 19:30 to 20:30 that includes

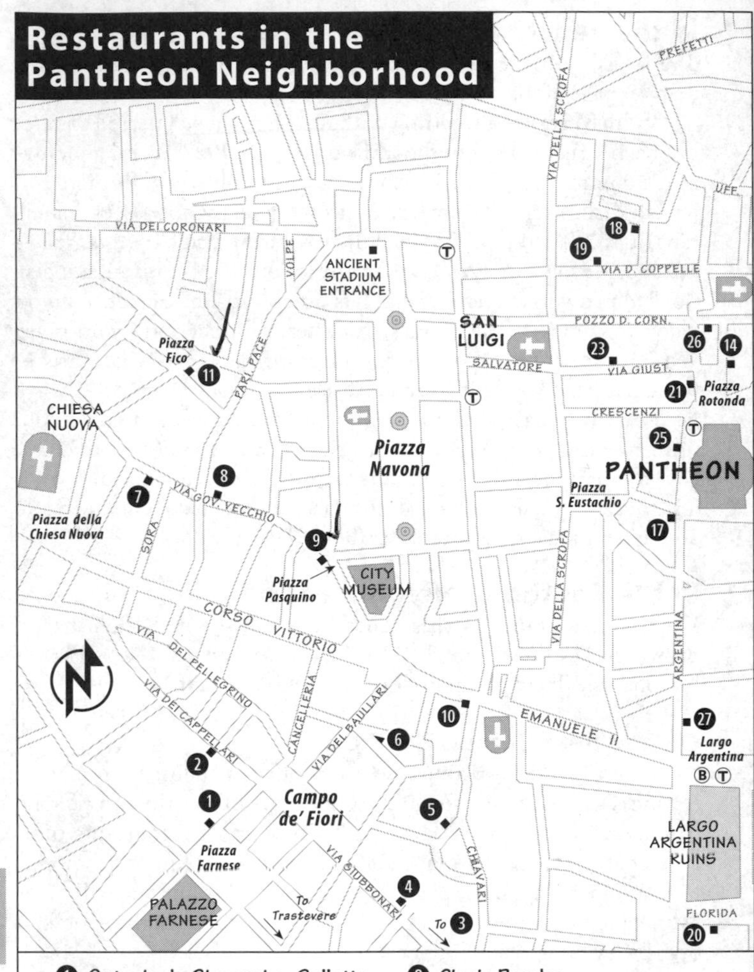

1. Osteria da Giovanni ar Galletto
2. Osteria Enoteca al Bric
3. To Vineria Salumeria Roscioli
4. Filetti di Baccalà
5. Trattoria der Pallaro
6. Pizzeria da Baffetto 2
7. Pizzeria da Baffetto
8. Ciccia Bomba
9. Cul de Sac & L'Insalata Ricca
10. L'Insalata Ricca
11. Rist. Pizzeria "da Francesco"
12. L'Antica Birreria Peroni
13. Rist. Pizzeria Sacro e Profano

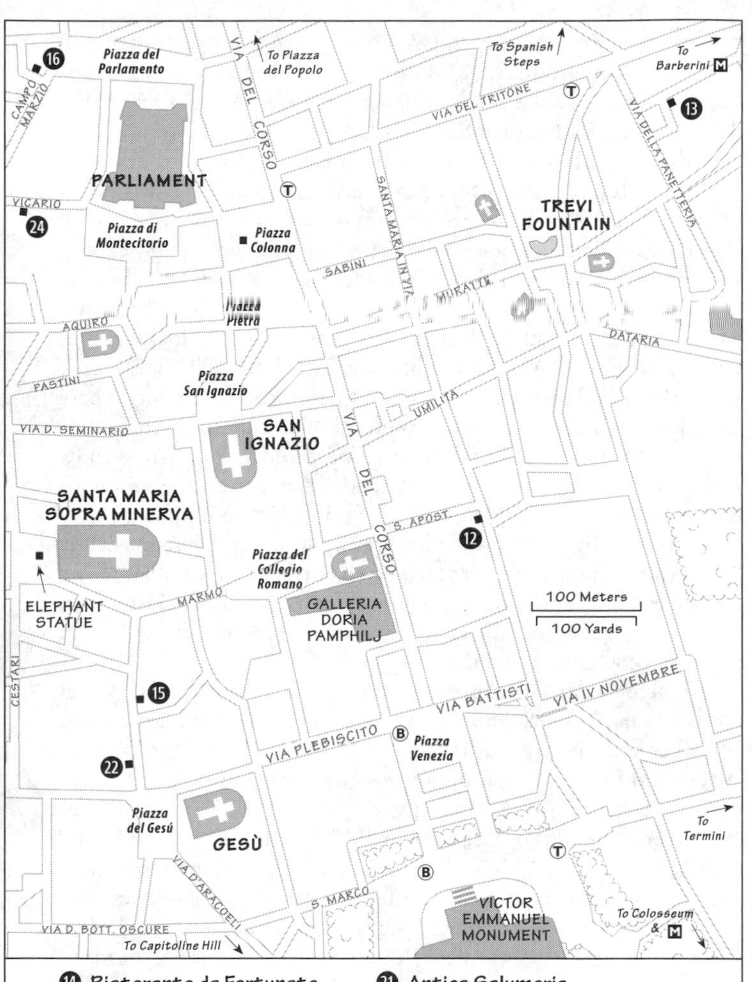

⓮ Ristorante da Fortunato
⓯ Ristorante Enoteca Corsi
⓰ Trattoria dal Cav. Gino
⓱ Miscellanea
⓲ Osteria da Mario
⓳ Taverna le Coppelle
⓴ Pizzeria Florida
㉑ Antica Salumeria
㉒ Super Market Carrefour Express
㉓ Supermercato Despar
㉔ Gelateria Caffè Pasticceria Giolitti
㉕ Crèmeria Monteforte
㉖ Gelateria San Crispino
㉗ Bar Pascucci

a plate of cheeses and meats, two glasses of good wine, water, and bread (Tue-Sun from 19:30 for dinner, closed Mon, reserve if dining after 20:30, can be pricey, 100 yards off Campo de' Fiori at Via del Pellegrino 51, tel. 06-687-9533).

Vineria Salumeria Roscioli is an elegant *enoteca* that's a hit with local foodies, so reservations are a must. While it's just a salami toss away from touristy Campo de' Fiori, you'll dine with classy locals, and feel like you're sitting in a romantic (and expensive) deli after hours. They have a good selection of fine cheeses, meats, local dishes, and top-end wines by the glass (€15-25 plates, Mon-Sat 12:30-16:00 & 19:00-24:00, closed Sun, 3 blocks east of Campo de' Fiori at Via dei Giubbonari 21, tel. 06-687-5287).

Filetti di Baccalà is a cheap and basic Roman classic, where nostalgic regulars cram into wooden tables and savor their old-school favorites—fried cod finger-food fillets (€5 each) and raw *puntarelle* greens (slathered with anchovy sauce in spring and winter). Study what others are eating, and order from your grease-stained server by pointing at what you want. Sit in the fluorescently lit interior or try to grab a seat out on the little square, a quiet haven a block east of Campo de' Fiori (Mon-Sat 17:30-23:00, closed Sun, cash only, Largo dei Librari 88, tel. 06-686-4018). If you're not into greasy spoons, avoid this place.

Trattoria der Pallaro, an eccentric and well-worn eatery that has no menu, has a slogan: "Here, you'll eat what we want to feed you." Paola Fazi—with a towel wrapped around her head turban-style—and her gang dish up a five-course meal of homey Roman food. You have three menu choices: €25 for the works; €20 for appetizers, *secondi*, and dessert; or €15 for appetizers and pasta. Any option is filling, includes wine and coffee, and is capped with a thimble of mandarin juice. While the service can be odd and the food is rustic, the experience is fun (daily 12:00-16:00 & 19:00-24:00, reserve if dining after 20:00, cash only, indoor/outdoor seating on quiet square, a block south of Corso Vittorio Emanuele, down Largo del Chiavari to Largo del Pallaro 15, tel. 06-6880-1488).

Pizzeria da Baffetto 2 makes pizza Roman-style: thin crust, crispy, and wood-fired. Eat in the cramped informal interior, or outside on the busy square (€7-9 pizzas, daily 18:30-24:00, Sat-Sun also open for lunch 12:30-15:30, a block north of Campo de' Fiori at Piazza del Teatro di Pompeo 18, tel. 06-6821-0807).

Near Piazza Navona

Piazza Navona is the quintessential setting for dining on a Roman square. Whether you eat here or not, you'll want to stroll the piazza before or after your evening meal. This is where many people fall in love with Rome. The tangled streets just to the west are lined with popular eateries of many stripes.

Ciccia Bomba is a traditional trattoria where Gianpaolo, Gianluca, and their crew serve up tasty homemade pasta, wood-fired pizza, and other Roman specialties (consider their daily-special sheet)—all at a good price. While you can sit at a table on ancient pavement next to your own column, I like the ambience upstairs (€7 pastas, €9 *secondi*, Thu-Tue 12:30-15:00 & 19:00-24:00, closed Wed, Via del Governo Vecchio 76, a block west of Piazza Navona, just north from Piazza Pasquino, tel. 06-6880-2100).

Cul de Sac, a corridor-wide trattoria lined with wine bottles, is packed with an enthusiastic crowd enjoying a wide-ranging menu, from pasta to homemade pâté. They have fun tasting-plates of *salumi* and cheese, more than a thousand different wines, and fine outdoor seating. It's small, and they don't take reservations—come early to avoid a wait (€7-15 plates, daily 12:00-16:00 & 18:00-24:00, a block off Piazza Navona on Piazza Pasquino, tel. 06-6880-1094).

Ristorante Pizzeria "da Francesco," bustling and authentic, has a 50-year-old tradition, a hardworking young waitstaff, great indoor seating, and classic outdoor seating on a cluttered little square that makes you want to break out a sketchpad. Their blackboard explains the daily specials (€9 pizzas and pastas, €15 *secondi*, open daily 12:00-15:00 & 19:00-24:00 except closed Tue at lunch, 3 blocks west of Piazza Navona at Piazza del Fico 29, tel. 06-686-4009).

Pizzeria da Baffetto, buried deep in the old quarter behind Piazza Navona, is a Roman favorite, offering tasty pizza but rude service. Its tables are tightly arranged amid the mishmash of photos and sketches littering the walls. The pizza-assembly kitchen keeps things energetic, and the pizza oven keeps the main room warm (you can opt for a table on the cobbled street). Come early or late, or be prepared to wait (€7 pizzas, daily from 18:30, cash only; order "P," "M," or "D"—small, medium, or large; west of Piazza Navona on the corner of Via Sora at Via del Governo Vecchio 114, tel. 06-686-1617).

L'Insalata Ricca is a popular local chain that specializes in healthy, filling €8 salads and less-healthy pastas and main courses (daily 12:00-15:45 & 18:45-24:00). They have a handy branch on Piazza Pasquino (next to the recommended Cul de Sac, tel. 06-6830-7881) and a more spacious and enjoyable location a few blocks away, on a bigger square next to busy Corso Vittorio Emanuele (near Campo de' Fiori at Largo dei Chiavari 85, tel. 06-6880-3656).

Near the Trevi Fountain

L'Antica Birreria Peroni is Rome's answer to a German beer hall. Serving hearty mugs of the local Peroni beer and lots of just plain fun beer-hall food and Italian classics, the place is a hit with Romans for a cheap night out (Mon-Sat 12:00-24:00, closed Sun, midway between Trevi Fountain and Capitoline Hill, a block off Via del Corso at Via di San Marcello 19, tel. 06-679-5310).

Ristorante Pizzeria Sacro e Profano fills an old church with spicy southern Italian (Calabrian) cuisine and satisfied tourists. Run with enthusiasm by Emiliano and friends, this is just far enough away from the Trevi mobs. Their pizza oven is wood-fired, and their hearty €15 *antipasti* plate is a filling montage of Calabrian taste treats (Mon-Sat 12:00-15:00 & 18:00-23:00, closed Sun, a block off Via del Tritone at Via dei Maroniti 29, tel. 06-679-1836).

Close to the Pantheon

Eating on the square facing the Pantheon is a temptation, and I'd consider it just to relax and enjoy the Roman scene. But if you walk a block or two away, you'll get less view and better value. Here are some suggestions.

Ristorante da Fortunato is an Italian classic, with fresh flowers on the tables and white-coated, black-tie career waiters politely serving good meat and fish to politicians, foreign dignitaries, and tourists with good taste. Don't leave without perusing the photos of their famous visitors—everyone from former Iraqi Foreign Minister Tariq Aziz to Bill Clinton seems to have eaten here. All are pictured with the boss, Fortunato, who, since 1975, has been a master of simple edible elegance. (His son Jason is now on the team.) The outdoor seating is fine for watching the river of Roman street life flow by, but the real atmosphere is inside. For a dressy night out, this is a reliable and surprisingly reasonable choice—but be sure to reserve ahead (plan to spend €45 per person, daily 12:30-15:30 & 19:30-23:30, a block in front of the Pantheon at Via del Pantheon 55, tel. 06-679-2788).

Ristorante Enoteca Corsi is a wine shop that grew into a thriving lunch-only restaurant. The Paiella family serves straightforward, traditional cuisine at great prices to an appreciative crowd of office workers. Check the blackboard for daily specials (gnocchi on Thursday, fish on Friday, and so on). Friendly Giuliana, Claudia, Sara, and Manuela welcome eaters to step into their wine shop and pick out a bottle. For the cheap take-away price, plus €2-4 (depending on the wine), they'll uncork it at your table. With €9 pastas, €13 main dishes, and fine wine at a third of the price you'd pay in normal restaurants, this can be a good value. And guests with this book finish their meal with a free glass of homemade *limoncello* (Mon-Sat 12:00-15:30, closed Sun, no reservations possible, a block toward the Pantheon from the Gesù Church at Via del Gesù 87, tel. 06-679-0821).

Trattoria dal Cav. Gino, tucked away on a tiny street behind the Parliament, has been a favorite since 1963. Photos on the wall recall the days when it was the haunt of big-time politicians. Grandpa Gino shuffles around grating the parmesan cheese while his English-speaking children Carla and Fabrizio serve up traditional Roman favorites and make sure things run smoothly. Reserve ahead, even for lunch, as you'll be packed in with savvy locals (€8 pastas, €11 *secondi,* cash only, Mon-Sat 13:00-14:45 & 20:00-22:30, closed Sun, fish on Friday, behind Piazza del Parlamento and just off Via di Campo Marzio at Vicolo Rosini 4, tel. 06-687-3434).

Miscellanea is run by much-loved Mikki, who's on a mission to keep foreign students well-fed. Welcoming travelers as well as locals, he offers hearty €4 sandwiches and a long list of €7 salads, along with pasta and other staples. Mikki (and his son Romeo) often tosses in a fun little extra, including—if you have this book on the table—a free glass of Mikki's "sexy wine" (from *fragoline*—strawberry-flavored grapes). While basic, it's convenient and inexpensive (daily 8:00-24:00, indoor/outdoor seating, facing the rear of the Pantheon at Via della Palombella 34, tel. 06-6813-5318).

Osteria da Mario, a homey little mom-and-pop joint with a no-stress menu, serves traditional favorites in a fun dining room or on tables spilling out onto a picturesque old Roman square (€8 pastas, €10 *secondi,* Mon-Sat 13:00-15:30 & 19:00-23:00, closed Sun; from the Pantheon walk 2 blocks up Via del Pantheon, go left on Via delle Coppelle, and take first right to Piazza delle Coppelle 51; tel. 06-6880-6349, Marco).

Taverna le Coppelle is simple, basic, family-friendly, and inexpensive—especially for pizza—with a checkered-tablecloth ambience (€9 pizzas, daily 12:30-15:00 & 19:30-23:30, Via delle Coppelle 39, tel. 06-6880-6557, Alfonso).

Pizzeria Florida, about four blocks south of the Pantheon, offers cheap pizza slices and sandwiches to go (daily 10:00-22:00, Via Florida 25, across from cat sanctuary, tel. 06-6880-3236).

Picnicking Close to the Pantheon

It's fun to munch a picnic with a view of the Pantheon. (Remember to be discreet.) Here are some options.

Antica Salumeria is an old-time *alimentari* (grocery store) on the Pantheon square. While they hustle most tourists into premade €5 sandwiches, you can make your own picnic. Find your way to the back to buy artichokes, mixed olives, bread, cheese, and meat (daily 8:00-21:00, mobile 334-340-9014).

Supermarkets near the Pantheon: Food is relatively cheap at Italian supermarkets. **Super Market Carrefour Express** is a convenient place for groceries a block from the Gesù Church (Mon-Sat 8:00-21:00, Sun 9:00-19:30, 50 yards off Via del Plebiscito at

Via del Gesù 59). Another place, **Supermercato Despar,** is half a block from the Pantheon toward Piazza Navona (daily 8:30-22:00, Via Giustiniani 18).

Gelato Close to the Pantheon

Three fine *gelaterie* and bars specializing in fresh-fruit smoothies are within a five-minute walk of the Pantheon.

Gelateria Caffè Pasticceria Giolitti, Rome's most famous and venerable ice-cream joint, has reasonable take-away prices and elegant Old World seating (daily 7:00-24:00, just off Piazza Colonna and Piazza Monte Citorio at Via Uffici del Vicario 40, tel. 06-699-1243).

Crèmeria Monteforte is known for its traditional, quality gelato and super-creamy sorbets *(cremolati).* The fruit flavors are especially refreshing—think gourmet slushies (Tue-Sun 10:00-24:00, off-season closes earlier, closed Mon and Dec-Jan, faces the west side of the Pantheon at Via della Rotonda 22, tel. 06-686-7720).

Gelateria San Crispino serves small portions of particularly tasty gourmet gelato using creative ingredients. Because of their commitment to natural ingredients, the colors are muted; gelato purists consider bright colors a sign of unnatural chemicals used to attract children. They serve cups, but no cones (daily 12:00-24:00, a block in front of the Pantheon on Piazza della Maddalena, tel. 06-6889-1310).

Bar Pascucci is a hole in the wall that's been making refreshing fruit *frullati* and frappés (like smoothies and shakes) for more than 75 years. Add a sandwich or fruit salad to make a healthy light meal (Mon-Sat 6:00-23:00, closed Sun, near Largo Argentina at Via di Torre Argentina 20, tel. 06-686-4816).

In North Rome: Near the Ara Pacis and Spanish Steps

To locate these restaurants, see the "Dolce Vita Stroll" map on page 383.

Ristorante il Gabriello is inviting and small—modern under medieval arches—and provides a peaceful and local-feeling respite from all the top-end fashion shops in the area. Claudio serves with charisma, while his brother Gabriello cooks creative Roman cuisine using fresh, organic products from his wife's farm. Italians normally just trust their waiter and say, "Bring it on." Tourists are understandably more cautious, but you can be trusting here. Simply close your eyes and point to anything on the menu. Or invest €45 in "Claudio's Extravaganza" (not including wine), and he'll shower you with edible kindness. Specify whether you'd prefer fish, meat, or both. (Romans think raw shellfish is the ultimate in fine dining. If you differ, make that clear.) When finished, I stand up, hold my belly, and say, *"Ahhh, la vita è bella"* (€10 pastas, €15 *secondi,* dinner only, Mon-Sat 19:00-23:00, closed Sun, reservations smart, air-con, dress respectfully—no shorts please, 3 blocks from Spanish Steps at Via Vittoria 51, tel. 06-6994-0810).

Osteria Gusto is thriving with trendy locals. While pricey, it's untouristy, gives a glimpse of today's Roman scene, and is fine for a glass of good wine over an artisanal cheese plate or a complete dinner (€13 pastas, €18 *secondi,* daily 12:30-15:30 & 19:00-24:00, opens at 18:30 for drinks and appetizers only, reservations recommended after 20:00 and on weekends, on the corner of Via Soderini at Via della Frezza 16, tel. 06-3211-1482). Their more expensive *ristorante* and more casual wine bar (which offers lighter bites) are directly adjacent.

L'EnotecAntica, an upbeat, atmospheric 200 plus-year-old *enoteca,* has around 60 Italian-only wines by the glass (€4-10, listed on a big blackboard) and a fresh €14 *antipasti* plate of veggies, *salumi,* and cheese. Very crowded on summer evenings, it comes with wonderful ambience both inside and out; its outside tables are set on a quiet cobbled street (daily 12:00-24:00, Via della Croce 76b, tel. 06-679-0896).

Palatium Enoteca Regionale is a crisp, modern restaurant funded by the region of Lazio (home to Rome) to show off its finest agricultural fare. Surrounded by locals, you'll enjoy generous, shareable plates of cheeses and *salumi,* a limited menu of pasta and meat, and a huge selection of local wine (€12-16 dishes, Mon-Sat 12:30-15:30 & 19:30-23:00, closed Sun, 5 blocks in front of the Spanish Steps at Via Frattina 94, tel. 06-6920-2132).

In Ancient Rome: Near the Colosseum and Forum

You'll find good views but poor value at the restaurants directly behind the Colosseum. To get your money's worth, eat at least a block away. Here are several handy eateries, all shown on the map on page 336: one at the foot of Via Cavour, two at the top of Terme di Tito (a long block uphill from the Colosseum, near St. Peter-in-Chains church—of Michelangelo's *Moses* fame; for directions, see page 161), and two a couple of blocks to the east.

Enoteca Cavour 313 is a wine bar with a mission: to offer good wine and quality food with an old-fashioned commitment to value and friendly service. It's also a convenient place for a good lunch near the Forum and Colosseum. Angelo and his three partners enjoy creating a mellow ambience under lofts of wine bottles (limited menu of daily specials and fine wines by the glass, daily 12:30-14:45 & 19:00-24:00, 100 yards off Via dei Fori Imperiali at Via Cavour 313, tel. 06-678-5496).

Hostaria da Nerone is a traditional place serving hearty classics, including tasty homemade pasta dishes. Their *antipasti* plate—with a variety of veggies, fish, and meat—is a good value for a quick lunch. While the *antipasti* menu indicates specifics, you can have a plate of whatever's out—just direct the waiter to assemble the €9 *antipasti* plate of your lunchtime dreams (€10 pastas, €12 *secondi*, Mon-Sat 12:00-15:00 & 19:00-23:00, closed Sun, indoor/outdoor seating, Via delle Terme di Tito 96, tel. 06-481-7952, run by Teo and Eugenio).

Caffè dello Studente, next door to Hostaria da Nerone, is popular with engineering students attending the nearby University of Rome. Pina, Mauro, and their perky daughter Simona (who speaks English) give my readers a royal welcome and serve average, microwaved *bar gastronomia* fare—toasted sandwiches, salads, and mixed bruschetta. If it's not busy, show this book when you order at the bar and sit without paying extra at a table (Mon-Sat 7:30-22:30, April-Oct Sun 9:00-22:30, Nov-March closed Sun, Via delle Terme di Tito, tel. 06-488-3240).

Trattoria Luzzi is a well-worn, no-frills eatery serving simple food in a high-energy environment (as they've done since 1945). With good prices, big portions, and proximity to the Colosseum, it draws a crowd—reserve or expect a short wait at lunch and after 19:30 (€6 pastas, €7 pizzas, €9 *secondi*, Thu-Tue 12:00-24:00, closed Wed, Via San Giovanni in Laterano 88, tel. 06-709-6332).

La Taverna dei Quaranta, a casual neighborhood favorite, is a bit more refined than nearby Luzzi, but still far from pretentious. In the evening, they fire up the wood oven for pizza, to go along with a basic menu of Roman classics and seasonal specialties. As the place caters mostly to locals, service can be a bit slow and straightforward—but it's a good bet in this touristy area (€8 pastas, €13 *secondi*, daily 12:00-15:30 & 19:00-24:00, Via Claudia 24, tel. 06-700-0550).

Near Termini Station

These restaurants are near my recommended hotels on Via Firenze. Several are clustered on Via Flavia, others are nearby (Target, etc.), and a few, such as Bar Tavola Calda, are good options for quick meals.

On (or near) Via Flavia

To easily check out a fun and varied selection of eateries within a block of each other, walk to Via Flavia (a block behind the Church

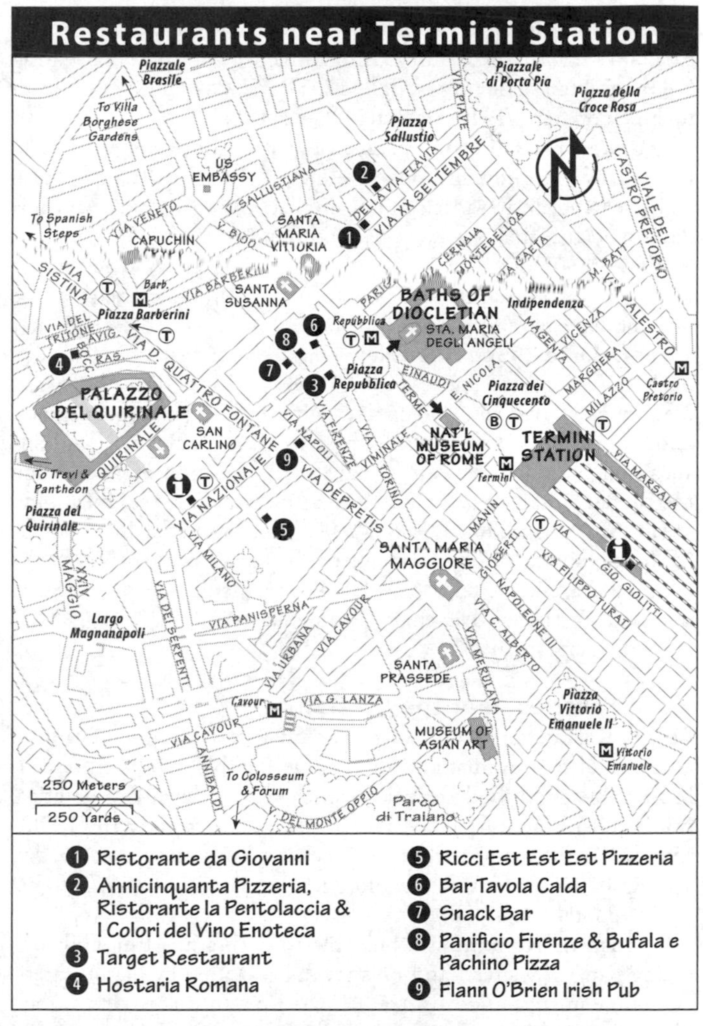

of Santa Maria della Vittoria of *St. Teresa in Ecstasy* fame) and survey these choices—an old-time restaurant, a good pizzeria, a small romantic place, and a friendly wine bar.

Ristorante da Giovanni, well-worn and old-fashioned, makes no concessions to tourism or the modern world—just hard-working cooks and waiters serving standard dishes at great prices to a committed clientele. It's simply fun to eat in the middle of this high-energy, Roman time warp (€6-10 pastas and *secondi*, daily specials, Mon-Sat 12:00 15:00 & 19:00-22:00, closed Sun and Aug, corner of Via XX Settembre at Via Antonio Salandra 1, tel. 06-485-950).

Annicinquanta Pizzeria, big and classic, serves the neighborhood's favorite pizzas in a calm ambience with outdoor seating (€8 Neapolitan-style pizzas, daily 12:15-15:30 & 19:30-24:00 except no lunch on Sat, Via Flavia 3, tel. 06-4201-0460).

Ristorante la Pentolaccia, pricier and more romantic than the nearby Da Giovanni, is a dressy, tourist-friendly place with tight seating and traditional Roman cooking—consider their daily specials. This is a local hangout, and reservations are smart (daily 12:00-15:00 & 17:30-23:00, a block off Via XX Settembre at Via Flavia 38, tel. 06-483-477). To start things off with a free bruschetta, leave this book on the table.

I Colori del Vino Enoteca is a modern wine bar that feels like a laboratory of wine appreciation. It has woody walls of bottles, a creative menu of meats and cheeses with different regional themes, and a great list of fine wines by the glass. Helpful, English-speaking Marco carries on a long family tradition of celebrating the fundamentals of good nutrition: fine wine, cheese, meat, and bread (Mon-Fri 12:00-15:00 & 17:30-23:00, closed Sat-Sun because Marco doesn't cater to noisy weekend drinkers, corner of Via Flavia and Via Aureliana, tel. 06-474-1745). Remember Shakespeare's sage warning about drinking: "It provokes the desire, but it takes away the performance."

More Eateries near the Station

Target Restaurant seems to be the favorite recommendation of every hotel receptionist and tour guide for this neighborhood. It has reliably good food, a sleek look, capable service, and practical prices (€8-12 salads, pastas, and pizzas; €20 *secondi,* daily 12:00-15:00 & 19:00-24:00 except no lunch on Sun, reserve to specify seating outside or inside—avoid getting seated in basement, Via Torino 33, tel. 06-474-0066).

Hostaria Romana is a busy bistro with a hustling and fun-loving gang of waiters, and noisy walls graffitied by happy eaters. As its menu specializes in traditional Roman dishes, it's a good place to try *saltimbocca alla romana* or *bucatini all'amatriciana* (see "Roman Cuisine," earlier in this chapter). Their €10 *antipasti* plate, with a variety of vegetables and cheeses, makes a hearty start to your meal (€9 pastas, €14 *secondi*, Mon-Sat 12:15-15:00 & 19:15-23:00, closed Sun, reservations smart, a block up the lane just past the entrance to the big tunnel near the Trevi Fountain at Via del Boccaccio 1, tel. 06-474-5284).

Ricci Est Est Est Pizzeria, a venerable family-run pizzeria, has plenty of historical ambience, good €8 pizzas, and dangerously tasty *fritti,* such as fried *baccalà* (cod) and zucchini flowers (Tue-Sun 19:00-24:00, closed Mon and Aug, Via Genova 32, tel. 06-488-1107).

Fast, Simple Meals near the Station

Bar Tavola Calda is a workers' favorite for a quick, cheap lunch. They have good, fresh, hot dishes ready to go for a fine price. Head back past the bar to peruse their enticing display, point at what you want, then grab a seat and the young waitstaff will serve you (Mon-Sat 6:00-18:00, closed Sun, Via Torino 40).

Snack Bar puts out a lunchtime display of inexpensive pastas, colorful sandwiches, fresh fruit, and salad. Their loyal customers appreciate the fruit salad with yogurt (daily 6:00-24:00, Via Firenze 33, mobile 339-393-1356, Enrica).

Panificio Firenze makes hearty sandwiches, has a selection of well-priced wine, and stocks other goodies for a picnic to go (sandwiches priced by weight, Mon-Fri 7:00-19:00, Sat 7:00-14:00, closed Sun, Via Firenze 51-52, tel. 06-488-5035, Giovanni).

Bufala e Pachino Pizza is a convenient place for pizza by the slice *(al taglio)* and priced by weight—just point and tell them how much you'd like. Their *supplí* (fried rice balls filled with mozzarella), at just €1 each, make for cheap, filling snacks (daily 10:00-23:00, Via Firenze 54).

Flann O'Brien Irish Pub is an entertaining place for a light meal of pasta...or something *other* than pasta, such as grilled meats and giant salads, served early and late, when other places are closed. They have Irish beer, live sporting events on TV, and perhaps the most Italian crowd of all. Walk way back before choosing a table. Live bands often play on Friday evenings (daily 7:00-24:00, Via Nazionale 17, at intersection with Via Napoli, tel. 06-488-0418).

Near Vatican City

Avoid the restaurant-pushers handing out fliers near the Vatican: They're hawking places with bad food and expensive menu tricks. Try any of these instead (see map on page 342).

Handy Lunch Places near Piazza Risorgimento

These are a stone's throw from the Vatican wall, located halfway between St. Peter's Basilica and the Vatican Museum. They're all fast and cheap, with a good *gelateria* next door.

Hostaria dei Bastioni, run by Antonio while Emilio cooks, has noisy street-side seating and a quiet interior (€8 pastas, €12 *secondi*, Mon-Sat 12:00-15:30 & 18:30-23:00, closed Sun, at corner of Vatican wall at Via Leone IV 29, tel. 06-3972-3034).

L'Insalata Ricca is another branch of the popular chain that serves salads and pastas (daily 12:30-15:30 & 18:30-23:45, across from Vatican walls at Piazza Risorgimento 5, tel. 06-3973-0387).

Duecento Gradi is a good bet for fresh and creative €5 sandwiches. Munch your lunch on a stool or take it away (daily 11:00-24:00, Piazza Risorgimento 3, tel. 06-3975-4239).

Gelato: **Gelateria Old Bridge** scoops up hearty portions of fresh gelato for tourists and nuns alike—join the line (daily 10:00-23:00, just off Piazza Risorgimento across from Vatican walls at Via Bastioni 3).

Other Good Options in the Vatican Area

The first three listings—the restaurant, the streets with pizza shops, and the covered market—are near the Vatican Museum. The Borgo Pio eateries are near St. Peter's Basilica.

La Rustichella serves tasty wood-fired pizza and the usual pasta in addition to their sprawling *antipasti* buffet (€8 for a single plate). Arrive when it opens at 19:00 to avoid a line and have the pristine buffet to yourself. Do like the Romans do—take a moderate amount and make one trip only (Tue-Sun 12:30-15:00 & 19:00-24:00, closed Mon, near Metro: Cipro, opposite church at end of Via Candia, Via Angelo Emo 1, tel. 06-3972-0649). Consider the fun and fruity **Gelateria Millennium** next door.

Viale Giulio Cesare and ***Via Candia:*** These streets are lined with cheap *pizza rustica* shops, self-serve places, and basic eateries.

Covered Market: As you collect picnic supplies, turn your nose loose in the wonderful **Mercato Trionfale** covered market. It's one of the best in the city, located three blocks north of the Vatican Museum (Mon-Sat roughly 7:00-14:00, Tue and Fri some stalls stay open until 19:00, closed Sun, corner of Via Tunisi and Via Andrea Doria). If the market is closed, try several nearby supermarkets; the most convenient is **Carrefour Express** (Mon-Sat 8:00-20:00, Sun 9:00-20:00, Via Sebastiano Veniero 16).

Along Borgo Pio: The pedestrians-only Borgo Pio—a block from Piazza San Pietro—has restaurants worth a look, such as **Tre Pupazzi** (Mon-Sat 12:00-15:00 & 19:00-23:00, closed Sun, at corner of Via Tre Pupazzi and Borgo Pio, tel. 06-686-8371). At **Vecchio Borgo,** across the street, you can get pasta, pizza slices, and veggies to go (Mon-Sat 9:00-21:00, closed Sun, Borgo Pio 27a, tel. 06-8117-3585).

ROME WITH CHILDREN

Sorry, but Rome is not a great place for little kids. Parks are rare. Kid-friendly parks are rarer. Most of the museums are low-tech and lack hands-on fun.

But there is some good news. Rome's many squares are traffic-free, with plenty of space to run and pigeons to feed while Mom and Dad enjoy a coffee at an outdoor table. Italians are openly fond of kids, so you'll probably get lots of friendly attention from locals. And you won't get many complaints about the cuisine: pizza and gelato.

Sights and Activities

Ancient Sites, Churches, and Museums

While some ancient sites, such as the **Colosseum,** are naturally fascinating for kids, others, like the Roman Forum, may be a snooze. To keep them engaged, consider picking up a copy of *Rome: Past and Present,* a book with plastic overlays showing how the ruins used to look. It's available at stalls near the entrance of ancient sites (prices are soft, so negotiate).

For a fun overview of the city, the topless double-decker **Trambus 110 tour** offers a two-hour swing past all of the major sights (see page 41).

The spooky tunnels of the **catacombs** are goblin-pleasers (the Catacombs of Priscilla offer half-off entry for kids 15 and under; for catacombs, see pages 73 and 95). The macabre **Capuchin Crypt,** decorated with bones, fascinates children and adults alike (see page 69).

In Vatican City, the climb to the top of **St. Peter's** is great for its dizzy railing view into the church from halfway up the dome—

Family Travel Tips

- Ask at Rome's TIs about kid-friendly activities. TIs often have a helpful "kid's pack."
- Don't overdo it. Tackle only one or two key sights a day (Vatican Museum, or Colosseum and Forum), and mix in a healthy dose of fun activities, like exploring Rome's great public sights (Piazza Navona, Trevi Fountain, and Villa Borghese Gardens).
- Rome's hotels often give price breaks for kids. (Air-conditioning can be worth the splurge.)
- Eat dinner early (around 19:00), and you'll miss the romantic crowd. While kids may do best in self-serve cafeterias or even fast-food places, if you eat early you'll find that children are comfortable and welcome in better restaurants. Eating *al fresco* is great with kids. For ready-made picnics that can please adults and kids, try the *rosticcerie* (delis). *Pizza rustica* shops sell cheap take-out pizza; kids like *margherita* (tomato and cheese) and *diavola* (similar to pepperoni).

- Public WCs are hard to find: Try museums, bars, gelato shops, and fast-food restaurants.
- Follow this book's crowd-beating tips. Kids don't want to stand in a long line for a museum (which they might not even want to see).
- Give your kids a business card from your hotel, along with your contact information, just in case you get separated.
- Any person under 39 inches tall travels free on Rome's public transit.
- If you're taking the train to another city, check for family discounts; see page 476 for information.

plus the hike will tire out young tots (see page 205). The **Vatican Museum** comes with mummies, cool statues, and has an audioguide designed for families. Nearby, **Castel Sant'Angelo**—with Vatican views and weapon displays—appeals to young knights (see page 65).

The **Church of San Ignazio,** with its false dome, fascinates kids and adults (see page 180). Your children can get a whiff of Egypt by visiting Rome's funky little **pyramid** (free and always viewable, Metro: Piramide—see page 85). Check out the cat hospice in the adjacent park and climb on the chunk of old Roman wall across the street.

Bocca della Verità, the legendary "Mouth of Truth" at the Church of Santa Maria in Cosmedin, is fun for kids and parents with cameras (see page 49). Liars beware.

Several museums are particularly enjoyable for kids. The **Montemartini Museum,** in an old power plant, features ancient statuary, with art at kids' level and no crowds (see page 89). The **Planetarium** and **Astronomical Museum** (especially the "Machine of Space and Time") at the Museum of Roman Civilization in E.U.R. also appeal to kids (see page 93).

Explora, a children's museum, is a hands-on wonderland for kids 12 and under. Descriptions are in Italian, but younger kids probably won't care (kids 1-3-€3, kids 4-99-€7, parent must accompany child; four 2-hour self-guided sessions/day: Tue-Sun at 10:00, 12:00, 15:00, and 17:00; closed Mon, confirm session times in advance by checking website—www.mdbr.it—or calling 06-361-3776, helpful English-speaking staff; 10-minute walk from Piazza del Popolo at Via Flaminia 82, Metro: Flaminio).

Outdoor Fun

The **Villa Borghese Gardens** are Rome's sprawling central park. The best kids' zones are near Porta Pinciana, where you'll find rental bikes, pony rides, and other amusements (Metro: Barberini or Spagna). Summer weekends at the gardens, sure to be a hit with kids, include classic Roman puppet shows at Teatro dei Burattini. Rome's **zoo,** Bioparco, in the northeast section of the park, houses about 900 animals—including the endangered black lemur, pygmy hippopotamus, Gila monster, and painted hunting dog (kids under 3-free, kids 4-12-€11, adults-€13, daily April-Oct 9:30-18:00, Nov-March 9:30-17:00, last entry one hour before closing, café and picnic areas, Piazzale del Giardino Zoologico 1, Metro: Flaminio, tel. 06-360-8211, www.bioparco.it).

Older children may want to **rent a bike** at the Ancient Appian Way (✪ see Ancient Appian Way Tour chapter); use the bike/pedestrian path to avoid the traffic.

Rome has a big water park called **Hydromania** (€16.50 Mon-Fri, €18 Sat-Sun, cheaper for kids 12 and under and anyone arriving after 14:00; open June-Aug daily 9:30-18:30, Sat-Sun until 19:00, closed Sept-May; Vicolo del Casale Lumbroso 200, exit 33 off ring freeway west of the city, tel. 06-6618-3183, www.hydromania.it).

Aquapiper, another water park, is near Tivoli (€16, June-Aug daily 9:00-19:00, closed Sept-May, Via Maremmana Inferiore, in Guidonia, 15-minute drive east of Rome, tel. 0774-326-538, www.aquapiper.it); ask about the free shuttle bus from the center of Rome (leaves from Piazza della Repubblica).

Rome feels safe at night, and you can easily take your kids on the **walks** suggested in this book, such as the "Dolce Vita Stroll" on page 382. On the Heart of Rome Walk, children like slurping up chocolate gelato at the Tre Scalini *gelateria* on Piazza Navona and tossing coins in the Trevi Fountain. Consider letting your child act as tour guide for an hour by leading one of the walks. *Buona fortuna!*

SHOPPING IN ROME

Traditionally, shops are open from 9:00 to 13:00 and from 15:30 or 16:30 to 19:00 or 19:30. They're often closed on Sundays, summer Saturday afternoons, and winter Monday mornings. But in the city center, you'll find that many are now staying open through lunch (generally 10:00-19:00).

For information on VAT refunds and customs regulations, see page 14.

If all you need are souvenirs, a surgical strike at any souvenir shop will do. Otherwise, try...

Department Stores

To conveniently peruse clothes, bags, shoes, and perfume at several major Italian chain stores, wander the shopping complex under Termini train station (most stores open daily 8:00-22:00).

Large department stores offer relatively painless one-stop shopping. A good upscale department store is **La Rinascente** (like Nordstrom or Macy's). Its main branch is on Piazza Fiume, and a smaller store is on Via del Corso in the **Galleria Alberto Sordi,** an elegant 19th-century "mall" (across from Piazza Colonna). **UPIM** is a popular mid-range department store (many branches, including inside Termini train station, Via Nazionale 111, Piazza Santa Maria Maggiore, and Via del Tritone 172). **Oviesse,** a cheap clothing outlet, is near the Vatican Museum (on the corner of Via Candia and Via Mocenigo, Metro: Cipro).

Shopping Neighborhoods

An affordable shopping area is all along **Via del Corso,** with prices increasing as you head toward Piazza di Spagna. **Via Nazionale** also features a range of reasonably priced shops, especially for clothes and shoes. Near the bottom of Via Nazionale, **Via**

Boschetto and **Via dei Serpenti** are more unique, with a mix of clothing shops and designer bric-a-brac. **Via Cola di Rienzo**, near the Vatican, is good for mid-range clothes. Cheapskates scrounge through the junky but dirt-cheap shops in the gritty area around **Piazza Vittorio.**

Boutiques

For top fashion, stroll the streets around the Spanish Steps, including **Via Condotti, Via Borgognona** (for the big-name shops), and **Via del Babuino** (more big names and a few galleries). For antiques and vintage items, wander **Via dei Coronari** (between Piazza Navona and the bend in the river), **Via Giulia** (between Campo de' Fiori and the river), **Via dei Banchi Vecchi** (parallel to Via Giulia), and **Via Margutta** (classier, with art galleries too, from Spanish Steps to Piazza del Popolo). For funkier, unique finds, try **Via Giubbonari**—it's packed with artsy little boutiques—and other streets near Campo de' Fiori.

Flea Markets

For antiques and fleas, the granddaddy of markets is the **Porta Portese** *mercato delle pulci* (flea market). This Sunday-morning market is long and spindly, running between the actual Porta Portese (a gate in the old town wall) and the Trastevere train station. Starting at Porta Portese, walk through the long, tacky parade of stalls selling cheap bras and shoes. Along the way, check out the con artists with the shell games. Each has shills in the crowd "winning big money" to get suckers involved. Hang on to your wallet—literally, in your front pocket, or better yet, use a money belt and make sure it's safely tucked under your clothes. This is a den of thieves. The heart of the market for real flea-market junk (hiding a few little antique treasures) is the square in the center near Via Cesare Pascarella. I find that a slow stroll through the entire market and back to the Porta Portese takes about an hour and a half. While the shopping gets old (and the vendor food will make you sick), the people-watching is endlessly entertaining (6:30-13:00 Sun only, on Via Portuense and Via Ippolito Nievo; to get to the market, catch bus #75 from Termini train station or tram #8 from Largo Argentina, get off the bus or tram on Viale di Trastevere, and walk toward the river—and the noise).

At the **Via Sannio** market, you'll find new and used clothing and leather goods, some handicrafts, and random items that were probably stolen. You won't find antiques (Mon-Sat 9:00-13:30, closed Sun, behind Coin department store, a couple of blocks south of San Giovanni in Laterano, Metro: San Giovanni).

Open-Air Produce Markets

Rome's outdoor markets provide a fun and colorful dimension of the city that even the most avid museumgoer should not miss. Wander through the easygoing neighborhood produce markets that clog certain streets and squares every morning (7:00-13:00) except Sunday. Consider the huge **Mercato Trionfale** (three blocks north of Vatican Museum at Via Andrea Doria). Another great food market is the **Mercato Esquilino** (Via Turati near Piazza Vittorio). Smaller but equally charming slices of everyday Roman life are at markets on these streets and squares: **Piazza delle Coppelle** (near the Pantheon), **Via Balbo** (near Termini train station and recommended hotels off Via Nazionale), and **Via della Pace** (near Piazza Navona). The covered **Mercato di Testaccio** sells mostly produce and is a hit with photographers and people-watchers (Metro: Piramide). And **Campo de' Fiori,** despite having become quite touristy, is still a fun scene.

Fiumincino Airport

Rome's main airport (a.k.a. Leonardo da Vinci Airport) sells Italian specialty foods vacuum-packed to clear US customs. Most shops are near the departure gates (after you check your bags and pass through security). Try *parmigiano reggiano* cheese, dried porcini mushrooms or peppers, and better olive oil than you can buy at home. Don't bother buying any salami or prosciutto unless it's canned; you're not allowed to bring fresh meat into the US. Remember, if you're flying to the US and transferring before your final destination, you'll likely be required to pack purchased liquids in your checked luggage after clearing customs (a potential recipe for disaster).

NIGHTLIFE IN ROME

Romans get dressed up and eat out in casual surroundings for their evening entertainment. For most visitors, the best after-dark activity is simply to grab a gelato and stroll the medieval lanes that connect the romantic, floodlit squares and fountains. Head for Piazza Navona, the Pantheon, Campo de' Fiori, Trevi Fountain, Spanish Steps, Via del Corso, Trastevere (around the Santa Maria in Trastevere Church), or Monte Testaccio.

✪ See my Heart of Rome Walk chapter and "Dolce Vita Stroll" (later in this chapter).

Performances

Get a copy of the entertainment guide *Evento* (free at TIs and many hotels). Look at the current listings of concerts, operas, dance, and films. Posters around town also advertise upcoming events. For the most up-to-date events calendar, check these English-language websites: www.inromenow.com, www.wantedinrome.com, and http://rome.angloinfo.com.

Music: Music lovers will seek out the mega-music complex of the Rome **Auditorium** (Auditorium Parco della Musica), designed by contemporary architect Renzo Piano (€20-60 tickets, check availability in advance—concerts often sell out, Viale Pietro de Coubertin 30, take Metro to Flaminio and then catch tram #2, box office tel. 06-8024-1281, www.auditorium.com). Nicknamed the Park of Music, it's a place where many Romans go just for the scene—music store, restaurants, cafés, and fresh modern architecture with three state-of-the-art auditoriums (known as "the beetles" for their appearance). If you want to see today's Rome enjoying today's culture, an evening here is the best you'll do. As it's a ways out of the city center, shuttle buses get everyone back downtown after the concerts are over.

The *Passeggiata*

Throughout Italy, early evening is time to stroll. While elsewhere in Italy this is called the *passeggiata,* in Rome it's a cruder, big-city version called the *struscio* (meaning "to rub").

Unemployment among Italy's youth is very high; many stay with their parents even into their thirties. They spend a lot of time being trendy and hanging out. Like American kids gathering at the mall, working-class suburban youth *(coatto)* converge on the old center, as there's little to keep them occupied in Rome's dreary outskirts (which lack public spaces). The hot *vroom-vroom* motor scooter is their symbol; haircuts and fashion are follow-the-leader.

In a more genteel small town, the *passeggiata* comes with sweet whispers of *"bella"* and *"bello"* ("pretty" and "handsome"). In Rome, the admiration is stronger, oriented toward consumption—they say *"buona"* and *"buono"*—meaning roughly "tasty." But despite how lusty this all sounds, you'll see just as many chunky, middle-aged Italians out and about as hormone-charged youth.

Classical Music and Opera: The **Teatro dell'Opera** has an active schedule of opera and classical concerts. In the summer, the productions move to the Baths of Caracalla, where ancient ruins make an evocative backdrop. You'll see locals in all their finery, so pull your fanciest outfit from your backpack (near Via Firenze/Via Nazionale hotels at Via Firenze 72, tel. 06-4816-0255, www.operaroma.it).

Musical events at the Episcopal **Church of St. Paul's Within the Walls** range from orchestral concerts (usually Tue and Fri) to full operatic performances, which are usually on Saturdays (€20-30, performances at 20:30, arrive 30-45 minutes early for a good seat, lasts between 1.5 and 2.5 hours, Via Napoli 58, near Termini train station and recommended hotels, tel. 06-482-6296, www.imusiciveneziani.com). On Sunday evenings at 18:30, the church occasionally hosts hour-long candlelit *Luminaria* concerts (€10-20, buy tickets at the church on Sunday, www.stpaulsrome.it).

Movies

Movies in their original language are hard to come by in Rome (look for "V.O."—*versione originale*). The one reliable cinema is the **Nuovo Olimpia** (3 blocks north of Piazza Colonna, just off Via del Corso at Via in Lucina 16, tel. 06-686-1068). For movie listings, check out www.inromenow.com (includes English-language film showings) and www.romereview.com.

Nightclubs

An interesting place for club-hopping is **Monte Testaccio.** After 21:00, ride the Metro to the Piramide stop and follow the noise. Monte Testaccio, once an ancient trash heap, is now a small hill whose cool caves house funky restaurants and trendy clubs. (It stands amid a pretty rough neighborhood, though.)

Other Evening Activities

Some **museums** have later opening hours (especially on Sat in summer), offering a good chance to see art in a cooler, less-crowded environment. See the "Rome at a Glance" sidebar on page 56, and ask the TI if any museums are currently open late.

The **Scuderie del Quirinale** stays open late when it's hosting major art exhibitions (Sun-Thu 10:00-20:00, Fri-Sat 10:00-22:30, last entry one hour before closing, Via XXIV Maggio 16, tel. 06-696-271, www.scuderiequirinale.it).

Pub crawls, offered year-round by several companies, attract a boisterous crowd. I tried one and had never seen 50 young, drunk people having so much fun. Look for fliers locally. Late on Friday and Saturday evenings, entire quarters of old Rome seem to be overtaken by young beer-drinking revelers. Campo de' Fiori becomes one big, rude street party.

▲▲Dolce Vita Stroll

This is the city's chic stroll, from Piazza del Popolo (Metro: Flaminio) down a wonderfully traffic-free section of Via del Corso, and up Via Condotti to the Spanish Steps. It takes place from around 17:00 to 19:00 each evening (Fri and Sat are best), except on Sunday, when it occurs earlier in the afternoon. Leave before 18:00 if you plan to visit the Ara Pacis (Altar of Peace), which closes at 19:00 and is closed Monday.

As you stroll, you'll see shoppers, people-watchers, and flirts on the prowl filling this neighborhood of some of Rome's most fashionable stores (some open after siesta 16:30-19:30). While both the crowds and the shops along Via del Corso have gone downhill recently, elegance survives in the grid of streets between here and the Spanish Steps. If you get hungry during your stroll, see page 366 for descriptions of neighborhood wine bars and restaurants.

To reach **Piazza del Popolo,** where the stroll starts, take Metro line A to Flaminio and walk south to the square. Delightfully car-free, Piazza del Popolo is marked by an obelisk that was brought to Rome by Augustus after he conquered Egypt. (It used to stand in the Circus Maximus.) In medieval times, this area was just inside Rome's main entry (for more background on the square, see page 71).

If starting your stroll early enough, the Baroque church of

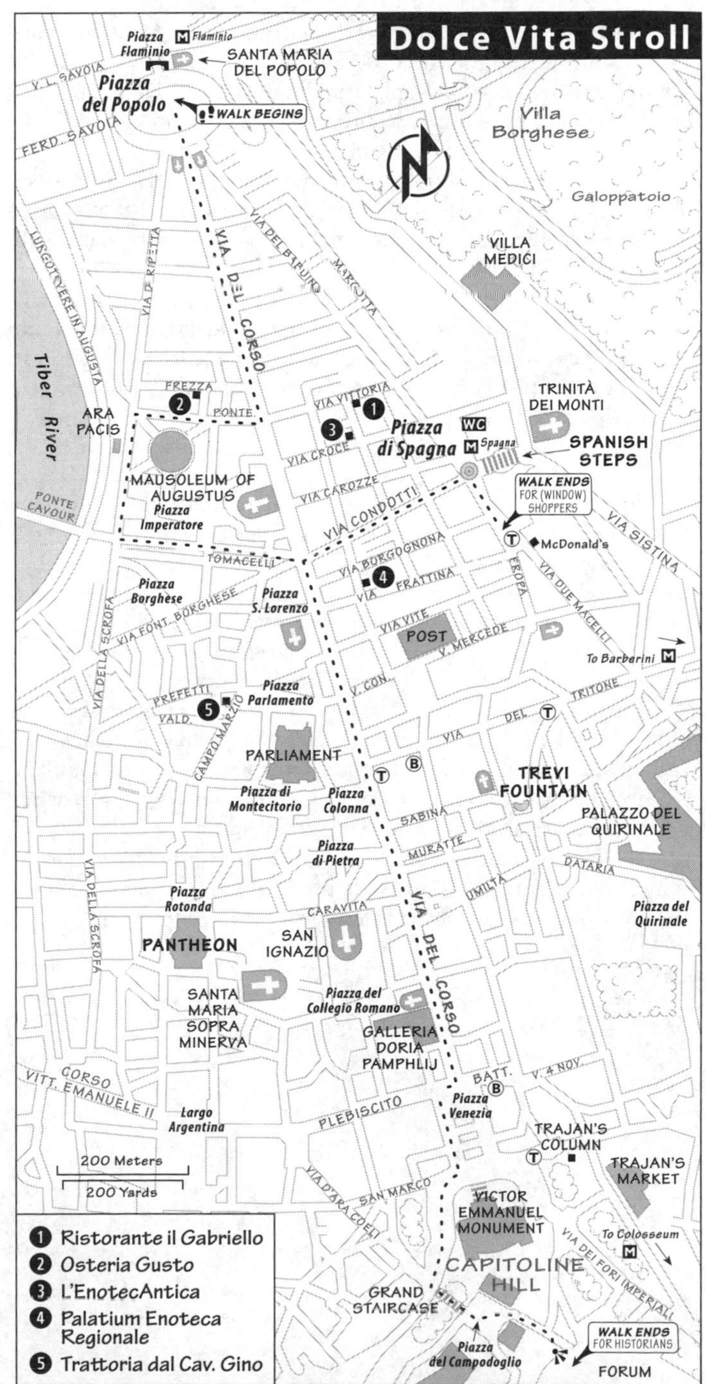
Dolce Vita Stroll
Piazza Flaminio
Flaminio
SANTA MARIA DEL POPOLO
Piazza del Popolo
WALK BEGINS
Villa Borghese
Galoppatoio
VILLA MEDICI
VIA DEL CORSO
VIA DEL BABUINO
MARGUTTA
LUNGOTEVERE IN AUGUSTA
VIA DI RIPETTA
Tiber River
FREZZA
PONTE
ARA PACIS
MAUSOLEUM OF AUGUSTUS
Piazza Imperatore
PONTE CAVOUR
VIA VITTORIA
Piazza di Spagna
WC
Spagna
TRINITÀ DEI MONTI
SPANISH STEPS
WALK ENDS FOR (WINDOW) SHOPPERS
VIA CROCE
VIA CAROZZE
VIA CONDOTTI
TOMACELLI
VIA BORGOGNONA
VIA FRATTINA
McDonald's
VIA SISTINA
VIA DUE MACELLI
EUROPA
Piazza Borghese
Piazza S. Lorenzo
VIA FONT. BORGHESE
VIA DELLA SCROFA
VIA VITE
POST
V. MERCEDE
To Barberini
PREFETTI
VALD
CAMPO MARZIO
Piazza Parlamento
V. CON.
VIA DEL TRITONE
PARLIAMENT
Piazza di Montecitorio
Piazza Colonna
TREVI FOUNTAIN
PALAZZO DEL QUIRINALE
SABINA
MURATTE
DATARIA
Piazza di Pietra
UMILTÀ
Piazza del Quirinale
Piazza Rotonda
CARAVITA
PANTHEON
SAN IGNAZIO
SANTA MARIA SOPRA MINERVA
Piazza del Collegio Romano
GALLERIA DORIA PAMPHLIJ
CORSO VITT. EMANUELE II
BATT.
V. 4 NOV.
Piazza Venezia
PLEBISCITO
Largo Argentina
TRAJAN'S COLUMN
TRAJAN'S MARKET
200 Meters
200 Yards
VIA D'ARA COELI
SAN MARCO
VICTOR EMMANUEL MONUMENT
To Colosseum
VIA DEI FORI IMPERIALI
CAPITOLINE HILL
GRAND STAIRCASE
Piazza del Campodoglio
WALK ENDS FOR HISTORIANS
FORUM
1 Ristorante il Gabriello
2 Osteria Gusto
3 L'EnotecAntica
4 Palatium Enoteca Regionale
5 Trattoria dal Cav. Gino

Santa Maria del Popolo is worth popping into (Mon-Sat until 18:30, Sun until 19:30, next to gate in old wall on north side of square). Inside, look for Raphael's Chigi Chapel (KEE-gee, second chapel on left) and two paintings by Caravaggio (in the Cerasi Chapel, left of altar; see listing on page 72).

From Piazza del Popolo, shop your way down **Via del Corso.** With the proliferation of shopping malls, many chain stores lining Via del Corso are losing customers and facing hard times. Still, this remains a fine place to feel the pulse of Rome at twilight.

Historians side-trip right down Via Pontefici past the fascist architecture to see the massive, rotting, round-brick **Mausoleum of Augustus,** topped with overgrown cypress trees. Beyond it, next to the river, is Augustus' **Ara Pacis,** enclosed within a protective glass-walled museum (see the self-guided tour on page 75). From the mausoleum, walk down Via Tomacelli to return to Via del Corso and the 21st century.

From Via del Corso, window-shoppers should take a left down **Via Condotti** to join the parade to the **Spanish Steps.** The streets that parallel Via Condotti to the south (Borgognona and Frattina) are more elegant and filled with high-end boutiques. A few streets to the north hides the narrow Via Margutta. This is where Gregory Peck's *Roman Holiday* character lived (at #51); today it has a leafy tranquility and is filled with pricey artisan shops.

Historians: Ignore Via Condotti and forget the Spanish Steps. Stay on Via del Corso, which has been straight since Roman times, and walk a half-mile down to the Victor Emmanuel Monument. Climb Michelangelo's stairway to his glorious (especially when floodlit) square atop Capitoline Hill. Stand on the balcony (just past the mayor's palace on the right), which overlooks the Forum. As the horizon reddens and cats prowl the unclaimed rubble of ancient Rome, it's one of the finest views in the city.

ROME CONNECTIONS

Rome is well-connected with the rest of the planet: by train, bus, plane, car, and cruise ship. This chapter addresses your arrival and departure from the city. It explains the various options and gives a rundown on their points of departure.

By Train

Rome's main train station is the centrally located **Termini** train station, which has connections to the airport. Rome's other major station is the **Tiburtina** bus/train station, which is starting to get some high-speed rail connections. Smaller stations include **Ostiense** (useful for going to South Rome and Testaccio, also may have some high-speed rail) and its neighbor, **Porta San Paolo** (with connections to Ostia Antica). If you're staying near the Vatican and taking a regional train, it saves time to get off at the **San Pietro** train station rather than at Termini. Cruise-ship passengers coming from Civitavecchia on a day trip usually use Ostiense or San Pietro.

Minimize your time in the station—the banks of Trenitalia's user-friendly automated ticket machines (marked *Biglietto Veloce/Fast Ticket*) are handy but cover Italian destinations only. They take euros and credit cards, display schedules, issue tickets, and even make reservations for railpass holders. Still, it can be quicker to get tickets and train info from travel agencies in town. For more on train travel in Italy—including your ticket-buying options—see page 470.

Termini Train Station

Termini, Rome's main train station, is a buffet of tourist services. While information desks are jammed with travelers, very handy

red info kiosks at the head of the tracks can answer your simple questions. The Customer Care window near the main entrance and ticket booths can also be helpful for schedule questions.

Along track 24, about 100 yards down, you'll find the **TI** (daily 8:00-21:00), a **post office** (Mon-Fri 8:30-14:00, Sat 8:30-13:00, closed Sun), a **hotel booking** office, and **car rental** desks. The **baggage storage** *(deposito bagagli)* is downstairs (€5/5 hours, then cheaper, daily 6:00-24:00).

The **"Leonardo Express" train** to Fiumicino Airport runs from track 24 (see "By Plane," later). A good self-service **cafeteria,** Ciao, is near the head of track 24, upstairs, with fine views (daily 11:00-22:30). For **sandwiches** to go, try VyTA in the atrium across from track 1.

Near track 1, you'll find a **pharmacy** (daily 7:30-22:00); along the same track is a **waiting room** and **Despar Express**, selling everything from groceries to electronics (daily 7:00-21:30). If you can't find what you're looking for there, try downstairs at **Conad** (daily 6:00-24:00) or one of the many other specialty shops.

Elsewhere in the station are **ATMs,** late-hours banks, and 24-hour thievery. In the station's main entrance lobby, **Borri Books** sells books in English, including popular fiction, Italian history and culture, and kids' books, plus maps upstairs (daily 7:00-23:00).

Termini is also a local transportation hub. The city's two Metro lines (A and B) intersect downstairs at Termini Metro station. Buses (including Rome's hop-on, hop-off bus tours—see page 41) leave across the square directly in front of the main station hall. The Metro and bus areas are under construction until sometime in 2013—look for signs directing you to the Metro platform or bus stop. Taxis queue in front; avoid con men hawking "express taxi" services in unmarked cars (only use cars marked with the word *taxi* and a phone number). To avoid the long taxi line, simply hike out past the buses to the main street and hail one.

From Termini, most of my recommended hotels are easily accessible by foot (for those near this train station) or by Metro (for those in the Colosseum and Vatican neighborhoods).

The station has some sleazy sharks with official-looking business cards; avoid anybody selling anything unless they're in a legitimate shop at the station.

Since nearly all of the most convenient connections for travelers depart from Termini, I've listed those below. But as a precaution, it's always smart to confirm whether your train departs from

Termini or Tiburtina.

From Rome's Termini Station by Train to: Venice (roughly hourly, 3.75 hours, overnight possible), **Florence** (at least hourly, 1.5 hours, some stop at Orvieto en route), **Siena** (1-2/hour, 1 change, 3-4 hours), **Orvieto** (hourly, 1.25 hours), **Assisi** (hourly, 2-3.5 hours, 5 direct, most others change in Foligno), **Pisa** (hourly, 3-4 hours, many change in Florence), **La Spezia** (8/day direct, more with transfers in Pisa, 3-4.5 hours), **Milan** (hourly, 3-8 hours, overnight possible), **Milan's Malpensa Airport** (1 direct express/ day, 4.5 hours), **Naples** (at least hourly, 1.25 hours on Frecciarossa trains, otherwise 2 hours), **Civitavecchia** cruise-ship port (2-3/ hour, 1-1.5 hours), **Brindisi** (6/day, 3 direct, 6-9 hours, overnight possible), **Amsterdam** (6/day, 20 hours), **Interlaken** (5/day, 6.5-8 hours), **Frankfurt** (6/day, 11-12 hours), **Munich** (5/day, 10-11.5 hours, 1 direct night train, 11.5 hours), **Nice** (7/day, 8.75-10.5 hours,), **Paris** (4/day, 10.75-12.75 hours; 1 night train, 14 hours, transfer in Milan, important to reserve ahead at www.thello.com), **Vienna** (2/day, 11.75 hours, 1 direct night train, 12 hours).

Tiburtina Train and Bus Station

Tiburtina, Rome's second-largest train station, is located in the city's northeast corner. In general, slower trains (from Milan, Bolzano, Bologna, Udine, and Reggio di Calabria) and some night trains (from Munich, Milan, Venice, Innsbruck, and Udine) use Tiburtina, as does the night bus to Fiumicino Airport. Direct night trains from Paris and Vienna use Termini train station instead.

Tiburtina has been newly redeveloped for high-speed rail, including some Eurostar Italia trains and the new Italo service (run by a private operator). Some Italo trains may also stop at Ostiense Station. A separate "Casa Italo" area in each station has dedicated service counters, red ticket machines, and waiting areas. You can also book Italo tickets by phone (tel. 06-0708) or online (www.italotreno.it). Because this is a new company, it's hard to predict the level of service or even its long-term survival; for more information see page 472.

Tiburtina is also known as a hub for bus service to destinations all across Italy. Buses depart from the piazza in front of the station. Ticket offices are located in the piazza and around the corner on Circonvallazione Nomentana (just beyond the elevated freeway).

The Tiburtina Station is on Metro line B, with easy connections to Termini (a straight shot, four stops away) and the entire Metro system. Or take bus #492 from Tiburtina to various city-center stops (such as Piazza Barberini, Piazza Venezia, and Piazza Cavour) and the Vatican neighborhood.

From Rome's Tiburtina Station by Train to: Florence (8/day, 1.5 hours), **Milan** (8/day, 3.5 hours), **Naples** (5/day, 1.25 hours).

By Bus

Long-distance buses (such as from Siena and Assisi) arrive at Rome's **Tiburtina Station** (described above).

From Rome by Bus to: Assisi (2/day, 3 hours—the train makes much more sense), **Siena** (8/day, 3 hours), **Sorrento** (1-2/day, 4 hours; this is a cheap and easy way to go straight to Sorrento).

By Plane

Rome's two airports—**Fiumicino** (a.k.a. Leonardo da Vinci, airport code: FCO) and the small **Ciampino** (airport code: CIA)—share the same website (www.adr.it).

Fiumicino Airport

Rome's major airport has a TI (in Terminal 3, daily 9:00-18:30), ATMs, banks, luggage storage, shops, and bars. The Rome Walks website (www.romewalks.com) has a useful video on options for getting into the city from the airport.

The slick, direct **"Leonardo Express" train** connects the airport and Rome's central Termini train station in 30 minutes for €14. Trains run twice hourly in both directions from roughly 6:00 to 23:00 (leaving the airport at :07 and :37). From the airport's arrival gate, follow signs to the train car icon or *Stazione/Railway Station*. Buy your ticket from a machine, the Biglietteria office, or a newsstand at the platform; then validate it in a yellow machine near the track. Make sure the train you board is going to the central "Roma Termini" station, not "Roma Orte" or others.

Going from Termini train station to the airport, trains depart at about :22 and :52 past the hour, from track 24. Check the departure boards for "Fiumicino Aeroporto"—the local name for the airport—and confirm with an official or a local on the platform that the train is indeed going to the airport (€14, buy ticket from any tobacco shop or a newsstand in the station, or at the self-service machines, Termini-Fiumicino trains run 5:52-22:52). Read your ticket: If it requires validation, stamp it in the yellow machine near the platform before boarding. From the train station at the airport, you can access most of the terminals. American airlines flying direct to the US depart from Terminal 5, which is a separate building not connected to the rest of the terminals. If you arrive by train, catch the T5 shuttle bus *(navetta)* on the sidewalk in front of Terminal 3—it's too far to walk with luggage.

Allow lots of time going in either direction; there's a fair amount of transportation involved, including moving walkways, escalators, and walking (e.g., getting from your hotel to Termini, from Termini to the train platform, the ride to the airport, getting from the airport train station to check-in, etc.). Flying to the US involves an extra level of security—plan on getting to the airport even earlier than normal (I like to arrive 2.5 hours ahead of my flight).

The **Terravision Express bus** connects Fiumicino and Termini train station, departing every 40 minutes (€6 one-way, €11 round-trip, leaves the airport from Terminal 3, leaves Termini Station from Via Marsala—just outside the exit closest to track 1; one hour, www.terravision.eu). The **SIT Bus Shuttle** also connects Fiumicino and Termini (€8 one-way, €15 round-trip, similar schedule and info to Terravision, tel. 06-592-3507, www.sitbusshuttle.com). While cheaper than the train, the buses take twice as long and can potentially fill up (allow plenty of extra time).

Shuttle van services run to and from the airport and can be economical for one or two people. It's cheaper from the airport to downtown, as several companies compete for this route; by surveying the latest deals, you should be able to snare a ride into town for around €10. To get from your hotel to the airport, consider Rome Airport Shuttle (€25/1 person, extra people-€6 each, by reservation only, tel. 06-4201-4507 or 06-4201-3469, www.airportshuttle.it).

A **taxi** between Fiumicino and downtown Rome takes 45 minutes in normal traffic (for tips on taxis, see page 37). If you're catching a taxi at the airport, be sure to wait at the taxi stand. Avoid unmarked, unmetered taxis; these guys will try to tempt you away from the taxi-stand lineup by offering an immediate (rip-off) ride. Rome's and Fiumicino's official taxis have a fixed rate to and from the airport (€48 for up to four people with bags).

Cabbies not based in Rome or Fiumicino are allowed to charge €70 for the ride. That sign is posted next to the €48-fare sign—confusing many tourists and allowing dishonest cabbies to overcharge. It's best to use a Rome city cab, with the "SPQR" shield on the door. They can only charge €48 for the ride to anywhere in the historic center (within the old city walls, where most of my recommended hotels are located).

If your cab driver tries to charge you more than €48 from the airport into town, say, *"Quarant'otto euro—è la legge"* (kwah-RAHNT-OH-toe AY-oo-roh—ay lah LEJ-jay; which means, "Forty-eight euros—it's the law"), and they should back off.

To get from the airport into town cheaply by taxi, try teaming up with any tourist also just arriving (most are heading for hotels near yours in the center). When you're departing Rome, your hotel can arrange a taxi to the airport at any hour.

ROME CONNECTIONS

For **airport information,** call 06-65951. To inquire about flights, call 06-6595-3640.

Ciampino Airport

Rome's smaller airport (tel. 06-6595-9515) handles charter flights and some budget airlines (including all Ryanair and some easyJet flights).

To get to downtown Rome from the airport, you can take the Cotral bus, which leaves every 40 minutes (€5, 20-minute ride, toll-free tel. 800-174-471, www.cotralspa.it), to the Anagnina Metro stop, where you can connect by Metro to the stop nearest your hotel. Rome Airport Shuttle also offers service to and from Ciampino (€25/1 person, listed earlier). The Terravision Express Shuttle connects Ciampino and Termini train station, leaving every 20 minutes (€4 one-way, €8 round-trip, www.terravision.eu). The SIT Bus Shuttle also connects Termini to Ciampino (€4, about 2/hour, 45 minutes, runs 7:45-23:15 Ciampino to Termini, 4:30-21:30 Termini to Ciampino, pickup on Via Marsala just outside the train exit closest to track 1, tel. 06-592-3507, www.sitbusshuttle.it). A taxi should cost €30 to downtown (within the old city walls, including most of my recommended hotels).

By Car

Driving and Parking in Rome

The Grande Raccordo Anulare circles greater Rome. This ring road has spokes that lead you into the center. Entering from the north, leave the autostrada at the Settebagni exit. Following the ancient Via Salaria (and the black-and-white *Centro* signs), work your way doggedly into the Roman thick of things. This will take you along the Villa Borghese Gardens and dump you right on Via Veneto in downtown Rome. Avoid rush hour and drive defensively: Roman cars stay in their lanes like rocks in an avalanche.

Parking in Rome is dangerous. Park near a police station or get advice at your hotel. The Villa Borghese underground garage is handy (Metro: Spagna). Garages charge about €24 per day.

Consider this: Your car is a worthless headache in Rome. Avoid a pile of stress and save money by parking at the huge, easy, and relatively safe lot behind the train station in the hill town of Orvieto (follow *P* signs from autostrada) and catching the train to Rome (hourly, 1-1.5 hours).

If you absolutely must drive and park a car in Rome, try to avoid commuter traffic by arriving Friday evening, or anytime during the weekend, and by leaving town during the weekend. Park your car at Tiburtina Station (€1/hour, www.atac.roma.it) and take a 10-minute ride on the Metro line B into the center.

For more information on car rental and driving in Italy, see page 481.

By Cruise Ship

Hundreds of cruise ships—including Carnival, Royal Caribbean, Princess, and Celebrity lines—dock each year at the port of **Civitavecchia,** about 45 miles northwest of Rome. If your trip includes cruising beyond Rome, consider my new guidebook, *Rick Steves' Mediterranean Cruise Ports*. Port facilities include a TI (tel 0766-1892-667), ATMs, Internet access, bag storage, and cafés.

To get from your ship to Civitavecchia's train station, take the free shuttle bus to the port entrance (some shuttles may take you all the way to the station—ask). From the shuttle-bus stop, walk through the security checkpoint at the port gate, and then walk about 10 minutes straight ahead up the main road with the sea on your right-hand side. After about three blocks, at Hotel de La Ville, bear left and uphill through a long parking lot to the pale-orange train station (marked *Civitavecchia*); if you get turned around, look for signs to *Stazione FF. SS.*

Taxis also wait at the port gate, attempting to extort €15 for the very short ride to the train station (tel. 076-626-121). A local bus to the train station only saves you a few minutes of walking; take one only if you're carrying heavy bags or have limited mobility. **Buses** #B, #C, and #D go from just above the port gate on Largo Plebiscito (Viale Garibaldi stop) one stop to the train station (Stazione FF. SS. stop; €1, 3-4/hour, 5 minutes, buy ticket at a tobacco shop before you board).

Getting Between Civitavecchia and Downtown Rome

The traffic between Civitavecchia and Rome is terrible, making trains faster and more economical than a taxi (which can run €110-150 one-way). Recommended driver Ezio of Autoservizi Monti Concezio takes cruise travelers to Rome in a private car (€130/2 people, €20 for each additional person) and offers full-day tours of the city (€380/2 people, €30 for each additional person; see "Car and Minibus Tours" on page 42). Beware of unlicensed taxis offering a huge price break; local police sometimes follow these "gypsy" cabs in a scam that imposes hefty fines on both the driver and the passengers (the driver later gets a kickback from the cop).

Keep in mind that it takes approximately 1.5 hours each way to get between your ship and downtown Rome—so you'll need to mentally subtract at least three hours from the time you have in port.

ROME CONNECTIONS

Frequent trains (2-3/hour) connect Civitavecchia with several stations in Rome. Depending on your sightseeing plans, you'll likely be best off heading either to **Ostiense Station** (with a handy Metro station, just two stops from the Colosseum) or **San Pietro Station** (15 minute walk or a couple stops on bus #64 to get to St. Peter's Basilica). **Termini Station,** the main hub for the city's transit and for shuttle trains to the airport, overshoots the key city-center sights a bit.

Regional trains (marked *REG*) head into Rome roughly twice an hour, stopping at San Pietro and Ostiense stations on their way to Termini (40-55 minutes to San Pietro, 55-70 minutes to Ostiense, 80 minutes to Termini). The **Intercity train** (marked *IC*) is somewhat faster (50 minutes to Ostiense, 60 minutes to Termini), but doesn't stop at San Pietro Station, and isn't covered by the good-value BIRG ticket (described next). When there are enough ships in port to justify it, there's also a special **express "Seatrain"** to San Pietro Station, offering one daily round-trip designed for cruise travelers.

If you're taking a regional train, save money by getting the wonderful BIRG ticket: a €12 day pass covering second-class, round-trip train travel between Civitavecchia and Rome as well as unlimited travel on Rome's buses, Metro, and trams—a great convenience (not valid on fast Intercity trains or the express Seatrain). Otherwise, expect to pay about €4.50 each way for regional trains or €9.50 on the Intercity. All train tickets must be validated in the yellow box before getting on the train.

The Civitavecchia train station has five main platforms (*binario,* or *bin*; numbered 1 through 5), connected by an underground tunnel. There are also two "short" *(tronco)* platforms, 1T and 2T, at the far-right end of the station as you face the tracks; these are *not* the same as tracks 1 and 2. Be sure you're waiting at the correct platform. For a useful video on taking the train from the port into the city, check out the Rome Walks website (www.romewalks.com).

Getting Between Civitavecchia and Fiumicino Airport

You'll need to take two **trains** to link Civitavecchia and Fiumicino Airport: one between Civitavecchia and Rome's Termini train station, and another between Termini and the airport. See "By Plane," earlier.

Shuttle van services run between the port and Rome's Fiumicino Airport. Try **Rome Airport Shuttle** (€90/1-2 people, €15 each additional person up to 8, share with others and save, much more for pickup between 21:00 and 7:00, tel. 06-4201-4507 or 06-4201-3469, www.airportshuttle.it). A **taxi** costs about €120 one-way between Civitavecchia and Fiumicino Airport.

Rome Tours from Civitavecchia

A tiny company called **Can't Be Missed** offers Rome tours from the port (€59 plus €19 for Vatican Museum admission, small groups, mobile 329-129-8182, www.cantbemissedtours.com, info@cantbemissedtours.com). Your guide first meets you at the Civitavecchia train station, leads you on a walk through Rome's ancient city center, gives you a tour of the Vatican Museum, and then takes you to St. Peter's Basilica before putting you on a train back to the port.

Many of Civitavecchia's private limousine companies and the Rome Airport Shuttle also offer Rome tours. Look for a tour that is a minimum eight hours in length: six hours for sightseeing and two-plus hours of travel time. On shorter tours you'll see most of Rome from the bus window. Plan to spend about €300 for three or four people.

DAY TRIPS FROM ROME

There's so much to see and do in Rome that you could easily fill a vacation without ever leaving the city limits. But here are several nearby sights that might match your particular interest.

Ostia Antica is similar to Pompeii, but without the crowds. This excavated ancient Roman city is located an easy 45 minutes by Metro and train from Rome.

Tivoli is less accessible (consider seeing it via private tour), but you're rewarded with the ruins of Hadrian's Villa and with the

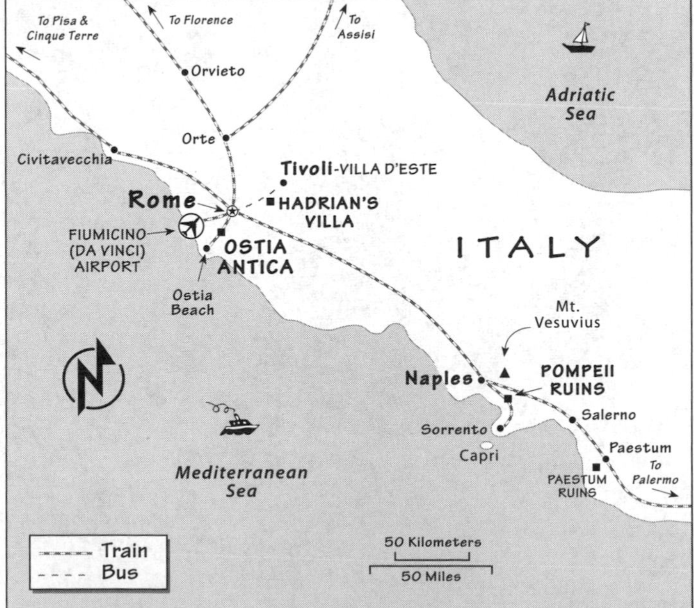

lush gardens and restored fountains of a Renaissance mansion, the Villa d'Este.

Thanks to Italy's excellent train system, it's 1.25 hours to **Naples** on a direct high-speed train (or 2 hours on cheaper trains), landing you right in the middle of town. Visit Roman statues and mosaics at the wonderful Archaeological Museum, stroll colorful Spaccanapoli street, and have lunch in the city where pizza was born, sampling the exotic chaos of southern Italy.

History hounds can venture an hour farther south of Naples to see the ultimate in ruined Roman cities—**Pompeii**—frozen in time by the eruption of Mt. Vesuvius.

Arrive back in Rome for a late dinner at a sidewalk café to recount your busy day over a glass of wine.

Italy's fast trains put other cities within day-trip range, including **Orvieto** (1.25 hours by train), **Assisi** (2-3.5 hours), and **Florence** (1.5 hours). For in-depth information on Orvieto and Assisi, see *Rick Steves' Italy,* and for Florence, see *Rick Steves' Florence & Tuscany.*

OSTIA ANTICA DAY TRIP

For an exciting day trip, pop down to the Roman port of Ostia, which is similar to Pompeii but a lot closer and, in some ways, more interesting. Because Ostia was a working port town, it shows a more complete and gritty look at Roman life than wealthier Pompeii. Wandering around today, you'll see warehouses, apartment flats, mansions, shopping arcades, and baths that served a once-thriving port of 60,000 people.

Orientation

Cost: €8.50 for the site and museum.

Hours: April-Oct Tue-Sun 8:30-19:00, Nov-Feb Tue-Sun 8:30-17:00, March Tue-Sun 8:30-18:00, closed Mon year-round, last entry one hour before closing. The museum closes from 13:30 to 14:30 for lunch.

Getting There: Getting to Ostia Antica from downtown Rome is a snap—it's a 45-minute combination Metro/train ride. (Since the train is part of the Metro system, it only costs one Metro ticket each way—€3 total round-trip.)

From Rome, take Metro line B to the Piramide stop, which is also the Roma Porta San Paolo train station. The train tracks are just a few steps from the Metro tracks: Follow signs to *Lido*—go up the escalator, turn left, and go down the steps into the Roma-Lido station. All trains depart in the direction of Lido, leave every 15 minutes, and stop at Ostia Antica along the way. The lighted schedule reads something like, *"Prossima partenza alle ore 13.25, bin 3,"* meaning, "Next departure at 13:25 from track 3." Look for the next train, hop on, ride for about 30 minutes (no need to stamp your Metro ticket again, but keep it handy in case they decide to check), and get off at the Ostia Antica stop.

Leaving the train station in Ostia Antica, cross the road via the blue skybridge and walk straight down Via della Stazione di Ostia Antica, continuing straight until you reach the parking lot. The entrance is to your left. (If you don't have a ticket to get back, purchase one at the ticket window at the station, or from the nearby snack bar.)

Tip: If you're using the Metro and want to maximize sightseeing efficiency on your Ostia day trip, consider visiting the sights in south Rome on your return. The Piramide Metro stop—where you'll change trains—really *is* next to a pyramid, and is on the edge of the Testaccio neighborhood, which has several interesting sights. Other south Rome sights include St. Paul's Outside the Walls, E.U.R., and the Montemartini Museum (for more on all of these, see page 89).

Information: A map of the site with suggested itineraries is available for €2 from the ticket office. Tel. 06-5635-0215. Helpful websites include www.ostia-antica.org and http://archeoroma.beniculturali.it/en.

Audio Tour: Although you'll see little audioguide markers throughout the site, there are no audioguides for rent. But you can download this chapter as a free Rick Steves audio tour (see page 27).

Length of This Tour: Allow two hours inside the site. Add in your round-trip train rides, and it's at least a four-hour excursion from Rome.

Cuisine Art: A good cafeteria—with the site's only WC—is next to Ostia's museum.

History

Located at (and named for) the mouth *(ostium)* of the Tiber, Ostia was founded in the fourth century B.C. Gobbled up early by Rome, its main industry was the salt—precious preserver of meat in ancient times—gleaned from nearby salt flats. Often called Rome's first colony, Ostia served as a naval base, protecting Rome from any invasion by river. By 150 B.C., when Rome controlled the Mediterranean, Ostia's importance became commercial rather than military. Rome eventually outgrew the port of Ostia, and a vast new port was dug nearby (where Rome's airport now stands). But Ostia remained a key administrative and warehousing center, busy with the big business of keeping more than a million Romans fed and in sandals.

Eventually things really soured for Ostia. Rome fell. The river changed course. The port was abandoned, silted up, became a malaria-infested swamp, and was eventually forgotten. The mud

that buried Ostia actually protected it from the ravages of time—and stone-scavenging medieval peasants.

The Tour Begins

Overview

Consider your visit a three-part affair:

1. Follow this tour, which leads you straight down Decumanus Maximus (the town's main drag), with a couple of slight detours, finishing at the forum (the main square).

2. Pop into the museum, and consider getting a bite to eat at the cafeteria.

3. Explore the back lanes—going on a visual scavenger hunt—as you wander your way back to the entry point.

• *Find the map (30 yards inside the gate, on the right) for an orientation. The pale green shows the ancient coast and course of the river—which eventually abandoned its city. Notice how the core of Ostia is a rectangular Roman military camp, with two major roads crossing at the forum. One of four city gates lies ahead, and on your left is the...*

❶ Necropolis

Ancient Romans buried their dead outside the city walls. Ostia was a famously pagan town, slow to become Christian. To a pagan, the closest thing to an afterlife was to be remembered. If their families could afford it, they'd have the tomb on the roadside with a thumbnail bio carved into the stone that all could read as they came and went (for example, "My name was Caius. I was a baker."). This area was called a necropolis (city of the dead); Christians preferred the term cemetery (from the Greek for resting place). Detour to find family sepulchers (marked by arches)—private open-air rooms lined with niches for ash-filled urns. Until the first century A.D., cremation was common. In the second and third centuries A.D., the Romans here buried their dead in marble and terra-cotta sarcophagi in tombs.

• *Ahead (where the road narrows) you enter the ancient city of Ostia through the scant remains of the gate called...*

❷ Porta Romana

Just as Rome's Porta San Paolo faced Ostia, Ostia's Porta Romana faced Rome. Inside the gate (which was locked at night) you'd find a place to leave your animal (on the left) and a warehouse (on the right). To the left (under the big tree), you can see on the gate the bits of the Latin inscription that proclaimed to all who entered: "The Senate and the people of the colony of Ostia constructed the walls." The "colony" reference is a reminder that Ostia was the first bit of the Roman Empire. The big basin, once fed by a fountain, was where animals could be watered. Information panels like the one here are generally helpful only for the artist's reconstruction of the sight. The verbiage is what locals refer to as *aria fritta* (fried air—greasy and heavy but containing nothing of value).

From the gate, Ostia's main street (named Decumanus Maximus) leads straight to the forum, where this walk ends. Note that this road was elevated above some buildings' foundations. Over the centuries, Ostia's ground level rose. You can actually identify buildings from the republic (centuries before Christ) and the empire (centuries after Christ) by their level. Anything you walk down into is from the earlier period.

• *Just inside the gate and to the right are the...*

❸ Republican Warehouses (Magazzini Repubblicani)

The first century B.C. was busy with activities relating to the river port. Walking along the main street, you pass vast warehouses on the right. The goods of the port, such as grain from Sicily, Egypt, and all of North Africa, were processed and stored in warehouses here (which had elevated floors to keep things dry) before being consumed by Rome.

Ahead, a series of stubby brick columns are the remains of a roofed portico that provided a shaded walkway into town. Notice the bricks—generally, rough bricks are original, while smooth bricks are part of the reconstruction. Ostia has been picked clean since ancient times. The ports' treasures ended up gracing buildings as far away as Constantinople.

• *Continue straight ahead about 100 yards. The little well in the road is medieval—a remnant from Middle Age squatters who found shelter in these ruins. From here, you'll see a viewpoint (with railings, above on the right). Climb up for a view of the...*

❹ Baths of Neptune (Terme di Nettuno)

Examine the fine mosaic depicting Neptune riding four horses through the sea. Apart from the cupid riding the dolphin, the sea looks frightening—which it was. The large square to the left of the mosaic would have been busy with people wrestling, stretching, doing jumping jacks, and getting rubdowns. The niches that ring the square housed small businesses. The row of umbrella pines in the distance marks the original channel of the river before it changed course, abandoning the town.

• *Climb back down to the main drag, and continue to the right until you reach the theater on your right. Enter the theater through its main central gate.*

❺ Theater (Teatro)

The scant remains of the stucco decor under the entry arch hint at the elegance of this place 2,000 years ago. At the end of the tunnel, men would bid farewell to their women (before the women went to sit in the higher seats—typical of the gender division in public Rome).

Before you is a typically Roman complex mixing religion, business, and entertainment: a grand theater facing a temple surrounded by a commercial square. Up to 4,000 residents could gather in this theater. Plays were rowdy daytime events—like going to a day game at the ballpark—with lots of audience participation. And heaven help a bad actor. The three rows of marble steps near the orchestra were reserved for the chairs of big shots. In its day, a wall rose behind the stage, enclosing the theater. Even today, this place—one of the oldest brick theaters anywhere—is used for concerts. Climb to the top of the theater for a fine view.

• *From the theater, continue (farther away from the main street) behind the stage into the big square. Head to the right and walk counterclockwise around the square, ending up back at the theater. Most of the notable mosaics line the right side of the square.*

❻ Square of the Guilds (Piazzale delle Corporazioni)

This grand square evolved from a simple place where businessmen would stroll and powwow together to a monumental square lined with more than 60 offices of ship owners and traders. This was the bustling center of Rome's import-export industry. Along the sidewalk, second-century A.D. mosaics advertise the services offered by the various shops. Walking counterclockwise, circle the square to "read" the mosaics that advertised in Latin and in pictograms for illiterate or non-Latin-reading sailors. The most common symbol—the lighthouse—was the sign of the port of Ostia. Grain containers are reminders that grain was the major import of Ostia. The elephant marking the office of the Sabratans (a place in present-day Libya) symbolized the sale of ivory or perhaps of exotic animals (great for parties and private spectacles and

Colosseum events). The fine mosaic in the corner shows the innovative Roman ships. When ship technology enabled boats to tack and sail against the wind, commerce moved more readily, making the Mediterranean a thriving Roman free-trade zone.

Statues of notable local guild members and business leaders decorated the courtyard. The temple in the center was likely related to Ceres, the goddess of harvest and abundance (prosperity from good business).

At the end of the square, as you leave, notice the small white altar on the right. This would have been used to sacrifice animals—such as the rams carved into the corners—to ask for favor from the gods. The entrails would be read to divine the future and to determine whether the gods were for or against a particular business venture. This altar is a copy; the original is in Rome. (Consider the burden on Italy of protecting and preserving what is actually the cultural heritage of all of Europe against illegal digging, exportation, vandalism, weather, and pollution. There's a special branch of the Carabinieri dedicated to art theft.)

• *Continue down the main street. About two blocks down (look for Tempio Repubblicano on the corner to the right), Via dei Molini marks the wall of the original military* castrum *(rectangular camp). Before continuing straight into that oldest part of Ostia, turn right, down Via dei Molini. Walk about a block and a half until you see Molino del Silvano on the left. (Don't take the left onto Via Casa di Diana—we'll get to that next.)*

❼ Mill (Molino)

This mill and bakery building *(panificio)* dates from A.D. 120. The lava millstones in front of you were used to grind grain. Study the workings: A bowl-like lower structure carefully cupped a moving upper section. Grain would be sprinkled in from a sack hanging from the ceiling. Mules or workers would power the grinding by walking in circles, pushing inserted wood poles. Powdery flour (with not much grit) would eventually tumble out of the bottom of the mill, ready to be made into bread.

• *Now, backtrack half a block down Via dei Molini in the direction of the main street. At the big tree, take the first right onto...*

❽ Via Casa di Diana

There are two places of interest along this street: a tavern (just over halfway down on the left) and a typical apartment building with

stairs leading to a commanding rooftop view (across the street from the tavern, on the right).

At the **Insula of the Thermopolium,** step past the grooved threshold—which once held a sliding wooden door—and belly up to the tavern's bar. You'll see display shelves with food and drinks for sale, a small sink, and a cute fresco advertising food, drink, and music. Too smoky and noisy? Step out back and enjoy the quiet courtyard with the fountain.

The **Insula of the Paintings** is across the street. Climb all the way to the open rooftop for a good view and a chance to imagine life as an apartment dweller in ancient Rome. An *insula* was a multistoried tenement complex where the lower middle-class lived. In ancient times, the lower classes lived in miserable, cramped apartment buildings up to 10 floors high (the average was 5 floors). To reach their rooms on the higher floors, people climbed treehouse-type stairs. Plumbing didn't exist. It was stinky. "Windows" covered with just shutters or cloth curtains dipped in grease did little to cut the street din.

Buildings were made cheaply of wood, with weak foundations, so many burned or collapsed. The apartments had no heat and no kitchen, so residents cooked or purchased food elsewhere. They tossed garbage out the windows. Because chariot and cart traffic was allowed only after dark, there was lots of night noise.

The wealthier classes, on the other hand, lived in sprawling and luxurious homes. These were generally built on one floor, with a series of rooms facing a central open courtyard. Decorative pools collected rainwater. Statues, mosaics, and frescoes were everywhere. Rome's wealthy were as comfortable as the poor were wretched.

From this rooftop perch, find the museum (the modern building). Behind the museum, see modern pleasure boats where today's Tiber leaves Ostia. The temporary arched roofing protects rooms warehousing lots of ancient bits and pieces (worth a look).

• *Now, walk (from street level, of course) to the end of the street, toward the high brick wall and then left into Ostia's...*

⑨ Forum

Whenever possible, Rome imposed a grid road plan on its conquered cities. After Rome conquered Ostia in about 400 B.C., it built a military camp, or *castrum*—a rectangular fort with east, west, north, and south gates and two main roads converging on the forum. Throughout the empire, Romans found comfort in this familiar city plan. While people found it no fun to be conquered, the empire brought order and stability to their lives through laws and the creation of grid-planned cities and grand squares such as this one.

Ostia's main square became a monumental forum in the imperial period. And dominating this square, as in most Roman towns, was the **grand temple** (from A.D. 120). The marble veneer was scavenged in the Middle Ages, leaving only the core brickwork. Note the reinforcement arches in the brick. The temple, called the Capitolium (after the original atop Capitoline Hill in Rome), was dedicated to the pagan trinity of Jupiter, Juno, and Minerva. A forum dominated by a Capitolium temple was a standard feature of colonies throughout the empire. The purpose: to transport the Roman cult of Jupiter, Juno, and Minerva to the newly conquered population.

On the opposite side of the square, distinguished by its sawed-off column, is the Temple of Roma and Augustus. Its position is powerfully symbolic. The power of the emperor stands equal, facing the power of the Capitolium Triad.

The basilica also faces the forum square. Dating from about A.D. 100, this was where legal activities and commercial business took place. (With your back to the Capitolium temple, it's to your right and consists of little more than the footprint of the building.) Its central nave and two side aisles lead to the "high altar" where the judge sat.

Behind the Capitolium temple—and a little to the right—the pink modern building houses the fine little Ostia Museum. Behind that is a shop and a modern cafeteria. From the forum, the Decumanus Maximus continues into a vast urban expanse, great for simply wandering (see "Archaeological Scavenger Hunt" at the end of this chapter).

• *But first, make one more stop. Walk to the front left corner of the Temple of Roma and Augustus. As you're facing it, look left for a street marked by a grand arch. This leads to Ostia's best and largest baths (entrance on right).*

⑩ Forum Baths (Terme del Foro)

As you wander around this huge complex, try to imagine it peopled, steaming, and busy. Government-subsidized baths were a popular social and business meeting place in any Roman city. Roman engineers were experts at radiant heat. A huge furnace heated both the water and air that flowed through pipes under the floors and in the walls (you can see the hollow bricks in the walls). Notice the fine marble steps—great for lounging—that led into the pools. Bathers used olive oil rather than soap to wash, so the water needed to be periodically skimmed by servants. Like a high-end spa, there was a *laconicum* (sweating room), two *tepidaria* (where Romans were rubbed down by masseuses), and the once-steamy *caldarium* with three pools.

From the baths (across the street and a bit to the right from the entry), find the 20-hole latrine. You can still see the pivot hole in the floor that once supported its revolving door. The cutout below each seat was to accommodate the washable sponge on a stick, which was used rather than toilet paper. Rushing water below each seat (brought in by aqueduct) did the flushing. So much for privacy—even today, there's no word in Italian for it.

⓫ Ostia Museum

This small museum offers a delightful look at some of Ostia's finest statuary. Without worrying too much about exactly what's what, just wander and imagine these fine figures—tangled wrestlers, kissing cupids, playful gods—adorning the courtyards of wealthy Ostian families. Most of the statues are second- and third-century A.D. Roman pieces inspired by rare and famous Greek originals. The portrait busts are of real people—the kind you'd sit next to in the baths (or on the toilets).

Roman sculptors excelled at realistic busts. Roman religion revered the man of the house (and his father and grandfather). Statues of daddy and grandpa were common in the corner of any proper house. And with the emperor considered a god, you'd find his bust in classrooms, at the post office, and so on. The sarcophagi (marble coffins) generally show mythological scenes.

Perhaps the most interesting room (to the left as you enter, just before the steps) features statuary from religions of foreign lands. Being a port town, Ostia accommodated people (and their worship needs) from all over the known world. The large statue of a man sacrificing a bull is a Mithraic altarpiece (see page 288).

The **cafeteria, WC,** and **shop** are in a modern building just behind the museum.

Archaeological Scavenger Hunt

As you return to the entry gate, get off the main drag and explore Ostia's back streets. Wandering beyond the forum and then taking the back lanes as you return to the entry, see if you can find:

- Tarp- and sand-protected mosaic flooring.
- White cornerstones put into buildings to fend off wild carts and reflect corners in the dark.
- Fast-food fish joint (on Decumanus Maximus, just beyond the forum)
- Hidden bits of fresco (clue: under hot tin roofs).
- Republican buildings and buildings dating from the empire.
- Stucco roughed up for fresco work (before applying the wet plaster of a fresco, the surface needs to be systematically gouged so the plaster can grip the wall).
- Millstones for grinding grain (Ostia's big industry).
- Floor patterns made colorful with inlaid marble.
- A *domus*—a single-family dwelling facing a fancy, central open-air courtyard.

TIVOLI DAY TRIP

At the edge of the Sabine Hills, 18 miles east of Rome, sits the medieval hill town of Tivoli, a popular retreat since ancient times. Today, it's famous for two very different villas: Hadrian's Villa, a Versailles-like seat of government from which the emperor ruled (outside but still near the capital), and the restored Villa d'Este, the lush and watery 16th-century residence of a cardinal in exile.

The town of Tivoli, with Villa d'Este in its center, is about 2.5 miles from Hadrian's Villa ("Villa Adriana" in Italian). Pick up a map and bus schedule at the TI on Largo Garibaldi, near the bus stop (Tue-Sun 9:30-17:30, closed Mon, tel. 0774-313-536).

Note that Hadrian's Villa is open daily, and Villa d'Este is closed on Monday.

Several Rome tour companies—including Context Rome, Rome Walks, and Through Eternity—offer private tours of the villas (see their respective websites for specifics; tour companies listed on page 41).

Getting to Tivoli

Reaching the town of Tivoli and Villa d'Este is easy. Getting to Hadrian's Villa is more of a challenge—you'll go into Tivoli, then backtrack on another bus—but many find it well worth the trouble (see map on page 395). To return to Rome from Tivoli, simply reverse the connections—*no problema*. If visiting both villas, see Villa d'Este first, then head straight back to Rome after Hadrian's Villa.

From Rome, take a Metro/bus combination. Ride Metro line B to Ponte Mammolo, and then catch the local blue Cotral bus to Tivoli (€2, 3/hour, 45 minutes, at Ponte Mammolo buy bus tickets at the bar or newsstand downstairs, buses leave upstairs—and can be crowded, be prepared to stand, direction: Tivoli).

For **Villa d'Este,** get off in downtown Tivoli, near the central square and the big park with the playground (start paying attention as the bus winds up the hill; ask the driver, "Villa d'Este?"). The TI kiosk is just uphill to the right; the entrance is to the left, past the modern arch. Follow the signs (for about a block) that lead to the villa.

To get to **Hadrian's Villa** from downtown Tivoli, catch orange "CAT" city bus #4 or #4X. Buy your ticket at a nearby tobacco shop (€1, bus stop is near the playground, every 10 minutes, 10-minute ride and then 10-minute walk, infrequent on Sun). A taxi is about €15 (look for one near the arch in the main square).

When you're ready to leave Hadrian's Villa, catch bus #4 or #4X in the direction of Tivoli. To continue on to Rome, get off at the main road, Via Tiburtina, and change to a Cotral bus (ask the bus driver for help—he knows what you need to do). Departures after 16:30 can be sparse.

It's also possible to walk (about 15 minutes) from the bus stop near Hadrian's Villa to Via Tiburtina. The way is not well-signed, so don't be shy about asking locals for directions.

Villa d'Este

Ippolito d'Este's grandfather, Alexander VI, was the pope. Ippolito was fast-tracked for church service from birth and became a cardinal. His claim to fame: his pleasure palace at Tivoli. In the 1550s, he destroyed a Benedictine monastery to build this fanciful late-Renaissance palace. Like Hadrian's Villa, it's a large residential estate. But this one features hundreds of Baroque fountains, all gravity-powered. The Aniene River, frazzled into countless threads, weaves its way entertainingly through the villa. At the bottom of the garden, the exhausted little streams once again team up to make a sizable river. Pirro Ligorio, Tivoli's architect, was also the archaeologist in charge of excavating Hadrian's Villa, and that sight provided much in both inspiration and raw material for the fancy fountains of Tivoli. Ligorio could basically use Hadrian's Villa as a quarry to provide statuary and decorative stonework for his vision in making Tivoli.

The cardinal had a political falling-out with Rome, and he was exiled. With this watery wonderland on a cool hill with fine views, he made sure Romans would come to visit. It's symbolic of the luxury and secular interests of the cardinal.

After years of neglect, the villa has been completely restored. All the most eye-popping fountains have been put back in

operation, and—with the exception of the two highest jets of the central fountain, which are electric-powered—everything still operates on natural hydraulics. A terrace restaurant has been installed on the highest level of the garden, opportunely placed to catch cool afternoon sea breezes coming in across the plain of Rome. Expect lots of stairs.

Cost and Hours: €8, audioguide-€4, April-Sept Tue-Sun 8:30-19:30, closed Mon, closes earlier off-season, last entry one hour before closing, tel. 0774-312-070, www.villadestetivoli.info. Upon arrival, note the posted schedule listing when the water organ *(l'organo ad acqua)* will play—a cute five-minute performance every two hours.

Hadrian's Villa

Built at the peak of the Roman Empire by Hadrian (ruled A.D. 117-138), this was a retreat from the political complexity of court life. The Spanish-born Hadrian—an architect, lover of Greek culture (nicknamed "The Little Greek"), and great traveler—envisioned the site as a microcosm of the lands he ruled as emperor, which at that point stretched from England to the Euphrates and encompassed countless diverse cultures. In the spirit of Legoland, Epcot, and Las Vegas, he re-created famous structures from around the world, producing a kind of diorama of his empire in the form of the largest and richest Roman villa anywhere. Just as Louis XIV governed France from Versailles rather than Paris, Hadrian ruled Rome from this villa of more than 300 evocative acres. He basically spent his last decade here.

Start your visit at the plastic model of the villa, a 10-minute walk up the main path (the WC is nearby, hidden underground). Find the Egyptian Canopus (sanctuary of the god Serapis, a canal lined with statues), the Greek Pecile (from Athens), and the Teatro Marittimo (a circular palace, Hadrian's favorite retreat on an island, where he did his serious thinking). Regrettably, this "Versailles of Ancient Rome" was plundered by barbarians and Renaissance big shots who all wanted something classical in their courtyards. They burned the marble to make lime for cement. The art was scavenged and wound up in the Vatican Museum, the Louvre, and other museums throughout Europe. Today, Hadrian's Villa is a harmonious blend of nature and ruins—ideal for wandering while pondering the legacy of a great civilization.

Cost and Hours: €8, €11 with special exhibitions, audioguide-€5, April-Sept daily 9:00-19:00, closes earlier off-season, last entry 1.5 hours before closing, tel. 0774-382-733.

NAPLES and POMPEII DAY TRIP

While the Eternal City can keep you busy for ages, here are two excuses to leave Rome for a day. The trip south to Naples and Pompeii is demanding (four to five hours of train travel round-trip). But you'll be rewarded for your time, given the chance to wander ancient Rome's most evocative ruins and go on an urban safari in what is perhaps Europe's most intense city.

If you have a week in Rome and are interested in maximum travel thrills, take a day trip to Naples and Pompeii. (See map on page 395.) Note that Naples' Archaeological Museum is closed on Tuesday. Pompeii is open daily.

Naples (Napoli)

If you like Italy as far south as Rome, go farther south—it gets better. If Italy is getting on your nerves, don't go farther. Italy intensifies as you plunge deeper. Naples is Italy in the extreme—its best (birthplace of pizza and Sophia Loren) and its worst (home of the Camorra, Naples' "family" of organized crime).

Neapolis ("new city") was a thriving Greek commercial center 2,500 years ago. Today, it remains southern Italy's leading city, offering a fascinating collection of museums, churches, and eclectic architecture. But more than anything, it has a brash and vibrant street life—"in your face" in ways both good and bad. Walking through its colorful Old Town is one of my favorite sightseeing experiences anywhere in Italy.

Naples—Italy's third-largest city, with more than one million people—has almost no open spaces or parks, which makes its position as Europe's most densely populated city plenty evident.

Watching the police try to enforce traffic sanity is almost comical in Italy's grittiest, most polluted, and most crime-ridden city. But Naples surprises the observant traveler with its impressive knack for living, eating, and raising children in the streets with good humor and decency. Overcome your fear of being run down or ripped off long enough to talk with people. Enjoy a few smiles and jokes with the man running the neighborhood tripe shop, or the woman taking her day-care class on a walk through the traffic.

The pulse of Italy throbs in Naples. Like Cairo or Mumbai, it's appalling and captivating at the same time, the closest thing to "reality travel" that you'll find in Western Europe. But this tangled mess still somehow manages to breathe, laugh, and sing—with a joyful Italian accent.

Planning Your Time

A blitz visit to Naples and Pompeii looks something like this:

7:35	Catch the express train from Rome to Naples, where you'll transfer to the commuter train to Pompeii.
10:00	Tour Pompeii, grab a quick lunch (it's best to bring a picnic), then catch the commuter train back to Naples.
14:30	Visit Naples' Archaeological Museum during the heat of the day (closed Tue).
15:30	Take my self-guided "Slice of Neapolitan Life" walk.
18:30	Finish with a pizza dinner as the city comes to life in the early evening.
20:30	Hop on the train back to Rome.
22:30	Arrive in Rome.

Orientation to Naples

Naples is set deep inside the large and curving Bay of Naples, with Mount Vesuvius looming just five miles away. Although Naples is a sprawling city, its fairly compact core contains the most interesting sights. The tourist's Naples is a triangular shape, from Centrale train station to the east, the Archaeological Museum to the west, and Piazza del Plebiscito (Royal Palace) and the port to the south. Within this triangle are unusual churches and a very straight street. Rising above this historic core are hills and mountains, some capped with mighty fortresses (such as San Martino).

Tourist Information

Naples has several different TI organizations. The most convenient—and least helpful—is in the **Centrale train station** and is operated by a private agency (daily 9:00-19:00, near track 23, tel. 081-268-779). The regional TI has two branches: one at the **Galleria Umberto I shopping mall** (across from the entrance to the Teatro di San Carlo; Mon-Sat 9:00-19:00, Sun 9:00-14:00, tel. 081-402-394) and another across from the **Church of Gesù Nuovo** (same hours as Galleria Umberto I, tel. 081-551-2701). The city of Naples operates a main TI on **Piazza del Plebiscito** (at #14, to the right of the church entrance, Mon-Fri 9:00-19:00, closed Sat-Sun, tel. 081-795-6162), plus two kiosks with limited hours—one near the Museo Metro stop in the park next to the **National Archaeological Museum**, and another at **Piazza de Nicola** a few blocks in front of the train station (both Mon-Fri 10:30-14:00, closed Sat-Sun). For cruise-ship passengers, as you exit the **cruise terminal** complex, you'll pass through a little checkpoint (marked *Molo Angioimo*) that has a small TI with maps.

At any TI, pick up a map and ask for the *Qui Napoli* booklet, which lists the latest museum hours, events, and transportation info (due to funding cuts, the booklet is often out of print; if so, ask if they have an old one). The best overall website is www.inaples.it.

Arrival in Naples

By Train: There are several Naples train stations, but all trains coming into town stop at either Napoli Centrale or Garibaldi—essentially the same stop, one on top of the other.

Centrale is the busiest station, facing Naples' main square, Piazza Garibaldi. You'll find all the administrative facilities in Centrale, including a TI (near track 23), an ATM (at Banco di Napoli near track 24), and a baggage check (€5/5 hours, then €0.70/hour, daily 7:00-23:00, marked *deposito bagagli,* near track 5). Note that services in this station tend to change location frequently.

Garibaldi is a subway station used by trains to make a quick stop as they barrel through. It's connected to Centrale Station by escalators. The Circumvesuviana stop, where you can catch a commuter train to Sorrento and Pompeii, is also on this level.

Continuing to Pompeii on the Circumvesuviana

Naples and Pompeii are connected by a **commuter train**—the Ferrovia Circumvesuviana—handy for tourists, commuters...and

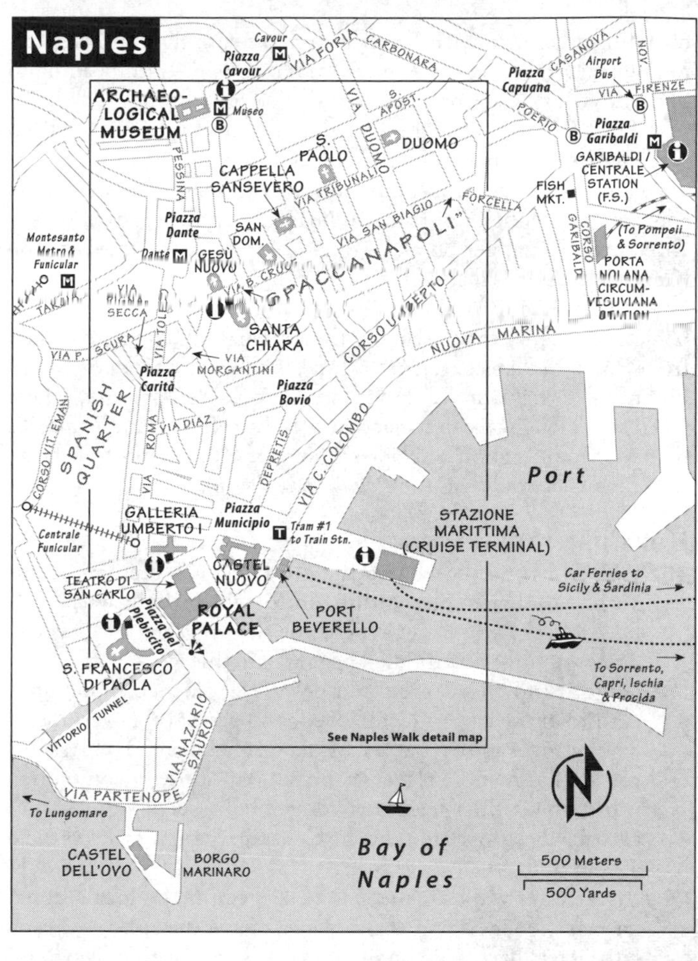

pickpockets (www.vesuviana.it).

At Naples' Centrale train station, follow the signs to the Circumvesuviana (across from track 13, downstairs, and down the corridor to the left), where you'll find the ticket office and info booth. There are two trains per hour to Pompeii (about 45 minutes, €2.80 one-way, final destination: Sorrento, not covered by railpasses). There's no round-trip discount, and all-day passes are generally not worthwhile, except on weekends when they're roughly half-price. When you buy your ticket, purchase a round-trip ticket if you'll be returning to Naples: Ask for *"Pompeii, andata e ritorno"* (ahn-DAH-tah ay ree-TOR-noh). Ask which track your train will depart from (*"Quale binario?"*; KWAH-lay bee-NAH-ree-oh). Just beyond, you'll find the gate where you insert your ticket. The train platforms are downstairs. Before boarding, check the schedule carefully or confirm with a native to make sure the train is going to Pompeii (you want the *Pompei Scavi* stop); any train heading to Sorrento will stop at Pompeii.

The Circumvesuviana also has its own terminal (called Napoli P. Nolana, one Circumvesuviana stop or a 10-minute walk beyond Centrale Station), but there's no reason to use it unless you're nearby. When returning to Naples' Centrale Station on the Circumvesuviana, get off at Garibaldi—the next-to-the-last stop (Centrale Station is just up the escalator).

If you're coming **from Rome,** note that a different (non-Circumvesuviana) train—run by the national rail company—goes from Rome to Naples, then continues to the ugly modern city of Pompei. There is almost no reason to go to Pompei city, where you'll face a long walk to the actual site. Therefore, from Rome, it's better to simply get off at Naples' Centrale Station and transfer to the Circumvesuviana (to the *Pompei Scavi* stop).

Helpful Hints

Theft Alert: Err on the side of caution. Don't venture into neighborhoods that make you uncomfortable. Walk with confidence, as if you know where you're going and what you're doing. Assume able-bodied beggars are thieves.

Stick to busy streets and beware of gangs of hoodlums. A third of the city is unemployed, and past local governments have set an example that the Mafia would be proud of. Assume con artists are more clever than you. Any jostle or commotion is probably a thief-team smokescreen. To keep bags safe, it's probably best to store them at Centrale Station or keep them at your hotel.

Always walk on the sidewalk (even if the locals don't) and carry your bag on the side away from the street—thieves on scooters have been known to snatch bags as they swoop by. The less you have dangling from you (including cameras and necklaces), the better.

Perhaps your biggest risk of theft is while catching or riding the Circumvesuviana commuter train. If you're connecting from a major train, you'll be stepping from a relatively secure compartment into a crowded Naples subway filled with thieves hunting disoriented tourists with luggage. While I ride the Circumvesuviana comfortably and safely, each year I hear of many who get ripped off on this ride. You won't be mugged—but you may be conned or pickpocketed. Especially late at night, the Circumvesuviana train is plagued by intimidating ruffians. For maximum safety and peace of mind, sit in the front car, where the driver will double as your protector.

Con artists may say you need to "transfer" by taxi to catch

the Circumvesuviana; you don't. Anyone offering to help you with your bags is likely a thief, despite displayed credentials. There are no porters at Centrale Station or in the lower level where the Circumvesuviana station is located. Wear your money belt, hang on to your bag, and don't display any valuables.

Traffic Safety: In Naples, red lights are discretionary, and pedestrians need to be wary, particularly of motor scooters. Smart tourists jaywalk in the shadow of bold and confident locals, who generally ignore crosswalks. Wait for a break in traffic, cross with confidence, and make eye contact with approaching drivers. The traffic will stop.

Travel Agency: Ontano Tours books train and boat tickets from a small office just inland from the new Galleria del Mare shopping center at Molo Beverello (Mon-Sat 8:30-20:00, closed Sun, tel. 081-580-0340, www.ontanotour.it).

Tours: Convenient for cruise-ship passengers, the **"Can't Be Missed" tour** company gives you a quick look at Naples, Sorrento, and Pompeii with a small group and local guide for €65 (meet at 8:30 in front of port, bus leaves at 9:00, returns at 17:15, Pompeii ticket extra, mobile 329-129-8182, www.cantbemissedtours.com).

Local Guides: Pina Esposito specializes in art and archaeology, and does fine tours of Naples' excellent but somewhat hard-to-appreciate Archaeological Museum (€120/2 hours, 10 percent off with this book, confirm one week in advance, sometimes available on shorter notice, mobile 349-596-8251, annamariaesposito1@virgilio.it). The team at **Mondo Guide** offers private tours of the museum and city (€50/hour, €320/4 hours, tel. 081-751-3290, www.mondoguide.it, info@mondoguide.it). Both Pina and Mondo Guide also lead tours of Capri, Pompeii, and the surrounding area, and can provide drivers.

Getting Around Naples

By Subway: Naples' slow-moving subway, the Metropolitana, has two lines. Line 2, the main line, runs from Centrale Station (catch it downstairs at the Garibaldi stop) through the center of town (direction: Pozzuoli), stopping at Piazza Cavour (a five-minute walk from the Archaeological Museum) and Montesanto (top of Spanish Quarter and Spaccanapoli street, and base of funicular up to San Martino). Line 1 runs from the central Dante stop, stopping at the Museo station, near the Archaeological Museum (near Line 2's Piazza Cavour subway stop), then looping through town out to Piscinola/Scampia (suburbs). While the Cavour and Museo subway stops are near each other, they aren't connected (but are at

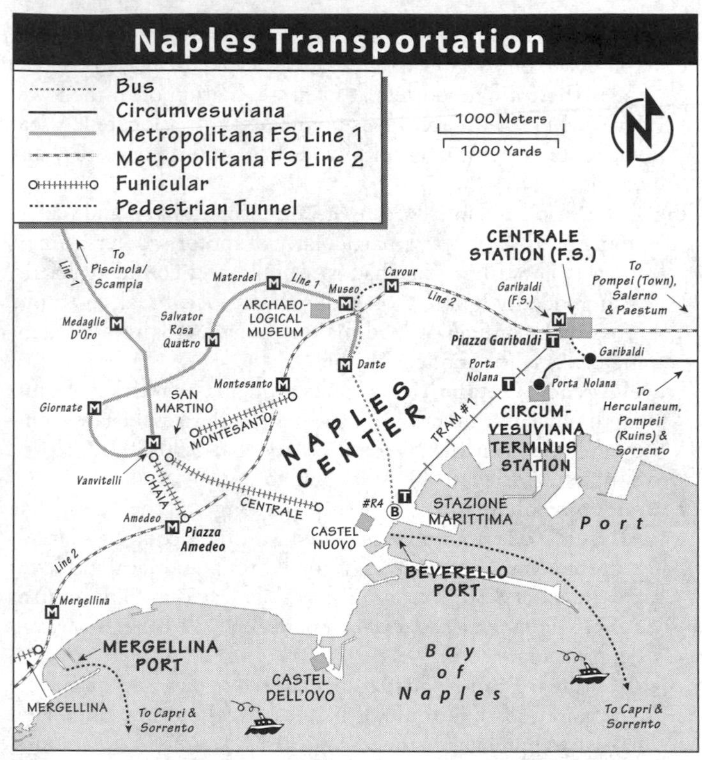

opposite ends of the same park, about a five-minute walk). Tickets cost €1.20 and are good for 1.5 hours. All-day tickets cost €3.60 (or €3 on weekends). Validate tickets in the small yellow boxes you'll see before you reach the track.

By Taxi: Taxi drivers in Naples are notorious for overcharging. A short ride in town should cost €10-12; figure on €12-15 from downtown to the port. Ask for the *tariffa predeterminata* (a fixed rate). There are some legitimate extra charges (baggage fees, €2 supplement after 22:00, €1.50 supplement on Sun and holidays).

By Bus: Buses are handy for getting between the port and train station. If you need to curtail my self-guided walk, you can hop a bus to the station. Tickets cost €1.20 at tobacco shops; validate the ticket in the yellow box on the bus as you board.

On a Hop-on, Hop-off Bus Tour: The "Sightseeing Napoli" tour bus makes several different loops through the city, allowing riders to get on and off to explore, but Naples' most interesting areas are the gritty side-streets where buses can't go (€22, tickets good for 24 hours, buy from driver or from kiosk in front of Castel Nuovo near the port, scant recorded narration; for details, see the brochure at hotels and TI, www.napoli.city-sightseeing.it).

Sights in Naples

▲▲▲Archaeological Museum (Museo Archeologico)

For lovers of antiquity, this museum alone makes Naples a worthwhile stop. Considering its popularity and the importance of the collection, it's remarkable how ramshackle, unkempt, and dumpy its displays are. Still, if you can overlook the dust bunnies, this museum offers the best possible peek into the artistic jewelry boxes of Pompeii and Herculaneum. When Pompeii was excavated in the early 1800s, Naples' Bourbon king bellowed, "Bring me the best of what you find!" The actual sites are impressive but barren; the finest art and artifacts ended up here.

Cost and Hours: €6.50, but often €10 with mandatory charge for special exhibits, cash only, Wed-Mon 9:00-19:30, closed Tue, last entry 30 minutes before closing. A few less-important collections close early (generally around 12:30)—but none of the items on my self-guided tour are affected. Early and temporary closures are noted on a board near the ticket office.

Getting There: To take the subway from Centrale Station, follow signs to the Metro, called *Metropolitana*, located downstairs at the Garibaldi subway station (across from track 13). Buy your ticket at the newsstand or a tobacco shop. Validate your ticket in the small yellow boxes near the escalator going down to the tracks. You're looking for trains heading in the direction of Pozzuoli (generally depart from track 4). Hop on any train that comes through (confirm by its sign or with a local that it's going to Pozzuoli), and ride the subway one stop. As you leave the Metro, exit and hike five minutes uphill through the park along the busy street. Look for a grand old red building located up a flight of stairs at the top of the block.

If taking the Metro back to Centrale Station, exit the museum to the left, and continue downhill to the Cavour stop, passing the Museo station (which is on a different line).

Figure on €12 for a taxi from the train station to the museum.

Information: The shop sells a worthwhile *National Archaeological Museum of Naples* guidebook—at €12, it's still a better value than the audioguide. Tel. 081-442-2149.

Tours: For the basics, you can follow my self-guided tour (below). If you want a **guided tour,** you may see Pina Esposito at the museum (see "Local Guides," earlier; €120/2-hour tour, 10 percent less with this book; help her assemble a group of up to 10 to split the fee; it's more reliable to book her in advance). **Audioguides,** which haven't been updated for years, cost €5 (at ticket desk).

Baggage Check: Bag check is obligatory and free.

Photography: Photos are allowed without a flash.

Renovations: The museum seems to be in constant chaos due to ongoing renovations. If you can't find a particular work, ask a museum custodian, *"Dov'è?"* (DOH-vay, meaning "Where is?"), followed by the item's name.

Self-Guided Tour: Overview

Entering the museum, stand at the base of the grand staircase. To your right, on the ground floor, are larger-than-life statues from the Farnese Collection, starring the *Toro Farnese* and *Farnese Hercules.* Up the stairs on the mezzanine level (turn left at the lion) are mosaics and frescoes from Pompeii, including the *Battle of Alexander* and the Secret Room of erotic art. On the top floor is a scale model of Pompeii and bronze statues from Herculaneum (a nearby town destroyed in the same eruption that devastated Pompeii). You'll find WCs by circling behind the staircase.

• *From the base of the grand staircase, turn right and head to the far end, angling a bit to reach the farthest room.*

Ground Floor: The Farnese Collection

The museum's ground floor alone has enough Greek and Roman art to put any museum on the map. Its highlight is the Farnese Collection, a grand hall of huge, bright, and wonderfully restored statues excavated from Rome's Baths of Caracalla.

The tangled ***Toro Farnese*** depicts a woman being tied to a bull. At 13 feet, it's the tallest ancient marble group ever found, and the largest intact statue from antiquity. A third-century A.D. copy of a lost bronze Hellenistic original, it was carved out of one piece of marble. Michelangelo and others "restored" it at the pope's request—meaning that they integrated surviving bits into a new work. Panels on the wall show which pieces were actually carved by Michelangelo (in blue on the chart): the head of the woman in back, the torso of the aunt under the bull, and the dog. (Imagine how the statue would stand out if it was thoughtfully lit and not surrounded by white walls.)

Here's the story behind the statue: Once upon an ancient Greek time, King Lycus was bewitched by Dirce. He abandoned his pregnant wife, Antiope (standing regally in the background). The single mom gave birth to twin boys (shown here). When they grew up, they killed their deadbeat dad and tied Dirce to the horns of a bull to be bashed against a mountain. Captured in marble, the action is thrilling: cape flailing, dog snarling, hooves in the air. You can almost hear the bull snorting. And in the back, Antiope oversees this harsh ancient justice with satisfaction.

At the far end of the hall stands the ***Farnese Hercules.*** The great Greek hero is exhausted. He leans wearily on his club (draped with his lion skin) and bows his head. He's just finished the daunting Eleventh Labor, having traveled the world, fought men and gods, freed Prometheus from his rock, and carried Atlas' weight of the world on his shoulders. Now he's returned with the prize: the golden apples of the gods, which he cups behind his back. But, after all that, he's just been told he has to return the stolen apples and do one final labor: Descend into Hell itself.

The 10-foot colossus is a third-century A.D. Roman marble copy (signed by "Glykon") of a fourth-century B.C. Greek bronze original (probably by Lysippos). The statue was enormously famous in its day. Dozens of copies—some marble, some bronze—have been found in Roman villas and baths. This version was unearthed in Rome's Baths of Caracalla in 1546, along with the *Toro Farnese.*

The *Farnese Hercules* was equally famous in the 16th-18th centuries. Tourists flocked to admire it, art students studied it from afar in prints, Louis XIV made a copy for Versailles, and petty nobles everywhere put small-scale knock-offs in their gardens. This curly-haired version of Hercules became the modern world's image of the Greek hero.

Behind Hercules is a series of small rooms lined with precious stones. In the farthest one, in a freestanding glass case, is the sumptuous **Farnese Cup** (*Tazza Farnese,* second century B.C., from Egypt). This large, ancient cameo made of agates looks more like a cereal bowl than a cup. Its decorations are both Egyptian (the Nile toting a lush cornucopia) and, on the flip side, Greek (Medusa's head).

• Backtrack to the main entry hall, then head up to the mezzanine level (turning left at the lion).

Mezzanine: Pompeiian Mosaics and the Secret Room

Most of these mosaics—of animals, musicians, and geometric designs—were taken from Pompeii's House of the Faun (see page 447). Walk through several rooms and look for the 20-inch-high statue in a freestanding glass case: the house's delightful centerpiece, the ***Dancing Faun.*** This rare surviving Greek bronze statue (from the fourth century B.C.) is surrounded by some of the best mosaics of that age.

A museum highlight, just beyond the statue, is the grand ***Battle of Alexander,*** a second-century B.C. copy of the original Greek fresco, done a century earlier. It decorated a floor in the House of the Faun and was found intact; the damage you see occurred as this treasure was moved from Pompeii to the king's collection here. Alexander (left side of the scene, with curly hair and sideburns) is about to defeat the Persians under Darius (central figure, in chariot with turban and beard). This pivotal victory allowed Alexander to quickly overrun much of Asia (331 B.C.). Alexander is the only one without a helmet...a confident master of the battlefield while everyone else is fighting for their lives, eyes bulging with fear. Notice how the horses, already in retreat, add to the scene's propaganda value. Notice also the shading and perspective, which Renaissance artists would later work so hard to accomplish. (A modern reproduction of the mosaic is now back in the House of the Faun.)

The **Secret Room *(Gabinetto Segreto)*** contains a sizable assortment of erotic frescoes, well-hung pottery, and perky statues that once decorated bedrooms, meeting rooms, brothels, and even shops at Pompeii and Herculaneum. These bawdy statues and frescoes—many of them once displayed in Pompeii's grandest houses—were entertainment for guests. (By the time they made it to this museum, in 1819, the frescoes could be viewed only with permission from the king—see the letters in the glass case just outside the door.) The Roman nobles commissioned the wildest scenes imaginable. Think of them as ancient dirty jokes.

At the entrance, you're enthusiastically greeted by big stone penises that once projected over Pompeii's doorways. A massive phallus was not necessarily a sexual symbol, but a magical amulet used against the "evil eye." It symbolized fertility, happiness, good luck, riches, straight A's, and general well-being.

Circulating counterclockwise through this section, look for: a faun playfully pulling the sheet off a beautiful woman, only to be grossed out by a hermaphrodite's plumbing (perhaps the original *"Mamma mia!"*; #12); horny pygmies from Africa in action (#27); a toga with an embarrassing bulge (#34); a particularly high-quality statue of a goat and a satyr illustrating the act of sodomy (#36); and, watching over it all with remarkable aplomb, Venus, the patron goddess of Pompeii (#39).

The next room is furnished and decorated the way an ancient brothel might have been. The 10 frescoes on the wall functioned as both a menu of services offered and as a kind of *Kama Sutra* of sex positions. The glass cases contain more phallic art.

• *So, now that your travel buddy is finally showing a little interest in art...finish up your visit by climbing the stairs to the top floor.*

Top Floor: Statues, Artifacts, and a Model of Pompeii

At the top of the stairs, go through the center door to enter a grand, empty hall. This was the **great hall** of the university (17th and 18th centuries) until the building became the royal museum in 1777. The sundial (from 1791) still works. At noon, a sunray strikes the spot, indicating today's date...if you know your zodiac.

To your right (look for the *La Villa dei Papiri* sign) is an exhibit of **bronze statues** that once decorated the Herculaneum holiday home of Julius Caesar's father-in-law. The statues depict racers, dancers, fauns, and lots of disembodied heads (first-century B.C. copies of fourth-century B.C. originals). In the second room (labeled *tablinum*), look into the lifelike blue eyes of the intense *Corridore* (athletes), bent on doing their best. The *Five Dancers,* with their inlaid-ivory eyes and graceful poses, decorated a portico. The next room (marked *rectangular peristyle*) has more fine works: *Resting Hermes* (with his tired little heel wings) is taking a break. Nearby, the *Drunken Faun* (singing and snapping his fingers to the beat, a wineskin at his side) is clearly living for today—true to the *carpe diem* preaching of the Epicurean philosophy. Caesar's father-in-law was an Epicurean philosopher,

and his library—containing 2,000 papyrus scrolls—supported his outlook.

Return to the grand hall and continue to the other side, passing through several rooms of vases, statuettes, spoons, glassware, and other objects found at Pompeii. Keep going to the far end, where you'll find a **scale model** of the archaeological site of Pompeii, circa 1879 *(plastico di Pompeii)*. Belly up to the railing and find the Porta Marina entrance and the large rectangle of the town's Forum. Another model on the wall shows the site in 2004, after more excavations.

The Rest of the Museum

After years in restoration, the museum's large collection of **frescoes** taken from the walls of Pompeii villas is back (in Rooms LXVI to LXXVIII—at the end of the great hall and on the left). Pompeiians loved to decorate their homes with scenes from mythology (Hercules' Labors, Venus and Mars in love), landscapes, everyday market scenes, and faux architecture. The display is roughly chronological.

For extra credit, visit ***Doriforo.*** (Ask a guard, *"Dov'è il Doriforo?"* He was last spotted on the ground floor, in the hall to the left, as you face the staircase—on the way to the exit.) This seven-foot-tall "spear-carrier" (the literal translation of *doriforo)* just stands there, as if holding a spear. What's the big deal about this statue, which looks like so many others? It's a marble replica made by the Romans of one of the most-copied statues of antiquity, a fifth-century B.C. bronze Greek original by Polyclitus. This copy once stood in a Pompeii gym, where it inspired ancient athletes by showing the ideal proportions of Greek beauty. So full of motion, and so realistic in its *contrapposto* pose (weight on one foot), the *Doriforo* would later inspire Donatello and Michelangelo, triggering the Renaissance. And so the glories of ancient Pompeii, once buried and forgotten, live on today.

Self-Guided Walk

▲▲▲A Slice of Neapolitan Life

Take this three-part walk from the Archaeological Museum through the heart of town and back to the Centrale train station. Allow at least three hours, plus time for pizza and sightseeing stops. If you have limited time, do a shorter, 1.5-hour-long version by walking briskly and skipping Part 2.

Naples, a living medieval city, is its own best sight. Couples

"A Slice of Neapolitan Life" Walk

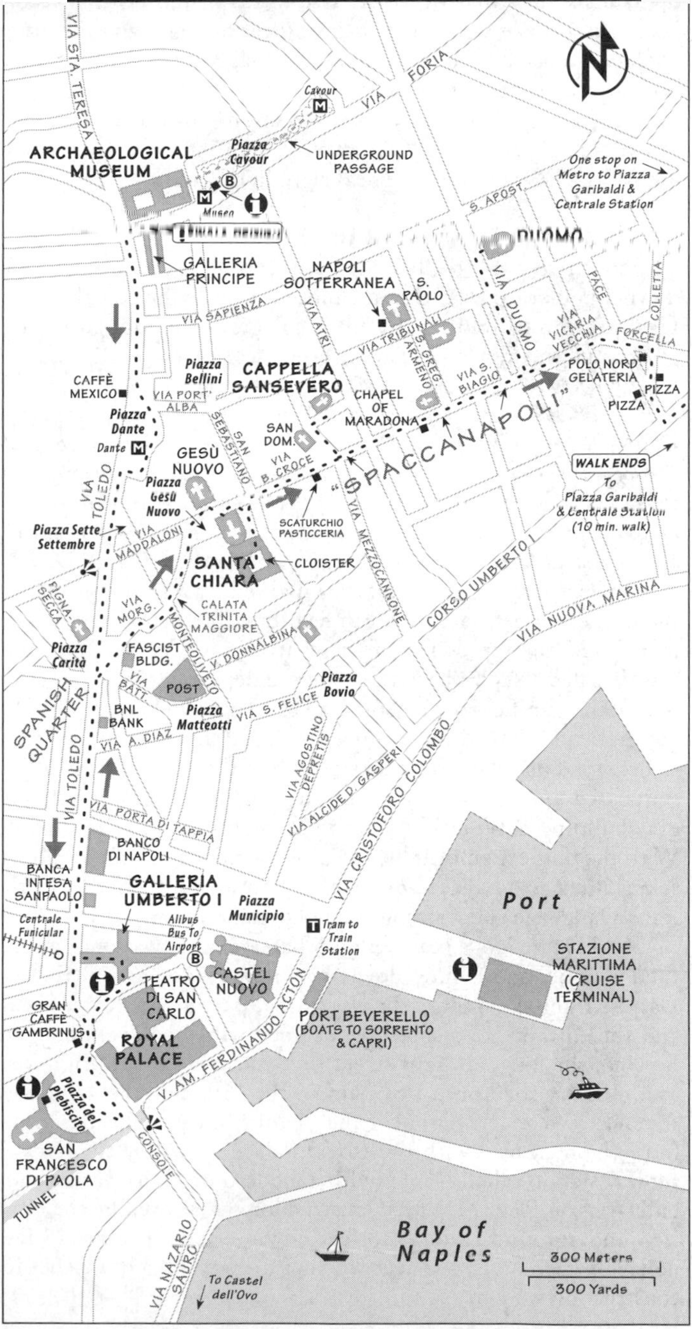

artfully make love on Vespas surrounded by more fights and smiles per cobblestone than anywhere else in Italy. Rather than seeing Naples as a list of sights, visit its one great museum and then capture its essence by taking this walk through the core of the city. Should you become overwhelmed or lost, step into a store and ask for directions: "Where is Centrale Station?" in Italian is *"Dov'è la stazione Centrale?"* (DOH-vay lah staht-zee-OH-nay chen-TRAH-lay). Or point to the next sight in this book.

Part 1: Piazza Dante and Via Pessina

The first two parts of this walk are a straight one-mile ramble down a boulevard to Galleria Umberto I, near the Royal Palace. Ideally, begin by touring the Archaeological Museum (at the top of Piazza Cavour, Metro: Cavour or Museo).

• *Leaving the Archaeological Museum, turn right and go one block, to the head of Via Pessina. Follow this busy street downhill to Piazza Dante—see his statue in the distance. (Alternatively, to avoid the traffic-clogged Via Pessina, when you leave the museum, you can cross the street, cut through the fancy Galleria Principe mall—only the second-most-impressive gallery we'll see on this walk, then continue out the bottom end and two more blocks, jogging right to reach Piazza Dante.)*

Piazza Dante: This square is marked by a statue of Dante, the medieval poet. Here you can feel Italy...but many Neapolitans merely feel the repression of the central state. When Napoleon was defeated, Naples became its own independent kingdom. But with Italian unification in 1861, Naples went from being a thriving cultural and political capital to a provincial town, its money used to help establish the industrial strength of the north. Originally, a statue of a Spanish Bourbon king stood here. The grand red-and-gray building is typical of Bourbon structures from that period. With the unification of Italy, the king, symbolic of Italy's colonial subjugation, was replaced by Dante—considered the father of the Italian language and a strong symbol of nationalism.

Old Dante looks out over an urban area that was once grand, then chaotic, and is now slowly becoming grand again. Behind Dante's right shoulder is the Port'Alba, part of Naples' old wall and the entrance to a small street lined with book vendors. Via Pessina, the long, straight street that you're walking, originated as a military road built by Spain in the 16th century. It skirted the old town wall to connect the Spanish military headquarters (now the museum) with the Royal Palace (down by the bay). A subway station called Dante (with a modern-art flair) was recently built here on Piazza Dante. Construction was slowed by the city's rich underground history: 13 feet down—Roman ruins; 23 feet down—Greek ruins; and every inch of the way—big headaches for construction workers.

Across the street, **Caffè Mexico** (at #86) is an institution known for its espresso, which is served already sweetened—ask for *senza zucchero* if you don't want sugar (pay first, then take receipt to the counter; locals tip €0.10). Most Italians agree that Neapolitan coffee is the best anywhere.

Continue walking downhill, remembering that here in Naples, red traffic lights are considered "decorations." When crossing a street, try to tag along with a native. The people here are survivors: A long history of corrupt and greedy colonial overlords has taught Neapolitans to deal creatively with authority. Many credit this aspect of Naples' past for the advent of organized crime here.

Via Pessina becomes Via Toledo (another reminder of Spanish rule), Naples' principal shopping street. In 1860, from the white marble balcony of the Neoclassical building overlooking Piazza Sette Settembre, the famous revolutionary Giuseppe Garibaldi declared Italy united and Victor Emmanuel II its first king. Not until 1870, when Rome fell to the unification forces, was the dream of Italian unity fully realized.

• *Continue straight on Via Toledo. About three blocks below Piazza Dante and a block past Piazza Sette Settembre, you'll come to the long, straight, and narrow street called...*

Spaccanapoli: Before crossing the street—whose name translates as "split Naples"—look left. Look right. Since ancient times, this thin street has bisected the city. It changes names several times: Via Maddaloni (as it's called here), Via B. Croce, Via S. Biagio dei Librai, Forecella, and Vicaria. We'll return to this intersection later.

• *If you want to abbreviate this walk, turn left here and skip ahead to "Part 3." Part 2—described next—is a bit of a detour, and requires backtracking uphill later. But if you have time, it's worth the effort.*

NAPLES

Part 2: Via Toledo, the Spanish Quarter, and Piazza del Plebiscito

• *Stay on Via Toledo, which runs through...*

Piazza Carità: Surrounded by fascist architecture from 1938, this square is full of stern, straight, obedient lines. (For the best fascist architecture in town, take a slight detour from here—with your back to Via Toledo, leave Piazza Carità downhill on the right-hand corner and walk a block to the Poste e Telegrafi building. There you'll see several government buildings with stirring reliefs singing the praises of a totalitarian society.)

If you're feeling adventurous, head up one of Naples' most

colorful open-air market streets: **Via Pignasecca.** It's the first street you pass on the right as you enter Piazza Carità (angling sharply back the way you came). Strolling this chaotic strip, you'll pass meat and fish stalls, produce stands, street-food vendors, and much more. The action continues for several blocks, all the way up to the Montesanto station, where you can access the Metro or the funicular up to San Martino.

• *From Piazza Carità, continue south down Via Toledo for a few blocks, looking to your left for more...*

Fascist Architecture (Banks): You can't miss the two big, blocky bank buildings. First comes the chalky-white BNL Bank. A bit farther down, try robbing the Banco di Napoli (Via Toledo 178). Step across the street and check out its architecture: typical fascist arches and reliefs, built to celebrate the bank's 400th anniversary (est. 1539—how old is *your* bank?).

• *On the next block (marked Banca Prossima) is the...*

Banca Intesa Sanpaolo: This fills an older palace—take a free peek at the opulent interior. In the lobby you can buy a ticket for the **Galleria d'Italia Palazzo Zevallos Stigliano,** a small collection located in the upper two floors. The gallery's only piece worth seeing—on the second floor—is a great late Caravaggio painting. *The Martyrdom of Saint Ursula* shows a terrible scene: His marriage proposal rejected, the king of the Huns shoots an arrow into Ursula's chest. Blood spurts, Ursula is stunned but accepts her destiny sweetly, and Caravaggio himself—far right, his last self-portrait—screams to symbolize the rejection of evil. The rest of the second floor holds opulent chandeliered apartments, a few Neapolitan landscapes, and little else. The first floor has fine temporary exhibits (€4, Tue-Sun 10:00-18:00, closed Mon, entry includes 40-minute audioguide, fine WC, Via Toledo 185, tel. 800-1605-2007, www.palazzozevallos.com).

• *Feeling bold? From here, side-trip uphill a couple of blocks into the...*

Spanish Quarter: This is a classic world of *basso* (low) living. In such tight quarters, families generally do it in the road. This is *the* cliché of life in Naples, as shown in so many movies. The Spanish Quarter is Naples at its rawest, poorest, and most characteristic. The only predictable things about this Neapolitan tide pool are the ancient grid plan of its streets (which survives from Greek times), the friendliness of its shopkeepers, and the boldness of its mopeds. Concerned locals will tug on their lower eyelids, warning you to be wary. Hungry? Pop into a grocery shop and ask

the man to make you his best prosciutto and mozzarella sandwich (the price should be about €4).

• *Return to Via Toledo (clogged with more people than cars) and work your way down. Near the bottom of the street, on the right, notice the station for the* ***Centrale funicular.*** *If you have extra time and enjoy city views, this can take you sweat-free up to the top of San Martino, the hill with a fortress and a monastery/museum looming over town (covered by regular €1.20 transit ticket, separate entrance fees for fortress and museum).*

But for now, keep heading down the main drag to the immense...

Piazza del Plebiscito: This square celebrates the 1861 vote (*plebiscito,* plebiscite), when Naples chose to join Italy. Dominating the top of the square is the **Church of San Francesco di Paola,** with its Pantheon-inspired dome and broad, arcing colonnades. If it's open, step inside to ogle the vast interior—a Neoclassical recreation of one of ancient Rome's finest buildings (free, daily 8:30-12:00 & 16:00-19:00).

• *Opposite is the...*

Royal Palace (Palazzo Reale): Having housed Spanish, French, and even Italian royalty, this building displays statues of all those who stayed here. Look for eight kings in the niches, each from a different dynasty (left to right): Norman, German, French, Spanish, Spanish, Spanish, French (Napoleon's brother-in-law), and, finally, Italian—Victor Emmanuel II, King of Savoy. The statues were done at the request of V. E. II's son, so his dad is the most dashing of the group.

This huge, lavish palace welcomes the public (€4, more with special exhibits, includes painfully dry audioguide, Thu-Tue 9:00-20:00, closed Wed, last entry one hour before closing, tel. 848-800-288). The palace's grand Neoclassical staircase leads up to a floor with 30 plush rooms. You'll follow a one-way route (with some English descriptions) featuring the palace theater, paintings by "the Caravaggio Imitators," Neapolitan tapestries, fine inlaid-stone tabletops, chandeliers, gilded woodwork, and more. The rooms do feel quite grand, but lack the personality and sense of importance of Europe's best palaces. Don't miss the huge, tapestry-laden Hercules Hall. On the way out, stop into the chapel, with a fantastic nativity scene—a commotion of 18th-century ceramic figurines.

The **Gran Caffè Gambrinus,** facing the piazza, takes you back to the elegance of 1860. It's a classic place to sample a unique Neapolitan treat called *sfogliatella* (crispy scallop shell-shaped pastry filled with sweet ricotta cheese). Or you might prefer the mushroom-shaped, rum-soaked bread-like cakes called *babà,* which come in a huge variety. Stand at the bar *(banco),* pay double to sit *(tavola),* or just wander around as you imagine the café buzzing with the ritzy intellectuals, journalists, and artsy bohemian types who munched on *babà* here during Naples' 19th-century heyday (daily 7:00-24:00, Piazza del Plebiscito 1, tel. 081-417-582).

• *Continue 50 yards past the Royal Palace (toward the trees) to enjoy a...*

Fine Harbor View: While boats busily serve Capri and Sorrento, Mount Vesuvius smolders ominously in the distance. Look back to see the vast "Bourbon red" palace—its color inspired by Pompeii. On the hilltop above Piazza del Plebiscito is Naples' Carthusian Monastery and the Castle of St. Elmo. This street continues to Naples' romantic harborfront—the fishermen's quarters (Borgo Marinaro)—a fortified island connected to the mainland by a stout causeway, with its fanciful Castel dell'Ovo (castle of the egg) and trendy harborside restaurants. Farther along the harborfront stretches the Lungomare promenade and Santa Lucia district. (The long harborfront promenade, Via Francesco Caracciolo, is a delightful people-watching scene on balmy nights.)

• *Head back to the piazza and go behind the palace, where you can peek inside the Neoclassical...*

Teatro di San Carlo: Built in 1737, 41 years before Milan's La Scala, this is Europe's oldest opera house and Italy's second-most-respected (after La Scala). The theater burned down in 1816, and was rebuilt within the year. Guided 35-minute visits basically just show you the fine auditorium with its 184 boxes—each with a big mirror to reflect the candlelight (€5, tours every 40 minutes, Mon-Sat 10:00-16:00, closed Sun, tel. 081-553-4565, www.teatrosancarlo.it).

Beyond Teatro di San Carlo and the Royal Palace is the huge, harborfront **Castel Nuovo,** which houses government bureaucrats and the **Civic Museum.** It feels like a mostly empty shell, with a couple of dusty halls of Neapolitan art, but the views over the bay from the upper terraces are impressive (€6, Mon-Sat 9:00-19:00, closed Sun, last entry one hour before closing, tel. 081-795-7722).

Across the street from Teatro di San Carlo, go through the tall yellow arch into the Victorian iron and glass of the 100-year-old shopping mall, **Galleria Umberto I,** which was built in 1892 to reinvigorate the district after a devastating cholera epidemic here. Gawk up.

• *For Part 3 of this walk, double back up Via Toledo to Piazza Carità, veering right (just above the first big fascist-style building we saw earlier) on Via Morgantini through Piazza Monteoliveto; cross the busy street, then angle up Calata Trinità*

Maggiore to the fancy column at the top of the hill. (To avoid the backtracking and uphill walk, catch a €10 taxi to the Church of Gesù Nuovo—JAY-zoo noo-OH-voh.)

Part 3: Spaccanapoli Back to the Station

You're back at the straight-as-a-Greek-arrow Spaccanapoli, formerly the main thoroughfare of the Greek city of Neapolis.

• *Stop at...*

Piazza Gesù Nuovo: This square is marked by a towering 18th-century Baroque monument to the Counter-Reformation. Although the Jesuit order was powerful in Naples because of its Spanish heritage, locals never attacked Protestants here with the full fury of the Spanish Inquisition.

• *Now visit two bulky old churches, starting with the austere, fortress-like, 17th-century...*

Church of Gesù Nuovo: The unique pyramid-grill facade survives from a fortified 15th-century noble palace. Step inside for a brilliant Neapolitan Baroque interior (free, daily 7:00-13:00 & 16:00-19:30). The second chapel on the right features a much-adored **statue of Giuseppe Moscati** (1880-1927), a Christian doctor famous for helping the poor. In 1987, Moscati became the first modern doctor to be canonized. Sit and watch a steady stream of Neapolitans taking turns to kiss and touch the altar, then hold the good doctor's highly polished hand.

Continue on to the third chapel and enter the **Sale Moscati.** Look high on the walls of this long room to see hundreds of "Ex Votos"—tiny red-and-silver plaques of thanksgiving for prayers answered with the help of St. Moscati (each has a symbol of the ailment cured). Naples' practice of using Ex Votos, while incorporated into its Catholic rituals, goes back to its pagan Greek roots. Rooms from Moscati's nearby apartment are on display, and a glass case shows possessions and photos of the great doctor. As you leave the Sale Moscati, notice the big bomb casing that hangs in the left corner. It fell through the church's dome in 1943, but caused almost no damage...yet another miracle.

• *Head across the street, to the simpler...*

Church of Santa Chiara: Dating from the 14th century, this church is from a period of French royal rule under the Angevin dynasty. Consider the stark contrast between this church (Gothic) and the Gesù Nuovo (Baroque). Notice the huge inlaid-marble Angevin coat of arms on the floor. The faded Trinity on the back wall (on the right as you face the door), shows a dove representing the Holy Spirit between the heads of God the Father and Christ (c. 1414). This is an example of the fine frescoes that once covered the walls. Most were stuccoed over during Baroque times or destroyed in 1943 by World War II bombs. The altar is adorned with four finely carved Gothic tombs of Angevin kings. A chapel stacked with Bourbon royalty is just to the right (daily 7:00-13:00 & 16:30-20:00). The cloistered courtyard and sleepy museum behind the church are not worth the time or €5 to visit.

• *Now return to the main drag, turn right, and continue straight down traffic-free Via B. Croce. A good little lunch spot,* ***Trattoria da Titina e Gennaro,*** *is just down the street across from the church (Via Santa Chiara 6).*

Since this is a university district, you'll see lots of students and bookstores. This neighborhood is also extremely superstitious. Look for incense-burning women with carts full of good-luck charms for sale.

• *Farther down Spaccanapoli, you'll see the next square...*

Piazza San Domenico Maggiore: This square is marked by an ornate 17th-century monument built to thank God for ending the plague. But more important is the well-loved **Scaturchio Pasticceria,** another good place to try *sfogliatella* (€1.70 to go, costs double at a table in the square, daily 7:20-20:40, tel. 081-551-7031).

• *From this square, detour left along the right side of the castle-like church, then follow yellow signs, taking the first right and walking one block to...*

Cappella Sansevero: This small chapel is a Baroque explosion mourning the body of Christ, who lies on a soft pillow under an incredibly realistic veil. It's also the personal chapel of Raimondo de Sangro, an eccentric Freemason, containing his tomb and the tombs of his family. Raimondo was a grand master of the Freemasons of the Kingdom of Naples. His chapel—filled with Freemason symbolism—is a complex ensemble, with statues representing virtues such as self-control, religious zeal, and the Freemason philosophy of freedom through enlightenment. Though it's a pricey private enterprise, it's worth a visit (€7, buy tickets at office at the corner, Mon and Wed-Sat 10:00-18:00, Sun 10:00-13:30, closed Tue, last entry 20 minutes before closing, no photos but postcards sold in gift shop, Via de Sanctis 19, tel. 081-551-8470, www.museosansevero.it). Good English explanations are posted throughout; when you buy your ticket, pick up the floor plan, which identifies each of the statues lining the nave.

Study the incredible ***Veiled Christ*** in the center. Carved out of marble, it's like no other statue I've seen (by Giuseppe "Howdeedoodat" Sammartino, 1753). The Christian message (Jesus died for our salvation) is accompanied by a Freemason message (the veil represents how the body and ego are obstacles to real spiritual freedom). As you walk from Christ's feet to his head, notice how the expression on Jesus' face goes from suffering to peace.

Raimondo's mom and dad are buried on either side of the

main altar. To the right of the altar, marking his father's tomb, a statue representing *Despair* or *Disillusion* struggles with a marble rope net (carved out of a single piece of stone), symbolic of a troubled mind. The flames on the head of the winged boy represent human intellect—more Freemason symbolism, showing how knowledge frees the human mind. To the left of the main altar is a statue of *Modesty*, marking the tomb of Raimondo's mother (who died young, at 20). The veiled woman fingers a broken tablet, symbolizing an interrupted life.

Raimondo de Sangro lies buried in a side altar (on the right) An inventor, he created the deep-green pigment used on the ceiling fresco. The inlaid M. C. Escher-esque maze on the floor around de Sangro's tomb is another Freemason reminder of how the quest for knowledge gets you out of the maze of life. This tilework once covered the floor of the entire chapel.

Your Sansevero finale is downstairs: two mysterious...skeletons. Perhaps another of the mad inventor's fancies: Inject a corpse with a fluid to fossilize the veins so that they'll survive the body's decomposition. While that's the legend, it was most likely created to illustrate how the circulatory system works.

• *Return to Via B. Croce (a.k.a. Spaccanapoli), turn left, and continue your cultural scavenger hunt. At the intersection of Via Nilo, find the...*

Statue of the Nile (on the left): A reminder of the multiethnic make-up of Greek Neapolis, this statue is in what was the Egyptian quarter. Locals like to call this statue *The Body of Naples,* with the overflowing cornucopia symbolizing the abundance of their fine city. (I once asked a Neapolitan man to describe the local women, who are famous for their beauty, in one word. He replied simply, "Abundant.") This intersection is considered the center of old Naples.

• *Directly opposite the statue, between the two doors of Bar Nilo, is the...*

"Chapel of Maradona": The small "chapel" on the wall is dedicated to Diego Maradona, a soccer star who played for Naples in the 1980s. Locals consider soccer almost a religion, and this guy was practically a deity. You can even see a "hair of Diego" and a teardrop from the city when he went to another team for more money. Unfortunately, his reputation has since been sullied by problems he's had with organized crime, drugs, and police. Perhaps inspired by Maradona's example, the coffee bar has posted a quadrilingual sign (though strangely, not in English) threatening that those who take a picture without buying a cup of coffee may find their camera damaged...*Capisce*? (Note that this "chapel" is removable—if it's raining or they're just feeling grumpy, it may be gone.)

• *As you continue, you'll begin to see shops selling...*

***Presepi* (Nativity Scenes):** A few blocks farther along Spaccanapoli, at the tiny square, Via San Gregorio Armeno leads left into a colorful district (and also to the underground Napoli Sotterranea archaeological site). This has the highest concentration of shops that sell tiny components of fantastic *presepi,* including figurines caricaturing local politicians and celebrities. Just as many Americans keep an eye out year-round for Christmas-tree ornaments, Italians regularly add pieces to the family *presepe,* the centerpiece of their holiday celebrations.

• *Back on Spaccanapoli, as Via B. Croce becomes Via S. Biagio dei Librai, notice the...*

Gold and Silver Shops: Some say stolen jewelry ends up here, is melted down immediately, and gets resold in some other form as soon as it cools. The inimitable Sr. Grassi runs the Ospedale delle Bambole (doll hospital) at #81.

• *Cross busy Via Duomo. If you have time and aren't churched out, consider detouring five minutes north (left) up Via Duomo to visit the...*

Duomo: Naples' historic cathedral was built by imported French Anjou kings in the 14th century. The breathtaking Neo-Gothic facade is the result of a 19th-century renovation. Step into the vast interior to see the mix of styles along the side chapels—from pointy Gothic arches to rounded Renaissance ones to gilded Baroque decor (free, Mon-Sat 8:30-13:30 & 14:30-20:00, Sun 8:30-13:30 & 16:30-19:30).

Explore the two largest side-chapels—each practically a church in its own right. On the left, the Chapel of St. Restituta stands on the site of the original, early-Christian church that predated the cathedral (at the far end, you can pay €1.50 to see its sixth-century baptismal font under mosaics, and go downstairs to see its even earlier foundations). On the right is the Chapel of San Genarro—dedicated to the beloved patron saint of Naples—decorated with silver busts of centuries of bishops and seven paintings done on bronze.

Back out in the main nave, the altar at the front is ringed by carved wooden seats, filled three times a year by clergy to witness the Miracle of the Blood. Thousands of Neapolitans cram into this church for a peek at two tiny vials with the dried blood of San Genarro. As the clergy roots—or even jeers—for the miracle to occur, the blood temporarily liquefies. Neapolitans take this ritual with deadly seriousness, and believe that if the blood does not become liquid, it's terrible luck for the city. Sure enough, on the rare occasion that the blood has remained solid, locals can point to a terrible event soon after—such as an earthquake or an eruption of Mount Vesuvius.

The stairs beneath the altar take you to a crypt with the relics of San Genarro and (across the room) a statue of the bishop who rescued the relics from a rival town and returned them to Naples.

• *Whether or not you visit the Duomo, continue straight along Via Vicaria. As you stroll, ponder Naples' vibrant...*

Street Life, Past and Present: Here, the street and side-street scenes along Via Vicaria intensify. This is known as a center of the Camorra (organized crime). Paint a picture with these thoughts: Naples has the most intact street plan of any ancient Roman city. Imagine this city during those times (and retain these images as you visit Pompeii), with streetside shop fronts that close up after dark, turning into private homes. Today, it's just one more page in a 2,000-year-old story of a city: all kinds of meetings, beatings, and cheatings; kisses, near misses, and little-boy pisses.

You name it, it occurs right on the streets today, as it has since ancient times. People ooze from crusty corners. Black-and-white death announcements add to the clutter on the walls. Widows sell cigarettes from buckets. For a peek behind the scenes in the shade of wet laundry, venture down a few side streets. Buy two carrots as a gift for the woman on the fifth floor if she'll lower her bucket to pick them up. The neighborhood action seems best at about 18:00.

A few blocks on, at the tiny fenced-in triangle of greenery, hang out for a few minutes to just observe the crazy motorbike action and teen scene.

• *From here, veer right onto Via Forcella (which leads to the busy boulevard that takes you to Centrale Station). A block down, a tiny, fenced-in traffic island protects a chunk of the ancient Greek wall of Neapolis (fourth century* B.C.*). Turn right here on Via Pietro Colletta, walk 40 yards, and step into the North Pole, at the...*

Polo Nord Gelateria: The oldest *gelateria* in Naples has had four generations of family working here since 1931. Before you order, sample a few flavors, including their *bacio* or "kiss" flavor (chocolate and hazelnut)—all are made fresh daily (Mon-Sat 10:00-23:00, Sun 10:00-14:00 & 17:00-23:00, Via Pietro Colletta 41, tel. 081-205-431). Via Pietro Colletta leads past Napoli's two most competitive **pizzerias** (see "Pizza in Naples" sidebar, later) to Corso Umberto I.

• *Turn left on the grand boulevard-like Corso Umberto I. From here to Centrale Station, it's at least a 10-minute walk (if you're tired, hop on a bus; they all go to the station). To finish the walk, continue on Corso Umberto I—past a gauntlet of purse/CD/sunglasses salesmen and shady characters hawking stolen mobile phones—to the vast, ugly Piazza Garibaldi. On the far side is the station. You made it.*

Pizza in Naples

Naples—whose pizzerias bake just the right combination of fresh dough, mozzarella, and tomatoes in traditional wood-burning ovens—is the birthplace of pizza. Drop by one of the two most venerable pizzerias in town (both a few long blocks from the station, at the end of my "A Slice of Neapolitan Life" self-guided walk).

Antica Pizzeria da Michele is for pizza purists. Filled with locals (and tourists), it serves just two varieties: *margherita* (tomato sauce and mozzarella) and *marinara* (tomato sauce, oregano, and garlic, no cheese). Come early to sit and watch the pizza artists in action. A pizza with beer costs €6-7 (Mon-Sat 10:30-24:00, closed Sun; look for the vertical red *Antica Pizzeria* sign at the intersection of Via Pietro Colletta and Via Cesare Sersale at #1; tel. 081-553-9204). As this place is often jammed with a long line, arrive early or late to get a seat. If there's a mob, head inside to get a number. If it's too crowded, the less-exceptional Pizzeria Trianon (described next) generally has room.

Pizzeria Trianon, across the street, has been da Michele's archrival since 1923. It offers more choices, slightly higher prices (€5-7), air-conditioning, and a cozier atmosphere. For less chaos, head upstairs. While waiting for your meal, you can survey the transformation of a humble wad of dough into a smoldering bubbly feast in their entryway pizza kitchen (daily 11:00-15:30 & 19:00-23:00, Via Pietro Colletta 42, tel. 081-553-9426, Giuseppe).

Porta Nolana Open-Air Fish Market

For those with a little more time, Naples' fish market squirts and stinks as it has for centuries under the Porta Nolana (gate in the city wall) immediately in front of Napoli P. Nolana Station and four long blocks from Centrale Station. Of the town's many boisterous outdoor markets, this will net you the most photos and memories. From Piazza Nolana, wander under the medieval gate and take your first left down Vico Sopramuro, enjoying this wild and entirely edible cultural scavenger hunt (Tue-Sun 8:00-14:00, closed Mon).

Two other markets with more clothing and less fish are at Piazza Capuana (several blocks northwest of Centrale Station and tumbling down Via Sant'Antonio Abate, Mon-Sat 8:00-18:00, Sun 9:00-13:00) and a similar cobbled shopping zone along Via Pignasecca (just off Via Toledo, west of Piazza Carità, described on page 428).

Pompeii

Stopped in its tracks by the eruption of Mount Vesuvius in A.D. 79, Pompeii offers the best look anywhere at what life in Rome must

have been like around 2,000 years ago. A once-thriving commercial port of 20,000, Pompeii (worth ▲▲▲) grew from Greek and Etruscan roots to become an important Roman city. Then, on August 24, A.D. 79, everything changed. Vesuvius erupted and began to bury the city under 30 feet of hot volcanic ash. For the archaeologists who excavated it centuries later, this was a shake-and-bake windfall, teaching them volumes about daily Roman life. Pompeii was accidentally rediscovered in 1599; excavations began in 1748.

Orientation to Pompeii

Cost: €11, cash only.

Hours: Daily April-Oct 8:30-19:30, Nov-March 8:30-17:00 (last entry 1.5 hours before closing).

Closures: Be warned that some buildings and streets are bound to be closed for restoration when you visit.

Crowd-Beating Tips: On busy days, there can be a line of up to 30 minutes to buy a ticket. If you anticipate lines, buy your ticket at the "info point" kiosk at the train station (same price as at the site, credit cards accepted).

Getting There: Pompeii is roughly midway between Naples and Sorrento on the Circumvesuviana train line (2/hour, €2.80 and 40 minutes from Naples, one-way, not covered by railpasses, www.vesuviana.it). Get off at the Pompei Scavi, Villa dei Misteri stop; from Naples, it's the stop after Torre Annunziata. The DD express trains bypass several of the suburban stations but stop at the site, making the trip slightly faster. The "info point" kiosk at the station is a private agency selling tours (not a real TI), but they can provide some information and sell tickets for the site. From the Pompei Scavi train station, it's just a short five-minute walk to the site entrance: Turn right and walk down the road about a block to the entrance (first left turn). Parking is available at Camping Zeus near the Circumvesuviana train station (€2.50/hour); several other campgrounds/parking lots are nearby.

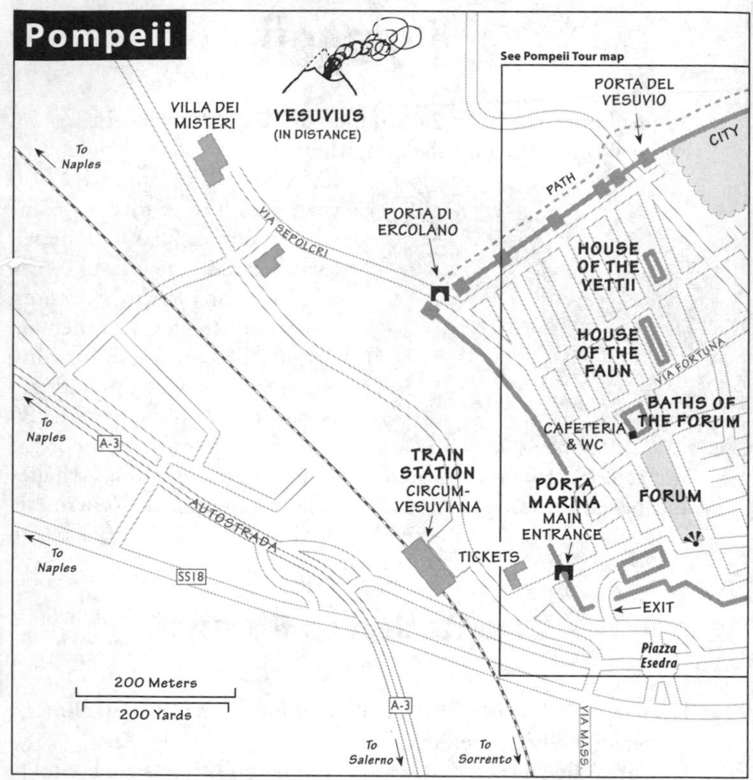

Information: A good map and a helpful information booklet (which describes the most important stops within the site), when available, are included with your admission, but you must pick them up at the information window (to the left of the WCs). Tel. 081-857-5347, www.pompeiisites.org.

The bookshop sells the small Pompeii and Herculaneum *Past and Present* book. Its plastic overlays allow you to re-create the ruins (€13 in bookstores, pay no more than that if you buy from a street vendor; look for the current year's edition).

Tours: My self-guided tour in this chapter covers the basics and provides a good framework for exploring the site on your own. You can download this chapter as a free Rick Steves **audio tour**; see page 27.

Live guides (around €110/2 hours) of varying quality—there really is no guarantee of what you're getting—cluster near the ticket booth and may try to herd you into a group with other travelers, which makes the price more reasonable for you. For a private tour, consider **Gaetano Manfredi,** who

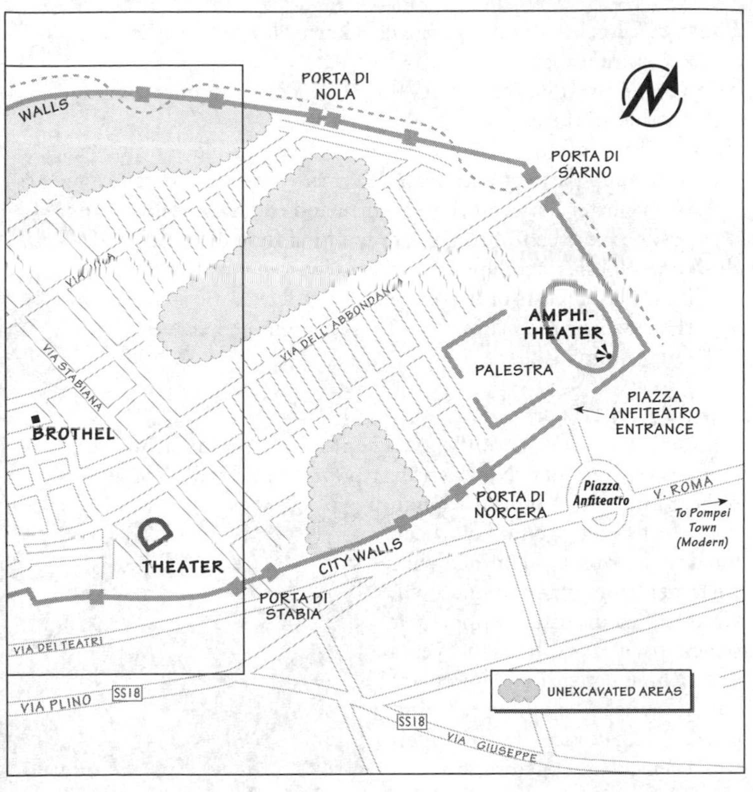

is pricey but brings energy and theatricality to his tours (€120-220 for 8-10 people, book in advance—best by email, mobile 338-725-5620, www.pompeiitourguide.com, gaetanoguide@hotmail.it). **Antonio Somma** also specializes in the site and does tours of the surrounding region (€115, book in advance, mobile 339-891-9489, www.pompeitour.com, info@pompeitour.com). The Naples-based guides listed on page 417 can also guide you at Pompeii. Parents, note that the ancient brothel and its sexually explicit frescoes are included on tours; let your guide know if you'd rather skip that stop.

Audioguides are available from a kiosk near the ticket booth at the Porta Marina entrance (€6.50, €10/2 people, ID required), but they offer basically the same info as your free booklet.

Length of This Tour: Allow two hours, or three if you visit the theater and amphitheater.

With Limited Time: If you're short on time, focus on the Forum, the Baths of the Forum, the House of the Faun, the House of the Vettii (if it's open), and the brothel.

Baggage Check: A free baggage check is near the turnstiles at the site entrance.

Services: The site has two WCs—one near the entrance and another in the cafeteria.

Eating: The cafeteria within the site serves edible sandwiches, pizza, and pasta at a reasonable price. A few mediocre restaurants cluster between the entrance and the train station. Your best bet may be to bring your own food for a discreet picnic.

Starring: Roofless (collapsed) but otherwise intact Roman buildings, plaster casts of hapless victims, a few erotic frescoes, and the dawning realization that these ancient people were no different from us.

Background

Pompeii, founded in 600 B.C., eventually became a booming Roman trading city. Not rich, not poor, it was middle class—a perfect example of typical Roman life. Most streets would have been lined with stalls and jammed with customers from sunup to sundown. Chariots vied with shoppers for street space. Two thousand years ago, Rome controlled the entire Mediterranean—making it a kind of free-trade zone—and Pompeii was a central and bustling port.

There were no posh neighborhoods in Pompeii. Rich and poor mixed it up as elegant houses existed side by side with simple homes. While nearby Herculaneum would have been a classier place to live (traffic-free streets, fancier houses, far better drainage), Pompeii was the place for action and shopping. It served an estimated 20,000 residents with more than 40 bakeries, 30 brothels, and 130 bars, restaurants, and hotels. With most of its buildings covered by brilliant white ground-marble stucco, Pompeii in A.D. 79 was an impressive town.

POMPEII

As you tour Pompeii, remember that its best art is in the Archaeological Museum in Naples (described earlier in this chapter).

Self-Guided Tour

• *Just past the ticket-taker, start your approach up to the...*

❶ Porta Marina

The city of Pompeii was born on the hill ahead of you. This was the original town gate. Before Vesuvius blew and filled in the har-

bor, the sea came nearly to here. Look to the left (near the tall cypress tree) to see the stone rings where ships tied up to the dock. Also notice the two openings in the gate (ahead, up the ramp). Both were left open by day to admit major traffic. At night, the larger one was closed for better security.

• *Pass through the Porta Marina and continue up to the top of the street, pausing at the three large stepping-stones in the middle.*

❷ Pompeii's Streets

Every day, Pompeiians flooded the streets with gushing water to clean them. These stepping-stones let pedestrians cross without getting their sandals wet. Chariots traveling in either direction could straddle the stones (all had standard-size axles). A single stepping-stone in a road means it was a one-way street, a pair indicates an ordinary two-way, and three (like this) signifies a major thoroughfare. The basalt stones are the original Roman pavement. The sidewalks (elevated to hide the plumbing) were paved with bits of broken pots (an ancient form of recycling) and studded with reflective bits of white marble. These "cats' eyes" helped people get around after dark, either by moonlight or with the help of lamps.

• *Continue straight ahead, don your mental toga, and enter the city as the Romans once did. The road opens up into the spacious main square: the Forum. Stand at the near end of this rectangular space and look toward Mount Vesuvius.*

❸ The Forum (Foro)

Pompeii's commercial, religious, and political center stands at the intersection of the city's two main streets. While it's the most ruined part of Pompeii, it's grand nonetheless. Picture the piazza surrounded by two-story buildings on all sides. The pedestals that line the square once held

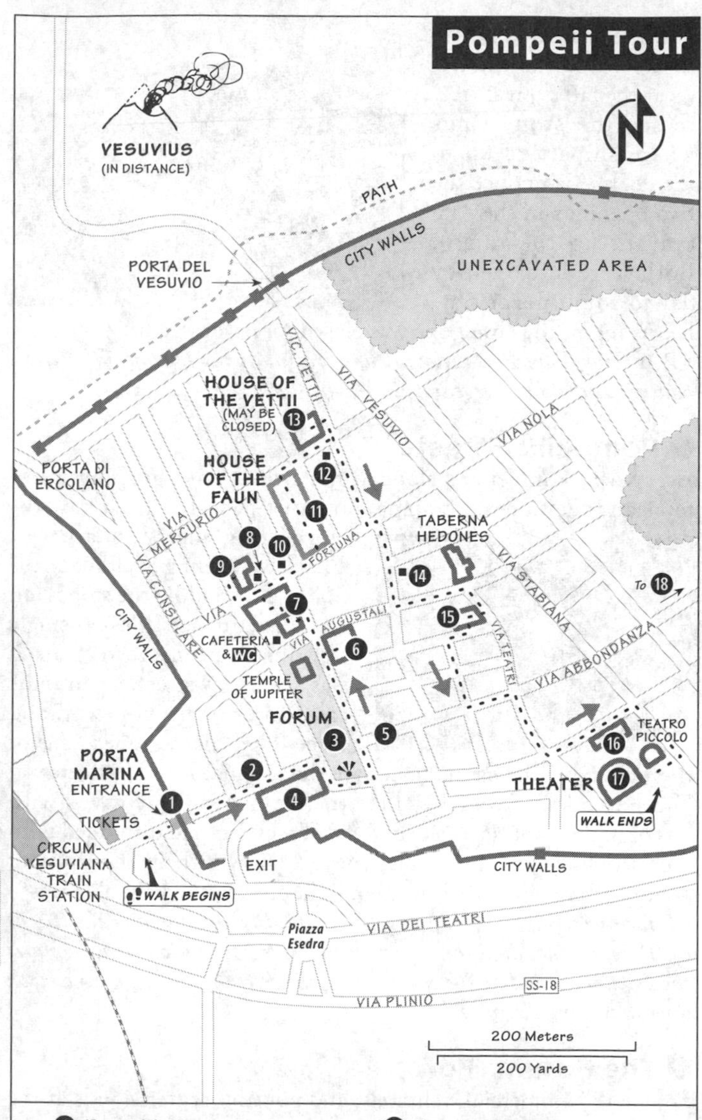

1. Porta Marina
2. Pompeii's Streets
3. Forum
4. Basilica
5. Via Abbondanza
6. Fish & Produce Market; Plaster Casts of Victims
7. Baths of the Forum
8. Fast-Food Joint
9. House of the Tragic Poet
10. Aqueduct Arch
11. House of the Faun
12. Original Lead Pipes
13. House of the Vettii
14. Bakery & Mill
15. Brothel
16. Temple of Isis
17. Theater & Piccolo Theater
18. To Amphitheater

statues (now safely displayed in the museum in Naples). In its heyday, Pompeii's citizens gathered here in the main square to shop, talk politics, and socialize. Business took place in the important buildings that lined the piazza.

The Forum was dominated by the **Temple of Jupiter,** at the far end (marked by a half-dozen ruined columns atop a stair-step base). Jupiter was the supreme god of the Roman pantheon—you might be able to make out his little white marble head at the center-rear of the temple.

At the near end of the Forum (behind where you're standing) is the **curia,** or city hall. Like many Roman buildings, it was built with brick and mortar, then covered with marble walls and floors. To your left (as you face Vesuvius and the Temple of Jupiter) is the **basilica,** or courthouse.

Since Pompeii was a pretty typical Roman town, it has the same layout and components that you'll find in any Roman city—main square, curia, basilica, temples, axis of roads, and so on. All power converged at the Forum: religious (the temple), political (the curia), judicial (the basilica), and commercial (this piazza was the main marketplace). Even the power of the people was expressed here, since this where they gathered to vote. Imagine the hubbub of this town square in its heyday.

Look beyond the Temple of Jupiter. Five miles to the north looms the ominous backstory to this site: **Mount Vesuvius.** Mentally draw a triangle up from the two remaining peaks to reconstruct the mountain before the eruption. When it blew, Pompeiians had no idea that they were living under a volcano, since Vesuvius hadn't erupted for 1,200 years. Imagine the wonder—then the horror—as a column of pulverized rock roared upward, and then ash began to fall. The weight of the ash and small rocks collapsed Pompeii's roofs later that day, crushing people who had taken refuge inside buildings instead of fleeing the city.

• *As you face Vesuvius, the basilica is to your left, lined with stumps of columns. Step inside and see the layout.*

❹ Basilica

Pompeii's basilica was a first-century palace of justice. This ancient law court has the same floor plan later adopted by many Christian churches (which are also called basilicas). The big central hall (or nave) is flanked by rows of columns marking off narrower side aisles. Along the side walls are traces of the original marble.

The Eruption of Vesuvius

At about 1:00 in the afternoon on August 24, A.D. 79, Mount Vesuvius erupted, sending a mushroom cloud of ash, dust, and rocks 12 miles into the air. It spewed for 18 hours straight, as winds blew the cloud southward. The white-gray ash settled like a heavy snow on Pompeii, its weight eventually collapsing roofs and floors, but leaving the walls intact. While most of Pompeii's 20,000 residents fled that day, about two thousand stayed behind.

Although the city of Herculaneum was closer to the volcano—about four miles away—it had largely escaped the rain of ash, due to the direction of the wind. However, 12 hours after Vesuvius awoke, the type of eruption suddenly changed. The column of hot gas and rock collapsed, creating a superheated avalanche of ash, pumice, and gas. This red-hot "pyroclastic flow" sped down the side of the mountain at nearly 100 miles per hour, engulfing Herculaneum. Several more flows over the next few hours further entombed Herculaneum, burying it in nearly 60 feet of hot material that later cooled into rock, freezing the city in time. Then around 7:30 in the morning, another pyroclastic flow headed south and struck Pompeii, dealing a fatal blow to those who'd remained behind.

The columns—now stumps all about the same height—were not ruined by the volcano. Rather, they were left unfinished when Vesuvius blew. Pompeii had been devastated by an earthquake in A.D. 62, and was just in the process of rebuilding the basilica when Vesuvius erupted 17 years later. The half-built columns show off the technology of the day. Uniform bricks were stacked around a cylindrical core. Once finished, they would have been coated with marble dust stucco to simulate marble columns—an economical construction method found throughout Pompeii (and the Roman Empire).

Besides the earthquake and the eruption, Pompeii's buildings have suffered other ravages over the years, including Spanish plunderers (c. 1800), 19th-century souvenir hunters, WWII bombs, wild vegetation, another earthquake in 1980, and modern neglect. The fact that the entire city was covered by the eruption of A.D. 79 actually helped preserve it, saving it from the sixth-century barbarians who plundered many other towns into oblivion.

• *Exit the basilica and cross the short side of the square, where the city's main street hits the Forum.*

❺ Via Abbondanza

Look down Via Abbondanza, Pompeii's main street. Lined with shops, bars, and restaurants, it was a lively, pedestrian-only zone.

The three "beaver-teeth" stones are traffic barriers that kept chariots out. On the corner (just to the left), take a close look at the dark travertine column standing next to the white one. Notice that the marble drums of the white column are not chiseled entirely round—another construction project left unfinished when Vesuvius erupted.

• *Head toward Vesuvius, walking along the right side of the Forum. Immediately to the right of the Temple of Jupiter (just before the four round arches), a door leads into the market hall, where you'll find two glass cases.*

❻ Fish and Produce Market—Plaster Casts of Victims

As the frescoes on the wall (just inside on the left) indicate, this is where Pompeiians came to buy their food—fish, bread, chickens, and so on. These fine examples of Roman art—with their glimpses of everyday life and mastery of depth and illusion—would not be matched until the Renaissance, a thousand years after the fall of Rome.

The glass cases hold casts of Pompeiians, eerily captured in their last moments. They were quickly suffocated by a superheated avalanche of gas and ash, and their bodies were encased in volcanic debris. While excavating, modern archaeologists detected hollow spaces underfoot, created when the victims' bodies decomposed. By gently filling the holes with plaster, the archaeologists were able to create molds of the Pompeiians who were caught in the disaster.

• *Continue on, leaving the Forum through an arch behind the Temple of Jupiter. Here you'll find a pedestrian-only road sign (ahead on the right corner, above the* REG VII INS IV *sign) and more "beaver-teeth" traffic blocks. The modern cafeteria is the only eatery inside the archaeological site (with a coffee bar and WC). Twenty yards past the cafeteria, on the left-hand side at #24, is the entrance to the...*

❼ Baths of the Forum (Terme del Foro)

Pompeii had six public baths, each with a men's and a women's section. You're in the men's zone. The leafy courtyard at the entrance was the gymnasium. After working out, clients could relax with a hot bath *(caldarium)*, warm bath *(tepidarium)*, or cold plunge *(frigidarium)*.

The first big, plain room you enter served as the **dressing room.** Holes on the walls were for pegs to hang clothing. High up, the window (with a faded Neptune underneath) was originally covered with a less-translucent Roman glass. Walk over the non-slip mosaics into the next room.

The ***tepidarium*** is ringed by mini-statues or *telamones* (male caryatids, figures used as supporting pillars), which divided the lockers. Clients would undress and warm up here, perhaps stretching out on one of the bronze benches near the bronze heater for a massage. Look at the ceiling—half crushed by the eruption and half intact, with its fine blue-and-white stucco work.

Next, admire the engineering in the steam-bath room, or ***caldarium***. The double floor was heated from below—so nice with bare feet (look into the grate to see the brick support towers). The double walls with brown terra-cotta tiles held the heat. Romans soaked in the big tub, which was filled with hot water. Opposite the big tub is a fountain, which spouted water onto the hot floor, creating steam. The lettering on the fountain reminded those enjoying the room which two politicians paid for it...and how much it cost them (5,250 *sestertii*). To keep condensation from dripping annoyingly from the ceiling, fluting (ribbing) was added to carry water down the walls.

• *Today's visitors exit the baths through the original entry. If you're a bit hungry, immediately across the street is an ancient...*

❽ Fast-Food Joint

After a bath, it was only natural to want a little snack. So, just across the street is a fast-food joint, marked by a series of rectangular marble counters. Most ancient Romans didn't cook for themselves in their tiny apartments, so to-go places like this were commonplace. The holes in the counters held the pots for food. Each container was like a thermos, with a wooden lid to keep the soup hot, the wine cool, and so on. Notice the groove in the front doorstep and the holes out on the curb. The holes likely accommodated cords for stretching awnings over the sidewalk to shield the clientele from the hot sun, while the grooves were for the shop's folding accordion doors. Look at the wheel grooves in the pavement, worn down through centuries of use. Nearby are more stepping-stones for pedestrians to cross the flooded streets.

• *Just a few steps uphill from the fast-food joint, at #5 (with a locked gate), is the...*

❾ House of the Tragic Poet (Casa de Poeta Tragico)

This house is typical Roman style. The entry is flanked by two family-owned shops (each with a track for a collapsing accordion door). The home is like a train running straight away from the street: atrium (with skylight and pool to catch the rain), den (where deals were made by the shopkeeper), and garden (with rooms facing it and a shrine to remember both the gods and family ancestors). In the entryway is the famous "Beware of Dog" *(Cave Canem)* mosaic.

Today's visitors enter the home by the back door (circle around to the left). On your way there, look for the modern exposed pipe on the left side of the lane; this is the same as ones used in the ancient plumbing system, hidden beneath the raised sidewalk. Inside the house, the grooves on the marble well-head in the entry hall (possibly closed) were formed by generations of inhabitants dragging the bucket up by rope. The richly frescoed dining room is off the garden. Diners lounged on their couches (the Roman custom) and enjoyed frescoes with fake "windows," giving the illusion of a bigger and airier room. Next to the dining room is a humble BBQ-style kitchen with a little closet for the toilet (the kitchen and bathroom shared the same plumbing).

• *Return to the fast-food place and continue about 10 yards downhill to the big intersection. From the center of the intersection, look left to see a giant arch, framing a nice view of Mount Vesuvius.*

❿ Aqueduct Arch—Running Water

Water was critical for this city of 20,000 people, and this arch was part of Pompeii's water-delivery system. A 100-mile-long aqueduct carried fresh water down from the hillsides to a big reservoir perched at the highest point of the city wall. Since overall water pressure was disappointing, Pompeiians built arches like the brick one you see here (originally covered in marble) with hidden water tanks at the top. Located just below the altitude of the main tank, these smaller tanks were filled by gravity, and provided each neighborhood with reliable pressure.

• *If you're thirsty, fill your water bottle from the modern fountain. Then continue straight downhill one block (50 yards) to #2 on the left.*

⓫ House of the Faun (Casa del Founo)

Stand across the street and marvel at the grand entry with *"HAVE"* (hail to you) as a welcome mat. Go in. Notice the two shrines above the entryway—one dedicated to the gods, the other to this wealthy family's ancestors.

You are standing in Pompeii's largest home, where you're

greeted by the delightful small bronze statue of the *Dancing Faun,* famed for its realistic movement and fine proportion. (The original, described on page 422, is in Naples' Archaeological Museum.) With 40 rooms and 27,000 square feet, the House of the Faun covers an entire city block. The next floor mosaic, with an intricate diamond-like design, decorates the homeowner's office. Beyond that is the famous floor mosaic of the *Battle of Alexander.* (The original is also at the museum in Naples.) In 333 B.C., Alexander the Great beat Darius and the Persians. Romans had great respect for Alexander, the first great emperor before Rome's. While most of Pompeii's nouveau riche had notoriously bad taste and stuffed their palaces with over-the-top, mismatched decor, this guy had class. Both the faun (an ancient copy of a famous Greek statue) and the Alexander mosaic show an appreciation for history.

The house's back courtyard leads to the exit in the far-right corner. It's lined with pillars rebuilt after the A.D. 62 earthquake. Take a close look at the brick, mortar, and fake marble stucco veneer.

• *Sneak out of the House of the Faun through its back door and turn right. (If this exit is closed, return to the entrance and make a U-turn left, around to the back of the house.) Thirty yards down, along the right-hand side of the street are metal cages protecting...*

⓬ Original Lead Pipes

These 2,000-year-old pipes (made of lead imported from Britannia) were part of the city's elaborate water system. From the aqueduct-fed water tank at the high end of town, three independent pipe systems supplied water to the city: one for baths, one for private homes, and one for public water fountains. If there was a water shortage, democratic priorities prevailed: First the baths were cut off, then the private homes. The last water supply to go was the public fountains, where all citizens could get drinking and cooking water.

• *If the street's not closed off, take your first left (on Vicolo dei Vettii), walk about 20 yards, and find the entrance (on the left) to the next stop. (If the street is closed, turn right down the street marked* REG VI INS XIV *and skip down to the next set of directions.)*

⓭ House of the Vettii (Casa dei Vettii)

Pompeii's best-preserved home has been completely blocked off for years; unfortunately it's unlikely to reopen in time for your

visit. The House of the Vettii was the bachelor pad of two wealthy merchant brothers. If you can see the entryway, you may spot the huge erection. This is not pornography. There's a meaning here: The penis and the sack of money balance each other on the goldsmith scale above a fine bowl of fruit. Translation: Only with a balance of fertility and money can you have abundance.

If it's open, step into the atrium with its ceiling open to the sky to collect light and rainwater. The pool, while decorative, was a functional water-supply tank. It's flanked by large money boxes anchored to the floor. The brothers were certainly successful merchants, and possibly moneylenders, too.

Exit on the right, passing the tight servant quarters, and go into the kitchen, with its bronze cooking pots (and an exposed lead pipe on the back wall). The passage dead-ends in the little Venus Room, which features erotic frescoes behind glass.

Return to the atrium and pass into the big colonnaded garden. It was replanted according to the plan indicated by the traces of roots that were excavated from the volcanic ash. Richly frescoed entertainment rooms ring this courtyard. Circle counterclockwise. The dining room is finely decorated in black and "Pompeiian red" (from iron rust). Study the detail. Notice the lead humidity seal between the wall and the floor, designed to keep the moisture-sensitive frescoes dry. (Had Leonardo da Vinci taken this clever step, his *Last Supper* in Milan might be in better shape today.) Continuing around, you'll see more of the square white stones inlaid in the floor. Imagine them reflecting like cats' eyes as the brothers and their friends wandered around by oil lamp late at night. Frescoes in the Yellow Room (near the exit) show off the ancient mastery of perspective, which would not be matched elsewhere in Europe for nearly 1,500 years.

• *Facing the entrance to the House of the Vettii, turn left and walk downhill one long block (along Vicolo dei Vettii) to a T-intersection (Via della Fortuna), marked by a stone fountain with a bull's head for a spout. Intersections like this were busy neighborhood centers, where the rent was highest and people gathered. With the fountain at your back, turn left, then*

immediately right, walking along a gently curving road (Vicolo Storto). On the left side of the street, at #22, find four big stone cylinders.

⓮ Bakery and Mill (Forno e Mulini)

The brick oven looks like a modern-day pizza oven. The stubby stone towers are flour grinders. Grain was poured into the top, and donkeys or slaves pushed wooden bars that turned the stones. The powdered grain dropped out of the bottom as flour—flavored with tiny bits of rock. Each neighborhood had a bakery like this.

Continue to the next intersection (Via degli Augustali, where there's another fast-food joint, at #32) and turn left. As you walk, look at the destructive power of all the vines, and notice how deeply the chariot grooves have worn into the pavement. Deep grooves could break wagon wheels. The suddenly ungroovy stretch indicates that this road was in the process of being repaved when the eruption shut everything down.

• *Head about 50 yards down this (obviously one-way) street to #44 (on the left). Here you'll find the Taberna Hedones (with a small atrium, den, and garden). This bar still has its original floor and, deeper in, the mosaic arch of a grotto fountain. Just past the tavern, turn right and walk downhill to #18, on the right.*

Possible detour: If the road past the tavern is blocked off, here's another way to reach the next stop: First, backtrack to the Forum—go back the way you came, turn left at the bull's-head fountain, then turn left again at the aqueduct arch. Back in the Forum, head down to the far end and turn left onto the main street, Via dell'Abbondanza (which we looked down earlier—remember the beaver teeth?). Follow this, turning left up the second street (after the fountain, marked REG VII INS I, *with a small* Vicolo del Lupanare *sign). This leads to the entrance of the...*

⓯ Brothel (Lupanare)

You'll find the biggest crowds in Pompeii at a place that was likely popular 2,000 ago, too—the brothel. Prostitutes were nicknamed *lupe* (she-wolves), alluding to the call they made when trying to attract business. The brothel was a simple place, with beds and pillows made of stone. The ancient graffiti includes tallies and exotic names of the women, indicating the prostitutes came from all corners of the Mediterranean (it also served as feedback from satisfied customers). The faded frescoes above the cells may have been a kind of menu for services offered. Note the idealized women (white, which was considered beautiful; one wears an early bra) and the rougher men (dark, considered horny). The bed legs came with little disk-like barriers to keep critters from crawling up.

• *Leaving the brothel, go right, then take the first left, and continue going downhill two blocks to the intersection with Pompeii's main drag, Via dell'Abbondanza. The Forum—and exit—are to the right, for those who may wish to opt out from here.*

The huge amphitheater—which is certainly skippable—is 10 minutes to your left. But for now, go left for 60 yards, then turn right just beyond the fountain, and walk down Via dei Teatri. Turn left before the columns, and head downhill another 60 yards to #28, which marks the...

⓰ Temple of Isis

This Egyptian temple served Pompeii's Egyptian community. The little white stucco shrine with the modern plastic roof housed holy water from the Nile. Isis, from Egyptian myth, was one of many foreign gods adopted by the eclectic Romans. Pompeii must have had a synagogue, too, but it has yet to be excavated.

• *Exit the temple where you entered, and go right. At the next intersection, turn right again, and head downhill to the adjacent theaters. Your goal is the large theater down the corridor at #20, but if it's closed, look at the smaller but similar theater (Teatro Piccolo) just beyond at #19.*

⓱ Theater

Originally a Greek theater (Greeks built theirs with the help of a hillside), this was the birthplace of the Greek port here in 470 B.C.

During Roman times, the theater sat 5,000 people in three sets of seats, all with different prices: the five marble terraces up close (filled with romantic wooden seats for two), the main section, and the cheap nosebleed section (surviving only on the high end, near the trees). The square stones above the cheap seats once supported a canvas rooftop. Take note of the high-profile boxes, flanking the stage, for guests of honor. From this perch, you can see the gladiator barracks—the colonnaded courtyard beyond the theater. They lived in tiny rooms, trained in the courtyard, and fought in the nearby amphitheater.

• *You've seen Pompeii's highlights. When you're ready to leave, backtrack to the main road and turn left, going uphill to the Forum, where you'll find the main entrance/exit.*

However, there's much more to see—three-quarters of Pompeii's

164 acres have been excavated, but this tour has covered only a third of the site. After the theater—if you still have energy to see more—go back to the main road, and take a right toward the eastern part of the site, where the crowds thin out. Go straight for about 10 minutes, likely jogging right after a bit (just follow the posted maps). You'll wind up passing through a pretty, forested area. At the far end is the...

⓲ Amphitheater

If you can, climb to the upper level of the amphitheater (though the stairs are often blocked). With Vesuvius looming in the background, mentally replace the tourists below with gladiators and wild animals locked in combat. Walk along the top of the amphitheater and look down into the grassy rectangular area surrounded by columns. This is the **Palaestra,** an area once used for athletic training. (If you can't get to the top of the amphitheater, you can see the Palaestra from outside—in fact, you can't miss it, as it's right next door.) Facing the other way, look for the bell tower that tops the roofline of the modern city of Pompei, where locals go about their daily lives in the shadow of the volcano, just as their ancestors did 2,000 years ago. *HAVE!*

• *If it's too crowded to bear hiking back along uneven lanes to the entrance, you can slip out the site's "back door," which is next to the amphitheater. Exiting, turn right and follow the site's wall through nondescript neighborhoods all the way back to the entrance.*

ROMAN HISTORY

Three Millennia in Seven Pages

History in a Hurry

Ancient Rome lasted a thousand years (500 B.C.-A.D. 500), half as an expanding republic, half as a dominating empire. When Rome

fell to invaders, all of Europe suffered a thousand years of poverty and ignorance (A.D. 500-1500), though Rome's influence could still be felt in the Catholic Church. Popes rebuilt Rome for pilgrims—in Renaissance, then Baroque and Neoclassical styles (1500-1800). As capital of a newly united Italy, Rome followed fascist Mussolini into World War II (and lost), but rebounded in Italy's postwar economic boom.

Want more?

Legendary Birth (1200-500 B.C.)

Aeneas flees burning Troy (1200 B.C.), wanders like Odysseus, and finally finds a home along the Tiber. His descendants, Romulus and Remus—orphaned at birth, suckled by a she-wolf, and raised by shepherds—grow up to steal wives and build a wall, thus founding Rome (753 B.C.).

Closer to fact, the local

agrarian tribes were dominated by more sophisticated neighbors to the north (Etruscans) and south (Greek colonists). Their convenient location on the Tiber was perfect for a future power.

Sights

- Romulus' "huts" and wall (Palatine Hill)
- She-Wolf statue (Capitoline Museums)
- Frescoes of Aeneas and Romulus (National Museum of Rome)
- Bernini's Aeneas statue (Borghese Gallery)
- Etruscan wing (Vatican Museum)
- Etruscan Museum (in Villa Borghese Gardens)
- Etruscan legacy (the original Circus Maximus, the drained Forum)

The Republic (509-27 B.C.)

The city expands throughout the Italian peninsula (500-300 B.C.), then defeats Hannibal's North African Carthaginians (the Punic Wars, 264-146 B.C.) and Greece (168 B.C.). Rome is master of the Mediterranean, and booty and captured slaves pour in. Romans bicker among themselves over their slice of the pie, pitting the wealthy landowners (the ruling Senate) against the working class (plebs) and the rebellious slaves (Spartacus' revolt, 73 B.C.). In the chaos, charismatic generals like Julius Caesar, who can provide wealth and security, become dictators. Change is necessary...and coming.

Sights

- Forum's Curia, Temple of Saturn, Temple of Castor and Pollux, Rostrum, Basilica Aemilia, Temple of Julius Caesar, and Basilica Julia (all rebuilt later)
- Appian Way built, lined with tombs
- Aqueducts, which carry water to a growing city
- Portrait busts of citizens (National Museum of Rome)
- The republic's "S.P.Q.R." monogram and motto, seen today on statues, buildings, and even manhole covers: *Senatus Populusque Romanus*, or the "Senate and People of Rome." (Some northern Italians, who feel the South is dragging them down, translate S.P.Q.R. as *Sono Porci Questi Romani*—"These Romans Are Pigs.")

The Empire—The "Roman Peace," or Pax Romana (A.D. 1-200)

After Julius Caesar is killed by disgruntled republicans, his adopted son Augustus takes undisputed control, ends the civil wars, declares himself emperor, and adopts a family member to succeed him, setting the pattern of rule for the next 500 years.

Rome rules an empire of 54 million people, stretching from England to Africa, from Spain to Turkey. The city, with more than a million inhabitants, is decorated with Greek-style statues and monumental structures faced with marble...it is the marvel of known world. The empire prospers on a (false) economy of booty, slaves, and trade, surviving the often turbulent and naughty behavior of emperors such as Caligula and Nero. You can see Roman history in the faces of the emperors by reading the ✪ National Museum of Rome Tour chapter.

Sights

- Colosseum
- Forum
- Palatine Hill palaces
- Ara Pacis ("Altar of Peace")
- Augustus' house (House of Livia and Augustus) on Palatine Hill
- Pantheon
- Trajan's Column and Forum
- Greek and Greek-style statues and emperors' busts (National Museum of Rome, Vatican Museum, Capitoline Museums)
- Piazza Navona (former stadium)
- Hadrian's Villa (Tivoli) and tomb (now Castel Sant'Angelo)

Rome Falls (200-476)

Corruption, disease, and the constant pressure of barbarians pecking away at the borders slowly drain the unwieldy empire.

Despite Diocletian's division of the empire and Constantine's legalization of Christianity (313), the city is sacked (410), and the last emperor checks out (476). Rome falls like a huge column, kicking up dust that will plunge Europe into a thousand years of darkness.

Church Architecture

History comes to life when you visit a centuries-old church. Even if you wouldn't know your apse from a hole in the ground, learning a few simple terms will enrich your experience. Note that not every church has every feature, and that a "cathedral" isn't a type of church architecture, but rather a designation for a church that's a governing center for a local bishop.

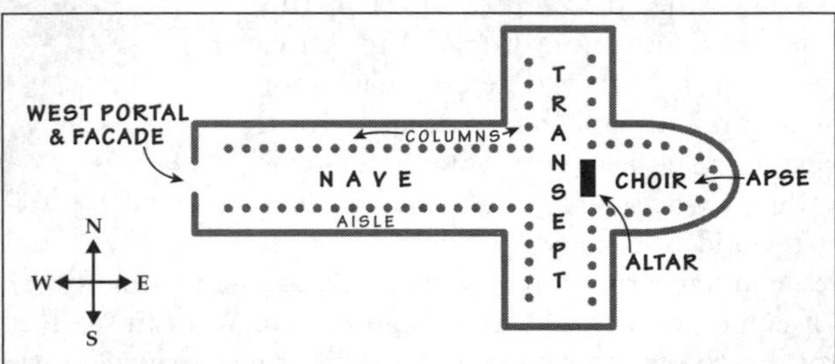

Aisles: The long, generally low-ceilinged arcades that flank the nave.

Altar: The raised area with a ceremonial table (often adorned with candles or a crucifix), where the priest prepares and serves the bread and wine for Communion.

Apse: The space beyond the altar, generally bordered with small chapels.

Barrel Vault: A continuous round-arched ceiling that resembles an extended upside-down U.

Choir: A cozy area, often screened off, located within the church nave and near the high altar, where services are sung in a more intimate setting.

Cloister: A square-shaped series of hallways surrounding an open-air courtyard, traditionally where monks and nuns got fresh air.

Facade: The outer wall of the church's main (west) entrance, viewable from outside and generally highly decorated.

Groin Vault: An arched ceiling formed where two equal barrel vaults meet at right angles. Less common usage: term for a medieval jock strap.

Narthex: The area (portico or foyer) between the main entry and the nave.

Nave: The long, central section of the church (running west to east, from the entrance to the altar) where the congregation stood through the service.

Transept: The north-south part of the church, which crosses (perpendicularly) the east-west nave. In a traditional Latin cross-shaped floor plan, the transept forms the "arms" of the cross.

West Portal: The main entry to the church (on the west end, opposite the main altar).

Sights

- Arch of Constantine
- The Forum's Basilica of Constantine
- Baths of Diocletian
- Old Roman Wall (gates at Via Veneto or Piramide)

Medieval Rome (500-1500)

The once-great city of a million people dwindles to a rough village of 50,000, with a corrupt pope, forgotten ruins, and malaria-carrying mosquitoes. Cows graze in the ruined Forum, and wolves prowl the Vatican at night. During the 1300s, even the popes leave Rome to live in France. What little glory Rome retains is in the pomp, knowledge, and wealth of the Catholic Church.

Sights

- The damage done to ancient Roman monuments, caused by disuse, barbarian looting, and pillaging for pre-cut stones
- Early Christian churches built before Rome fell (Santa Maria Maggiore, San Giovanni in Laterano, and San Clemente)
- Churches of Santa Maria sopra Minerva and Santa Maria in Trastevere
- Castel Sant'Angelo

Renaissance and Baroque Rome (1500-1800)

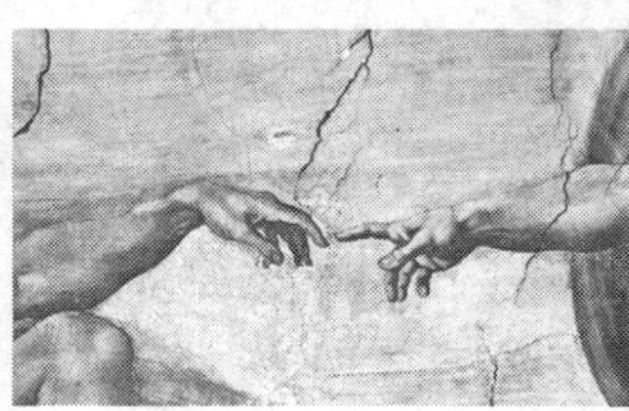

As Europe's economy recovers, energetic popes rebuild Rome to attract pilgrims. The best artists decorate palaces and churches, carve statues, and build fountains. The city is not a great political force, but as the center of Catholicism during the struggle against Protestants (c. 1520-1648), it is an influential religious and cultural capital.

Renaissance Sights

- Michelangelo's Sistine Chapel (Vatican Museum), dome of St. Peter's, *Pietà* (St. Peter's), *Moses* (St. Peter-in-Chains Church), Christ statue (Santa Maria sopra Minerva), Piazza del Campidoglio (Capitoline Hill Square), Santa Maria degli Angeli church (in former Baths of Diocletian)
- Raphael's *School of Athens* and *Transfiguration* (Vatican Museum)

Rome in World War II

By 1943, as bombs began falling just outside the walls of Rome, it was clear to all that Italy's alliance with Nazi Germany was a huge mistake, leading the country to ruin. The fascist Grand Council dismissed Mussolini, and the king ordered his arrest. The ex-dictator fled north, and fascism collapsed without violence. Rome was declared an "open city" (meaning a city with no military bases). Italy surrendered to the Allies. The king fled to Allied-occupied southern Italy, abandoning Rome to Nazi forces, which occupied it for nine terrible months. The Roman people and the Vatican joined forces to save some citizens from the Nazis.

The Gestapo demanded 50 kilos of gold from the Roman Jews, who, with great difficulty and help from non-Jews, succeeded in providing it. Regardless, more than 2,000 Jews were deported to concentration camps. After Italian partisans planted a bomb near the Trevi Fountain that killed 32 Germans, more than 300 people randomly chosen from Rome's prison were killed in retaliation. As the Allies marched closer, they bombed Rome and its surroundings, but avoided striking the center.

Thankfully, Hitler granted the occupying Nazi troops permission to leave the city, which he declared a "place of culture" that should not be "the scene of combat operations." Pope Pius XII agreed, declaring, "Whoever raises a hand against Rome will be guilty of matricide to the whole civilized world and in the eternal judgment of God." Finally, the Germans marched out, the Americans marched in (through the gate of San Giovanni) on June 4, 1944, and the exhausted city welcomed them with joy and relief.

- Paintings by Raphael, Titian, and others (Borghese Gallery)

Baroque Sights

- St. Peter's Square and interior (largely by Bernini)
- Bernini statues (at Borghese Gallery; also *St. Teresa in Ecstasy* at Santa Maria della Vittoria church) and fountains (Piazza Navona, Piazza Barberini)
- Ancient obelisks erected in squares (Piazza del Popolo, Piazza Navona)
- Trevi Fountain and Spanish Steps
- Gesù and San Ignazio churches
- Caravaggio's *Calling of St. Matthew* (San Luigi dei Francesi Church) and other paintings (Borghese Gallery and Vatican

Museum)
- Baroque paintings (Borghese Gallery)
- Borromini's facade of Santa Agnese Church (Piazza Navona)

Modern Rome (1800-present)

Rome becomes the capital of a newly reunited Italy (1870) under King Victor Emmanuel II, is modernized by fascist Mussolini, and survives the destruction of World War II to become a republic. Italy's postwar "economic miracle" makes Rome a world-class city of cinema, banking, and tourism.

Sights

- Victor Emmanuel II Monument, which honors modern Italy's first (democratic) king
- Mussolini: the balcony he spoke from (at Palazzo Venezia, on Piazza Venezia), his planned city (E.U.R.), grand boulevards (Via dei Fori Imperiali, Via della Conciliazione), his home (Villa Torlonia), and Olympic Stadium
- Cinecittà film studios and Via Veneto nightlife, which have faint echoes of Fellini's *La Dolce Vita*
- Subway system, broad boulevards, smog

Rome Today

After surviving the government-a-year turbulence and Mafia-tainted corruption of the postwar years, Rome is stabilizing. Today, the average Roman makes more money than the average Englishman. The city is less polluted and more organized. Several years ago, in celebration of the millennium, the Eternal City gave its monuments a facelift. The world turned its attention on Rome once again in 2005, as the Vatican mourned the death of a pope... and elected a new one. In 2010, Rome opened MAXXI, its new state-of-the-architecture museum of modern art. In 2011, Pope John Paul II was beatified, one step away from being named a saint. Today's Rome is ready for pilgrims, travelers, and you to come and make more history.

APPENDIX

Contents

Tourist Information

The Italian national tourist offices **in the US** are a wealth of information. Before your trip, scan their website (www.italia.it), or contact the nearest branch to briefly describe your trip and request information. They'll mail you a general-interest brochure, and you can download many other brochures free of charge. If you have a specific problem, they're a good source of sympathy.

In New York: Tel. 212/245-5618, fax 212/586-9249, newyork@enit.it; 630 Fifth Ave. #1965, New York, NY 10111.

In Chicago: Tel. 312/644-0996, fax 312/644-3019, chicago@enit.it; 500 N. Michigan Ave. #506, Chicago, IL 60611.

In Los Angeles: Tel. 310/820-1898, fax 310/820-6357, losangeles@enit.it; 12400 Wilshire Blvd. #550, Los Angeles, CA 90025.

In Rome, your best first stop is generally the tourist information office (abbreviated **TI** in this book). TIs are good places to get a city map, advice on public transportation (including bus and train schedules), walking-tour information, tips on special events, and recommendations for nightlife. Many are scattered throughout Rome (listed on page 25; http://en.turismoroma.it or www.060608.it). Other useful websites include www.vatican.va (St. Peter's Basilica), http://mv.vatican.va (Vatican Museum), and www.inromenow.com.

While the TI is eager to book you a room, use its room-finding service only as a last resort. They are unable to give hard opinions on the relative value of one place over another. The accommodations stakes are too high to go potluck through the TI. Even if there's no "fee," you'll save yourself and your host money by going direct with the listings in this book.

Communicating

Hurdling the Language Barrier

Many Italians—especially those in the tourist trade and in big cities such as Rome—speak English. Still, you'll get better treatment if you learn and use Italian pleasantries. In smaller, non-touristy towns, Italian is the norm. For a list of survival phrases, see page 499.

Note that Italian is pronounced much like English, with a few exceptions, such as: c followed by e or i is pronounced ch (to ask, *"Per centro?"*—To the center?—you say, pehr CHEHN-troh). In Italian, ch is pronounced like the hard c in Chianti (*chiesa*—church—is pronounced kee-AY-zah). Give it your best shot. Italians appreciate your efforts.

Telephones

Smart travelers use the telephone to reserve or reconfirm rooms, get tourist information, reserve restaurants, confirm tour times, or phone home. This section covers dialing instructions, phone cards, and types of phones (for more in-depth information, see www.ricksteves.com/phoning).

How to Dial

Calling from the US to Italy, or vice versa, is simple—once you break the code. The European calling chart on page 466 will walk you through it.

Dialing Domestically Within Italy

Italy has a direct-dial phone system (no area codes). To call anywhere within Italy, just dial the number. For example, the number of one of my recommended Rome hotels is 06-482-4696. That's the number you dial whether you're calling it from Rome's main train station or from Milan.

These instructions apply to dialing from a landline (such as a pay phone or your hotel-room phone) or an Italian mobile phone.

If you're making calls within Italy using your US mobile phone, you may need to dial as if it's a domestic call, or you may need to dial as if you're calling from the US (see "Dialing Internationally," next). Try it one way, and if it doesn't work, try it the other way.

Italy's land lines start with 0 and mobile lines start with 3. The country's toll-free lines begin with 80. These 80 numbers—called *freephone* or *numero verde* (green number)—can be dialed free from any phone without using a phone card. Note that you can't call Italy's toll-free numbers from the US, nor can you count on reaching American toll-free numbers from Italy. Any Italian phone number that starts with 8 but isn't followed by a 0 is a toll call, generally costing €0.10-0.50 per minute.

Italian phone numbers vary in length; a hotel can have, say, an eight-digit phone number and a nine-digit fax number.

Dialing Internationally to or from Italy

If you want to make an international call, follow these steps:

• Dial the international access code (00 if you're calling from Europe, 011 from the US or Canada). If you're dialing from a mobile phone, you can replace the international access code with +, which works regardless of where you're calling from. (On many mobile phones, you can insert a + by pressing and holding the 0 key.)

• Dial the country code of the country you're calling (39 for Italy, or 1 for the US or Canada).

• Dial the local number. Note that in most European countries, you have to drop the zero at the beginning of the local number—but in Italy, you dial it. (The European calling chart lists specifics per country.)

Calling from the US to Italy: To call the recommended hotel in Rome from the US, dial 011 (the US international access code), 39 (Italy's country code), then 06-482-4696.

Calling from any European country to the US: To call my office in Edmonds, Washington, from anywhere in Europe, I dial 00 (Europe's international access code), 1 (the US country code), 425 (Edmonds' area code), and 771-8303.

Mobile Phones

Traveling with a mobile phone is handy and practical.

Using Your Mobile Phone: Your US mobile phone works in Europe if it's GSM-enabled, tri-band or quad-band, and on a calling plan that includes international calls. Phones from T-Mobile and AT&T, which use the same GSM technology that Europe does, are more likely to work overseas than Verizon or Sprint phones (if you're not sure, ask your service provider). Most US providers charge $1.29-1.99 per minute while roaming internationally to make or receive calls, and 20-50 cents to send or receive text messages.

You'll pay cheaper rates if your phone is electronically "unlocked" (ask your provider about this); then in Europe, you can simply buy a tiny **SIM card,** which gives you a European phone number. SIM cards are sold at mobile-phone stores and some newsstand kiosks for about $5-15, and generally include several minutes' worth of prepaid domestic calling time. When you buy a SIM card, you may need to show ID, such as your passport.

Insert the SIM card in your phone (usually in a slot on the side or behind the battery), and it'll work like a European mobile phone. Before purchasing a SIM card, always ask about fees for domestic and international calls, roaming charges, and how to check your credit balance and buy more time. When you're in the SIM card's home country, domestic calls average 10-20 cents per minute, and incoming calls are free. You'll pay more if you're roaming in another country.

Buying a European Mobile Phone: Mobile-phone shops all over Europe sell basic phones. Many airports and train stations have hole-in-the-wall shops. The mobile-phone desk in a big department store is another good place to check. Phones that are "locked" to work with a single provider start around $40; "unlocked" phones (which allow you to switch out SIM cards to use your choice of provider) start around $60. You'll also need to buy a SIM card and prepaid credit for making calls. (My Italian friends tell me that TIM is a reliable Italian mobile-phone company.)

Renting a European Mobile Phone: Car-rental companies and mobile-phone companies offer the option to rent a mobile phone with a European number. While this seems convenient, hidden fees (such as high per-minute charges or expensive shipping costs) can really add up—which usually makes it a bad value. One exception is Verizon's Global Travel Program, available only to Verizon customers.

Data Downloading on a Smartphone: Many smartphones, such as the iPhone, Android, and BlackBerry, work in Europe (though some older Verizon iPhones don't work abroad). For voice calls and text messaging, smartphones work the same as other US mobile phones (explained earlier). But beware of sky-high rates of about $20 per megabyte for data downloading (checking email, browsing the Internet, streaming videos, and so on). The best solution: Disable data roaming entirely, and only use your device to access the Internet when you find free Wi-Fi. You can ask your mobile-phone service provider to cut off your account's data-roaming capability, or you can manually turn it off on your phone (look under the "Network" menu).

If you want Internet access without being limited to Wi-Fi, you'll need to keep data roaming on—but you can take steps to reduce your charges. Consider paying extra for a limited international data-roaming plan through your carrier, then use data roaming selectively (if a particular task gobbles bandwidth, wait until you're on Wi-Fi). In general, ask your provider in advance how to avoid unwittingly roaming your way to a huge bill. If your smartphone is on Wi-Fi, you can use certain apps to make cheap or free voice calls (see "Calling over the Internet," next).

Calling over the Internet

Some things that seem too good to be true...actually are true. If you're traveling with a laptop, tablet, or smartphone, you can make free calls over the Internet to another wireless device, anywhere in the world, for free. (Or you can pay a few cents to call a telephone from your device.) The major providers are Skype (www.skype.com, also available as a smartphone app), Google Talk (www.google.com/talk), and FaceTime (this app is preloaded on most Apple devices). You can get online at a Wi-Fi hotspot and use these apps to make calls without ringing up expensive roaming charges (though call quality can be spotty on slow connections). You can make Internet calls even if you're traveling without your own mobile device: Many European Internet cafés have Skype, as well as microphones and webcams, on their terminals—just log on and chat away.

Landline Telephones

As in the US, these days most Italians do most of their phoning on mobile phones. But for those sticking with landlines, here are the different places from which to make landline calls.

Calling Options

Hotel-Room Phones: Calling from your hotel room can be great for local calls and for calls using cheap international phone cards (described later). Otherwise, hotel-room phones can be an almost criminal rip-off for long-distance and international calls. Many hotels charge a fee for dialing local and sometimes even "toll-free" numbers—always ask for the rates before you dial. Incoming calls are free, making this a cheap way for friends and family to stay in touch (provided they have a good long-distance plan with good international rates—and a list of your hotels' phone numbers).

Public Pay Phones: Coin-op phones are virtually extinct. Most pay phones require an insertable phone card, described below.

Metered Phones: In Italy, some call shops have phones with meters. You can talk all you want, then pay the bill when you

European Calling Chart

Just smile and dial, using this key:
AC = Area Code, LN = Local Number.

European Country	Calling long distance within...	Calling from the US or Canada to...	Calling from a European country to...
Austria	AC + LN	011 + 43 + AC (without the initial zero) + LN	00 + 43 + AC (without the initial zero) + LN
Belgium	LN	011 + 32 + LN (without initial zero)	00 + 32 + LN (without initial zero)
Bosnia-Herzegovina	AC + LN	011 + 387 + AC (without initial zero) + LN	00 + 387 + AC (without initial zero) + LN
Britain	AC + LN	011 + 44 + AC (without initial zero) + LN	00 + 44 + AC (without initial zero) + LN
Croatia	AC + LN	011 + 385 + AC (without initial zero) + LN	00 + 385 + AC (without initial zero) + LN
Czech Republic	LN	011 + 420 + LN	00 + 420 + LN
Denmark	LN	011 + 45 + LN	00 + 45 + LN
Estonia	LN	011 + 372 + LN	00 + 372 + LN
Finland	AC + LN	011 + 358 + AC (without initial zero) + LN	999 (or other 900 number) + 358 + AC (without initial zero) + LN
France	LN	011 + 33 + LN (without initial zero)	00 + 33 + LN (without initial zero)
Germany	AC + LN	011 + 49 + AC (without initial zero) + LN	00 + 49 + AC (without initial zero) + LN
Gibraltar	LN	011 + 350 + LN	00 + 350 + LN
Greece	LN	011 + 30 + LN	00 + 30 + LN
Hungary	06 + AC + LN	011 + 36 + AC + LN	00 + 36 + AC + LN
Ireland	AC + LN	011 + 353 + AC (without initial zero) + LN	00 + 353 + AC (without initial zero) + LN

European Country	Calling long distance within…	Calling from the US or Canada to…	Calling from a European country to…
Italy	LN	011 + 39 + LN	00 + 39 + LN
Montenegro	AC + LN	011 + 382 + AC (without initial zero) + LN	00 + 382 + AC (without initial zero) + LN
Morocco	LN	011 + 212 + LN (without initial zero)	00 + 212 + LN (without initial zero)
Netherlands	AC + LN	011 + 31 + AC (without initial zero) + LN	00 + 31 + AC (without initial zero) + LN
Norway	LN	011 + 47 + LN	00 + 47 + LN
Poland	LN	011 + 48 + LN	00 + 48 + LN
Portugal	LN	011 + 351 + LN	00 + 351 + LN
Slovakia	AC + LN	011 + 421 + AC (without initial zero) + LN	00 + 421 + AC (without initial zero) + LN
Slovenia	AC + LN	011 + 386 + AC (without initial zero) + LN	00 + 386 + AC (without initial zero) + LN
Spain	LN	011 + 34 + LN	00 + 34 + LN
Sweden	AC + LN	011 + 46 + AC (without initial zero) + LN	00 + 46 + AC (without initial zero) + LN
Switzerland	LN	011 + 41 + LN (without initial zero)	00 + 41 + LN (without initial zero)
Turkey	AC (if there's no initial zero, add one) + LN	011 + 90 + AC (without initial zero) + LN	00 + 90 + AC (without initial zero) + LN

- The instructions above apply whether you're calling a land line or mobile phone.
- The international access code (the first numbers you dial when making an international call) is 011 if you're calling from the US or Canada. It's 00 if you're calling from virtually anywhere in Europe (except Finland, where it's 999 or another 900 number, depending on the phone service you're using).
- To call the US or Canada from Europe, dial 00, then 1 (the country code for the US and Canada), then the area code and number. In short, 00 + 1 + AC + LN = Hi, Mom!

leave—but be sure you know the rates before you have a lengthy conversation. Note that charges can be "per unit" rather than per minute; find out the length of a unit.

Types of Telephone Cards

Insertable phone cards work only at pay phones, while international phone cards can be used with any type of phone (and will save you plenty of money, especially on overseas calls). Both types of phone cards are good only in Italy. If you have a live card at the end of your trip, give it to another traveler to use.

Insertable Phone Cards: These types of cards, usable only at pay phones, are sold by Italy's largest phone company, Telecom Italia. They give you the best deal for calls within Italy and are reasonable for international calls. You can buy Telecom cards (in €5 or €10 denominations) at tobacco shops, post offices, and machines near phone booths (many phone booths have signs indicating where the nearest phone-card sales outlet is located).

Rip off the perforated corner to "activate" the card, and then physically insert it into a slot in the pay phone. It displays how much money you have remaining on the card. Then just dial away. The price of the call is automatically deducted while you talk.

International Phone Cards: With these cards, phone calls from Italy to the US can cost less than a nickel a minute. They can also be used to make local calls, and they work from any type of phone, including your hotel-room phone or a mobile phone with a European SIM card. To use the card, dial a toll-free access number, then enter your scratch-to-reveal PIN number. If you're calling from a hotel, be sure to dial the *freephone* number (starts with "80") provided on your card rather than the "local access" number (which would incur a charge).

You can buy the cards at small newsstand kiosks, *tabacchi* (tobacco) shops, Internet cafés, hostels, and hole-in-the-wall long-distance phone shops. Because there are so many brand names, ask for an international phone card (*carta telefonica prepagata internazionale,* KAR-tah teh-leh-FOHN-ee-kah pray-pah-GAH-tah in-ter-naht-zee-oh-NAH-lay). Tell the vendor where you'll be making most calls (*"per Stati Uniti"*—to America), and he'll select the brand with the best deal.

Buy a lower denomination in case the card is a dud. I've had good luck with the Europa card, which offers up to 350 minutes from Italy to the US for €5. Since you don't need the actual card to use the account, you can write down the access number and code and share it with friends.

US Calling Cards: These cards, such as the ones offered by AT&T, Verizon, or Sprint, are a rotten value and are being phased out. Try any of the options outlined earlier.

Useful Phone Numbers

Emergency Needs

English-Speaking Police Help: 113
Ambulance: 118
Road Service: 116

Embassies

US Embassy: 24-hour emergency line—tel. 06-46741, non-emergency—tel. 06-4674-2420 answered Mon-Fri 15:00-17:00 (passport services Mon-Fri 8:30-12:00, Via Vittorio Veneto 121, www.usembassy.it)
Canadian Embassy: Tel. 06-854-441 (Mon-Fri 9:00-12:00, closed Sat-Sun, Via Zara 30, www.italy.gc.ca)

Travel Advisories

US Department of State: Tel. 202/647-5225, www.travel.state.gov
Canadian Department of Foreign Affairs: Canadian tel. 800-267-6788, www.international.gc.ca
US Centers for Disease Control and Prevention: Tel. 800-CDC-INFO (800-232-4636), www.cdc.gov/travel

Directory Assistance

Telephone Help (in English; free directory assistance): 170
Directory Assistance (for €0.50, an Italian-speaking robot gives the number twice, very clearly): 12

Internet Access

It's useful to get online periodically as you travel—to confirm trip plans, check train or bus schedules, get weather forecasts, catch up on email, blog or post photos from your trip, or call folks back home (explained earlier, under "Calling over the Internet").

Your Mobile Device: The majority of accommodations in Rome offer Wi-Fi, as do many cafés, making it easy for you to get online with your laptop, tablet, or smartphone. Access is often free, but sometimes there's a fee.

Some hotel rooms and Internet cafés have high-speed Internet jacks that you can plug into with an Ethernet cable. A cellular modem—which lets your laptop access the Internet over a mobile phone network—provides more extensive coverage, but is much more expensive than Wi-Fi (in Italy, www.wind.it and www.tim.it offer pay-as-you-go mobile broadband).

Public Internet Terminals: Many accommodations offer a computer in the lobby with Internet access for guests. If you ask politely, smaller places may sometimes let you sit at their desk for a few minutes just to check your email. If your hotelier doesn't have access, ask to be directed to the nearest place to get online.

Security: Whether you're accessing the Internet with your own device or at a public terminal, using a shared network or computer comes with the potential for increased security risks. Be careful about storing personal information online, such as passport and credit-card numbers. If you're not convinced a connection is secure, avoid accessing any sites that could be vulnerable to fraud (e.g., online banking).

Mail

You can mail one package per day to yourself worth up to $200 duty-free from Europe to the US (mark it "personal purchases"). If you're sending a gift to someone, mark it "unsolicited gift." For details, visit www.cbp.gov and search for "Know Before You Go."

Mail service in Italy has improved over the last few years, but even so, mail nothing precious from an Italian post office (though Vatican City's post offices are reliable). For quick transatlantic delivery (in either direction), consider services such as DHL (www.dhl.com).

Transportation

By Car or Train?

If your trip will cover more of Italy than just Rome, you'll need to decide whether to rent a car or take trains. Cars are best for three or more traveling together (especially families with small kids), those packing heavy, and those scouring the countryside. Trains and buses are best for solo travelers, blitz tourists, and city-to-city travelers. While a car gives you the ultimate in mobility and freedom, enables you to search for hotels more easily, and carries your bags for you, the train zips you effortlessly from city to city, usually dropping you in the center and near the TI.

Trains

To travel by train cheaply in Italy, you can simply buy tickets as you go. Ticket machines work well and are easy to use (see "Buying Tickets," later), so you can usually avoid long lines at ticket windows. Pay all ticket costs in the station before you board, or you'll pay a penalty on the train.

Types of Trains: Most trains in Italy are operated by the state-run Trenitalia company (a.k.a. Ferrovie dello Stato Italiane or FS). Since ticket prices depend on the speed of the train, it pays to know

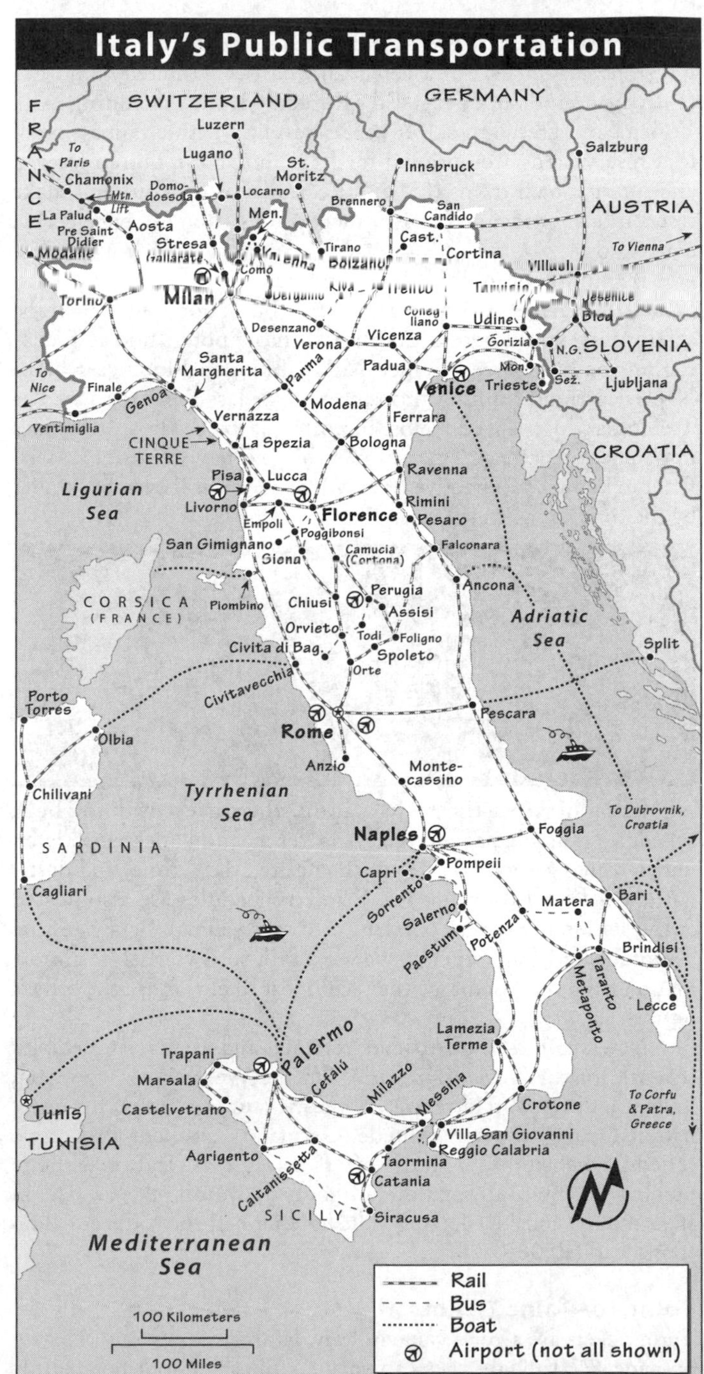

Italy's Public Transportation
SWITZERLAND
GERMANY
FRANCE
AUSTRIA
SLOVENIA
CROATIA
CORSICA (FRANCE)
SARDINIA
SICILY
TUNISIA
Ligurian Sea
Adriatic Sea
Tyrrhenian Sea
Mediterranean Sea
Luzern
Lugano
St. Moritz
Innsbruck
Salzburg
To Paris
Chamonix
Mtn. Lift
Domodossola
Locarno
Brennero
San Candido
La Palud
Pre Saint Didier
Aosta
Men.
Stresa
Tirano
Cast.
Cortina
To Vienna
Como
Milan
Torino
Coneg liano
Udine
Bled
Desenzano
Verona
Vicenza
Gorizia
N.G.
Padua
Mon.
To Nice
Finale
Santa Margherita
Parma
Venice
Trieste
Sež.
Ljubljana
Genoa
Modena
Ventimiglia
Vernazza
Ferrara
CINQUE TERRE
La Spezia
Bologna
Pisa
Lucca
Ravenna
Livorno
Rimini
Florence
Empoli
Pesaro
Poggibonsi
San Gimignano
Camucia (Cortona)
Falconara
Siena
Ancona
Piombino
Chiusi
Perugia
Assisi
Orvieto
Todi
Foligno
Civita di Bag.
Spoleto
Split
Orte
Civitavecchia
Porto Torres
Pescara
Olbia
Rome
Anzio
Montecassino
Chilivani
To Dubrovnik, Croatia
Naples
Foggia
Pompeii
Capri
Cagliari
Sorrento
Matera
Bari
Salerno
Potenza
Paestum
Brindisi
Taranto
Metaponto
Lecce
Lamezia Terme
Palermo
Trapani
Cefalù
Milazzo
Marsala
Messina
Crotone
To Corfu & Patra, Greece
Castelvetrano
Tunis
Villa San Giovanni
Reggio Calabria
Agrigento
Taormina
Caltanissetta
Catania
Siracusa
100 Kilometers
100 Miles
Rail
Bus
Boat
Airport (not all shown)

the different types of trains: pokey R *(regionali)*, medium-speed RV *(regionali espresso)*, and E *(espresso)*; fast IC (Intercity) and EC (Eurocity); and super-fast ES (Eurostar Italia, including Alta Velocità and Frecciarossa). If you're traveling with a railpass, note that reservations are optional for IC trains, but required for EC and international trains (€5) and ES trains (€10). You can't make reservations for regional trains, such as most Rome-Civitavecchia connections.

Beginning in mid-2012, a brand-new, private train company called Italo began running fast trains on major routes in Italy, attempting to challenge Trenitalia's monopoly. Italo is focusing on the high-speed Venice-Milan-Bologna-Florence-Rome-Naples corridor, running trains at more or less the same speed as Trenitalia's high-speed trains, but often at lower fares. Italo does not currently accept railpasses. As this is a new venture, it's difficult to know how effective Italo will be—or if it'll even be around by the time you visit.

Schedules: At the train station, the easiest way to check schedules is at a handy automated ticket machine (described later, under "Buying Tickets"). Enter the desired date, time, and destination to see all your options. Printed schedules are also posted at the station (departure posters are always yellow). Be aware that Trenitalia and Italo don't cooperate at all, so if you ask for information from one company, they will most likely ignore the other's options.

Newsstands sell up-to-date regional and all-Italy timetables (€5, ask for the *orario ferroviaro*). On the Web, check www.trenitalia.it and www.italotreno.it (domestic journeys only); for international trips, use www.bahn.de (Germany's excellent all-Europe schedule website). Trenitalia offers a single all-Italy telephone number for train information (24 hours daily, toll tel. 892-021, in Italian only, consider having your hotelier call for you). For Italo trains, call tel. 06-0708.

Point-to-Point Tickets

Train tickets are a good value in Italy. Fares are shown on the map on page 477, though fares can vary for the same journey, mainly

Deciphering Italian Train Schedules

At the station, look for the big yellow posters labeled *Partenze*—Departures (ignore the white posters, which show arrivals).

Schedules are listed chronologically, hour by hour, showing the trains leaving the station throughout the day. Each schedule has columns:

- The first column *(Ora)* lists the time of departure.
- The next column *(Treno)* shows the type of train.
- The third column *(Classi Servizi)* lists the services available (first- and second-class cars, dining car, *cuccetta* berths, etc.) and, more importantly, whether you need reservations (usually denoted by an R in a box). Note that all Eurostar Italia (ES) and Alta Velocita (AV) trains, many InterCity (IC) and EuroCity (EC) trains, and most international trains require reservations.
- The next column lists the destination of the train *(Principali Fermate Destinazioni),* often showing intermediate stops, followed by the final destination, with arrival times listed throughout in parentheses. Note that your final destination may be listed in fine print as an intermediate destination. For example, if you're going from Rome to Orvieto, scan the schedule and you'll notice that regional trains that go to Florence usually stop in Orvieto en route. Travelers who read the fine print end up with a far greater choice of trains.
- The next column *(Servizi Diretti e Annotazioni)* has pertinent notes about the train, such as "also stops in..." *(ferma anche a...),* "doesn't stop in..." *(non ferma a...),* "stops in every station" *(ferma in tutte le stazioni),* "delayed..." *(ritardo...),* and so on.
- The last column lists the track *(Binario)* the train departs from. Confirm the *binario* with an additional source: a ticket-seller, the electronic board that lists immediate departures, TV monitors on the platform, or the railway officials who are usually standing by the train unless you really need them.

For any odd symbols on the poster, look at the key at the end. Some of the phrasing can be deciphered easily, such as *servizio periodico* (periodic service—doesn't always run). For the trickier ones, ask a local or railway official, try your *Rick Steves' Italian Phrase Book & Dictionary*, or simply take a different train.

You can also check schedules—for trains anywhere in Italy, not just from the station you're currently in—at the handy ticket machines. Enter the date and time of your departure (to or from any Italian station), and you can view all your options.

Open or Non-Reserved Ticket—Need to Validate

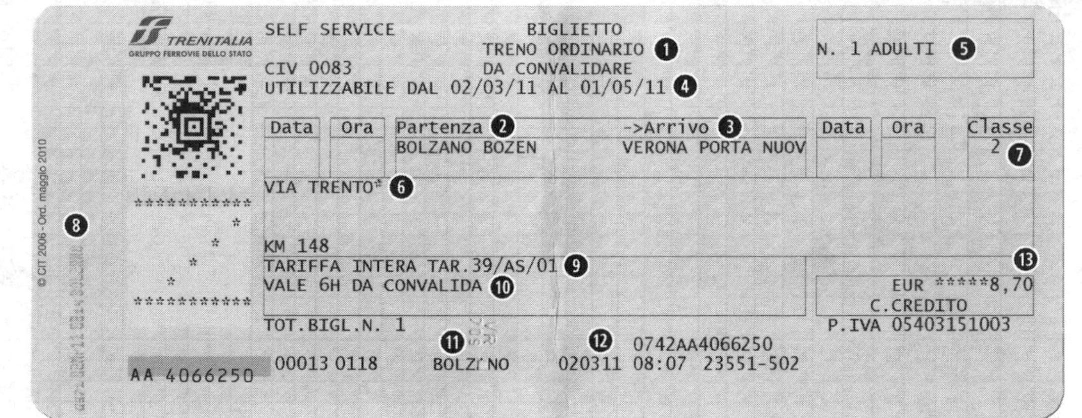

1. Open ticket for non-express trains, must be validated
2. Point of departure
3. Destination
4. Validity of ticket (use once within 2 months of purchase)
5. Number of passengers
6. Route
7. Class of travel (1 = 1st; 2 = 2nd)
8. Validation stamp
9. Full fare for non-express train
10. Once stamped, ticket is good for 1 trip within 6 hours
11. Location of ticket sale
12. Date ticket was purchased
13. Ticket cost

Reserved Ticket (Fast Train)—Need Not Validate

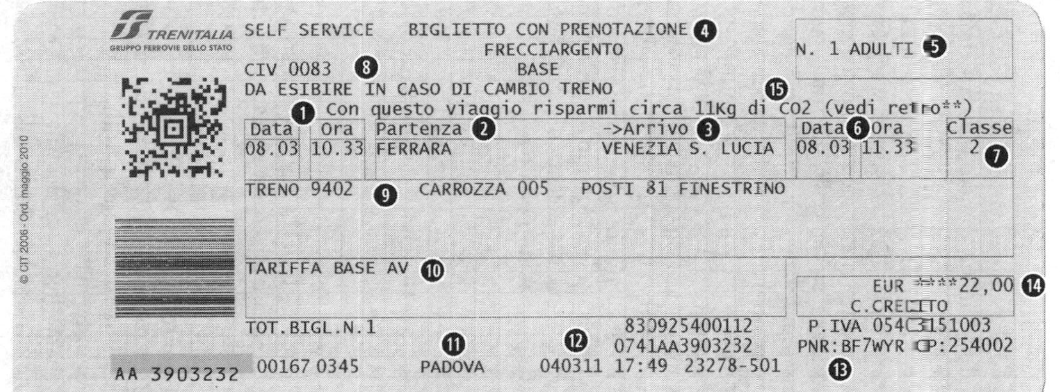

1. Departure date & time
2. Point of departure
3. Destination
4. "Ticket with reservation"
5. Number of passengers
6. Arrival date & time
7. Class of travel (1 = 1st; 2 = 2nd)
8. "Present to official if changing trains"
9. Train #, train car # & seat # (finestrino = window seat)
10. Fast-train fare (other types of trains can be cheaper and don't require reservations)
11. Location of ticket sale
12. Date ticket was purchased
13. Booking ID
14. Ticket cost
15. Amount of CO^2 usage reduced by this train trip

depending on the time of day, the speed of the train, and more. **First-class** tickets cost 50 percent more than **second-class.** While second-class cars go as fast as their first-class neighbors, Italy is one country where I would consider the splurge of first class. The easiest way to "upgrade" a second-class ticket once on board a crowded train is to nurse a drink in the snack car.

Speed vs. Savings: For point-to-point tickets, you'll pay more the faster you go. Spending a modest amount of extra time in transit can save money. For example, a round-trip ticket between Rome and Civitavecchia costs €14-17 on an ES train (45 minutes each way), but €9 on a regional train (1.25 hours each way). On longer, mainline routes, fast trains save more time and provide most of the service. For example, super-fast Venice-Rome trains run hourly, cost €76 in second class, and make the trip in 3.75 hours, while less-frequent InterCity options cost €45 and take 6.5 hours.

Discounts: Families with young children can get price breaks—kids ages 4 and under travel free; ages 4-11 at half-price. Ask for the "Offerta Familia" deal when buying tickets at a counter (or, at a ticket machine, choose "Yes" at the "Do you want ticket issue?" prompt, then choose "Familia"). With the discount, families of three to five people with at least one kid (age 12 or under) get 50 percent off the child fare and 20 percent off the adult fare. The deal doesn't apply to all trains at all times, but it's worth checking out.

Discounts for youths and seniors require purchase of a separate card (Carta Verde for ages 12-26 costs €40; Carta Argento for ages 60 and over is €30), but the discount on tickets is so minor (10-15 percent respectively for domestic travel), it's not worth it for most.

Buying Tickets: Avoid train station ticket lines whenever possible by using the automated ticket machines in station halls. You'll be able to easily purchase tickets for travel within Italy (not international trains), make seat reservations, and even book a *cuccetta* (koo-CHEHT-tah; overnight berth).

Trenitalia's automated ticket machines (usually green and white, marked *Biglietto Veloce/Fast Ticket*) are user-friendly and found in all but the tiniest stations in Italy. You can pay by cash (they give change) or by debit or credit card (even for small amounts). Select English, then your destination. If you don't immediately see the city you're traveling to, keep keying in the spelling until it's listed. You can choose from first- and second-class seats, request tickets for more than one traveler, and (on the high-speed Eurostar Italia trains) choose an aisle or window seat. If the machine prompts you—"Fidelity Card?"—choose no. Don't select a discount rate without being sure that you meet the criteria (for example, Americans are not eligible for certain EU or resident

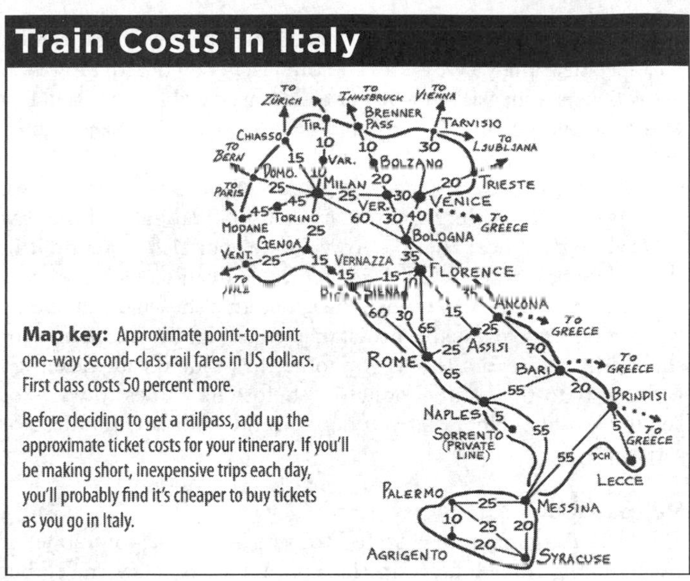

Map key: Approximate point-to-point one-way second-class rail fares in US dollars. First class costs 50 percent more.

Before deciding to get a railpass, add up the approximate ticket costs for your itinerary. If you'll be making short, inexpensive trips each day, you'll probably find it's cheaper to buy tickets as you go in Italy.

discounts). Railpass-holders can use the machines to make seat reservations. If you need to validate your ticket, you can do it in the same machine if you're boarding your train right away.

For nearby destinations only, you can also buy tickets from the older, gray-and-blue machines marked *Rete regionale* (cash only, push button for English).

It's possible, but generally unnecessary, to buy Trenitalia tickets in advance online at www.trenitalia.it. Because most Italian trains run frequently and there's no deadline to buy tickets, you can keep your travel plans flexible by buying tickets as you go, or buy several tickets at one station when you are ready to reserve.

To buy tickets for high-speed **Italo** trains, look for a dedicated service counter (in most major rail stations), or a red automated ticket machine labeled *Italo*. You can also book Italo tickets by phone (tel. 06-0708) or online (www.italotreno.it).

Note that if you buy a ticket for one train line, you must travel with only that company—your ticket is not valid on the competitor's train line. Survey your options carefully before you choose.

Be aware that you can't buy international tickets from machines; for this and anything else that requires a real person, try a local travel agency, a good alternative to the ticket windows at the station. They also sell domestic tickets and make reservations. The cost is only a little more (agencies charge a small fee); it can be more convenient (if you find yourself near a travel agency while you're sightseeing); there are no crowds; and the language barrier can be smaller than at the station's ticket windows.

Validating Tickets: If your ticket includes a seat reservation on a specific train, you're all set and can just get on board. However, many tickets (especially for slower trains) are flexible—not tied to a particular train or specific reserved seat—and so must be validated before you board. You always need to validate the small, paper-slip tickets that you buy from newsstands or older ticket machines. Tickets from the newer machines must also be validated if they say *"Da convalidare"* near the top. To validate your ticket, stamp it in the yellow box near the platform. Once you validate a ticket, you must complete your trip within the timeframe shown on the ticket (within 6 hours for medium-distance trips; within 1.25 hours for short rides under 6 miles). If you forget to validate your ticket, go right away to the train conductor—before he comes to you—or you'll pay a fine. Note that you don't need to validate a railpass or e-ticket.

Railpasses

The **Italy Pass** for Italian State Railways may save you money if you're taking three long train rides or prefer first-class travel, but don't count on it for hop-on convenience on every train. Use the price map opposite to add up your ticket costs (ticket prices on the map are for the fastest trains on a given route, many of which have reservation costs built in). Note that railpasses are not valid on high-speed Italo trains.

Railpass travelers must make separate seat reservations for the fastest trains between major Italian cities (€10-15 each). Railpass travelers can just hop on InterCity trains (optional €5 reservation) and regional trains (no reservations possible). Making a reservation at a train station or travel agency is the same as the process to buy a ticket, so you may need to stand in line either way. Reservations for berths on overnight trains cost extra, aren't covered by railpasses, and aren't reflected on the ticket cost map.

A 23-country **Eurail Global Pass** can work well for an all-Europe trip, but is a bad value for travel exclusively in Italy. A cheaper version, the **Eurail Select Pass,** allows you to tailor a pass to your trip, provided you're traveling in three, four, or five adjacent countries directly connected by rail or ferry. For instance, with a three-country pass allowing 10 days of train travel within a two-month period (about $730 for a single adult in 2012), you could choose France-Italy-Greece or Germany-Austria-Italy. A **France and Italy Pass** combines just those two countries. (If your route includes a connection in Switzerland, you'll pay extra—so the Select Pass is a better choice if you want to see the Alps.) Note that none of these passes cover direct day or night trains between Italy and Paris, which require a separate ticket. Before you buy a Select Pass or France and Italy Pass, consider how many travel days

Railpasses

Prices listed are for 2012 and are subject to change. For the latest prices, details, and train schedules (and easy online ordering), see my comprehensive *Guide to Eurail Passes* at www.ricksteves.com/rail.

"Saver" prices are per person for two or more people traveling together. "Youth" means under age 26. The fare for children 4–11 is half the adult individual fare or Saver fare. Kids under age 4 travel free.

ITALY PASS

	Individual 1st Class	Individual 2nd Class	Saver 1st Class	Saver 2nd Class	Youth 2nd Class
3 days in 2 months	$274	$223	$234	$192	$183
Extra rail days (max 7)	31-38	25-31	26-33	20-27	20-25

ITALY RAIL & DRIVE PASS

Any 3 rail days and 2 car days in 2 months.

Car Category	1st Class	2nd Class	Extra Car Day
Economy 2-Door	$384	$326	$69
Economy 4-Door	392	335	77
Compact	413	356	98
Intermediate	441	384	126
Economy Automatic	422	364	107
Premium	548	490	233
Extra rail days (max 3)	31	25	

Prices are per person, two traveling together. Solo travelers pay about 20 percent more. To order a Rail & Drive pass, call your travel agent or Rail Europe at 800-438-7245. *This pass is not sold by Europe Through the Back Door.*

FRANCE–ITALY PASS

	Individual 1st Class	Individual 2nd Class	Saver 1st Class	Saver 2nd Class	Youth 2nd Class
4 days in 2 months	$411	$353	$353	$300	$268
Extra rail days (max 6)	45-50	38-40	38-40	31-37	28-30

Be aware of your route. Direct Paris–Italy trains (day and overnight) and trains via Switzerland aren't covered by this pass.

GREECE–ITALY PASS

	Individual 1st Class	Individual 2nd Class	Saver 1st Class	Saver 2nd Class	Youth 2nd Class
4 days in 2 months	$384	$309	$327	$263	$252
Extra rail days (max 6)	38-40	30-32	32-34	25-27	25-27

Covers deck passage on overnight Superfast Ferries between Patras, Greece and Bari or Ancona, Italy (starts use of one travel day). Or 30-50% discount on Hellenic Mediterranean Line ferry with basic cabin Patras-Corfu-Brindisi (does not use a travel day). Does not cover travel to or on Greek islands, except a 30% discount on Blue Star Ferries. Very few trains run in Greece.

SELECTPASS

This pass covers travel in three adjacent countries. Please visit **www.ricksteves.com/rail** for four- and five-country options.

	Individual 1st Class	Saver 1st Class	Youth 2nd Class
5 days in 2 months	$486	$413	$317
6 days in 2 months	536	456	350
8 days in 2 months	633	539	413
10 days in 2 months	734	624	478

you'll really need. Use the pass only for travel days that involve long hauls or several trips. Pay out of pocket for tickets on days you're taking only short, cheap rides.

For a summary of railpass deals and the latest prices, check my Guide to Eurail Passes at www.ricksteves.com/rail. If you decide to get a railpass, this guide will help you know you're getting the right one for your trip.

Train Tips

This section contains information on making seat reservations, storing baggage, avoiding theft, and dealing with strikes.

Seat Reservations: Trains can fill up, even in first class. If you're on a tight schedule, you'll want to reserve a few days ahead for fast trains (see "Types of Trains," earlier). Purchasing tickets or passholder reservations on board a train comes with a nasty penalty. Buying them at the station can be a time-waster unless you use the automatic ticket machines.

If you don't need a reservation, and if your train originates at your departure point (e.g., you're catching the Rome-Assisi train in Rome), arriving at least 15 minutes before the departure time will help you snare a seat.

Some major stations have train composition posters on the platforms showing where first- and second-class cars are located when the trains arrive (letters on the poster are supposed to correspond to letters posted over the platform, but they don't always). Since most trains now allow you to make reservations up to the time of departure, conductors are no longer marking reserved seats with a card—instead, they simply post a list of the reservable and non-reservablc scat rows (sometimes in English) in each train car's vestibule. This means that if you board a crowded train and get one of the last seats, you may be ousted when the reservation-holder comes along.

Baggage Storage: Many stations have *deposito bagagli* where you can safely leave your bag for about €8 per 12-hour period (payable when you pick up the bag, double-check closing hours). Due to security concerns, no Italian stations have lockers.

Theft Concerns: Italian trains are famous for their thieves. Never leave a bag unattended. Police do ride the trains, cutting down on theft. Still, for an overnight trip, I'd feel safe only in a *cuccetta* (a bunk in a special sleeping car with an attendant who keeps track of who comes and goes while you sleep—approximately €21 in a six-bed compartment, €26 in a less-cramped four-bed compartment, €50 in a more private, double compartment).

Strikes: Strikes, which are common, generally last a day. Train employees will simply explain, "*Sciopero*" (strike). But in actuality, sporadic trains, following no particular schedule, lumber down the tracks during most strikes. When a strike is pending, travel agencies (and Web-savvy hoteliers) can check the Internet for you to see when the strike goes into effect and which trains will continue to run. Revised schedules may be posted in Italian at stations, and station personnel still working can often tell you what trains are expected to run. If I need to get somewhere and know a strike is imminent, I leave early (heading off the strike, which often begins at 9:00), or I just go to the station with extra patience in tow and hop on anything rolling in the direction I want to go.

Renting a Car

If you're renting a car in Italy, bring your driver's license. You're also technically required to have an International Driving Permit—an official translation of your driver's license (sold at your local AAA office for $15 plus the cost of two passport-type photos; see www.aaa.com). While that's the letter of the law, I've often rented cars in Italy without having—or being asked to show—this permit.

Rental companies require you to be at least 21 years old and have held your license for one year. Drivers under the age of 25 may incur a young-driver surcharge, and some rental companies do not rent to anyone 75 and over. If you're considered too young or old, look into leasing (described later), which has less-stringent age restrictions.

Research car rentals before you go. It's cheaper to arrange most car rentals from the US. Call several companies and look online to compare rates, or arrange a rental through your hometown travel agent.

Most of the major US rental agencies (including National, Avis, Budget, Hertz, and Thrifty) have offices throughout Europe. Also consider the two major Europe-based agencies, Europcar and Sixt. It can be cheaper to use a consolidator, such as Auto Europe or Europe by Car, which compares rates at several companies to get you the best deal. However, my readers have reported problems with consolidators, ranging from misinformation to unexpected fees; because you're going through a middleman, it can be more challenging to resolve disputes that arise with the rental agency.

Regardless of the car-rental company you choose, always read the contract carefully. The fine print can conceal a host of common add-on charges—such as one-way drop-off fees, airport surcharges, or mandatory insurance policies—that aren't included in the "total price," but can be tacked on when you pick up your car. You may need to query rental agents pointedly to find out your actual cost.

For the best rental deal, rent by the week with unlimited mileage. To save money on gas, ask for a diesel car. I normally rent the smallest, least-expensive model with a stick shift (cheaper than an automatic). An automatic transmission adds about 50 percent to the car-rental cost. Almost all rentals are manual by default, so if you need an automatic, you must request one in advance; beware that these cars are usually larger models (not as maneuverable on narrow, winding roads).

Roads and parking spaces are narrow in Italy, so you'll do yourself a favor by renting the smallest car that meets your needs. For a three-week rental, allow $900 per person (based on two people sharing a car), including insurance, tolls, gas, and parking. For trips of this length, consider leasing (see page 484); you'll save money on insurance and taxes.

You can sometimes get a GPS unit with your rental car or leased vehicle for an additional fee (around $15/day; be sure it's set to English and has all the maps you need before you drive off). Or, if you have a portable GPS device at home, consider taking it with you to Europe (buy and upload European maps before your trip). GPS apps are also available for smartphones, but downloading maps on one of these apps in Europe could lead to an exorbitant data-roaming bill.

Big companies have offices in most cities; ask whether they can pick you up at your hotel. Small local rental companies can be cheaper but aren't as flexible. Compare pickup costs (downtown can be less expensive than the airport) and explore drop-off options. When choosing where to pick up or drop off your car, don't trust the agency's description of "downtown" or "city center." In some cases, a "downtown" branch can be on the outskirts of the city—a long, costly taxi ride from the center. Before choosing, plug the address into a mapping website to compare locations. You may find that the "train station" location is handier. Returning a car at a big-city train station or downtown agency can be tricky; get precise details on the car drop-off location and hours. Note that rental offices usually close from midday Saturday until Monday.

When you pick up the rental car, check it thoroughly and make sure any damage is noted on your rental agreement. Find out how your car's lights, turn signals, wipers, and fuel cap function, and know what kind of fuel the car takes. When you return the car, make sure the agent verifies its condition with you.

If you want a car for only a couple of days, a rail-and-drive pass (such as a EurailDrive, Select Pass Drive, or Italy Rail and Drive) can be put to thoughtful use. The basic Italy Rail and Drive Pass, which includes theft insurance and CDW (described next), comes with two days of car rental and three days of rail in two months. While rail-and-drive passes are convenient, they're also pricey, particularly for solo travelers.

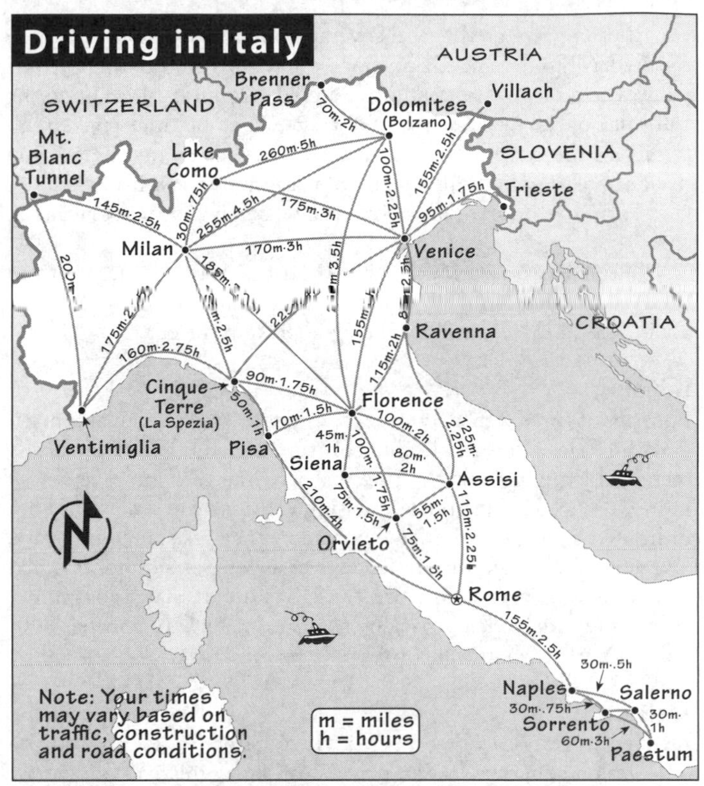

Car Insurance Options

Accidents can happen anywhere, but when you're on vacation, the last thing you need is stress over car insurance. When you rent a car, you're liable for a very high deductible, sometimes equal to the entire value of the car. Limit your financial risk in case of an accident by choosing one of these two options: Buy Collision Damage Waiver (CDW) coverage from the car-rental company (figure roughly 30 percent extra), or get coverage through your credit card (free, but more complicated).

In Italy, most car-rental companies' rates automatically include CDW coverage. Even if you try to decline CDW when you reserve your Italian car, you may find when you show up at the counter that you must buy it after all.

While each rental company has its own variation, basic CDW costs $15-35 a day and reduces your liability, but does not eliminate it. When you pick up the car, you'll be offered the chance to "buy down" the basic deductible to zero (for an additional $10-30/day; this is sometimes called "super CDW").

If you opt for credit-card coverage, there's a catch. You'll technically have to decline all coverage offered by the car-rental company, which means they can place a hold on your card for up to the full value of the car). In case of damage, it can be time-consuming to resolve the charges with your credit-card company. Before you decide on this option, quiz your company about how it works.

For more on car-rental insurance, see www.ricksteves.com/cdw.

Theft Insurance: Note that theft insurance (separate from CDW insurance) is mandatory in Italy. The insurance usually costs about $15-20 a day, payable when you pick up the car.

Leasing

For trips of three weeks or more, consider leasing (which automatically includes zero-deductible collision and theft insurance). By technically buying and then selling back the car, you save lots of money on tax and insurance. Leasing provides you a new car with unlimited mileage and a 24-hour emergency assistance program. You can lease for as little as 21 days to as long as six months. Car leases must be arranged from the US. One of many companies offering affordable lease packages is Europe by Car (US tel. 800-223-1516, www.ebctravel.com).

Driving

Driving in Italy can be scary—a video game for keeps, and you only get one quarter. Italian drivers can be aggressive. They drive fast and tailgate as if it were required. They pass where Americans are taught not to—on blind corners and just before tunnels. Roads have narrow shoulders or none at all. Driving in the countryside is less stressful than driving through urban areas, but stay alert. On one-lane roads, larger vehicles have the right-of-way. If you're on a truckers' route, stifle your Good Samaritan impulse when you see provocatively dressed women standing by camper-vans at the side of the road; they're not having car trouble.

Road Rules: Stay out of restricted traffic zones, or you'll risk huge fines. Car traffic is restricted in many city centers, including Rome. Don't drive or park anywhere with signs reading *Zona Traffico Limitato* (*ZTL*, often shown above a red circle, see image). If you do, your license plate will likely be photographed and a hefty (€100-plus) ticket mailed to your home without your ever having met a cop. Bumbling in and out of these zones can net you multiple fines. If your hotel is within a restricted area, it's best to ask your hotelier where to park outside the zone. (Although

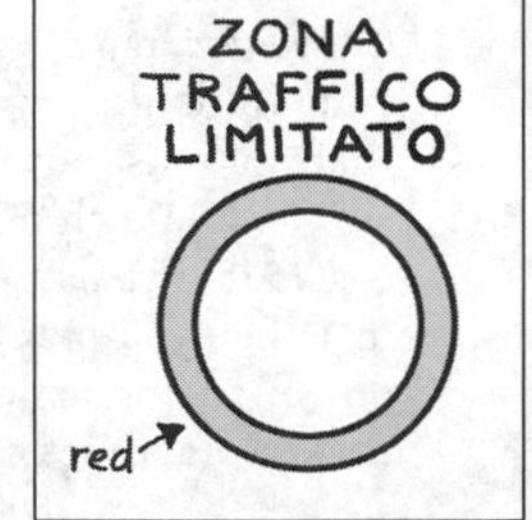

APPENDIX

your hotelier can register your car as an authorized vehicle permitted to enter the zone, this usually isn't worth the hassle.)

As for other road rules, seatbelts are mandatory, and you should keep headlights on at all times outside of urban areas. It's illegal to use your mobile phone without a hands-free headset while driving. In Europe, you're not allowed to turn right on a red light, unless there is a sign or signal specifically authorizing it. Ask your car-rental company about additional rules, or check the US State Department website (www.travel.state.gov, click on "International Travel," then specify your country of choice, and click "Traffic Safety and Road Conditions").

Tolls: Italy's freeway system, the autostrada, is as good as our interstate system, but you'll pay about a dollar for every 10 minutes of use. While I favor freeways because I feel they're safer, cheaper (saving time and gas), and less nerve-racking than smaller roads, savvy local drivers know which toll-free *superstradas* are actually faster and more direct than the autostrada. For more information, visit www.autostrade.it.

Fuel: Gas is expensive—often about $8.50 per gallon. Diesel cars are more common in Europe than back home, so be sure you know what type of gas your car takes before you fill up. Gas pumps are color-coded for unleaded *(senza piombo)* or diesel *(gasolio).* Autostrada rest stops are self-service stations open daily without a siesta break. Many 24-hour-a-day stations are entirely automated. Small-town stations are usually cheaper and offer full service but shorter hours.

Maps and Signage: A good map is essential. Learn the universal road signs (explained in charts in most road atlases and at service stations). Although roads are numbered on maps, actual road signs don't list route numbers. Instead, roads are indicated by blue signs with a city name on them (for example, if you want to take a road heading east out of Rome—marked route S-5 on your map—you'd follow signs to Tivoli, the next town along this road). The signs are inconsistent: They may direct you to the nearest big city or simply the next town along the route.

STOP AND LEARN THESE ROAD SIGNS

50
Speed Limit (km/hr)
Yield
No Passing
End of No Passing Zone
One Way
Intersection
Main Road
Freeway
Danger
No Entry
No Entry for cars
All Vehicles Prohibited
P
Parking
No Parking
Customs
Peace

Theft: Cars are routinely vandalized and stolen. Thieves easily recognize rental cars and assume they are filled with a tourist's gear. Try to make your car look locally owned by hiding the "tourist-owned" rental-company decals and putting an Italian newspaper in your back window. Be sure all of your valuables are out of sight and locked in the trunk, or even better, with you or in your room.

Parking: White lines generally mean parking is free. Yellow lines mean that parking is reserved for residents only (who have permits). Blue lines mean you'll have to pay—usually €1.50 per hour (use machine, leave time-stamped receipt on dashboard). If there's no meter, there's probably a roving attendant who will take your money. Study the signs. Often the free zones have a 30- or 60-minute time limit. Signs showing a street cleaner and a day of the week indicate which day the street is cleaned; there's a €100 tow-fee incentive to learn the days of the week in Italian.

Zona disco has nothing to do with dancing. Italian cars come equipped with a time disk (a cardboard clock), which you set at your arrival time and lay on the dashboard so the attendant knows how long you've been parked. This is a fine system that all drivers should take advantage of. (If your rental car doesn't come with a *zona disco,* pick one up at a tobacco shop or just write your arrival time on a piece of paper and place it on the dashboard.)

Garages are safe, save time, and help you avoid the stress of parking tickets. Take the parking voucher with you to pay the cashier before you leave.

Cheap Flights

If you're considering a train ride that's more than five hours long, a flight may save you both time and money. When comparing your options, factor in the time it takes to get to the airport and how early you'll need to arrive to check in.

The best comparison search engine for both international and intra-European flights is www.kayak.com. For inexpensive flights within Europe, try www.skyscanner.com or www.hipmunk.com.

Most budget airlines—such as easyJet, Ryanair, and Air Berlin—serve Rome. If you're not sure who flies to your destination, check its airport's website for a list of carriers.

Be aware of the potential drawbacks of flying on the cheap: nonrefundable and nonchangeable tickets, minimal or nonexistent customer service, treks to airports far outside of town, and stingy baggage allowances with steep overage fees. If you're traveling with lots of luggage, a cheap flight can quickly become a bad deal. To avoid unpleasant surprises, read the small print before you book.

Resources

Resources from Rick Steves

Books: *Rick Steves' Rome 2013* is one of many books in my series on European travel, which includes country guidebooks, city guidebooks (Venice, Florence, Paris, London, etc.), Snapshot guides (excerpted chapters from my country guides), Pocket Guides (full-color little books on big cities, including Rome), and my budget-travel skills handbook, *Rick Steves' Europe Through the Back Door.* Most of my titles are available as ebooks. My phrase books—for Italian, French, German, Spanish, and Portuguese—are practical and budget-oriented. My other books include *Europe 101* (a crash course on art and history), *Mediterranean Cruise Ports* (how to make the most of your time in port), and *Travel as a Political Act* (a travelogue sprinkled with tips for bringing home a global perspective). A more complete list of my titles appears near the end of this book.

Video: My public television **series,** *Rick Steves' Europe,* covers European destinations in 100 shows, with 17 episodes on Italy, including three on Rome. To watch episodes online, visit www.hulu.com; for scripts and local airtimes, see www.ricksteves.com/tv.

Audio: My weekly public radio show, *Travel with Rick Steves,* features interviews with travel experts from around the world. I've also produced free, self-guided audio tours of the top sights in Rome. All of this audio content is available for free at Rick Steves Audio Europe, an extensive online library organized by destination. Choose whatever interests you, and download it for free via the Rick Steves Audio Europe smartphone app, www.ricksteves.com/audioeurope, iTunes, or Google Play.

Maps

The black-and-white maps in this book are concise and simple, designed to help you locate recommended places and get to local TIs, where you can pick up more in-depth maps of cities or regions (usually free). Better maps are sold at newsstands and bookstores. Before you buy a map, look at it to be sure it has the level of detail

Begin Your Trip at www.ricksteves.com

At ricksteves.com, you'll discover a wealth of free information on European destinations, including fresh monthly news and helpful tips from thousands of fellow travelers. You'll find my latest guidebook updates (www.ricksteves.com/update), a monthly travel e-newsletter (easy and free to sign up), my personal travel blog, and my free Rick Steves Audio Europe smartphone app (if you don't have a smartphone, you can access the same content via podcasts). You can even follow me on Facebook and Twitter.

Our **online Travel Store** offers travel bags and accessories that I've designed specifically to help you travel smarter and lighter. These include my popular carry-on bags (rollaboard and backpack versions), money belts, totes, toiletries kits, adapters, other accessories, and a wide selection of guidebooks, planning maps, and DVDs.

Choosing the right **railpass** for your trip—amid hundreds of options—can drive you nutty. We'll help you choose the best pass for your needs and ship it to you for free.

Want to travel with greater efficiency and less stress? We organize **tours** with more than three dozen itineraries and more than 500 departures reaching the best destinations in this book...and beyond. Our Italy tours include "the best of" in 17 days, Village Italy in 14 days, South Italy in 13 days, Sicily in 10 days, Venice-Florence-Rome in 10 days, the Heart of Italy in 9 days, and a week-long Rome tour. You'll enjoy great guides, a fun bunch of travel partners (with small groups of generally around 24-28), and plenty of room to spread out in a big, comfy bus. You'll find European adventures to fit every vacation length. For all the details, and to get our Tour Catalog and a free Rick Steves Tour Experience DVD (filmed on location during an actual tour), visit www.ricksteves.com or call us at 425/608-4217.

you want. Drivers will want to pick up a good, detailed map in Europe (I'd recommend a 1:200,000- or 1:300,000-scale map).

Other Guidebooks

If you're like most travelers, this book is all you need. But if you're heading beyond my recommended neighborhoods and destinations, $40 for extra maps and books can be money well-spent. If you'll be traveling elsewhere in Italy, consider *Rick Steves' Italy, Rick Steves' Venice,* or *Rick Steves' Florence & Tuscany*.

The following books are worthwhile but not updated annually, check the publication date before you buy. The tall, green Michelin guide to Rome has solid, encyclopedic coverage of sights, customs, and culture, though very little on hotels and restaurants (also sold in English in Italy). The Access guide to Rome is well-researched, organized by neighborhood, and color-coded for sights, hotels, and restaurants. Focusing mainly on sights, the colorful Eyewitness guide to Rome is fun for its great graphics and photos, but it's relatively skimpy on content and weighs a ton. You can buy it in Rome (no more expensive than in the US) or simply borrow it for a minute from other travelers at certain sights to make sure you're aware of that place's highlights. *Let's Go Rome, Venice & Florence* is youth-oriented, with good coverage of hostels and nightlife.

For a book of city walking tours, try *City Secrets: Rome* (Kahn) or *City of the Soul: A Walk in Rome* (Murray). For a list of bookstores in Rome, see page 27.

Recommended Books and Movies

To learn more about Rome past and present, check out a few of these books or films.

Nonfiction

Written in the 18th century, Edward Gibbon's *Decline and Fall of the Roman Empire* is considered *the* classic history of ancient Rome from its peak to its downfall.

Originally published as a series of *New Yorker* articles in the 1950s, *Rome and a Villa* reads as if it's Eleanor Clark's journal. Of Paul Hofmann's multiple books about Italy, *The Seasons of Rome* is the favorite among readers. Another good Americans-in-the-Eternal-City memoir is *As the Romans Do* (Epstein). A third of Elizabeth Gilbert's spiritual memoir/travelogue *Eat, Pray, Love* takes place in Rome.

The holy center of Christendom has plenty of worthwhile books documenting its history. *Saints & Sinners* (Duffy) is a warts-and-all illustrated guide to the popes. In *When in Rome,* Robert Hutchinson writes as a lapsed (sometimes irreverent) Catholic discovering the roots of Christianity in Vatican City. *Michelangelo and the Pope's Ceiling* (King) describes the drama behind the masterpiece. *The Pope's Elephant* (Bedini), written by a historian from the Smithsonian, tells the story of Pope Leo X's favorite pet.

A Literary Companion to Rome (Varriano) also includes 10 self-guided walking tours. Kids (and adults who like cool pictures) enjoy David Macaulay's two books about Rome: *Rome Antics* and *City: A Story of Roman Planning and Construction* (both for ages nine and up).

Fiction

No modern crime drama or soap opera can top the world of ancient Roman politics. Colleen McCullough—who also wrote *The Thorn Birds*—describes the early days of the Roman Republic in her work of historical fiction, *The First Man in Rome.* Robert Graves wanders from Caesar Augustus to Caligula and beyond in *I, Claudius*.

Ancient Rome makes a great backdrop for mysteries, as shown in *Roman Blood* (Saylor) and *The Silver Pigs* (Davis), both the first in a series. *Cabal,* by Michael Dibdin, takes place in modern Rome. In the blockbuster book *Angels and Demons,* written by *The Da Vinci Code* author Dan Brown, murders are linked by Rome's Bernini statues.

For a literary take on Rome, try *Open City: Seven Writers in Postwar Rome* (edited by William Weaver).

Films

Two masterpieces of Italian Neorealism—set in the bleak, post-WWII years—take place in Rome: Roberto Rossellini's *Open City* (1945) and Vittorio De Sica's touching, heartbreaking film *Bicycle Thieves* (1949).

A feel-good love story, *Roman Holiday* (1953) made a star out of Audrey Hepburn. *Three Coins in the Fountain* (1954) is another romantic crowd-pleaser.

During the era of epics, Hollywood couldn't get enough of ancient Rome. *Quo Vadis* (1951) contains three hours of religious-historic drama. *Ben-Hur* (1959) is a campy mash-up of Christianity, Charlton Heston, and chariot races. *Spartacus* (1960) casts Kirk Douglas as a rebel fighting Rome. In 2000, *Gladiator* turned Hollywood's attention back to ancient Rome, winning five Academy Awards for its portrayal of life in the bloody arena.

La Dolce Vita (1961) is Federico Fellini's seductive masterpiece. (His 1972 film *Roma* seems tacky in comparison.)

The warm-hearted Italian epic *Best of Youth* (2003) takes place in several Italian locations, including Rome; this story of two brothers gives you a good sense of the last several decades of Italian history.

Originally a BBC miniseries, *I, Claudius* (1976) puts Derek

Jacobi and John Hurt at the center of a pulpy classic. The HBO miniseries *Rome* (2005-2007) gives an *Upstairs-Downstairs* look at the lives and loves of Julius Caesar and Augustus.

The 2009 film *Angels and Demons,* based on the book by *The Da Vinci Code* author Dan Brown, is set in Rome. Banned from filming in Vatican City, cameramen disguised themselves as tourists to gather some of the shots. The 2010 film version of *Eat, Pray, Love,* starring Julia Roberts, was filmed partly in Rome and Naples.

Holidays and Festivals

In Italy, holidays seem to strike without warning. For instance, every town has a festival honoring its patron saint. The Vatican Museum closes for a multitude of Catholic holidays; check its schedule at http://mv.vatican.va.

This list includes selected festivals in Rome, plus national holidays observed throughout Italy. Many sights and banks close on national holidays—keep this in mind when planning your itinerary. Before gearing your trip around a festival, make sure you verify its dates by checking the festival's website or TI sites (www.italia.it and http://en.turismoroma.it); www.whatsonwhen.com also lists many festival dates.

In Rome, hotels get booked up on Easter weekend (from Good Friday through Monday), April 25 (Liberation Day), May 1 (Labor Day), June 29 (Sts. Peter and Paul), November 1 (All Saints' Day), and on Fridays and Saturdays year-round. Some hotels require you to book the full three-day weekend around a holiday.

Jan 1	New Year's Day
Jan 6	Epiphany
March 17	Rome Marathon (www.maratonadiroma.it)
March 31	Easter Sunday
April 1	Easter Monday
April 21	City Birthday
April 25	Italian Liberation Day
May 1	Labor Day
June 2	Anniversary of the Republic
May 30	Feast Day of Corpus Christi
June 24	St. John the Baptist's Day
June 29	Sts. Peter and Paul's Day
July	Trastevere's Noantri Festival
Aug 10	St. Lawrence's Day
Aug 15	Assumption of Mary (Ferragosto)
Nov 1	All Saints' Day
Dec 8	Feast of the Immaculate Conception

2013

JANUARY

S	M	T	W	T	F	S
		1	2	3	4	5
6	7	8	9	10	11	12
13	14	15	16	17	18	19
20	21	22	23	24	25	26
27	28	29	30	31		

FEBRUARY

S	M	T	W	T	F	S
					1	2
3	4	5	6	7	8	9
10	11	12	13	14	15	16
17	18	19	20	21	22	23
24	25	26	27	28		

MARCH

S	M	T	W	T	F	S
					1	2
3	4	5	6	7	8	9
10	11	12	13	14	15	16
17	18	19	20	21	22	23
24/31	25	26	27	28	29	30

APRIL

S	M	T	W	T	F	S
	1	2	3	4	5	6
7	8	9	10	11	12	13
14	15	16	17	18	19	20
21	22	23	24	25	26	27
28	29	30				

MAY

S	M	T	W	T	F	S
			1	2	3	4
5	6	7	8	9	10	11
12	13	14	15	16	17	18
19	20	21	22	23	24	25
26	27	28	29	30	31	

JUNE

S	M	T	W	T	F	S
						1
2	3	4	5	6	7	8
9	10	11	12	13	14	15
16	17	18	19	20	21	22
23/30	24	25	26	27	28	29

JULY

S	M	T	W	T	F	S
	1	2	3	4	5	6
7	8	9	10	11	12	13
14	15	16	17	18	19	20
21	22	23	24	25	26	27
28	29	30	31			

AUGUST

S	M	T	W	T	F	S
				1	2	3
4	5	6	7	8	9	10
11	12	13	14	15	16	17
18	19	20	21	22	23	24
25	26	27	28	29	30	31

SEPTEMBER

S	M	T	W	T	F	S
1	2	3	4	5	6	7
8	9	10	11	12	13	14
15	16	17	18	19	20	21
22	23	24	25	26	27	28
29	30					

OCTOBER

S	M	T	W	T	F	S
		1	2	3	4	5
6	7	8	9	10	11	12
13	14	15	16	17	18	19
20	21	22	23	24	25	26
27	28	29	30	31		

NOVEMBER

S	M	T	W	T	F	S
					1	2
3	4	5	6	7	8	9
10	11	12	13	14	15	16
17	18	19	20	21	22	23
24	25	26	27	28	29	30

DECEMBER

S	M	T	W	T	F	S
1	2	3	4	5	6	7
8	9	10	11	12	13	14
15	16	17	18	19	20	21
22	23	24	25	26	27	28
29	30	31				

Dec 25 Christmas
Dec 26 St. Stephen's Day

Conversions and Climate

Numbers and Stumblers

- Europeans write a few of their numbers differently than we do. 1 = 1, 4 = 4, 7 = 7.
- In Europe, dates appear as day/month/year, so Christmas is 25/12/13.
- Commas are decimal points and decimals commas. A dollar and a half is 1,50, and there are 5.280 feet in a mile.
- When pointing, use your whole hand, palm down.
- When counting with fingers, start with your thumb. If you hold up your first finger to request one item, you'll probably get two.

- What Americans call the second floor of a building is the first floor in Europe.
- On escalators and moving sidewalks, Europeans keep the left "lane" open for passing. Keep to the right.

Roman Numerals

In the US, you'll see Roman numerals—which originated in ancient Rome—used for copyright dates, clocks, and the Super Bowl. In Italy, you're likely to observe these numbers chiseled on statues and buildings. If you want to do some numeric detective work, here's how: In Roman numerals, as in ours, the highest numbers (thousands, hundreds) come first, followed by smaller numbers. Many numbers are made by combining numerals into sets: V = 5, so VIII = 8 (5 plus 3). Roman numerals follow a subtraction principle for multiples of fours (4, 40, 400, etc.) and nines (9, 90, 900, etc.). The number four, for example, is written as IV (1 subtracted from 5), rather than IIII. The number nine is IX (1 subtracted from 10).

Rick Steves' Rome 2013 would translate as *Rick Steves' Rome MMXIII.* Big numbers such as dates can look daunting at first. The easiest way to handle them is to read the numbers in discrete chunks. For example, Michelangelo was born in MCDLXXV. Break it down: M (1,000) + CD (100 subtracted from 500, or 400) + LXX (50 + 10 + 10, or 70) + V (5) = 1475. It was a very good year.

M = 1000
CM = 900
D = 500
CD = 400
C = 100
XC = 90
L = 50
XL = 40
X = 10
IX = 9
V = 5
IV = 4
I = duh

Metric Conversions (approximate)

A kilogram is 2.2 pounds, and one liter is about a quart, or almost four to a gallon. A kilometer is six-tenths of a mile. I figure kilometers to miles by cutting them in half and adding back 10 percent of the original (120 km: 60 + 12 = 72 miles, 300 km: 150 + 30 = 180 miles).

1 foot = 0.3 meter
1 yard = 0.9 meter
1 mile = 1.6 kilometers
1 centimeter = 0.4 inch
1 meter = 39.4 inches
1 kilometer = 0.62 mile
1 square yard = 0.8 square meter
1 square mile = 2.6 square kilometers
1 ounce = 28 grams
1 quart = 0.95 liter
1 kilogram = 2.2 pounds
32°F = 0°C

Clothing Sizes

When shopping for clothing, use these US-to-European comparisons as general guidelines (but note that no conversion is perfect).

- Women's dresses and blouses: Add 30
  (US size 10 = European size 40)
- Men's suits and jackets: Add 10
  (US size 40 regular = European size 50)
- Men's shirts: Multiply by 2 and add about 8
  (US size 15 collar = European size 38)
- Women's shoes: Add about 30
  (US size 8 = European size 38-39)
- Men's shoes: Add 32-34
  (US size 9 = European size 41; US size 11 = European size 45)

Rome's Climate

First line—average daily high; second line—average daily low; third line—average days without rain. For more detailed statistics for Rome (as well as the rest of the world), check www.worldclimate.com.

J	F	M	A	M	J	J	A	S	O	N	D
52°	55°	59°	66°	74°	82°	87°	86°	79°	71°	61°	55°
40°	42°	45°	50°	56°	63°	67°	67°	62°	55°	49°	44°
13	19	23	24	26	26	30	29	25	23	19	21

Temperature Conversion: Fahrenheit and Celsius

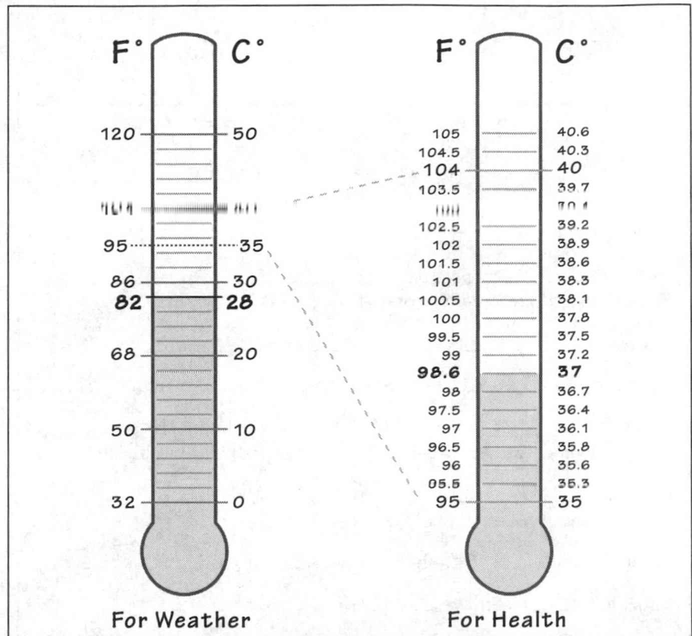

Europe takes its temperature using the Celsius scale, while we opt for Fahrenheit. For a rough conversion from Celsius to Fahrenheit, double the number and add 30. For weather, remember that 28°C is 82°F—perfect. For health, 37°C is just right.

Hotel Reservation

To: _______________ _______________
hotel ***email or fax***

From: _______________ _______________
name ***email or fax***

Today's date: _____ /_____ /_____
day ***month*** ***year***

Dear Hotel _______________________________,
Please make this reservation for me:

Name: _______________________________

Total # of people: _______ # of rooms: _______ # of nights: _______

Arriving: _____ /_____ /_____ My time of arrival (24-hr clock): _______
day ***month*** ***year*** (I will telephone if I will be late)

Departing: _____ /_____ /_____
day ***month*** ***year***

Room(s): Single___ Double ___ Twin___ Triple___ Quad___

With: Toilet ___ Shower___ Bath ___ Sink only___

Special needs: View___ Quiet___ Cheapest ___ Ground Floor___

Please email or fax confirmation of my reservation, along with the type of room reserved and the price. Please also inform me of your cancellation policy. After I hear from you, I will quickly send my credit-card information as a deposit to hold the room. Thank you.

____
Name

____
Address

____
City ***State*** ***Zip Code*** ***Country***

Before hoteliers can make your reservation, they want to know the information listed above. You can use this form as the basis for your email, or you can photocopy this page, fill in the information, and send it as a fax (also available online at www.ricksteves.com/reservation).

Packing Checklist

Whether you're traveling for five days or five weeks, here's what you'll need to bring. Pack light to enjoy the sweet freedom of true mobility. Happy travels!

- ❑ 5 shirts: long- and short-sleeve
- ❑ 1 sweater or lightweight fleece
- ❑ 2 pairs pants
- ❑ 1 pair shorts
- ❑ 1 swimsuit
- ❑ 5 pairs underwear and socks
- ❑ 1 pair shoes
- ❑ 1 rainproof jacket with hood
- ❑ Tie or scarf
- ❑ Money belt
- ❑ Money—your mix of:
  - ❑ Debit card (for ATM withdrawals)
  - ❑ Credit card
  - ❑ Hard cash (in easy-to-exchange $20 bills)
- ❑ Documents plus photocopies:
  - ❑ Passport
  - ❑ Printout of airline eticket
  - ❑ Driver's license
  - ❑ Student ID and hostel card
  - ❑ Railpass/car rental voucher
  - ❑ Insurance details
- ❑ Daypack
- ❑ Electronics—your choice of:
  - ❑ Camera (and related gear)
  - ❑ Computer/mobile devices (phone, MP3 player, ereader, etc.)
  - ❑ Chargers for each of the above
  - ❑ Plug adapter
- ❑ Empty water bottle
- ❑ Wristwatch and alarm clock
- ❑ Earplugs
- ❑ Toiletries kit
  - ❑ Toiletries
  - ❑ Medicines and vitamins
  - ❑ First-aid kit
  - ❑ Glasses/contacts/sunglasses (with prescriptions)
- ❑ Sealable plastic baggies
- ❑ Laundry soap
- ❑ Clothesline
- ❑ Small towel
- ❑ Sewing kit
- ❑ Travel information (guidebooks and maps)
- ❑ Address list (for sending postcards)
- ❑ Postcards and photos from home
- ❑ Notepad and pen
- ❑ Journal

If you plan to carry on your luggage, note that all liquids must be in 3.4-ounce or smaller containers and fit within a single quart-size sealable baggie. For details, see www.tsa.gov/travelers.

Italian Survival Phrases

Good day.	**Buon giorno.**	bwohn JOR-noh
Do you speak English?	**Parla inglese?**	PAR-lah een-GLAY-zay
Yes. / No.	**Si. / No.**	see / noh
I (don't) understand.	**(Non) capisco.**	(nohn) kah-PEES-koh
Please.	**Per favore.**	pehr fah-VOH-ray
Thank you.	**Grazie.**	GRAHT-seeay
You're welcome.	**Prego.**	PRAY-go
I'm sorry.	**Mi dispiace.**	mee dee-speeAH-chay
Excuse me.	**Mi scusi.**	mee SKOO-zee
(No) problem.	**(Non) c'è un problema.**	(nohn) cheh oon proh-BLAY-mah
Good.	**Va bene.**	vah BEHN-ay
Goodbye.	**Arrivederci.**	ah-ree-vay-DEHR-chee
one / two	**uno / due**	OO-noh / DOO-ay
three / four	**tre / quattro**	tray / KWAH-troh
five / six	**cinque / sei**	CHEENG-kway / SEHee
seven / eight	**sette / otto**	SEHT-tay / OT-toh
nine / ten	**nove / dieci**	NOV-ay / deeAY-chee
How much is it?	**Quanto costa?**	KWAHN-toh KOS-tah
Write it?	**Me lo scrive?**	may loh SKREE-vay
Is it free?	**È gratis?**	eh GRAH-tees
Is it included?	**È incluso?**	eh een-KLOO-zoh
Where can I buy / find...?	**Dove posso comprare / trovare...?**	DOH-vay POS-soh kohm-PRAH-ray / troh-VAH-ray
I'd like / We'd like...	**Vorrei / Vorremmo...**	vor-REHee / vor-RAY-moh
...a room.	**...una camera.**	OO-nah KAH-meh-rah
...a ticket to ____.	**...un biglietto per ____.**	oon beel-YEHT-toh pehr
Is it possible?	**È possibile?**	eh poh-SEE-bee-lay
Where is...?	**Dov'è...?**	DOH-veh
...the train station	**...la stazione**	lah staht-seeOH-nay
...the bus station	**...la stazione degli autobus**	lah staht-seeOH-nay DAYL-yee OW-toh-boos
...tourist information	**...informazioni per turisti**	een-for-maht-seeOH-nee pehr too-REE-stee
...the toilet	**...la toilette**	lah twah-LEHT-tay
men	**uomini, signori**	WOH-mee-nee, seen-YOH-ree
women	**donne, signore**	DON-nay, seen-YOH-ray
left / right	**sinistra / destra**	see-NEE-strah / DEHS-trah
straight	**sempre diritto**	SEHM-pray dee-REE-toh
When do you open / close?	**A che ora aprite / chiudete?**	ah kay OH-rah ah-PREE-tay / keeoo-DAY-tay
At what time?	**A che ora?**	ah kay OH-rah
Just a moment.	**Un momento.**	oon moh-MAYN-toh
now / soon / later	**adesso / presto / tardi**	ah-DEHS-soh / PREHS-toh / TAR-dee
today / tomorrow	**oggi / domani**	OH-jee / doh-MAH-nee

In an Italian-speaking Restaurant

I'd like...	**Vorrei...**	vor-REHee
We'd like...	**Vorremmo...**	vor-RAY-moh
...to reserve...	**...prenotare...**	pray-noh-TAH-ray
...a table for one / two.	**...un tavolo per uno / due.**	oon TAH-voh-loh pehr OO-noh / DOO-ay
Non-smoking.	**Non fumare.**	nohn foo-MAH-ray
Is this seat free?	**È libero questo posto?**	eh LEE-bay-roh KWEHS-toh POH-stoh
The menu (in English), please.	**Il menù (in inglese), per favore.**	eel may-NOO (een een-GLAY-zay) pehr fah-VOH-ray
service (not) included	**servizio (non) incluso**	sehr-VEET-seeoh (nohn) een-KLOO-zoh
cover charge	**pane e coperto**	PAH-nay ay koh-PEHR-toh
to go	**da portar via**	dah POR-tar VEE-ah
with / without	**con / senza**	kohn / SEHN-sah
and / or	**e / o**	ay / oh
menu (of the day)	**menù (del giorno)**	may-NOO (dayl JOR-noh)
specialty of the house	**specialità della casa**	spay-chah-lee-TAH DEHL-lah KAH-zah
first course (pasta, soup)	**primo piatto**	PREE-moh peeAH-toh
main course (meat, fish)	**secondo piatto**	say-KOHN-doh peeAH-toh
side dishes	**contorni**	kohn-TOR-nee
bread	**pane**	PAH-nay
cheese	**formaggio**	for-MAH-joh
sandwich	**panino**	pah-NEE-noh
soup	**minestra, zuppa**	mee-NEHS-trah, TSOO-pah
salad	**insalata**	een-sah-LAH-tah
meat	**carne**	KAR-nay
chicken	**pollo**	POH-loh
fish	**pesce**	PEH-shay
seafood	**frutti di mare**	FROO-tee dee MAH-ray
fruit / vegetables	**frutta / legumi**	FROO-tah / lay-GOO-mee
dessert	**dolci**	DOHL-chee
tap water	**acqua del rubinetto**	AH-kwah dayl roo-bee-NAY-toh
mineral water	**acqua minerale**	AH-kwah mee-nay-RAH-lay
milk	**latte**	LAH-tay
(orange) juice	**succo (d'arancia)**	SOO-koh (dah-RAHN-chah)
coffee / tea	**caffè / tè**	kah-FEH / teh
wine	**vino**	VEE-noh
red / white	**rosso / bianco**	ROH-soh / beeAHN-koh
glass / bottle	**bicchiere / bottiglia**	bee-keeAY-ray / boh-TEEL-yah
beer	**birra**	BEE-rah
Cheers!	**Cin cin!**	cheen cheen
More. / Another.	**Ancora un po.' / Un altro.**	ahn-KOH-rah oon poh / oon AHL-troh
The same.	**Lo stesso.**	loh STEHS-soh
The bill, please.	**Il conto, per favore.**	eel KOHN-toh pehr fah-VOH-ray
tip	**mancia**	MAHN-chah
Delicious!	**Delizioso!**	day-leet-seeOH-zoh

For more user-friendly Italian phrases, check out *Rick Steves' Italian Phrase Book & Dictionary* or *Rick Steves' French, Italian, and German Phrase Book.*

INDEX

INDEX

N

O

INDEX

U

V

MAP INDEX

Join
a Rick
Steves
tour
Enjoy Europe's
warmest welcome...
with the flexibility and
friendship of a small group
getting to know Rick's
favorite places and people.
It all starts with our free
tour catalog and DVD.
Great guides, small
groups, no grumps.
See more than three dozen itineraries throughout Europe
ricksteves.com

Start your trip at

Free information and great gear to

▸ Plan Your Trip

Browse thousands of articles and a wealth of money-saving tips for planning your dream trip. You'll find up-to-date information on Europe's best destinations, packing smart, getting around, finding rooms, staying healthy, avoiding scams and more.

▸ Eurail Passes

Find out, step-by-step, if a railpass makes sense for your trip—and how to avoid buying more than you need. Get free shipping on online orders

▸ Graffiti Wall & Travelers Helpline

Learn, ask, share—our online community of savvy travelers is a great resource for first-time travelers to Europe, as well as seasoned pros.

Rick Steves' Europe Through the Back Door, Inc.

ITALY
Audio Tours

Credits

Researchers

To update this book, Rick relied on the help of...

Ben Cameron

Ben experienced his first taste of European travel when he was three, exploring medieval castles with his parents. Returning after graduation, he was hooked and has spent much of his time since exploring Europe independently and leading tours for Rick Steves. When not living out of his backpack, Ben splits his time between Rome and Seattle.

Cameron Hewitt

Cameron writes and edits guidebooks for Rick Steves, specializing in Eastern Europe. For this book, he swung through the urban jungle of Naples, in search of the city's best pizza, viewpoints, and churches. When he's not traveling, Cameron lives in Seattle with his wife Shawna.

Avalon Travel
a member of the Perseus Books Group
1700 Fourth Street
Berkeley, CA 94710, U.S.A.

Printed in Canada by Friesens
First printing August 2012

ISBN 978-1-61238-373-6
ISSN 1527-4780

For the latest on Rick's lectures, guidebooks, tours, public radio show, and public television series, contact Europe Through the Back Door, Box 2009, Edmonds, WA 98020, tel. 425/771-8303, fax 425/771-0833, www.ricksteves.com, rick@ricksteves.com.

Europe Through the Back Door
Managing Editor: Risa Laib
Editors: Jennifer Madison Davis, Glenn Eriksen, Tom Griffin, Cameron Hewitt, Suzanne Kotz, Cathy Lu, Gretchen Strauch
Editorial Intern: Michael Maloy
Researchers: Ben Cameron, Cameron Hewitt
Graphic Content Director: Laura VanDeventer
Maps & Graphics: David C. Hoerlein, Twozdai Hulse, Lauren Mills, Laura VanDeventer

Avalon Travel
Senior Editor and Series Manager: Madhu Prasher
Associate Editor: Jamie Andrade
Assistant Editor: Nikki Ioakimedes
Copy Editor: Naomi Adler Dancis
Proofreader: Megan Mulholland
Indexer: Laura Welcome
Production & Typesetting: McGuire Barber Design
Cover Design: Kimberly Glyder Design
Maps & Graphics: Lohnes and Wright, Kat Bennett, Mike Morgenfeld

Front Matter Color Photos: p. i, Victor Emmanuel Monument © Michael Potter
Front Cover Photo: Pietà, St. Peter's Basilica, Vatican City © Cameron Hewitt
Additional Photography: Wikimedia Commons, Rick Steves, Gene Openshaw, Dominic Bonuccelli, David C. Hoerlein, Laura VanDeventer, Cameron Hewitt, Bruce VanDeventer, Michael Potter, Ben Cameron, Anne Jenkins, Robyn Cronin, Amanda Scotese, Risa Laib
Sistine Chapel photo, page 231, © Erich Lessing / Art Resource, NY

Want More Italy?

Maximize the experience with Rick Steves as your guide

Guidebooks

Florence, Venice and Italy guides make side-trips smooth and affordable

Phrase Books

Rely on Rick's Italian Phrase Book and Dictionary

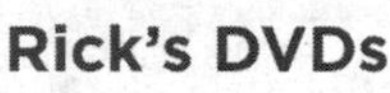

Rick's DVDs

Preview where you're going with 13 shows on Italy

Free! Rick's Audio Europe™ App

Get free audio tours for Rome's top sights

Small-Group Tours

Rick offers several great itineraries through Italy

For all the details, visit ricksteves.com